COOKING FOR COMPANY

Other cookbooks by *Farm Journal*

FARM JOURNAL'S COUNTRY COOKBOOK
FARM JOURNAL'S TIMESAVING COUNTRY COOKBOOK
FREEZING & CANNING COOKBOOK
FARM JOURNAL'S COMPLETE PIE COOKBOOK
LET'S START TO COOK

By the Food Editors of FARM JOURNAL

Cooking for Company

Edited by NELL B. NICHOLS

FARM JOURNAL *Field Food Editor*

•

Photography supervised by

AL J. REAGAN

ART DIRECTOR OF *The Farmer's Wife*

DOUBLEDAY & COMPANY, INC.

GARDEN CITY, NEW YORK

CONTENTS

COLOR ILLUSTRATIONS

WHAT THIS COOKBOOK IS ABOUT

Memories of company dinners in the country start city cliff dwellers to daydreaming. They see feasts of golden, crisp-coated fried chicken, feather-light yeast rolls, homemade ice cream, butter-rich layer cakes, juicy apple pies, sizzling hot sausage patties, new potatoes from the garden and corn-on-the-cob so fresh that milky goodness spurts from the kernels when you press them. . . .

But country meals are more than food bounty—friendliness and warm welcomes are the setting. So are happy people around an attractive table —perhaps on an airy porch or in a comfortable family room. Analyze country hospitality further and you'll discover that what makes it memorable is the desire of the host and hostess to share the fruits of their land and to exchange news and ideas with friends. It's this willingness to give and to receive that sheds a special luster over countryside social gatherings.

Many busy women, pressed for time, sometimes ask themselves: Why have company? Is it worth the effort? Deep in their hearts, thoughtful parents know that guests contribute much to a family. Most mothers and fathers appreciate that entertaining teaches children to extend hospitality and to become outgoing through their opportunities to meet and talk with many kinds of interesting people.

It's still fashionable in the country to be neighborly. And neighborhoods are growing bigger—they're reaching far places. In this jet travel age and with foreign student exchanges increasing, there are chances to give visitors from faraway countries a close-up picture of American family life.

As the speed of travel quickens, more Americans now travel and eat meals native to the countries they visit. Today's young people go to foreign lands in military service and via International Farm Youth Exchanges. No wonder the interest in the food specialties of many nation-alities is on the upgrade. The more boys and girls learn about different types of people and their customs, including their favorite foods, the better they will fit into the places they visit and the more they'll enjoy meals they eat on foreign shores.

If you get acquainted with some of the best dishes of millions, you'll know what they are when you run across them. And you'll experience some fine eating adventures.

Awareness of this food trend led us to include in the pages of this cookbook recipes from many nations, altered slightly by American in-gredients, kitchen equipment and our food likes. Look for these in-ternational treats—you'll discover such tasty dishes as South-of-the-Border Enchiladas, Indian Curry, Finnish Shortbread, Spanish Chilled Vegetable Soup (*gazpacho*), Chinese Chicken with Walnuts, French Cheese Pie, Czechoslovakian Poppy Seed Cake and Hungarian Chicken Paprika. We suggest that you serve the Hearty Italian Dinner, contributed by one of the testers in FARM JOURNAL Kitchens, who is of Italian descent. Make it for special occasions—the Lasagne Roll-Ups that resemble little pillows with ruffled edges, Pork Roast with Flavor Pockets and Pears Cardinale, one of the simplest but most delicious desserts you'll ever run across.

You will notice the recipe section begins with "Hearty Main Dishes"—our biggest chapter. We put it first because most women, when planning menus, begin by deciding what meat or main dish they will serve. After main dishes, our recipe chapters follow in meal-planning order: vege-tables, salads, breads, desserts. We've added specialty chapters on Bev-erages and Snacks, Cooking for a Crowd and Cooking over Coals. And at the back of the book, you will find a special section called "Hostess How-to"—it includes menus for all occasions; etiquette rules for serving sit-down dinners, buffets, teas, even co-operative potlucks; suggestions for garnishes, table settings, centerpieces, party favors—and accepted table manners!

Children exposed to neatly set and appealing tables for company meals will someday have the same kind in their homes. So enlist the help and interest of your daughters and sons. Ask the girls to help fix the food, arrange the centerpiece, set the table and make the party favors if you plan to use them (complete directions in the Hostess How-to sec-tion). This makes the assignment easy for your young helpers—and challenging. Suggest that your husband ask the boys to assist him when he serves the first course in the living room. They can pass the food and look out for the guests' needs. All this is valuable social training.

Consider the host as well as the children when you entertain. Many men in urban families get home from work in time to relax before guests arrive. Farmers frequently work up to the last minute, and come to the house tired after a long day's work. The clever wife faces the situation and tactfully refrains from insisting that her weary husband assume all the host's duties with enthusiasm. You, the hostess, often will be wise to take over some of the hosting—at least make the host's responsibilities as easy as possible. You will find many ideas in this cookbook that will help you do this.

If you serve the first course in the living room, for instance, guests will sip, dip, eat and visit and not be too concerned if their host is delayed. Just fix our Snack Tree and let people pick their appetizers from it. They'll be so interested in this novel way of helping themselves that they'll not notice the passage of time. There are many other good meal beginnings in this book that you can use.

If your husband isn't fond of carving and serving foods at the table, have a buffet meal and eliminate these duties. Or if you want to have a sit-down dinner around the table, select a menu of easy-serve dishes. You might choose one of our astonishingly good bake and carve-ahead roasts that you reheat quickly at mealtime in their pan juices. Roast Veal or Lamb with Sweet Onions, Deep-Peppered Pork and Braised Beef in Sour Cream are good examples. Ducks, roasted and cut in fourths for individual servings, taste marvelous when you reheat them in Lemon-Carrot Sauce. Garnished with orange and banana slices, the duck looks as good as it tastes.

To maintain your poise and avoid anxiety when you fear your meal must wait for a tardy host or guest, select dishes that do not deteriorate if you do not serve them promptly. Oven stews are ideal for such situations. Beef 'n' Rigatoni Stew does not require immediate service. And what a superior company dish it is. Barbecued Chicken in Foil is just one of the many extra-good chicken specialties that are patient waiters if you can't serve the meal on time. The big chapter on Hearty Main Dishes contains many other tasty treats that bring the hostess cheer when she is confronted with a dinner delay.

Before you leave the giant Main Dish chapter, look at the superb collection of distinctive chicken recipes, which prove that country kitchens (where many of these recipes originated) have not lost their talent in chicken cookery. You'll find a recipe for Chicken Pizza that especially pleases youngsters. Other members of the poultry family have recipe representation—turkey, goose and wild and tame ducks. Mingling with them are sea food and fish recipes. Salmon Loaf with Shrimp Sauce, for instance, shows how a hostess can make a good everyday canned fish loaf glamorous with a new sauce. Pause with the unusual fish sauces —at least briefly. You'll want to use them to dress up fish dinners for discriminating guests.

We've made a point of presenting recipes for dishes you can fix ahead because they make entertaining much easier than it used to be. For instance, you'll run across recipes for Heat-and-Eat Frozen Potatoes. A tremendous variety of make-ahead salads awaits you—refrigerated, frozen and molded. Some you fix in a skillet or casserole to serve hot; others you toss at the last minutes. You'll see many recipes for the molded gelatin beauties so popular in the country, including Three-Row Garden Salad, which is molded in a loaf pan and ideal for toting to a share-the-load meal. When you slice this salad and serve it on individual plates, it's a festive red, green and orange striped ribbon. Really refreshing.

We've given country breads—the kinds guests compliment—a whole chapter. You'll want to make square doughnuts, coffee cakes and rolls of many kinds for coffee parties, fruit-nut loaves for party sandwiches and pancakes of many descriptions. Included also are sour dough biscuits and pancakes, along with the recipe for the starter that leavens and flavors them. If you're hostess-minded, the dainty teatime sandwiches or the delicate Caramel Twists will delight you—and your guests.

It's not surprising that it took two chapters to introduce the dessert recipes that were too good to omit from this cookbook—Country-Best Cakes, Cookies and Pies and Great Country Desserts. Among our dessert recipes are such inviting tempters as butter-rich cakes, prune cakes from prune growers' wives, date and other fruit cakes. And all kinds of cookies and country pies that can't be surpassed—Strawberry Satin Pie, for instance (see picture in this cookbook—it's a luscious beauty). There are dasher-turned ice creams, cobblers, dumplings, custards and other too-good-to-forget meal endings. Be sure to notice one homemaker's way of successfully hostessing a dessert buffet or Tart Bar—perfect kind of service for a group of 12 or more.

Outdoor chefs have their own chapter in this book. Cooking over Coals presents menus, recipes and tips on how to have success with this kind of cooking. You'll read how to give a summer pig roast—an idea borrowed from Hawaii by an Illinois farm couple who used it to entertain 80 guests.

No whistle-stop journey through this book would be complete without at least a reference to Chapter 1, How to Make Food Taste Wonderful. In the final analysis, it's taste that's of prime importance. Fine flavors in food have no substitute. The recipes in this book will enable you to serve meals and refreshments that taste exceptionally good. You'll get ideas for flavor boosters and some unusual seasoners. In Chapter 1 we offer a description of all the seasonings you will want to get acquainted with if they're new to you.

Because country women frequently plan, fix and serve food for a group of people, we include large-quantity recipes in a separate chapter, Cooking for a Crowd. In addition to our own recipes, we feature about 50 recipes from a famous Indiana home economist, Veronica Morrissey, who has successfully managed tearooms, restaurants and club dining rooms in different sections of the country. For several years she was a consultant to eating establishments stretching across country from California to Virginia. It was her responsibility to improve the food and to attract new customers. In her travels and experiences, Miss Morrissey collected ideas and from them developed superior quantity recipes which yield beautiful food that tastes wonderful. We are proud to present these recipes that produce dishes that met a real test—they sold well and received praise from people who paid for the privilege of eating them.

The number of servings in these recipes varies—from 8 to 12 up to 100 or more. If the recipe you select is not as big as you need, we suggest you make it twice rather than doubling it—there's less chance for error in multiplying ingredients. This is a good rule to follow in doubling other recipes in this book, too—make them twice.

Other home economists, now homemakers across the country, also contributed recipes they use when entertaining. All are locally recognized for the excellent food they serve guests. County extension home economists also share with you in this cookbook their favorites when they are hostessing, and also some of the specialties of good cooks in their respective counties. Many of the exciting recipes in this cookbook come from our own Test Kitchens, of course.

And as with all FARM JOURNAL cookbooks, farm and ranch women helped by sharing their best recipes for company and community co-operative meals. Especially did 500 FARM JOURNAL Test Group members and 1000 alumnae share their compliment-getting recipes.

We produced *Cooking for Company,* the sixth FARM JOURNAL cookbook,* because sharing food and hospitality has such a featured place in the interests of FARM JOURNAL readers, as it has in our magazine. Every country hostess wishes to put her best food forward with food she serves guests in her home, at picnics, covered dish meals, church and club suppers and for other occasions.

We hope that you and your guests will enjoy the food that you fix with recipes in this cookbook and that our other suggestions will make your entertaining easier and merrier. Excellent food combined with friendliness and a talent for making guests feel that their comfort and pleasure are uppermost in your thoughts will bring you a reputation as an outstanding hostess.

NELL B. NICHOLS
FARM JOURNAL Field Food Editor

* The five other FARM JOURNAL cookbooks are: COUNTRY COOKBOOK, TIMESAVING COUNTRY COOKBOOK, FREEZING & CANNING COOKBOOK, COMPLETE PIE COOKBOOK, and LET'S START TO COOK.

COOKING FOR COMPANY

CHAPTER 1

HOW TO MAKE FOOD TASTE WONDERFUL

Taste is something like the smell of a rose—difficult to describe. Think of the foods you've eaten and you'll discover the ones you remember most have one thing in common: superlative taste! So good that they're unforgettable. A hostess wants most of all to serve this kind of memorable food to company. And that's exactly what the recipes in this cookbook are designed to help you do.

Many country foods are flavor-rich from the start because they are so fresh. Capitalize on this in your menus—use eggs, milk and cream in custard-type and other desserts, for instance; whisk vegetables from the garden to the pan, for example. Give young, tender peas you gather from the vines an important place in your meals. (That's what we did in Chicken with Peas—see Index.) Team tiny, succulent Summer Squash and Sausage for another pleasant surprise (see Index).

Taste as you cook. And check the seasonings in a dish before you take it to the table. Just a dash of salt, sugar or herb can make a world of difference in the perfection of a dish.

You will meet many flavor boosters in this chapter. Herbs and spices are the two main types. Get acquainted with them and the other seasoners and let them help you. A good way to start is to use recipes in this cookbook such as Dilly Potato and Carrot-Chive salads and tomato dishes to which basil adds its charms. Notice, too, what a bit of tarragon does to chicken and green salads. Country cooks are in luck because they can grow many herbs near the kitchen door for fast use during the growing season and to put in the freezer for the remainder of the year. Browse in the supermarkets at the displays of dried herbs, spices and other seasoners; try some kinds that are still new to you.

This chapter is a short course on how to make food taste good. Use the ideas in it and your guests will take home with them memories of food too delicious to forget.

Get Acquainted with Taste Secrets

Hostesses agree that the food they fix for company must taste exceptionally good. There's simply no substitute for fine flavor. How do you capture it in the dishes you fix? No one answer will help you, but many. Here are some of those we find most important in FARM JOURNAL Test Kitchens:

• Start with top quality food. If you live in the country, you're in luck. You'll use many foods that grow on your own or neighbors' farms—juicy berries ripened in the patch, the choicest fruits you can gather from orchards, succulent vegetables hurried from the garden shortly before cooking and plentiful supplies of farm-fresh eggs, milk, cream and butter. Your freezer holds superior meats, poultry, vegetables and fruits which you package and put away with care. And likely, there's a well-stocked supermarket nearby where you shop for food not available in the farming community.

• Distinguish between top quality and high cost. A tender herb-flavored pot roast with rich brown gravy, even though less expensive, is a far better dish to serve your guests than a tough rib roast.

• Make use of foods in season; plan your time and menu so you can. Share with your guests the finest flavors, at their peak of goodness.

• If food comes from the freezer, follow directions in recipes for thawing it. Many foods, like fruits and berries, are most delicious when only partly thawed. When you put food in the freezer for future use, sort out the choicest packages and label them for special occasions.

• Cook food to the right degree of doneness. For instance, watch that you don't overcook vegetables; they're usually best when tender but still crisp. Select tested recipes and follow them. If the recipe says keep your heat low—don't let food boil away its goodness. Always bake food at the temperature the recipe specifies. Be sure your oven temperature control is accurate—check it occasionally with an oven thermometer.

• Remember that serving temperature affects taste. Serve hot foods hot, not lukewarm. If you entertain a lot, an electric food warmer is a big help. Leave cold foods in the refrigerator until you're ready to serve.

• Taste while you cook, and correct the seasoning before serving a dish.

• Add seasoners with discretion. It's easy to correct the taste when you use too little—but almost impossible when you use too much. Your purpose is to enhance natural flavors, never to hide them. American kitchens have such superior food that it's a pity to cover their taste. Roast beef, for instance, is so tasty that you might better pass sauces for it and let guests help themselves if they wish extra seasoning.

• Give flavors a chance to blend and mellow—some dishes taste better if not served immediately after cooking. Notice references in recipes about when to serve a dish after you fix it.

• Keep a list of combinations of foods

that improve each other, like oranges and coconut, sweet potatoes and ham, roast pork and apricots, cabbage and corned beef, turkey and cranberries, strawberries and cream.

• Avoid getting in a rut; try new recipes. Experiment with seasoners.

• Get acquainted with the vast array of seasoning helps you can keep in your cupboard or refrigerator. This chapter contains a sampler—everything from salt to meat sauces to mini-recipes for flavored butters. In this chapter you'll also find a handy glossary of spices and herbs, and suggestions for using them. When you've read about them, you'll want to browse around your supermarket, just to see how many good tastes you've been overlooking.

Seasoners to Keep in Your Cupboard

You'll find that an intelligent addition of these taste and aroma carriers boosts many dishes into the gourmet class. Here are the five important seasoner families:

Herbs: They are the leaves, never the stems, of low-growing annual and perennial plants that grow in temperate zones. You use them in three forms: fresh, dried and frozen. (See Country Herb Gardens.)

Seeds: The seeds such as mustard, caraway or poppy of some annual plants, both whole and ground, add character to many dishes. (See Seed Seasoners.)

Spices: They are the bark (cinnamon), roots (ginger), fruit or berry (allspice, nutmeg, pepper) and buds (cloves) of perennial plants that usually grow in the tropics. (See Spice Seasoners.) You can buy whole and ground spices.

Vegetable Spices: Among the best examples of these seasoners are: garlic (dried, powder and salt), green pepper (green pepper flakes), chili peppers, red peppers, cayenne, horseradish, onions (salt, powder, instant minced, instant toasted and shredded green), powdered mushrooms and paprika. (The fresh vegetables are excellent seasoners when available.)

Paprika, because of its bright color and mild flavor, makes a decorative garnish. Hungarian cooks use paprika to add zip to many of their famous dishes. The paprika in their kitchens has more "bite" than the kind in our cupboards. You can make paprika, similar to the Hungarian kind, by adding a dash of red pepper or cayenne to the mild American variety.

Seasonings: This is a general name for blends of spices and/or herbs and/or seeds and/or salt. Usually experts make the blend for a special purpose, but clever women find many uses for each blend. Examples of these blends are: chili powder, curry powder, poultry seasoning, Italian seasoning, pumpkin pie spice, apple pie spice, shrimp spice and barbecue spice. These blends are timesavers, for they cut down on measuring.

How to Treat Spices and Dried Herbs in Your Kitchen

• Store spices and dried herbs away from heat and light in a dry place to cut down on flavor losses. Never store near the range. Keep lids on containers when not in use. If you live in a warm or humid climate, store paprika and pepper blends, like chili powder, in the refrigerator.

· Jot down date of purchase on packages of spices and dried herbs. Time destroys their color, flavor and aroma. Herbs usually lose flavor faster than spices. Whole spices hold their flavor almost indefinitely. Ground spices and herbs need to be replenished once or twice a year even if you have to discard some unused portions. Smell them. If the scent has disappeared, spices and herbs have lost their value.

· Use whole spices in slow long-cooking stews and other dishes. Add them at the beginning of the cooking so the simmering can extract their full flavor and aroma. Add ground spices to cooked foods about 15 minutes before serving time.

· If you do not use dried herbs fast, buy the leaf form and crush before using. The flavor and aroma last longer when the leaves are whole and are sealed tightly.

Country Herb Gardens

Herb growing fascinates many farm women. It's a hobby they enjoy. The plants perfume the breezes, form attractive backgrounds for blossoms in flower arrangements and contribute enchanting tastes to many dishes.

Herbs are among a hostess's best friends. They give her a chance to serve foods that have an elusive something that makes them special.

"Bouquets of pink sweetheart roses and perky sprays of mint and lemon balm, on the tables at a luncheon party," says a country woman, "intrigued me so much that I decided to start an herb garden. My venture was a success. Every year I use more kinds of the aromatic leaves in my cooking. Added wisely, and that means sparingly, they provide interesting flavors and scents."

What grows in country herb gardens? Here are some of the most praised plants that FARM JOURNAL readers cultivate, along with some of of the ways they use the leaves to season foods. You'll notice that many recipes in this cookbook list herbs among the ingredients.

ABC List of Country Garden Herbs and Vegetable Spices —Ways to Use Them

Basil, Sweet and Bush: The flavor of the leaves is delicate, faintly suggestive of cloves. "Tomato herb" is one name for basil. Use it to season tomato juice, salad and other tomato dishes. Since basil is a mild herb, you can add it a little more generously than many others. You can experiment with it. This herb gives character to spaghetti sauces, macaroni and cheese and French dressing.

Burnet: Its faint cucumber taste improves green salads.

Chervil: The leaves, which are beautiful and fernlike, taste somewhat like anise, but are slightly peppery. They're excellent in potato, chicken, egg and green salads. They add a subtle, delicious flavor to vegetable soups.

Chives: Chopped chives sprinkled on dairy sour cream or whipped cream cheese mixed with dairy sour cream are a favorite baked potato go-with. The herb has a mild onion taste that also contributes flavor to most vegetable soups and cottage and cream cheese.

Garlic Chives: For a change, substitute this herb, which has a mild garlic flavor, for regular chives.

Dill: This herb does wonders for cheese dips, tomato and chicken soups, cottage cheese, creamed chicken, cucumber, potato and cabbage salads, cream sauce for fish and tartar sauce. It's excellent sprinkled on lamb and cooked beets.

Lemon Balm: As its name suggests, this herb has a strong lemon flavor. It's marvelous in iced tea and cold fruit drinks.

Lovage: The leaves have a pronounced celery taste. Toss a few of them in green and other salads, such as tuna and potato. Add them to soups and any dish where a suggestion of the celery flavor is good.

Sweet Marjoram: Here's the herb with hundreds of kitchen uses. It's good in potato soup, stuffings for turkey, hot cheese dishes, scrambled eggs, peas, carrots, scalloped potatoes, coleslaw and broccoli, to name a few. Season roast beef and lamb with it. The flavor is piquant and the leaves are fragrant.

Mint: Peppermint and spearmint are the two kinds of mint that grow most commonly in country gardens. The leaves have a refreshing taste most acceptable in fruit salads, compotes and drinks—also in tea, both hot and cold.

Parsley: This decorative herb needs no introduction. It's a top-ranking garnish. But it also adds tastiness to vegetable soups, cottage cheese, chicken, egg and green salads. Snip the leaves fine with scissors for chopped parsley.

Peppergrass: A very few of the strong, peppery leaves add interest to green salads. Use with a light hand.

Roquette: The leaves taste like peanuts. Chop and mix a few of them into mayonnaise and spread on bread for distinctive sandwiches.

Rosemary: While this herb grows best in Southern gardens, it makes an ideal potted plant on sunny window sills. If used sparingly in cooking, it has a remarkably good flavor. Sprinkle it on chicken and lamb before roasting; use it to season beans and peas. The leaves impart superior flavor to many soups. And do add a little rosemary to fat when French-frying potatoes.

Sage: All women who cook know the flavor of this herb is positive. While sage is much enjoyed as a seasoning for pork, try it also in cheese spreads for sandwiches and for poultry stuffings. Many women like to add a bit of sage to chicken casseroles and to breads, such as biscuits, to serve with chicken or pork. Some country women call sage the "sausage seasoning."

Sorrel, French: The young, rather tart leaves perk up green salads.

Summer Savory: This is the savory that also comes dried in packages for year-round sale. (Winter savory has stronger flavor.) Its nickname is "the bean herb." That's because it deliciously seasons fresh, frozen and dried beans. When making bean salads, a dash of savory adds an extra-special taste. Savory also is a pleasing seasoning for chicken soup and scrambled eggs.

Tarragon: Its characteristic, fresh taste is slightly like that of licorice or anise. Toss a few leaves in the green salad and add them, chopped, to mayonnaise for fish salads. Tarragon gets top billing as a seasoner for chicken casseroles, beets, peas, egg and tomato dishes. Fold a few leaves into shrimp salad for a gourmet touch. Vinegar, flavored with tarragon, is a prime favorite in many kitchens, especially where Creole cooking is the rule. One New Orleans custom is to sprinkle broiled fish, just before serving, with a few drops of tarragon vinegar.

Thyme: Whenever possible, add this moderately strong-flavored herb the last 10 minutes of the cooking period. A dash of thyme is tasty in stuffings for fish, chicken and meat dishes. Sprinkle it sparingly over fish chowders and oyster stew just before serving. Add it to cream soups, green salads, tomatoes, peas and carrots.

Dried Herbs in Packages

Women who do not have herb gardens, as well as some who do, use them dried, from packages available in supermarkets. Among the herbs listed in Country Garden Herbs that are available nationally in dried form are: basil, chervil, marjoram, mint, parsley, rosemary, sage, savory, tarragon and thyme.

Some of the herbs popular in our kitchens do not grow commonly in our country herb gardens. Here are the important omissions.

Bay Leaf: These leaves of a laurel that grows in Mediterranean coun-

tries are a favorite addition to stews, pot roast gravy, soups, fish, poultry and practically all meats. Good cooks use them often, but with discretion, because their flavor is pronounced.

Filé: Powdered, dried sassafras leaves are important in Creole cooking, especially in Louisiana, where they answer to the name gumbo filé. They thicken and flavor soups (gumbos) and were introduced to early settlers by the Indian squaws, who seasoned foods with them for centuries.

Orégano: This herb is also called the "pizza herb." That's because good cooks sprinkle it over pizzas for the final touch of flavor. It enhances all tomato and many egg and cheese dishes. Do use it sparingly, for it has a potent flavor. Add a dash of orégano to hamburgers, chili con carne, spaghetti sauce, lamb stews and the melted butter to pour over sea food. It's an excellent seasoner for dried beans, broccoli and cabbage. And it's good on pork and lamb roasts. Rub leg of lamb with a cut clove of garlic and sprinkle on a little orégano before roasting. The Spanish explorers brought orégano, a Mediterranean herb, to Mexico, where it now grows wild. South of the border it's often called Mexican sage.

Make Your Own Herb Combinations

Fines Herbes: Among the fresh herbs good cooks usually combine are parsley, tarragon, basil, chervil, rosemary and bay leaf. Chop each herb separately, combine them and sprinkle over stews, soups, omelets and many other dishes just before serving. Parsley, chives and chervil are a favored trio.

Bouquet Garni: This is the name given to assorted herbs, fresh or dried, tied together in a small cheesecloth bag and dropped into stews, soups, chicken fricassee and other dishes. Discard the herbs after cooking. Parsley, marjoram, thyme and bay leaf are a good combination. For lamb stew, try a thyme and bay leaf and a whole clove.

How to Use Fresh and Dried Herbs

• Beware of overseasoning. Start out adding very small quantities, a pinch for 4 servings. Add more the next time if you like. A general rule is to allow ¼ tsp. dried herbs to 4 servings of a food, more if the herbs are fresh. The common ratio is: three times as much chopped fresh as dried herbs, which have more intense flavors.

• Measure dried herbs and then crush them in your hand before adding to food you are seasoning.

• Avoid overcooking fresh and dried herbs. Add them, when possible, to such foods as soups and stews, during the last 45 minutes of cooking. Add them to salad dressings, fruits and juices an hour or longer before serving to give the flavors time to blend.

• Experiment. One good way to do this is to use some of the recipes in this cookbook that call for herbs. They've been tested and approved by a critical taste panel.

How to Freeze Fresh Herbs

Herb gardeners select young lush sprays of herbs and freeze them to save trips to the garden when in a hurry, and for winter use. Here is the way to freeze and use them.

• Dip herbs in and out of cold water to wash; then blanch them in boiling water 10 seconds—no longer. Plunge them immediately into ice water to chill quickly. Pat dry with paper towels.

• Seal enough of an herb, or a mixture of herbs, for special recipes in aluminum foil packages or in small freezer bags (the same kind of herb or mixture of herbs in each packet). Label, place in a large plastic bag and freeze.

• To use, snip unthawed herbs with scissors into the dish they are to season.

ABC List of Seed Seasoners —Ways to Use Them

Anise: These seeds taste something like licorice. Stir them into the dry ingredients for sugar cookies; add a touch of grated lemon peel for a treat. Add them to cakes, sweet rolls and Swedish rye bread. Sprinkle a few seeds over fruit salads, cups and compotes.

Caraway: These savory seeds are an important ingredient in many rye breads. They're also good in cabbage salads, pickled beets, cooked cabbage and sauerkraut. Many country women like to add a few seeds to cooked turnips. Surprisingly, they're a happy addition to apple pie filling.

Cardamom: That marvelous flavor of true Danish pastry comes from these seeds, ground. Ground cardamom also pleasingly flavors many coffee cakes and cookies. A touch of it enhances grape jelly. Try Swedish Cardamom Toast for a change. Make it like Cinnamon Toast, but use ground cardamom instead of cinnamon, ¼ tsp. to ½ c. sugar. Cardamom seeds are included in all curry powder. You can buy ground or whole seeds.

Celery: The tiny seeds are from a plant that grows mainly in France and India; it is different from our vegetable by the same name. Use the whole seeds in tomato juice, potato salad, cheese dishes, salad dressings, sauces, soups, stews, meat loaves, cheese and egg dishes. When ground, the seeds are mixed with salt and sold as celery salt.

Coriander: Some people think these seeds taste like a mixture of lemon peel and sage. Add whole seeds to Spanish rice; add ground seeds to apple desserts, gingerbread, buns, cookies and cakes. They're an excellent seasoning for scrambled eggs.

Cumin: It's the salty, sweet taste that makes these seeds popular in kitchens. They are an important ingredient in chili powders. Use the whole seeds in chili con carne, tamales, soups, meat and rice dishes. The ground seeds add a tasty note to deviled eggs (mixed in the yolks), hamburgers and cheese spreads. Dust ground cumin over cooked rice just before serving for an extra-special taste.

Dill: Seeds of the dill plant are sold only in the whole form. They are excellent in pickles, rye and pumper-nickel breads, beet soup (borsch), potato salad, cucumber salad, cheese spreads and dips, sauerkraut, cabbage, broccoli, turnips, cauliflower, tomato dishes, cottage cheese and spaghetti. Many women sprinkle a few seeds over coleslaw and potato salad for a final touch of flavor. Scatter a few seeds over lamb chops near the end of the broiling; add them to apple pie filling for an unusual taste delight.

Fennel: These seeds taste something like anise or licorice. Sprinkle them over apple pie filling, on top of sea food and chicken casseroles, green salads, baked fish, cooked potatoes, onions and cabbage. Scatter a few seeds on the roast duck. Only the whole seeds are available in markets.

Mustard: You can buy the seeds in three forms: whole, powdered (ground) and in a sauce (prepared mustard). Add whole seeds to cabbage, coleslaw, sauerkraut, relishes, potato salad and pickles. Ground seeds add zip to soups, egg, cheese (macaroni and cheese) and sea food dishes, and salad dressings for fruits and vegetables. Add a smidgen of prepared mustard to cheese sauce to give it a flavor lift.

Poppy: The fragrant, blue-black seeds have a delicate, nut-like flavor. Sprinkle them on breads, coffee cakes and rolls. Add them to buttered noodles and soups. (Many women cook the seeds in butter until the butter turns a light golden brown before adding them to cooked noodles, cabbage, new potatoes, carrots, summer squash, green beans and fish. The cooking develops their flavor.) Poppy seed cake is a favorite in many homes. (See recipe in Index.)

Sesame: Toasting sesame seeds develops their almond or nut-like flavor. You can use them, when toasted, in almost any recipe in place of nuts. Always toast them before adding them to batters and doughs, sprinkling them on cooked noodles or green salads. To toast them, spread the seeds in a shallow baking pan and bake in a moderate oven (350°) until they turn a pale brown, about 20 minutes. Sprinkle untoasted seeds (the form in which you buy them) on sugar cookies and bake. The seeds have a crisp, crunchy texture when browned. Sprinkle them untoasted on any food that will brown during cooking, such as: crumb-topped chicken casseroles, buns and breads. Sesame seeds are a great seasoner in Oriental dishes, especially in cookies and candies.

Spice Seasoners—Ways to Use Them

Allspice: The only spice native to the Western Hemisphere, allspice tastes like a blend of cinnamon, nutmeg and cloves. Use the whole spice in pickle making, gravies, meat and fish dishes; the ground spice in cakes, cookies, pudding, *especially plum pudding,* relishes, tomato sauce, mincemeat, pumpkin pie, etc. Sprinkle a dash of it on fruit salad. Add ¼ tsp. allspice and ¼ tsp. nutmeg to yellow cake batter. Makes a truly delicious cake.

Cinnamon: There are hundreds of ways to use this spice. Cinnamon sticks make flavorful stirrers for hot chocolate, cocoa, tea, punch and coffee. Add the sticks when cooking spiced, fresh and dried fruits—espe-

cially tasty with prunes. Add the ground spice to baked apple dishes; combine with sugar for cinnamon toast. Sprinkle lightly on pineapple dishes, bananas and grapefruit. Season cakes, cookies, puddings and apple pie with cinnamon—and add a touch of it to pastry for apple pie. Stir a little of this favorite spice into chocolate cake batter. And do try cinnamon ice cream on sliced or baked peaches, baked apples and apple crisps. To make it, blend 1 tsp. ground cinnamon into 1 qt. vanilla ice cream and freeze.

Cassia buds are from a type of cinnamon native to China. They're wonderful in sweet pickles, but are now in scarce supply.

Cloves: Cloves are the most fragrant of all spices. Use the nail-shaped flower buds, the whole spice, to decorate and season baked ham and pork roasts. Stick a few in a whole onion and bake in the pot with dried beans or cook with chili con carne. Add the ground spice to baked foods, chocolate pudding, beets, potato soup and stews. Sprinkle it on broiled grapefruit halves and season all sweet yellow vegetables with it—sweet potatoes, for instance; also pumpkin and winter squash. Cloves make cranberry juice cocktail something special. But always *use this spice with a light hand,* for it is pungent.

Ginger: The root of an Oriental, lily-like plant, ginger is one of the world's greatest spices. It comes whole and ground. Use the whole spice in pickling solution when making spiced fruits. Cook whole ginger at least a half hour to obtain its best flavors. (It's the whole root that is candied.) Use the ground spice in cakes, cookies and gingerbread. Add it to stews, pot roasts and chicken and fish dishes. Sprinkle a little ground ginger on cold melon just before serving, on grapefruit halves, but chill them before serving. Add a few shakes of it to apple and prune juices. Ginger gives a touch of mystery to macaroni and cheese, many other cheese dishes, chicken casseroles and carrots. Sprinkle a suggestion of the spice on fried and baked chicken. And stir a dash of it into applesauce.

Mace: Mace is the dried pulp around nutmeg seeds; it tastes much like nutmeg, although its flavor is more potent. Use this sweet but warm and spicy ground spice discreetly in chicken fricassee. Add a dash to cherry pie filling and vanilla pudding. *It's the perfect spice for pound cake.* Stir mace into whipped cream for dessert toppings. Sprinkle it over canned cherries and other fruits to step up flavor. It's lighter in color than nutmeg. Use it instead of nutmeg when brown nutmeg flecks are undesirable. Team it with grated lemon peel in flavoring sugar cookies.

Nutmeg: Certainly this was the favorite spice of old-time cooks, who grated the nuts. Today, the convenient ground spice is almost universally used. Sprinkle it on baked custards, custard pie, cooked cabbage, cauliflower and spinach. Scatter a little on eggnog. Add to whipped cream toppings for dessert and to rice for custard-type puddings. Follow the custom of Swedish cooks and add a pinch of it to meat balls and creamed spinach—just a suggestion of the spice. Slice bananas, pour on light cream and dust with nutmeg for a pleasing dessert. Perk up rhubarb pie

filling and stewed rhubarb with a bit of nutmeg.

Pepper: This is the world's most popular spice; it has thousands of uses in the kitchen. It comes in three forms: whole, cracked (coarsely ground) and ground. Add the whole berries, called peppercorns, to stews and soup stocks, the cracked pepper to salads. An increasing number of women use pepper mills to grind peppercorns instead of using packaged ground pepper. The flavor is different. Black and white peppercorns grow on the same vines. The black berries are picked before they are quite ripe, the white ones ripen before they are gathered. Black pepper has the stronger flavor. Use ground white pepper when black dots of pepper are not desirable.

Saffron: This is the world's most costly spice. It consists of handpicked pistils of crocus blossoms and it takes thousands of dried flowers to make a quarter pound of saffron. Use it sparingly, just a few strands to give rice dishes yellow color, flavor and aroma. Some nationalities add saffron to breads, rolls and cakes, but few American cooks use it in baking. Be sure to rub the strands before adding saffron to rice or other foods.

Turmeric: A root of the ginger family, turmeric has a mild but slightly bitter taste. It's an important seasoner for curries, mustard pickles and mustard sauce (prepared mustard). A dash of it is good in creamed and scrambled eggs, corned beef hash and with lamb. Add a trace of it to the yolks of deviled eggs and to chicken and potato salads. Because it is used in making prepared mustard, people say turmeric tastes like mustard.

Seasoning with Butter

The taste of butter, as country cooks know so well, is a treat—especially in cakes, cookies and frostings. You can buy butter flavoring, but farm women use the yellow pats or sticks from the refrigerator. Butter is the prime flavoring for salted, cooked vegetables. To butter a hot vegetable, add from 1 to 3 tblsp. butter for every 2 c. vegetable. It's the clever woman who combines the butter flavor with other seasoners to give her cooked vegetable dishes, fish and meats distinctive flavor overtones. Here are some examples:

Brown Butter Sauces for Vegetables: Pass these sauces in a small pitcher for guests to pour over cooked vegetables. Melt ¼ c. butter to light golden brown and add the following:
• Celery—Stir in 1 tsp. celery seeds. Good on potatoes and carrots.
• Cheese—Stir in 2 tblsp. grated Parmesan cheese. Pour over broiled or fried fish, cooked cauliflower, parsnips or peas.
• Garlic—Stir in 1 small clove garlic, cut in half. Let stand a few minutes in a warm place. Remove garlic before serving. Good on fish and most vegetables.
• Horse-radish—Stir in 1 tblsp. prepared horse-radish. Excellent on beets.
• Lemon-Chive—Add grated peel of ½ lemon, 2 tblsp. lemon juice, 1 tblsp. finely snipped chives and ⅛ tsp. each of salt and pepper. Serve over hot boiled new potatoes (enough for 6 potatoes).

Drawn Butter Sauce: Melt ¼ c. butter. Combine 2 tblsp. flour, ½ tsp. salt, ⅛ tsp. paprika and ⅛ tsp. cayenne; stir into butter to make a smooth paste. Add 1 c. cold water. Stir and cook until sauce thickens. Remove from heat. Stir in 1 tsp. lemon juice. Serve on broiled or fried fish and green vegetables.

VARIATIONS

• Lemon-Parsley—Add 1 tblsp. lemon juice and 1 tblsp. snipped parsley to Drawn Butter Sauce.
• Olive—Add ¼ c. finely chopped pimiento-stuffed olives to Drawn Butter Sauce.
• Egg-Chive—Add 1 c. chopped hard-cooked egg and 1 tblsp. finely snipped chives to Drawn Butter Sauce

Mustard Butter: To melted butter add a dash of dry mustard and spread over hot, sizzling steaks.

Blue Cheese Butter: Mash crumbled blue cheese with butter and add a few drops of Worcestershire sauce. Spread on hot steaks just out of the broiler.

Crumb Sauce: Combine ½ c. fine, dry bread crumbs and ¼ c. butter. Heat and stir until crumbs are a light golden brown. Spoon over top of hot, cooked and salted cabbage, cauliflower, asparagus, green beans, onions and other vegetables.

Black Butter: Heat ⅓ c. butter until it froths and turns golden brown. Add 1 tblsp. lemon juice and ⅛ tsp. salt. Serve at once on hot cooked carrots, green beans or cabbage.

Honey Butter: Whip ½ c. (¼ lb.) soft butter until light and fluffy.

Gradually add ¼ c. honey; beat until smooth. Stir in 1 to 1½ tsp. grated orange peel if you like. Serve over cooked beets or carrots and on waffles and pancakes.

Almond Butter Sauce: Sauté ¼ c. chopped almonds in ¼ c. butter to a light golden brown. Add ¼ tsp. salt and 2 tsp. lemon juice. Serve over hot grilled or fried fish, cooked green beans or other green vegetables.

Cashew Nut Butter: Sauté ¼ c. chopped cashew nuts in ¼ c. butter until light golden brown. Toss with cooked green beans.

Seasoning with Cream

Along with butter, country women depend on cream—both sweet and sour—to flavor foods deliciously. Many cooks like to add heavy cream to cooked vegetables without thickening it. It's the ideal taste dress-up for peas, tiny new potatoes and many other vegetables.

Dairy sour cream is gaining popularity in farm kitchens, now that it's widely available. It adds a zesty flavor to many dishes. Here are a few simple directions to heed when using it:

Handle dairy sour cream with care to maintain its smooth texture; overstirring may thin it. Heat but do not boil it—it curdles if it gets too hot. You'll notice that many recipes in this cookbook specify that you add sour cream at the last minute, just before you serve the hot dish in which it is an ingredient.

Don't be upset if dairy sour cream

becomes thin when you add it to sauces and salad dressings that contain lemon juice, vinegar or other acid foods. It thickens again when refrigerated.

You can whip dairy sour cream just as you do heavy sweet cream. It takes about 5 minutes. The cream thins out at first, and it never gets as thick as whipped sweet cream. It doubles in volume.

Sour Cream-Horse-radish Glaze: Add 1 tsp. drained prepared horse-radish to 1 c. dairy sour cream. Spread over beef pot roast when it is browned and tender. Return to oven 3 to 5 minutes to form a glaze on the meat.

Sour Cream with Chives: Spoon 1 tblsp. or more dairy sour cream on the openings in baked potatoes. Sprinkle on finely snipped chives, green onion or parsley. (If you add the chives, onion or parsley to the sour cream, it may become thin.)

Seasoning with Cheese

The three kinds of cheese that American women like best in their cooking are: Cheddar, grated Parmesan and process cheese and spreads. Swiss cheese also is a seasoning favorite in some dishes, such as the classic fondue. For uncooked dishes, cream cheese is a blue ribbon selection and blue cheese has an enthusiastic following. See Index for natural cheeses that are fast becoming dessert favorites on their own, following European custom. Remember that their flavor is best when you serve them at room temperature rather than chilled.

Staple Seasoners—Ways to Use Them

Salt: Though every cook knows the value of this, the No. 1 seasoner, there are far too many dishes that get to the table undersalted or oversalted. Measure the correct amount as given in the recipe instead of shaking it in—and always taste before serving. Seasoned or seasoning salt, which is a blend of salt, spices and herbs, also comes in shakers. Try it.

Sugar: A touch of sweetness improves the flavor of many foods. Add ½ tsp. sugar to gravy and 1 tsp. or more to vegetables, like tomatoes, green peas and sauerkraut. Use just enough to bring out the natural sweetness of vegetables.

Monosodium Glutamate: This white, crystalline substance boosts the natural flavors of foods; it has no flavor of its own. Chinese cooks use it in their finest dishes. Add it before or during cooking. Some suggested amounts are: 1 tsp. per chicken, 1 tsp. per lb. of ground beef, ½ tsp. per lb. of roast meats, ½ tsp. sprinkled on each side of large steaks and 1 tsp. for 6 servings vegetables.

Honey: A few drops or spoonfuls of honey give delightful flavor to many dishes—salad dressings, carrots, squash and other vegetables, for instance. Notice how frequently honey appears in the list of ingredients in this cookbook; that's because it's a country favorite.

Molasses: The tangy taste of molasses in cakes, cookies, candies, puddings, baked beans and many other dishes rates high in country kitchens.

Corn Syrup: It is convenient to add when you want to give a food, such as cooked vegetables (corn, tomatoes and peas) a touch of sweetness.

Maple and Maple-Blended Syrups: These sweeteners are delightful poured over ice creams and the whipped cream on pumpkin pies. They flavor and sweeten candies, frostings and many other confections.

Vinegar: Cider vinegar is a faithful standby, but don't stop with it. Try the flavored varieties—malt, tarragon (fragrant with the herb), wine (made with table wine), garlic-wine (wine vinegar with garlic added), basil, mixed herb and spice vinegars, to name a few. Use tarragon vinegar with fish, chicken and meats and in salad dressings; garlic vinegar with spinach and cooked greens, and in pickled beets. Many good cooks make salad dressings with basil vinegar to serve over tomatoes.

Some FARM JOURNAL readers with herb gardens make fresh herb vinegars. One woman does it this way: Combine 1 c. coarsely chopped tarragon leaves, ½ c. sugar and 2 c. cider vinegar in a saucepan. Stir and heat mixture over high heat until sugar dissolves; then stir and bring mixture to a boil over medium heat. Pour this into a hot sterilized pint jar and adjust cap as the manufacturer directs. Store this vinegar in a cool, dry place at least a month or 6 weeks before using. You can make dill vinegar the same way, substituting 2 sprigs fresh dill for the tarragon—it's a good potato salad vinegar.

Flavorings—Ways to Use Them

Flavoring Extracts: Along with the trio of great favorites, vanilla, almond and lemon extracts, there's a wide selection of flavorings you can keep in your kitchen. Take a look on the shelves in your supermarket—you'll find extracts of cherry, orange, peppermint, pineapple, wintergreen and many others. When you have a collection of them in your kitchen, be sure to keep the bottles closed tightly to retain the flavors. And when possible, add flavoring extracts to cooled, rather than hot, foods for best results. Experiment with combinations of flavoring extracts to get intriguing tastes—vanilla and almond, orange and almond, orange and lemon, peppermint and vanilla (for chocolate cakes). One FARM JOURNAL reader says she likes to flavor fudge cake with ¼ tsp. peppermint extract and 1 to 1½ tsp. vanilla. She uses orange extract or half-and-half orange and almond extracts in coconut cakes, and almond extract in orange cake.

Grated Orange and Lemon Peels: A touch of orange peel improves most dishes that call for orange extract, grated lemon peel improves those that specify lemon extract. The peels give a fresh orange or lemon taste. But these grated peels, along with lime peel, are flavorings in their own right. Orange peel, for instance, is wonderful in cooked beets and sweet potatoes.

Maraschino Cherry Juice: Tints foods, such as cake frostings and angel food cake, a gorgeous pink and provides interesting flavor.

Sherry, Rum and Brandy Flavorings: Cooking sherry contains considerable salt, which means you need to reduce the amount of salt in a recipe that was not designed for the addition of the sherry. Sherry, rum and brandy flavorings are unsalted—they are pure flavorings. They're festive flavors for desserts and other dishes.

Imitation Extracts: Some of the imitation flavorings available are banana, black walnut, cherry, coconut, maple, peach, pineapple, raspberry and strawberry flavors.

Wine: The European custom of flavoring dishes with wine is on the increase in kitchens on this side of the Atlantic. While the food cooks, the alcohol in the wine evaporates, leaving the wine flavor. Some recipes in this cookbook list wine with the ingredients, but we also give alternates.

Specialty Seasoners, Bottled and Packaged —Ways to Use Them

Instant Coffee: Add this brown powder to obtain the coffee taste in a jiffy. Try it in whipped cream for topping desserts, in confectioners sugar frostings and for flavoring gingerbread and cake.

Candied Ginger: Chop it and sprinkle over whipped cream on top of gingerbread, pumpkin pie, baked apples and any dessert in which the ginger taste pleases. We know an adventuresome cook who adds a little chopped candied ginger to biscuits she makes to serve with chicken.

Flavored Instant Tenderizer: This powder seasons as well as tenderizes the less tender meats and poultry. Follow label directions when you use it on meats, poultry and game birds. It also cuts down on shrinkage and the cooking time. Since it is salty, do not add salt to meats and poultry you tenderize.

Bottled Meat Sauces: In addition to your own canned sauces, there are many kinds on market shelves. Try using them. Here are a few that you'll find mentioned in our recipes: Tabasco, ketchup, chili sauce, thick steak sauce and Worcestershire.

Bottled Barbecue Sauce and Hickory-Smoke-Flavored Sauces: These sauces add exciting flavors to many foods, like hamburgers, frankfurters, stews, meat loaves, fish dishes, meats, poultry and sea food.

Sauce Mixes: Use these products as labels on envelopes direct. (You add milk, water or other liquid to them and heat.) They are expertly seasoned and are quick to use. Among our favorites are: gravy mixes, cheese, curry, sour cream, white, meat loaf, a la king, chili, stroganoff and spaghetti sauces.

Canned Tomato Sauce: Many recipes in this cookbook call for this sauce.

It is comparatively inexpensive and has fine flavor. It's made with ripe tomatoes and seasonings of salt, spices and herbs. And it's a great time-saver.

Canned White Sauce: Some markets carry this sauce, along with canned hollandaise and cheese sauces. Just a turn of the can opener and they are ready to use.

Canned Condensed Soups and Soup Mixes: While these often end up in soup bowls, they also are the base for many sauces now made in country kitchens. You thin the condensed soup with water, milk or other liquid to the desired consistency and heat. The result is a smooth, flavorful sauce. Notice the many recipes in this cookbook in which these soups appear. The mixes also are wonderful seasoners. Just sprinkle them in the dish you are fixing or rub them over meats before cooking.

Salad Dressing Mixes: Envelopes of mixes, beautifully seasoned, make superior salad dressings when you shake them with water and vinegar and then with salad oil. There are many kinds, such as garlic, Italian, blue cheese, Parmesan and cheese-garlic. Some good cooks sprinkle the dry mixes directly on food to season it— the garlic mix on chicken for frying and on sliced tomatoes instead of salad dressing.

Bottled Salad Dressings: Use them on salads, of course, but also to flavor meats and poultry. For instance, brush fish and beef steaks with French dressing before broiling.

CHAPTER 2

HEARTY MAIN DISHES

Country women know that main dishes are the focus around which to build good company meals. They decide on them first when planning menus, knowing that their husbands and guests frequently judge the success of a meal by the tenderness and taste of the meat. Farmers are meat eaters and they know top quality when they cut into it and taste.

Roasts are so popular that along with new recipes, like Country-Style Beef Wellington, a beef roast in a pastry jacket, this chapter also gives directions for basic perfect beef roasts. Our Glazed Pork Roast, golden and glistening with apricot glaze, is a FARM JOURNAL special. Our Marinated Lamb and Veal Stew with Dumplings win compliments.

You'll notice that many of the meat and poultry dishes are the type that take care of themselves in the oven while they cook. What a blessing this is to any woman getting a company meal! Stuffed Pork Pockets and Parmesan Chicken are just two examples. Many recipes in this chapter produce dishes that travel successfully. You'll want to tote them to covered-dish suppers.

We're especially proud of the chicken recipes, many of which are from recipe files in farm kitchens known for good meals. Golden Chicken Casserole is such a dish—offer it at your next buffet supper. Our Roast Young Chickens are as unusual as they are good. You precook them half an hour, cool and freeze. When you take them from the freezer, you put the chickens in a hot oven—an hour later you carry them sizzling and beautifully browned to the table. Our Chicken Pizza has a big following too, especially among young people.

If you think tuna recipes dominate the fish and sea food section, just remember how cans of it in the cupboard guarantee wonderful company dishes on short notice. Do try our tuna recipes—they're special. Taste-testers said of our Shrimp Marengo: "The best shrimp dish I ever ate." Our delicious fish sauces add a gourmet touch to the fish platter.

The guests you have when you serve dishes made from the main-dish recipes in this chapter will be lucky.

Roast Beef for Company

Plan a guest meal around a standing rib beef roast and you'll have a head start in popularity. Everyone likes it. And it's simple to get ready and to cook. If you select a large roast you may be lucky enough to have leftovers to make our special Beef Stroganoff (see Index for recipe).

We give you three recipes for roast beef, the classic standing rib, today's country version of Beef Wellington and Tender Sirloin Tip. The Duke of Wellington's chef, according to historians, wrapped roasted beef tenderloin, spread with liver pâté, in pastry and baked it for the English general's victory dinner after Waterloo. You'll also like it in your celebration dinners.

For filling sandwiches, we team roast sirloin tip slices with big crusty rolls. How men like them!

BEEF-EATERS' FAVORITE ROAST

Watch men's pleased expression when they see this big, tender roast on the table

1 (3-rib) standing rib roast,
   about 8 lbs.

• Stand roast, fat side up, on a rack in a shallow pan. Add no water. Insert roast-meat thermometer into center of roast, making sure point rests on meat, not in or on fat, gristle or bone.
• Roast uncovered in a slow oven (325°) until thermometer registers the doneness you like (140° for rare,

160° for medium and 170° for well-done meat). Time estimates are not accurate, but are a guide. It takes from 3½ to 5 hours for an 8-lb., 3-rib roast that measures 6″ from tip of rib to backbone. (A longer cut roasts in less time.)
• When the thermometer registers 5 to 10 degrees lower than the desired temperature you want, remove the roast from the oven. Place it on a large warm platter with the broader cut surface down. The cooking will continue to the right temperature while you handle the last-minute details before dinner. The meat "sets" and carves easier.
• To serve, place the roast in front of the carver with the ribs to his left and the rib ends pointing toward him.
• Slice as desired. For big, king-size servings, cut so each rib makes 1 serving and the meat between two ribs makes 2 servings, or 7 servings in all; or slice thinly for 16 average-size servings.

Note: You can sprinkle the roast with salt, pepper and monosodium glutamate before cooking, but the seasonings do not penetrate the meat.

TENDER SIRLOIN TIP ROAST

Several thin slices of this roast in a big crusty roll make a sandwich hard to surpass. Serve with relishes

1 (4 lb.) sirloin tip roast
Seasoned instant meat tenderizer

• Sprinkle the roast with tenderizer as the label directs. Then cook it like

Beef-Eaters' Favorite Roast (standing rib). It takes about 2¼ hours for a 4-lb. sirloin tip to roast rare, 2¾ hours for medium and 3¼ hours for well-done meat. The temperatures, if you use a roast-meat thermometer, are 140° for rare, 160° for medium and 170° for well-done.
• Serve warm or cold. If you wish to serve the roast cold in sandwiches, cook it a day ahead, cool and chill without slicing.
• When ready to make sandwiches, slice the cold meat very thin and place it in large buttered crusty rolls. The thinner you slice it, the tenderer the meat seems. Makes enough for 8 generously filled sandwiches.

COUNTRY-STYLE BEEF WELLINGTON

Company-special roast beef in a crust—roast the meat a day ahead. See photo elsewhere in this book

6 to 8 lb.	whole tenderloin of beef (fold rib end under sirloin), or 5 lb. center cut of filet, or 6 lb. rib eye roast
1	(4 oz.) can mushrooms, drained and finely chopped
½ c.	finely chopped onion
2 tblsp.	melted butter
1	(8 oz.) pkg. liverwurst
3 c.	sifted flour
1 tsp.	salt
3 tblsp.	chopped parsley
1½ tsp.	celery seeds
⅔ c.	shortening
½ c. plus 2 tblsp.	cold water
1	egg, slightly beaten

• Tie meat securely if you use a folded filet. Insert meat thermometer into center of meat; roast uncovered in slow oven (325°) until thermometer reaches 140° (rare). Cool, wrap and refrigerate.
• Next day, sauté mushrooms and onion in butter until onion is tender. Combine with liverwurst, and mix. Chill until ready to use.
• To make crust, mix flour, salt, parsley and celery seeds. Cut in shortening until mixture is consistency of tiny peas. Sprinkle on cold water, 1 tblsp. at a time, tossing mixture lightly with a fork.
• Shape dough into a ball and roll out in a rectangle about ⅛" thick, measuring 2" wider than the length of the roast, 2" longer than its circumference. Save pastry scraps.
• Remove strings from cold roast. Pat liverwurst mixture on roast, covering top and sides only.
• Place roast, coated side down, on pastry rectangle. Fold up pastry to meet along center top and ends. Trim off extra pastry, moisten edges and press together firmly to seal well.
• Place pastry-covered roast, sealed edges down (pâté side is now turned up), in a greased shallow pan.
• Roll pastry scraps and cut out 3 flowers, 3 leaves and 3 stems. Brush pieces with beaten egg and seal to top of roast in an attractive design. Brush entire surface with beaten egg; prick with a fork.
• Bake in moderate oven (375°) 1 hour, or until crust is golden brown. Remove roast from pan; let stand 15 minutes before carving. Makes about 12 servings.

CALIFORNIA POT ROAST

Tastes and looks different from most pot roasts—it always wins praises

4 to 5 lb. chuck or rump pot roast
3 tblsp. fat or salad oil
2 tsp. salt
¼ tsp. pepper
½ c. water
1 (8 oz.) can tomato sauce
3 medium onions, thinly sliced
2 cloves garlic, minced
2 tblsp. brown sugar
½ tsp. dry mustard
¼ c. lemon juice
¼ c. vinegar
¼ c. ketchup
1 tblsp. Worcestershire sauce

• Brown roast well on both sides in fat in heavy pan or Dutch oven. Add salt, pepper, water, tomato sauce, onions and garlic. Cover tightly and simmer over low heat about 1½ hours.
• Combine brown sugar, mustard, lemon juice, vinegar, ketchup and Worcestershire sauce and pour over meat. Cover and continue cooking until meat is fork tender, about 1½ hours.
• Remove meat to warm platter; make gravy. Serve roast cut in thin slices with the gravy, or shred the meat and mix it with the gravy to serve on halves of warm buns. Makes 8 to 10 servings.

Gravy: Skim off most of the fat; measure the broth. Add water to make 3 c. Pour in cooking pan or Dutch oven. Mix 6 tblsp. flour with ½ c. water to make a smooth paste; stir into broth. Return to heat and cook over low heat, stirring constantly, until gravy bubbles all over. Check seasonings by tasting, adding more salt if needed. Cook and stir about 5 minutes longer. Makes about 3 cups.

New Carve-Ahead Roasts

Good news for men who dislike to carve roasts at the table with everyone watching! You can roast and carve meats ahead and cover them with sauce. Then all you have to do at mealtime is bake them 10 minutes, or until heated thoroughly. You'll find the meats are juicy and moist—basted with a delectable sauce after carving—and that they're hotter than most just-carved roasts. The host will be free to give extra attention to guests when you eliminate carving.

We give you the recipe here for beef to carve ahead and reheat; elsewhere in this chapter are recipes for Roast Veal or Lamb with Sweet Onions, Deep-Peppered Pork and Roast Duckling in Carrot Sauce (see Index).

BRAISED BEEF IN CREAM

Use plenty of garlic to support beef flavor—two big cloves are just right

1 (4 lb.) boneless pot roast
    (sirloin tip, bottom round,
    rump or chuck)
2 tblsp. shortening (about)
Salt
Pepper
½ c. water
½ c. butter (¼ lb.)
2 c. heavy cream
2 large cloves garlic
4 tblsp. lemon juice
1½ tsp. salt (about)
¾ tsp. pepper (about)
Watercress or parsley (finely
    chopped and sprigs)

• In Dutch oven or heavy casserole with cover, slowly brown meat on all sides in hot shortening. Season generously with salt and pepper. Add water; cover and simmer 2½ to 3 hours, or until meat is tender. Remove from kettle; allow to stand 20 minutes, then slice thinly.

• Pour off pan juices and save for another use. Heat butter in kettle until it bubbles and browns. Add cream, garlic, lemon juice, about 1½ tsp. salt and ¾ tsp. pepper. Cook over medium heat, stirring, about 3 minutes, or until sauce reduces slightly.

• Spoon half the sauce over bottom of a shallow heat-proof serving platter. Arrange meat slices, slightly overlapping, in sauce. Pour remaining sauce over top. Near serving time, bake in moderate oven (350°) 10 minutes, or until heated through. Spoon sauce over meat; sprinkle generously with watercress; garnish with watercress sprigs. Makes about 8 servings.

PANNED STEAK STRIPS

Borrow a trick from the Chinese and cook beef fast over high heat. Get everything ready—then start cooking

1 flank steak (about 1½ lbs.), thinly sliced across the grain into strips no thicker than ⅛″ (slices best when partially frozen)
4 tsp. cornstarch
4 tsp. vinegar
1 tblsp. sugar
½ tsp. salt
¼ tsp. freshly ground pepper
4 slices bacon, cut into thin strips

1 large head iceberg lettuce, or romaine, cut across the head into ½″ thick slices
2 green onions with green tops, thinly sliced
8 very thin slices fresh lemon (with peel), cut into quarters

• Toss steak strips with cornstarch, vinegar, sugar, salt and pepper, and allow to stand 30 minutes.

• In a large skillet, slowly cook bacon until almost crisp; remove bacon from pan, and remove from skillet any bacon fat in excess of 4 tblsp. Heat remaining bacon fat in skillet until very hot.

• Add beef and cook over very high heat for just a few minutes, tossing lightly to stir, just until browned; lift meat from pan.

• Add lettuce, onions and lemon to pan and cook, tossing, for just a minute or two, until barely wilted and tender-crisp.

• Return beef and bacon to skillet and just heat through. Garnish with sliced green onions. Serve immediately. Makes 4 big servings.

Note: You may want to make two skilletfuls for 8 servings.

SWEET-SOUR BEEF

Treat your guests with this Chinese-American supper dish. Serve on rice

1 (1½ to 2 lb.) flank steak, cut in slivers against the grain
¾ c. soy sauce
3 green peppers, cut in narrow strips (about 2 c.)
3 tblsp. salad oil
Juice drained from pineapple

1 (1 lb. 4 oz.) can pineapple
   tidbits, drained
3 tblsp. cornstarch
1 tblsp. soy sauce
3 tblsp. vinegar
6 tblsp. water
½ c. sugar

• Put steak slivers in a shallow dish. Add ¾ c. soy sauce; mix well so all the beef will marinate in the liquid. Allow to stand at least 30 minutes.

• Cook pepper strips in salad oil until limp and glazed; do not overcook. Remove from pan.

• Add beef to skillet in which peppers cooked and cook over high heat, stirring occasionally. Reduce heat to low; add pineapple juice (from tidbits) and cook slowly about 10 minutes. Add pineapple tidbits and peppers.

• Mix together cornstarch, 1 tblsp. soy sauce, vinegar, water and sugar, blending well. Add to meat and cook until sauce thickens, stirring constantly. Serve on cooked rice. Makes 6 to 8 servings, depending on size of the steak.

COMPANY CORNED BEEF

When guests taste this, compliments come easy. Delicious hot or cold

4 to 5 lbs. corned beef
2 bay leaves
5 peppercorns
2 sprigs parsley
1 stalk celery, cut in chunks
1 small onion, sliced
Whole cloves
2 tblsp. butter or margarine
1 tblsp. prepared mustard
⅓ c. brown sugar
⅓ c. ketchup
3 tblsp. vinegar
3 tblsp. water

• Wash corned beef thoroughly to remove brine. Place in a large kettle and cover with cold water. Add bay leaves, peppercorns, parsley, celery and onion. Cover and simmer 3 to 3¾ hours (about 45 minutes to a pound), or until tender.

• Remove hot beef to shallow baking dish. Insert whole cloves in it to decorate and season.

• Melt butter; add remaining ingredients and mix thoroughly. Cook over medium heat until ingredients are well blended.

• Pour sauce over corned beef and bake in moderate oven (350°) 30 minutes, basting with the sauce several times. Serve hot or cold. Makes 8 to 10 servings.

French-Style Beef Specials

From two California home economists, who are homemakers, come recipes for beef flavored with Burgundy wine. During the cooking, the alcohol evaporates, leaving only the mellow flavor of the grapes. If you do not wish to use Burgundy, you can substitute beef bouillon, but the flavor will be different.

These hostess dishes are popular with many women because they are well received by their guests. *And they can be cooked one day, cooled and refrigerated and then reheated the next day just before serving time.* Here are the recipes, which are different, yet similar in some ways. One of them makes 8 servings, the other 4 servings, but you can double the recipe.

BURGUNDY BEEF

Serve in a chafing dish or casserole over candle warmer—rice is go-with

1   lb. round steak, cut in long
        thin strips (¼ × 2")
Salt
Pepper
Flour
¼   c. shortening
2   carrots, grated
1   clove garlic
1   stalk celery, finely sliced
½   medium white onion, minced
½   c. red Burgundy wine (or
        beef bouillon)
1½ c. water
¼   tsp. dried rosemary

• Season meat strips with salt and pepper; then dredge in flour. Brown in shortening. Place in a 1½-qt. casserole; add carrots, garlic, celery and onion, mixing lightly. Add Burgundy, water and rosemary, and stir.
• Cover and bake in moderate oven (350°) 1½ to 2 hours, adding a little water during the baking when needed to prevent dryness. Serve on rice. Makes 4 servings.

BEEF BOURGUIGNON

Men like to find this French dish on the buffet when they're guests

1   c. sliced white onions
¼   c. butter
3   lbs. round steak, cut in 1½"
        cubes
3   tblsp. flour
1   tsp. salt
¼   tsp. pepper
½   tsp. dried thyme
½   tsp. dried marjoram
3   drops garlic juice
2   c. beef bouillon

1   c. red Burgundy wine
1   lb. button mushrooms

• Sauté onions in butter in a heavy saucepan until tender; add meat and brown on all sides. Add flour, salt, pepper, herbs and garlic juice, stirring until smooth.
• Add 1½ c. bouillon and ½ c. wine. Simmer 3 hours. Add mushrooms; continue cooking 1 more hour, adding remaining bouillon and wine as needed. Makes 8 servings.

Note: The wine may be omitted and another cup of bouillon used in its place, but the wine gives the dish marvelous flavor (all the alcohol evaporates during the cooking).

RANCHER'S BEEF STEW

Snow peas are the something new in this hearty beef-vegetable stew

2   lbs. beef chuck, cubed
¼   c. flour
¼   c. shortening
1   medium onion, chopped
2   c. tomato juice
2   bay leaves
½   tsp. marjoram
1   tblsp. sugar
2   tsp. salt
½   tsp. pepper
1   tsp. dried parsley
1   c. water
4   medium potatoes, quartered
4   carrots, cut in strips
½   c. celery, diced
1   pt. frozen pea pods, partially
        defrosted

• Dredge meat cubes in flour.
• Melt shortening, sauté onion; remove from skillet. Brown meat.
• Add tomato juice, browned onions, seasonings, parsley and water.

• Cover and cook over low heat 1 hour, or until meat is tender.
• Add potatoes, carrots and celery. Cover. Continue to cook until vegetables are almost tender, about 30 minutes.
• Add pea pods. Cover and cook until all vegetables are tender, about 5 to 7 minutes. Remove bay leaves. Makes 6 servings.

Pine Nuts Add Rich Flavor

Among the nuts used extensively for food by Western American Indians are pine nuts. These seeds of piñon pine trees are very rich and sweet-flavored; today they are popular across country. You'll find them in the fancy nut shops of big cities and in food markets, large and small throughout the West, either shelled or unshelled. Indian tribes, especially the Utes and Navajos, gather them every autumn in large quantities for winter use.

It's the taste of small, elongated pine nuts that gives this rice pilaf distinction, making it a favorite company dish of a Western home economist and her friends.

RICE PILAF WITH PINE NUTS

Perfect companion for beef and lamb

1 ½ c. raw long grain white rice
1   large onion, chopped
½   c. butter or margarine
2   tblsp. chopped parsley
1 ½ cans condensed beef
        consommé
1   c. water
¾   to 1 c. shelled pine nuts

• Sauté rice and chopped onion in butter in skillet until rice is golden. Combine with parsley, consommé and water; pour into a greased 2-qt. casserole.
• Cover and bake in moderate oven (350°) until rice feels tender between fingers and water is absorbed, about 30 minutes. Uncover immediately.
• To serve, fluff up rice with a fork. Spoon onto a large tray and sprinkle with pine nuts. Makes 6 servings.

MEAT BALL STEW

Try this stew of brown meat balls and vegetables—new use for ground beef

1 ½ lbs. ground beef
1 ½ tsp. salt
⅛   tsp. pepper
1   egg
1   tblsp. minced onion
½   c. soft bread crumbs
1   tblsp. salad oil
3   tblsp. flour
1   (1 lb.) can tomatoes
1   c. water
½   tsp. salt
2   tsp. sugar
1   tsp. crushed dried basil
3   medium potatoes, peeled
        and diced
4   small carrots, peeled and
        diced
1   onion, coarsely chopped
1   stalk celery, sliced

• Mix ground beef with 1½ tsp. salt, pepper, egg, minced onion and bread crumbs. Form into balls the size of walnuts. Brown in hot oil.
• Remove meat balls from skillet; pour off all fat except 3 tblsp. Blend in flour. Stir in remaining ingredients. Bring mixture to a boil; simmer over low heat 10 minutes, adding more

water if necessary. Pour over meat balls in a 2-qt. casserole.
• Bake, covered, in moderate oven (350°) 1 hour, or until vegetables are tender. Makes 6 servings.

BEEF 'N' RIGATONI STEW

This is an unusually attractive company stew—bakes with little attention

1   c. dried prunes
¼   c. flour
1   tsp. salt
1 ½ lbs. lean chuck beef, cut in 1 ½" cubes
2   tblsp. salad oil
1   medium onion, coarsely chopped
1   clove garlic, minced
2   tsp. salt
¼   tsp. pepper
½   tsp. dried orégano
4   drops Tabasco sauce
1   (8 oz.) can tomato sauce
Hot water
½   (1 lb.) pkg. rigatoni, or other large macaroni

• To make pitting easier, stew prunes 5 minutes in 2 c. water. Drain and cool, then pit and set aside. (The pitted prunes now available do not require precooking.)
• In a plastic bag containing flour and 1 tsp. salt, shake beef cubes, a few at a time, until they are well coated.
• Brown beef in hot oil in deep 4-qt. Dutch oven. Add onion, garlic, 2 tsp. salt, pepper, orégano and Tabasco sauce.
• Add tomato sauce and enough hot water to keep liquid 1" above meat (about 3 c.). Stir well.
• Cover tightly and bake in slow oven (300°) 2 hours.

• Add rigatoni and prunes. Add enough hot water to cover (about 2 c.). Bake 1 hour longer. Makes 6 servings.

AFTER-CHURCH STEW

Let stew bake 3 hours in slow oven while you're at church. Add potatoes when you get home and bake ¾ hour

1 ½ lbs. lean beef, cut in 1 ½" cubes (chuck, round or top sirloin)
2   tsp. salt
½   tsp. dried basil
¼   tsp. pepper
2   stalks celery, cut in diagonal slices
4   carrots, cut in halves lengthwise and crosswise
2   onions, cut in ½" slices
1   (10 ½ oz.) can condensed tomato soup
½   soup can water
3   potatoes peeled and cubed

• Place beef (no need to brown it) in 3-qt. casserole. Sprinkle with salt, basil and pepper. Top with celery, carrots and onions.
• Combine soup and water. Pour over meat and vegetables, coating all pieces.
• Cover tightly and bake in slow oven (300°) 3 hours.
• Add potatoes and bake 45 minutes longer. Makes 5 servings.

Note: Double this recipe if you need more than 5 servings.

Slim pretzel sticks take the place of toothpicks for serving cubes of cheese or meat as hors d'oeuvres. Guests like these edible holders.

SAVORY STEW

Cook stew one day, reheat the next—lets the flavors mellow and blend

⅓ c. flour
1 tsp. salt
2 lbs. lean beef chuck, cut in
    1½″ cubes
4 slices bacon
12 small white onions, peeled
4 carrots, peeled and cut in
    halves crosswise and
    lengthwise
1 clove garlic, minced
1 (10½ oz.) can condensed
    beef bouillon
2 c. cranberry juice cocktail
1 tblsp. sugar
6 crushed peppercorns
4 whole cloves
1 bay leaf
1 tsp. salt
½ tsp. marjoram
¼ tsp. dried thyme

• In a plastic bag with flour and 1 tsp. salt, shake beef cubes, a few at a time, until they are well coated.

• Fry bacon until it begins to brown. Cut in 1″ pieces and place in heavy 3-qt. casserole.

• Brown beef cubes quickly in bacon fat; place in casserole. Add onions and carrots.

• Sauté garlic in drippings 2 or 3 minutes. Add bouillon; bring to a boil and stir from bottom to loosen particles. Add cranberry juice, sugar and seasonings; bring to boil again. Pour over meat and vegetables. Cover tightly and bake in slow oven (300°) 2 hours. Cool and refrigerate overnight.

• Next day, lift congealed fat from top. Pour liquid into saucepan and heat. Make thin paste of ¼ c. flour and water; add slowly to hot liquid, stirring and cooking until mixture thickens and comes to a boil. Pour over meat and vegetables in casserole. Heat in slow oven (300°) 30 minutes. Makes 6 servings.

When the recipe calls for Creole mustard, you are likely to find it in supermarkets in Louisiana, Texas and other Southern states, but only in gourmet food shops in other areas. Dijon mustard is more widely available. Both of these prepared mustards are spicy and hot.

Dependable Ground Beef

Farm women invent more new company dishes with ground beef than with all other meats put together. Some of them are extremely simple, like the numerous hamburger mixes that teen-agers fix in sandwiches when they have guests. Other combinations are somewhat more elaborate—Roundup Beef Rolls, for instance, which come from the ranch kitchen of a Kansas member of FARM JOURNAL's Family Test Group.

Adaptations of international ground beef dishes, which we include, lead to good eating. A good example is what another member of our Test Group does with Swedish meat balls. Being of Swedish descent, she fixes the meat as her mother and grandmother taught her. To please her husband, who is of German descent, she makes the gravy with gingersnaps as one of the ingredients.

ROUNDUP BEEF ROLLS

If your friends like hamburgers, they will enjoy these pinwheels—herbed biscuits around seasoned ground beef

Filling:
2   tblsp. shortening
1   lb. ground beef
¾   c. minced onion
½   c. finely diced celery
½   tsp. salt
¼   tsp. pepper
⅔   c. tomato sauce

Crust:
1 ½ c. sifted flour
2   tsp. baking powder
½   tsp. salt
⅛   tsp. dried marjoram
¼   tsp. dried sage
3   tblsp. shortening
⅓   c. tomato sauce plus water
     to make ½ c. liquid

• Melt shortening in skillet; add ground beef, onion and celery. Cook over medium heat until beef is browned. Add salt, pepper and ⅔ c. tomato sauce. Cook until thickened. Set aside while making crust.
• Sift together flour, baking powder and salt. Add herbs and mix well. Cut in shortening until mixture resembles coarse cornmeal. Add tomato sauce mixture and mix just until flour is moistened. Knead dough gently about 4 times on a lightly floured surface. Roll out to make a 13 × 9″ rectangle.
• Spread beef mixture on dough; roll like a jelly roll starting at the 9″ edge. Place on ungreased baking sheet. Bake in moderate oven (375°) 30 to 35 minutes. Cut in slices and serve with ketchup, chili sauce, speedy or fresh Mushroom Sauce or Mushroom-Cheese Sauce. Serves 6.

Speedy Mushroom Sauce: Stir 1 c. milk or dairy sour cream into 1 can condensed cream of mushroom soup; heat. Do not let sauce containing sour cream come to a boil.

Fresh Mushroom Sauce: Melt 5 tblsp. butter or margarine in skillet. Add ½ lb. fresh mushrooms, sliced. Sprinkle with 1 tblsp. flour. Toss and cook over medium heat, stirring occasionally, until tender, 8 to 10 minutes. Season with salt or stir in 1 tsp. soy sauce. Slowly stir in ¾ c. light cream. Cook and stir until mixture thickens.

Mushroom-Cheese Sauce: Stir ⅓ c. milk into 1 can condensed cream of mushroom soup. Add ½ c. shredded sharp Cheddar cheese. Heat and stir until cheese melts.

SWEET-SOUR MEAT BALLS

You bake the meat balls while you make the unusual Sweet-Sour Sauce

5   slices dry bread
2   lbs. ground beef
½   c. grated onion
½   tsp. garlic salt
¼   tsp. pepper
1   tsp. salt
2   eggs, slightly beaten
Sweet-Sour Sauce

• Cut bread in cubes. Soak in a little cold water until soft. Squeeze out water. Combine with remaining ingredients except Sweet-Sour Sauce. Shape in balls the size of walnuts (1½″); place in 15½ × 10½ × 1″ jelly roll pan. (Or brown balls in skillet containing a little hot fat.)
• Bake in very hot oven (450°) 15 to 18 minutes.
• Place balls in Sweet-Sour Sauce and simmer 10 minutes. If balls are made

ahead, add sauce to them and heat in the oven. Makes about 36 meat balls, 8 to 9 servings.

SWEET-SOUR SAUCE

A surprise ingredient—gingersnaps—make this sauce different

1 (1 lb. 12 oz.) can tomatoes (about 3½ c.)
1 c. brown sugar, firmly packed
¼ c. vinegar
½ tsp. salt
1 tsp. grated onion
10 gingersnaps, crushed

· Combine all ingredients. Cook to boiling. Add baked meat balls and simmer 10 minutes. Makes enough sauce for 36 (1½") meat balls.

MEAT BALL KABOBS

Exciting, elegant, new way to fix ground beef for company. The Kansas rancher's wife who shares this recipe expands it to fit her guest list

Kabobs:
1 lb. ground beef
½ c. quick-cooking rolled oats, uncooked
1 egg, beaten
1 tsp. salt
¼ tsp. pepper
3 large carrots, cut in chunks
6 small white onions
6 small potatoes
3 slices bacon, cut in halves
1 large green pepper, cut into squares

Sauce:
2 (8 oz.) cans tomato sauce
½ c. water
2 tsp. Worcestershire sauce
¼ tsp. garlic salt

· Mix ground beef, rolled oats, egg and seasonings. Form into small meat balls.
· Parboil carrots, onions and potatoes until almost tender (about 10 minutes).
· Thread vegetables, meat balls, folded bacon slices and green pepper squares onto 6 small skewers. Brown in electric skillet.
· Mix all ingredients for sauce. Pour over kabobs in electric skillet. Simmer, covered, 30 to 45 minutes. Serve as is, or over hot, cooked rice. Makes about 6 servings.

South-of-the-Border Main Dishes

To our good neighbors south of the Rio Grande, tortillas are as important as bread to us. Tacos are their sandwiches. Mighty good, too!

The recipe for Enchiladas is for the classic rolled kind. You also can make the simpler New Mexican type for an informal luncheon or supper. You heat the tortillas, which look like thin corn pancakes, in oil until they are speckled with brown. Next you dip them in the sauce and stack two or three together with lots of grated cheese between. You put "the stacks" on a baking sheet in a slow oven to keep warm and melt the cheese. And if there are men or boys among your guests, you top the enchiladas with fried eggs, sunny side up. Just before serving the stacks, spoon on Enchilada Sauce.

ENCHILADAS

Here's a great hostess main dish from our Southwest and South-of-the-Border. Do try it

Salad oil
12 tortillas
1 lb. ground beef
½ clove garlic, minced
1 tsp. salt
⅛ tsp. pepper
1 large onion, finely chopped
½ c. chopped ripe olives (optional)
¾ lb. mild Cheddar cheese, shredded
Enchilada Sauce

• Heat a small amount of oil in a skillet. Brown tortillas lightly on both sides, allowing about 30 seconds per side (only a few seconds for canned tortillas). Do not allow them to become crisp, as they need to be rolled. Remove tortillas to absorbent paper to drain.

• Brown ground beef with garlic, salt and pepper in a small amount of oil. Keep beef hot.

• On each tortilla place 2 tblsp. browned ground beef, 1 tblsp. chopped onion, 2 tsp. chopped ripe olives and 1½ tblsp. shredded cheese. Roll up tortillas.

• Spread 1 c. Enchilada Sauce over bottom of a greased 15½ × 10½ × 1″ jelly roll pan. Place tortillas, folded side down, in sauce. Spoon 2 tblsp. Enchilada Sauce over each tortilla and sprinkle with remaining cheese.

• Bake in moderate oven (350°) about 20 minutes, or until sauce starts to bubble. Serve at once. Makes 6 large servings.

Note: You can double this recipe for 12 servings, and freeze the filled and rolled tortillas. Add the sauce and shredded cheese topping when you bake them.

ENCHILADA SAUCE

A North-of-the-Border variation—it gives zip to filling and tortillas

1 medium onion, chopped
3 tblsp. butter or margarine
½ medium green pepper, chopped
2 (8 oz.) cans tomato sauce
1 c. water
⅛ tsp. Tabasco sauce
1 tblsp. chili powder

• Sauté onion in butter until clear. Add green pepper, sauté about 1 minute longer. Stir in tomato sauce, water, Tabasco and chili powder. Simmer over low heat about 30 minutes. Makes about 3 cups.

TACOS

Children like these crunchy tortillas filled with ground meat, chopped lettuce, tomatoes and cheese

1 lb. ground beef
½ clove garlic, minced
2 tblsp. grated onion
½ tsp. Worcestershire sauce
1½ tsp. salt
1 tsp. chili powder
Salad oil
16 canned or frozen tortillas
1 c. shredded mild Cheddar cheese
½ c. chopped onion
2 c. finely shredded lettuce
1 c. finely chopped fresh tomato
Taco Sauce

• Mix together ground beef, garlic, onion, Worcestershire sauce, salt and chili powder; brown in skillet in small amount of oil (meat mixture should be moist). Keep hot.

• Pour oil about ¼″ deep in skillet and heat; fry tortillas quickly, one at a time. Fry on one side a few seconds, just until it starts to puff in center but is not crisp. Turn to second side and fold into a half-moon shape, making a pocket for filling. Hold the top side of tortilla down with a spatula or wooden spoon and fry until crisp on one side. Turn to other side and fry until crisp, holding top with a spoon. Drain shells. Stack shells, open side up, in a baking pan and keep hot in warm oven (200°).

• When all tortillas are fried, fill each with 1 to 2 tblsp. hot ground beef mixture (depending on size of tortilla). Top meat mixture in each shell with shredded cheese, chopped onion, shredded lettuce and tomato. Spoon about 2 tsp. hot Taco Sauce on each. Eat from the hand over large plates. Makes 8 servings.

Taco Sauce: Heat together 1 c. tomato juice, 3 tblsp. ketchup, ⅛ tsp. Tobasco sauce and ½ tsp. Worcestershire sauce. Makes enough sauce for 16 Tacos.

LASAGNE

A fine hot dish to tote to a supper meeting. Ask two women each to make the recipe—enough to serve 18

2 tblsp. salad oil
½ c. finely chopped onion
1 clove garlic, minced
1 lb. ground beef
1 (1 lb.) can tomatoes

1 (8 oz.) can tomato sauce
1 tsp. salt
½ tsp. pepper
¼ tsp. crushed dried basil
½ tsp. dried orégano
2 tsp. sugar
9 lasagne noodles
2 eggs
1 lb. ricotta cheese
¼ lb. mozzarella cheese, cut in thin slices
¼ c. grated Parmesan cheese

• Heat oil in skillet; add onion and garlic. Cook until onion and garlic are tender but not browned. Add ground beef and cook slowly, stirring occasionally until beef loses its red color. Add tomatoes, tomato sauce, seasonings and sugar. Simmer, uncovered, 30 minutes, or until sauce is thick but not dry.

• Cook noodles according to directions on package.

• In a separate bowl, beat eggs; blend in ricotta cheese.

• In a greased 2-qt. casserole (square or rectangular, if available), layer half of meat sauce, 3 lasagne noodles, half of ricotta cheese and half of mozzarella cheese. Add more layers in this order: noodles, meat sauce, noodles, ricotta and mozzarella cheese. Sprinkle on Parmesan cheese. Bake in moderate oven (350°) until bubbly and golden, about 35 to 40 minutes. Cut into squares. Makes 9 servings.

If your recipe calls for 1 c. canned tomatoes, you can use fresh tomatoes from your garden. Peel and cut up fresh tomatoes to make 1⅓ c. Simmer 10 minutes. You should have 1 cupful.

LASAGNE ROLL-UPS

Individual servings of lasagne look like little pillows with ruffled edges

Sauce:

1 ½   lbs. ground beef
⅓   c. salad oil
⅓   c. finely chopped onion
1 ½   large cloves garlic, minced
2   tsp. salt
¼   tsp. pepper
2   whole cloves
½   dried bay leaf
2   (1 lb. 1 ½ oz.) cans plum
        tomatoes, pressed through
        strainer
2   (6 oz.) cans tomato paste
1 ¼   c. water
1   tsp. orégano
¼   tsp. monosodium glutamate
2   tsp. sugar

Filling:

2   lbs. ricotta cheese
½   tsp. salt
⅛   tsp. pepper
½   tsp. ground nutmeg
¼   lb. mozzarella cheese,
        shredded
4   tblsp. grated Parmesan or
        Romano cheese
1   tblsp. chopped parsley
1   (1 lb.) pkg. lasagne noodles

• To make sauce, partially brown ground beef in oil. Add onion, garlic, salt, pepper, cloves and bay leaf. Continue to brown over medium heat about 10 minutes, until well browned.

• Stir in remaining ingredients for sauce. Let come to a boil, then simmer gently, loosely covered, about 1 hour. Stir occasionally.

• To make filling, whip ricotta cheese. Add seasonings, mozzarella cheese, grated cheese and parsley. Set aside.

• Cook lasagne noodles according to package directions. Rinse with cold water; drain well. Lay noodles on clean towels.

• On each lasagne noodle spread ¼ c. filling. Fold over 1″ and continue to fold, making a slightly flat roll.

• Place 1 c. meat sauce in each of two 2-qt. rectangular baking dishes. Place roll-ups, seam side down, in baking dishes. Add ⅓ c. hot water to each dish and enough meat sauce almost to cover roll-ups. Reserve rest of sauce.

• Bake in moderate oven (350°) 35 minutes, or until sauce bubbles in center of dish.

• Serve with rest of meat sauce and grated Parmesan or Romano cheese. Makes about 16 party rolls; 9 main-dish servings or 16 servings if served as an accompaniment with a roast or chicken.

Beef Loaves to Tote

Our three beef loaf recipes have one thing in common—cheese helps season them. And most delightfully! Cottage cheese shows up in the two Italian-type loaves, Roman and Parmesan. Cheddar cheese does the honors in Glazed Beef Loaf, a really attractive number. Good travelers they are and welcome, too, when they reach their destination at the church or other community supper.

GLAZED BEEF LOAF

Wonderful way to tote ground beef to church suppers or any potluck meal

2   eggs, beaten
⅔   c. milk

2 tsp. salt
¼ tsp. pepper
3 slices bread, cut in small
cubes
⅔ c. finely chopped onion
⅔ c. shredded raw carrot
1 ½ c. shredded Cheddar cheese
2 lbs. ground beef
¼ c. brown sugar
¼ c. ketchup
1 tblsp. prepared mustard

• Stir together eggs, milk, salt, pepper and bread. Beat until bread is broken up. Add onion, carrot, cheese and beef, mixing well.
• Form into a loaf in center of a 13 × 9 × 2″ baking pan. Bake in moderate oven (350°) 1 hour and 15 minutes.
• Combine brown sugar, ketchup and mustard. Spread over beef loaf and continue baking 15 minutes. Makes 10 servings.

ROMAN MEAT LOAF

Something new and tasty in meat loaves—beef with an Italian accent

1 c. cracker crumbs
1 ½ lbs. ground beef
1 (6 oz.) can tomato paste
2 eggs, beaten
1 c. finely chopped onion
⅓ c. finely chopped green
pepper
¾ tsp. salt
⅛ tsp. pepper
1 ½ c. small curd cottage cheese
1 (4 oz.) can mushroom pieces
1 tsp. dried parsley, or 1
tblsp. chopped fresh
parsley
¼ tsp. orégano

• Combine ½ c. cracker crumbs with beef, tomato paste, eggs, onion, green pepper, salt and pepper. Pat half of mixture in bottom of an 8 × 8 × 2″ pan.
• Combine remaining ½ c. cracker crumbs with cottage cheese, mushroom pieces, parsley and orégano. Spread over meat mixture in pan. Top with remaining meat mixture.
• Bake in moderate oven (350°) 1 hour. Let stand 10 minutes before cutting. Makes 8 servings.

PARMESAN MEAT LOAF

An interesting company loaf—tastes good, bakes quick—it's only 1″ thick

1 lb. ground beef
1 c. small curd creamed
cottage cheese
½ c. quick-cooking rolled oats
1 egg
¼ c. ketchup
1 tsp. prepared mustard
2 tblsp. chopped onion
1 tsp. salt
⅛ tsp. pepper
¼ c. grated Parmesan cheese

• Mix together all the ingredients except Parmesan cheese. Lightly pack into a greased 8 × 8 × 2″ pan, taking care not to press down. Leave the top rough-textured.
• Bake in moderate oven (350°) 30 minutes. Sprinkle Parmesan cheese on top and bake 10 minutes longer. (You can use grated Cheddar instead of the Parmesan cheese.)
• Let stand 5 minutes when removed from oven, before cutting in squares. Makes 6 servings.

Note: Bake 2 pans of meat loaf if you need more servings.

Recommended for Hungry Boys

Hospitable mothers like to keep a ready-to-go hamburger mix in the freezer. Here's what a county extension home economist says: "I heat Multipurpose Hamburger Mix, spoon it—or let the boys spoon it—over split buns when they and friends drive in after a football or basketball game. You should see them pitch in and eat. The sandwiches really fill them up. Quite an accomplishment when boys are at the fast-growing stage!"

MULTIPURPOSE HAMBURGER MIX

Sure way to please: Heat mix when car full of hungry boys stops in yard

4   medium onions, chopped
4   lbs. ground beef
2   c. chopped celery
4   tsp. salt
½   tsp. pepper
2   (14 oz.) bottles ketchup

• Pan-fry onions and ground beef in a large kettle or electric skillet. Add celery and cook until soft (do not brown). Add seasonings and ketchup. Simmer 20 minutes.
• Skim off excess fat. Cool, package and freeze. Makes 10 cups.
• To serve, heat and spoon over split buns.

COLORADO SLOPPY JOE'S

They'll all want second helpings of these de luxe "loose hamburgers"

1 ½   lbs. ground beef
3   tblsp. shortening

1   stalk celery, chopped
1   large onion, chopped
1   green pepper, chopped
½   can condensed tomato soup
1   c. ketchup
1   tblsp. celery seeds
1 ½   tsp. salt
¼   tsp. pepper
2   tblsp. flour
1   tblsp. brown sugar
1   tblsp. vinegar
1   tblsp. prepared mustard
    (optional)

• Brown meat in shortening if meat is lean; otherwise brown beef in its own fat. Add celery, onion and green pepper and simmer until tender. Add remaining ingredients.
• Cook slowly 1 hour. Serve 1 tblsp. (or more) mixture in split hamburger bun. Makes 15 to 18 Sloppy Joe's, depending on size of buns and amount of hamburger mixture used in each.

MIXER-MADE MEAT LOAF

Three ways to use this—in a big loaf or individual loaves, or in patties— all are good. Hot or cold, loaves are moist but easy to slice

2   eggs
1   (10½ oz.) can tomato purée
1   c. water
6   slices bread
¼   c. dried or fresh minced onion
4   tsp. salt
½   tsp. pepper
2   tsp. Worcestershire sauce
3   lbs. lean ground beef

• Beat eggs until frothy in large bowl of electric mixer. Reduce speed to very low; blend in tomato purée and water. Tear bread into pieces and gradually drop into turning mixer bowl; mix thoroughly. Add onion and seasonings.

• Slowly add beef. If mixture climbs beaters before all beef is added, add water, a tablespoonful at a time. Shape into a loaf in a 13 × 9 × 2" baking pan. Bake in slow oven (300°) 1¼ hours, or until pink color in center disappears. Makes 15 servings.

VARIATIONS

Beef Patties: Measure meat loaf mixture into ½ c. portions. Flatten and pan-fry or broil until no longer pink in the center, about 15 minutes. Makes 18 generous patties. (Keep a supply, uncooked, in the freezer for quick dinners.)

Little Meat Loaves: Pack meat loaf mixture into muffin-pan cups. Bake in very hot oven (450°) 15 minutes. Makes about 30—count on at least 2 for each adult serving.

BASIC BEEF MIX

When you entertain children, count on them liking either pizza or spaghetti. They'll also enjoy Quick Pizzaburgers

5 lbs. ground beef
2 c. chopped onions
3 (6 oz.) cans tomato paste
3 (8 oz.) cans tomato sauce
2 tblsp. salt
2 tblsp. sugar
1 tsp. garlic powder
½ tsp. orégano

• Cook beef and onions, uncovered, until beef loses pink color. Stir together remaining ingredients. Pour over meat; simmer 5 minutes.

• Cool; divide mixture into thirds

(about 4 c. each) and refrigerate up to a week, or freeze. Makes about 3 quarts.

VARIATIONS

Quick Pizzaburgers: Spoon ¼ to ⅓ c. Beef Mix on half a split hamburger bun. Bake in moderate oven (350°) 10 minutes, or until meat is hot. Top with a (1 oz.) slice process Cheddar cheese; return to oven for 5 minutes, or until cheese melts. Serve with other half of bun. Makes 16 servings.

Boys' Spaghetti: Heat 4 c. Beef Mix. Stir into 8 oz. spaghetti, cooked and drained. Sprinkle with grated Parmesan cheese. Makes 7 servings.

Hearty Mealtime Pizza: Dissolve 1 pkg. active dry yeast in ¼ c. lukewarm water. Combine 1½ tsp. sugar, 2 tsp. salt and ¾ c. scalded milk; cool to lukewarm, then stir into dissolved yeast. Beat in 1 c. sifted flour until smooth. Add more sifted flour (about 1½ c.) to make a stiff dough. Knead until smooth. Divide dough in half; press each half into a greased 13 × 9 × 2" pan. Top each with 2 c. Beef Mix and sprinkle with 1 c. grated Cheddar cheese. Let rise 30 minutes. Bake in moderate oven (350°) until crust is brown, about 35 minutes. Makes 16 servings. Has a "bready" base—children can eat out of hand.

Consider Beef Casseroles

Beef casseroles, expertly seasoned, are tasty fare. Some of them you can get ready to bake ahead and refrigerate or freeze, to tuck in the oven when it's time to get the meal. And once they're in the oven, they free time for the hurried hostess during that zero hour, the last minutes before you invite your guests to the buffet or table.

Some country women collect interesting casseroles to dress up the food they bake in them. A good idea to remember when you browse around the housewares department in your stores and antique shops!

HAMBURGER CHEESE BAKE

Wonderful main dish to tote to potluck suppers—it's easy to fix and really good

1   (8 oz.) pkg. noodles
2   lbs. ground beef
1 ½ tsp. salt
¼   tsp. pepper
1   medium onion, chopped
2   tblsp. chopped green pepper
½   tsp. garlic salt
2   (8 oz.) cans tomato sauce
1   tsp. orégano
1   (8 oz.) pkg. cream cheese
½   c. dairy sour cream
1 ½ c. cottage cheese

• Cook noodles by package directions; drain. Brown beef with salt, pepper, onion, green pepper and garlic salt added. Stir in tomato sauce and orégano. Set aside.

• Soften cream cheese at room temperature; blend with sour cream; add cottage cheese, mixing well.

• Place half the cooked noodles in a 13 × 9 × 2″ pan. Cover with the cheese mixture. Spread remaining noodles over the top. Pour on the beef mixture.

• Bake in moderate oven (350°) about 20 minutes, or until piping hot. Makes 12 servings.

Note: To make 6 servings, use half of all ingredients except cheese; use 1 (3 oz.) pkg. cream cheese. Use 1 small onion instead of a medium-size onion.

MAZETTI

A Southern hostess favorite that wins praise—serve it hot from the oven

2   lbs. ground beef
2 ½ c. finely chopped celery with leaves (about ½ bunch)
2   c. chopped onions
2   cloves garlic, finely chopped
1   tblsp. water
1   (8 oz.) pkg. medium-fine noodles
2   cans condensed tomato soup
1   (6 oz.) can mushrooms and liquid
2   tsp. salt
½   tsp. pepper
½   lb. grated sharp Cheddar cheese (2 c.)

• Brown meat in skillet. Add celery, onions, garlic and water. Cover and steam until vegetables are tender. Remove from heat.

• Cook noodles according to package directions; drain. Add noodles to beef mixture; mix in soup, undrained mushrooms, salt and pepper.

• Spread mixture in a 3-qt. casserole. Sprinkle cheese on top. (Dish may be refrigerated up to 24 hours, or frozen before cooking.)

• Place in cold oven; set at very slow (250°). Bake uncovered until bubbly, about 1 hour. Makes 10 to 12 servings.

MACARONI MEDLEY

New carry-along dish wins praises

1 (8 oz.) pkg. large elbow
   macaroni
1 large onion, diced
½ green pepper, diced
3 tblsp. butter
2 lbs. ground beef
1 tsp. salt
2 (8 oz.) cans tomato sauce
2 c. water
1 (1½ oz.) pkg. spaghetti sauce
   mix (Italian style with
   mushrooms)
1 (4½ oz.) can chopped ripe
   olives
½ lb. Cheddar cheese, grated
   coarsely

• Cook macaroni in salted, boiling water, as directed on package. Drain.
• Sauté onion and green pepper in butter until soft, but do not brown. Add beef and brown. Drain off fat. Add salt, tomato sauce and water; stir in spaghetti sauce mix and simmer 10 minutes.
• Mix olives and cheese with macaroni, saving out 1 c. cheese.
• Place half of the macaroni mixture in a greased 13 × 9 × 2″ pan; cover with half the meat mixture. Repeat.
• Bake in moderate oven (350°) 40 minutes, sprinkling on the 1 c. reserved cheese the last 10 minutes of baking. Makes 8 to 10 servings.

Add color and flavor to salads with onion rings marinated in leftover pickle juice. Pickled beet juice gives most color. Chill onion rings in liquid 24 hours before using.

QUICK TAMALE PIE

Let teen-age cooks fix this Southwestern dish for after-game suppers

2 lbs. ground beef
2 cans condensed tomato soup
2 cans condensed chili beef
   soup
1 tblsp. instant onion
1 tsp. salt
2 (6 oz.) pkgs. corn chips
   (7 c.)
½ lb. shredded sharp process
   cheese

• Brown ground beef in a large skillet. Drain off excess fat. Stir in soups, onion and salt; heat.
• Place 2 c. corn chips in bottom of a 3-qt. casserole. Top with half of beef mixture and half of cheese. Top with 2 c. corn chips, then remaining meat mixture. Then top with remaining corn chips and remaining cheese.
• Bake in moderate oven (350°) 25 minutes. Makes 8 servings.

POTATO-WIENER SUPPER

Potaoes and hot dogs in a new dish sure to please the young guests

2 (12 oz.) pkgs. frozen hash
   brown potatoes, thawed
1 (3½ oz.) can fried onion rings
½ c. butter or margarine, melted
1 tsp. salt
⅛ tsp. pepper
1 can condensed cream of
   celery soup
1 (1 lb.) pkg. all-meat wieners

• Combine potatoes, crumbled onion rings, reserving a few rings for topping, butter, salt and pepper in a casserole. Mix celery soup with 1 can water. Pour about three fourths of

the soup over potato mixture and mix thoroughly.
• Cut wieners in halves and arrange on top of casserole. Top with a few onion rings and pour on remaining soup.
• Bake in moderate oven (375°) 25 minutes. Makes 6 servings.

Pork for Company

Today's pork has many virtues. It's less fat than ever before, because of developments in hog breeding. And there's great variety in cuts. You'll find many of them in our new and tempting dishes.

Our pork parade starts with golden-coated Glazed Pork Roast. What a beauty! The apricot glaze makes the roast sparkle on the platter and adds fruity flavor that's so good with pork. Do have this roast for a special guest dinner soon. It's guaranteed to please.

GLAZED PORK ROAST

Pamper your guests with this regal roast that glistens with apricot glaze. For a bonus, make sauce from the extra glaze to spoon over carved, tender pork

    4   to 5 lb. pork loin roast
Salt
Pepper
    ⅔   c. brown sugar, firmly
          packed
2 ½   tsp. dry mustard
    2   tblsp. cornstarch
    2   c. apricot nectar
    4   tsp. cider vinegar

• Rub roast well with salt and pepper; score fat on roast in a diamond pattern.
• Place roast, fat side up, on a rack in an open roasting pan. Insert meat thermometer into the center of roast so it does not touch bone or rest in fat.
• Roast meat in a slow to moderate oven (325 to 350°) until meat thermometer indicates an internal temperature of 170°. Times vary with type of loin cut; center loin roast, roast about 30 to 35 minutes per pound; blade loin or sirloin roast, roast about 40 to 45 minutes per pound.
• About ½ hour before roast is done, mix brown sugar, mustard and cornstarch in a saucepan. Stir in apricot nectar and cider vinegar. Place over medium heat and cook, stirring constantly, until slightly thickened. Remove roast from oven and spoon about ½ c. glaze over it (reserve rest of glaze). Replace meat in oven until done. Remove roast from oven 20 minutes before serving for easier carving. Makes 8 servings.

Apricot Sauce: Mix about 3 tblsp. brown drippings from roasting pan with remaining apricot glaze. Heat and serve as a sauce to spoon over the roast pork.

PORK ROAST
WITH FLAVOR POCKETS

Seasonings make the difference— treat guests to this superior roast

    1   (8 lb.) pork loin roast
    1   tsp. dried fennel seeds,
          rubbed between palms of
          hands to bring out aroma
    2   tsp. salt

¼ tsp. pepper
½ tsp. monosodium glutamate
½ tsp. dried orégano, crushed
½ dried bay leaf, crushed
⅛ tsp. nutmeg
⅛ tsp. ground cloves
2 tblsp. chopped parsley
1 tsp. minced onion
1 clove garlic, minced

• Place pork roast, fat side up, on rack in open roasting pan just large enough to hold roast. Mix remaining ingredients well with fingers.
• Make flavor pockets in roast— pierce meat with a knife to a depth of 1". Move tip of knife from side to side to enlarge pocket. Make pockets at 2 to 3" intervals over top side of roast.
• Place ½ tsp. flavor mixture in each pocket and press it deep into the pocket with fingers. Close pocket with fingers. Rub remaining flavor mixture over roast.
• Roast meat, uncovered, in slow oven (325°), allowing about 30 minutes per pound, or until meat thermometer registers 170°.
• Remove roast from oven about 20 minutes before serving. Make gravy with drippings in roasting pan. Makes about 8 servings.

FRESH PORK POT ROAST WITH DUMPLINGS

Serve guests this man-approved dish

½ fresh pork leg or shoulder
   (about 5 lbs.)
2 tsp. salt
½ tsp. dried thyme
1 large bay leaf, crushed
Dumplings

• Trim excess fat from meat. Rub

meat with mixture of salt, thyme and bay leaf. Refrigerate 2 hours.
• Brown meat in fat trimmings in heavy deep pan or Dutch oven. Add water to depth of 2". Cover, and simmer on top of range until well done (20 to 25 minutes per pound). Add more water if needed.
• Remove meat from pan; set aside, keeping it warm. Makes 6 to 8 servings.

Gravy: Skim fat from drippings. Measure ¾ c. drippings into pan; stir in ½ c. flour; cook until bubbly. Stir in 4 c. water to make thin gravy; season with salt and pepper; simmer about 5 minutes.

Dumplings: Sift together 1½ c. sifted flour, 2 tsp. baking powder, ¾ tsp. salt and ⅛ tsp. ground sage. Cut in 3 tblsp. shortening. Combine 1 egg, slightly beaten, and ⅔ c. milk; stir in dry ingredients until all are moistened. Drop by spoonfuls into boiling gravy. Cover; cook 15 minutes. Serve with sliced meat and gravy.

ROAST FRESH HAM

For a change, bake a fresh ham basted with apple juice or cider

1 (12 lb.) fresh ham
3 cloves garlic
1 tblsp. salt
½ tsp. pepper
1 tsp. caraway seeds, crushed
4 medium onions, sliced
2 medium carrots, sliced
   lengthwise
2 bay leaves
3 whole cloves
½ c. water
1 c. apple juice (about)

• Score fat or skin of ham in diamond

pattern. Rub well with one cut garlic clove, salt and pepper. Sprinkle with caraway seeds.

• Place roast, fat side down, on bed of onions, carrots, remaining garlic cloves, bay leaves and cloves. Add water.

• Roast, uncovered, 1 hour in slow oven (325°). Turn fat side up; insert meat thermometer. Roast to internal temperature of 185°, or total of 30 minutes per pound. During last 2 hours, baste frequently with apple juice to make skin crisp and brown (cover loosely with foil if roast begins to get too brown). Remove meat and vegetables from pan and keep hot while making gravy. Serve garnished with spiced crab apples. Makes 16 to 20 servings.

Gravy: Strain meat juices in pan and skim off fat. Return ¼ c. drippings to pan. Stir in ¼ c. flour mixed with ¼ c. water; cook over direct heat until smooth. Add 1 c. apple juice, 1 tsp. salt and ¼ tsp. pepper. Just before serving, reduce heat, stir in 2 c. dairy sour cream; heat but do not boil. If too thick, thin with apple juice.

DEEP-PEPPERED PORK

Serve this gourmet carve-ahead treat in a shallow casserole with its own pan juices—potatoes add to heartiness

1 (4 lb.) boneless rolled pork
   roast
Coarsely ground black pepper
Salt
Fresh garlic (optional)
1 lemon
8 medium potatoes
Thin lemon slices

• With a sharp knife, pierce surface of pork about 1½″ deep in about ten places. With your forefinger, press into each hole about ⅛ tsp. pepper, about ⅟₁₆ tsp. salt, ¼ clove garlic and a thin strip of lemon peel (yellow part only). Rub surface of roast with lemon juice, salt and pepper.

• Place pork on rack in roasting pan; insert meat thermometer. Bake in slow oven (300°) until meat thermometer registers 185°, or about 40 minutes per pound.

• Meanwhile, peel potatoes and cut in halves; cook until just tender; drain.

• Remove roast from oven, allow to stand at least 20 minutes, then slice, saving meat juices. Loosen crusty drippings from roasting pan. Arrange pork slices, slightly overlapping, in a deep platter or shallow casserole; spoon over meat juices and enough roast drippings to moisten (avoid excess fat) and remaining juice from lemon.

• Coat potatoes with roast drippings; arrange around pork slices. Bake in slow oven (300°) 20 to 30 minutes, or until pork is heated through, basting once or twice with pan juices. Garnish with lemon slices. Serve very hot. Makes about 8 servings.

Tender Pork Chops in New Ways

You can count on tender meat when you entertain if you fix pork chops by the recipes in this cookbook. Notice the flavor surprises. These blend beautifully with the taste of browned pork. Remember that browning pork produces exceptionally fine flavor—looks good, too. So take time to brown the chops as the recipes direct.

STUFFED PORK CHOPS

To keep the pockets full of stuffing, cut pork chops by this Iowa method, developed by a pork producer's wife

6   pork chops, at least 1"
    thick for stuffing
2   tblsp. butter or margarine
2   tblsp. finely chopped onion
¼   tsp. ground sage
¼   tsp. crushed dried basil
1   tblsp. dried or chopped
    fresh parsley
1 ½ c. small dry bread cubes
¼   c. dry onion soup mix
½   c. water

• Cut pork chops along the bone, about halfway through, then cut toward outside to make a pocket.
• Melt butter; add onion, sage, basil and parsley. Sauté until onion is golden. Toss with bread cubes. Stuff mixture into pork chop pockets.
• Brown chops in small amount of fat; place in 13 × 9 × 2" casserole or baking pan. Sprinkle dry onion soup mix over chops. Pour on ½ c. water and cover.
• Bake in slow oven (325°) about 1 hour, or until chops are tender. Makes 6 servings.

HONEYED PORK CHOPS

Hostess adaptation of an old Chinese dish—delicious, fascinating flavors

6   pork chops, ¾" thick
¼   c. soy sauce
1   tblsp. ketchup
½   c. water

3   tblsp. honey
1   small onion, finely chopped
¼   tsp. ground ginger
⅛   tsp. pepper
1   tblsp. toasted sesame seeds

• Brown chops in small amount of fat; place in a 13 × 9 × 2" baking pan. (Don't salt chops; soy sauce does the job.)
• Combine remaining ingredients except sesame seeds. Pour over chops, sprinkle on sesame seeds.
• Cover baking pan and bake in slow oven (325°) about 1 hour, or until chops are tender. Makes 6 servings.

PORK CHOPS WITH APPLES

Sliced apple rings with cherry centers bake atop tender, browned chops

9   loin pork chops, ¾" thick
Salt
Pepper
3   tart red apples, unpeeled
1 ½ tblsp. butter
9   maraschino cherries
6   tblsp. brown sugar
1   tsp. cinnamon
½   tsp. ground ginger

• Brown chops slowly in heavy skillet; place in shallow baking dish one layer deep. Sprinkle generously with salt and pepper.
• Core unpeeled apples and slice in ½" thick rings. Add butter to skillet in which chops were browned, and sauté apple rings until slightly tender. Place one ring on top of each chop. Cover, and bake in slow oven (300°) 30 minutes.
• Remove from oven. Place cherry in center of each apple ring; sprinkle all with mixture of brown sugar, cinnamon and ginger. Baste with drip-

pings to moisten sugar. Finish baking, uncovered, in moderate oven (350°) 15 to 20 minutes. Makes 9 servings.

PORK CHOPS WITH ORANGE RICE

Orange juice and peel add flavor; orange slices decorate casserole

6   pork chops, ¾" thick
Salt
Pepper
⅔   c. uncooked rice
¾   tsp. salt
1   tsp. sugar
¼   c. raisins
1   tblsp. grated orange rind
1½   c. boiling water
⅔   c. orange juice
6   half slices orange
3   tsp. brown sugar

• Brown chops well; drain off fat. Season with salt and pepper.
• Mix rice, ¾ tsp. salt, sugar, raisins and grated rind in 3-qt. casserole. Pour on boiling water and orange juice.
• Cover casserole and place in moderate oven (350°) 10 minutes. Remove from oven, stir rice. Lay chops on top of rice; top each chop with a half slice of orange and ½ tsp. brown sugar.
• Bake in a moderate oven (350°) 45 minutes to 1 hour, or until chops are tender. Makes 6 servings.

When baking a ham, slit the rind lengthwise on the underside before placing it in the roasting pan. As the ham bakes, the rind will pull away and can be removed easily, without lifting the ham.

MOCK FILET MIGNON

Use this dish for a very special occasion. Serve with spiced peaches or crab apples

9   lean loin pork chops, boned, 1" thick, or 9 pork tenderloin slices, 1" thick
9   slices bacon
9   large whole mushrooms, stemmed
3   tblsp. butter

• Shape boned chops into rounds. Circle each with a strip of bacon and secure with toothpicks.
• Place in flat baking dish, cover. Bake in slow oven (300°) 1 hour. Uncover; brown under broiler.
• Sauté mushrooms in butter until brown and tender. Top each filet with a mushroom. Makes 9 servings.

STUFFED PORK POCKETS

This platter treat cooks in the oven without attention—guests really like it

1   c. canned whole kernel corn, well drained
3   slices bread, toasted and cubed
¼   c. diced celery
2   tblsp. chopped onion
¼   tsp. nutmeg
1   tsp. salt
⅛   tsp. pepper
1   egg, beaten
3   tblsp. light cream
8   double loin pork chops, cut with pocket
1   tblsp. fat or drippings
Salt
Pepper
2   chicken bouillon cubes
1½   c. hot water

• Put corn, toast cubes, celery, onion, nutmeg, 1 tsp. salt and ⅛ tsp. pepper into a bowl. Add egg and cream. Mix lightly.
• Stuff into chops; secure opening with skewers or toothpicks.
• Brown chops on both sides in hot fat. Sprinkle lightly with salt and pepper.
• Arrange in baking pan. Mix bouillon cubes and hot water; pour over pork chops. Cover (with aluminum foil if pan has no lid). Bake in slow oven (325°) 1½ hours. Makes 8 servings.

GLAZED SPARERIBS WITH APPLES

Ask several women to bring a pan of these ribs to the potluck supper. They'll serve a crowd to perfection

5 to 6 lbs. lean meaty spareribs
½ c. apricot jam
2 tblsp. prepared mustard
6 firm baking apples
½ c. brown sugar
½ c. hot water

• Arrange ribs in large shallow pan. Place in very hot oven (450°) 15 to 20 minutes, or until brown. Remove from oven and pour off fat. Reduce oven heat to moderate (350°).
• Mix together jam and mustard; spread this over the top of the ribs.
• Core apples and peel the top half. Fill centers with brown sugar; place in baking pan around ribs. Pour hot water into baking pan.
• Bake 1 hour in moderate oven (350°). Makes 6 servings.

PARTY PORK ROLLS

Doubly delicious with ham, fresh and smoked. See photo in this book

3 slices fresh ham steak, ½" thick

Ham Stuffing:
2 c. ground cooked smoked ham
⅛ tsp. pepper
½ c. dry bread or cracker crumbs
1 egg, slightly beaten

Bread Stuffing:
¼ c. finely chopped onion
⅓ c. butter or margarine
½ c. finely chopped celery
2 tsp. salt
1 tsp. poultry seasoning
¼ tsp. pepper
1 c. dry bread crumbs
¼ c. hot water

• Mix together thoroughly all ingredients for ham stuffing.
• To make bread stuffing, cook onions in butter until golden. Add remaining ingredients for bread stuffing and mix.
• Bone steak; pound to flatten. Brown lightly in 2 tblsp. butter.
• Spread steaks with ham stuffing. Cover evenly with a layer of bread stuffing. Roll as for jelly roll and tie securely with string.
• Bake in covered pan in moderate oven (350°) 30 minutes. Remove from oven; spread pork rolls with a glaze of ½ c. orange marmalade mixed with 2 tsp. maraschino cherry juice. Bake, uncovered, 15 to 20 minutes longer. Remove strings; slice each roll into 2" slices. Makes 6 servings.

Note: You can double this recipe to make 12 servings.

Glamorous Glazed Ham

When you're trying to decide what to have for a company dinner on Easter, or for any other day, consider a whole baked ham. You can serve it hot or cold. And you can make it glisten with a glaze. It's an ideal choice for a buffet-style meal. Our Honey-Glazed Ham is handsome. You start with a fully cooked whole ham and heat it in the oven to bring out the rich, mellow flavors before you drizzle the honey on it.

HONEY-GLAZED HAM

A beautiful ham calls for guests

- 1 (10 to 12 lb.) fully cooked bone-in ham
- 2 c. apple juice or cider
- ¾ tsp. whole allspice
- 1 tsp. whole cloves
- ½ tsp. cracked ginger
- 3 (2") cinnamon sticks
- 1 c. honey
- Whole cloves
- Paprika

• Place ham, fat side up, on rack in shallow pan. Insert meat thermometer into center, using care not to touch bone.

• Heat apple juice with allspice, 1 tsp. whole cloves, ginger and stick cinnamon in saucepan, bringing to a boil. Cover and boil 5 minutes. Remove from heat and brush a little of this mixture over ham.

• Bake ham in slow oven (325°) 1½ to 2 hours, basting every 15 minutes with the spiced apple juice mixture.

• Drizzle ½ c. honey over ham. Bake 30 minutes longer. Remove from oven, and drizzle on remaining ½ c. honey. Bake 30 minutes, or until thermometer registers 160°, or until ham glistens and is golden.

• Remove from oven and cool 30 minutes. Score fat, stud with whole cloves and sprinkle lavishly with paprika. Place on platter. For the Christmas holidays, garnish platter with a few small holly sprays; at other seasons, garnish with pickled peaches, drained and tucked in nests of parsley. Makes 20 to 22 servings.

ROSY HAM RING

Letters from women, praising this pretty loaf, prompt us to reprint the recipe from our Freezing & Canning Cookbook

- 3 lbs. ground smoked ham
- 1 lb. ground pork
- 2 eggs
- 1 ¾ c. graham cracker crumbs
- 1 ½ c. milk
- ½ tsp. ground allspice
- Tomato Basting Sauce

• Combine all ingredients except sauce; mix well. In a 16 × 11" baking pan, shape with hands to make a ring (or loaf) about 10" across. Pour over half of sauce.

• Bake in moderate oven (350°) 45 minutes; pour over remaining sauce and bake 45 minutes longer, basting several times with sauce. Makes 12 to 14 servings.

Tomato Basting Sauce: Combine 1 can condensed tomato soup, ½ c. vinegar, ½ c. brown sugar and 1½ tsp. prepared mustard.

Note: You can mix this loaf a few days early and freeze it. Allow a little longer cooking time. At serving time fill the center of the ring with buttered peas, corn or succotash.

HAM STEAK COUNTRY STYLE

Fork-tender pork in well-seasoned sauce—country skillet food at its best

3 slices fresh ham steak, ½″ thick
½ c. flour
½ tsp. salt
⅛ tsp. pepper
½ c. butter or margarine
3 medium onions, sliced
1 can condensed cream of mushroom soup
1 c. light cream
½ tsp. Worcestershire sauce
¼ tsp. garlic powder
¼ tsp. salt
¼ tsp. pepper
½ c. dairy sour cream
1 (4 oz.) can sliced mushrooms, drained

• Trim fat from steaks. Cut into serving-size pieces; pound to flatten. Rub with mixture of flour, ½ tsp. salt and ⅛ tsp. pepper. Brown in ¼ c. melted butter. Place in shallow baking dish.
• Melt remaining ¼ c. butter in same skillet. Add onions and cook until tender. Arrange over meat.
• Combine soup, light cream, Worcestershire sauce, garlic powder, salt and pepper; heat. Add a little of hot soup mixture to sour cream; stir until smooth. Stir into remaining soup mixture. Pour over meat and onions. Sprinkle with mushrooms. Bake, uncovered, in moderate oven (350°) about 40 minutes. Makes 6 servings.

COMPANY HAM BAKE

Guests won't suspect they're eating a quick-and-easy dish—this is so tasty

2 (10 oz.) pkgs. frozen Brussels sprouts
3 to 4 c. finely cubed canned ham
½ c. mayonnaise
1 can condensed cream of chicken soup
1 tsp. wine vinegar
½ c. bread crumbs, buttered
½ c. grated sharp Cheddar cheese

• Cook Brussels sprouts by package directions; drain. Place in a shallow 2-qt. baking dish. Top with ham.
• Mix mayonnaise, soup and vinegar and pour over the ham mixture.
• Mix bread crumbs and cheese and sprinkle evenly over the top.
• Bake in moderate oven (350°) 25 minutes, or until top is browned. Makes 6 servings.

HAM STUFFED PEPPERS

The superior filling makes these stuffed peppers a company special

8 medium green peppers
2 tsp. salt
1 medium onion, chopped (1 c.)
⅓ c. finely chopped celery
3 tblsp. butter
1 lb. ground ham
3 medium tomatoes
3 slices bread
½ tsp. salt
1 c. shredded Cheddar cheese

• Cut thin slice from top of each pepper; remove seeds. Boil, covered, in water with 2 tsp. salt added, 5 minutes; drain.

• Meanwhile, cook onion and celery in butter until soft (do not brown). Stir in ham and cook 1 minute. Add tomatoes, peeled and chopped, bread, cut in tiny cubes, and salt; mix thoroughly. Heat 3 minutes.

• Spoon into peppers. Set peppers in muffin-pan cups. Sprinkle top of ham stuffing with cheese. Bake in moderate oven (350°) 25 to 30 minutes. Makes 8 servings.

Sausage—Meat and Seasoners

Sausage is no newcomer to country kitchens, but our main dishes made with it are new. In them pork sausage provides meat and seasonings (herbs and spices). Carry Sausage-Bread Loaves to the club or church supper. They will stir up a lot of conversation.

SAUSAGE-BREAD LOAVES

Sausage bakes in hollowed-out bread loaf—wrap in foil to tote

½ lb. bulk pork sausage
½ lb. ground beef
1 medium onion, chopped
    (⅔ c.)
2 loaves brown-and-serve French bread, or 1 loaf regular French bread
⅓ c. water
1 egg, slightly beaten
2 tblsp. prepared mustard
2 tblsp. chopped parsley
½ tsp. salt
¼ tsp. orégano
1 small clove garlic, crushed
2 tblsp. melted butter

• Brown sausage in skillet. Add beef and onion; brown lightly.

• Cut ends from loaves of bread, hollow out, leaving a thin shell.

• Mix bread crumbs with water, egg, mustard, parsley, salt and orégano. Add meat; toss lightly.

• Pack meat mixture into bread shells; replace ends of loaves and hold in place with skewers. Add garlic to butter; brush on bread.

• Bake on baking sheets in hot oven (400°) 15 to 20 minutes. To serve, cut in 2″ slices. Makes 6 servings.

Note: Bake as many loaves as you need.

SUMMER SQUASH AND SAUSAGE

Pick squash young from the vines. You may need to adjust seasonings to the spicing of your sausage

1½ lbs. fresh (bulk) pork sausage
2 tblsp. butter or margarine
2 lbs. summer squash (zucchini, crookneck or pattypan), coarsely shredded
Juice of 1 lemon
¾ tsp. crumbled dried basil
½ tsp. salt
⅛ tsp. pepper

• Form sausage into 8 flat patties and slowly brown on both sides in a large skillet; remove from pan, pour off any fat in excess of 2 tblsp. Loosen pan drippings; add butter and melt.

• Add squash, and season with lemon juice, basil, salt and pepper; top with browned sausage patties. Cover and cook over medium heat about 8 minutes, or until squash is tender-crisp; stir once. Makes 4 generous servings.

Note: You may want to make two skilletfuls for 8 servings.

SWEET POTATO MAIN DISH

There are sweet potatoes, apples, sausage and maple syrup in this supper special. No wonder it tastes so good

4 c. thinly sliced, unpeeled tart
      apples
4 c. thinly sliced, uncooked
      sweet potatoes
2 tsp. instant minced onion
2 tsp. salt
½ c. maple-blended syrup
½ c. apple juice
¼ c. melted butter
1 lb. pork sausage
⅓ c. dry bread crumbs

• Arrange alternate layers of apple and sweet potato slices in greased 2-qt. casserole, sprinkling each layer with onion and salt.

• Combine syrup, apple juice and butter; blend and pour over all. Cover and bake in moderate oven (350°) 1 hour.

• Meanwhile, crumble sausage into skillet and brown. Drain; mix with bread crumbs.

• After an hour, uncover sweet potato-apple dish and spread with sausage mixture. Bake uncovered 20 minutes. Makes 6 servings.

TWO-RICE CASSEROLE

Wild rice is expensive, so a smart Texas ranch woman stretches it by mixing with regular rice. Good idea

1 lb. bulk pork sausage
1 c. chopped onions
2 (4 oz.) cans mushroom
      pieces, drained
¾ c. mixed long grain white
      and wild rice
½ tsp. salt

2½ c. water
½ tsp. poultry seasoning
2 c. chicken broth (13¾ oz.
      can)
¼ c. flour
½ c. toasted slivered almonds

• Cook sausage, onions and mushrooms in skillet until sausage is browned and onion is soft. Drain off the fat. Put sausage mixture in a greased 2-qt. casserole.

• Meanwhile combine rice (your own mixture or packaged long grain and wild rice mix) with ½ tsp. salt if you make your own mix, or with the seasonings in packaged rice mix. Add water, cover and bring quickly to a boil. Cover tightly and cook over low heat until all the water is absorbed, 25 to 30 minutes. When rice is cooked, add poultry seasoning.

• In a saucepan, combine a little chicken broth with flour and stir to make a smooth paste. Add remaining chicken broth and cook, stirring constantly, until thickened.

• Stir rice and broth into the sausage mixture in casserole. Top with almonds. Bake in moderate oven (350°) 30 minutes. Makes 8 servings.

Gourmet-Type Pork Dishes

When you feel the urge to fix company food on the gourmet side, try Pork Cantonese or Parslied Tomato Pork. Exquisite flavor blends are common to both dishes. It's a good idea to know your guests' tastes before you serve them these dishes. If they like only meat, potatoes and other standard country food, save these recipes to try on some of your friends who travel around to different places and countries. They often become more adventurous with foods and acquire a liking for many kinds.

PORK CANTONESE

Ring fluffy rice on platter and fill with this Chinese-inspired pork dish

2   lbs. boneless lean pork, cut
        in 1" pieces
2   tblsp. salad oil
1   (14 oz.) can pineapple
        chunks
1   (4 oz.) can mushrooms
⅓   c. unsulphured molasses
¼   c. vinegar
2   green peppers, cut in strips
2   onions, sliced and separated
        in rings
1 ½ tblsp. cornstarch
2   tblsp. water

• Brown pork on all sides in hot salad oil in skillet.
• Drain pineapple and mushrooms, reserving liquids. Combine liquids and add enough water to make 2 c. Add liquid to pork; cover and simmer until tender, about 45 minutes.
• Stir in molasses and vinegar until blended. Add pineapple, mushrooms, green peppers and onions; cover and cook 10 minutes. (Vegetables retain a little crispness.)
• Blend together cornstarch and water. Stir into hot mixture and cook until slightly thickened. Serve over hot rice. Makes 8 servings.

Borrow a trick from Swedish kitchens when you make lamb gravy. Use a little coffee, with cream and a little sugar added, for part of the liquid.

PARSLIED TOMATO PORK

Chick-peas instead of potatoes are a new note in this dish festive with tomato pieces and chopped parsley

1 ½ lbs. lean boneless pork slices,
        cut about ¼" thick (use
        leg or loin)
3   tblsp. salad oil
1   medium onion, minced
1   (1 lb.) can chick-peas
        (garbanzos), drained
3   medium tomatoes, cut into
        wedges (sixths)
¼   c. chopped fresh parsley
¾   tsp. salt
¾   tsp. garlic salt
¾   tsp. pepper

• In a large skillet, sauté pork slices over medium heat in salad oil until browned and tender. Pour off any oil in excess of 1½ tblsp. Add onion and sauté just until limp.
• Add chick-peas, tomatoes and parsley; season with salt, garlic salt and pepper. Cover and simmer 10 minutes; stir once or twice. Makes 6 servings.

Note: You may want to make two skilletfuls for 12 servings.

Distinctive Lamb Treats

Give the man-of-the-house a break and serve Marinated Lamb Roast for your next company dinner. It's a dish that always pleases the host. Not only because it tastes good, but also because it comes from the oven sliced and ready to serve. Guests like it.

Lamb takes kindly to barbecue sauces. The member of our Family

Test Group who shares her recipe for Barbecued Lamb Shanks says when she serves them she gives guests paper bibs and napkins. Helps to make eating fun, she finds.

Northwestern Lamb Stew is a favorite of an Oregon county home agent. She features it in after-the-game buffet suppers. The dish is especially appropriate in autumn when both cranberries and lamb are most plentiful. Another merit of this dish is that you can fix it ahead, refrigerate and quickly reheat.

MARINATED LAMB ROAST

Guests will like this precarved, new-style roast that comes from oven ready to serve. Lemon and onion slices and tangy tomato sauce flatter meat's flavor

4 to 5 lb. presliced square
    shoulder of lamb
1 medium onion, sliced
1 lemon, sliced
2 cloves garlic
1 tblsp. salt
½ tsp. pepper
½ tsp. dried orégano
1 bay leaf, crushed
¼ c. salad oil
¼ c. water
½ c. vinegar
1 (8 oz.) can tomato sauce
2 drops Tabasco

• Have meatman cut lamb shoulder into 1" chops with hand saw; then tie together with cord into original shape.
• Tuck onion and lemon slices in between chops. Crush garlic into salt; add remaining ingredients; pour over lamb in large shallow bowl.
• Cover and marinate at least 6 hours,

or overnight, in refrigerator, turning occasionally.
• Roast on rack in shallow pan in slow oven (325°), allowing 30 minutes per pound. Baste with marinade during last hour of roasting. Cut string to serve. Makes 8 servings.

Note: Try our marinade with a boned and rolled shoulder roast—perfect for rotisseries. Follow range manufacturer's directions. Insert meat thermometer to get correct degree of doneness: 175° for medium, 180° for well done.

BARBECUED LAMB SHANKS

Try this company supper special of a California Test Group member

8 lamb shanks
½ c. flour
1 tsp. salt
½ c. salad oil or shortening
½ c. brown sugar
2 tsp. dry mustard
½ tsp. salt
½ tsp. pepper
1 c. ketchup
2 tblsp. vinegar
1 (1 lb.) can tomatoes

• Roll lamb shanks in mixture of flour and 1 tsp. salt. Brown several at a time in salad oil in large Dutch oven or kettle. When browned, remove from kettle and brown other shanks. Pour off all fat.
• Meanwhile combine brown sugar, dry mustard, ½ tsp. salt and pepper. Stir in ketchup and vinegar. Pour over lamb shanks in Dutch oven. Then pour tomatoes over.
• Cover and bake in moderate oven (350°) 1½ to 2 hours, until meat is tender. Or simmer gently on top of range. Makes 8 servings.

NORTHWESTERN LAMB STEW

Colorful, hearty and winning at after-football-game suppers—stew may be made ahead, chilled and reheated

4   lbs. boneless lamb shoulder, cut in 1" cubes
3   tblsp. salad oil
3   tsp. salt
¼   tsp. pepper
1 ½ c. chopped onions
2   cloves garlic, sliced
2   (6 oz.) cans tomato paste
1 ½ c. apple juice, or dry red wine
1   c. water
½   tsp. ground ginger
½   tsp. orégano
1 ½ c. whole cranberry sauce
3   tblsp. cornstarch
½   c. water

• Brown meat in salad oil in large kettle or Dutch oven. Pour off all excess fat.
• Add salt, pepper, onions, garlic, tomato paste, apple juice and 1 c. water. Cover and simmer 45 minutes.
• Add ginger, orégano and cranberry sauce. Cover and simmer until meat is tender, about 45 minutes.
• Blend together cornstarch and ½ c. water. Stir into meat mixture and stir until bubbly and slightly thickened. Serve over cooked rice. Makes 12 servings.

Note: Cranberry sauce gives this lamb stew a slightly sweet, fruity taste.

VARIATION

Middle Eastern Lamb: Omit the cranberry sauce and follow recipe for Northwestern Lamb Stew.

Change of Pace with Veal

Bring out the kettle, if it's a cold day and friends are coming to dinner, and fix a country-style veal stew with plump dumplings. Along with the veal and dumplings, cook succulent vegetables. What a stew! Certainly the seasonings show the influence of an expert cook. Also try Company-Special Veal. Perfect for buffets, but also a good dish to carry to the covered dish suppers in a casserole.

COMPANY-SPECIAL VEAL

Count on compliments when you serve this veal—seasonings are the secret

½   lb. fresh mushrooms, sliced
2   tblsp. butter or margarine
½   c. flour
1 ½ tsp. salt
¼   tsp. pepper
1   tsp. paprika
1 ½ lbs. boneless veal, cut in ½ × ½ × 1" strips
¼   c. butter or margarine
1   clove garlic, minced
1   green pepper, cut in strips
1   onion, thinly sliced
1 ½ c. chicken broth
1 ½ c. processed rice, cooked (about 6 c.)
⅓   c. sliced pimiento-stuffed olives

• Brown mushrooms in 2 tblsp. butter. Remove from skillet and reserve. Combine flour, salt, pepper and paprika in paper bag. Shake veal in seasoned flour and brown in ¼ c. butter along with minced garlic. Add green pepper, onion and 1 c. chicken

broth; cover and simmer 30 minutes, or until veal is tender.
• Blend remaining ½ c. chicken broth with 3 tblsp. flour from paper bag. (If not enough seasoned flour is left, add enough flour to make 3 tblsp.) Add to veal mixture and cook, stirring until thickened. Add mushrooms to veal. Serve over hot rice, cooked by package directions, with sliced pimiento-stuffed olives folded into the rice. Makes 8 servings.

Note: If more convenient, cook rice, add olives and place in bottom of a 3-qt. greased casserole. Top with veal mixture, cover and bake in moderate oven (350°) 30 minutes. This makes a good and easy-to-serve company dish, but the rice is fluffier if veal mixture is spooned over it at serving time.

VEAL STEW WITH DUMPLINGS

Feather-light dumplings and tomato sauce share honors in this country-style stew

Stew:

2   lbs. veal, cut in 1″ cubes
¼   c. flour
¼   c. shortening
2½ c. hot water
1   c. diced potatoes
1   c. diced carrots
1   c. green lima beans or peas
½   c. chopped celery
½   c. chopped onion
2   bay leaves
1   tsp. Worcestershire sauce
2   tsp. salt
⅛   tsp. pepper
1   (8 oz.) can tomato sauce

Dumplings:

1½ c. sifted flour
2¼ tsp. baking powder
¾   tsp. salt
¾   c. milk
3   tblsp. melted shortening

• Roll meat in flour; brown in hot shortening. Add hot water; cover and cook slowly 1 hour, or until tender. Add vegetables and seasonings; continue cooking for 30 minutes.
• Meanwhile make dumplings. Sift dry ingredients together; stir in milk and shortening to make a soft dough.
• Add tomato sauce to stew; bring to a boil. Drop dumpling batter from spoon in 10 or 12 mounds on top of stew. Cover tightly and steam without lifting cover, 12 to 15 minutes. Makes 8 servings.

ROAST VEAL WITH SWEET ONIONS

Be sure the sweet onion rings are fine and crisp—they're the exceptionally good garnish for this carve-ahead roast

1   (4 lb.) boneless veal roast
    (rolled shoulder or leg)
⅔   c. salad oil
6   tblsp. wine vinegar
1½ tsp. salt
½   tsp. pepper
1   sweet onion, very thinly
    sliced

• Place meat on rack in roasting pan; insert meat thermometer. Roast in slow oven (325°) until meat thermometer registers 170°, or about 40 minutes per pound. Remove from oven and allow to stand about 20 minutes, then slice, saving juices.

• Shake or beat together oil, vinegar, salt and pepper. Remove any excess fat and burned drippings from roasting pan; loosen drippings. Add meat juices and the oil-vinegar mixture; stir to blend.

• Arrange meat slices, slightly overlapping, in roasting pan; spoon on juices to moisten well. Cover with foil. Before serving, place in moderate oven (350°) 10 minutes, or until heated through. Arrange meat slices on a warm serving platter; top with onions separated into rings.

• Quickly heat remaining roasting pan juice mixture; pass as a sauce. Makes about 8 servings.

VARIATION

Roast Lamb with Sweet Onions: Follow recipe for the roast veal, substituting 1 (4 lb.) boneless rolled leg of lamb (4 to 6 lbs. before boning) for the veal. Roast until meat thermometer registers 160°, about 35 minutes per pound. The lamb will make about 6 generous servings.

Main-Dish Custard Pies

You can call the main dish an unsweetened cheese custard pie or by its French name, *quiche* (pronounced keesh). It's good by either name, and an excellent choice for a company supper.

Cooks in France created this great dish. It's not surprising, for the French, from the beginning of their fame as good cooks to this day, have appreciated the value of fresh country eggs, cream, butter and cheese in the kitchen. In the provinces of Lorraine and Alsace, where the quiche originated, the first crusts were of bread dough, similar to pizza crusts. Pastry is the rule today. Many French country women fit the rolled pastry into the pans with their knuckles, which they insist are cooler than fingers.

We give you the basic recipe for the rich crust, the unsweetened custard and several fascinating fillings. Home economists adapted all of them to American tastes. We do include the famous Quiche Lorraine. You will notice that it is made with well-aged natural Swiss or Gruyère cheese and that bacon contributes flavor to the pie.

If you want to serve more than six people, you will want to bake more than one pie. If there are leftovers, refrigerate them. You can serve them cold or reheated on a baking sheet until piping hot. One of our men readers says he likes to eat the scraps as an accompaniment to a glass of cold tomato juice.

MAIN-DISH CUSTARD PIE

The crust of this open-face pie is rich with butter, filling is rich with cream. Serve with hot soup and a green salad

Crust:
1 ½ c. sifted flour
¼ tsp. salt
½ c. butter
1 egg, lightly beaten

Custard:
3 eggs
1 c. heavy cream

• Sift together flour and salt. Cut in butter with a pastry blender until the mixture resembles coarse cornmeal.

Add the egg and toss with a fork to mix.

• Gather dough into a ball and chill. Roll out on a well-floured board. Fit pastry into a 10" pie pan (or a 10" fluted tart pan).

• Measure the depth of the pan and trim the pastry 1" wider. Fold the dough over and press it firmly against the pan sides. Arrange the filling ingredients in the crust (see Variations).

• Beat the eggs for the custard and beat in the cream. Pour the custard over the filling in the crust.

• Bake in a hot oven (425°) 10 minutes; reduce heat to a slow oven (325°) and continue baking about 30 minutes or until the custard is set. To test for doneness, insert a knife in the center of the pie. If it comes out almost clean, remove the pie from the oven. It will set completely in a few minutes. Cut in wedges and serve warm. Makes 6 to 8 servings.

VARIATIONS

Ham-Cheese Custard Pie: Sprinkle ¼ lb. shredded Cheddar cheese and ¾ c. finely diced cooked ham in the crust. Blend 1 tsp. Worcestershire sauce, ¼ tsp. salt, ¼ tsp. dry mustard and ⅛ tsp. black pepper into the custard. Pour over the cheese-ham mixture. If you like caraway seeds, sprinkle 1 tsp. of them over the pie before baking.

Chicken-Cheese Custard Pie: Sprinkle ¼ c. grated Parmesan cheese in the crust. Top with 1 c. finely diced cooked chicken and 2 small green onions with tops, finely chopped. Add ¼ tsp. salt, ⅛ tsp. dry mustard and ⅛ tsp. black pepper to the custard and pour it over the chicken-onion

mixture. Sprinkle top of pie with ¼ c. sliced almonds and ¼ c. grated Parmesan cheese and bake.

Cheese-Spinach Custard Pie: Cook 1 (10 oz.) pkg. frozen chopped spinach (or 1 c. finely chopped fresh spinach leaves) until tender. Drain and squeeze dry. Cook 4 small green onions with tops, thinly sliced, in 1 tblsp. butter until soft. Remove from heat and combine with the spinach and ¼ c. finely chopped (or snipped with scissors) parsley. Blend ½ tsp. salt, ½ tsp. ground sage and ⅛ tsp. black pepper into the custard and stir into it the spinach mixture. Pour into the crust. Sprinkle top of pie with ¼ c. grated Parmesan cheese and bake.

Quiche Lorraine: Sprinkle ¼ lb. shredded, well-aged natural Swiss or Gruyère cheese and 8 slices crisp cooked bacon, drained well and crumbled, in the crust. Pour in the custard. Sprinkle lightly with nutmeg and bake.

WOODSTOCK

You can also serve this colorful dish over fluffy rice or baked potato

½ lb. sharp Cheddar cheese, cut in cubes
2 c. Thick White Sauce
6 hard-cooked eggs, sliced
1 (6 oz.) can whole mushrooms and liquid
2 tblsp. sliced pimiento
¼ c. thinly sliced green pepper
1 (5½ oz.) can chow mein noodles

• Add cheese to white sauce and heat in double boiler over boiling water until cheese is melted. Add eggs, undrained mushrooms, pimiento and green pepper. Heat. Serve over crisp noodles. Makes about 6 servings.

Thick White Sauce: For a thick sauce use ¼ c. butter and ¼ c. flour to 1 c. milk. Double this amount to make 2 cups thick sauce.

Note: Double this recipe to serve a crowd.

Unforgettable Garden Row Soup

Women who have gardens especially like to serve the end-of-the-season vegetables to guests in a farewell to summer. Garden Row Soup is a classic example of a gourmet dish that's almost a whole meal in itself— a meal in which the late vegetables take the spotlight.

This recipe was developed by the husband of one of FARM JOURNAL's food editors, who worked out the duplicate of a soup he remembered from boyhood days in Texas. He couldn't forget the big bowls of clear beef stock seasoned with spices and herbs, simmering with good-sized pieces of vegetables, none of them soft and mushy from overcooking.

Each vegetable contributes its own special flavor to the hearty soup. The pink, partly ripe tomatoes that appear on vines most abundantly at the end of the season help keep the soup clear and add a pungent flavor. The pieces of corn on the cob are a conversation piece. Guests enjoy the old Mexican custom of picking up the corn to eat out of hand.

FARM JOURNAL readers who have adopted the soup for a favorite in early autumn entertaining make the beef stock one day and refrigerate it. Then it's easy to lift off the fat with a spoon and finish making the soup the day company is coming. Keep the rest of the menu simple (see How to Plan Company Menus).

BEEF STOCK OR BROTH
The foundation for superior soup

4 lbs. beef soup bones (pieces)
2½ qts. cold water

• Remove meat from bones; cut it in small pieces. Put meat, bones and water in a kettle. Do not cover. Simmer (do not boil) 3 hours. Strain. Save the meat to chop and use later in hash, sandwiches and other dishes. *To remove fat from stock:* Skim off with a metal spoon lowered to the surface of the stock. Or lay a piece of paper towel on surface of fat. When it's saturated, remove and replace with another piece of paper towel. Repeat until the fat is removed. Or wrap a cube of ice in paper towel and draw across the top of the stock. Change paper as needed. Or refrigerate the stock overnight; you can then lift off the congealed fat with a spoon. *To clarify stock:* Crush an eggshell; mix with 1 egg white and ¼ c. cold water. Stir into lukewarm defatted stock. Heat to boiling; let stand about 5 minutes and strain through two thicknesses of cheesecloth or a fine wire sieve. Makes 2 quarts.

GARDEN ROW SOUP

Get out soup bowls and invite guests
to share this end-of-the-garden special

2 qts. beef stock, clarified
2 tsp. salt
½ tsp. orégano
½ tsp. marjoram
½ tsp. celery seeds
⅛ tsp. ground cuminseed
6 peppercorns
1 clove garlic, crushed
1 large onion, chopped
¼ c. chopped parsley
4 carrots, scraped and sliced
1 large green pepper, scalded, skinned and cut in strips
1 c. green beans, cut in pieces
1 zucchini, cut in ¾" slices
3 ears sweet corn, cut in 3" lengths
2 large pink tomatoes, skinned and quartered

• Simmer stock with salt, spices and garlic for 30 minutes.
• Add onion, parsley, carrots, green pepper and beans; simmer 20 minutes.
• Add zucchini and corn; simmer 15 minutes. Add tomatoes; simmer 15 minutes. Makes 8 servings.

Note: If you like, cut the corn in thin slices—they will look like rosettes in the soup.

CRAB BISQUE

This rich soup is an excellent supper
main dish. An electric skillet helps

1 can condensed cream of tomato soup
1 can condensed cream of celery soup
1 can condensed cream of mushroom soup
1 can condensed green pea soup
5 c. milk
1 (7½ oz.) can crabmeat
1 tsp. salt
Paprika
¼ c. chopped parsley

• Combine soups and blend. Gradually add milk. Stir in undrained crab and salt.
• Heat slowly, stirring constantly, until just hot enough to serve. (This must be stirred while heating, because it scorches easily.)
• Serve sprinkled with paprika and garnished with parsley. Makes about 11 cups.

HERBED POTATO SOUP

With this hearty soup in the freezer
you're always ready for supper guests

8 medium potatoes, peeled
2 onions, chopped or 2 tblsp. minced dry onion
4 tblsp. butter
2 tblsp. chopped parsley
½ tsp. crushed dried basil
4 tblsp. flour
2 tsp. salt
½ tsp. pepper
2 c. cold milk
4 c. scalded milk
2 c. hot potato water

• Cook potatoes and onions together until potatoes are tender. Drain; save potato water. Put the potatoes through a ricer or coarse strainer.
• While potatoes cook, melt the butter in a heavy 6-qt. saucepan. Add chopped parsley and basil.
• Blend in flour, salt and pepper; gradually stir in the cold milk. Add scalded milk and potato water. Cook

over medium heat; stir constantly, until mixture thickens slightly. Stir in potatoes and onions; heat. Serve in bowls; sprinkle soup with chopped parsley, or dust with paprika. This soup freezes successfully. Makes 12 cups.

SPAGHETTI SOUFFLÉ

A hearty colorful supper dish—it's surprising how remarkably good it is

2 c. soft bread crumbs
½ c. melted butter
6 eggs, separated
2 c. drained, cooked spaghetti
    (about 5 oz. uncooked,
    broken in 2" lengths)
2 tblsp. chopped parsley
2 tblsp. chopped pimiento
2 tblsp. chopped green pepper
2 tblsp. chopped onion
1½ tsp. salt
2 c. milk
Mushroom Sauce

· Combine bread crumbs and melted butter in mixing bowl. Stir in egg yolks and all other ingredients except egg whites and Mushroom Sauce.
· Beat egg whites until stiff but not dry. Fold into spaghetti mixture.
· Pour into a 2-qt. casserole or soufflé dish. Bake in moderate oven (350°) 1 hour, or until set in center. Serve with Mushroom Sauce. Makes 6 to 8 servings.

Mushroom Sauce: Sauté 1 (4 oz.) can drained mushroom stems and pieces in 3 tblsp. butter. Stir in 2 tblsp. flour, ¼ tsp. salt and ⅛ tsp. pepper. Gradually add 1 c. milk, stirring until smooth. Cook over medium heat, stirring constantly, until of medium thickness. Makes 1¼ cups.

Sunday-Best Country Chicken

To sort out good chicken recipes from our Test Kitchen files is a real chore. The problem is which ones to leave out. You run across so many distinctive and delicious chicken treats that you wish you could fill a whole cookbook with them. But, here are some of the most praised ones.

The recipe for Roast Young Chickens comes from a Santa Fe County, New Mexico, friend. You precook the chickens briefly, cool and freeze them. Then, when you want to have chicken for dinner, you hurry the birds into a hot oven or place them over glowing coals to thaw, finish cooking and brown. You can baste them with barbecue sauce or lemon juice while they cook. Either addition brings out interesting flavors. Incidentally, weight-watching guests rejoice that there's no stuffing to tempt them. Also try the other recipes that start with uncooked chicken—Parmesan, Fried Pecan, Sesame, Romano and Honey-Sauced Chicken, for instance. And for a more unusual taste delight, fix Chicken Kiev.

ROAST YOUNG CHICKENS

Keep partially roasted chickens in the freezer ready to brown in the oven or over coals—saves time

2 (2½ to 3 lbs.) broiler-fryers
1 tblsp. salt
¼ tsp. pepper
⅓ c. melted butter

· Rinse chickens in cold water; drain and pat dry with paper towels or a clean cloth. Rub the cavity in each bird with ½ tsp. salt. Fasten neck skin to back with skewers. Tie legs together.

• Rub outside of birds with remaining salt and pepper; brush with melted butter.

• Place chickens, breast side down, on rack in a shallow baking pan.

• Roast in a very hot oven (450°) 30 minutes; cool quickly. Wrap and freeze. Freeze pan drippings separately. Freezer storage time: up to 1 month.

• To serve, place frozen chickens on rack in shallow pan, breast side up. Roast in a hot oven (400°) about 1 hour, or until drumstick joints move easily. Baste with the thawed drippings (from freezer) several times during the roasting. Makes 6 to 8 servings.

VARIATIONS

Roast Chicken without Freezing: Prepare broiler-fryers as in the preceding recipe. Roast in moderate oven (375°) on rack in uncovered pan; allow 30 minutes per pound.

Southern Barbecued Chicken: Instead of basting precooked, frozen broiler-fryers with pan drippings, baste them with this sauce: Mix and bring to a boil 2½ c. water, 1 tblsp. brown sugar, 2½ tsp. pepper, 2 tblsp. pan drippings or salad oil, ¼ c. vinegar, 2½ tsp. salt, 2 tblsp. Worcestershire sauce, 2 tblsp. finely chopped onion, 1 tsp. dry mustard, 2 tsp. chili powder, ½ tsp. Tabasco and 1 clove garlic.

Lemon Barbecued Chicken: To the pan drippings (from the freezer) add ½ c. lemon juice for each broiler-

fryer. Use to baste frozen precooked chickens while roasting, instead of plain pan drippings.

OVEN-FRIED PECAN CHICKEN

Crisp-coated, golden brown chicken has a rich, pecan taste and it's much easier to fix than skillet frying

1 c. prepared biscuit mix
½ tsp. salt
2 tsp. paprika
½ tsp. poultry seasoning
½ c. finely chopped pecans
1 (2½ to 4 lb.) broiler-fryer, cut in serving pieces
½ c. evaporated milk
½ c. melted butter or margarine

• Combine biscuit mix, seasonings and pecans. Dip chicken into evaporated milk; then coat well with the flour mixture. Place in a 13 × 9 × 2" baking pan.

• Pour melted butter over the chicken, completely covering every piece. Bake in moderate oven (375°) 1 hour or in a slow oven (200°) for 2 hours, or until chicken is fork tender. Makes 4 to 5 servings.

PARMESAN CHICKEN

The coating on the chicken turns golden—its flavor can't be surpassed

1⅓ c. herb stuffing mix
½ c. shredded Parmesan cheese
¼ tsp. garlic salt
1¼ tsp. salt
⅛ tsp. pepper
1¼ tsp. monosodium glutamate
¾ c. butter (1½ sticks)
16 pieces chicken (breasts, thighs and legs)

• Roll stuffing mix to make fine

crumbs; put in pie pan. Mix in cheese and dry seasonings.
• Melt ½ c. butter (1 stick) in shallow pan. Dip chicken pieces, one at a time, into butter and then roll in crumbs to coat all over.
• Arrange chicken pieces in a large, shallow baking pan lined with aluminum foil. Do not overlap pieces. Dot chicken with remaining butter, breaking it in bits.
• Bake, uncovered, in moderate oven (350°) 1 hour. Makes 8 servings.

Note: To oven-fry chicken for 8 to 10 servings, double the recipe and arrange chicken pieces in 2 (13 × 9 × 2″) baking pans. Bake, uncovered, on 2 racks in a moderate oven (375°) 30 minutes; reverse position of pans on shelves in oven and bake 30 minutes longer, or until chicken is tender.

CHICKEN BARBECUED IN FOIL

You can fix as many silvery packages of chicken as your oven will hold

3 tblsp. butter
1 tblsp. brown sugar
¾ c. chopped onion
1 tsp. vinegar
2 tblsp. Worcestershire sauce
1 tsp. prepared mustard
¼ c. lemon juice
½ c. ketchup
1 (2½ to 3 lb.) broiler-fryer, cut in half

• Combine all ingredients except the chicken. Bring to a boil; reduce heat and simmer, uncovered, 15 minutes.
• Meanwhile, rub chicken with salt and pepper. Place each half on a piece of heavy aluminum foil, large enough for a drugstore wrap. Put half

of the sauce on each chicken half. Wrap.
• Bake in moderate oven (350°) 1 hour, or a very slow oven (200°) for 2 hours. Carefully open packages to avoid burns from escaping steam; turn back the foil.
• Broil chicken until browned. Remove from foil and serve with sauce. Makes 2 generous servings.

CHICKEN KIEV

These boned, stuffed and fried chicken breasts are an elegant guest special. Serve them on important occasions

4 large chicken breasts, boned and cut in half lengthwise
Salt
½ c. softened butter
½ c. chopped onion
½ c. chopped parsley
Flour
1 egg, well beaten
1 tblsp. water
½ c. fine bread crumbs

• Remove skin from chicken breasts; pound with wooden mallet or rolling pin to flatten to ¼″ thickness. Sprinkle with salt.
• Cream butter; add onion and parsley. Divide mixture into 8 even portions. Spread butter mixture at the end of each chicken breast. Roll as for jelly roll; tuck in sides of meat. Press to seal; fasten with toothpicks, or tie with string to secure.
• Dust each chicken roll with flour; dip into egg beaten with the water, and roll in bread crumbs. Chill at least 1 hour.
• Fry two chicken rolls in hot deep fat (360°) until golden brown, about 15 minutes. Drain on paper towels.

Repeat. Remove toothpicks or string. Serve hot. Makes 6 to 8 servings.

Note: You can pan-fry the chicken rolls instead of frying them in deep fat. Melt ¼ c. butter or margarine in a skillet; brown the chicken rolls on all sides. Cover and cook gently 12 minutes; uncover and cook 5 minutes longer, or until crisp, turning the rolls once.

SESAME CHICKEN

A sophisticated main dish that's tasty. It will impress your guests. Try it

Breasts, thighs and legs of
    2 broiler-fryers
1 tblsp. butter, melted
1 tsp. prepared mustard
2 tblsp. lemon juice
1 tsp. salt
2 tblsp. flour
⅓ c. sesame seeds, toasted
1 (⅝ oz.) pkg. cheese-flavored
    dry salad dressing mix
¾ c. evaporated milk
1½ c. prepared pancake flour
1 tblsp. paprika
½ c. vegetable shortening

• Wash chicken; pat dry with paper towels. Mix butter, mustard, lemon juice, salt, flour, sesame seeds and salad dressing mix to make a paste. Spread on the chicken to coat pieces.
• Dip chicken in milk, then in flour mixed with paprika. Lightly brown in hot shortening; turn carefully with tongs.
• Place in a 13 × 9 × 2″ baking pan. Cover pan with aluminum foil. Bake in moderate oven (375°) 35 minutes. Then bake uncovered 25 minutes, or until chicken is tender. Makes 6 servings.

CHICKEN ROMANO

*Specialty of a Maryland farm woman
—equally good hot or cold*

2 (2½ lb.) broiler-fryers,
    quartered
½ c. grated Romano or
    Parmesan cheese
¾ c. evaporated milk
¼ c. flour
1 tsp. salt
¼ c. cornmeal
⅓ c. butter, melted
1 tblsp. dried rosemary

• Wash chicken; pat dry. Rub on cheese. Dip chicken in milk and then in combined dry ingredients. Lightly brown in hot butter in heavy skillet.
• Arrange chicken quarters in a 13 × 9 × 2″ baking pan. Sprinkle with rosemary. Cover with aluminum foil.
• Bake in moderate oven (375°) 30 minutes. Remove the foil; bake 35 minutes more. Makes 4 to 6 servings.

HONEY-SAUCED CHICKEN

Honey and lemon give the not too sweet sauce a wonderful flavor

2 (3 lb.) broiler-fryers, cut in
    serving pieces
2 c. flour
½ c. bread crumbs
4 tsp. salt
½ tsp. pepper
¼ c. paprika
1½ c. butter
½ c. honey
½ c. lemon juice

• Roll chicken in mixture of flour, bread crumbs, salt, pepper and paprika.
• Put 1 c. butter in a 13 × 9 × 2″

baking pan; place in hot oven (400°) a few minutes to melt butter (do not let it brown). Remove from oven and arrange chicken in a single layer in the pan; turn chicken to coat with the melted butter.
• Bake 30 minutes, skin side down, in hot oven (400°). Turn chicken. Mix the remaining ½ c. butter, melted, honey and lemon juice. Pour over the chicken. Bake 30 minutes longer, or until chicken is fork-tender, basting frequently with the honey sauce. Makes 8 servings.

DRUMSTICKS IN BASKET

Offer guests sauce in which to dip their golden, crisp-coated chicken

24	chicken legs (broiler-fryers)
½	c. butter or margarine
½	c. flour
2¾	tsp. salt
¼	tsp. pepper
2	tsp. paprika

• Dip chicken legs in melted butter to coat; then roll them in a mixture of flour, salt, pepper and paprika. Arrange 12 legs in each of two buttered large, shallow pans. (Make 2 pans of heavy aluminum foil, each 13 × 9 × 1"; set each on a baking sheet.) Do not let chicken pieces touch. Pour any remaining butter over chicken.
• Place pans of chicken on two shelves in hot oven (425°) and bake, uncovered, 30 minutes. Turn chicken pieces and reverse position of chicken pans in oven (change shelves). Bake about 15 minutes longer, or until chicken is fork-tender and golden brown.
• Put paper frills on ends of chicken

legs; place in basket, frilled ends out. Place on buffet surrounded by sauces to ladle on serving plates. Makes 8 to 10 servings.

Assorted Sauces for Drumsticks

Apricot Sauce: In saucepan combine 1 (12 oz.) jar apricot preserves (1 c.) with ¼ c. prepared mustard and ¼ c. prepared horse-radish. Heat. Serve warm. Makes about 1½ cups.

Peppy Pineapple Sauce: Make like Apricot Sauce, substituting 1 (12 oz.) jar pineapple preserves for apricot preserves. Makes about 1½ cups.

Hot Tomato Sauce: Combine 1 c. bottled hot ketchup with 2 tblsp. prepared mustard. Stir to mix, but do not beat. Makes about 1 cup.

Sour Cream-Dill Sauce: Combine 1 c. dairy sour cream, 2 tblsp. mayonnaise and 2 tsp. dried dill. Chill several hours. Serve very cold. Makes about 1 cup.

Chicken, Hungarian Style

Many hostesses specialize in serving American adaptations of great world dishes. Chicken Paprika, borrowed from the Hungarians, is a typical example. After you fix it, you let the dish stand an hour to blend the flavors. This hour just before serving a company meal eases the before-dinner stress. You reheat last minute.

While Poppy Seed Noodles are the

traditional Chicken Paprika go-with, many country cooks prefer buttered Homemade Noodles, or, to the delight of the men, fluffy mashed potatoes.

Hungarian paprika has more "bite" than the kind available in most supermarkets. If you like a more pronounced seasoning, see Vegetable Spices in Index for the way to add more zip to American paprika.

CHICKEN PAPRIKA

A world-famous way to fix chicken—take a taste and you'll understand why

8   slices bacon
½   c. chopped onion
2   (3 to 4 lb.) broiler-fryers
1   c. flour
2   tsp. salt
2   tsp. paprika
2   tblsp. chicken broth

Gravy:
3   tblsp. flour
1   c. chicken broth
⅔   c. milk
1 ½ tsp. paprika
½   tsp. salt
1 ½ c. dairy sour cream

• Chop bacon and cook in large skillet or kettle until crisp. Remove bacon from skillet. Add onion to bacon fat and cook until soft (do not brown). Remove and set aside.
• Cut chickens in serving pieces. Reserve giblets and necks for other use.
• Combine flour, salt and paprika in a paper bag. Shake chicken pieces, a few at a time, in bag to coat with flour mixture. Brown chicken in bacon fat, adding more fat (about 2 tblsp.) if necessary. Spoon 2 tblsp. chicken broth over browned chicken; cover

and cook over low heat 25 minutes, or until tender.
• To make gravy, remove chicken from skillet. Stir flour into the fat in skillet to make a smooth paste. Add chicken broth and milk and cook, stirring constantly, until thick and bubbly. Stir in paprika, salt and reserved onion and bacon. Add sour cream, stirring over low heat, just until cream is blended in and gravy is heated (do not let boil).
• Return chicken to sour cream mixture, spooning sauce over each piece. Cover, remove from heat and let stand 1 hour to blend flavors.
• To serve, reheat (do not boil) and serve with buttered Homemade Noodles, Poppy Seed Noodles or mashed potatoes. Makes about 8 servings.

HOMEMADE NOODLES

Fascinate guests with these ribbons of egg dough cooked in chicken broth

3 egg yolks
1 egg
3 tblsp. cold water
1 tsp. salt
2 c. flour

• Beat egg yolks and egg until very light; beat in water and salt. Stir and work flour in with the hands to make a stiff dough.
• Divide into three parts. Roll each part out on a cloth-covered board as thinly as possible—paper thin. Place each piece of dough between towels until partially dry (it will look like a chamois skin).
• Roll each piece up like a jelly roll and cut with a sharp knife to make strips ⅛″ wide for fine noodles, ½″ for broad noodles. Shake out the

strips and let them dry before cooking. Makes 6 cups.

Note: Noodles freeze successfully if packaged in airtight containers.

POPPY SEED NOODLES

Heat poppy seeds in chicken fat instead of butter if you have it

2 (8 oz.) pkgs. noodles
4 tblsp. poppy seeds
6 tblsp. butter or margarine
2 tsp. salt
¼ tsp. black pepper

· Cook noodles by package directions; drain.
· Heat poppy seeds in butter until butter starts to brown. Add salt and pepper. Toss lightly with hot noodles. Makes 8 to 10 servings.

VARIATION

Poppy Seed-Almond Noodles: Heat ¾ c. slivered, blanched almonds with the poppy seeds.

CHICKEN-HAM BAKE

You'll be glad, when you make this, that a North Carolina home agent sent us her favorite recipe

4 chicken breasts, cut in halves
½ c. flour
1 tsp. salt
¼ tsp. pepper
½ tsp. seasoned salt
½ c. butter
4 center slices ham, ¼" thick
1 c. chopped onion
2 (4 oz.) cans mushroom pieces, drained
1 tblsp. snipped parsley
½ tsp. salt

½ tsp. pepper
½ tsp. ground mace
2 tsp. brown sugar
1 c. chicken broth, or ½ c. dry sherry wine and ½ c. chicken broth
½ c. orange juice

· Shake chicken breasts in paper bag containing mixture of flour, 1 tsp. salt, ¼ tsp. pepper and seasoned salt. Brown on all sides in skillet containing ¼ c. butter. (Add 2 tblsp. more butter during browning if necessary.)
· Trim fat from ham. Cut slices in lengthwise halves. Wrap one slice of ham around each piece of chicken breast and tie with string or heavy thread. Brown lightly. Place in a 13 × 9 × 2″ pan.
· Add remaining butter to skillet. Add onion and cook until soft. Add mushrooms and remaining ingredients; heat. Spoon over chicken-ham rolls. Cover pan with aluminum foil.
· Bake in slow oven (325°) 1 hour. Cut and remove string before serving. Makes 8 servings.

CHICKEN-RICE BAKE

Put this in the oven when you leave for church—you can get dinner fast

1½ c. regular rice
1 can condensed cream of mushroom soup
1 can condensed cream of chicken soup
1 can condensed cream of celery soup
1¾ c. milk
1 (3½ to 4 lb.) broiler-fryer, cut up
1 (1⅜ oz.) pkg. onion-soup mix

- Grease the bottom of a 13 × 9 × 2″ pan; add rice to make the bottom layer.
- Combine soups and milk; heat and pour over rice.
- Lay chicken pieces on top. Scatter on soup mix. Cover with aluminum foil.
- Bake in slow oven (325°) 2 hours. Makes 7 servings.

Note: Make 2 pans of this Chicken-Rice Bake for 12 to 14 servings.

CHICKEN WALNUT
American version of Chinese favorite

2 c. regular rice
1 c. walnut halves or large pieces
¼ c. salad oil
3 chicken breasts, skinned and cut in narrow strips (or 2 breasts and 2 thighs)
1 c. diced onion
1 c. diagonally sliced celery (¾″ pieces)
2 (5 oz.) cans water chestnuts, drained and thinly sliced
1 c. chicken broth
2 tblsp. soy sauce
3 tblsp. cornstarch
¼ c. water or cold chicken broth

- Put rice on to cook, using your favorite method.
- Cook walnuts in salad oil in skillet until yellow. Stir frequently and watch carefully to prevent burning. Remove nuts from skillet.
- Add chicken strips (2 c.), onion, celery and water chestnuts to skillet. Cook 5 minutes, stirring frequently. Add broth and soy sauce. Cover and simmer 5 minutes.

- Combine cornstarch with water (or cold broth). Stir into chicken mixture. Cook and stir until mixture is bubbly and thickened.
- Serve on rice; top with walnuts. Makes 8 servings.

CHICKEN BREASTS WITH SESAME
A happy discovery—this dish so easy to fix and serve, and so good to eat

6 large chicken breasts, boned
2 eggs, slightly beaten
1 tblsp. water
1 tblsp. soy sauce
1 tsp. salt
¼ tsp. pepper
¼ c. flour
½ c. sesame seeds
½ c. butter or margarine
Creamy Mushroom Sauce

- Remove skin from chicken breasts. Blend together eggs, water, soy sauce, salt and pepper in a shallow dish. Dip chicken into flour, then into egg mixture and next in sesame seeds.
- Melt butter in 13 × 9 × 2″ pan. Add chicken and turn to coat with butter.
- Bake in hot oven (400°) until golden brown and tender, 40 to 50 minutes. Serve with Creamy Mushroom Sauce. Makes 6 servings.

Creamy Mushroom Sauce: Sauté 1 (4 oz.) can mushrooms, drained, in ¼ c. butter until golden. Cover and simmer 5 minutes. Blend in ¼ c. flour; slowly add 1 can condensed chicken bouillon, stirring until smooth. Stir in ½ c. light cream and 2 tblsp. chopped parsley. Season with ⅛ tsp. pepper. Heat just until mixture simmers.

Note: A half pound fresh mushrooms may be substituted for the canned mushrooms. Add ¼ tsp. salt.

YELLOW RICE AND CHICKEN

Put this in oven 2 hours before meal-time and forget it until time to serve

1 ½ c. saffron-tinted rice
3   chicken breasts
6   chicken thighs
1   tsp. salt
¼   tsp. pepper
1   can condensed cream of
      chicken soup
1   can condensed cream of
      celery soup
1   can condensed cream of
      mushroom soup
2 ½ c. milk
1 ½ c. crushed potato chips
½   c. melted butter or
      margarine
⅛   tsp. paprika

• Place rice in bottom of well-greased 13 × 9 × 2″ baking pan. (Regular white rice may be used, but yellow rice is attractive.)
• Cut chicken breasts in halves. Arrange chicken pieces over rice, preferably in one layer. Sprinkle with salt and pepper.
• Blend the three kinds of soup together with milk. Pour over chicken; top with potato chips and then pour butter over all. Sprinkle with paprika.
• Bake in slow oven (325°) 2 hours or until tender. Makes 8 servings.

A TV tray set beside the hostess place at the table can hold rolls or relishes to be passed during the meal. Use the tray also in serving dessert or coffee.

CHICKEN-SPAGHETTI SUPPER

Chicken, spaghetti and cheese unite with expert seasonings in this dish

⅓   c. fat or salad oil
1   (4 to 5 lb.) stewing chicken,
      cut up
1 ¼ tsp. salt
1   medium onion, finely
      chopped
½   green pepper, finely chopped
½   tsp. paprika
½   c. diced pimiento (canned)
1   (1 lb.) pkg. spaghetti
1   c. pitted ripe olives, cut in
      halves
½   lb. process American cheese,
      grated
Salt
Pepper

• Melt ¼ c. fat or salad oil in heavy saucepan or Dutch oven. Add chicken pieces and turn often to brown on all sides. Cover with boiling water; add 1¼ tsp. salt and simmer about 3 hours, or until tender.
• Remove chicken from broth in which it cooked and cool. Measure broth; add enough water to make 2 quarts. Remove chicken from bones; cut in small pieces and return to the broth.
• Lightly brown onion and green pepper with paprika in remaining fat. Add to broth with pimiento. Bring to a boil; add spaghetti and cook until tender, about 15 to 20 minutes. Add olives and half the cheese, and simmer gently over low heat, stirring constantly, until cheese is melted.
• Check for seasonings, adding more salt and pepper if needed.
• To serve, pour into a large bowl or

heap on a platter and sprinkle with the remaining cheese. Makes 10 to 12 servings.

GOLDEN CHICKEN CASSEROLE

Its popularity shows up at buffets—guests keep coming back for helpings

- 1 large stewing chicken (4 to 5 lbs.)
- 1 large onion, quartered
- 1½ tsp. salt
- ½ c. chicken fat, butter or margarine
- ½ c. flour
- 2 (4 oz.) cans mushrooms, drained
- 1 c. evaporated milk
- 1 tsp. salt
- ⅛ tsp. pepper
- ½ tsp. turmeric
- ½ tsp. crushed orégano
- 1 c. rice
- 2½ c. boiling water
- 1½ tsp. salt
- 1 tblsp. butter
- ½ c. chopped green onions
- ½ c. shredded mild cheese

- Cook chicken until tender in water to cover with onion and 1½ tsp. salt added. Cool chicken (reserving broth); remove skin and cut chicken meat in small pieces with kitchen scissors.
- Melt chicken fat in saucepan. Stir in flour; add 4 c. liquid (juice drained from mushrooms and chicken broth) and evaporated milk. Cook and stir until sauce is thick and smooth. Add 1 tsp. salt, pepper, turmeric and orégano.
- Combine rice with boiling water; add 1½ tsp. salt and butter. Cover and bake in hot oven (400°) 30 minutes, or until tender.

- Spread rice in bottom of a large casserole or baking dish. Top with chicken, then with green onions, sauce and mushrooms; sprinkle cheese over top.
- Bake in moderate oven (350°) 30 minutes. Makes 10 to 12 servings.

CHICKEN-NUT CASSEROLE

A well-seasoned company casserole. Nuts and celery add crunchiness

- 1 stewing chicken (3½ lbs. or more), simmered, covered, in water until tender
- 1 c. chopped celery
- 1 c. walnuts, pecans or almonds, chopped
- 2 tblsp. minced onion
- 1 can condensed cream of mushroom soup
- 1 c. mayonnaise
- 2 tblsp. lemon juice
- ¾ tsp. salt
- ¼ tsp. pepper
- Fine buttered bread crumbs, or crushed potato chips
- Paprika

- Remove chicken meat from bones and chop. Mix with remaining ingredients, except bread crumbs and paprika.
- Turn chicken mixture into buttered 2-qt. casserole. Top with buttered bread crumbs, and sprinkle with paprika.
- Bake, uncovered, in moderate oven (350°) until bubbly, about 20 minutes. Makes 6 to 8 servings.

Note: This casserole may be wrapped and frozen before or after baking.

Chicken-Vegetable Skillet

Farm women with gardens are in luck. They have a real opportunity to share prime, succulent vegetables with friends. Here is an example of a simple but gourmet dish that features peas fresh from the vines, new potatoes, chicken and distinctive seasonings. Town people especially appreciate such country feasts.

SUMMER CHICKEN WITH PEAS

Garden Glory—one name for this main dish. Use care not to overcook peas, destroying their bright color

    6 tblsp. butter or margarine
    1 frying chicken (about 2½ lbs.)
        cut in serving pieces
    1 lb. small new potatoes,
        scrubbed, with a strip
        peeled around the centers
Salt
Freshly ground pepper
    2 tblsp. fresh lemon juice
    3 green onions with tops,
        thinly sliced
    1 lb. fresh peas, shelled
        (about 1 c.), or 1 (10 oz.)
        pkg. frozen peas
    ¼ c. chopped fresh parsley
    1 c. dairy sour cream
    1 tsp. crumbled dried thyme
    ½ tsp. salt
    ¼ tsp. pepper
Additional parsley

• Melt butter in a large skillet. Add chicken and potatoes and brown slowly on all sides; season with salt and pepper. (Be generous with pep-

per.) Sprinkle chicken with lemon juice; reduce heat, cover pan and simmer 30 minutes.
• Add green onions to butter in bottom of skillet; sprinkle peas and parsley over chicken and potatoes; cover again and simmer 10 minutes more, or until chicken and potatoes are tender.
• Remove chicken and vegetables to serving platter; keep warm.
• Remove skillet from heat. Add sour cream, thyme, ½ tsp. salt and ¼ tsp. pepper; stir to mix well and to loosen pan drippings.
• Pour over chicken or pass as sauce. Garnish with additional parsley; serve immediately. Makes 4 servings.

Note: You may want to make two skilletfuls for 8 servings.

Chicken with Curry

Chicken and curry powder are like peaches and cream—good companions. Perhaps you think of real Chicken Curry as a strange dish that only people in faraway India or neighboring places enjoy. That's scarcely true today when so many Americans travel extensively. Many a boy in military service tastes dishes on other shores that he learns to like. When he returns home, he brings along his fondness for them.

Why not get acquainted with international dishes that are world masterpieces and introduce your friends to them? It's a timely way to introduce interest in food when you entertain.

If you make Chicken Curry, it's a good idea to start out with the smaller amount of curry powder specified in the recipe. You can add the larger measurement next time, if you like.

Country Captain, a combination of fried chicken and curry, is truly American. Its birthplace is Georgia, where golden peach pickles are the favored accompaniment. It's a dish that many hostesses across country now feature in company meals. Give it a trial run and see if it doesn't please.

CHICKEN CURRY

You can make the curry sauce ahead, refrigerate and reheat at mealtime. Serve with bowls of condiments

1 (3 to 4 lb.) broiler-fryer,
    cut in pieces
1 large onion, chopped
¼ c. butter
3 c. chicken broth
6 tblsp. flour
1 tsp. to 1 tblsp. curry powder
Cooked rice

• Drop chicken pieces into boiling salted water to cover. Simmer, covered, until tender. Remove from broth and cool. Strain and reserve broth.

• Remove chicken from bones and cut in bite-size pieces.

• In a large saucepan, sauté onion in melted butter until clear (do not brown). Add 2 c. strained chicken broth; heat.

• Make a thin paste of flour and 1 c. cold broth or water, and slowly add to heated chicken broth, stirring constantly until smooth. Continue cooking and stirring until sauce is of medium thickness.

• Place curry powder in a small bowl. Gradually stir in a cup of the thickened broth, then return it to the saucepan. Add chicken and heat.

• To serve, spoon chicken curry over rice. Let people help themselves to condiments such as raisins, finely chopped almonds or peanuts, chopped hard-cooked egg, chopped sweet pickles, chutney, chopped fresh tomatoes or sliced green onions. Makes 6 generous servings.

Note: You can double this recipe to make 12 servings.

COUNTRY CAPTAIN

Delicious company dish you can put in oven and forget for 2½ hours. Fried and curried chicken combined

1 (3½ to 4 lb.) broiler-fryer,
    cut in serving pieces
¼ c. flour
1 tsp. salt
⅛ tsp. pepper
¼ c. shortening or salad oil
¾ c. finely chopped onion
1 green pepper, cut in strips
1 small clove garlic, minced
2 tblsp. butter or margarine
5 c. canned tomatoes
½ c. dark raisins
1½ tsp. salt
½ tsp. pepper
1 tblsp. curry powder
1 tblsp. butter or margarine
½ c. blanched, slivered almonds
½ leaf thyme, crushed
1 tblsp. chopped parsley

• Coat chicken pieces with flour mixed with 1 tsp. salt and ⅛ tsp. pepper. Brown in hot shortening; set aside.

• In a clean skillet, sauté onion, green pepper and garlic in 2 tblsp. butter. Add tomatoes, raisins, salt, pepper

and curry powder. Simmer 10 minutes.
• Place chicken in a 3-qt. casserole. Pour on the sauce. Cover; bake in moderate oven (350°) 1 hour, or in very slow oven (250°) 2½ hours, or until chicken is fork tender.
• Melt 1 tblsp. butter in a small skillet; add almonds and stir over medium heat until nuts are delicately browned.
• Sprinkle thyme, almonds and chopped parsley on chicken just before serving. Makes 6 servings.

SEVILLE RICE AND CHICKEN

Sea food, chicken and rice are main ingredients in this Spanish-style dish

  4   chicken breasts, halved
Salt
Pepper
  ¼   c. butter or margarine, melted
Paprika
  ½   c. sherry (optional)
  ⅓   c. olive or salad oil
  2   cloves garlic, minced
  1   medium onion, chopped
  1½ c. raw, long grain rice
  1   green pepper, chopped
  2   c. clam broth plus 1 c. chicken broth (or 3 c. chicken broth)
  1   (1 lb.) can tomatoes
  1   tsp. salt
  1   tsp. sugar
  1   lb. fresh or frozen raw shrimp, shelled and deveined
  ¾   c. pimiento-stuffed green olives, halved
  ⅛   tsp. red pepper

• Place chicken breasts, skin side up, in greased baking pan. Season with salt and pepper, brush with melted butter and sprinkle liberally with paprika. Bake, covered, in moderate oven (350°) 30 minutes. If you use sherry, uncover and pour it over the chicken; continue to bake until chicken is tender and nicely browned, about 15 minutes.
• In the meantime, heat oil in a large skillet; add garlic, onion and rice. Cook, stirring constantly, until rice is golden. Add green pepper, broth, tomatoes, salt and sugar. Cover; boil gently 20 minutes, or until rice is tender. Stir occasionally.
• Stir in shrimp, ½ c. olives and red pepper. Continue cooking, covered, about 5 minutes, until shrimp are cooked through and liquid is absorbed.
• Spoon rice onto large heated platter or plate, garnish with ¼ c. olive halves. Arrange chicken around rice. Makes 8 servings.

When you serve cold sandwiches, offer your guests cups of hot chicken broth, tomato juice or soup . . . a change from hot tea or coffee.

Cooked Chicken from the Freezer

Keeping cooked chicken in the freezer ready to use is a farm custom. So many marvelous chicken dishes begin with it and the broth, which country women freeze separately.

This collection of recipes illustrates how good these chicken treats can be. Chicken Pizza, by the way, is a young people's favorite.

CHICKEN CASSEROLE WITH BISCUITS

This main dish comes from Kentucky bluegrass country, an area of fine food

½   c. chopped onion
½   c. chopped celery
½   c. chopped green pepper
¼   c. butter or margarine
4   tblsp. flour
½   tsp. salt
¼   tsp. pepper
¼   tsp. garlic salt
2½ c. chicken broth
3   c. cubed cooked chicken
2   c. biscuit mix
⅔   c. milk
¾   c. grated Cheddar cheese
½   c. sliced ripe olives (optional)
⅛   tsp. paprika

• Cook onion, celery and green pepper in butter until soft. Blend in flour, salt, pepper and garlic salt. Add chicken broth and cook over medium heat, stirring constantly, until mixture is thickened and bubbly.

• Combine onion mixture with chicken and pour into a greased 2-qt. casserole. Place in hot oven (425°) to heat while you make the biscuits.

• Prepare biscuit mix, using ⅔ c. milk, as directed on package. Turn onto surface lightly dusted with biscuit mix and knead a few times. Roll out to make an 8″ square; sprinkle with cheese and olives. Then roll as for jelly roll, sealing edges. Cut 8 slices 1″ thick. Place biscuit pinwheels on top of hot chicken mixture in casserole, sprinkle with paprika and bake until biscuits are lightly browned about 25 minutes. Makes 8 servings.

Note: You can sprinkle ½ c. chopped

pimiento-stuffed instead of ripe olives on rolled dough if you like.

CHICKEN ROLLS WITH SAUCE

Flaky pastry swirls around moist chicken filling—the sauce is unusual and tasty

2   c. sifted flour
2   tsp baking powder
1   tsp. salt
½   c. plus 2 tblsp. shortening
¼   c. milk
1   egg, slightly beaten
2   c. chopped cooked chicken
2   tblsp. finely chopped parsley
¾   c. finely chopped celery
¼   c. chopped pimiento
1   can condensed cream of
      mushroom soup
½   c. dairy sour cream
½   c. milk

• Sift together dry ingredients. Cut in shortening. Add milk to egg; stir into dry mixture. Shape into two balls, wrap in waxed paper and refrigerate.

• Combine chicken, parsley, celery and pimiento. Stir in ½ can soup. Divide mixture in half.

• Roll half the dough into a 13 × 9″ rectangle. Spread with half the chicken mixture. Roll up like a jelly roll. Repeat with remaining dough and chicken mixture.

• Place the rolls on a greased baking sheet. Bake in moderate oven (375°) 30 minutes or until golden brown. Slice to serve.

• Blend remaining soup and sour cream; stir in milk and heat over medium heat (do not boil). Serve hot over each chicken roll slice. Makes 8 servings.

CHICKEN PIZZA

Youngsters say this is the best use for leftover chicken. Grownups agree

1 (6 oz.) can tomato paste
1 can condensed cream of
   mushroom soup
1 pkg. plain pizza mix
½ tsp. salt
Pepper
5 c. chopped cooked chicken
Grated Parmesan cheese

· Combine tomato paste, soup, sauce from pizza mix, salt and pepper. Simmer about 20 minutes.
· Prepare pizza crust by package directions and pat into a pizza pan. Add chicken to sauce; spread evenly on crust; sprinkle with cheese.
· Bake in a moderate oven (375°) 30 minutes, or until crust is browned. Makes 6 to 8 servings.

Note: If you do not have a pizza pan, pat the pizza crust into 3 (9") pie pans.

CALIFORNIA CHINESE CHICKEN

Excellent main dish for a crowd. May be combined and frozen to bake later

3 cans condensed cream of
   mushroom soup
2 c. finely sliced green onions
2 c. thinly sliced celery
1 (1 lb.) can bean sprouts,
   drained
4 c. diced cooked chicken
2 c. slivered toasted almonds
1 (4 oz.) can pimiento, chopped
¼ c. soy sauce
2 (5½ oz.) cans fried Chinese
   noodles

· Combine all ingredients except Chinese noodles in large mixing bowl.

Spread in greased 13 × 9 × 2" baking pan. Top with noodles.
· Bake in moderate oven (350°) 1 hour. Makes 10 to 12 servings.

VARIATION

California Hostess Turkey: Substitute cooked turkey for the chicken.

CHICKEN-BROCCOLI

Luncheon main dish—serve with a molded cranberry or other fruit salad

2 c. diced cooked chicken
1 (10 oz.) pkg. frozen broccoli
   stalks, cooked by package
   directions
½ tsp. salt
1 can condensed cream of
   chicken soup
½ c. mayonnaise
2 tsp. lemon juice
¼ tsp. curry powder

· Place chicken and broccoli in bottom of 1½-qt. casserole. Sprinkle with salt. Combine remaining ingredients and spread over top of chicken-broccoli mixture.
· Bake, uncovered, in moderate oven (350°) until bubbling hot, about 30 minutes. Serve hot. Makes 4 servings.

Note: To make 8 servings, bake 2 casseroles of Chicken-Broccoli.

DEEP-DISH ASPARAGUS AND CHICKEN PIE

Watch your guests take second helpings—better make two of these pies

Pastry for 1-crust pie
18 to 20 asparagus spears
   (about 1 lb.)
3 c. cut-up cooked chicken
6 (4 × 4") slices Swiss cheese

2 tblsp. Parmesan cheese
1 can condensed cream of
    chicken soup
½ c. liquid from cooked
    asparagus

• Cook asparagus in boiling, salted water 10 to 20 minutes, or until just tender; drain (reserve liquid). Cut spears into 1″ lengths.
• In a greased 2-qt. oblong baking dish, layer half of chicken, asparagus pieces and cheese slices. Sprinkle with 1 tblsp. Parmesan cheese. Repeat, using remaining chicken, asparagus and cheese slices. Sprinkle with remaining Parmesan cheese.
• Dilute soup with ½ c. asparagus liquid. Pour over layers.
• Roll out pastry in oblong shape; fit over chicken-asparagus layers.
• Bake in moderate oven (350°) 30 to 45 minutes, or until crust is nicely browned. Makes 6 to 8 servings.

RICE PILAF

Serving chicken or sea food and want a distinctive go-with? Well, here it is

1   medium onion, finely
    chopped
¾   c. thinly sliced celery
1 ½ c. long grain rice
¼   c. butter or margarine
1 ½ tsp. salt
¼   tsp. pepper
½   tsp. dried thyme
3 ½ c. chicken broth or bouillon

• Sauté onion, celery and rice in butter over low heat until vegetables are transparent and rice is golden. Add salt, pepper, thyme and chicken broth.
• Cover skillet with a tight fitting lid

and cook over low heat until broth is absorbed, about 20 to 25 minutes. Makes 8 servings.

Broken flower stems, mended with cellophane tape, last as long as unbroken ones.

Roast Goose
Is on the Platter

The New Mexico hostess who shares her recipe for roasting goose likes to use a stuffing containing fruits. She and her husband grow geese and select young birds for their company dinners. Weights of geese vary greatly, from about 4 to 14 lbs. ready-to-cook weight. Young goose has tender meat and cooks more quickly than a mature goose. Whatever kind you choose for your company dinner, allow from 1 to 1½ lbs. ready-to-cook weight per person.

The adobe home of the woman who graciously contributed this recipe is located in a high altitude area (7000 feet). For that reason, she roasts goose at a higher temperature (350°) than the one given in our recipe. She turns it breast side up, and bastes it every 15 to 20 minutes with apple cider and drippings, which give the bird a dark brown color. She also occasionally pricks the skin with a fork to encourage the fat to escape. Her husband, who says goose is harder to carve than turkey or chicken, suggests that it's a good idea to show the whole bird to the guests to tempt them, and then to carve it in the kitchen.

ROAST GOOSE
WITH FRUIT STUFFING

It's the fruited stuffing that's distinctive. Adds a tangy taste which is equally good in turkey or chicken

2 geese, each 6 to 8 lbs.
    ready-to-cook weight
Goose giblets
1 qt. water
2 (8 oz.) pkgs. prepared
    poultry stuffing
2 c. fresh cranberries, washed
    and mashed
¼ lb. fresh mushrooms, wiped
    and chopped, or 2 (4 oz.)
    cans mushrooms, drained
1 (1 lb.) can sweetened plums,
    drained, pitted and
    quartered (reserve ½ c.
    juice)
1 tblsp. salt
¼ tsp. freshly ground pepper

· Simmer giblets in water until tender, about 1 hour. Time will vary with age of the goose. Reserve ½ c. cooking broth from giblets. Chop giblets finely.

· Mix together prepared poultry stuffing, mashed cranberries, mushrooms, plums and ½ c. plum juice, salt, pepper, chopped giblets and ½ c. broth from cooked giblets.

· Remove any pinfeathers from geese and singe off hairs. Fill neck and body cavities with stuffing, skewer shut and truss.

· Place breast side down on rack in a large roasting pan. Roast uncovered in slow oven (325°) 3 to 4 hours for goose 6 to 8 lbs. ready-to-cook weight. (Fat drains to pan, rather than into breast meat.) Turn bird breast side up about two thirds of the way through the roasting time. During roasting, fat may be spooned or siphoned off as it accumulates in the pan so that it will not overbrown (use it for shortening in cooking).

· Test for doneness by moving the drumstick up and down. The joints should yield readily and the drumstick meat should feel very soft (do not undercook goose). Makes about 12 servings.

Roast Turkey
for Many Occasions

Turkey, roasted buttery-brown, holds its claim to supremacy on the Thanksgiving platter, but today's hostesses feature it in company meals the year round. One reason is that almost everybody enjoys it. Then, it's handsome and showy on the platter. If you wish to shorten the roasting time, cook the stuffing and turkey separately (see our Roasting Guide). For picnics, a whole turkey, roasted (without stuffing) a day ahead and chilled, is a true delight.

PERFECT ROAST TURKEY

Prepare the Turkey:

· Thaw bird if frozen. Let it thaw unwrapped in refrigerator 2 to 4 days, depending on size. Or if package is watertight, place it under running cold water until bird is pliable, 2 to 6 hours. Rinse inside and out with cold water, drain and pat dry with paper towel. Stuff if you wish. Shake bird to settle stuffing, but do not pack it. Truss turkey; brush with fat.

To Roast Turkey:

In Open Pan: Place breast side up on rack in shallow pan. Do not cover pan or add water. Cover turkey loosely with foil; then press the foil tightly at ends of drumsticks and neck; do not let foil touch top or sides of bird. Cook in slow oven (325°), basting occasionally with fat (optional). This way of cooking gives the most attractive roast turkey for carving at the table.

• When turkey is two thirds done (see Roasting Guide), cut band of skin or cord that holds drumsticks against turkey. This shortens cooking time by letting heat penetrate to inside of thighs. If you use a meat thermometer, insert it now (see directions) and continue roasting.

In Covered Pan: Some cooks like to omit the foil and cover the pan with a lid. Turkey cooked with a cover on has a steamed taste. Remove cover when turkey has an hour longer to cook so it will brown. The type of pan affects the roasting time. Turkey roasted in a shiny, light-colored pan may take as much as an hour longer than one cooked in a dark enameled or dull metal roaster.

In Foil: This is a good way to cook large turkeys, 16 to 24 lbs., for church or other community meals when carving is done in the kitchen. The high temperature shortens cooking time.

• Place turkey breast side up in center of wide, heavy foil that's at least 12" longer than the bird. (For big bird, put two widths together with drugstore fold and press to make leakproof seal.)

• Bring one end of foil up over turkey; then bring up other end, lapping it over first end by 2 to 3". Fold tightly. Fold foil down snugly over greased breast and legs. Press remaining sides up to hold drippings. Package will not be airtight.

• Place wrapped turkey in shallow pan without rack. Roast in very hot oven (450°). Remove pan from oven 30 to 40 minutes before turkey should be done (see Roasting Guide). Slit foil open and fold away from turkey to edge of pan. Insert meat thermometer if you use one. Return to oven until done.

To Insert Thermometer: Push it into thickest part of inside thigh muscle; do not touch bone.

Tests for Doneness:

1) Always make the pinch test: Protecting your thumb and forefinger with paper or cloth, pinch thickest part of inside thigh muscle; do not touch bone.

2) Turkey should be done when thermometer reads 185 to 190°.

ROASTING GUIDE

Ready-to-Cook Weight	Approximate Oven Times	
	In Pan at 325° (Stuffed)	In Foil at 450° (Unstuffed)
	Hours	Hours
6–8 lbs.	3½–4	1½–2
8–12 lbs.	4–4½	2–2½
12–16 lbs.	4½–5½	3–3¼
16–20 lbs.	5½–7	3¼–3½
20–24 lbs.	7–8½	3½–4

SAVORY TURKEY STUFFING

Vegetables, nuts make the difference

1 c. minced onion
1 c. finely chopped celery
1 c. shredded carrots
1 c. slivered almonds
1 c. shortening
12 c. dry bread cubes
    (about ¼")
1 tblsp. poultry seasoning
½ tsp. pepper
1 tblsp. salt
1 c. beef bouillon

· Sauté vegetables and slivered almonds 5 minutes in shortening (do not brown).
· To bread cubes add poultry seasoning, pepper and salt. Add vegetable mixture and broth to moisten; toss lightly to mix. Cool completely. Then stuff turkey, or bake it in a pan 1 hour. Makes enough stuffing for a 12 to 14 lb. turkey.

Note: If you have a large turkey, add 1 c. bread cubes for each additional pound of turkey. It is not necessary to change other ingredients unless turkey weighs more than 18 pounds.

ROAST DUCKLINGS
IN CARROT SAUCE

Garnish with orange and banana slices

2 (5 lb.) ducklings
½ lemon
Salt
Pepper
Lemon-Carrot Sauce
2 oranges, peeled and sliced

3 bananas, peeled, cut in 1"
    diagonal slices and
    brushed with lemon juice
4 tblsp. chopped fresh parsley

· Rub skin of ducklings with lemon; rub cavities with salt and pepper; close cavities with skewers. Place on rack in roasting pan; roast in moderate oven (350°) about 1½ hours, or until leg joints move easily.
· Remove ducks from oven and cut into quarters with poultry shears or electric slicing knife. Replace in whole-duck shape on heat-proof serving platters. Spoon about ⅓ Lemon-Carrot Sauce over ducks; surround with orange and banana slices.
· Bake in moderate oven (350°) 10 minutes, or until heated through. Sprinkle with parsley. Serve a duck quarter with orange and banana slices to each person; pass remaining hot Lemon-Carrot Sauce. Makes 8 servings.

LEMON-CARROT SAUCE

Delightful coating for roast duck

1 medium onion, finely chopped
2 large carrots, peeled and
    grated
4 tblsp. butter (or part butter,
    part duck drippings)
2 tblsp. cornstarch
2 c. chicken broth
3 tblsp. lemon juice
⅓ c. sugar
Salt
Pepper
3 tblsp. chopped fresh parsley

· Sauté onion and carrots in butter until limp.
· Blend cornstarch into ¼ c. chicken broth. Stir into butter mixture. Add

remaining broth, lemon juice and sugar. Season to taste with salt and pepper.

· Cook over medium heat, stirring, for about 5 minutes or until sauce is clear and slightly thickened. Stir in 3 tblsp. chopped fresh parsley. Makes enough sauce for two 5-lb. ducklings.

Country Game and Fish Favorites

Game and fish dinners have a special appeal in farm homes, especially if the men (or women) in the family like to hunt and fish. Farmers take pride in their quarry. They like to share their prizes with friends.

We give you choice recipes for game and fish from farm and ranch kitchens. Be sure to try our fish sauces. They are exceptional. And for good measure, we include some sea food specialties.

BRAISED RABBIT IN WINE SAUCE
Gourmets praise rabbit fixed this way

2 rabbits, cut into pieces
Flour
Salt
Pepper
Butter
¼ c. dry white wine
1 c. hot water
1 c. chopped celery
½ c. chopped parsley
1 bay leaf
¼ tsp. paprika

· Roll rabbit pieces in flour. Season with salt and pepper. In a large skillet, sauté rabbit pieces in ½" butter until well browned.

· Add remaining ingredients; cover

and simmer over low heat until tender, about 1 hour. (Add more water to sauce if necessary.) Remove bay leaf before serving. Serve with buttered noodles, glazed parsnips, lettuce wedges and cranberry pie. Makes 8 to 10 servings.

Six Good Ways to Cook Wild Ducks

Wild ducks are better eating than ever. That's what many farmers, who like to shoot ducks, and their wives, who take pride in cooking the prizes their husbands bring home, tell us. The main reason for the improvement, they say, is that the ducks themselves eat better. They get more corn, wheat and other small grains left in the fields by mechanical harvesters.

When the food editors of FARM JOURNAL wanted to find the best ways to cook wild duck, they went directly to the homes of men who like to hunt and who, with their families and friends, consider duck dinners special treats. One wild duck makes 1 or 2 servings, depending on its size. Most farmers insist that their wives cook as many ducks as people around the table.

Here are six recipes, all different, that are the result of the quest. They come from the four major duck flyways—Atlantic, Mississippi, Central and Pacific. Home economists in our Test Kitchens used mallards, each weighing about 1¾ pounds, to test the recipes. You can adjust the cooking time to the size of the birds you have and to their age. When you're in doubt about age, or think the ducks lost fat during a long flight, it's a good plan to wrap the birds individually in foil when roasting them.

There are some men who like duck cooked very rare, about 22 minutes in a hot oven (400°). Our recipe for California Rare Duck is a compromise between the very-rare and the well-done versions. It was the favorite of men editors on FARM JOURNAL who shoot ducks. Several readers have written that they never liked wild duck until they tasted Texas Barbecued Duck (see picture in this cookbook).

TEXAS BARBECUED DUCK

Roasting ducks in foil is a safe bet—it tenderizes and keeps birds moist

2 wild ducks
2 tblsp. salad oil
Barbecue Sauce

• Rub ducks with oil; brown under broiler. Brush ducks with half the Barbecue Sauce; place 1 tblsp. sauce in cavity. Wrap each bird closely in heavy foil; bake in shallow pan in slow oven (325°) 1 hour, or until tender. Remove foil last 15 minutes, and spoon over remainder of sauce.

To Grill Outdoors: Proceed as above, browning over hot coals and finishing over slow coals.

Barbecue Sauce: Sauté 2 tblsp. chopped onion in ¼ c. butter. Add ½ c. ketchup, ½ c. lemon juice, ¼ tsp. paprika, ½ tsp. salt, ¼ tsp. pepper, ¼ tsp. red pepper, 2 tblsp. brown sugar and 2 tblsp. Worcestershire sauce. Simmer 15 minutes.

WILD DUCK IN SOY MARINADE

Favorite of an Arkansas man who hunts on his cotton and rice farm

2 wild ducks, quartered
1 (13½ oz.) can pineapple tidbits
½ c. soy sauce
1 tsp. ground ginger
¼ c. shortening or bacon drippings
1 (3 oz.) can mushrooms, drained

• Marinate ducks overnight in mixture of pineapple, soy sauce and ginger.
• Wipe meat; brown in fat. Place in shallow casserole; pour on marinade and mushrooms. Bake, covered, in moderate oven (350°) 1½ hours, or until tender (add water, if necessary).

DUCK FILETS

Some Arkansas farm women fix these for church suppers. They cook filets at home, layer them in electric roasters—they're easy to tote and reheat

1 wild duck
Instant meat tenderizer
2 slices bacon
2 tblsp. salad oil

• With sharp knife, remove skin from duck. Cut meat from breast in 2 filets.
• Use meat tenderizer as directed on the package. Wrap each filet loosely with bacon slice; fasten with toothpicks.
• Cook filets in hot oil over moderate heat until browned and tender, about 15 minutes per side. Serve on hot platter surrounded by ribbons of cooked bacon.

VARIATION

Duck Patties: Omit tenderizer. Pound filets; dip in mixture of salt, pepper and flour. Round into patties; wrap bacon strip around edge; fasten with toothpick. Cook in hot oil over moderate heat until browned and tender, about 15 minutes on each side.

CALIFORNIA RARE DUCK

Ducks roasted this way are tender and moist—glaze makes skin crisp, shiny. Pink flesh tastes like beef

1 wild duck
1 tsp. salt
½ tsp. pepper
¼ tsp. garlic salt

• Rub cavity and outside of duck with seasonings. Bake on rack in shallow pan, uncovered, in extremely hot oven (500°) 25 to 35 minutes.

To Glaze: Ten to 15 minutes after placing duck in oven, brush several times with mixture of 2 tblsp. light or dark corn syrup and 1 tsp. bottled gravy flavoring.

SPICY ROAST DUCK

Serve ducks in foil packages; let everyone open his own and enjoy the fragrance of allspice and bay leaf

1 wild duck
2 tblsp. flour
½ tsp. salt
⅛ tsp. pepper
1 tblsp. whole allspice, cracked
1 bay leaf, crumbled

• Rub duck inside and out with mixture of flour, salt, pepper and allspice.
• Sprinkle bay leaf pieces over top.
• Place on rack in roaster (arranging several ducks close together helps prevent drying). Bake, covered, in slow oven (325°) 2½ to 3 hours, or until tender. It's a good idea to wrap each duck in foil the last hour of roasting.

In making sauces, 1 tblsp. cornstarch has about the same thickening power as 2 tblsp. flour.

BASTED DUCK WITH OYSTER STUFFING

In Maryland's oyster country, many cooks fill ducks with oyster stuffing

1 duck
1 tsp. salt
¼ tsp. pepper
1 qt. bread stuffing (your favorite)
1 c. oysters
¼ c. melted butter
¼ c. lemon juice
¼ tsp. paprika
⅛ tsp. dried thyme

• Season duck cavity and outside of bird with salt and pepper.
• To your favorite bread stuffing, add 1 c. oysters, drained and chopped. Use oyster liquor as a part of liquid to moisten stuffing.
• Lightly stuff duck; put the remainder of the stuffing in a pan to bake with duck (baste with duck drippings).
• Place duck on a rack in a roasting pan; cover and bake in a slow oven (325°) about 2½ hours. Remove cover to brown.
• Baste often during roasting with mixture of butter, lemon juice, paprika and dried thyme.

BROILED LAKE TROUT

There's no greater platter treat than grilled fish expertly seasoned

4   large filets of lake trout
Salt
Pepper
¼ c. finely chopped onion
1¼ tsp. dried dill weed
1   c. melted butter or
      margarine
Juice of 1 lemon

• Place 4 large fish filets in 2 lightly greased 15½ × 10½ × 1″ jelly roll pans.
• Sprinkle with salt, pepper, onion and dill weed. Drizzle on ½ c. melted butter.
• Mix remaining ½ c. melted butter with juice of 1 lemon.
• Preheat broiler. Place one pan about 5″ from broiler unit. Broil about 10 minutes, or until fish flakes easily. Drizzle on lemon-butter mixture as the fish broils. Keep trout hot while you broil the other pan of fish. Makes 8 generous servings.

HALIBUT AU GRATIN

Pretty served from a casserole but also when baked in individual shells

1   lb. fresh or frozen halibut
4   slices onion
2   bay leaves
4   tblsp. butter or margarine
4   tblsp. flour
2   c. milk
½ lb. Cheddar cheese, shredded
Salt
Pepper
½ c. buttered bread crumbs
Parsley
Paprika

• Top halibut with onion slices and broken bay leaves. Steam in a covered pan 30 minutes.
• Meanwhile, melt butter, stir in flour, add milk and stir and cook until sauce thickens and is smooth.
• Add cheese and stir until it is melted; then season to taste with salt and pepper.
• Break halibut into serving-size pieces, discard bay leaves and place fish in buttered 1½-qt. casserole. Top with cheese sauce and sprinkle with buttered bread crumbs, chopped parsley and paprika.
• Bake in moderate oven (350°) 30 minutes. Makes about 4 servings.

Note: This is a recipe you can double successfully or make 2 recipes if you wish to serve the dish to more than 4.

Quartet of Superb Fish Sauces

Good cooks around the world trade recipes for their favored nationality dishes. Since Europeans often are experts in handling fish in their kitchens, we asked a home economist for their secrets which she scouted when she visited France, Spain and Portugal. The four sauces that dress up fish and make it taste better than ever are the result. They're just what a hostess wants when she plans to have fish for a company meal.

You can use fresh or frozen white fish of any kind—fresh or salt water varieties from the supermarket or what the fisherman in your family brings home. Serve these sauces on such fish as halibut, swordfish, sea bass, butterfish, cod, haddock, sole, flounder, perch, mackerel, lake trout or catfish. If you use frozen fish, defrost it overnight or at least several hours in the refrigerator.

Cook the fish until it loses its translucency and breaks apart in flakes when you test it with a fork or the tip of a knife. The secret is not to cook fish too long, for that makes the flesh dry. Season it lightly with salt and pepper before adding the sauce.

Our recipes make enough sauce for 2 pounds of fish, about 6 servings. You may want to prepare the recipe twice if you are serving more people. It won't be a burden, for these sauces are easy and quick to make.

CHEESE-PIMIENTO WHIP

This bright-with-color sauce makes fried and broiled fish exciting

1 (3 oz.) pkg. cream cheese, softened
1 tsp. lemon juice
⅛ tsp. salt
⅛ tsp. pepper
½ c. heavy cream, softly whipped
1 (2 oz.) jar pimientos, drained and sliced
3 tblsp. minced green onions with part of green tops

· Beat cream cheese, lemon juice, salt and pepper together until creamy; fold into whipped cream along with pimientos and green onions.
· Drop spoonfuls of whip on servings of hot, cooked fish. Let it melt down and turn into a sauce. Makes enough whip for 2 pounds of fish, about 6 servings.

If your church group serves lunches at farm sales in a tent or garage, here's how to add temporary shelves for food. Place 2 stepladders a short distance apart; rest boards between them on the steps. Use this extra space for such things as pieces of pie and cake. Everything is within plain sight of the waitresses, too.

VEGETABLE-EGG SAUCE

Chopped green vegetables and yellow and white hard-cooked eggs decorate the platter of fish and add flavor

1 tblsp. butter
1 c. heavy cream
½ tsp. garlic salt
½ tsp. dry mustard
¼ tsp. pepper
⅛ tsp. salt
2 tblsp. finely chopped parsley
2 hard-cooked eggs, grated or finely chopped
½ c. cooked peas or frozen peas, thawed to separate
1 (10½ oz.) can asparagus tips, drained

· Combine butter, cream, garlic salt, dry mustard, pepper and salt in a saucepan; bring to a boil, then simmer just a few minutes, to reduce slightly.
· Add remaining ingredients; heat through, stirring gently to blend.
· Spoon over hot, cooked fish; sprinkle with additional parsley. Makes enough sauce for 2 pounds of fish, about 6 servings.

FISH SAUCE PROVENÇALE

Use this colorful sauce when you want to show guests how tasty fish can be

4   medium tomatoes, cut in
    sixths, seeded and peeled
    if you wish
½   tsp. sugar
⅓   c. finely sliced green onions
    (white part only)
2   tblsp. butter
1 ½ tblsp. lemon juice
½   c. butter
½   tsp. garlic salt
¼   tsp. salt
¼   tsp. pepper
4   tblsp. finely chopped parsley

• Sprinkle tomatoes with sugar.
• In large frying pan, sauté green onions in the 2 tblsp. butter, just until limp. Add tomatoes and gently cook and turn just until heated through.
• Add remaining ingredients. Gently shake and tilt pan over heat to mix ingredients and just melt butter. (Butter should be of a thick creamy consistency; do not let it melt down to a thin liquid.)
• Spoon over hot, cooked fish. Makes enough sauce for 2 pounds of fish, about 6 servings.

CUCUMBER MAYONNAISE

Especially for baked and broiled fish. Make sauce with dill once, next time with tarragon—both enhance fish

½   c. mayonnaise
1   tsp. finely crumbled dried
    tarragon, or ½ tsp. dried
    dill weed
1   tsp. lemon juice
½   tsp. scraped onion
⅛   tsp. salt
⅛   tsp. pepper
1   large cucumber, peeled and
    coarsely grated

• Mix together thoroughly mayonnaise, tarragon or dill, lemon juice, onion, salt and pepper. Squeeze excess moisture from cucumber; fold into mayonnaise mixture. Chill thoroughly. Makes enough sauce for 2 pounds of fish, about 6 servings.

BUTTERED SHRIMP AND PINEAPPLE

Unusual food combination makes this pretty main dish a conversation piece

4   tblsp. butter or margarine
1   large green pepper, seeded
    and cut crosswise into ¼"
    thick rings
1 ½ lbs. large uncooked shrimp
    (fresh shrimp or frozen,
    thawed), shelled and
    deveined
1   (1 lb. 4 oz.) can pineapple
    slices, drained, or 8
    slices fresh pineapple
¾   tsp. salt
⅛   tsp. pepper
2   tsp. chili powder
Lime or lemon wedges

• Melt butter in a large skillet over medium heat. Add green pepper, shrimp and pineapple; season with salt and pepper, and generously with chili powder.
• Sauté, turning gently, just until shrimp turn pink and green pepper is tender-crisp—about 10 minutes. Serve immediately with lime or lemon wedges and steamed rice. Makes 4 servings.

Note: You may want to make two skilletfuls for 8 servings.

SHRIMP CREOLE

What a color-bright main dish—plump pink shrimp and bright green pea pods

2	tblsp. butter
½	medium green pepper, chopped
2	medium onions, chopped
½	c. chopped celery
1	(1 lb. 4 oz.) can tomatoes
1½	tsp. salt
¼	to ½ tsp. black pepper
⅛	tsp. red pepper
1	c. water
1	tblsp. flour
1	tsp. sugar
2	c. cooked shrimp
1	pt. frozen pea pods (snow peas), partially defrosted

• Melt butter in skillet; sauté green pepper, onions and celery until tender. Add tomatoes, salt, black pepper, red pepper and water. Cover and cook about 10 minutes.

• Combine flour and sugar; add enough water to make a smooth paste and stir into tomato mixture. Cook and stir until slightly thickened. Add shrimp and pea pods; cook until pea pods are tender, about 5 minutes. Serve with fluffy rice. Makes 6 servings.

SHRIMP MARENGO

Simply delicious, taste-testers voted

3	lbs. fresh or frozen shrimp
8	slices bacon
1	c. chopped onion
1	clove garlic, minced
2	(8 oz.) cans mushroom stems and pieces, undrained
2	(1 lb.) cans tomatoes (4 c.)
1	(6 oz.) can tomato paste
1	can consommé
1	tsp. dried basil
1¼	tsp. dried orégano
1	tsp. salt
1	tsp. monosodium glutamate
1	tblsp. sugar
3	tblsp. prepared mustard
3	drops Tabasco
½	c. flour
½	c. water
Fluffy Rice	

• Clean shrimp. Fry bacon, cut in pieces, until crisp; drain. Set bacon aside. To bacon drippings add onion and cook lightly. Add garlic, shrimp, undrained mushrooms, tomatoes, tomato paste, consommé, basil, orégano, salt, monosodium glutamate, sugar, mustard and Tabasco. Cook gently 10 minutes.

• Combine flour and water to make a smooth paste. Stir into shrimp mixture and cook 1 minute, stirring all the time. Add bacon. Serve on Fluffy Rice. Makes 16 cups, or 16 servings.

Fluffy Rice: For 16 servings, bring to a boil 7½ c. water. Add 3 c. long grain converted rice and 3 tsp. salt. Cover and simmer until all the water is absorbed, about 25 minutes.

Keep Canned Fish in Your Cupboard

Cans of fish, like salmon and tuna, are insurance that you can make a good company main dish on short notice. Here are some splendid examples of hearty, tasty combinations. In one of them, Salmon Loaf with

Shrimp Sauce, you fix a treat for your guests by making a sauce from canned, frozen cream of shrimp soup.

SALMON LASAGNE

Keep makings on hand and you can fix a good main dish in a hurry

½ c. chopped onion
½ c. chopped green pepper
¼ c. butter or margarine
2 (6 oz.) cans tomato paste
1½ c. water
1 tsp. dried basil
½ tsp. salt
⅛ tsp. pepper
2 (1 lb.) cans salmon
1 (8 oz.) pkg. lasagne
    noodles, cooked
1 (6 oz.) pkg. mozzarella
    cheese slices
½ c. grated Parmesan cheese

• Cook onion and green pepper in butter until tender, but do not brown. Add tomato paste, water, seasonings and salmon.
• Grease a 13 × 9 × 2″ baking pan; alternate layers of noodles, salmon mixture and cheeses, making three layers of each, with cheeses on top.
• Bake in moderate oven (375°) 25 minutes. Makes 12 to 14 servings.

SALMON LOAF
WITH SHRIMP SAUCE

Makings for this superb dish come from cupboard, refrigerator, freezer

2 (1 lb.) cans salmon
¼ c. finely minced onion
¼ c. chopped parsley

¼ c. lemon juice
½ tsp. salt
½ tsp. pepper
½ to 1 tsp. ground thyme
2 c. coarse cracker crumbs
About ½ c. milk
4 eggs, well beaten
¼ c. butter, melted
Shrimp Sauce

• Drain salmon, saving liquid.
• Flake salmon into bowl; add onion, parsley, lemon juice, seasonings and cracker crumbs; mix lightly.
• Add salmon liquid plus enough milk to make 1 cup; add eggs and melted butter. Mix lightly.
• Spoon into greased 2-qt. loaf pan or casserole. Bake in moderate oven (350°) 1 hour or until loaf is set in center. Makes 8 servings.

Shrimp Sauce: Heat a can of frozen condensed cream of shrimp soup according to directions on label. Add ¼ c. milk, stir until smooth. Spoon onto hot salmon loaf.

SALMON NOODLE CASSEROLE

At its best for supper on a cold day. Most kitchens have all the makings

1 (7¾ oz.) can salmon
1 (10 oz.) pkg. frozen peas,
    cooked by package
    directions and drained
½ (8 oz.) pkg. noodles, cooked
    by package directions
    and drained
1 tblsp. chopped onion
½ c. salad dressing
¼ c. milk

Keep the ingredients for Salmon Loaf with Shrimp Sauce (*recipe, above*) on hand in your pantry and freezer and you're deliciously ready for guests. This well-flavored loaf with its easy sauce makes a first-rate company dish.

1 can condensed cream of
celery soup
¼ c. Parmesan cheese

• Mix salmon, peas, noodles and onion together.
• Stir salad dressing and milk into
soup; pour over noodle mixture, tossing together lightly.
• Spread in a greased flat 13 × 9 × 2″
baking dish and sprinkle the top with
cheese.
• Bake in moderate oven (350°) 25
to 30 minutes. Makes 6 servings.

Tuna Stars in Many Dishes

Look at the tuna recipes that follow. You'll agree, we believe, that
they make a splendid collection. It's
smart to keep on hand the necessary
ingredients for making two or three
of these superior main dishes.

TUNA CALIFORNIAN

Mighty fine eating—and so different

1 (8 oz.) pkg. elbow macaroni
2 c. dairy sour cream (1 pt.)
1 tsp. orégano
3 (9½ oz.) cans tuna
1 c. sliced ripe olives
1 (8 oz.) can mushrooms,
undrained
¾ c. chopped green pepper
½ c. chopped cashews
2 c. grated Cheddar cheese
2 (7 oz.) pkgs. frozen onion
rings

• Cook macaroni in boiling salted water by package directions. Drain.

• Mix together all ingredients, except
cheese and onion rings. Turn into a
greased 13 × 9 × 2″ baking pan.
Sprinkle with cheese. Lay thawed onion rings on top.
• Bake in moderate oven (350°) 30
minutes. Slip under broiler a minute,
or long enough to brown onion rings.
Makes 12 to 14 servings.

CASHEW TUNA LUNCHEON

*A distinctive tuna casserole—luncheon
guests will ask for the recipe*

1 (3 oz.) can chow mein
noodles
1 can condensed cream of
mushroom soup
¼ c. water
1 (7 oz.) can chunk-style tuna
¼ lb. cashew nuts, salted or
unsalted
1 c. finely diced celery
1 tblsp. chopped green pepper
¼ c. minced onion
⅛ tsp. salt (if cashews are
unsalted)
⅛ tsp. pepper (optional)

• Combine all the ingredients in a
1½-qt. casserole, saving out ½ c.
chow mein noodles. Sprinkle reserved
noodles over the top.
• Bake, uncovered, in slow oven
(325°) 40 minutes. Makes 5 servings.

Note: You can double this recipe for
10 servings. Combine ingredients in
a 3-qt. casserole and bake about 50
minutes. If you want to keep the
casserole warm, turn to a very slow
oven (170°) until serving time. Cover
if holding time is more than 1 hour.

The surprise in Party Pork Rolls (*recipe, page 41*) is the blended flavors of
both fresh and smoked ham. Spread fresh ham steak with ground smoked
ham and bread stuffing; roll like a jelly roll, bake, glaze with marmalade.

TUNA ORIENTAL

Extremely easy to fix and very good

1   (5½ oz.) can chow mein
        noodles
2   (7 oz.) cans tuna
2   cans condensed cream of
        mushroom soup
1⅓ c. cashews
2   c. diced celery
½   c. minced onion
Salt
Pepper
Mandarin orange slices, drained

• Combine half of noodles with the tuna, flaked, soup, cashews, celery and onion. Season with salt and pepper. Mix well and put into a greased 3-qt. casserole. Top with remaining noodles.
• Bake in moderate oven (350°) 30 to 40 minutes. Garnish with mandarin orange slices. Makes 10 servings.

Note: If you use salted cashews, do not add more salt.

TUNA ROMANOFF

Depend on this to bring compliments

2   c. cottage cheese
2   c. dairy sour cream (1 pt.)
¼   c. minced onion
¼   c. chopped pimiento
4   tsp. Worcestershire sauce
⅛   tsp. Tabasco
3   (9½ oz.) cans tuna
1   (12 oz.) pkg. noodles,
        cooked and drained
2   (4 oz.) cans mushrooms,
        undrained
1   c. sliced ripe olives
1   tsp. salt
1   c. bread crumbs
¼   c. butter

• Mix cottage cheese, sour cream, onion and pimiento; add Worcestershire sauce and Tabasco. Stir in tuna, hot noodles, mushrooms, olives and salt; turn into a greased 13 × 9 × 2″ baking pan. Sprinkle bread crumbs over top and dot with butter.
• Bake in moderate oven (350°) 30 minutes. Makes 12 to 14 servings.

SUNDAY SUPPER CASSEROLE

With this in the oven, relishes and dessert on hand, you're ready to ask stop-by friends to stay for supper

1   (12½ oz.) can tuna
1   can condensed cream of
        mushroom soup
1   can condensed cream of
        chicken soup
2   c. water
½   c. regular rice
½   c. chopped celery
1½ c. potato chips

• Combine all ingredients except potato chips. Pour into greased 10 × 6″ glass baking dish.
• Crush potato chips and sprinkle over the top. Bake in moderate oven (350°) 1½ hours. Makes 6 to 8 servings.

TUNA-CHEESE PIE

The home economist who shares this recipe keeps pies on hand for suppers

4   tblsp. butter
½   c. chopped green pepper
½   c. chopped onion
2   cans condensed cream of
        celery soup
1   c. shredded sharp process
        cheese
4   (6½ oz.) cans chunk-style
        tuna

½ c. chopped pimiento
1 c. frozen peas
Cheese Pastry

• In butter, pan-fry green pepper and onion until soft. Blend in soup and cheese; stir in tuna, pimiento and peas, thawed enough to separate. Spoon into 4 (8″) aluminum foil pie pans, or 8 (4½″) foil pie pans.
• Meanwhile make Cheese Pastry (recipe below), roll and place on top of pies. Flute edges and cut vents in crust. Bake in hot oven (400°) 30 to 35 minutes. Makes 8 servings.

Frozen Tuna-Cheese Pie: Reduce onions to ¼ c. Follow recipe for Tuna-Cheese Pie, but do not bake. Freeze. To serve, place frozen pies in hot oven (400°), bake 40 to 45 minutes.

CHEESE PASTRY

You can use plain pastry, but cheese adds flavor that's good with tuna

2 c. sifted flour
1 tsp. salt
¾ c. vegetable shortening
½ to 1 c. grated process Cheddar cheese
4 to 5 tblsp. water

• Combine flour and salt in mixing bowl. Cut in shortening until mixture resembles coarse cornmeal. Add cheese.
• Sprinkle on cold water, 1 tblsp. at a time, tossing mixture with a fork. The dough should be just moist enough to hold together when pressed

gently with a fork. It should not be sticky.
• Divide in 4 or 8 parts, depending on size of pans you are using. Roll each part about 1½″ bigger than top of pan. Place on top of pies and bake as directed.

TUNA-CAULIFLOWER FIESTA

Company casserole is colorful as confetti—good for buffet service

2 (7 oz.) cans chunk-style tuna
2 (10 oz.) pkgs. frozen cauliflower
¼ c. green pepper, cut in strips
¼ c. tuna oil or salad oil
¼ c. flour
1 tsp. salt
⅛ tsp. pepper
1½ c. milk
¼ c. pimiento, cut in strips
⅔ c. grated sharp Cheddar cheese

• Drain tuna, reserving oil.
• Cook cauliflower as directed on package until just tender-crisp; drain. Place in well-greased, shallow 2-qt. casserole. Layer tuna chunks over cauliflower.
• Cook green pepper in oil until tender; blend in flour and seasonings. Gradually add milk and cook over medium heat until thickened; stir constantly. Add pimiento; pour sauce over tuna. Top with cheese.
• Bake in moderate oven (350°) 30 to 35 minutes. Makes 6 servings.

CHAPTER 3

VEGETABLES COUNTRY-STYLE

Farm women with gardens are in luck with vegetables. They can "catch them young" and serve them when they're at their most succulent, tender best. Capitalize on this advantage, especially when you entertain town guests. What tastes better than corn on the cob rushed from patch to kettle and hurried piping hot to the table? Or juicy, dead-ripe tomatoes, chilled, in salads? And while vegetables are at their flavor peak, the forward-looking hostess puts a supply in the freezer to treat her guests when winter comes.

Keep your kitchen door open to some of the less common vegetables, such as Italian green beans. You'll find several recipes in this chapter that call for them. Eggplant is not new, but in many homes it rarely appears on the table. Try Italian Eggplant, a recipe from a California ranch woman of Italian descent. We've yet to find anyone who doesn't praise this pizza-like dish.

Potatoes, as any farmer will tell you, are country favorites. That's why we give them a place at the beginning of this chapter. We hope you'll please your guests with the Heat-and-Eat Potato Treats developed in our Test Kitchens. One secret is that you transfer them from freezer to oven without thawing. They're perfect for entertaining.

While vegetables usually play the supporting role to meat, poultry or fish, do give them the spotlight when they are in season. This is an especially fine way to please guests without gardens. You'll find excellent suggestions—Summer Chicken with Peas, and Summer Squash and Sausage, for instance—in our collection of main-dish recipes (see Index).

Surprise your company with new vegetable combinations. Frosty Vegetable Soup, borrowed from Spain, really refreshes on a hot day.

Many of our vegetable dishes include a dash of herbs for distinctive flavor. Of our recipes for frozen and canned vegetables, we wouldn't want you to miss Southwestern Corn Bake and Broccoli and Rice. They're hostess and guest favorites.

Gentlemen Prefer Potatoes

When you collect recipes for vegetable dishes with men guests in mind, start with potatoes. Of all the garden treats, nothing interests the masculine world so much as the humble spud. Since this cookbook features choice foods for country entertaining, we start the vegetable section with potatoes. It's no secret that most women, and this includes hostesses, do a lot of cooking to please men.

BUFFET CHEESE-POTATOES

You can make these potatoes in a ring mold, but a loaf is easier to unmold without breaking

6 c. cooked, cubed potatoes
    (6 to 7)
½ tsp. salt
¼ tsp. pepper
4 tblsp. butter or margarine
4 tblsp. flour
½ tsp. salt
⅛ tsp. pepper
½ tsp. dry mustard
2 c. milk
½ lb. sharp Cheddar cheese,
    shredded
2 tblsp. crushed round buttery
    crackers
½ c. grated Cheddar cheese
1 to 2 tblsp. milk

• Combine potatoes, ½ tsp. salt and ¼ tsp. pepper in mixing bowl.
• Melt butter in saucepan, blend in flour, ½ tsp. salt, ⅛ tsp. pepper and dry mustard. Add milk and cook over low heat until sauce is thickened. Stir in shredded cheese and continue cooking until cheese melts. Remove from heat.
• Mix just enough of cheese sauce into potatoes to hold them together, about 2 c. Place in a well-greased 9 × 5 × 3″ loaf pan. Cover and refrigerate several hours or overnight.
• Refrigerate remaining cheese sauce.
• To serve, run knife carefully around edges of pan. Place ovenproof platter or baking sheet on top of loaf pan. Invert and let stand a few minutes. Tap gently to loosen potatoes. Remove loaf pan. Sprinkle potatoes with cracker crumbs and grated cheese. Bake in hot oven (400°) about 25 minutes, until potatoes are lightly browned and heated through.
• Serve with remaining cheese sauce. To heat sauce, add 1 to 2 tblsp. milk to cold sauce and place over medium heat, stirring frequently. Makes 8 servings.

OVEN-CREAMED POTATOES

Perfect to serve with steak or roast beef, and easier than spuds creamed on range top—no watching or turning

2 c. chopped onions
⅔ c. chopped green pepper
½ c. chopped celery
½ c. butter or margarine
6 tblsp. flour
4 c. milk
2 tsp. salt
¼ tsp. pepper
6 c. cubed, cooked potatoes
    (about 6 medium potatoes)
1 c. shredded Cheddar cheese

• Cook onions, green pepper and celery in butter until soft (do not brown). Stir in flour. Add milk and cook, stirring constantly, until mixture comes to a boil and is thickened. Stir in salt and pepper.

· Place potatoes in a greased 3-qt. casserole. Pour sauce over. Top with cheese. Bake in moderate oven (350°) until hot and bubbly, about 30 minutes. Makes 10 to 12 servings.

POTATOES CHANTILLY

Mashed potatoes go fancy—they're topped with whipped cream and cheese, then baked

10   medium potatoes (about
       4 lbs.)
1½ tsp. salt
1   c. warm milk
¼   c. butter
¼   tsp. pepper
½   c. heavy cream, whipped
1   c. grated sharp cheese

· Peel potatoes; cook in water to cover with ½ tsp. salt added, until just tender. Drain thoroughly. Add warm milk, remaining salt, butter and pepper to potatoes and beat with electric mixer until light and fluffy.

· Pour into buttered 2½-qt. casserole. Spread with whipped cream; sprinkle with cheese.

· Bake in moderate oven (350°) about 20 minutes, or until lightly browned and puffy on top. Makes 12 servings.

POTATOES AU GRATIN

Carry these country-style potatoes scalloped with eggs and ham to the next community supper

1   c. chopped onion
½   c. chopped celery
¼   c. butter or margarine
¼   c. flour
2½ c. milk

2   tblsp. chopped parsley
       (optional)
1   tsp. salt
¼   tsp. pepper
2   c. shredded Cheddar cheese
4   c. cooked, cubed potatoes
       (about 4 medium
       potatoes)
3   hard-cooked eggs, sliced
3   c. cubed cooked ham

· Cook onion and celery in butter (in large skillet) until soft; do not brown. Stir in flour. Add milk and cook, stirring constantly, until mixture boils and is thickened.

· Stir in parsley, salt, pepper and 1 c. cheese. Combine potatoes, eggs and ham in a 3-qt. casserole. Pour sauce over; mix lightly. Top with remaining cup of cheese.

· Bake in moderate oven (350°) 35 minutes, or until hot and bubbly. Makes 8 servings.

CHEESE 'N' POTATO CASSEROLE

You needn't peel the potatoes for this dish from a Southern Test Group member. Try Fancy-Top variation

6   medium potatoes, scrubbed
       but not peeled
¼   tsp. salt
⅛   tsp. pepper
1   c. grated cheese
1   can condensed cream of
       mushroom soup
3   tblsp. butter or margarine
¾   c. milk

· Slice potatoes thinly. Layer in greased 2-qt. casserole: half of potato slices, seasonings, grated cheese and soup. Dot with half of butter. Make second layer of potatoes, seasonings

and soup. Dot with remaining butter.
• Rinse soup can with milk; pour over top of casserole. Cover and bake in moderate oven (350°) 1 hour, or until potatoes are tender.
• Remove cover; sprinkle on remaining ½ c. grated cheese. Return to oven just until cheese is melted. Makes 6 to 8 servings.

VARIATION

Fancy-Top Cheese 'n' Potato Casserole: For company or a main-dish supper casserole, top with 2 tblsp. chopped pimiento before baking. After casserole has baked 1 hour, top with 3 sliced hard-cooked eggs and remaining ½ c. grated cheese. Return to oven just until cheese is melted.

NONESUCH POTATO CASSEROLE

Makes a bright color spot on table

7   slices bacon
4   c. diced raw potatoes
3   c. canned tomatoes
1   tsp. salt
⅛   tsp. pepper
¼   tsp. dried orégano
3   small onions, thinly sliced

• Fry 3 slices of bacon until partially cooked but not crisp; drain. Cut remaining 4 slices uncooked bacon into small pieces.
• Layer in a 2-qt. casserole: half the potatoes, tomatoes, uncooked bacon pieces, seasonings and sliced onions. Make second layer, repeating ingredients. Top with the 3 slices of partially cooked bacon.
• Bake in moderate oven (350°) 1½ hours, or until potatoes are tender. Makes 6 to 8 servings.

STUFFING-POTATO CASSEROLE

Mashed potatoes and stuffing go together in the same appetizing dish

¼   c. butter or margarine
1   medium onion, chopped
2   c. dried bread cubes
¼   tsp. sage
¼   tsp. thyme
1   tblsp. dried parsley flakes
4   c. mashed potatoes, unsalted
      (leftover or instant)
2   eggs, beaten
1   tsp. salt
¼   tsp. pepper
1   c. milk

• Melt butter in skillet; sauté chopped onion until golden. Add bread cubes, sage, thyme and parsley flakes. Toss with butter and onion.
• In a separate bowl, combine potatoes, eggs, salt, pepper and milk. (If mashed potatoes have been salted, add only ¼ tsp. salt.) Stir in bread and onion mixture. Place in buttered 2-qt. casserole.
• Bake, uncovered, in moderate oven (350°) until heated through, 20 to 30 minutes. Makes 8 to 10 servings.

BROWNED CREAM POTATOES

Definitely rich and delicious—men especially like spuds fixed this way

6   tblsp. butter
2   tsp. flour
2   c. heavy cream
2¼ tsp. salt
1   tsp. black pepper
¼   c. finely chopped onion
¼   tsp. nutmeg
8   potatoes, boiled or baked,
      peeled and finely chopped

• Melt 4 tblsp. butter in saucepan;

stir in flour. Gradually add cream and cook, stirring constantly until sauce bubbles and thickens. Add salt, pepper, onion and nutmeg; blend thoroughly.
· Add potatoes to the sauce; mix well. Pour into a lightly greased 2-qt. baking dish. Dot top with remaining 2 tblsp. butter.
· Bake in moderate oven (350°) about 45 minutes, until browned. Makes 6 to 8 servings.

CHEESE POTATO PUFF

Mashed potatoes a tasty new way— men will be asking for more

12   medium potatoes
 6   tblsp. butter or margarine
2 ¼ c. grated Cheddar cheese
 1   to 1 ¼ c. milk
 ¾   to 1 tsp. salt
 2   eggs, beaten

· Peel potatoes; cook in salted water until tender. Drain and mash thoroughly.
· Add butter, cheese, milk and salt, and beat over low heat until butter and cheese are melted.
· Fold in eggs and pour into a greased 13 × 9 × 2″ baking pan or dish. Bake in moderate oven (350°) 30 to 45 minutes, or until puffy and golden brown. Makes 10 servings.

OVEN FRENCH FRIES

A wise selection for a fast-fix meal

Potatoes, cut in ⅜″ strips, or
    into ⅜″ slices
Melted butter
Salt
Corn flake crumbs

· Dip potatoes in melted butter, sprin-

kle with salt and roll in crumbs. Place in baking dish, one layer deep. Bake in moderate oven (375°) 45 minutes, or until done.

Note: Allow 1 medium potato for each serving.

BROWN POTATOES

Perfect companion for roast beef

12 medium potatoes
 2 c. chopped beef suet
Salt
Pepper

· Peel potatoes and cut in lengthwise halves. Boil 8 minutes in salted water; drain.
· Place beef suet in shallow pan; melt in oven.
· One hour before dinner, add potatoes and bake in slow oven (325°) about 1 hour, or until tender. Turn occasionally to brown potatoes evenly. Season with salt and pepper. Makes 8 servings.

Note: If you're roasting beef and do not have room in oven for a pan of potatoes, you can boil peeled whole medium-size potatoes 15 minutes, drain and put in pan around roast to cook 45 minutes. Turn occasionally to brown evenly.

BAKED POTATO SAUCE

Nothing tastes better on hot baked potatoes—get it ready the day before company comes. Serve it cold

1   c. dairy sour cream
1   c. mayonnaise
2   tblsp. lemon juice
3   tblsp. chopped chives
¼   tsp. salt
⅛   tsp. pepper

• Combine all ingredients; cover and chill 24 hours before serving. Pass in a bowl to spoon on baked potatoes. Makes 2 cups.

Heat-and-Eat Potato Treats from Your Freezer

Many FARM JOURNAL readers have asked our food editors how to freeze potatoes when they're at their peak quality so they will store successfully in their freezers. This was the incentive that initiated work in our Test Kitchens to determine the best way to do it. We discovered how to handle potatoes so you can freeze them successfully for up to two months.

The trick is to cook the potatoes and freeze them in ready-to-use shapes so they go directly from freezer to range or oven. It's important not to let the potatoes thaw before heating; thawing softens them and makes them mushy.

Many homemakers now use our recipes to stock their freezers with several meals of hashed browns and fluffy mashed potatoes. Frequently they cook double amounts, use one portion and freeze the other. Here are the directions:

FROZEN HASHED BROWN POTATOES
Cook two skilletfuls of these golden, crisp-crusted potatoes for 8 or 9

To Freeze:
• Boil baking-type potatoes in their jackets until just tender but still firm (10 to 15 minutes). Drain, cool and peel. Grate potatoes on a coarse grater.
• Line a 10" skillet with aluminum foil, bringing foil up to cover sides. Mix 1½ tsp. salt with 4 c. grated potatoes. Pack in foil-lined skillet, pressing down firmly. Remove from skillet with foil. Seal, label and freeze. Repeat to stock your freezer.

To Cook:
• Heat ½ c. shortening over medium heat (350° in electric skillet) in same skillet in which potatoes were shaped for freezing. Remove foil and add the disk of frozen potatoes (shortening will spatter, so quickly cover the skillet). Cook 5 minutes over medium heat. Uncover and continue cooking 10 to 12 minutes, or until potatoes are browned on the bottom. Cut into 4 wedges; turn each piece separately with spatula or pancake turner. Continue cooking 5 minutes, or until attractively browned. Makes 4 generous servings.

BASIC MASHED POTATOES
Freeze these plain or make into one of our five interesting variations

4 lbs. boiling potatoes
1 c. milk (amount varies with moisture in potatoes)
¼ c. butter
1½ tsp. salt

• Peel potatoes. Boil until soft; drain. Press potatoes through a ricer or mash.
• Heat milk, butter and salt together. Gradually whip in until the potatoes are smooth and fluffy.
• Form into shapes that are ready to use with no thawing. Freeze by directions in variations that follow.

VARIATIONS

Potato Puffs: Add ½ c. grated Cheddar cheese or 2 egg yolks to Basic Mashed Potatoes. Chill. Form into balls; roll into a mixture of ¾ c. corn flake crumbs and 3 tblsp. toasted sesame seeds. Freeze on tray until firm. Package, label and return to freezer. Makes 48 small or 24 medium balls.
To Serve: Place frozen puffs on baking sheet. Brush lightly with melted butter. Bake in hot oven (400°) 20 minutes for small puffs and 30 minutes for medium puffs. To serve without freezing, omit brushing with butter and bake puffs only until they brown, 5 to 10 minutes.

Snowcaps: Add 2 egg yolks to Basic Mashed Potatoes. Spoon hot potatoes in mounds on baking sheet. Cool; freeze until firm. Remove from baking sheet; place in plastic bags. Seal, label and return to freezer. Use to top meat and vegetable casseroles. Makes 24 snowcaps.

Pimiento Nests: Add ½ c. chopped, drained pimiento to Basic Mashed Potatoes. Line a 1½-qt. casserole with aluminum foil. Spoon half the potato mixture into casserole. Shape into a nest, building up the sides to top of casserole. Remove from casserole with foil to hold shape of the nest. Reline casserole with foil and shape remaining potato mixture. Cool; freeze nests until firm. Remove from freezer; package, seal and label. Return to freezer. Serve with chicken filling (see recipe for Potato-Chicken Casserole).

Cheese Nests: Add ½ c. grated Cheddar cheese to hot Basic Mashed Potatoes; omit the pimiento and proceed as for Pimiento Nests. Serve with onion filling (see recipe for Cheese-Onion Pie).

Potato Nests: Omit the pimiento and shape like Pimiento Nests.

CHICKEN IN POTATO NEST

For company you can use two Pimiento Nests and double the other ingredients

1 frozen Pimiento Nest
4 tblsp. melted butter or
      margarine
2 tblsp. flour
1 c. chicken broth
Salt
Pepper
1 (4 oz.) can sliced mushrooms,
      drained
½ c. diced celery
1 c. diced cooked chicken

• Remove wrapper from frozen Pimiento Nest. Place in casserole in which it was shaped originally. Drizzle with 2 tblsp. melted butter. Cover and bake in hot oven (400°) 30 minutes. Uncover and bake 30 minutes.
• In the meantime, combine remaining 2 tblsp. butter and flour in heavy saucepan. Slowly add broth; stir constantly until sauce is smooth and thick. Season with salt and pepper. Add remaining ingredients; heat. Spoon hot mixture into baked Pimiento Nest. Makes 6 servings.

CHEESE-ONION PIE

Potatoes make the crust for this pie—serve with fish, ham or fried chicken

1 frozen Cheese Nest
2 tblsp. melted butter

1 beef bouillon cube
½ c. boiling water
2 c. chopped onions
¼ c. butter or margarine
3 tblsp. flour
1 c. milk
Salt
Pepper

• Remove wrapper from frozen Cheese Nest. Place in casserole in which it was shaped originally. Drizzle with 2 tblsp. melted butter. Cover and bake in hot oven (400°) 30 minutes. Uncover and bake 30 minutes.
• In the meantime, dissolve bouillon cube in boiling water. Add onions, cover and simmer until tender; drain.
• Melt ¼ c. butter in heavy saucepan. Add flour to make a smooth paste. Add milk slowly; stir constantly until white sauce is smooth and thick.
• Season with salt and pepper. Add drained onions. Spoon onion mixture into baked Cheese Nest for serving. Makes 6 servings.

Sweets Are Potatoes in the South

"When we speak of potatoes in the South," says FARM JOURNAL's Southern home economist, "we refer to those yellow-orange sweets. Irish potatoes are the white ones."

Regardless of where you live in the United States, you owe a debt of gratitude to Southern kitchens for their wonderful ways with sweet potatoes. Here are three excellent examples of superior dishes from a Georgia farm woman. (See Index for other tasty dishes made with this vegetable.)

CRUNCH-CRESTED SWEETS

The crunch comes from browning marshmallows and corn flakes on top orange-scented mashed sweet potatoes

¼ c. butter, melted
1 tsp. grated orange peel
½ tsp. salt
⅛ tsp. pepper
3 c. cooked, mashed sweet potatoes
1½ c. presweetened corn flakes (sugar-coated)
⅔ c. miniature marshmallows

• Reserve 2 tblsp. melted butter. Mix remaining butter, orange peel, salt, pepper and sweet potatoes; spoon into a buttered 1½-qt. casserole.
• Sprinkle with corn flakes; drizzle with reserved 2 tblsp. melted butter and top with marshmallows. Bake in slow oven (325°) 30 minutes. Makes 6 servings.

SWEET POTATO CASSEROLE

Double the recipe for a crowd. Can be made ahead, baked at last minute

6 medium sweet potatoes or yams, boiled in skins
1 egg, beaten
½ c. heavy cream
5 tblsp. sugar
1 tsp. salt
½ tsp. nutmeg
1 tsp. rum extract (optional)
2 tsp. finely grated orange peel
1 tblsp. melted butter

• Peel, mash and whip sweet potatoes until smooth, or put through ricer (you should have 3 c. potatoes after mashing).
• Add beaten egg, heavy cream,

sugar, salt, nutmeg and rum extract. Beat until light and fluffy.
· Put in buttered 1½-qt. casserole. Sprinkle evenly with orange peel. Drizzle the melted butter on top.
· Place in hot oven (400°) 30 minutes, or until lightly browned. Makes 6 servings.

BANANA-SWEET POTATO BAKE

Excellent take-along dish—pretty, too

3   c. mashed cooked sweet
       potatoes (6 medium)
2   ripe bananas, mashed
1   tsp. salt
¼ to ½ c. light cream
1   c. miniature marshmallows

· Combine hot sweet potatoes (mashed until smooth) and bananas. Add salt and sufficient cream to make a soft, fluffy mixture.
· Place in buttered 1-qt. casserole. Dot top with marshmallows. Heat in slow oven (325°) long enough to brown marshmallows, about 45 minutes. Serve piping hot. Makes 6 servings.

Note: You can make 2 casseroles of this vegetable treat for 10 to 12 servings.

ASPARAGUS—THE GARDEN'S FIRST GIFT

Farm women have a great respect for asparagus and have their own idea on how to handle it successfully for company meals. Some even plant an asparagus bed near the kitchen door so they can cut it quickly just before cooking. They like to rush it from patch to table.

During the spring season, they cut the tender, green spears daily and cook or freeze them. When spring surrenders to summer and warm weather arrives, they let the shoots grow into fernlike plants which they use in flower arrangements.

Here are country-kitchen-approved directions for fixing asparagus after it is cut: Grasp each stalk with both hands and break it—it will snap at the tender line. Wash the tip ends in hot water, agitating them about 3 minutes to remove the sand and silt. Next, rinse the asparagus in cold water and let it stand in the cold bath for 10 minutes, or until the stalks are crisp.

To cook asparagus, use a large utensil, such as a skillet (an electric one is fine), and prop the tip ends on a piece of crumpled aluminum foil. This will hold them out of the hot cooking water, while water covers the ends by about 2". Salt the water, ½ tsp. salt to 1 c. water. Cook the asparagus, covered, just until tender, from 10 to 20 minutes, and drain it.

BAKED ASPARAGUS-CHEESE SANDWICH

You may need to bake two dishes of the hot sandwiches—depends on how many people you're having for supper

6   thick (¾") slices firm-textured
       bread (like home-baked)
6   (3½" square) slices process
       Swiss cheese
4   eggs
2   c. milk
1   tsp. salt
⅛ tsp. pepper
¼ tsp. nutmeg

1 tblsp. finely chopped onion
18 cooked asparagus spears
½ c. shredded Cheddar cheese

· Trim crusts from bread slices. Arrange bread slices in bottom of 13 × 9 × 2″ pan or glass dish. Top each bread slice with a slice of process Swiss cheese.
· In a bowl, beat eggs slightly; add milk, stir in seasonings and onion. Pour this mixture over sandwiches and bake in slow oven (325°) 25 minutes.
· Remove from oven. Top each bread slice with 3 cooked asparagus spears. Sprinkle on shredded Cheddar cheese. Return dish to oven and continue to bake 10 to 15 minutes, until custard sets and top is golden. Allow to stand 5 minutes before serving. Makes 6 servings.

SPRING ASPARAGUS AND EGG BAKE

You may need to make this recipe twice to have enough for a company main dish

18 asparagus spears
¼ c. butter or margarine
¼ c. flour
½ tsp. salt
1 ½ c. milk
1 c. shredded Cheddar cheese
⅛ tsp. red pepper
4 hard-cooked eggs, sliced
½ c. cracker crumbs
¼ c. melted butter or margarine

· Cook asparagus spears in boiling, salted water 10 to 20 minutes, or until just tender.
· In a saucepan, melt butter and stir in flour and salt; blend in enough

milk to make a smooth paste. Stir in remainder of milk and cook over medium heat until white sauce is thick, stirring constantly. While white sauce is hot, stir in shredded cheese and red pepper. Stir until cheese is melted.
· In a greased 1½-qt. baking dish layer half of asparagus, sliced eggs and white sauce. Repeat ingredients to make a second layer. Top with cracker crumbs mixed with butter.
· Bake in moderate oven (350°) 30 minutes, or until mixture bubbles. Place under broiler for 2 minutes to brown top. Makes 5 servings.

Note: For 10 servings, bake 2 casseroles of this asparagus and egg treat, or double recipe and bake 45 to 50 minutes in a 3-qt. casserole.

WINTER TAKE-ALONG CASSEROLE

This tasty dish is popular at potluck suppers in the country

2 (10 oz.) pkgs. frozen asparagus
1 c. chopped onion
¼ c. butter or margarine
6 tblsp. flour
3 c. milk
2 tsp. salt
¼ tsp. pepper
4 hard-cooked eggs, sliced
½ c. shredded Cheddar cheese
½ c. dry bread crumbs

· Cook asparagus as directed on package until barely tender; drain.
· In a large skillet, cook onion in butter until tender (not brown). Stir in flour. Add milk and cook, stirring constantly, until thickened. Mix in salt, pepper, eggs and asparagus.

· Turn into a 2-qt. casserole. Top with cheese and crumbs. Bake in moderate oven (350°) until hot and bubbly, about 30 minutes. Makes 8 servings.

HERB-BUTTERED GREEN BEANS

Seasonings make this a company special—and so quick to do

2 (15½ oz.) cans green beans
¼ c. butter
1 tblsp. instant minced onion
¼ c. minced celery
1 tblsp. sesame seeds
¾ tsp. salt
¼ tsp. dried basil
¼ tsp. crushed dried rosemary
    leaves

· Heat beans.
· Melt butter in saucepan; add the onion, celery, sesame seeds, salt, basil and rosemary. Simmer a few minutes to cook celery.
· Toss with beans in a warm serving dish. Makes 8 servings.

INDIANA SUCCOTASH

Green beans very finely cut team with corn in this expertly seasoned dish

1½ lbs. green beans
1½ tsp. salt
1½ c. green onions with tops
6   tblsp. butter
2   (1 lb. 1 oz.) cans whole
       kernel corn, drained
¾   tsp. paprika
¾   tsp. celery salt
1   tsp. sugar

· Cut beans in rounds about the size of the yellow corn kernels; cook with ½ tsp. salt in water to cover about 15 minutes, or just until tender. Drain.
· Sauté green onions in butter until transparent (do not brown); add corn, 1 tsp. salt, paprika, celery salt and sugar, then beans.
· Simmer, covered, about 10 minutes to blend seasonings and heat thoroughly. Makes 12 servings.

Note: Fresh corn, cut from the top, may be used when available instead of canned corn.

NEW-STYLE GREEN BEANS
WITH TOMATOES

Better make two casseroles for company—fresh flavors and bright colors make this vegetable dish a success

1   lb. fresh green beans, cut
2   tblsp. shortening
½   c. chopped onions
2   tblsp. flour
¼   tsp. salt
⅛   tsp. pepper
1   c. milk
2   c. grated sharp cheese
2   ripe tomatoes, sliced

· Cook beans in boiling salted water until tender; drain, and keep hot.
· Melt shortening in saucepan; add onions and sauté until golden. Stir in flour, salt and pepper to make a smooth paste. Add milk gradually and cook, stirring until thickened. Add cheese; stir until melted.
· Place hot green beans in a greased 1½-qt. casserole. Pour on three fourths of cheese sauce. Cover beans with tomato slices. Sprinkle lightly with salt. Top with rest of cheese sauce.
· Place under broiler for 5 minutes, until tomatoes are tender and cheese

sauce bubbling and golden brown. Makes 4 to 6 servings.

TWO-BEAN CASSEROLE

Simple dress-up for common vegetables—mix ahead, chill and heat at mealtime

2 c. cut green beans (canned or frozen)
2 c. cut yellow beans (canned or frozen)
½ c. tomato sauce
1 (1 ½ oz.) pkg. onion-soup mix
⅛ tsp. pepper

• Combine drained beans in 1½-qt. baking dish. Mix tomato sauce, soup mix and pepper; pour over beans.
• Cover and bake in moderate oven (375°) 20 minutes, or until hot and bubbly. Garnish with hard-cooked egg. Makes 6 to 8 servings.

GREEN BEANS WITH CHEESE

Ideal vegetable dish for buffet service

3 tblsp. melted butter
2 tblsp. flour
1 tsp. salt
¼ tsp. pepper
1 tsp. sugar
½ tsp. grated onion
1 c. dairy sour cream
2 (12 oz.) pkgs. frozen French-style green beans, cooked
½ lb. grated Cheddar cheese
½ c. corn flake crumbs

• Combine 2 tblsp. butter and flour; cook gently. Remove from heat; stir in salt, pepper, sugar, onion and sour cream. Fold in beans cooked by package directions. Place in a shallow 2-qt. casserole.

• Cover with cheese, then with corn flake crumbs mixed with 1 tblsp. butter. Bake in moderate oven (350°) 30 minutes. Makes 12 servings.

GREEN BEANS WITH ALMONDS

Nuts add crunchy texture and flavor

3 (10 oz.) pkgs. quick-frozen French-style green beans
3 tblsp. butter
¾ c. sliced almonds
6 tblsp. butter

• Cook beans in boiling salted water by package directions. Add 3 tblsp. butter and toss to mix.
• Sauté almonds in 6 tblsp. butter until lightly brown. Toss into beans. Makes 8 servings.

GREEN BEANS GOLDENROD

A delicious egg sauce tops this popular vegetable. Makes a pretty dish

2 (10 oz.) pkgs. frozen cut green beans
2 hard-cooked eggs
2 tsp. butter
2 tsp. flour
¼ tsp. salt
⅛ tsp. pepper
½ c. milk
½ c. mayonnaise

• Cook beans in boiling salted water by package directions.
• Chop egg whites; press yolks through sieve.
• While beans cook, make sauce by melting butter in saucepan; blend in flour, salt and pepper. Gradually stir in milk. Cook over medium heat, stirring constantly until thickened. Stir in chopped egg whites. Remove from heat; stir in mayonnaise.

· Drain beans; place in serving dish. Spoon on sauce; sprinkle top with sieved egg yolks. Makes 8 servings.

New Ways to Fix Italian Green Beans

One of the most pleasing ways to vary vegetables in a company meal is to serve a vegetable that is not universally grown in home gardens. Italian green beans, for instance. Their flat, broad pods are tender, meaty and stringless. And they both look and taste different from the more common kinds of green beans.

Our three recipes that call for Italian green beans are from the hostess collection of a Minnesota reader of FARM JOURNAL, known among her circle of friends for the wonderful food she serves when she entertains.

ITALIAN GREEN BEANS WITH TOMATOES

Savory tomato sauce enhances flavor of these beans—do try them soon

¼ c. chopped onion
2 tblsp. butter
2 c. stewed tomatoes
½ tsp. salt
⅛ tsp. pepper
1 bay leaf
2 whole cloves
1 pt. Italian green beans

· Sauté onion in butter until golden. Add tomatoes and seasonings and simmer, uncovered, 15 minutes. Remove bay leaf and cloves.
· In a covered saucepan, cook Italian green beans in small amount of boiling salted water until tender, about 5 to 8 minutes. Drain.
· Add to tomato mixture. Makes 4 servings.

Note: You may want to double this recipe for 8 servings.

ITALIAN GREEN BEANS PARMESAN

Cheese adds flavorful touch-up to these broad beans—easy to fix

1 pt. Italian green beans
2 tblsp. butter
Grated Parmesan cheese

· In a covered saucepan, cook Italian green beans in a small amount of boiling salted water until tender, about 5 to 8 minutes. Drain excess liquid.
· Add butter and mix lightly. Sprinkle with cheese. Makes 4 servings.

Note: You may want to double this recipe for 8 servings.

ITALIAN GREEN BEANS WITH WATER CHESTNUTS

Special-occasion dish; water chestnuts give crunchy texture that makes beans unusual and company-pleasing

½ c. canned water chestnuts, drained and sliced
2 tblsp. butter
1 pt. Italian green beans
⅓ c. water

· In a heavy saucepan sauté water chestnuts in butter. Add Italian green beans and water.
· Cover, bring to a boil and simmer until beans are tender, approximately 5 to 8 minutes. Makes 4 servings.

Note: You may want to double this recipe to make 8 servings.

Across-Country Baked Beans

The hostess who lives on Cape Cod has no problem deciding what to have for supper when she has guests on Saturday. A pot of baked beans is the traditional main dish. Guests expect it. Women in other areas find this old-time favorite equally popular. There's something friendly about the aroma of beans baking that permeates the house on a snowy evening.

We give you treasured bean recipes from three regions in the United States: Massachusetts, where baked beans originated (adapted from the Indians); Michigan's Saginaw Valley, where a large percentage of our nation's dry beans grow; and the West, where a medley of different kinds of beans cook together for barbecues, cookouts and picnics the year around. And for the hostess who wants to serve baked beans, even though she has little time for cooking, we include Saucy Baked Beans (made from canned beans as are Western Beans), with two exciting variations.

All baked beans are at their best when every bean is tender and juicy without being mushy. If you are cooking dry beans, taste for doneness while they cook. When they're done, remove them from the oven. If necessary, you can reheat them shortly before suppertime.

While a bean pot is ideal for baking beans and adds a homey touch to the buffet or table, you can use a casserole if you don't have a pot. Deep casseroles, those nearest the shape of bean pots, are best choice.

BOSTON BAKED BEANS

Stick a few whole cloves in the onion for subtle spicy taste—really good

1 lb. dry navy beans (2 c.)
6 c. cold water
1 tsp. salt
¼ lb. salt pork
1 medium onion, peeled
2 tsp. dry mustard
⅓ c. brown sugar
¼ c. molasses

· Wash beans and add cold water to them. Cover and let soak overnight. Or bring to a boil and simmer 2 minutes, remove from heat, cover and let stand 1 hour.
· Add the salt to the beans and liquid and simmer until *tender,* about 1 hour. Drain, reserving liquid. Measure 1¾ c. bean liquid; add water if necessary.
· Cut a slice from the salt pork and put it in the bottom of the bean pot. Add the beans and place the onion in the center of the beans.
· Mix the mustard, sugar and molasses in the bean liquid and pour over the beans.
· Cut 3 gashes in the remaining salt pork and place on the beans, rind side on top.
· Cover and bake 5 to 7 hours in a slow oven (300°), adding more water as needed. Remove the cover from the bean pot the last half hour of baking so the pork rind will brown and become crisp. Makes 6 servings.

When you prepare deviled eggs in large quantities, put yolks through a ricer or food mill. It's faster than mashing them with a fork.

BAKED BEANS MICHIGAN

It's easy to understand why this is a favorite of bean growers' families. Apples are the unusual tasty addition

2 lbs. dry navy beans
9 c. water
1 lb. salt pork, diced
3 tart apples, peeled, cored and coarsely cut
1 medium onion, chopped
½ c. brown sugar
½ c. molasses
3 tsp. dry mustard
3 tblsp. vinegar
¼ tsp. pepper

• Wash the beans and soak overnight in the water. Add the salt pork and cook in a kettle until beans are tender, about 1 hour.
• Pour the bean mixture into a bean pot, add the remaining ingredients and bake, covered, 6 hours in a slow oven (300°). Add more warm water during cooking if necessary. Makes 10 servings.

WESTERN BAKED BEANS

Four-in-one baked beans. Use 1 cup sugar for beans on the sweet side

8 slices bacon
4 large onions, peeled and separated in rings
½ to 1 c. brown sugar
1 tsp. dry mustard
½ tsp. garlic powder (optional)
1 tsp. salt
½ c. cider vinegar
2 (15 oz.) cans dried lima beans, drained
1 (1 lb.) can green lima beans, drained

1 (1 lb.) can dark red kidney beans, drained
1 (1 lb. 11 oz.) jar New England style baked beans, undrained

• Pan-fry bacon until crisp, drain on paper towels and set aside.
• Place onion rings in a large skillet and add the sugar, mustard, garlic powder, salt and vinegar. Cover and cook 20 minutes.
• Add onion mixture to the beans and stir in the bacon, crumbled. Pour into a 3-qt. casserole.
• Bake, covered, ½ hour in a moderate oven (350°). Uncover and bake ½ hour longer. Makes 12 servings.

SAVORY BAKED BEANS

Here is a baked bean recipe that's a favorite in Rocky Mountain area

2 (1 lb. 13 oz.) cans pork and beans
1 lb. lean bacon, cut in pieces
2 medium onions, cut in chunks
2 large green peppers, cut in chunks
2 tsp. Worcestershire sauce
1 c. ketchup
1 c. brown sugar

• Combine all ingredients and put into 2 medium-size or 1 large casserole.
• Bake, covered, in slow oven (325°) 3 hours, stirring occasionally. Uncover the last 30 minutes of cooking. Makes about 20 servings.

Note: You can use less bacon, but a full pound makes these baked beans unforgettable and a conversation piece whenever served.

SAUCY BAKED BEANS

The recipe to use when you're pressed for time. Don't miss the variations

2 strips lean bacon, cut in
    pieces
2 (1 lb.) cans baked beans in
    tomato sauce
1 small onion, peeled and
    chopped
2 tblsp. prepared mustard
¼ c. dark molasses
1 tblsp. brown sugar
¼ tsp. allspice
2 tsp. Worcestershire sauce

• Brown the bacon lightly, drain and crumble. Combine all the ingredients and pour into a 1½-qt. casserole or 2-qt. bean pot. Cover.
• Bake in a moderate oven (350°) 1½ hours. Uncover the last half hour to brown beans. Makes 8 servings.

VARIATIONS

Pineapple Baked Beans: Add 1 (13½ oz.) can drained pineapple chunks to the bean mixture and bake.

Cheese Baked Beans: Omit bacon from Saucy Baked Beans. Add ½ c. grated sharp Cheddar cheese and 1 c. cooked ham or salami, cut in cubes, to the bean mixture and bake.

LIMA BEANS WITH CHEESE

Try Gruyère cheese instead of the Cheddar or Swiss for a flavor change

3 (10 oz.) pkgs. quick-frozen
    lima beans
1½ c. grated Cheddar or Swiss
    cheese
¾ c. snipped parsley
¾ c. milk

• Cook beans in boiling salted water as directed on packages. Drain.
• Add cheese, parsley and milk. Mix gently until cheese melts. Serve at once. Makes 9 servings.

PINEAPPLE BEETS

Pleasing way to perk up beets when you serve them often. Good flavor blend

1 (13½ oz.) can pineapple
    chunks
½ c. water
⅓ c. cider vinegar
4 tblsp. brown sugar
1 tblsp. cornstarch
½ tsp. salt
⅛ tsp. ground ginger
2 (1 lb.) cans sliced beets,
    drained (4 c.)

• Drain syrup from pineapple and mix with water and vinegar. Mix brown sugar, cornstarch, salt and ginger; add vinegar mixture. Cook until thickened, stirring constantly. Add beets, then heat to boiling. Just before serving, mix pineapple into hot mixture. Makes 8 servings.

BROCCOLI PLATTER

Easy sauce is a new touch, but peanuts sprinkled on top are the surprise

2 tblsp. minced onion
2 tblsp. butter or margarine
1 c. dairy sour cream
½ tsp. poppy seeds
½ tsp. paprika
¼ tsp. salt
⅛ tsp. cayenne pepper
2 lbs. cooked broccoli, salted
⅓ c. chopped salted peanuts

• Saute onion in butter; remove from heat. Stir in sour cream, poppy seeds, paprika, salt and cayenne pepper; heat over boiling water.

• Arrange hot broccoli on heated platter; pour warm sauce over top. Sprinkle with peanuts (or cashews for company). Makes 6 to 8 servings.

CREAMY LIMA BEANS AND BROCCOLI

Ideal casserole for a company buffet

3 tblsp. butter
¼ tsp. curry powder (if desired)
2 c. bite-size rice cereal biscuits
1 (10 oz.) pkg. frozen lima beans
1 (10 oz.) pkg. frozen chopped broccoli
1 can condensed cream of mushroom soup
1 can condensed cream of celery soup

• Melt butter; add curry powder and cereal. Stir over low heat about 5 minutes to coat the cereal.
• Cook vegetables separately. Combine beans with soups and 1 c. cereal mixture. Stir in broccoli. Place in buttered 2-qt. baking dish. Top with remaining cereal mixture.
• Bake in moderate oven (350°) 30 minutes. Makes 8 servings.

BROCCOLI AND RICE

If you use frozen chopped broccoli stir lightly just before serving

2 c. hot water
1 (1 to 1½ oz.) pkg. onion-soup mix
1⅓ c. packaged precooked rice
2 tblsp. butter
1 tsp. salt
¼ tsp. pepper
1 tblsp. lemon juice
1 (10 oz.) pkg. frozen broccoli (chopped or whole stalks)

• Add hot water to onion-soup mix. Stir; add rice, butter, salt, pepper and lemon juice.
• Place frozen broccoli in greased 2-qt. casserole. Pour rice mixture over.
• Cover with a tight-fitting lid and bake in moderate oven (375°) 45 minutes. Makes 4 servings.

Note: Bake as many casseroles of Broccoli and Rice as needed to serve your guests.

BRUSSELS SPROUTS WITH LEMON

Lemon brings out a garden-fresh taste

1½ qts. Brussels sprouts
¾ c. butter
Salt
Pepper
Lemon slices

• Trim sprouts, removing any imperfect leaves. Pour boiling salted water (1 tsp. salt to 1 qt. water) over them to cover; let stand 5 minutes; drain.
• Melt butter in heavy skillet; add sprouts. Cover tightly and cook over very low heat just until they are tender, 10 to 20 minutes. Test for tenderness with a kitchen fork.
• Add salt and pepper to taste. Serve garnished with thin lemon slices. Makes 8 servings.

Petunias planted in a tube cake pan make a lovely centerpiece for an outdoor umbrella table. The umbrella can be inserted through the openings in the pan and table.

½ tsp. ground ginger
½ c. orange juice
4 tblsp. butter

Carrots Make Colorful Dishes

Artistic women frequently select carrots for guest meals on account of their brilliant color. Nutritionists choose them because they are a good-for-you food. Most hostesses include them in their special-occasion meals for both reasons and also because the vegetable is almost always available and tastes so fine. Carrots are especially delicious when fixed by the recipes that follow.

CANDIED GARDEN CARROTS

This is something like candied sweets —use young carrots if available

8 or 10 peeled whole carrots
½ tsp. salt
2 tblsp. butter
6 tblsp. brown sugar

• Cook carrots in ½" water with ½ tsp. salt added, until just tender. Drain.
• In a small skillet, melt butter. Add brown sugar and stir until dissolved. Add carrots and cook over low heat, turning until well glazed. Makes about 8 servings.

ORANGE CARROTS

Orange in color and in flavor—ginger adds zest and a big taste bonus

10 medium carrots, peeled and sliced
2 tblsp. sugar
2 tsp. cornstarch
½ tsp. salt

• Slice carrots crosswise on the bias about ½" thick. Cook, covered, in a little boiling salted water (½ tsp. salt to 1 c. water) until just tender, about 20 minutes. Drain.
• Meanwhile, combine sugar, cornstarch, salt and ginger in a small saucepan. Add orange juice; cook, stirring constantly, until mixture thickens and bubbles. Boil 1 minute. Stir in butter. Pour over hot carrots and toss to coat with orange sauce. Makes 8 servings.

WALNUT CARROTS

Walnuts add crunchy note and flavor to bright carrots, expertly seasoned

5 c. (3") carrot sticks (32 young carrots)
1 ½ c. water
½ tsp. salt
½ c. melted butter or margarine
2 tsp. honey
½ tsp. salt
¼ tsp. coarse pepper
2 tblsp. lemon juice
¼ tsp. grated lemon peel
½ c. coarsely broken walnuts

• Cook carrots (peeled) in water with ½ tsp. salt added, just until tender. Drain thoroughly.
• Meanwhile, heat remaining ingredients except the walnuts. Pour this topping over the hot carrots. Toss in the walnuts. Makes 8 servings.

Give cooked, buttered lima beans a flavor lift by stirring in a few celery seeds.

SCALLOPED CARROTS

Serve guests this new vegetable dish
—from a good cook's recipe files

4 c. cooked, mashed carrots
1⅓ c. water in which carrots
     were cooked
16 soda crackers, rolled fine
3 tblsp. finely chopped onion
⅔ c. grated Cheddar cheese
3 tblsp. light cream
Salt
Pepper

· Mix ingredients in order listed.
Taste to check salt and pepper, add
more if you wish.
· Pour into a greased 2-qt. casserole.
Bake in moderate oven (350°) 25
minutes. Makes 8 servings.

HONEYED CARROTS

One taste is enough to start a run
on this color-bright vegetable dish

5 c. carrots, peeled and sliced
     ½" thick
¼ c. butter or margarine
¼ c. honey
2 tblsp. brown sugar
2 tblsp. chopped parsley
¼ tsp. salt
⅛ tsp. pepper

· Cook carrots in boiling salted water
until just tender. Drain.
· Melt butter; add honey, brown
sugar, parsley, salt and pepper. Blend.
· Place carrots in greased 1½-qt.
casserole. Pour sauce over. Cover
with foil and bake in moderate oven
(350°) 20 to 30 minutes. Makes 8
servings.

Note: If more convenient, simply heat
cooked carrots in the sauce, but it

often is easier to get them ready in
advance and heat in oven just before
the meal is served.

ITALIAN EGGPLANT

One of the best eggplant dishes ever
invented—pizza-like with yellow and
red top. For a true Italian flavor,
use ⅓ c. each olive and salad oil

1 medium eggplant
Salt
1 egg, slightly beaten
1 c. corn flake or bread crumbs
⅔ c. salad oil
¼ tsp. pepper
2 tblsp. chopped parsley
¼ c. grated Parmesan cheese
6 slices mozzarella cheese
     (6 oz.)
1 (8 oz.) can tomato sauce

· Peel eggplant if desired; cut in ½"
slices. Sprinkle with salt. Dip in egg
and then in crumbs. Dry on rack a
few minutes.
· Pour oil into skillet to the depth
of ⅛" and heat. Brown eggplant
slices on both sides in hot oil. Place
slices in a shallow baking pan, overlapping if necessary. Sprinkle with
pepper, parsley and Parmesan cheese;
top with mozzarella cheese slices.
Pour tomato sauce over all.
· Bake in moderate oven (350°) 20
to 25 minutes. Makes 6 servings.

Note: Make two panfuls of Italian
Eggplant if there will be 8 to 12
people around the table.

CHEESE-ONION SCALLOP

Delicious way with onions. You can
mix foods ahead and refrigerate to
bake when getting supper

4 c. sliced onions
1 c. condensed Cheddar cheese
soup
½ c. milk

• Separate onion slices into rings. Combine soup and milk; mix with onion rings in 1½-qt. baking dish.
• Bake uncovered in moderate oven (375°) 30 minutes, or until hot and bubbly. Garnish with pimiento or a light sprinkling of cayenne pepper (red pepper). Makes 8 servings.

GLAZED ONIONS

Excellent choice for a turkey dinner

18 small white onions, peeled
4 tblsp. butter
1 to 2 tsp. sugar

• Peel onions; cut slice from stem and root ends. Cook, covered, in salted water (½ tsp. salt to 1 c. water) until just tender, about 25 minutes. Drain.
• Melt butter in heavy skillet; add onions. Cook over medium heat, shaking pan so onions roll around and start to brown on all sides.
• Sprinkle with sugar and continue rolling skillet around so sugar will give onions a shiny glaze. Makes 6 to 8 servings.

CHEESE-CREAMED SPINACH

The kind of vegetable dish you'll be proud to offer guests—it's distinctive

3 (10 oz.) pkgs. frozen chopped spinach
1 (1 to 1½ oz.) envelope onion-soup mix
2 c. dairy sour cream
½ c. grated Cheddar cheese

• Cook spinach as directed on package; drain. Combine with onion-soup mix and dairy sour cream. Spoon into greased 2-qt. casserole. Top with cheese.
• Bake in moderate oven (350°) until heated throughout, about 25 minutes. Makes 8 to 10 servings.

America Gave the World Pod Peppers

When you drive along the highways of our Southwest in autumn, you see brilliant red pods of chili peppers, strung together, hanging by the sides of adobe houses to dry in the golden sunshine. And when you visit the vegetable counters in supermarkets west of the Mississippi River and elsewhere, you frequently see fresh green chili peppers, with pointed ends. Green chili peppers, canned, are even more widely available. The use of these seasoners is spreading across the country.

All pod peppers were unknown by people other than American Indians, before Europeans came to the New World. Early settlers learned from the natives how to use capsicum peppers. The name pepper is confusing, for they are not related to peppercorns, the dried Old World berries that are ground and used almost daily in our kitchens. Early Spanish explorers, who were not botanists, called them chili, an Aztec name. You'll find them listed among the ingredients of several recipes in this cookbook. They're important in Southwestern Corn Bake, which is truly delicious.

SOUTHWESTERN CORN BAKE

A vegetable dish that's highly prized by Southwestern hostesses—do try it

2 (16 to 17 oz.) cans cream
    style corn
2 eggs, beaten
¾ c. yellow cornmeal
1 tsp. garlic salt
6 tblsp. salad oil
1 (4 oz.) can green chili, finely
    cut
2 c. grated Cheddar cheese

· Mix together all ingredients except chili and cheese.
· Divide mixture in half. Place one half in a greased 8 × 8 × 2″ baking dish.
· Mix together chili and cheese; lay on top of corn mixture in dish. Cover with the remaining corn mixture.
· Bake in moderate oven (350°) 35 minutes. Makes 8 servings.

TEXAS GUMBO RICE

A new dish that complements meats

4 slices bacon
1 large onion, minced
6 medium tomatoes, cut up
1 green pepper, chopped
1 c. sliced okra
1 (16 oz.) can whole kernel
    corn (undrained)
2 tsp. salt
¼ tsp. pepper
½ tsp. chili powder
½ c. long grain rice

· Cook bacon in large skillet until crisp. Remove from pan and drain.
· Measure 3 tblsp. bacon fat into skillet; add onion and sauté until tender. Add remaining ingredients. Cover and

simmer 20 minutes, or until rice is tender. Place in serving dish; crumble bacon on top. Makes 6 servings.

CHEESE SCALLOPED CORN

A custard-like corn dish accented with cheese, onion and green pepper

2 eggs, beaten
2 (1 lb.) cans cream style corn
1 c. milk
1 c. cracker crumbs
½ c. chopped onion
½ c. chopped green pepper
1 c. grated Cheddar cheese
¼ tsp. salt
⅛ tsp. pepper

· Beat eggs in large mixing bowl; stir in remaining ingredients.
· Spoon into two greased 1-qt casseroles. Bake, uncovered, in moderate oven (350°) until set, about 35 minutes. Makes 8 to 10 servings.

Summer Squash with a Garden-Fresh Taste

Summer squash is no newcomer to home gardens or dinner tables, but new and better varieties appear every year. Just look in your seed catalogs and supermarkets. The flavor of these squashes is delicate and they're about the easiest vegetable to cook. Gather them young, when they're at their best, and you don't have to peel them (the skins are so tender) or remove the tiny seeds.

Here are recipes featuring summer squash, whatever variety you have or prefer—green like zucchini, yellow like the crookneck, or green-white like very young pattypans. Some of them make 4 or 6 servings, but you can double them if you're having company.

SUMMER SQUASH PARMESAN

Cook thin slices until just tender-crisp for good texture and taste

4   c. thinly sliced unpeeled, fresh or frozen summer squash
1   small onion, sliced
1   tblsp. water
2   tblsp. butter
½   tsp. salt
⅛   tsp. pepper
3   tblsp. Parmesan cheese

• Put all ingredients except cheese in a skillet. Cover and cook 1 minute over high heat. Uncover, continue to cook over low heat, turning with spatula, until barely tender.
• Sprinkle with cheese and serve. Makes 6 to 8 servings.

SQUASH AND VEGETABLE SAUTÉ

A different vegetable dish; tangy in flavor. Good with meat

3   tblsp. butter or margarine
3   c. sliced zucchini or yellow summer squash
3   c. shredded cabbage
¾   c. chopped green pepper
1½ tsp. salt
⅛   tsp. pepper
¼   tsp. crushed dried orégano
¼   tsp. crushed dried thyme
1   tblsp. vinegar

• Melt butter in skillet. Add squash and cabbage. Cover and cook over medium heat about 5 minutes. Uncover; add green pepper. Cook over low heat, turning occasionally with spatula, until squash is tender, about 10 minutes.
• Stir in remaining ingredients. Makes 6 servings.

SUMMER SQUASH WITH DILL

A zippy vegetable dish to perk up an otherwise bland meal

5   yellow summer squash
2   tsp. salt
¼   c. butter or margarine
⅔   c. finely chopped onion
1½ tsp. paprika
½   tsp. salt
¼   tsp. pepper
1   tsp. dried dill weed
2   tblsp. vinegar

• Cut squash in long thin strips. Sprinkle with 2 tsp. salt and let stand 1 hour. Drain off liquid and squeeze squash strips gently in a clean towel.
• Melt butter, add onion and sauté until golden. Stir in paprika, ½ tsp. salt, pepper, dill weed, vinegar and squash. Cook over medium heat until tender, about 15 minutes. Makes 6 servings.

PUFFED-UP ZUCCHINI

Light and tender—almost like a soufflé. Serve with roast meats

4   c. chopped zucchini
1   c. chopped onion
¼   c. water
2   tblsp. butter or margarine
½   tsp. salt
⅛   tsp. pepper
1   tblsp. grated horse-radish
1   egg, slightly beaten
1   c. coarse cracker crumbs
3   tblsp. butter or margarine

• Combine zucchini and onion in

saucepan. Add water, cover and cook until tender, about 15 minutes. Drain well. Mash zucchini; add butter, salt, pepper and horse-radish. Cool.

• Add egg and mix thoroughly. Pour into greased 1-qt. baking dish. Top with crumbs that have been browned in the 3 tblsp. butter.

• Bake in moderate oven (350°) 30 minutes. Makes 6 servings.

HERB-BAKED SQUASH AND CARROTS

This is a truly colorful vegetable dish with a wonderful flavor combination

3   tblsp. water
2   tblsp. salad oil
3   c. sliced summer squash
3   c. coarsely grated carrots
¾   c. chopped onion
¼   tsp. crushed dried thyme
¼   tsp. crushed dried orégano
1 ½ tsp. salt
⅛   tsp. pepper
1   tblsp. chopped parsley
1   tblsp. butter or margarine

• Pour water and oil into saucepan; add squash, carrots and onion. Cover and simmer 5 minutes.

• Add remaining ingredients, cover and cook, stirring occasionally, just until tender (do not overcook). Makes 6 servings.

BAKED ZUCCHINI

California cooks excel with zucchini— here's proof in a soufflé-like dish

3   c. sliced raw zucchini (¼")
1 ½ c. soda cracker crumbs
3   eggs, beaten
½   c. butter, melted
½   tsp. salt

1   (4 oz.) jar pimiento, diced
1   c. milk
2   c. shredded Cheddar cheese

• Mix all ingredients. Pour into greased 2-qt. casserole.

• Bake, uncovered, in slow oven (300°) 30 to 40 minutes, until golden brown. Makes 8 servings.

SQUASH MEDLEY

A highly praised FARM JOURNAL *vegetable casserole*

4   fresh medium unpeeled summer squash, or 4 c. frozen summer squash
½   green pepper, chopped
2   ripe tomatoes, peeled and chopped
6   slices bacon, fried and chopped
1 ½ c. shredded process cheese
⅓   c. chopped onion
½   tsp. salt
½   c. fine bread crumbs
2   tblsp. butter

• Parboil squash (zucchini for 3 minutes; yellow crooknecks or small white pattypans, 5 minutes; and white scallops, 15 to 20 minutes). If you use frozen squash, do not parboil.

• To make filling, combine remaining ingredients except crumbs and butter. Mix well.

• Slice parboiled squash thinly. Place in baking dish, alternating squash and filling. Top with bread crumbs and dabs of butter.

• Bake in moderate oven (375°) 35 minutes. Makes 6 to 8 servings.

Put a string of blinking Christmas lights in your jack-o'-lantern. He seems to wink as the colors change.

MAPLED ACORN SQUASH

Rosemary and maple syrup make this deliciously different. An autumn hit

4 acorn squash
Crushed dried rosemary leaves
Salt
⅓ c. maple-blended syrup

• Split squash; remove and discard seeds. Sprinkle cut side of each squash lightly with rosemary and salt. Turn cut side down in baking pan. Surround with ½″ hot water. Bake in hot oven (400°) until tender, about 45 minutes.

• Turn cut side up; spoon 2 tsp. maple syrup into each cavity and spread to coat all surfaces. Return squash to oven for 5 minutes. Makes 8 servings.

Autumn Brings Acorn Squash

Autumn brings many prized foods to the country kitchen—especially apples, pumpkins and acorn squash. The small green-coated squash with yellow interior is one of the season's gifts. Use it in your company meals in the fall, when the squash is at its best.

For a pretty and tasty dish, fill Mapled Acorn Squash at serving time with cooked and buttered frozen peas. Or omit the maple-blended syrup and add a slice of process yellow cheese to each squash half; then return to the oven for 5 minutes.

STUFFED ACORN SQUASH

Nice to fix with an oven meal

3 medium-size acorn squash
1½ c. soft bread crumbs
1 c. grated sharp cheese
¼ c. softened butter or margarine
3 tblsp. chopped green pepper
2 tblsp. chopped onion
1 tsp. salt
⅛ tsp. pepper

• Split squash; remove and discard seeds. Place cut side down in baking pan. Bake in hot oven (400°) 45 minutes, until tender.

• Remove from oven. When cool enough to handle, scoop out pulp, leaving shells about ¼″ thick. Mash pulp; add remaining ingredients. Pile lightly into shells and bake in moderate oven (350°) until lightly browned, about 30 minutes. Makes 6 servings.

Tomatoes Are Red, Ripe and Juicy

It's the home-grown touch that frequently gives country dishes their superior eating quality. Vegetable and fruit crops are bountiful some years —tomatoes, for instance. "If you have bushel-baskets and tubs filled with ripe tomatoes at their peak," an upstate New York gardener says, "you get busy and put some of them away to enjoy the rest of the year."

This farm woman developed a two-in-one canning idea. After each picking, she cooks the tomatoes and turns them into a couple of hostess-canned products that please family as well as guests. One is Tangy Tomato Cocktail, the other, Spicy Spaghetti Sauce. There are many ways to use these tomato specialties.

When home economists in our Test Kitchens tried out her methods, they and their taste-testers liked what they sampled. If you have a big supply of tomatoes, here are directions for two ways to salvage some of them. Better guest meals will result.

BASIC TOMATO MIXTURE

Both cocktail and sauce start with this

20 lbs. firm ripe tomatoes,
    about 60 medium-size
    tomatoes
2 tblsp. salt
1 tsp. celery salt
3 tblsp. Worcestershire sauce
2 tsp. onion powder
¼ tsp. Tabasco sauce

• Wash tomatoes, cut in halves and remove stem ends (no peeling necessary). Remove any spoiled or green spots (they can ruin the mixture).

• Place tomato halves in a large canning kettle over high heat. Add salt, celery salt, Worcestershire sauce, onion powder and Tabasco sauce. Bring to a full boil, stirring frequently to prevent sticking. Cook 5 minutes. Remove from heat and ladle mixture into a food mill, colander or large sieve. Strain off any liquid that pours through easily. Stir just enough to let the juice pour through. Use it to make the cocktail.

Tangy Tomato Cocktail: Taste the juice to make sure it is well seasoned. If you wish, add another 1 tsp. celery salt. If juice is too tart, add 1 to 2 tblsp. sugar. Heat mixture just until boiling, pour into quart canning jars, adjust lids and process in a boiling water bath 10 minutes. Makes about 4 quarts.

Spicy Spaghetti Sauce: Transfer the juicy tomato pulp into another container without passing through a food mill, colander or sieve. Add 1 tblsp. dried orégano leaves, 2 cloves garlic, peeled and quartered, and 2 tblsp. Worcestershire sauce. Place in the electric blender, about 2 c. at a time; blend until smooth. Make sure tomato skins are blended. (If you want to remove all the small bits of tomato skin and seeds, run this mixture through a colander, food mill or sieve after blending.) Heat mixture until boiling. Pour into pint canning jars, adjust lids and process 10 minutes in a boiling water bath. Makes about 7 pints.

TOMATO-LIMA BEANS

This tasty dish waits patiently in a slow oven if guests are late to supper

2 (10 oz.) pkgs. frozen lima
    beans
1 c. chopped onion
3 tblsp. butter or margarine
2 tblsp. flour
1 (1 lb.) can tomatoes
½ tsp. salt
½ tsp. celery salt
¼ tsp. pepper
1 c. shredded Cheddar cheese

• Cook beans by package directions until barely tender. Drain.

• Cook onion in butter until soft (not browned); stir in flour to make a smooth paste. Add tomatoes; cook until mixture thickens and bubbles. Add salt, celery salt and pepper. Stir in beans.

• Turn into a 1½-qt. casserole. Sprinkle with cheese. Bake in moderate oven (350°) until bubbly hot, 20 to 30 minutes. Makes 8 servings.

Note: You can heat this vegetable dish in a saucepan if more convenient than baking it.

SAVORY BAKED TOMATOES

Adornment for any plate and so tasty —juicy red tomato slices topped with crisp gold crumbs and herb magic

4 ripe tomatoes, cut in halves
Garlic salt
Finely crushed dried basil
¼ c. butter or margarine
½ c. coarse cracker crumbs
2 tsp. dried parsley flakes

• Place tomato halves, cut side up, in greased baking pan. Sprinkle tops with garlic salt and lightly with basil.
• Melt butter in a small skillet; add cracker crumbs and parsley. Sauté until crumbs are golden, stirring constantly. Spoon crumbs onto tomato halves.
• Bake in moderate oven (350°) 20 minutes, or until hot. Makes 8 servings.

VEGETABLE-CHEESE TOPPER

Spoon this vegetable medley on waffles or toast for a new supper dish

¼ c. butter or margarine
½ c. diced celery
¼ c. diced green pepper
4 tblsp. flour
1 tsp. salt
⅛ tsp. pepper
1 ½ c. milk
2 c. grated sharp cheese
¾ c. canned corn, drained
2 fresh tomatoes, peeled and chopped
Toast or waffles

• Melt butter in a saucepan; add celery and green pepper, and sauté just until tender-crisp. Stir in flour, salt and pepper to make a smooth paste. Add milk gradually and cook, stirring until thickened.
• Add cheese; stir until melted. Add corn and tomatoes. Heat and serve over waffles or toast. Makes 4 to 6 servings.

Fancy Tops for Casseroles: *Instead of buttered bread crumbs, cut buttered bread slices in cubes and arrange them checkerboard fashion on top of mixture in casserole. Or cut yellow process cheese in strips and arrange in the shape of V's (chevrons) on top of buttered crumbs on casserole mixture.*

End-of-Season Tomatoes

Before frost comes in autumn, country gardeners daily relieve tomato vines of their dead-ripe, juicy fruit. When company is coming to dinner and sliced tomatoes or tomato salad seems a little old-hat, you can sauté whole tomatoes in herb-seasoned butter for a superb hot vegetable dish. They add color and flavor to the meal and taste wonderfully good.

If you need more than 6 servings, which the following recipe makes, fix a second skillet of this autumn dish. That's the best way to double the recipe.

AUTUMN TOMATO SKILLET

Delicate herb seasoning guarantees a delicious hot vegetable dish

3 tblsp. butter or margarine
4 or 5 green onions, chopped

¼ tsp. dried thyme
¼ tsp. dried marjoram
6 peeled whole ripe tomatoes
Salt
Pepper

· Melt butter in skillet. Add onions and herbs. Sauté gently about 5 minutes.
· Arrange tomatoes in skillet; sprinkle lightly with salt and pepper. Cover skillet tightly; simmer 15 minutes.
· Carefully lift tomatoes onto serving platter. Makes 6 servings.

Frosty Vegetable Soup from Spanish Kitchens

Everyone who visits Spain when the weather is warm returns home with pleasant memories of refreshing cold *gazpacho*. And most women want to duplicate this vegetable soup in their own kitchens. We have worked out a recipe for it, knowing that many country women have the important makings in their gardens.

It takes time to chop the vegetables, but the results are worth the cost in minutes and effort. While you can use your blender for the chopping, you lose some of the desired texture. Also you can use salad oil instead of olive oil, but you get a different flavor from the truly great Spanish soup.

The ingredients are what we use in salads, but sipping your salad is different. Try this soup the next time you want something special to serve on a hot, humid day.

FROSTY SPANISH VEGETABLE SOUP

Make in morning to serve as evening meal on particularly sultry days

1 c. finely chopped peeled tomatoes
½ c. finely chopped green pepper
½ c. finely chopped celery
½ c. finely chopped peeled cucumber
¼ c. finely chopped onion
2 tsp. finely chopped or snipped fresh parsley
2 tsp. chopped or snipped chives
1 small clove garlic, minced
2½ tblsp. wine vinegar
2 tblsp. olive oil
1 tsp. salt
¼ tsp. ground pepper
½ tsp. Worcestershire sauce
2 c. tomato juice

· Combine all the ingredients in a glass bowl and stir to mix. Cover and chill thoroughly—several hours. Serve in chilled cups. Makes 6 servings.

Note: Double the recipe if you need more servings.

VARIATION

Quick Frosty Spanish Vegetable Soup: Chop the vegetables in a blender.

CHAPTER 4

COLORFUL SALADS AND SALAD DRESSINGS

Men no longer jest about salads tasting like fodder or rabbit food. The way they help themselves to the salad bowl on the buffet table and go back for seconds reveals a change in attitudes. Today's hostess relies heavily on salads to give color, texture and appetite appeal to guest meals.

What a splendid selection of salad recipes this chapter offers. There are crisp, crackling greens you toss in a bowl, and other salads you cook in casseroles and skillets. There are gorgeous gelatin molds to make ahead and chill in the refrigerator. Many of them are wonderful travelers, especially in cold weather. You'll find they're showpieces on the table.

Look through the pages that follow and notice salads for all seasons. Mint Julepeach, Cantaloupe, Fresh Blueberry pointed up with lime juice, and Superb Fruit Salad aglow with sunset colors—these are all summer delights. Party Egg and Tart Rhubarb salads come with spring. Hot Slaw with Apples suggests autumn, when orchards bear juicy fruit and gardens supply green cabbage. Canned and frozen fruits star in cheerful winter salads—like Jewels-in-a-Ring and Ginger Pear Salad.

Our chicken and potato salads deserve honorable mention, for they're unusually good—Dilly Potato and Regal Chicken salads are two examples. The first has a delicate dill taste, the second has two surprises: tarragon and salted peanuts.

The frozen salads in this chapter are extra-delicious. You'll find other remarkably good ones in the chapter on Cooking for a Crowd, for these are the salads a hostess often makes in big batches for party days.

To the salad dressings go much credit for the wonderful flavors they add. Do try Sherbet Salad Dressing on fruit salad. It's so luscious and color-bright. And if you're packing a picnic lunch, consider Refrigerator Sauerkraut Salad, a safe bet even in very hot weather, because of the brine content.

Toss Green Salads at the Last Minute

Some country hostesses boast that they never serve exactly the same tossed salads twice. That's because they make use of the tremendous variety of vegetables available today in gardens and supermarkets. Also they frequently switch flavors of salad dressings made easy by the packaged dry mixes and bottled dressings from the grocers' shelves. And sometimes they stir up their own dressings.

Making a top-notch green salad calls for strict attention to details. Here are a few of the most important:
· Wash greens, drain well and chill in plastic bags or vegetable crisper until they are crackling crisp.
· Tear or cut leaves in bite-size pieces (no smaller than size of half dollars).
· Cut raw nonleafy vegetables in chunks so everyone will know what he's eating. Minced and grated vegetables get lost in the salad bowl; small pieces of vegetables become limp quickly.
· Add the dressing just before you take the salad to the table or serve it in individual bowls or on plates.

GARDEN SALAD BOWLS

Spicy red beets and crisp greens produce picture-pretty individual salads

2 qts. mixed greens (leaf lettuce, romaine, escarole or tender beet greens)

½ c. onion slices
½ c. canned chick-peas, drained (optional)
1 c. pickled beet slices, well drained
Cottage Blue Cheese Dressing

· Wash and drain greens well; break into bite-size pieces before measuring.
· Toss together greens, onion slices and chick-peas (without dressing); divide into 8 or 10 salad bowls. Top each bowl with 4 beet slices and 2 tblsp. Cottage Blue Cheese Dressing.

COTTAGE BLUE CHEESE DRESSING

It's creamy with a mild cheese taste

2 tblsp. vinegar
⅛ tsp. salt
3 drops Tabasco sauce
⅔ c. mayonnaise
½ c. crumbled blue cheese
⅓ c. cottage cheese

· In a small bowl, blend vinegar, salt and Tabasco sauce; blend in mayonnaise and beat until smooth.
· Stir in blue cheese and cottage cheese. Makes 1⅓ cups.

CATALINA TOSSED SALAD

Perfect salad for the barbecue crowd —equally at home in indoor meals

2 qts. mixed greens (leaf or romaine lettuce, spinach leaves or tender beet greens)
3 tomatoes, cut in wedges
1 c. raw cauliflowerettes
½ c. crumbled blue cheese

It's the seasonings that make Summer Chicken with Peas so delectable (*see recipe, page 64*). You use lemon juice, green onions, sour cream, parsley, thyme and lots of freshly ground pepper in this Gourmet Special skillet meal.

½ c. crumbled cooked bacon
½ tsp. salt
¼ tsp. pepper
½ c. Honey French Dressing

• Wash and drain greens well; shake dry in a dish towel. Break into bite-size pieces before measuring.
• Add tomato wedges, cauliflower-ettes, blue cheese and bacon. Refrigerate until serving time.
• When ready to serve, add seasonings and dressing; toss to coat all the greens. Makes 8 to 10 servings.

HONEY FRENCH DRESSING

Honey is the magic in this dressing

1 tsp. salt
¼ tsp. pepper
1 tsp. dry mustard
⅓ c. cider vinegar
2 tblsp. honey
1 c. salad oil

• In a small bowl, mix salt, pepper and dry mustard; stir in vinegar and honey. Slowly add the salad oil while beating with a rotary beater or electric mixer. Makes about 1⅓ cups.

BERMUDA TOSSED SALAD

Sesame seeds and garlic croutons are the exciting flavor and texture accents

1 qt. lettuce (leaf or romaine)
1 qt. young spinach leaves
3 tomatoes, cut in wedges
½ c. sweet onion rings
3 tblsp. Toasted Sesame Seeds (see Index)
½ to 1 tsp. salt

¼ tsp. pepper
½ c. Honey French Dressing
1 to 3 c. Garlic Croutons

• Wash and drain leaves well; break into bite-size pieces before measuring.
• Add tomato wedges, onion rings and sesame seeds. Refrigerate until serving time.
• When ready to serve, add seasonings and dressing; top with croutons. Makes 8 to 10 servings.

Garlic Croutons: Trim crusts from 5 slices of day-old bread; cut into ½" cubes. In a heavy skillet, heat ⅓ c. salad oil and 1 crushed clove garlic. Add bread cubes; sauté until golden brown and crisp. Makes 3 cups.

BEST-EVER SALAD DRESSING

Toss your mixed green salad with this —you'll get coveted compliments

2 c. mayonnaise (1 pt.)
1½ tsp. anchovy paste
1 (8 oz.) bottle creamy French dressing
1 (1½ oz.) can grated Parmesan cheese
2 cloves garlic, crushed

• Combine a little mayonnaise with anchovy paste to blend thoroughly. Stir in remaining mayonnaise and other ingredients.
• Serve over your favorite mixed green salad, but first toss in a few crisp croutons or broken pieces of melba toast. Serve at once. Makes 2¾ cups.

Wild ducks are fine country eating when you fix them as Texas Barbecued Duck (*recipe, page 74*). For a company dinner, garnish platter with spiced pineapple or other fruit, and green grapes. You can cook ducks over coals.

Note: The garlic flavor strengthens if dressing is kept in refrigerator several days. If garlic cloves are stuck on toothpicks, they can be removed.

RED AND GREEN CABBAGE SALAD

Simple to fix, colorful salad that perks up meals featuring pork or ham

4 c. shredded green cabbage
4 c. shredded red cabbage
½ medium onion, minced
Sour Cream Dressing

· Toss cabbages and onion together with Sour Cream Dressing. Makes 8 to 10 servings.

SOUR CREAM DRESSING

2 c. dairy sour cream
6 tblsp. vinegar
¼ c. sugar
1 tblsp. salt
¾ tsp. dry mustard
Pepper (optional)

· Mix all ingredients together, adding pepper to taste. Makes about 2¼ cups dressing.

CONTINENTAL BEAN SALAD

Do try this bean salad garnished with deviled eggs and pimiento ribbons

2 (1 lb.) cans whole Blue Lake
      green beans (4 c.)
1 medium onion, thinly sliced
      and separated into rings
1 tsp. salt
½ tsp. pepper
⅓ c. lemon juice (or vinegar)
1 (2 oz.) can anchovy filets
2 tblsp. salad oil
4 hard-cooked eggs, deviled
Pimiento strips

· Drain beans thoroughly; add onion rings. Mix salt, pepper and lemon juice and sprinkle over bean-onion mixture.
· Mash anchovies to a paste with their own oil and the 2 tblsp. salad oil. Add to bean mixture and mix well by tossing lightly. Chill.
· Serve on lettuce; garnish each serving with one half egg, deviled, and pimiento strips. Makes 8 servings.

GREEN BEAN SALAD

Make-ahead special; flavors blend in the chilling. Good take-along salad

½ c. vinegar
¼ c. salad oil
1 tsp. salt
¼ tsp. pepper
1 tsp. sugar
4 c. cooked green beans
1 medium onion, finely chopped
Lettuce
3 slices fried bacon, crumbled

· Blend first 5 ingredients; pour over beans and onion. Chill well. Serve on lettuce; sprinkle on bacon just before serving. Makes 6 to 8 servings.

Herbs Perk Up Vegetable Salads

Something wonderful happens to vegetable salads when you season them with a snatch of herbs. Most country hostesses use only a dash of an herb in a salad because they want their guests to keep guessing what's responsible for the interesting taste.

The secret of many much-lauded country vegetable salads is in the garden corner where herbs grow. We give you seven examples of salads in which herbs and vegetables combine.

DILLY POTATO SALAD

Slices of hard-cooked eggs, sprinkled with paprika, make a tempting trim

5 c. cooked, cubed potatoes
4 hard-cooked eggs, chopped
¼ c. chopped dill pickle
½ c. chopped onion
¼ c. vinegar
1 tsp. salt
2 tsp. sugar
½ tsp. pepper
1 tsp. chopped fresh dill, or
    ¾ tsp. dried dill weed
½ c. mayonnaise

• Toss together potatoes, eggs, pickle and onion. Mix remaining ingredients and pour over the potatoes. Toss lightly. Sprinkle with paprika. Cover and chill. Makes 8 servings.

GARDEN PEA SALAD

For this "green" salad use tender peas rushed from garden and cooked quickly. Garnish with Cheddar cheese

¼ c. French dressing
¼ c. dairy sour cream
1 tblsp. prepared mustard
¼ c. diced sweet pickles
1 c. thinly sliced celery
1 tsp. sugar
½ tsp. salt
4 fresh marjoram leaves, finely
    chopped, or ¼ tsp. dried
    marjoram
3 c. cooked fresh peas
Cheddar cheese

• Add French dressing to sour cream; add mustard, pickles, celery, sugar,

salt and marjoram. (If dried marjoram is used, crumble it.) Mix well.
• Pour over peas; toss lightly. Chill at least 4 hours. Serve in shallow bowl; garnish with strips of yellow cheese. Makes 6 servings.

BABY BEET SALAD

New, attractive, tasty salad made by marinating beets in dressing. Use beets the size of ping-pong balls

1 c. French dressing
2 drops Tabasco sauce
½ tsp. minced fresh thyme
    leaves, or ¼ tsp. dried
    thyme leaves
3 c. cooked baby beets
Lettuce
2 hard-cooked eggs, chopped

• Mix French dressing, Tabasco and thyme in saucepan; simmer 5 minutes. Add beets, quartered, cover and refrigerate overnight. Drain.
• Arrange beets on lettuce or other crisp greens. Sprinkle with chopped eggs. Makes 6 servings.

RIPE TOMATO SALAD

This salad features famous teammates, juicy red tomatoes and basil

4 ripe tomatoes, cut in wedges
Salt
2 tblsp. finely chopped fresh
    basil leaves or ½ tsp.
    dried basil leaves
2 tblsp. salad oil
Juice of ½ lemon

• Sprinkle tomatoes with salt to season. Add basil to salad oil (if you use dried basil, crumble it). Sprinkle over tomatoes. Chill at least 1 hour.
• Squeeze lemon juice over top just

before serving. Serve on large plate or in shallow bowl. Lemon quarters and chopped parsley make an attractive garnish. Makes 6 to 8 servings.

CARROT-CHIVE SALAD

Brilliant colors—marvelous flavors

⅓ c. salad oil
¼ c. vinegar
½ tsp. salt
1 tblsp. chopped fresh chives,
    or ½ tsp. dried chives
2 tblsp. syrup drained from
    canned pineapple
3 c. coarsely shredded carrots
1 (13 ½ oz.) can pineapple
    tidbits

• Mix oil, vinegar, salt, chives and syrup drained from pineapple.
• Mix carrots and drained pineapple tidbits; pour over the oil-vinegar mixture. Toss lightly. Chill at least 4 hours. Serve in shallow bowl; garnish salad with chopped chives. Makes 6 to 8 servings.

HOT OR COLD GREEN BEAN SALAD

Some like it hot, some like it cold. Take your pick—it's good both ways

¼ c. salad oil
1 tblsp. vinegar
1 tsp. salt
⅛ tsp. black pepper
1 tsp. chopped fresh rosemary
    leaves, or ¼ tsp. dried
    rosemary leaves
1 clove garlic
3 c. cooked green beans

• Combine all the ingredients except the beans; beat well. Pour over the beans and toss lightly.
• Cover and chill at least 4 hours.

Remove garlic. Serve chilled, or heat 5 minutes before serving. Makes 6 servings.

LIMA BEAN SALAD

Green onions and basil make this special. Serve it to summer guests

¾ c. salad oil
½ c. vinegar
3 tblsp. finely chopped basil
    leaves, or 1 tsp. dried
    basil leaves
1 tsp. salt
1 tblsp. sugar
½ c. chopped green onion
6 c. cooked lima beans
Lettuce

• Mix oil, vinegar, basil, salt, sugar and onion. Pour over beans; mix lightly. Cover and chill at least 4 hours.
• Serve on crisp lettuce or other greens. Makes 8 servings.

Ready-to-Serve Salads Men Praise

You can keep this trio of tangy, sweet-sour salads, all of which have their start in the cabbage patch, on hand for several days. Sauerkraut Salad keeps even longer—a whole week. Just cover and store them in your refrigerator.

All three salads are hostess favorites in ranch and farm homes. One reason is the convenience of having them chilled and crisp—ready to serve on short notice. But the more important reason is their great appeal to men.

CABBAGE-ONION SALAD

Use green cabbage and white onions or white cabbage and red onions. It wilts slightly but has crisp texture

1 ½ qts. shredded cabbage
    (1 large head)
2 large onions, thinly sliced
    and separated in rings
1 c. sugar
1 c. vinegar
1 tsp. salt
1 tsp. celery seeds
1 tsp. dry mustard
¼ tsp. pepper
1 c. salad oil

• Alternate cabbage and onions in bowl, with onions for top layer.
• Combine sugar, vinegar, salt, celery seeds, mustard and pepper in saucepan. Bring to a boil. Remove from heat; add salad oil.
• Drip the hot mixture over cabbage and onions; do not stir. Cover and refrigerate 24 hours or longer before serving. Makes about 12 cups.

SAUERKRAUT SALAD

Ideal salad to tote to picnics—sauerkraut pickles the other vegetables and insures good keeping for hours

2 c. sauerkraut (1 lb. can)
½ c. sugar
½ c. thinly sliced celery
½ c. thin strips green pepper
½ c. shredded carrot
¼ c. chopped onion

• Cut sauerkraut strands in shorter pieces with scissors. Stir in sugar and let stand 30 minutes.
• Add remaining ingredients. Cover bowl tightly and chill in refrigerator at least 12 hours. Serve on lettuce

if you wish. Makes 8 servings (about ½ c. to each serving).

STAY-CRISP CABBAGE SALAD

This refrigerator salad does not wilt because gelatin coats the vegetables

8 c. shredded cabbage
2 carrots, shredded
1 green pepper, cut in thin
    strips
½ c. chopped onion
¾ c. cold water
1 envelope unflavored gelatin
⅔ c. sugar
⅔ c. vinegar
2 tsp. celery seeds
1 ½ tsp. salt
¼ tsp. black pepper
⅔ c. salad oil

• Shred cabbage fine with sharp knife. Mix with carrots, green pepper and onion. Sprinkle with ½ c. cold water; chill.
• Soften gelatin in ¼ c. cold water.
• Mix sugar, vinegar, celery seeds, salt and pepper in saucepan. Bring to a boil. Stir in softened gelatin. Cool until slightly thickened; beat well. Gradually beat in salad oil.
• Drain vegetables; pour dressing over top. Mix lightly until all vegetables are coated with the dressing. Serve immediately, or cover and store in refrigerator; stir just before serving to separate pieces. Makes 8 servings.

Serve Skillet Salads Hot

When it's cold and blustery outside, the country hostess often pampers her guests by serving a warm salad. Here are three excellent examples of salads to fix in and serve from a skillet instead of a bowl. You make them with ingredients widely available in cold weather. And they are as satisfying in winter as are frosty salads in July.

DUTCH POTATO SALAD

Try baked instead of boiled potatoes in this salad—gives a new taste

```
6    medium potatoes
4    slices bacon
1    medium onion, minced
2    tblsp. vinegar
1    c. dairy sour cream
1    tblsp. cream-style prepared
       mustard
1½   tsp. salt
¼    tsp. pepper
1    tblsp. chopped parsley
```

• Boil potatoes in their skins; peel and slice.
• Pan-fry bacon in skillet, drain and crumble. Pour off excess drippings, reserving ¼ c. in skillet.
• Sauté onion in bacon fat until tender. Stir in vinegar, sour cream, mustard, salt and pepper.
• Add potatoes, crumbled bacon and parsley; toss lightly in dressing. Heat until piping hot. Makes 8 servings.

HOT CHICKEN SALAD

Clever way to dress up leftover turkey or chicken to serve on cold days

```
4    tblsp. onion, minced
⅔    c. chopped green pepper
3    c. chopped celery
4    tblsp. butter
4    c. cooked chicken or turkey,
       cut into chunks
2    tblsp. lemon juice
2    tsp. salt
```

```
1    c. mayonnaise
½ to 1 c. toasted almonds,
       slivered
```

• Sauté onion, green pepper and celery in butter until tender, but do not brown.
• Stir in chicken, lemon juice and salt. Cover skillet and place over low heat until ingredients are hot. Just before serving, remove skillet from heat and lightly stir in the mayonnaise and almonds. Makes 8 to 10 servings.

VARIATION

Crisp-Topped Salad: Sprinkle the Hot Chicken Salad with 1½ c. crushed potato chips and ½ c. grated Swiss cheese. Heat under broiler until top of salad is golden brown. Makes 10 servings.

HOT SLAW WITH APPLES

Red and green, from skillet-to-table salad—tastes best served while warm

```
6    c. cabbage, finely shredded
3    tblsp. water
3    tblsp. lemon juice
2    tblsp. sugar
3    tblsp. butter or salad oil
1½   tsp. salt
½    tsp. caraway seeds, or 2
       tsp. toasted sesame seeds
1    large unpeeled apple,
       thinly sliced
```

• Place all ingredients except the apple slices in a skillet; cook, uncovered, over medium-high heat, stirring lightly, until the cabbage is tender-crisp, about 3 minutes.
• Reduce heat to low, add apple, cover and cook 1 minute longer. Serve at once. Makes 8 servings.

Main-Dish Potato Salad— A French Beauty

Few main dishes equal the appeal of Salad Niçoise (pronounced nee-swahz) on a warm evening. And few salads can meet the beauty standards this French potato salad sets.

For a French menu, serve the salad with French bread, cheese (see Index for Important Natural Cheeses) and fruit for dessert, and hot coffee. Serve it with hot rolls, coffee and lemon or pineapple sherbet for a more typically American meal.

It's a good plan to get the salad ready to serve before time to greet the guests. The recipe tells how.

SALAD NIÇOISE

Add this special potato salad to your recipe collection for company meals

9 medium potatoes, cooked and cut
1 c. Oil-Vinegar Dressing
½ c. chopped sweet onion
3 c. green beans
Salad greens
4 tomatoes
4 hard-cooked eggs
Pitted large ripe olives
Anchovy filets
1 or 2 (7 oz.) cans tuna

• Cook potatoes in their jackets. Just as soon as they can be handled, peel and cut in thin slices (⅛"). Put into a bowl and drizzle over ¼ c. Oil-Vinegar Dressing. Add the onion, toss gently and cover. Let stand at room temperature until cool; then refrigerate.

• Pour 3 tblsp. of the Oil-Vinegar Dressing over the hot, drained green beans; cover. Let stand at room temperature until cool; then refrigerate.

• To serve, toss green beans and potato slices together gently, adding more Oil-Vinegar Dressing to coat vegetables if needed. Mound in the center of a large chilled chop plate. Arrange crisp salad greens around the edges.

• Arrange tomatoes, peeled and quartered, and quartered eggs alternately around the potato salad. Tuck olives between tomatoes and eggs. Garnish top of salad with anchovy strips. Sprinkle salad with chopped fresh parsley, basil or savory. If not ready to serve, cover with foil and refrigerate.

• At serving time, turn chilled tuna onto a chilled plate and garnish with lemon quarters and greens. Or if you prefer, make clusters of tuna chunks with the tomatoes and eggs around the salad.

• Take a cruet of the Oil-Vinegar Dressing or a bowl of mayonnaise to the table. Pass so guests can add more dressing to the salad. Makes 8 to 12 servings.

Oil-Vinegar Dressing: Shake together in a covered jar or bottle ¾ c. salad oil (the French use olive oil), ¼ c. red wine vinegar, ¼ tsp. salt, ¼ tsp. dry mustard and ⅛ tsp. black pepper (freshly ground in pepper mill is traditional kind). Makes 1 cup.

For a tasty appetizer or salad, whip together in electric mixer 2 tblsp. Roquefort or blue cheese dressing and 1 lb. cottage cheese.

BAKED GERMAN POTATO SALAD

This ranch house special is in the oven when guests arrive—it's tasty

¾	c. diced bacon
1	c. chopped celery
1	c. chopped onion
3	tblsp. flour
1⅓	c. water
⅔	c. cider vinegar
⅔	c. sugar
3	tsp. salt
½	tsp. pepper
8	c. cooked cubed potatoes (about 8 medium)
1	c. sliced radishes
½	c. chopped dill pickle (optional)

• Cook bacon in large skillet; drain off fat. Measure fat and return ¼ c. to skillet. Add celery and onion; cook 1 minute. Blend in flour. Stir in water and vinegar; cook, stirring constantly, until mixture is thick and bubbly. Stir in sugar, salt and pepper.

• Pour mixture over potatoes and bacon in a greased 3-qt. casserole; mix lightly. Cover; bake in moderate oven (350°) 30 minutes.

• Remove from oven. Stir in radishes and dill pickle. Serve at once. Makes 10 to 12 servings.

REGAL CHICKEN SALAD

Best-ever chicken salad! The proof is in its taste, so make it soon

4	c. diced cooked chicken
1	(1 lb. 4½ oz.) can pineapple chunks, drained
2	c. seedless green grapes
1	c. chopped celery
⅔	c. coarsely chopped dry salted peanuts

	Salt
¼	tsp. dried tarragon
1	c. mayonnaise
2	tblsp. lemon juice
2	tblsp. juice drained from pineapple

• Combine chicken, drained pineapple (reserve juice), grapes, celery and peanuts. Taste for salt (salted nuts may furnish enough). Stir in tarragon.

• Combine mayonnaise, lemon juice and 2 tblsp. pineapple juice. Gently fold into chicken mixture. Serve on lettuce with parsley or small celery leaves for garnish. Makes 8 servings.

Note: If fresh grapes are not available, use 1 (1 lb.) can spiced grapes, drained.

BAKED CHICKEN SALAD

Fine selection for a women's lunch

2	(6 oz.) cans boned chicken, broken apart
1	c. macaroni shells, cooked and drained
1	c. diced celery
2	tblsp. minced onion
½	tsp. salt
¼	tsp. pepper
1	tblsp. wine vinegar
½	c. broken pecans
3	hard-cooked eggs, chopped
¾	c. crushed potato chips
¾	c. mayonnaise
1	c. condensed cream of chicken soup

• Put all ingredients except mayonnaise and soup in a large mixing bowl; mix gently. Add mayonnaise and soup and toss just until mixed.

• Turn into a buttered 2-qt. casserole. Bake in moderate oven (350°) 30 to

35 minutes, or until heated throughout. Makes 8 servings.

POTATO SALAD

Better double this recipe, for nearly everyone takes seconds. Be sure to add salad dressing to warm potatoes

    6   to 8 potatoes
    ⅔   c. salad dressing
    2   tblsp. vinegar
    1 ½ tsp. salt
    ⅛   tsp. cayenne pepper (more
        if you like it)
    ¼   c. chopped onion
    ½   c. diced celery
    2   tblsp. chopped green
        pepper
    2   tblsp. diced sweet pickle
    3   hard-cooked eggs, sliced

• Cook potatoes in jackets; let cool 15 to 30 minutes, until you can handle them.
• Meanwhile, mix together salad dressing, vinegar, salt and cayenne pepper.
• Peel and cube warm potatoes (should have about 6 c.); combine with remaining ingredients. Add salad dressing carefully, stirring in lightly. Let chill in refrigerator 2 to 4 hours before serving. Sprinkle lightly with paprika, if desired. Makes 6 to 8 servings.

Note: You can double this recipe for 12 to 16 servings.

Supper's Ready and Waiting

Supper for a guest or two on a sultry summer evening can be ready before the company arrives. If you have a hearty, main-dish salad, getting the meal is simple. Take our two recipes, for instance. You can fix Chicken Potato Salad in the cool of the morning and chill it all day. Molded Beef Salad is best when made in the evening and refrigerated overnight.

Fancy up the servings to give them special appeal. Unmold the salad on greens and add a fluffy topknot of parsley, a bouquet of sliced pimiento-stuffed olives or radish roses. For each individual serving of Molded Beef Salad, string a radish rose, then alternate slices of carrots and radishes on a small wooden pick. Insert one of these garnish kabobs in each salad.

Here are the recipes, developed in our Test Kitchens:

CHICKEN POTATO SALAD

Tangy dressing and thorough chilling produce a delightful flavor blend

    3   c. coarsely chopped cooked
        potatoes
    1 ½ c. cooked green lima beans
    ¾   c. prepared French dressing
    4   c. cut-up cooked chicken or
        turkey
    ¾   c. sandwich spread
    1   tsp. salt
    1   tsp. celery seeds
    ½   tsp. dry mustard
    ½   tsp. paprika
    ¼   c. finely chopped onion
    ½   c. chopped green pepper

• The night before you plan to serve this salad, stir together potatoes, beans and dressing. Marinate overnight.
• In the morning, mix with remaining ingredients. Pack firmly into a

2½-qt. glass bowl. Place a salad plate on mixture and weight with a quart of water.

• Chill several hours. Unmold on lettuce to serve. Makes 8 servings.

Note: If you serve salad from bowl, don't pack and weight it.

MOLDED BEEF SALAD

Demand for this salad soars with the temperature—a hot weather treat

1 can condensed beef consommé, boiling
1 envelope unflavored gelatin, softened in ½ c. cold water
2 tsp. seasoned salt
2 tblsp. Worcestershire sauce
1 c. dairy sour cream
1 c. grated raw carrots
1 c. diced celery
¼ c. chopped green onions and tops
3 c. diced cooked beef

• Stir consommé into gelatin until gelatin is dissolved. Refrigerate until partially thickened.

• Beat seasoned salt, Worcestershire sauce and sour cream into consommé until fluffy. Fold in remaining ingredients.

• Spoon into 6 oz. custard cups which have been rinsed with cold water. Cover; chill several hours. Unmold. Makes 6 servings.

PARTY EGG SALAD

For a warm spring day, arrange salad servings on platter with cold cuts

1 (3 oz.) pkg. lemon flavor gelatin
1 c. hot water
½ c. cold water
2 tblsp. vinegar
½ c. mayonnaise
½ tsp. salt
½ tsp. curry powder or dry mustard
4 hard-cooked eggs, finely chopped
½ c. diced celery
¼ c. diced green pepper
2 tblsp. chopped parsley

• Dissolve gelatin in hot water; add ½ c. cold water, vinegar, mayonnaise, salt and curry powder, beat well with rotary beater or blender.

• Pour into a metal loaf pan; chill in freezing unit or freezing compartment of refrigerator until mixture is firm about 1" from pan but is still soft in the center. (This will take about 20 minutes.) Remove from freezer, and beat with electric mixer or blender until mixture is fluffy and thick.

• Fold in eggs, celery, green pepper and parsley. Pour into an 11 × 7 × 2" glass dish. Chill in refrigerator until firm. Cut in individual servings. Serve on watercress or other greens. Makes 4 to 6 servings.

Note: This is an easy recipe to double if you need more servings.

Perfect Hard-Cooked Eggs: Use high-quality but not newly laid eggs. (Whites stick to the shells of newly laid eggs, making peeling difficult and the eggs unattractive.) Simmer in water about 15 minutes, or boil 8 minutes. Plunge the eggs in cold water at once and crack shells to hasten cooling. This prevents overcooking and reduces the formation of dark rings on yolks (caused by harmless iron sulfide).

TOMATO MACARONI SALAD

Young boys coming to the barbecue?
If so, use bow-tie macaroni in salad

½ lb. bow-tie or seashell
    macaroni
1   c. diced celery
1   green pepper, chopped
2   tblsp. finely chopped onion
3   tblsp. finely chopped fresh
    parsley, or 1 ½ tblsp.
    dried parsley flakes
1 ¼ tsp. salt
¼   tsp. pepper
½   tsp. celery seeds
¼   c. mayonnaise
⅓   c. creamy French dressing
4   large tomatoes, peeled and
    cut in wedges and
    sprinkled lightly with salt

• Cook macaroni in boiling salted
water; rinse under cold water, drain
and cool. Combine macaroni and all
ingredients except tomatoes. Cover
and chill until serving time. Fold in
tomato wedges, and serve on lettuce.
Makes 8 servings.

Glamorous Gelatin Salads

Gelatin salads often are party
show-offs. Sometimes it's their sparkling colors and fancy shapes that
draw attention. Or the charm is a
combination of jewel colors, interesting shapes and the exciting foods
captured in the gelatin.

What could be more handsome and
taste better at a spring party luncheon
than Avocado-Strawberry Ring or
more appetizing and beautiful on a
hot summer day than Mint Julepeach
Salad with balls of ripe peaches and

melons in shimmering lemon flavor
gelatin? And on a snowy winter evening, serve Sun Gold Fruit Salad to
put sunshine on the table.

MINT JULEPEACH SALAD

You'll be pleased with the way ginger
and mint enhance the peach-melon
flavors in this refreshing salad

2   (3 oz.) pkgs. lemon flavor
    gelatin
1 ½ c. hot water
½   c. frozen lemonade
    concentrate, undiluted
1   (7 oz.) bottle ginger ale,
    chilled
⅛   tsp. peppermint extract
2   c. fresh peach balls
1   c. honeydew melon balls
1   c. seedless green grapes,
    cut in halves

• Dissolve gelatin in hot water. Add
lemonade concentrate, ginger ale and
peppermint extract. Stir to dissolve.
Chill until partially set.
• Fold in remaining ingredients. Turn
into a 1½-qt. mold or 8 individual
molds. Chill. Makes 8 servings.

AVOCADO-STRAWBERRY RING

Beautiful salad for a buffet table

2   (3 oz.) pkgs. lemon or lime
    flavor gelatin
1   tsp. salt
2   c. boiling water
1 ¼ c. cold water
3   tblsp. lemon juice
2   ripe avocados, mashed
¼   c. mayonnaise
3   c. fresh strawberries
Honey Dressing

• Dissolve gelatin and salt in boiling

water. Add cold water and lemon juice. Chill until slightly thickened.
• Combine avocados and mayonnaise; blend well. Stir into gelatin thoroughly.
• Pour into 4-cup ring mold or 8 individual ring molds. Chill until firm. Unmold and fill center with strawberries. Serve with Honey Dressing. Makes 8 servings.

Honey Dressing: Combine ½ c. dairy sour cream, 3 tblsp. honey and ⅛ tsp. ground mace.

Frosted Jewel-Tone Fruit Salads

Fruit salads on the sweet side have many enthusiastic friends. Country hostesses serve these beauties with the main dinner course, or separately after dinner for dessert or evening refreshment.

The three glamorous salad molds that follow shimmer in jewel colors—emerald, topaz and ruby. They're brimful of lusciously juicy fruits. And each salad has its own special frosting that substitutes for salad dressing and highlights the fruity flavors.

Country women like to take these make-ahead salads to special "share-the-load" dinners and suppers to give their friends a treat. They like having no dressing to tote. And they find these salads are their own best show-offs, requiring no garnishes. Whenever they appear, they're eye-catchers that awaken interest—and appetites.

JEWELS-IN-A-RING

Emerald make-ahead salad holds fruits and has a rich cheese frosting

3   (3 oz.) pkgs. lime flavor
        gelatin
2½ c. boiling water
1   (1 lb. 4½ oz.) can
        pineapple chunks
1   (1 lb.) can peach slices
1   c. blueberries (optional)
¼   c. cold water
4   (3 oz.) pkgs. cream cheese

• Set aside 3 tblsp. gelatin. Dissolve remaining gelatin in boiling water. Drain fruit, and set aside ¼ c. of the liquid. Add fruit and remaining liquid to gelatin. Chill until syrupy. Spoon into a 2-qt. ring mold or a 12 × 7½ × 2" glass dish. Refrigerate overnight.
• About 2 hours before serving the salad, bring reserved fruit liquid and ¼ c. water to a boil; dissolve remaining gelatin (3 tblsp.) in boiling liquid. Chill until partially set.
• Meanwhile, beat softened cream cheese until fluffy. Gradually beat into the partially set gelatin mixture; be sure that mixture is smooth (no lumps). Refrigerate until of spreading consistency. (For a deeper green, tint with food color.)
• Unmold salad; if necessary, refrigerate until surface is firm. Frost with cheese mixture. Refrigerate until frosting sets, about 30 minutes. Makes 12 servings.

Note: If you make this salad in blueberry season, add 1 c. berries with the pineapple and peaches for interesting color and flavor touch. You can mold this salad in a deep 2-quart mold, such as a 2-quart mixing bowl.

Use ¼ to ⅓ c. less water in gelatin mixture to make unmolded salad more stable.

SUN GOLD FRUIT SALAD

You make salad one day and frost it the next—tastes every bit as good as it looks, and that means superb

2 (3 oz.) pkgs. orange flavor
    gelatin
2 c. boiling water
1½ c. cold water
1 (11 oz.) can mandarin
    oranges
1 (8¾ oz.) can apricot halves
1 c. seedless white grapes,
    fresh or canned
2 large bananas, sliced
Fluffy Topping
¼ c. grated American cheese

• Dissolve gelatin in boiling water; add cold water. Refrigerate until syrupy.

• Drain fruit, reserving 1 c. liquid. Fold fruit into gelatin mixture; pour into a 9 × 5 × 3″ loaf pan or a 12 × 7½ × 2″ glass dish. Refrigerate overnight.

• Unmold salad and frost with Fluffy Topping. Sprinkle top with cheese. Refrigerate until topping sets, about 1 hour. Makes 12 servings.

Fluffy Topping: Combine 6 tblsp. sugar and 2 tblsp. cornstarch in a heavy saucepan. Blend in 1 egg, slightly beaten, and the 1 c. reserved fruit liquid. Cook, stirring constantly, over low heat until thickened. Remove from heat; stir in 2 tblsp. butter and 1 tblsp. lemon juice. Cool. Whip 1 c. heavy cream, or 1 (2 oz.) pkg. dessert topping mix; fold into the cooled mixture.

FROSTED CRANBERRY SALAD

If it's easier, you can make this salad a few days ahead and freeze it

1 (8½ oz.) can crushed
    pineapple
1 (1 lb.) can whole cranberry
    sauce
2 (3 oz.) pkgs. raspberry flavor
    gelatin
1 (8 oz.) pkg. cream cheese
2 tblsp. salad dressing
1 c. heavy cream, or 1 (2 oz.)
    pkg. dessert topping mix,
    whipped
½ c. coarsely chopped walnuts
1 peeled and chopped tart
    apple

• Drain pineapple and cranberry sauce, reserving liquid; add enough water to make 2 c. liquid. Bring to a boil. Dissolve gelatin in hot liquid. Chill until partially set.

• Beat softened cream cheese (room temperature) and salad dressing together until fluffy. Gradually beat in gelatin; fold this mixture into the whipped cream or topping mix. Set aside 1½ c. of this mixture for topping. Add drained fruits, nuts and apple to the remaining cheese mixture. Pour into a 12 × 7½ × 2″ glass dish; refrigerate until surface sets, about 20 minutes.

• Frost with the reserved topping. Refrigerate several hours, or freeze. If frozen, remove salad to refrigerator 1 hour before serving. Makes 12 servings.

To give prunes new flavor, soak them in pineapple or other fruit juice instead of plain water. Allow them to stand, as usual, until plump and soft.

CANNED BLUEBERRY SALAD

If you enjoy blueberry pie, you'll like this unusual and luscious salad

1   (1 lb. 4 oz.) can blueberries
    (2½ c.)
2   (3 oz.) pkgs. cherry flavor
    gelatin
2   c. hot water
2½ c. dairy sour cream
Pineapple chunks
1   c. mayonnaise

• Open blueberries; do not drain. Dissolve gelatin in hot water; add blueberries and juice. Chill until mixture starts to thicken.
• Gradually add a little gelatin mixture to 2 c. sour cream; blend until all the gelatin has been added. (It does not blend perfectly.) Turn into a 1-qt mold and chill until firm.
• Unmold on lettuce. Garnish with pineapple chunks and mayonnaise with ½ c. sour cream folded in. Makes 8 to 10 servings.

FRESH BLUEBERRY SALAD

Lime juice points up blueberry flavor

3   c. large sweet blueberries
2   envelopes unflavored gelatin
1   c. cold water
1½ c. boiling water
⅔ c. sugar
⅛ tsp. salt
¼ c. fresh lime juice
Lettuce
1   c. mayonnaise
½ c. heavy cream, whipped

• Wash blueberries and drain.
• Place gelatin in a bowl; add cold water. When gelatin is softened, add boiling water; stir until gelatin is dissolved. Add sugar, salt and lime juice.

• Chill until mixture reaches the consistency of unbeaten egg whites; fold in blueberries. Pour into individual molds and chill until firm.
• Serve salads unmolded on lettuce or other greens; garnish with mayonnaise into which whipped cream is folded. Makes 8 to 10 servings.

Note: If blueberries are tart, add more sugar.

BLACK CHERRY SALAD

A black-red salad that always pleases

1   (1 lb.) can dark sweet cherries
Juice drained from cherries
1   (3 oz.) pkg. dark cherry
    flavor gelatin
1   (8½ oz.) can crushed
    pineapple
½ c. thinly sliced celery
½ c. chopped walnuts
Romaine (or other) lettuce
Whipped cream
Sprigs of fresh mint

• Drain cherries; measure juice and add enough water to make 1¾ c. Heat half of liquid and add to gelatin; stir until gelatin is dissolved. Add remaining liquid (mixture of water and cherry juice). Chill until mixture starts to thicken.
• Meanwhile, cut cherries in halves and combine with drained pineapple, celery and nuts. Fold into gelatin and turn into individual molds. Chill until firm.
• To serve, unmold on romaine lettuce, and garnish each salad with a spoonful of whipped cream (or dessert topping mix) and a sprig of fresh mint. Makes 9 servings.

CHERRY MIX SALAD

Color-gay with the taste of summer, a sparkling treat for winter holidays

1 (3 oz.) pkg. cherry flavor gelatin
1½ c. hot water
1 c. Frozen Cherry Mix, partly thawed (see Index)
1 c. diced peeled apples
½ c. chopped celery
¼ c. chopped pecans

• Dissolve gelatin in hot water. Chill until slightly thickened. Fold in remaining ingredients. Spoon into 8 individual molds.
• Chill until firm. Unmold on lettuce or other greens. Makes 8 servings.

LAYERED CHERRY SALAD

This colorful "sandwich" salad gets a royal welcome at women's luncheons

1 (1 lb.) can pineapple tidbits
1¾ c. pineapple liquid and water
1 (3 oz.) pkg. cherry flavor gelatin
1 (3 oz.) pkg. cream cheese
2 tsp. milk
1 (1 lb.) can sweet dark cherries
⅓ c. lemon juice
1 (3 oz.) pkg. orange flavor gelatin
½ c. sliced pimiento-stuffed olives
Greens
Mayonnaise

• Drain pineapple, reserving juice. Add enough water to juice to make 1¾ c. Heat to boiling and pour over cherry flavor gelatin; stir to dissolve gelatin. Chill until cold (do not let set); add pineapple and pour into an 8" square pan. Chill until firm.
• Combine cream cheese and milk; beat until smooth and fluffy. Spread over top of gelatin in pan. Return to refrigerator.
• Drain cherries; reserve juice. To cherry juice add ⅓ c. lemon juice and enough water to make 1¾ c. Heat to boiling and add to orange flavor gelatin; stir until gelatin is dissolved. Chill until cold (do not let set); add the cherries and olives. Spoon oven the cheese-topped gelatin. Chill until set.
• To serve, cut in rectangles, place on greens and place on one large plate or individual plates. Garnish each serving with spoonful of mayonnaise. Makes 9 servings.

GOOSEBERRY SALAD

Tart, just right to complement pork

2 (1 lb. 1 oz.) cans gooseberries
1 c. sugar
Cold water
2 (3 oz.) pkgs. lime flavor gelatin
1 c. crushed bananas
⅓ c. mayonnaise
Lettuce

• Drain berries and reserve syrup.
• Mix sugar with berries and place over low heat just to melt sugar.
• Add enough cold water to berry syrup to make 2 c.; bring to a boil and pour over gelatin. Stir until gelatin is dissolved; add 1½ c. water. Refrigerate until mixture thickens slightly.
• Fold in gooseberries and bananas. Pour into a 2-qt. mold, or 12 individual molds. Chill until firm. To

serve, unmold, chill 15 minutes. Spread thinly with mayonnaise and garnish with lettuce. Makes about 12 servings.

TART RHUBARB SALAD

Imaginative touch: Spoon sour cream on the salads and sprinkle on nutmeg

4   c. diced fresh rhubarb
1   c. water
¾   c. sugar
¼   tsp. salt
2   (3 oz.) pkgs. strawberry
      flavor gelatin
1 ¾ c. cold water
¼   c. lemon juice
1   c. diced celery
2   (11 oz.) cans mandarin
      oranges, drained
Dairy sour cream
Nutmeg

• Combine rhubarb, water, sugar and salt; bring to a boil. Reduce heat and simmer only until rhubarb loses crispness. Remove from heat and add the gelatin and stir until it is dissolved. Add cold water and lemon juice. Chill until partially thickened.
• Fold in celery and oranges; spoon into a shallow 2-qt. dish or 8 individual molds. Chill until firm.
• Serve on crisp lettuce topped with dairy sour cream; dust lightly with nutmeg. Makes 8 servings.

GOLDEN GLOW SALAD

As this picture-pretty salad chills, it separates into two distinct layers

24 marshmallows
½   c. pineapple juice (drained
      from crushed pineapple
      plus water)

1   (3 oz.) pkg. lemon flavor
      gelatin
1 ½ c. boiling water
¾   c. crushed pineapple,
      drained
¾   c. grated raw carrots
⅔   c. pineapple cream cheese
      (5 oz.)

• Melt marshmallows in pineapple juice over low heat, folding over and over until smooth.
• Dissolve gelatin in boiling water.
• Blend pineapple, carrots and cheese.
• When the gelatin is cool, blend together all the ingredients; pour into a 1-qt. ring mold. Serve garnished with watercress or lettuce and with salad dressing. Makes 6 servings.

HOSTESS SALAD FOR A DOZEN

Good-looking and good-tasting luncheon salad—requires no salad dressing

1   (3 oz.) pkg. lime flavor gelatin
1   (3 oz.) pkg. lemon flavor
      gelatin
2   c. hot water
1   (1 lb. 4 oz.) can crushed
      pineapple
1   c. dairy sour cream
1   c. small curd cottage cheese
1   c. thin pimiento-stuffed olive
      slices
1   c. chopped nuts

• Dissolve gelatins in hot water; add pineapple without draining. When mixture barely starts to congeal, mix in remaining ingredients.
• Turn into a 2-qt. ring mold or dish holding 2 quarts; chill until firm.
• Unmold on serving plate. Garnish with parsley. Makes 12 servings.

Note: At serving time, you can fill the center of the salad with creamed cottage cheese.

HOSTESS SALAD FOR 16

Tote this to church or potluck suppers—gelatins carry well in winter

2 (3 oz.) pkgs. lime flavor
    gelatin
1 (3 oz.) pkg. lemon flavor
    gelatin
4 c. hot liquid (water and
    pineapple juice)
1 (8 oz.) pkg. cream cheese
2 c. grated Cheddar cheese
2 (1 lb. 4½ oz.) cans crushed
    pineapple, drained
1½ c. chopped celery
1 c. heavy cream, whipped

• Dissolve gelatins in hot liquid (water plus juice drained from canned pineapple). Add a little of this warm mixture to the cream cheese, mashed, and blend with a fork (cheese does not blend completely with gelatin mixture), then blend cream cheese into gelatin. Chill until mixture starts to thicken; add Cheddar cheese, drained pineapple and celery. Fold in whipped cream.
• Pour into a 13 × 9 × 2" pan; refrigerate until firm. Cut in 16 servings. Serve on lettuce, without salad dressing.

STRAWBERRY SALAD

Guaranteed to please everyone who likes strawberries—it's luscious

2 (3 oz.) pkgs. strawberry flavor
    gelatin
2 c. hot water

2 (10 oz.) pkgs. frozen
    strawberries
1 (1 lb. 4½ oz.) can crushed
    pineapple, undrained
2 large bananas, mashed
1 c. dairy sour cream
1 (3 oz.) pkg. cream cheese (at
    room temperature)
Cream Mayonnaise

• Dissolve gelatin in hot water. Add frozen strawberries (unthawed) and stir until berries are separated. Add undrained pineapple and bananas. Pour half of mixture into 9 × 9 × 2" pan. Chill in refrigerator until set. Leave the other half at room temperature.
• Whip sour cream and cream cheese together; spread over firm gelatin in pan. Top with remaining half of gelatin mixture. Chill until firm.
• When ready to serve, cut salad in squares and serve on lettuce, topped with Cream Mayonnaise. Makes 12 servings.

Cream Mayonnaise: Add ½ c. heavy cream, whipped, to 1 c. mayonnaise or salad dressing.

ORANGE-ALMOND SALAD

Expertly and subtly seasoned, temptingly pretty salad—always a success

2 (11 oz.) cans mandarin
    oranges
1 (3 oz.) pkg. lemon flavor
    gelatin
1 tblsp. vinegar
1 tblsp. ketchup
½ c. slivered, blanched almonds
Salad dressing
Heavy cream, whipped

• Drain oranges, reserving liquid. Add

enough water to orange liquid to make 2 c. Heat half of the orange-water to boiling. Dissolve gelatin in hot liquid. Add remainder of liquid. Stir in vinegar and ketchup. Chill until mixture is partially thickened.

• Add orange segments and almonds. Pour into a 1-qt. ring mold or an 8 × 8 × 2″ pan. Chill until firm.

• Fold together equal parts salad dressing and whipped cream, and serve in center of ring or on top of individual servings. Makes 6 servings.

Note: Make 2 pans of this salad if you need more than 6 servings. Or double recipe and chill salad in a 2-qt. ring mold.

LIME SALAD BOUQUETS

Guest special from a Winsconsin hostess who frequently doubles the recipe

1 (3 oz.) pkg. lime flavor gelatin
1 c. boiling water
½ c. salad dressing
¼ c. light cream
¾ tsp. prepared horse-radish
1 (8 oz.) can crushed pineapple, undrained
1 c. cottage cheese
½ c. chopped walnuts

• Dissolve gelatin in boiling water. Chill until slightly thickened.

• Blend salad dressing, cream and horse-radish. Stir into gelatin. Stir in remaining ingredients.

• Spoon into molds and chill. Makes 6 servings.

Use small piggy banks as place cards for a child's party. Print each child's name on a bank and let him take it home as a favor.

PINEAPPLE-CHEESE SALAD

A church supper special that's also a winner in "at home" guest meals

2 pkgs. lemon flavor gelatin
2 c. boiling water
2 c. cold water
6 bananas, peeled and sliced
2 c. miniature or cut-up marshmallows
½ c. sugar
3 tblsp. cornstarch
2 (8½ oz.) cans crushed pineapple, undrained
1 c. heavy cream
1 c. shredded Cheddar cheese

• Dissolve gelatin in boiling water; add cold water and chill until syrupy. Stir in sliced bananas and marshmallows. Pour into 13 × 9 × 2″ pan. Chill until set.

• Mix sugar and cornstarch; add to undrained pineapple. Cook over medium heat, stirring constantly, until thickened. Cool.

• Whip heavy cream and fold into cooled pineapple mixture along with half of the shredded cheese. Spread mixture on congealed lemon gelatin.

• Sprinkle remainder of shredded cheese over top. Chill overnight. Cut into squares. Makes 12 to 15 servings.

CINNAMON APPLE SALAD

Country favorite with family friends

1 c. red cinnamon candies (red hots)
¼ c. sugar
2 c. hot water
2 (3 oz.) pkgs. raspberry flavor gelatin
2 c. cold water
2 or 3 drops red food color
2 c. diced unpeeled red apples

1 c. quartered orange slices
1 c. broken walnuts
Whipped cream or Cream
   Mayonnaise

• Dissolve candies and sugar in hot water and pour over gelatin; stir until gelatin is dissolved. Add cold water and food color. Chill until mixture thickens slightly; then stir in apples, oranges and nuts.

• Pour into a 2-qt. ring mold (or mold holding 2 quarts) and chill.

• To serve, unmold on lettuce and serve with whipped cream, lightly sprinkled with cinnamon, or Cream Mayonnaise (see Index). Makes 12 servings.

TOMATO ASPIC WITH VEGETABLES

An around-the-year salad—crunchy, bright and flavorful with vegetables

3 c. canned tomato juice
1 stalk celery
1 small onion, sliced
2 lemon slices
1 small bay leaf
1 tsp. salt
2 envelopes unflavored gelatin
⅔ c. cold tomato juice
¼ c. cider vinegar
⅛ tsp. salt
1 c. finely shredded cabbage
¼ c. chopped celery
¼ c. grated carrots
¼ c. chopped cucumber
2 tblsp. chopped onion (optional)

• Combine 3 c. tomato juice with celery stalk, onion slices, lemon slices, bay leaf and 1 tsp. salt. Simmer 10 minutes; strain.

• Meanwhile sprinkle gelatin over ⅔ c. tomato juice and vinegar in bowl. When softened, stir in hot tomato juice mixture and stir until gelatin is dissolved. Refrigerate, stirring occasionally, until mixture thickens to consistency of unbeaten egg whites.

• Sprinkle ⅛ tsp. salt on vegetables and fold them into the gelatin mixture. Pour into individual molds. Refrigerate until firm.

• Unmold on greens and serve with mayonnaise mixed with an equal amount of French dressing. Or serve with dairy sour cream. Spoon cream on salads. Makes 7 or 8 servings.

JELLIED EGG SALAD

Serve this tangy, tasty salad for the main dish in a light lunch

2 (3 oz.) pkgs. lemon flavor
   gelatin
1¼ c. boiling water
2 c. cold water
3 tblsp. lemon juice
1 c. mayonnaise
4 tblsp. pickle relish, drained
1 tsp. salt
¼ c. chopped onion
2 tblsp. chopped pimiento
6 hard-cooked eggs, chopped
   (reserve 1 egg yolk for
   garnish)

• Dissolve gelatin in boiling water. Add cold water and chill in refrigerator until syrupy. Stir in lemon juice, mayonnaise, pickle relish, salt, onion and pimiento. Fold in eggs.

• Spoon into a 2-qt. mold. Chill until firm. Serve on lettuce or watercress; garnish salad with sieved hard-cooked egg yolk. Makes 8 large servings.

THREE-ROW GARDEN SALAD

Color-bright, refreshing salad resembles striped ribbon when served

Orange Layer:

1 (3 oz.) pkg. orange flavor gelatin
1 c. boiling water
¾ c. pineapple juice
2 tblsp. lemon juice
1½ c. finely shredded carrots

Green Layer:

1 (3 oz.) pkg. lime flavor gelatin
1 c. boiling water
¾ c. pineapple juice
2 tblsp. lemon juice
1½ c. grated cabbage

Red Layer:

2 tsp. unflavored gelatin
½ c. cold water
1 (3 oz.) pkg. lemon flavor gelatin
½ tsp. salt
1 c. boiling water
2 tblsp. beet juice
2 tblsp. vinegar
1 c. finely diced cooked beets, well drained
1 tblsp. horse-radish
Cheese-Horse-radish Dressing

• Prepare layers separately, allowing about 15 minutes between each so that gelatins set at intervals.
• To make orange layer, dissolve orange flavor gelatin in boiling water. Add pineapple and lemon juice; chill until syrupy. Fold in carrots.
• To prepare green layer, dissolve lime flavor gelatin in boiling water. Add pineapple and lemon juices; chill until syrupy. Fold in cabbage.
• To make red layer, soften unfla-

vored gelatin in cold water. Dissolve lemon flavor gelatin and salt in boiling water; immediately stir in unflavored gelatin mixture. Add beet juice and vinegar; chill until syrupy. Fold in beets and horse-radish.
• Layer gelatins—orange, green, then red—in 9 × 5 × 3″ loaf pan. Allow each layer to set before adding second or third layer. Chill until firm.
• To unmold set pan in warm (not hot) water about 5 seconds; loosen around beet layer and turn out on platter. Garnish with green fresh carrot tops, young beet leaves or lettuce. Slice, then serve each person individual salad. Pass Cheese-Horse-radish Dressing. Makes 10 servings.

Cheese-Horse-radish Dressing: Soften 1 (3 oz.) pkg. cream cheese; beat until creamy. Blend in ¼ c. mayonnaise, 2 tblsp. light cream or milk, ½ tsp. celery salt and 2 tsp. horseradish. Fold in 2 tsp. chopped fresh or dried chives (optional). Makes ¾ cup.

Glazed Fruit Salad Glistens

Serving fruit in the main course is an old country custom. Remember how our grandmothers set a bowl of tart-sweet applesauce on the table? And how mixed dried fruits, cooked until plump and tender, were standard fare in ranch meals? Today's hostesses find that a medley of fruits, often leaning to the sweet side, brings compliments at buffets.

Glazed Fruit Salad is a splendid example. We first had it at the dinner table in the home of a Minnesota

Test Group member. One taste—we asked for the recipe. The luscious fruits not only brightened the meal with color, but they glistened. Our hostess served them in a low, large, yellow-green, footed compote, scalloped around the edges.

When we asked the hostess about the salad, she said one of its advantages is that you fix it a day ahead and refrigerate it so flavors blend. If you doubt that people like such a rather sweet, fruity salad, set a bowl of it on your buffet table. Watch how guests come back for second helpings, and listen to requests from women guests for the recipe.

GLAZED FRUIT SALAD

It's apricot pie filling that makes salad glisten—also adds fine flavor

1 (1 lb. 4 oz.) can pineapple
    chunks
1 (1 lb. 13 oz.) can fruit cocktail
2 (11 oz.) cans mandarin oranges
7 or 8 bananas, peeled, sliced
2 tblsp. lemon juice
1 (1 lb. 6 oz.) can apricot pie
    filling

• Drain the canned fruits thoroughly. Mix all the ingredients together and chill several hours, or overnight. Makes 12 servings.

SUPERB FRUIT SALAD

Summer salad with vivid sunset colors. Guests vote it tops in fruit salads

2 (11 oz.) cans mandarin
    oranges, drained
2 (13½ oz.) cans pineapple
    tidbits, undrained

2 c. miniature marshmallows
2 c. cantaloupe balls
2 c. watermelon balls
½ c. toasted slivered almonds
Fluffy Dressing

• Combine drained mandarin oranges, pineapple tidbits with their juice and marshmallows. Let stand in refrigerator at least 1 hour so marshmallows absorb some of the juice.
• Drain off excess juice; add melon balls and almonds.
• Serve in a large salad bowl, garnished with fresh mint. Let guests help themselves to salad and to Fluffy Dressing. Makes 8 cups.

FLUFFY DRESSING

Perfect with Superb Fruit Salad

2 eggs, beaten
2 tblsp. sugar
¼ c. light cream
4 tblsp. lemon juice
1 c. heavy cream, whipped

• Combine eggs, sugar and cream. Cook over hot water, stirring constantly, until slightly thickened. Beat in lemon juice with a rotary beater. (The eggs may start to coagulate on sides of pan; beating in the lemon juice with a rotary beater makes mixture smooth.) Remove from heat and chill.
• When ready to serve, fold in whipped cream. Serve in bowl with Superb Fruit Salad.

To dress up Waldorf or other fruit salads containing apples, peel red apples "round and round" in one piece. Arrange each peel of apple in a ring on lettuce-lined salad plate. Fill center with fruit salad.

COMBINATION FRUIT SALAD

Very easy and very good winter salad

1 c. cut-up dates
2 (11 oz.) cans mandarin
    oranges, drained
1 (1 lb. 4½ oz.) can pineapple
    chunks, drained
1 c. miniature marshmallows
2 tblsp. minced candied ginger
1 c. dairy sour cream

• Combine all ingredients; chill in refrigerator 2 to 4 hours before serving.
• To serve, spoon into lettuce cups and serve with crisp bread sticks (optional). Makes 8 servings.

GINGER-PEAR SALAD

Keep the makings for this wonderful fruit salad in your cupboard

1 (8½ oz.) can crushed
    pineapple
2 tblsp. minced candied ginger
1 or 2 drops green food color
    (optional)
1 (1 lb. 13 oz.) can pear halves
Lettuce
Mayonnaise
Candied ginger strips

• Combine crushed pineapple and minced candied ginger; add food color and heat slowly over low heat until ginger flavor is well blended with pineapple. Remove from heat and cool.
• Drain pears. Arrange in a flat dish, cut side up. Place a spoonful of cooled pineapple mixture on each pear half and let stand in refrigerator 1 to 2 hours.
• To serve, arrange a pear half, cut side down, on each lettuce-lined plate.

Spoon a little of the pineapple sauce over each pear.
• Top each salad with a fluff of mayonnaise, or mayonnaise with a little whipped cream added, and garnish with thin strips of candied ginger. Makes 8 servings.

CANTALOUPE SALAD

Cool-looking and cool-tasting—really refreshing on a sizzling day

2 medium cantaloupes, chilled
4 c. green seedless grapes
1 c. mayonnaise or salad
    dressing
⅓ c. frozen orange juice
    concentrate

• Cut cantaloupes lengthwise into 6 sections; remove seeds and peel off rind and all nonedible portions.
• Place each section on a crisp lettuce leaf and heap stemmed grapes around melon.
• Combine mayonnaise or salad dressing with frozen orange juice concentrate (undiluted); mix well and pass to ladle over salads. Makes 12 servings.

CRANBERRY-MARSHMALLOW SALAD

Refrigerate or freeze the salad— then it's ready before guests arrive

3 c. whole cranberries, fresh or
    frozen
¾ c. sugar
20 large marshmallows, cut in
    pieces, or 2⅓ c. miniature
    marshmallows
1 (8½ oz.) can crushed
    pineapple, drained
    (optional)
½ c. chopped nuts
1 c. heavy cream

• Put cranberries through the food chopper, using the coarse blade. (Frozen cranberries grind the best.) Add sugar and chill 2 hours. Add marshmallows, pineapple and nuts. Whip cream and fold into the cranberry mixture.

• Spoon into a bowl or mold, cover and refrigerate, or spoon into an 8" square baking pan, cover and freeze. Serve on or garnished with lettuce. Makes 6 to 8 servings.

BLOSSOM TIME ORANGE SALAD

A beautiful, low-calorie salad for afternoon bridge party refreshment

6 large oranges
1 (8 oz.) can pineapple tidbits, drained
1 large banana, diced
1 c. creamed cottage cheese
½ tsp. celery salt
2 tsp. chopped chives
Sprigs of watercress or fresh mint
Greens

• Wash oranges. Starting at stem end of each orange, make 6 equally spaced cuts through the skin to the pulp, to within 1" from bottom of orange. Carefully peel away from the pulp to form petals, which are attached at the base of the orange. Then carefully remove fruit pulp from the orange. Peel off white membrane and dice orange pulp.

• Toss orange pulp lightly with pineapple tidbits and diced banana. Spoon into orange shells.

• Blend cottage cheese with 2 tblsp. juice drained from pineapple, celery salt and chives. Spoon on top of fruit in orange shells and garnish with

sprigs of watercress or fresh mint. Serve on greens. Makes 6 servings.

Note: Double recipe to serve 12.

GRAPE-ORANGE SALAD

You can use 3 c. grapes and omit mandarin oranges, but they brighten salad. Really attractive on greens

2 c. seedless green grapes
1 (11 oz.) can mandarin oranges, drained
1 c. pecan halves
1 (3 oz.) pkg. cream cheese
1 tsp. sugar
¼ c. fresh orange juice (or reconstituted frozen concentrate)
Lettuce

• Combine grapes, oranges and pecans.

• Blend together cheese, sugar and enough orange juice (about ¼ c.) to make a mixture that will coat fruits and nuts. Stir into fruit and nut mixture. Chill. Serve on lettuce. Makes 8 servings.

POINSETTIA SALAD

So-easy-to-fix apple poinsettia makes stunning holiday fruit salad dress-up

2 c. diced unpeeled red apples
1 tblsp. lemon juice
1 c. sliced celery
1 c. grapes, halved and seeded
½ c. heavy cream, whipped
Lettuce
1 large unpeeled red apple
Walnuts, halves or chopped
1 c. miniature marshmallows
½ c. chopped walnuts

• Sprinkle diced apples with lemon juice. Combine with celery, grapes

(Tokay, green or white), marshmallows and chopped nuts. Chill. At serving time fold in whipped cream.

• Spoon salad into a lettuce-lined round *flat* bowl. Cut the *large* red apple into 16 wedges to represent poinsettia petals, removing core. (Dip in lemon juice to prevent discoloring.) Push them, red side up, into salad in a circle (they'll look like a poinsettia). Place walnuts, halves or chopped, for flower's center. Makes 8 to 10 servings.

Note: You can mix ½ c. salad dressing with fruits before chilling, but add the whipped cream at serving time.

SHERBET SALAD DRESSING

A wonderful frosty-cold dressing. Spoon it on your fruit salads

```
 2   tblsp. flour
 ¼   c. sugar
 ¼   tsp. salt
1⅓   c. fresh orange juice
 2   tblsp. fresh lemon juice
 2   egg yolks, slightly beaten
 1   tblsp. grated orange peel
 3   tblsp. salad oil
 ½   c. raspberry sherbet
```

• In top of double boiler combine flour, sugar and salt. Add orange and lemon juices. Cook, stirring constantly, until mixture thickens.

• Stir 2 tblsp. hot mixture into egg yolks; gradually add yolks to hot sauce. Stir and cook 1 minute. Remove from heat and stir in orange peel and salad oil. Cool and chill.

• Just before serving, fold in sherbet. Serve at once over fruit salad. Makes 2 cups.

Note: Use orange, pineapple, lemon, lime or any other flavor of sherbet.

Hostess Salads from Your Freezer

One reason why frozen fruit salads are hostess favorites is that they're make-aheads. But they have many other merits. They can eliminate one course because they are substantial enough to serve as both salad and dessert. And in some meals, their arctic temperature contrasts delightfully with the hot meats and vegetables.

Frozen fruit salads also are ideal for a women's salad or dessert luncheon. But, best of all, they're ready in the freezer when unexpected guests stop by and you want to serve a meal or refreshments. (See Index for other Frozen Salads that make more servings.)

FROZEN CRANBERRY SALAD

Freeze this pretty pink salad for Christmas holidays—so handy to have

```
 1   (3 oz.) pkg. cream cheese
 ¼   c. mayonnaise
 ¼   c. confectioners sugar
 1   (1 lb.) can whole cranberry
     sauce
 3   tblsp. lemon juice
 1   c. heavy cream, whipped
 1   c. coarsely chopped walnuts
```

• Combine cream cheese, mayonnaise and confectioners sugar in a bowl.

• Crush cranberry sauce with a fork; stir in lemon juice. Add to cheese mixture.

• Fold in whipped cream and nuts. Turn into an 8″ square pan. Freeze until firm.

• Serve cut in squares on lettuce.

Stuffed olives make a pretty garnish. Makes 8 servings.

Note: Sweeten the whipped cream lightly with sugar, if you like.

FROZEN FRUIT CHEESE SALAD

It has fewer calories than most frozen fruit salads and a new combination of flavors—a treat for your guests

2 c. small curd creamed
    cottage cheese, sieved
1 c. dairy sour cream
3 tblsp. confectioners sugar
¾ tsp. salt
1 c. drained canned pineapple
    tidbits
1 (11 oz.) can mandarin
    oranges, drained
1 c. pitted and chopped
    cooked prunes, drained
1 large banana, sliced
½ c. sliced maraschino cherries
½ c. chopped blanched almonds
Creamy Pink Dressing

• Blend cottage cheese lightly with sour cream, sugar, salt, pineapple, oranges, prunes, banana, cherries and almonds. Pour into 2 freezer trays which have been rinsed with cold water.

• Freeze until firm. Let stand a few minutes before cutting into serving pieces. Place on salad greens. Serve with Creamy Pink Dressing, and garnish each serving with a stemmed maraschino cherry and an orange section. Makes 12 servings.

Note: You can use diced fresh oranges instead of canned mandarin oranges.

Creamy Pink Dressing: Blend 1 c. dairy sour cream and 2 tblsp. mara-schino cherry juice together. Refrigerate until needed. Makes 1 cup.

CREAMY FROZEN SALAD

Simple to fix, luscious to eat, and fine to make ahead so you'll be ready with refreshments when guests arrive

2 c. dairy sour cream
2 tblsp. lemon juice
¾ c. sugar
⅛ tsp. salt
1 (9 oz.) can crushed pineapple,
    drained
¼ c. sliced maraschino cherries
¼ c. chopped pecans
1 banana, sliced

• Blend cream, lemon juice, sugar and salt. Stir in remaining ingredients.
• Pour into 1-qt. mold or liners for cupcakes or muffin-pan cups. Freeze. Makes 8 servings.

Special Deviled Eggs: *Substitute dairy sour cream for salad dressing in the egg yolk mixture.*

Wonderful New Marinated Salads

Marinate salads in their dressings and you'll discover that all the ingredients carry the full seasoning of the dressings. After you pour the dressing on the fruits and vegetables, you can chill them from 2 to 8 hours, whichever is more convenient.

These new salads are color-bright, simple to fix and intriguing in taste. And they look so tempting. Here is a quartet of recipes for gourmet salads you'll want to try soon.

PEACH-GRAPE COMPOTE SALAD

Good with roast chicken, ham or pork

3 c. sliced peeled fresh
    peaches, or canned sliced
    peaches, drained
1 ½ c. seedless grapes
Onion-Spice Dressing
Romaine leaves, or other lettuce

• Gently toss peaches and grapes with Onion-Spice Dressing. Cover and chill 2 hours or longer. To serve, turn into deep serving bowl, or spoon into small individual salad bowls. Tuck a few romaine leaves at sides to garnish. Makes 6 servings.

Onion-Spice Dressing: Shake or beat together ½ c. salad oil, 2 tblsp. wine or cider vinegar, 1 tblsp. lemon juice, 1 tblsp. brown sugar, 1 tsp. salt, ¾ tsp. ground cloves, ⅛ tsp. pepper and 1 tblsp. minced green onions with part of green tops.

FRUITED CUCUMBERS WITH BLACK PEPPER-LEMON DRESSING

Excellent to serve with roast chicken

1 cucumber, peeled and thinly
    sliced
3 c. (about) thin slices of fresh
    melon
Black Pepper-Lemon Dressing
Crisp lettuce
Finely chopped fresh parsley

• Gently toss cucumbers and fruit with Black Pepper-Lemon Dressing. Cover and chill 2 hours or longer. To serve, arrange on lettuce-lined chilled serving platter, or individual plates; spoon dressing over and sprinkle with chopped parsley. Makes 4 servings.

Note: Make 2 batches of this salad and dressing for more servings. When fresh melon is not in season, use fresh, or even canned, drained pears for the fruit.

Black Pepper-Lemon Dressing: Shake or beat together ½ c. salad oil, 3 tblsp. fresh lemon juice, ¾ tsp. Dijon-style mustard (or dry mustard), ½ tsp. salt, ½ tsp. freshly ground black pepper and ¼ tsp. crumbled dried rosemary.

TOMATO-MUSHROOM SALAD PLATTER

Wonderful with lamb, veal and beef

4 medium-large tomatoes
½ lb. fresh mushrooms
Basil Dressing
Crisp lettuce leaves

• Peel tomatoes if you wish; cut in ⅜" slices. Rinse and dry mushrooms and slice thinly.
• Layer vegetables in a shallow bowl, spooning Basil Dressing generously over each layer. Cover and chill 2 hours or longer, spooning dressing over vegetables occasionally or turning gently.
• To serve, arrange tomato and mushroom slices on lettuce-lined chilled serving platter, or individual salad plates; spoon on any remaining dressing. Makes 4 servings.

Note: Make this recipe and dressing twice for more servings.

Basil Dressing: Shake or beat together 1 c. salad oil, 6 tblsp. vinegar, 2 tblsp. fresh lemon juice, 2 tsp. crumbled dried basil, 1 tsp. salt, ½ tsp. garlic salt, ½ tsp. sugar and ¼ tsp. black pepper.

CUCUMBER-WALNUT SALAD BOWL

Just right with ham or smoked tongue

2 large cucumbers, peeled and
    thinly sliced
Onion Dressing
6 c. torn crisp lettuce (loosely
    packed to measure)
1 c. Toasted Chopped Walnuts

• Toss cucumbers thoroughly with half the Onion Dressing; cover and chill 2 hours or longer. Drain cucumbers well.

• In a chilled salad bowl, toss drained cucumbers, lettuce and finely chopped walnuts with remaining dressing; serve immediately. Makes 6 servings.

Onion Dressing: Shake or beat together ⅔ c. salad oil, ¼ c. wine vinegar, 1 tblsp. finely grated onion, 2 tsp. dry mustard and 1½ tsp. salt.

Toasted Chopped Walnuts: Sprinkle chopped walnuts on baking sheet; place in moderate oven (350°) until lightly browned, about 4 minutes; shake or stir occasionally.

CHAPTER 5

HOMEMADE COUNTRY BREADS

Farm kitchens are justly famous for breads that come hot and fragrant from their ovens. When a woman looks at her golden brown loaves, coffee cakes or rolls, she often steps to the telephone and asks a neighbor or two to come over for coffee and fresh bread while exchanging news. This is a part of today's life in the country.

The recipes in this chapter are for breads especially adapted to entertaining. Which one to bake and serve depends on your guest list and the occasion. If it's for supper on a wintry evening with men present, you won't go wrong on Sourdough Biscuits or Sourdough Silver Dollar Pancakes. These ranch breads need a starter for leavening. We tell you how to make it.

Doughnuts are another country treat. You may select Square Doughnuts, which always are the talk of a coffee party. Or you may prefer Colorado Spudnuts—the recipe comes from a member of FARM JOURNAL's Family Test Group who lives on a potato farm located in the shadow of tall mountains. They're special.

Feast your eyes on the pancake recipes and then feast your friends on the cakes they make. Which will you make first, delicate Crumb Pancakes or Pancake de Luxe that are almost a meal in themselves? Perhaps you'll prefer Chicken or Beef Filled Pancakes, or Apple or Shrimp Griddlecakes. We recommend them all.

Certainly the coffee cakes, like Mince-Streusel, Sugar-Top and Walnut Whirl, are coffee party delights. And the fruit and nut breads, both luscious and tasty, produce sandwiches that make hostesses proud, their guests happy. Pickle-Nut Confetti Loaf is unusually interesting and ideal for cream cheese sandwiches.

The hot yeast rolls in this chapter are the kind country women like to serve. If you want hard, crisp, French-type rolls, try Crusty Brown Rolls. Orange Pinwheels, Holly-Day Yeast Rolls and Caramel Twists are truly country-kitchen specials. And if you're having fried chicken, bake Sweet Potato Biscuits. Serve them hot with plenty of butter in true Southern style.

Yeast Rolls Hot from the Oven

Magic, to a country boy, may be pulling multicolored silk handkerchiefs from an empty hat. To his mother and sister, taking feathery, light rolls from the oven is a fitting definition.

"Certainly, what fragrant, brown rolls do for a rather ordinary company meal is magic," says a farm hostess. "They often turn a dinner or supper into a feast."

Many of our recipes for hot rolls come from farm kitchens, where they are favorites. Take your pick of recipes the next time you entertain.

Will it be Orange Pinwheels filled with Date or Herb Butter, Crusty Brown French Rolls or another kind? Just reading this bread section will make you want to invite friends to dinner or a coffee party.

Holly-Day Rolls Say Merry Christmas

A hospitable Iowa farm woman, a Guest Cook in our Test Kitchens, bakes what she calls Holly-Day Yeast Rolls for the Christmas season. (And at many other times of the year!) With a freezer supply of these yeast rolls, made with refrigerator dough and filled with seasoned butter, she's always ready for friends who stop by to visit.

She reheats the crescents filled with Date Butter and/or Cinnamon Rolls filled with Cinnamon-Nut Butter while the coffee percolates. For dinner guests, she enjoys serving her crescents filled with Herb Butter. She says they're exceptionally good with meat or poultry. Our taste-testers agree.

She keeps covered jars of the seasoned butters in the refrigerator; they're ready to use when it's baking time. This easy and friendly way to entertain helped make one country woman famous in her county for her hospitality. You'll find that her plan will work for you.

HOLLY-DAY YEAST ROLLS

Buttery fillings give these rolls place in special-occasion meals

Basic Dough:
- 2 pkgs. active dry yeast
- 2 c. warm water (105–15°)
- ½ c. sugar
- ¼ c. softened shortening
- 1 egg, slightly beaten
- 2 tsp. salt
- ⅔ c. nonfat dry milk (not reconstituted)
- 6 to 7 c. sifted flour
- Date Butter or Herb Butter

• Dissolve yeast in warm water. Stir in sugar, shortening, egg and salt. Mix in dry milk and flour with a spoon. The dough is soft and pliable.

• Place in a greased, covered bowl in the refrigerator. Let stand overnight. (Use within 3 days.)

• About 4 hours before baking, pinch off about one fourth the dough and roll into a circle on a lightly floured board. Cut into 16 wedges. (Or use half or three fourths of dough to make more rolls.) Spread 1 tsp. Date

Butter or Herb Butter on each wedge. Starting at the large end, roll up each wedge. Place 2" apart on a greased baking sheet, points underneath. Let rise until doubled, about 1½ to 2 hours.
• Bake in hot oven (400°) until golden brown, about 15 minutes. Makes 16 rolls.

Date Butter: Put ½ lb. pitted dates through food chopper, using the coarse blade. Follow with ¼ c. walnuts or pecans. Stir in ¼ lb. softened butter. Mix dates, nuts and butter well, cover and store in the refrigerator. Bring to room temperature before spreading on roll dough. Makes 1⅓ cups.

Herb Butter: Stir together ¼ lb. softened butter, 1 tsp. powdered sage, 1 tsp. crushed rosemary leaves, 1 tsp. dried parsley, ¼ tsp. salt and ⅛ tsp. freshly ground pepper. Refrigerate in covered container. Bring to room temperature before spreading on dough. Makes ½ cup.

VARIATION

Cinnamon Rolls: Roll one fourth of dough for Holly-Day Yeast Rolls in a rectangle about 16 × 8". (Use one half or more of the dough if you want to bake more rolls.) Spread with Cinnamon-Nut Butter. Roll dough lengthwise, as for jelly roll. Seal edge; cut in 1" slices. Place cut side down 1" apart in a greased 9 × 9 × 2" pan, or 2" apart on a greased baking sheet. Cover; let rise until doubled. Bake like Holly-Day Yeast Rolls.

Cinnamon-Nut Butter: Stir together ¼ lb. softened butter, ½ c. brown sugar, 1 tsp. cinnamon and ½ c. al-monds that have been spread in a pan and roasted in a moderate oven (350°) until a delicate brown, then finely chopped. Spread on dough for Cinnamon Rolls. Makes 1 cup.

Note: You can spread Date or Herb Butter on the dough and roll and bake as for Cinnamon Rolls.

Rolls Mother Used to Make

When a home economist friend, who is a homemaker and marvelous cook, sent this recipe, she wrote: "These are the best rolls I've ever eaten. My mother used to make them. She taught me her secrets—a soft dough and a long rising time."

12-HOUR RUM ROLLS
Sweet rolls that melt in your mouth

1   pkg. active dry yeast
¼   c. warm, not hot, water (110°)
¾   c. melted butter or margarine
¾   c. scalded milk
¾   c. sugar
3   eggs, beaten
¾   tsp. salt
3½ to 4 c. flour
¾   c. chopped raisins
Rum (or Vanilla) Icing

• Place yeast in large bowl; add water. Stir to dissolve. Combine ½ c. butter, scalded milk, cooled to lukewarm, ½ c. sugar, eggs and salt. Add to yeast mixture.
• Add flour to make a soft dough (still sticky). Cover and let rise 5 or 6 hours in a warm place.
• Turn dough onto a floured board

(it is very soft and should remain that way). Divide in half.

• Roll each half in an 18 × 12" rectangle. Spread with remaining ¼ c. melted butter and sprinkle with remaining ¼ c. sugar and the raisins. Roll very loosely (as for jelly roll) from the long side and pinch edges to seal.

• Cut each roll into 16 pieces; place, cut side down, in greased muffin pans. Cover and let rise 6 hours.

• Bake in moderate oven (375°) 12 to 15 minutes, or until done. As soon as rolls come from the oven, brush with Rum (or Vanilla) Icing.

Rum (or Vanilla) Icing: To 1 c. confectioners sugar add about 1 tblsp. water, just enough to make a spreadable mixture. Add ½ tsp. rum extract (or vanilla).

HOMEMADE HAMBURGER BUNS

What a difference homemade buns make: Plain hamburgers become extra-special

2 pkgs. active dry yeast
¼ c. sugar
½ c. warm, not hot, water
     (105–15°)
6 c. sifted flour
½ c. non-fat dry milk (not
     reconstituted)
1 tblsp. salt
2 c. water
2 eggs, beaten
½ c. salad oil or melted
     shortening
Sesame or poppy seeds

• Combine yeast, sugar and water and let stand until yeast softens. Stir to dissolve.

• Sift together flour, dry milk and salt into large bowl. Make well in center of dry ingredients and pour in the water, yeast mixture, eggs and oil. Mix well; cover and let rise in a warm place 1 hour.

• Turn dough onto well-floured board (dough may be sticky), turn a few times to coat dough well with flour. Pinch off pieces about the size of an egg; place, smooth side up, on a greased baking sheet, about 3" apart. Brush with mixture of beaten egg (or egg yolk) and a little milk; then sprinkle with sesame or poppy seeds.

• Let rise 20 minutes. Bake in hot oven (425°) 8 to 12 minutes, or until done. Makes about 30 buns.

OATMEAL ROLLS

A Wyoming Test Group member says her guests expect these rolls at her house—taste them; you'll know why

1 ¼ c. boiling water
⅓ c. shortening
⅓ c. brown sugar
1 tsp. salt
1 c. quick-cooking rolled oats
1 pkg. active dry yeast
¼ c. warm, not hot, water
     (105–15°)
4 c. flour
1 egg, beaten

• Pour boiling water over shortening, brown sugar, salt and rolled oats. Let stand until lukewarm.

• Meanwhile sprinkle yeast over warm water in bowl and stir until dissolved.

• Combine rolled oats mixture with yeast; add 2 c. flour and egg. Beat until well blended.

• Add remaining flour, a little at a time, to make a soft dough. Turn onto a lightly floured surface and knead until dough is smooth and elastic.

• Place in a greased bowl and invert dough so top is greased. Cover with a clean towel and let rise in warm place until doubled in bulk, about 1½ hours. Punch down and let rise again until doubled, about ½ hour.

• Shape into 1″ balls and place 3 balls in each greased muffin-pan cup (or shape as desired). Let rise until doubled, 20 to 30 minutes.

• Bake in moderate oven (375°) about 25 minutes, until lightly browned. Makes 32 rolls.

OVERNIGHT REFRIGERATOR ROLLS

Versatile—you can bake both puffy, light pan rolls and a gorgeous coffee cake from this dough (no kneading)

    2   pkgs. active dry yeast
    2½ c. warm water (105–15°)
    ¾   c. soft or melted shortening
    ¾   c. sugar
    2   eggs, well beaten
    8   to 8½ c. flour
    2½ tsp. salt

• Soften yeast in warm water. Add shortening, sugar, eggs, 4 c. flour and salt. Stir to mix and then beat until smooth, about 1 minute.

• Stir in remaining flour. (You may want to use your hands to mix in the last 2 cups.) This will be a soft dough.

• Place in a greased bowl and lightly grease surface of dough. Cover tightly. Store in the refrigerator overnight or until needed. (Dough will keep about 4 days, but punch it down daily. Count days from time dough is placed in refrigerator.) Makes 36 rolls

or 2 (9″) coffee cakes (baked in tube pan).

Pan Rolls: Punch down refrigerated dough and pinch off one third. Cover the remaining dough and put back in the refrigerator.

• Shape the one third dough into 12 rolls and place them in a greased 9 × 9 × 2″ baking pan. Cover with a clean towel and let rise until doubled, about 1 hour.

• Bake in a hot oven (400°) 15 to 20 minutes. Turn out on wire rack.

VARIATION

Golden Crown Coffee Cake: Combine ¾ c. sugar, 2 tsp. cinnamon, ½ c. chopped walnuts and ½ c. raisins.

• Use half of Overnight Refrigerator Rolls dough. Cut off pieces about the size of walnuts. Roll each piece in melted butter and then in the sugar mixture.

• Arrange the first layer of dough pieces in a well-greased 9″ tube pan; place a second layer over the spaces. Continue building layers until all dough pieces are used. Sprinkle remaining sugar mixture over the top.

• Cover with a clean towel and let rise in a warm place until doubled, about 1 hour. Bake in a moderate oven (350°) 40 to 55 minutes. Take from oven, cool 10 minutes and then remove from pan. Makes 12 servings.

Pinwheels for Guests

A Wisconsin hostess enjoyed entertaining so much that she decided to go into business and serve paying

The day before your party, roast and chill beef filet. Next day pat liverwurst paté on beef, wrap it in pastry, trim with pastry flowers and bake. You'll have a regal treat, Country-Style Beef Wellington (*recipe, page 18*).

guests in her gracious home. She gives them the same food her personal friends appreciated most before she started her tearoom.

Among her food much complimented are Orange Pinwheels— featherlight bread dough wound around an orange filling and baked to a tempting brown.

ORANGE PINWHEELS

Paying guests ask for these sweet rolls

Dough:

1 pkg. active dry yeast
¼ c. warm water (105–15°)
¾ c. milk
¼ c. sugar
1 tsp. salt
3 eggs
3 tblsp. soft butter
4 to 4½ c. flour

Orange Filling:

⅓ c. soft butter
½ c. sugar
2 tsp. grated orange peel

• To make dough, dissolve yeast in warm water in mixing bowl. Scald milk; cool to lukewarm. Add milk, sugar, salt, eggs, butter and half the flour to yeast mixture. Stir with a spoon until smooth. Mix in enough of the remaining flour to make a *soft* dough. (The consistency of the dough is important. When you first make these rolls, you may have difficulty handling the soft dough, but it's the softness that makes these rolls so very light and tender.)
• Knead on a lightly floured board

until smooth and elastic, about 5 minutes. Place in a greased bowl; turn over so greased side is up. Cover with a clean towel and let rise in a warm place until doubled, about 1½ hours. Punch down and let rise until almost doubled, about 30 minutes.
• Roll dough in a 15 × 9″ rectangle. Mix ingredients for Orange Filling and spread over the dough. Roll as for jelly roll, pinching edges together. Cut roll in 1″ slices.
• Place cut side down in a greased 13 × 9 × 2″ pan. Cover and let rise until doubled, 35 to 40 minutes. Bake in moderate oven (375°) 25 minutes, or until lightly browned. Makes 18.

CARAMEL TWISTS

These rolls will start conversation. Good with coffee for evening drop-ins

Dough:

4½ c. sifted flour
¼ c. sugar
1 tsp. salt
¾ c. butter or margarine
1 pkg. active dry yeast
¼ c. warm, not hot, water (105–15°)
3 egg yolks, beaten
1 c. milk, scalded and cooled to lukewarm

Caramel Coating:

⅔ c. butter or margarine
¼ c. light corn syrup
1½ c. light brown sugar, firmly packed
1 c. chopped walnuts

What better welcome to spring than fresh-cut asparagus for supper? Baked Asparagus-Cheese Sandwich—bread and cheese in velvety egg custard, topped with the tender green spears—is superior (*recipe, page 92*).

Filling:

½ c. brown sugar

1 tsp. cinnamon

· Combine flour, sugar and salt in mixing bowl. Cut in butter until size of small peas.

· Dissolve yeast in warm water. Add to flour mixture along with beaten egg yolks and milk. Beat until thoroughly mixed and smooth. Cover bowl and chill in refrigerator overnight.

· When ready to bake, prepare caramel coating by melting butter in a small saucepan. Stir in the syrup. Spread this mixture in bottoms of two 15½ × 10½ × 1″ jelly roll pans. Sprinkle ¾ c. brown sugar and ½ c. chopped nuts evenly in each pan.

· To make filling, mix the brown sugar and cinnamon. Divide into thirds.

· Cut dough in three equal parts for easy handling. Roll each third into a 15 × 10″ rectangle. Brush center lengthwise third of each rectangle with soft butter, then sprinkle with filling mixture.

· Fold a third of each rectangle over the center third and sprinkle with filling mixture (you'll use ⅓ of filling mixture for each rectangle of dough). Fold remaining third over two layers. Cut crosswise into strips 1″ wide.

· Grasp ends of strips firmly and twist in opposite direction; seal ends firmly in fan shape. Place dough strips in pans about 1″ apart. Allow to rise about 30 minutes in a warm place free from drafts.

· Bake in moderate oven (350°) about 25 minutes. Invert pans immediately on large sheets of foil. Allow pans to remain inverted about 1 minute before removing. Makes about 30 twists.

Crusty Brown Rolls for Company

Hard, chewy rolls, the kind that attract customers in Italian and other European-type restaurants, and that the best European bakeries sell, are not difficult to make at home. If you start the dough promptly after breakfast, the rolls will be out of the oven by noon. You can cool and freeze them to reheat when you entertain.

There are four important rules to heed in baking crusty rolls. Here they are.

· Use water for the liquid. Milk makes soft crusts.

· Brush rolls with water or Egg Wash during the rising and before baking. We give you directions for each type of roll.

· Bake rolls in a steam-filled oven (see recipe).

· Rub no shortening on the rolls before or after baking.

CRUSTY BROWN ROLLS

Crisp crust on the outside, and airy inside—perfect for spaghetti suppers. Bake them in many shapes and flavors

2 pkgs. active dry yeast

1 ¾ c. warm water (105–15°)

4 tsp. sugar

2 tsp. salt

2 tblsp. melted shortening

6½ to 7 c. flour

3 egg whites, beaten stiff

· Add yeast to warm water; let stand 5 minutes. Add sugar, salt, shortening and 2 c. flour; beat well. Add egg whites. Add remaining flour until dough leaves the side of the bowl when you stir it.

• Turn out on a lightly floured surface. Knead until dough is smooth and elastic and tiny blisters show on the surface (about 5 minutes).

• Place in a lightly greased bowl; then turn bottom side up. Cover with a damp cloth.

• Let rise in a warm place (85°) until doubled, about 1 hour. Punch down.

• You may shape the dough at this point. For superior results, let the dough rise again until doubled; then punch it down and shape.

• Follow directions for shaping given with each type roll (directions follow).

• Place rolls on greased baking sheets sprinkled lightly with cornmeal. Brush with Egg Wash or with water. Cover and let rise until doubled, about 20 minutes. Brush again with Egg Wash or water.

• Bake in a hot oven (425°) 20 minutes, or until brown and crusty. Place a large shallow pan of boiling water on the bottom of the oven to provide steam while the rolls bake. This makes the rolls crusty. Makes about 3 dozen rolls.

Egg Wash: Beat slightly 1 egg white with 1 tblsp. water. Brush on rolls.

HOW TO SHAPE ROLLS

French Rolls: Shape raised dough in 3″ balls; flatten under hands to make 4″ circles or 6″ tapered oblongs ¾″ thick. Use a very sharp knife or razor to make cuts on top. Place on baking sheet, brush with Egg Wash; sprinkle with poppy or sesame seeds. Let rise until doubled, brush again with Egg Wash and bake.

Onion Rolls: Shape raised dough in 3″ round rolls ½″ thick; make hollows in centers with fingers. Fill with an onion mixture made by soaking 3 tblsp. instant minced onion in 3 tblsp. cold water, then drained and mixed with 1 tblsp. poppy seeds. Brush with Egg Wash; let rise until doubled; brush again with Egg Wash. Bake.

Salty Caraway Crescents: Divide the raised dough into 4 portions. Roll each portion into a very thin 16″ square; cut each into 16 (4″) squares. Roll each, starting at a corner, diagonally to opposite corner; seal, curve ends and roll gently under the palms of the hands to lengthen slightly. Place on baking sheet. Brush with Egg Wash. Let rise until doubled; brush again with Egg Wash. Sprinkle with coarse salt crystals and caraway seeds. Bake 10 minutes; brush again with Egg Wash; bake 5 minutes more, or until browned.

Note: Table salt may be used, but coarse salt such as that used for pickling and curing meat gives better results. It is available in nearly all food stores.

Italian Bread Sticks: Divide raised dough into 4 portions; roll out each portion to a 4 × 7″ rectangle. Cut in ½″ strips. Roll under hands to make strips 8″ long. Place on baking sheet 1″ apart. Brush with water; let rise and brush again with water before baking.

Sprinkle a cup of raisins with 1 tsp. melted butter or salad oil and toss to coat. Then when you chop them, raisins will not stick to your knife or scissors.

Come on Over—
the Coffee Cake's Done

Country coffee cakes are, as their name implies, wonderful go-withs for company breakfasts and other meals. Their name also indicates they're like a cake in a meal and can appear as dessert with or without a fruit compote.

If you have a daughter she can help out by making Quick Coffee Cake with packaged refrigerator biscuits from the supermarket. She'll be proud when she takes it from the oven and serves it to guests. And so will you! All you'll have to do is make the coffee.

WALNUT WHIRL

You'll find this golden brown bread is at home with coffee and guests in midmorning, afternoon or evening

¼ c. sugar
1 tsp. salt
¼ c. soft butter or margarine
¾ c. milk, scalded
1 pkg. active dry yeast
¼ c. warm water (110°)
1 egg
3¼ to 3¾ c. flour
Walnut Filling

• Add sugar, salt and butter to milk and cool to lukewarm.
• Dissolve yeast in water.
• Stir egg and half the flour into milk mixture; stir in yeast; beat until smooth. Work in enough remaining flour to make dough handle easily.
• Turn onto floured surface; knead until smooth. Press ball of dough in greased bowl, turn greased side up. Cover with damp cloth. Let rise in warm place until doubled, about 1½ hours.
• Punch down dough; let rise again until almost doubled, about 30 minutes.
• Cover worktable with several thicknesses of newspaper, then with large dish towel taped down to hold taut.
• Roll out dough on floured towel to approximately 30 × 20″ rectangle; it will be very thin. With rubber spatula, gently spread Walnut Filling over dough—right to the edges. Starting at wide side, lift cloth and let dough roll up like a jelly roll. Pinch edges to seal.
• Coil roll loosely on greased baking sheet; cover and let rise until nearly doubled, about 45 minutes.
• Bake in slow oven (325°) 40 to 45 minutes. Remove from baking sheet to rack to cool. Makes about 18 servings.

Walnut Filling: Mix ⅓ c. soft butter or margarine, ¾ c. brown sugar and 1 egg. Stir in ⅓ c. milk, 1 tsp. vanilla, 1 tsp. cinnamon and 3 c. walnuts, coarsely ground.

VARIATION

Short-Cut Walnut Whirl: Make coffee cake with hot roll mix (use 14 oz. pkg.). Let dough rise, then roll it out as above.

MINCE-STREUSEL COFFEE CAKE

This is made of sugar and spice and everything nice. Serve with coffee

3 c. sifted flour
1½ c. sugar
½ tsp. salt
½ tsp. cinnamon

½ tsp. nutmeg
½ tsp. cloves
¾ c. shortening (half butter)
1 ½ tsp. baking soda
1 ¼ c. buttermilk
2 eggs, slightly beaten
1 c. mincemeat
½ c. chopped nuts

• Sift flour, sugar, salt and spices together in a large bowl; cut in shortening with a pastry blender until the mixture resembles coarse cornmeal. Reserve half of this crumb mixture for topping. Blend the baking soda into remaining mixture. Lightly stir in buttermilk and eggs.

• Spoon half of the batter into a well-greased 15½ × 10½ × 1″ jelly roll pan. Scatter mincemeat evenly over the batter; top with the remaining batter. Sprinkle evenly with reserved crumb mixture and the nuts.

• Bake in moderate oven (350°) 30 minutes, or until cake tests done. Serve warm. Makes 18 generous servings.

COFFEE CAKE RING

A dual-purpose, rich quick bread to serve as coffee cake or for dessert

¾ c. butter or margarine
1 ½ c. sugar
2 eggs
1 c. dairy sour cream
½ tsp. vanilla
¼ tsp. salt
1 tsp. baking powder
2 c. sifted cake flour
½ c. chopped pecans
2 tblsp. brown sugar
1 tsp. instant cocoa mix
½ tsp. cinnamon

• Cream butter and sugar; add eggs,

cream again. Fold in sour cream and vanilla.

• Sift together salt, baking powder and flour; fold into creamed mixture.

• Mix nuts, sugar, cocoa mix and cinnamon.

• Spoon batter into greased and floured 9″ tube pan; top with nut mixture.

• Bake in moderate oven (350°) 50 to 60 minutes. Cool cake in pan 20 minutes before removing. Makes 12 servings.

VARIATION

Layered Coffee Cake Ring: Pour half of batter for Coffee Cake Ring in pan; sprinkle with half the nut mixture. Then top with the remaining batter and nut mixture; bake.

SUGAR-TOP COFFEE CAKE

Better make a couple of these coffee cakes if you're serving more than six

1 egg
¾ c. sugar
1 tblsp. melted butter or margarine
1 c. dairy sour cream
1 tsp. vanilla
1 ½ c. sifted flour
2 tsp. baking powder
¼ tsp. baking soda
¾ tsp. salt
Brown Sugar Topping

• Beat egg until frothy; beat in sugar and butter. Cream until light and fluffy. Add sour cream and vanilla; blend well.

• Sift dry ingredients together; add to the sour cream mixture. Blend well. Pour into a greased 8″ square pan. Sprinkle with Brown Sugar Topping.

• Bake in moderate oven (375°) 25 to 30 minutes, or until cake tests done. Serve warm. Makes 6 servings.

Brown Sugar Topping: Mix ½ c. brown sugar, 2 tblsp. flour, ½ tsp. cinnamon and 2 tblsp. softened butter until crumbly.

QUICK COFFEE CAKE

Bake this bread after guests arrive for coffee. They'll enjoy both its aroma and warm-from-the-oven taste

    3 tblsp. butter
    ¼ c. jam
    ¼ c. coarsely chopped walnuts
    1 (8 oz.) pkg. refrigerator
        biscuits

• Melt butter in 8″ pie pan. Blend in jam; sprinkle with nuts. Place one biscuit in center of pan; arrange remaining biscuits around it. Bake in hot oven (400°) 12 minutes, or until biscuits are browned. Invert on plate. Serve warm. Makes about 6 servings.

TINY APPLE HALF-MOONS

Fancy rolls for coffee or tea parties

    1 pkg. refrigerator quick
        cinnamon rolls (8)
    6 tblsp. butter, melted
    ¼ c. brown sugar
    1 medium apple, cored and
        finely chopped (½ c.)
    ½ c. raisins, plumped in hot
        water
    1 tsp. cinnamon
    ½ tsp. ground cardamom
    ½ tsp. grated lemon peel
    1 tsp. lemon juice
    ⅛ tsp. salt

• Separate cinnamon rolls. Roll each out, stretching to make thin rectangle.
• Combine 4 tblsp. melted butter with remaining ingredients for filling. Place 1 tblsp. filling down the long edge of each rectangle. Roll up lengthwise and shape in half-moon on greased baking sheet. Seal edges firmly.
• With scissors make slits in each half-moon, cutting to the bottom edge but not cutting through. Brush with remaining 2 tblsp. melted butter.
• Bake in hot oven (400°) 12 minutes, or until evenly browned. Frost with tube of icing included in packaged rolls. Makes 8 pastries.

Bring on a Hot Quick Bread

Hot breads, in the kitchens of women who live south of the Mason and Dixon line, frequently are masterpieces. For example, Sweet Potato Biscuits—they're as Southern as fresh coconut cakes and magnolia blossoms. Do serve these biscuits hot; that's half the secret of successful quick breads.

Apple Muffins are the specialty of a Colorado member of FARM JOURNAL's Family Test Group and her two daughters, who bake them for company meals to help their mother.

SWEET POTATO BISCUITS

Serve piping hot with plenty of butter and jelly, or jam, or honey

    2 c. sifted flour
    4 tsp. baking powder
    1 tsp. salt
    ⅔ c. shortening
    1 c. cooked, mashed sweet
        potatoes
    3 tblsp. milk

• Sift together dry ingredients. Cut in shortening. Blend in sweet potatoes. Add enough milk to make a soft dough (this will depend on moisture in potatoes).

• Knead lightly. Roll ¾" thick on lightly floured board. Cut with floured 2" cutter.

• Place on ungreased baking sheet and bake in hot oven (400°) 20 minutes, or until brown. Makes about 15 biscuits.

Applesauce in Breads

Many an expert country cook cans or buys applesauce especially to use for a quick, convenient ingredient in baking for company. When the apple crop is short or the supply of sauce in the cupboard runs out, she switches to commercially canned applesauce.

Apple Muffins are one example of a country hot bread in which applesauce supplies excellent flavor. It also produces a moist muffin.

APPLE MUFFINS
Tender muffins with sugar and spice

2 c. flour, sifted
4 tsp. baking powder
½ tsp. salt
½ tsp. cinnamon
¼ tsp. ginger
¼ c. sugar
1 egg, beaten
⅓ c. salad oil or melted shortening
½ c. milk
⅔ c. sweetened applesauce

• Sift the dry ingredients together. Make a well in the center of the mixture.

• In a separate bowl, beat egg; stir in the oil, milk and applesauce. Pour into the well in dry ingredients. Stir only enough to mix dry and liquid ingredients. The batter will be lumpy. (Overmixing makes tunnels in muffins and peaks on their tops.)

• Spoon batter into muffin-pan cups that have been greased lightly only on bottoms; fill cups about two thirds full. Sprinkle with one of the toppings that follow.

• Bake in a hot oven (400°) 20 to 25 minutes. Serve hot. Makes 12 large (3") muffins or 18 medium-size (2½") muffins.

Cinnamon Topping: Mix 2 tblsp. sugar with ½ tsp. cinnamon.

Crunch Topping: Mix 2 tblsp. brown sugar, 2 tblsp. chopped nuts and ½ tsp. cinnamon.

REFRIGERATOR BRAN MUFFINS
For a crusty, spiced top sprinkle a bit of cinnamon and sugar over the batter just before baking

1 c. boiling water
3 c. whole bran cereal
2 c. buttermilk
1½ c. sugar
⅔ c. shortening
4 eggs
4 c. sifted flour
2½ tsp. baking soda
1 tsp. salt

• Pour boiling water over whole bran cereal. Mix well, cool; stir in buttermilk.

• Cream sugar and shortening until fluffy. Add eggs and beat well.

• Sift together flour, soda and salt.

• Stir cooled bran mixture into creamed mixture. Stir in dry ingredients just to barely moisten (batter will not be smooth). Don't overmix.

• Store in tightly covered container in refrigerator overnight, or until needed. Can be stored up to 3 days.

• Spoon batter into greased muffin-pan cups. Bake in hot oven (425°) about 20 minutes. Makes 3 dozen muffins.

Note: You can bake half of the batter (or any amount you want) at one time, the remaining batter later. Or, for 18 muffins, you can cut this recipe in two—just use half of all the ingredients.

CARAMEL CRESCENTS

With refrigerator biscuits on hand, you can fast-fix this coffee go-with when guests stop in to visit

1 (8 oz.) pkg. refrigerator
   biscuits
¼ c. butter
¼ c. maple-blended syrup

• Stretch biscuits into oblong shapes. Flatten slightly with rolling pin on floured board; cut each biscuit in half lengthwise.

• Meanwhile, set electric fry pan temperature control at 275°. Melt butter; add syrup. Place biscuit crescents in gently bubbling butter-syrup mixture. Cook about 3 minutes on each side; turn once with buttered turner. (Watch carefully, if butter-syrup mixture begins to scorch, add 1 tblsp. syrup and reduce pan temperature slightly.)

• Place crescents on waxed paper; drizzle with syrup remaining in pan. Let cool 1 minute, or until syrup sets. Serve warm. Makes 20.

Unforgettable Sourdough Breads

Sourdough breads had their heyday when pioneers were winning the West and adventurers searched for gold in the Klondike. They still have a loyal following, especially among men, who like their tangy taste. A steady flow of letters comes to FARM JOURNAL Test Kitchens asking how to make sourdough bread.

The success of sourdoughs depends primarily on the starter, a fermented batter of water, sugar and flour, which both leavens and flavors the breads. Originally starters were temperamental because they relied on wild yeast that fell into them when exposed to the air. Our home economists recommend a starter made with active dry yeast. In it, the kind and amount of yeast is under control and the sourdough has a consistent taste.

Two of the best-liked sourdoughs are biscuits and pancakes, traditionally the size of silver dollars. Here are recipes for them and for starter:

SOURDOUGH STARTER

A modern version that's dependable

½ pkg. active dry (1¼ tsp.)
   or ½ cake compressed
   yeast
2 c. unsifted flour
2 tblsp. sugar
2½ c. water

• Combine the ingredients in a stone crock or a bowl. Beat well. Cover with cheesecloth and let stand two days in a warm place.

SOURDOUGH BISCUITS

These biscuits are light and fluffy—
they have that marvelous tangy taste

1 ½ c. sifted flour
2   tsp. baking powder
¼   tsp. baking soda (½ tsp.
      if Starter is quite sour)
½   tsp. salt
¼   c. butter or margarine
1   c. Starter

• Sift dry ingredients together. Cut in
butter with pastry blender. Add
Starter and mix.
• Turn dough out on a lightly floured
board. Knead lightly until satiny.
• Roll dough ½" thick. Cut with
floured 2½" cutter. Place biscuits in
a well-greased 9 × 9 × 2" pan.
Brush with melted butter. Let rise
about 1 hour in a warm place.
• Bake in a hot oven (425°) 20
minutes. Makes 12 biscuits.

Note: To replenish Starter, stir in 2
c. warm (not hot) water and 2 c.
flour.

SILVER DOLLAR HOTCAKES

Serve with butter and lots of "lick,"
the cowboy's term for sweet syrup

1 c. Starter
2 c. unsifted flour
2 c. milk
1 tsp. salt
2 tsp. baking soda
2 eggs
3 tblsp. melted shortening
2 tblsp. sugar

• About 12 hours before mealtime,
mix Starter, flour, milk and salt; let
stand in a bowl covered with cheesecloth. Set in a warm place.

• Just before baking cakes, remove 1
c. batter to replenish sourdough in
crock. To the remaining batter in the
bowl, add baking soda, eggs, shortening and sugar. Mix well.
• Bake cakes the size of silver dollars
on a lightly greased, hot griddle. For
thinner hotcakes, add more milk to
the batter. Makes about 30 cakes.

Give muffins a crunchy top. Mix ⅓
c. chopped nut meats, ⅓ c. brown
sugar, firmly packed, and ½ tsp.
ground cinnamon. Sprinkle over muf-
fins just before baking.

Strawberries for Breakfast: *Pick out*
the prettiest berries; wash but do not
hull. Arrange berries on individual
plates, around a mound of confec-
tioners sugar and a spoonful of dairy
sour cream or whipped cream. Dip
berries and eat with fingers.

Bishop's Bread—
A Traveling Recipe

Trading good recipes is fun today
just as it was when our grandmothers
were young. That's one way favorite
dishes get around the country. Take
North Carolina Bishop's Bread, for
example. A Minnesota extension
home economist, who shares this
recipe, says she found it in Georgia,
where she met a home economist
from North Carolina.

The loaf makes a splendid Christmas gift. It's festive with color, and
brimful of delightful flavors. We
know people who prefer it to fruitcake. Certainly, it's easier to make.

NORTH CAROLINA BISHOP'S BREAD

Serve sliced bread on tray with Cheddar cheese for an evening snack

3   eggs, well beaten
1   c. sugar
1 ½ c. flour
1 ½ tsp. baking powder
½   tsp. salt
1   c. cut-up dates
1   (10 oz.) jar maraschino
     cherries, drained and
     cut up (1 c.)
1   (6 oz.) pkg. semisweet
     chocolate pieces
1   c. coarsely chopped nuts

· Combine eggs and sugar.
· Sift together flour, baking powder and salt; add to egg mixture. Stir in dates, cherries, chocolate pieces and nuts.
· Pour batter into a well-greased 9 × 5 × 3″ loaf pan. Bake in slow oven (325°) 1¼ hours, or until cake tester inserted in center of loaf comes out clean. Cool in pan 10 minutes; remove to wire rack to complete cooling. Wrap in aluminum foil when cool. Let stand overnight before slicing. Makes 1 loaf.

APPLE QUICK BREAD

Moist, fruity sandwich special. Wrap in foil and store in cold place at least a day for easier slicing

½   c. butter or margarine
1   c. sugar
2   eggs
1   tsp. vanilla
2   c. grated peeled apples
2   c. sifted flour
1   tsp. salt

1   tsp. baking soda
1   tsp. baking powder
1   tsp. cinnamon
½   tsp. cloves
¾   c. black walnuts, chopped
1   tblsp. grated lemon peel

· Cream butter and sugar. Beat in eggs, one at a time. Add vanilla. Stir in the apples.
· Sift together flour, salt, baking soda, baking powder and spices. Blend into the creamed mixture. Add nuts and lemon peel.
· Pour into a lightly greased 9 × 5 × 3″ loaf pan, lined with waxed paper. Bake in moderate oven (350°) 50 minutes. Cool in pan 15 minutes; remove from pan and cool thoroughly on rack. Wrap in aluminum foil and store.

PRUNE WALNUT BREAD

Slice this moist nut-fruit bread thin for de luxe bread and butter sandwiches. Splendid choice for afternoon tea or coffee

1 ½ c. chopped prunes
1   c. boiling water
⅓   c. strained honey
1   egg, beaten
1   tsp. vanilla
2 ¼ c. sifted flour
⅔   c. sugar
1   tsp. baking soda
1   tsp. salt
2   tblsp. melted butter or
     margarine
1   c. chopped walnuts

· Combine prunes and boiling water. Cover and let stand 20 minutes. Add honey, egg and vanilla.
· Sift together flour, sugar, soda and

salt; add prune mixture, melted butter and walnuts, mixing well.

· Pour into a greased 9 × 5 × 3" loaf pan. Bake in slow oven (325°) 1 hour, or until bread tests done. Cool in pan 10 minutes; remove from pan and cool thoroughly on rack before slicing.

PICKLE-NUT CONFETTI LOAF

Make party sandwiches with cream cheese and this color-dotted bread

3   c. flour
¾   c. sugar
4   tsp. baking powder
1   tsp. salt
½   c. butter or margarine
⅔   c. candied dill pickle strips, coarsely chopped
½   c. chopped pecans
2   tblsp. diced pimiento
¾   c. milk
2   eggs, well beaten

· Sift flour, sugar, baking powder and salt into a bowl. Cut in butter with pastry blender until mixture resembles coarse cornmeal. Stir in pickles (you can use candied dill chips), nuts and pimiento.

· Combine milk and eggs. Make a well in center of flour mixture; add egg mixture all at once. Stir just to moisten dry ingredients (batter will not be smooth). Do not beat.

· Spread in greased 9 × 5 × 3" loaf pan. Bake in moderate oven (350°) 55 to 60 minutes. Cool, wrap in waxed paper and store in refrigerator overnight before slicing. Or wrap cooled loaf in freezer paper or foil and freeze.

ARIZONA CHRISTMAS BREAD

Here's a fruit bread with that good yeasty flavor. Makes a nice gift

1   c. milk
¼   c. butter or margarine
½   c. sugar
1   tsp. salt
½   tsp. ground nutmeg
½   tsp. ground mace
¼   tsp. ground cloves
2   pkgs. active dry yeast
½   c. warm, not hot, water (105–15°)
5½ to 6 c. flour
2   eggs, beaten
½   c. seedless raisins
¼   c. candied red cherries, cut in fourths
¼   c. candied green cherries, cut in fourths
½   c. chopped nuts
Butter Frosting

· Scald milk, remove from heat, add butter and stir until it melts. Stir in sugar, salt and spices, and cool until lukewarm.

· Meanwhile sprinkle yeast over warm water in a large bowl. Stir to dissolve.

· Add milk mixture to dissolved yeast; stir in 3 c. flour and beat until smooth. Add eggs, raisins, cherries and nuts. Blend in remaining flour to make a soft dough you can knead.

· Turn onto lightly floured board. Knead until smooth, about 10 minutes.

· Place in greased bowl and invert dough so top is greased. Cover and let rise in a warm place until dough doubles in size, about 1½ hours. Punch down and let rise again until doubled, about 45 minutes.

· Turn dough out, cut in half and

round in two balls. Cover with a clean towel and let rest 10 minutes. Shape into two loaves and fit into 9 × 5 × 3" loaf pans.

• Cover and let rise in warm place until dough is ¼" from tops of pans. (Brush tops of loaves with melted butter if desired.)

• Bake in moderate oven (375°) 35 to 40 minutes, until browned. Remove from pans and place on racks.

• Glaze with Butter Frosting and if desired sprinkle with a few chopped nuts.

Butter Frosting: Cream together ¼ c. soft butter and 2 c. sifted confectioners sugar. Blend in ¼ tsp. vanilla and 2½ tblsp. milk.

HEIDELBERG RYE BREAD

Interesting and different rye bread

2   pkgs. active dry yeast
2   c. warm, not hot, water
    (105–15°)
⅓   c. molasses
2   c. sifted medium rye flour
¼   c. cocoa
1   tblsp. caraway seeds
1   tblsp. salt
1   tblsp. melted shortening
3¼ c. sifted white flour
Cornmeal

• Sprinkle yeast on water; stir to dissolve. Add molasses, rye flour, cocoa and caraway seeds. Beat until smooth. Add salt and shortening. Stir in white flour gradually until the dough cleans the bowl.

• Turn out on floured board or canvas. Let rest 10 minutes, then knead until smooth.

• Place in greased bowl; invert dough so top will be greased. Let rise until

doubled in bulk. Punch down; let rise again until doubled.

• Divide dough in half; shape each half in an oblong loaf. Taper ends by rolling them back and forth. Place on greased baking sheet sprinkled lightly with cornmeal. After somewhat raised, slash loaves lengthwise across top with a very sharp knife. Let rise until almost doubled.

• Set a pan of water on floor of oven. Bake loaves in moderate oven (375°) 35 to 40 minutes. Makes 2 loaves.

Note: You can glaze bread if desired, using the following: You'll need 1 tblsp. cornstarch and 1 c. cold water. Dissolve the cornstarch in a little water to make a smooth paste; add to remainder of water and cook, stirring until mixture is clear. When loaves are about half done, spread this glaze on them. Brush loaves again with glaze 10 minutes before taking bread from oven.

Pancakes Extend Warm Welcome

Sometimes on blustery, cold evenings the country hostess fixes an informal pancake supper for a foursome. For such homey occasions, oven-baked Pancake de Luxe is a most appropriate main dish. The puffy, slightly sweetened, folded pancake is unusual and flavorful. The recipe is shared by an Iowa farm woman who is a superb cook. If you are serving more than a quartet, you can make two pancakes.

Try some of our other interesting kinds—Chicken-Stuffed Pancakes, for instance. They have an added advantage in that you can make them ahead and freeze them for last-minute browning at mealtime.

PANCAKE DE LUXE

You fold this puffy, slightly sweetened pancake around and top it with pineapple sauce and cheese. This pancake-omelet is almost a meal by itself

Pancake:

    2 tblsp. vegetable shortening
    ½ c. sifted flour
    ¼ tsp. salt
    1 tblsp. sugar
    1 (13½ oz.) can pineapple
         tidbits
    4 eggs (at room temperature)

Sauce:

    1½ tsp. cornstarch
    1 tsp. grated lemon peel
    1 tblsp. butter
    1 tblsp. lemon juice
    1 c. grated Cheddar cheese

• To make pancake, preheat oven to moderate (350°). Melt shortening in heavy 10″ metal baking dish or skillet with heatproof handle.

• Sift together dry ingredients. Drain pineapple; reserve liquid.

• Separate eggs; beat whites until stiff. Beat yolks until thick; alternately beat in dry ingredients and ½ c. pineapple liquid. Fold mixture into beaten egg whites.

• Pour into sizzling shortening in dish or skillet. Bake in moderate oven (350°) about 15 minutes, or until lightly browned.

• Meanwhile, make sauce. In a heavy saucepan gradually stir ½ c. pineapple liquid (add water if necessary) into cornstarch. Cook over medium heat, stirring constantly, until clear and thickened. Remove from heat; stir in pineapple and remaining ingredients except the cheese.

• When the pancake is baked, leave it in the pan, or transfer to a heat-proof platter. Sprinkle half the grated cheese over pancake. Spread half of the pancake with half of the pineapple sauce. Using a narrow spatula or pancake turner, fold the other half of the pancake over the pineapple-covered half. Top with remaining pineapple sauce and sprinkle with remaining cheese.

• Return to over for 5 minutes, or until cheese begins to melt. Serve from pan. Makes 4 servings.

CHICKEN-STUFFED PANCAKES

Pancakes and chicken get together in a surprisingly good main dish

Pancakes:

    2 eggs and 2 egg yolks,
         beaten
    1 c. milk
    1 c. flour
    ⅛ tsp. salt
    2 tblsp. salad oil

Chicken Filling:

    ½ c. chopped onion
    2 tblsp. butter
    ½ tsp. salt
    ¼ tsp. pepper
    ½ tsp. dried thyme
    ¼ tsp. mace
    ¼ tsp. nutmeg
    ¼ c. flour
    ½ c. hot chicken stock (about)
    1 (4 oz.) can chopped
         mushrooms
    2 c. finely chopped cooked
         chicken

Coating:

¼ tsp. salt
¼ tsp. pepper
2 egg whites
½ c. fine dry bread crumbs

• Blend together all ingredients for pancakes until smooth. For each pancake, pour ¼ c. batter into preheated, lightly greased skillet. Tip pan so batter spreads evenly. When set, turn. Place baked pancakes on clean dish towels until ready to fill. You will have about 8 pancakes.

• To make filling, sauté onion in butter. Blend in seasonings and flour. Add enough chicken stock to liquid drained from mushrooms to make 1 c.; stir into onion mixture. Add mushrooms and chicken; cook until thick; stir constantly. Cool.

• Spoon filling on one half of pancake; roll, tucking in ends.

• For coating, beat together salt, pepper and egg whites until foamy.

• Dip pancakes in seasoned egg whites, then roll in bread crumbs. Place in buttered 13 × 9 × 2″ pan. Bake in moderate oven (350°) about 45 minutes, or until golden brown; baste frequently with melted butter. Makes 8 servings.

To Freeze Pancakes: After dipping rolled pancakes in egg white mixture and crumbs, place in a shallow pan lined with waxed paper. Cover tightly and freeze. To bake, place pancakes in buttered 13×9×2″ pan and bake in moderate oven (350°) about 60 minutes, or until golden brown. Baste frequently with melted butter while baking.

BEEF-FILLED PANCAKES

Husband-endorsed and company-approved dish from a California ranch hostess—good and hearty

Thin Pancakes:

3 eggs, beaten
1 c. milk
1 c. sifted flour
1 tblsp. sugar
2 tblsp. melted butter
⅛ tsp. salt

Filling:

2½ c. lean ground beef
1 medium onion, chopped
1 (4 oz.) can sliced mushrooms
2 tblsp. butter
¼ tsp. salt
1 tsp. dry mustard
½ c. ketchup
1 tblsp. steak sauce
½ tsp. dried parsley
½ tsp. dried rosemary
½ tsp. orégano
1 bay leaf, crumbled
2 c. shredded Cheddar cheese
1 c. grated Parmesan cheese
½ c. milk
6 thin slices mozzarella cheese

• To make pancakes, mix together ingredients in the order listed; blend until smooth. For each pancake, melt 1 tsp. butter in a heated 7″ skillet; add ¼ c. batter, tipping pan so batter spreads evenly.

• When batter is set, turn the pancake. Spread pancakes on clean towels; cool. Makes 8 large pancakes.

• To make filling, sauté beef, onion and mushrooms in butter; add remaining ingredients except cheese and milk. Simmer gently 15 minutes. Layer Cheddar and Parmesan cheese over the top. Heat until cheese is almost melted, but do not stir. Spoon off excess fat.

• Spread filling on pancakes; roll up and place in a 13 × 9 × 2" baking pan. Pour milk over the rolls and cover with mozzarella cheese.

• Bake, uncovered, in hot oven (400°) 20 minutes, or until hot and cheese melts. Makes 8 servings.

Southern Company Special: Cornmeal Griddle Cakes with Lacy Edges

The Southern hostess knows she can please guests with small, delicate, lacy-edged cornmeal griddle cakes. She often stacks these thin, hot batter cakes and tops them with country ham and oysters, or chicken or turkey hash. Other times she serves them with fried chicken alongside or with melted butter and honey or a sweet syrup.

Her important rule is to serve really hot cakes with really hot food spooned over them. You can bake and stack the cakes on baking sheets and place them in a very slow oven (200°). It's a good idea to cover them with a damp towel to prevent their drying out. Be sure to warm the serving plates.

Here's a basic recipe for Lacy-Edged Batter Cakes from a Virginia hostess, a home economist, along with directions for fixing Ham and Panned Oysters, a much-enjoyed topping. The recipes make 5 servings, but you can double them if you like. We also give you the recipe for a famous Southern chicken or turkey hash that's excellent on hot batter cakes. Also wonderfully good served on hot, crusty biscuits.

LACY-EDGED BATTER CAKES

Bake small griddle cakes; stack them high and serve them piping hot

2 c. white cornmeal
1 tblsp. baking powder
1 tblsp. sugar
1 tsp. salt
2 eggs, beaten
3 c. milk
4 tblsp. melted butter or margarine

• Sift cornmeal, baking powder, sugar and salt together.

• Combine eggs, milk and butter. Add to dry ingredients and blend thoroughly.

• Drop 2 tblsp. batter on a medium-hot greased griddle to make 4" cakes. Brown on both sides. To prevent cakes sticking to griddle and to make the edges lacy, add ½ tsp. or more bacon drippings or other fat to the griddle for each new baking.

• Serve hot. Makes about 30 (4") cakes, or 5 stacks, each containing 6 cakes.

HAM-OYSTER BATTER CAKES SUPREME

Ham: Cut 5 thin round slices ham (highly flavored cured ham is best). Remove most of the fat. Heat thoroughly in broiler, heavy skillet or griddle.

Panned Oysters: Drain 1 qt. oysters. Combine 2 tblsp. butter or margarine, 1 tblsp. Worcestershire sauce and ½ tsp. celery salt in heavy skillet over low heat.

• Add drained oysters and cook only until edges curl. Turn often and *do not overcook.* Top with generous sprinkling of paprika to add a touch of color to oysters and pan drippings. Drain, reserving juices. Makes 5 servings.

To Make Batter Cakes Supreme: For each serving, stack 6 Lacy-Edged Batter Cakes on a *warm* plate. Cover with hot ham slice. Top with Panned Oysters, covering ham. Spoon on a little of the heated pan juices. Garnish with parsley, lemon slices and fresh tomato quarters.
• Pass melted butter and extra pan juices to ladle over.

COUNTRY CHICKEN OR TURKEY HASH

Serve over a stack of 6 batter cakes for a memorable company main dish

4 tblsp. butter or margarine
½ c. chopped celery
¼ c. grated or finely minced onion
4 tblsp. flour
1 qt. chicken or turkey stock
3 c. diced chicken or turkey
Salt and pepper to taste

• Sauté celery and onion in butter in large skillet until soft. Stir in flour; mix until smooth. Add stock and stir until mixture is blended.
• Add diced meat and cook 10 to 15 minutes or until mixture is thick and well blended. Add seasonings if stock is unseasoned. Makes 4 to 5 cups, about 8 servings.

Make disposable ashtrays for large crowds from layers of heavy-duty aluminum foil. Use an ashtray as mold.

APPLE CORN CAKES

These hotcakes are twice as good when served with spiced applesauce and butter

1 egg, slightly beaten
2 tblsp. salad oil
1 c. buttermilk
1 c. cornmeal
½ tsp. baking soda
½ tsp. salt
1 tblsp. sugar
1 c. chopped peeled apples

• Stir together the egg, salad oil and buttermilk. Sift together the cornmeal, baking soda, salt and sugar; blend in the egg mixture. Add the apples.
• Bake on a preheated, lightly greased griddle. Makes about 20 (2″) cakes.

SHRIMP GRIDDLE CAKES

Imaginative—shrimp combined with pancakes. Add chopped shrimp to the batter and bake; serve with Quick Tomato Sauce

2 (4½ oz.) cans shrimp
1¾ c. sifted flour
1 tblsp. baking powder
¼ tsp. salt
1½ tsp. curry powder
¼ tsp. pepper
2 eggs, beaten
1⅓ c. milk
⅓ c. salad oil
Quick Tomato Sauce

• Rinse shrimp with cold water; drain. Chop coarsely.
• Sift dry ingredients together; stir in eggs, milk, salad oil and shrimp.
• Bake on a preheated, lightly greased griddle. Serve hot with Quick Tomato Sauce. Makes 15 (4″) cakes.

Quick Tomato Sauce: Blend 1 can condensed cream of tomato soup, ¼ c. butter and ½ c. light cream. Heat until butter melts. Serve in bowl or gravy boat for ladling over Shrimp Griddle Cakes.

VARIATIONS

Tuna Griddle Cakes: Substitute 1 (7 oz.) can tuna for the shrimp. Drain tuna and flake with a fork.

Chicken Griddle Cakes: Substitute 1 (5½ oz.) can boned chicken for the shrimp.

Store heavy glass cake plates and other special-occasion platters in a dish drainer. They won't chip so easily. And you can readily select those you want to use.

New-Fashioned Bread Crumb Pancakes

Today's clever hostess occasionally revives old-time country favorites to the enjoyment of her friends. Pancakes made with batter partly thickened and delicately flavored with bread crumbs are a good example.

Recipes for these griddle cakes are scarce now, but here is an heirloom revised in our Test Kitchens. Try it when you want pancakes that are somewhat different, and really good. Serve the first cakes hot, lightly buttered and with something tasty to spoon over—creamed dried beef, chicken or tuna, for instance. Then provide something sweet for the last pancakes, to take the place of dessert. This might be sparkling jellies and jams, a jar of honey or a pitcher of

maple or other sweet syrup. And do keep the coffee cups filled.

BREAD CRUMB PANCAKES

Bread crumbs, white or whole wheat, help thicken and flavor these cakes

1 c. flour
½ tsp. salt
1 tblsp. baking powder
1 tsp. sugar
4 slices white bread, or 3 slices whole wheat bread, one day old
2 eggs, separated
1 ⅓ c. milk
3 tblsp. melted butter

• Sift together flour, salt, baking powder and sugar. Add the bread, torn into fine crumbs.
• Beat egg yolks and milk together; stir into dry ingredients along with butter.
• Beat egg whites until soft peaks form. Gently fold into bread mixture.
• Bake on a preheated, lightly greased griddle. Serve hot. Makes about 15 (4") cakes.

Treat Guests to Doughnuts and Coffee

You're always ready for friends to stop by for coffee, a Colorado ranch woman says, when you have homemade raised doughnuts waiting in the freezer. She says they're a marvelous breakfast pickup when there's company, too.

We give you recipes for two kinds. Both are exceptionally light, and both are excellent coffee companions. Spudnuts, as their name implies, contain mashed potatoes. It's the shape of Square Doughnuts that first attracts the eye; the raisins are a pleasant surprise.

SQUARE DOUGHNUTS

Talk-of-the-coffee-crowd doughnuts

¾ c. milk
¼ c. sugar
1 tsp. salt
¼ c. butter or margarine
¼ c. lukewarm water (105–15°)
1 pkg. active dry yeast
1 egg, beaten
3¼ to 3½ c. unsifted flour

• Scald milk; stir in sugar, salt and butter. Cool until lukewarm.
• Measure lukewarm water into a large warm mixing bowl (warm by rinsing out bowl with hot water). Sprinkle in the yeast and stir until yeast dissolves.
• Add lukewarm milk mixture, egg and half of the flour. Beat until smooth. Stir in enough of remaining flour to make a soft dough. For lightness, add only enough flour to make a dough you can handle.
• Turn dough onto a lightly floured board or pastry cloth. Knead until smooth and elastic, about 5 to 10 minutes. (If dough sticks to the hands, grease them lightly with shortening or oil.)
• Place dough in a greased bowl, then turn the bottom side up. Cover with a damp cloth; let rise in a warm place until doubled, about 1 hour.
• Punch down dough. On a lightly floured surface, roll about ½" thick to make a rectangle 12 × 10". With a sharp knife, cut in 2½" squares

(cut in rounds if you prefer round doughnuts); cut holes in centers with a 1" cutter or bottletop. Place doughnuts on oiled baking sheets or waxed paper, about 2" apart. Cover with inverted baking pans (allow room for dough to rise), or with a cloth. Let rise until doubled, about 1 hour.
• About 15 minutes before end of rising period, heat fat in deep fryer or electric skillet to 375°. (You will be more confident of temperature if you use a deep fat frying thermometer.)
• Handle the dougnuts as gently as possible so they will not fall. Fry them, a few at a time, in deep fat 2 to 3 minutes, or until brown on both sides. Turn doughnuts only once. Drain them on absorbent paper; dip while still warm, in a glaze or granulated sugar. (You can fry the center cutouts.) Makes about 20 doughnuts.

VARIATION

Raisin Doughnuts: Follow the recipe for Square Doughnuts, except use 2 pkgs. active dry yeast instead of 1 pkg., and stir in 1 c. chopped raisins with the first half of the flour. The dough may rise a little more slowly.

GLAZES FOR DOUGHNUTS

Vanilla Glaze: Blend 2 c. confectioners sugar, ⅓ c. milk and 1 tsp. vanilla. Dip warm doughnuts into glaze and drain them on a rack over waxed paper. Reuse the glaze that drips off.

Spicy Glaze: Make like Vanilla Glaze, but omit the vanilla and add ½ tsp. cinnamon and ¼ tsp. nutmeg.

Orange Glaze: Follow recipe for Vanilla Glaze, but omit vanilla and substitute orange juice for milk.

To Glaze Doughnuts: Dip warm doughnuts in glaze and drain them on cooling racks over waxed paper. You can reuse the glaze that falls onto the waxed paper.

To Sugar Doughnuts: Drop drained, warm doughnuts into a paper bag of sugar and shake to coat. Or add 2 tsp. cinnamon to each ½ c. sugar when coating doughnuts.

COLORADO SPUDNUTS

Keep some of these potato doughnuts in the freezer to serve with coffee. They'll thaw while you make the coffee, or you can heat them

1 ¾ c. milk
½ c. shortening
½ c. sugar
½ c. mashed potatoes
1 pkg. active dry yeast
½ c. warm water (105–15°)
2 eggs, beaten
½ tsp. vanilla
6½ to 7 c. sifted flour
1 tsp. baking powder
2 tsp. salt

• Scald milk; stir in shortening, sugar and mashed potatoes. Cool to lukewarm (90°). Blend well. Sprinkle yeast over warm water and stir until yeast is dissolved. Add to lukewarm mixture. Stir in beaten eggs and vanilla.

• Sift 6½ c. flour with the baking powder and salt; add gradually to the lukewarm mixture. Mix well after each addition. Add another ½ c. flour if needed to make a *soft* dough you can handle (use no more than necessary). Turn into a greased bowl, then turn bottom side up. Cover and let rise in a warm place until doubled, about 1½ hours.

• Roll to ½″ thickness on a floured board or pastry cloth. Cut with floured doughnut cutter, reserving centers to make Pecan Rolls (recipe follows).

• Place cut-out doughnuts on waxed paper; cover with a cloth and let rise in warm place until doubled, about ½ hour.

• Fry a few doughnuts at a time in oil or fat heated to 375°. Drain on absorbent paper. Spread warm doughnuts with a thin glaze made of confectioners sugar and milk, or shake them in a bag containing sugar to coat them. Makes about 4 dozen.

Pecan Rolls from Spudnut Centers: Lightly grease 12 medium-size (2½″) muffin-pan cups. In the bottom of each cup, place 1 tsp. brown sugar, 1 tsp. light corn syrup, ½ tsp. water, 3 pecan halves and 3 or 4 raisins. Arrange 4 doughnut centers on top, cover with a cloth and let rise in a warm place until doubled, about ½ hour. Bake in moderate oven (350°) 25 to 30 minutes.

OVERNIGHT YEAST WAFFLES

Double recipe to make waffles for a crowd—the yeasty flavor is different

2 c. milk
½ c. warm water (105–15°)
1 pkg. active dry yeast
⅓ c. melted butter or margarine
1 tsp. salt
1 tsp. sugar
3 c. sifted flour
2 eggs
½ tsp. baking soda

• Scald milk; cool to lukewarm. Put

water in large bowl; sprinkle in yeast. Stir until yeast is dissolved.

· Add milk, butter, salt, sugar and flour; mix thoroughly with rotary beater until batter is smooth. Cover and let stand at room temperature overnight.

· When ready to bake, add eggs and baking soda. Beat well. Cook on waffle iron. Makes 6 to 8 waffles.

Teatime Open-Face Sandwiches

Tiny sandwiches for the tea party are so pretty that the work involved in making them is rewarding. Open-face sandwiches are especially attractive. Butter single slices of bread, crusts removed, and cut them in small, fancy shapes with a sharp knife or cookie cutters. Spread on one side with the filling, then garnish.

You don't need recipes for these fancies, but here are a few suggestions; they indicate how simple teatime sandwiches can be:

· Spread with currant, or other red jelly, and sprinkle with flaked coconut.

· Arrange thin slices pimiento-stuffed olives on small rounds of buttered bread. Put a little snipped parsley in the center.

· Spread bread with your favorite cheese spread; roll edges of sandwiches in finely snipped chives or parsley.

· Place small, thin cucumber slice on buttered rounds of bread; ring with thin red radish slice, cut in half.

· Spread half of sandwich with pineapple-cheese spread, the other half with deviled ham or jelly.

CUCUMBER SANDWICHES

American version of classic English teatime treat made with cucumbers

· With a very sharp knife, cut off both ends of long unsliced buns (Coney buns). Then carefully slice the buns thin. Spread one side of each slice with butter and then with mayonnaise. Cut a cucumber, peeled or unpeeled, as you like, in thin slices. Let stand in ice water until crisp. Drain and dry on towels. Place a cucumber slice between two slices of bread. If you have cucumbers in your garden, try to select them with the same diameter as that of the sliced rolls. If cucumber slices are too large, trim them to fit.

CUCUMBER-CHEESE SANDWICHES

Colorful open-face teatime sandwiches. They're small—dainty two-bite size

2 (3 oz.) pkgs. cream cheese
¼ c. milk
2 tsp. garlic salad dressing mix
48 slices cocktail rye bread
2 cucumbers
12 pimiento-stuffed olives

· Place cream cheese in small bowl; stir to soften. Add milk and salad dressing mix. Stir in mix thoroughly.

· Spread cheese mixture on little rye bread slices.

· Score chilled cucumbers with tines of fork and cut in thin slices. Cut olives crosswise, each in 4 slices.

· Lay cucumber slices on sandwiches and top with olive slices. Chill or serve at once, spread on tray or large plate or platter. Makes 4 dozen sandwiches.

VARIATION

Danish Cucumber-Cheese Sandwiches:
Substitute 6 tblsp. dairy sour cream
for the milk and blue cheese salad
dressing mix for the garlic.

COMPANY CINNAMON TOAST

Quick to fix when guests drop in—
it's rich, golden, luscious, tempting

6 slices bread, 1" thick
6 tblsp. sugar
2 tblsp. cinnamon
⅔ c. heavy cream
4 tblsp. melted butter or
   margarine

• Cut off crusts and cut each bread
slice in 3 strips.
• Mix sugar and cinnamon together in
a shallow dish. Pour the cream into
another shallow dish.
• Dip bread strips in cream to coat
both sides. Brush strip tops with butter; sprinkle all sides with the sugar-
cinnamon mixture to make a thick
covering.
• Place bread strips on rack in a
shallow baking pan. Bake in hot oven
(400°) 20 minutes. Serve hot. Makes
18 strips.

Toast for Company: *Spread warm*
toast slices liberally with dairy sour
cream and spoon on strawberry, cherry
or apricot jam. Try this on French
toast for a real treat.

Here's how to make a scallop trim on
party sandwiches. Cut stuffed olives
in half lengthwise; then cut in cross-
wise slices. Arrange slices, rounded
side out, around the edge of open-face
sandwiches.

YUGOSLAV KIFLE

These delicacies are yeast-leavened, a
cross between cookies and bread

2 c. sifted flour
½ tsp. salt
1 pkg. compressed yeast
½ c. butter
2 egg yolks, slightly beaten
½ c. dairy sour cream
1 egg white
¼ c. sugar
½ tsp. vanilla
½ c. finely chopped nuts
Confectioners sugar

• Sift flour with salt into large bowl.
Crumble in yeast. Cut in butter with
pastry blender or two knives. Add
egg yolks and sour cream. (If mixture
is crumbly, mix with your hand in
bowl until mixture cleans the bowl.)
• Turn out onto lightly floured board
and knead 5 minutes. Divide dough
into 4 equal parts and chill at least
1 hour.
• Meanwhile make filling by beating
egg white until stiff. Beat in sugar
and vanilla. Fold in chopped nuts.
• Sprinkle pastry board or cloth with
confectioners sugar and roll each ball
of dough to make a 10" circle. Cut
each circle in 8 wedges. Place 1 scant
tsp. filling on the wide end of each
wedge and roll up.
• Place on greased baking sheet, with
pointed end of roll on bottom. Bake
in moderate oven (375°) until lightly
browned, 20 to 25 minutes. Remove
hot rolls from baking sheet to rack
and dust with confectioners sugar.
Wonderful for tea and coffee parties.
Makes 32.

Note: Spread with confectioners sugar
frosting if you prefer.

CHEESE SANDWICH SPREAD

Recipe comes in handy to make hot sandwiches for unexpected guests.

2 tblsp. butter
1 tblsp. flour
1 c. milk
2 tblsp. sugar
⅛ tsp. pepper
1 tsp. dry mustard
2 egg yolks, slightly beaten
¾ lb. pasteurized process
      American cheese, grated
1 (4 oz.) can pimientos, drained
      and finely chopped
½ c. finely chopped dill pickles
1 tblsp. vinegar

• Melt butter in top of double boiler. Stir in flour; blend in milk. Cook, stirring constantly, over hot water until mixture thickens slightly, about 7 minutes. Blend hot mixture into sugar, pepper, dry mustard and beaten egg yolks. Stir in cheese. Cook, stirring occasionally, for 10 minutes, or until cheese melts and mixture thickens. Remove from heat; stir vigorously until spread is smooth. Stir in remaining ingredients. Refrigerate. Makes about 3½ cups.

VARIATIONS

Toasted Ham-Cheese Sandwiches: Spread about 1 tblsp. Cheese Sandwich Spread on a slice of bread; top with slice of cold ham and another slice of cheese-coated bread. Dip in this mixture: Beat together 2 eggs, 2 tblsp. milk and 1 tsp. prepared mustard (enough dip for 6 sandwiches). Brown sandwiches in butter.

Tuna-Egg Sandwiches: Combine ½ c. Cheese Sandwich Spread, ¼ c. mayonnaise, 1 (7 oz.) can tuna, or 1 c. finely chopped luncheon meat, and 3 hard-cooked eggs, chopped. Stir lightly to mix. Spread on 8 hamburger buns. Wrap in heavy aluminum foil. Heat in very slow oven (250°) 30 minutes.

Note: You can make sandwiches the night before for quick heating at serving time.

Hurry Sandwiches from the Oven

Mothers of teen-age youngsters like to keep sandwiches in the freezer ready to heat when the gang arrives hungry after skating or a game. Here are four examples of such sandwiches that will keep in the freezer up to 2 weeks. They're the kind young people like.

You'd better fix an extra sandwich for the man of the house, for men give these hot, hearty sandwiches their unstinted approval. Or serve them to grown-up guests who come over for an evening of cards or visiting.

BROILED TUNA SANDWICHES

Fun to serve for informal suppers. Increase recipe to fit size of crowd

6 hamburger buns
Butter or margarine, softened
1 (6½ or 7 oz.) can tuna,
      drained and flaked
1 c. cubed sharp Cheddar
      cheese
¼ c. diced green pepper
2 tblsp. minced onion
½ c. mayonnaise

• Spread split hamburger buns with

butter. Mix remaining ingredients. Spread mixture on cut sides of buns.
• (Freeze if desired in airtight wrap. Defrost 1 hour in wrap.)
• Place unwrapped buns, tuna side up, on baking sheet. Broil until hot and golden, about 5 minutes. Makes 6 servings.

HOT MEAT AND CHEESE DOGS

Fix ahead to bake after the gang arrives—a favorite with men and boys

8 Coney buns (long)
Butter or margarine, softened
1 (12 oz.) can luncheon meat, diced
½ c. diced process cheese spread
2 tblsp. pickle relish
3 tblsp. minced onion
1 tsp. poppy seeds
2 tsp. prepared mustard
2 tblsp. melted butter or margarine

• Spread buns with softened butter. Mix remaining ingredients and spoon into buttered buns. Wrap individually in foil.
• (Freeze if desired. Defrost 1 hour in foil.)
• Place foil-wrapped buns on baking sheet; heat in slow oven (300°) 20 minutes. Makes 8 servings.

BOLOGNA-CHEESE SUBMARINES

Easy way to please teen-age guests. Serve in foil so they'll stay hot

10 Coney buns (long)
Butter or margarine, softened
1 lb. bologna, ground
1 c. grated sharp Cheddar cheese
1 medium onion, chopped

⅓ c. sweet pickle relish, well drained
¼ c. prepared mustard
2 tblsp. mayonnaise

• Spread buns with butter. Combine remaining ingredients; spoon into buns.
• Wrap each bun in a piece of foil.
• (Freeze if desired. Defrost 1 hour in foil or place in oven, frozen.)
• Place foil-wrapped buns in slow oven (300°) 30 minutes. (If frozen, bake a total of 50 minutes.) Makes 10 servings.

PIZZA LOAF

Here's a new sandwich with the pizza look and taste. Serve it to company

1 long loaf French bread (1 lb.), or 4 long Italian rolls
Butter or margarine, softened
¾ lb. ground beef
½ c. grated Parmesan cheese
½ tsp. dried orégano leaves
1 tsp. salt
⅛ tsp. pepper
1½ tsp. minced onion
1½ (6 oz.) cans tomato paste
¼ c. sliced olives (optional)
2 ripe tomatoes, thinly sliced
8 slices process American cheese

• Cut bread loaf or rolls in halves lengthwise. Spread with butter.
• Combine beef, Parmesan cheese, seasonings, onion, tomato paste and olives. Spread mixture on cut sides of bread loaf or rolls.
• (If freezing for later use, cut each half loaf into good-size servings; wrap in foil or freezer wrap. Freeze. Defrost 1½ hours in wrap.)

· Place unwrapped loaves or servings, meat side up, on baking sheet. Top with tomato slices.

· Bake in moderate oven (350°) 20 minutes. Remove from oven; top with cheese slices. Return to oven until cheese is melted, about 5 minutes. Makes 8 to 10 servings.

CHAPTER 6

COUNTRY-BEST CAKES, COOKIES AND PIES

Country cakes, cookies and pies take an important place in hostesses' company meals. Many of the recipes in this chapter are country-kitchen originals like your mother and grandmother made. Home economists in our Test Kitchens brought them up to date, adapting them to today's ingredients and improved mixing methods without losing the exciting, memorable tastes of yesterday.

The cakes vary from the elaborate three-layer beauty queens, like Orange Butter and Fudge-Lemon cakes, to simple pudding cakes like Pumpkin, Rhubarb and Apple. Our Flower Wedding Cake (in chapter on Cooking for a Crowd) tastes as good as it looks—something not true of all wedding cakes. We want to call special attention to the dress-up toppings for angel food cakes. They add glamour and good flavor.

This chapter answers your questions about what cookies to bake for the Christmas cookie exchange, and for picnics. Nut-Crested Cookie Squares look like candy, but you bake them; they are praise-winners. For picnics, you'll have to search a long time for cookies that equal Best-Ever Butterscotch and Ranch House Raisin Cookies—similar to Boiled Raisin Cookies that Grandpa used to rave about. You'll want to keep some of the dough for Oatmeal Crisps in the refrigerator to bake and serve hot to guests who stop by to visit.

Most country hostesses tell us that homemade pies are their favorite company dessert. Many of our best pie recipes appear in *Farm Journal's Complete Pie Cookbook,* which you no doubt have. You'll find some new pie recipes in this chapter, however. Strawberry Satin Pie is almost too beautiful to eat, but it's too delicious to pass up. Spicy Apple Crunch Pie is something new and tasty in apple pies. Black and White Date Pie, the specialty of an Iowa farm woman who is a gracious hostess, is perfect with coffee for wintry evening refreshments.

Beautiful Butter Cakes

Many farm hostesses use packaged cake mixes, but most of them also bake butter cakes frequently, often for special occasions. We asked a country woman, famed among her friends for excellent butter cakes, why she sometimes bakes cakes "from scratch" when she entertains. Here's what she said: "They're getting to be unusual—they're not the same kind of cakes most everyone bakes. And they do have that heavenly butter flavor that can't be surpassed." Then she added: "I'm not saying they're better than all of the mix or other from-scratch cakes made with vegetable shortening, which I also bake, but butter cakes taste different. That I know."

Among the recipes for country butter cakes that follow are a couple of elegant three-layer cakes, Orange Butter and Fudge-Lemon, similar to the tall, glamorous cakes that once graced tables in Southern plantation homes. Their exquisite flavors match their beauty.

ORANGE BUTTER CAKE

Pineapple filling goes between cake layers and on top; whipped cream covers sides of this country treat

1 c. soft butter (room temperature)
2 c. sugar
4 eggs
3 c. sifted flour
3 tsp. baking powder
¼ tsp. baking soda
½ tsp. salt
1 c. milk
¼ c. orange juice
1 tsp. vanilla
1 tblsp. grated orange peel
Pineapple Filling

• Cream butter and sugar; beat in eggs one at a time.
• Sift dry ingredients together; add alternately with the remaining ingredients, except filling, to creamed mixture. (Do not pour orange juice and milk into the same cup.)
• Pour batter into 3 (9") paper-lined round layer cake pans. Bake in moderate oven (350°) about 35 minutes.
• Cool on rack about 5 minutes before removing from pans; complete cooling on wire racks. Put cooled layers together with Pineapple Filling. Spread filling on top of cake. Frost the sides with whipped cream.

PINEAPPLE FILLING

Orange and pineapple combination results in a flavor that complements the cake

¼ c. cornstarch
1 c. sugar
3 tblsp. orange juice
1 tsp. grated orange peel
½ c. butter
1 (1 lb. 4 oz.) can crushed pineapple, undrained

• Combine cornstarch, sugar and orange juice in saucepan. Stir in orange peel, butter and pineapple. Cook over low heat until thick and glossy; stir constantly.
• Cool before spreading on cake.

FUDGE-LEMON CAKE

High, handsome, rich, firm-textured

½ c. soft butter
2 c. sugar
4 eggs
4 squares unsweetened
      chocolate, melted
2 c. sifted flour
1 tsp. salt
2 tsp. baking powder
1¼ c. milk
2 tsp. vanilla
Chocolate-Lemon Frosting

• Cream butter and sugar until light and fluffy. Beat in eggs, one at a time. Add melted chocolate and blend.
• Sift dry ingredients together; add alternately with milk and vanilla to the creamed mixture.
• Grease the sides of 3 (9") round layer cake pans; dust with cocoa. Line bottoms of pans with ungreased paper. Divide batter evenly between the pans.
• Bake in moderate oven (350°) about 30 minutes, or until the cake is done.
• Cool on wire racks about 5 minutes; remove from pans and cool completely on racks. Frost with Chocolate-Lemon Frosting.

CHOCOLATE-LEMON FROSTING

Unusual lemon-chocolate flavor team turns cake into a fabulous dessert

½ c. soft butter
4 c. sifted confectioners sugar
3 squares sweet cooking
      chocolate, melted
1 egg
1 tsp. vanilla (optional)
¼ tsp. salt

Grated peel from 1 lemon (about
   1 tblsp.)
1 c. chopped nuts

• Cream butter with 1 c. confectioners sugar, melted chocolate and egg.
• Add 3 c. confectioners sugar, vanilla, salt and lemon peel. Beat until smooth. If frosting is too thick to spread, add a little milk. Stir in the nuts.
• Spread between cake layers and on top of the cake. Decorate with shaved chocolate pieces.

FUDGE CAKE

Guests praise this cake—a 5-star recipe reprinted from our Country Cookbook

¾ c. butter or margarine
2¼ c. sugar
1½ tsp. vanilla
3 eggs
3 (1 oz.) squares unsweetened
      chocolate, melted
3 c. sifted cake flour
1½ tsp. baking soda
¾ tsp. salt
1½ c. ice water

• Cream butter, sugar and vanilla with mixer. Add eggs, beating until light and fluffy. Add melted chocolate and blend well.
• Sift together dry ingredients; add alternately with water to chocolate mixture. Pour batter into three 8" layer pans which have been greased and lined with waxed paper. Bake in moderate oven (350°) 30 to 35 minutes. Cool. Put layers together with Date Cream Filling. Frost with Fudge Frosting.

DATE CREAM FILLING

1   c. milk
½   c. chopped dates
1   tblsp. flour
¼   c. sugar
1   egg, beaten
½   c. chopped nuts
1   tsp. vanilla

• Combine milk and dates in top of a double boiler.
• Combine flour and sugar and add beaten egg, blending until smooth. Add to hot milk. Cook, stirring, until thick. Cool.
• Stir in nuts and vanilla. Spread between layers.

FUDGE FROSTING

2   c. sugar
1   c. light cream
2   (1 oz.) squares unsweetened
        chocolate, grated

• Combine all ingredients in a heavy saucepan. Boil over high heat 3 minutes without stirring. Reduce heat and continue cooking until it reaches soft ball stage (234°). Cool.
• Beat until creamy and of spreading consistency. Add cream if too thick.
• Spread on sides of cake first and a little over the top edge; frost top last. Makes 8 to 10 servings.

MARBLED POUND CAKE

Cocoa makes this rich, moist cake taste different—no frosting needed

1 ¼ c. soft butter
2 ½ c. sugar
 5   eggs
2 ½ c. sifted flour
1 ¼ tsp. baking powder
 ½   tsp. salt

1   c. less 2 tblsp. milk
2   tsp. vanilla
¼   c. cocoa, sifted
Confectioners sugar

• Cream butter; gradually add sugar and beat until light and fluffy. Beat in eggs, one at a time, creaming well after each addition.
• Sift together flour, baking powder and salt. Add them alternately with the milk and vanilla to the creamed mixture.
• Take out 2 c. cake batter and blend the cocoa into it.
• Alternately spoon the light and chocolate batters into a greased and floured 10″ tube pan or a 10″ cast aluminum bundt-cake pan.
• Bake in slow oven (325°) 70 minutes for a 10″ tube pan, or 90 minutes for the heavier, bundt-cake pan, or until cake tests done.
• Cool in pan about 10 minutes. Invert cake on wire rack and remove the pan. Cool cake thoroughly. Sift on confectioners sugar.

BROWN MOUNTAIN CAKE

Perfect picnic loaf cake—easy to tote, slices neatly and tastes wonderful

1   c. soft butter
2   c. sugar
3   eggs
3   c. sifted flour
1   tsp. baking soda
½   tsp. salt
3   tblsp. cocoa
1   c. buttermilk
1   tsp. vanilla
½   c. warm water

• Cream butter and sugar until light and fluffy. Beat in the eggs, one at a time. Sift together the flour, baking

soda, salt and cocoa; add alternately with buttermilk to the creamed mixture. Stir in vanilla and warm water.
• Pour batter into a lightly greased and floured 13 × 9 × 2″ baking pan. Bake in moderate oven (350°) about 45 minutes, or until the cake tests done.
• Cool cake on rack. Frost with Chocolate Fudge Frosting or your favorite chocolate frosting.

Note: If you do not have buttermilk, use soured milk. Put 1 tblsp. vinegar into a 1-cup measuring cup and fill with sweet milk. Let stand a few minutes.

CHOCOLATE FUDGE FROSTING

No need trying to improve on this old-time treat—it's candy-good

2	squares unsweetened chocolate
1 ½	c. sugar
1 ½	tblsp. light corn syrup
⅛	tsp. salt
½	c. milk
½	c. butter
1	tsp. vanilla

• Combine chocolate, sugar, corn syrup, salt and milk in a medium saucepan. Cook over low heat; stir until the sugar dissolves and the chocolate melts.
• Bring to the boiling point over medium heat, stirring occasionally.
• Reduce heat to low and simmer, without stirring, to the soft ball stage (234°). If you test for doneness by dropping mixture into cold water, remove saucepan from heat to avoid overcooking.
• Remove from heat; add butter without stirring and cool until lukewarm

(110° on candy thermometer), or until bottom of pan feels lukewarm.
• Add vanilla and beat with spoon or portable electric mixer at medium speed until the frosting is creamy and barely holds its shape. Do not overbeat. (If frosting gets too stiff while beating, gradually add a little milk. If frosting gets too stiff while you are spreading it on the cake, set the saucepan in warm water to soften it.) Makes enough to frost a 13 × 9 × 2″ cake. To frost 8 or 9″ two-layer cake, double all ingredients except chocolate and vanilla, and use 3 squares chocolate and 1 tsp. vanilla. Cook frosting in a large 3-qt. saucepan.

Poppy Seed Cake— A Conversation Piece

One of the fascinations of American cookery is the many influences from other nations' kitchens. Most of them traveled across the seas with immigrants, who came to make new homes in the United States. The treasured recipes are handed from one generation to another and become heirlooms, but each generation makes adaptations. This recipe for Poppy Seed Cake is a good example.

Originally, this was a Czechoslovakian treat; now some of today's Americans add chocolate to the frosting. The homemaker and county extension home economist who contributes this recipe says the slightly bitter chocolate flavor complements the cake's sweetness.

The trick in making a cake containing poppy seeds is to keep the seeds evenly distributed in the layers during the baking. In this cake, the crunchy seeds stay where they belong, dotting the white layers with blue-black. It's work to make this cake, but worth the effort for a special occasion. Either freeze it or keep in the refrigerator until serving time so the fluffy whipped cream will stay in place.

POPPY SEED CAKE

This special-occasion cake is crunchy with poppy seeds—extra delicious

¾	c. milk
¾	c. poppy seeds
2¼	c. sifted flour
4	tsp. baking powder
½	tsp. salt
1½	c. sugar
½	c. vegetable shortening
1	tsp. vanilla
½	c. milk
3	large egg whites

Chocolate Whipped Cream
    Frosting

• Pour ¾ c. milk over poppy seeds; let stand in refrigerator overnight.

• Sift together flour, baking powder and salt.

• Cream sugar and shortening until light and fluffy. Add vanilla.

• Alternately add soaked poppy seed mixture, flour mixture and ½ c. milk to the creamed shortening and sugar. Beat egg whites until they stand in soft peaks; fold gently into batter. Pour batter into 2 greased and lightly floured 9″ round layer cake pans.

• Bake in moderate oven (350°) 30 minutes, or until cake tests done with cake tester or wooden pick. Cool 10 minutes in pans. Turn onto racks and complete cooling. When cool, spread Chocolate Whipped Cream Frosting between layers and on the sides and top of cake. Refrigerate until time to serve.

Chocolate Whipped Cream Frosting: Combine ½ c. sugar, ⅓ c. cocoa and 1½ c. heavy cream. Chill 1 hour or longer. Beat until stiff. Makes enough frosting to spread between cake layers and frost sides and top of a 2-layer 9″ cake.

VARIATION

Bohemian Poppy Seed Cake: Instead of putting layers together with Chocolate Whipped Cream Frosting, use Cream Filling. Then frost top and sides of cake with Chocolate Whipped Cream Frosting.

Cream Filling: (You'll use ¾ c. milk to make this.) Dissolve 1 tblsp. cornstarch in a little of the milk. Add remaining milk, ¼ c. plus 2 tblsp. sugar and 2 egg yolks, beaten. Beat slightly; cook slowly until mixture becomes thick. Remove from heat; add ½ c. chopped nut meats and ½ tsp. vanilla. Cool. Spread between cake layers.

Cakes Delicious with Fruit

When fruits and cake batters get together in country mixing bowls, something wonderful happens—delicious-tasting cakes. No one will insist that they are the world's best looking cakes, but neither does anyone underestimate their flavor, compared with more impressive layers and loaves.

We give you several recipes for

these cakes, to which apples, raisins, dates, prunes, pineapple and figs contribute their flavors. Nuts, too, are in many of them, usually pecans or walnuts.

From one end of the country to the other come these treasured recipes— prune cakes from California, apple cakes from Washington and fig cake from Alabama, for instance.

After you try these recipes, they'll become your treasures, too. They're that good. Lucky are the friends whom you invite to dinner, when you cut and serve them one of these farm specials.

AUTUMN FESTIVAL CAKE

A marvelous apple cake—ideal to have on hand for Thanksgiving house guests. Crisp topping bakes with cake

1   c. butter
¾   c. brown sugar, firmly
        packed
¾   c. sugar
4   eggs
1   c. grated peeled apples
1½ tsp. vanilla
1½ tsp. almond extract
2½ c. sifted flour
1½ tsp. baking powder
1   tsp. salt
2   tsp. nutmeg
½   tsp. mace
1   c. walnuts, chopped
1   c. raisins
1   tblsp. flour
¼   c. walnuts, chopped
2   tblsp. brown sugar

• Cream butter and sugars together until light and fluffy. Beat in eggs, one at a time. Beat in apples and flavorings.
• Sift together 2½ c. flour, baking powder, salt, nutmeg and mace; gradually blend into apple mixture.
• Comine 1 c. walnuts, raisins and 1 tblsp. flour, and mix into batter.
• Spoon into a well-greased 9″ tube pan. Combine ¼ c. walnuts and 2 tblsp. brown sugar; sprinkle over the batter. Bake in slow oven (325°) 1 hour and 30 minutes.
• Remove from oven, set pan on rack and let cake cool 15 minutes. Remove cake from pan and set on rack to cool completely.

MARSHMALLOW-APPLESAUCE CAKE

You push marshmallows into the batter of this applesauce cake; they'll rise to top during baking and make the frosting

2¾ c. unsifted flour
2   c. sugar
1½ tsp. baking soda
1½ tsp. salt
¼   tsp. baking powder
1   tsp. cinnamon
½   tsp. cloves
½   tsp. allspice
½   c. soft shortening
2   eggs
2   c. unsweetened applesauce
1   c. walnut halves
¼   lb. (20) large marshmallows

• Sift together flour, sugar, soda, salt, baking powder and spices.
• Add soft shortening, eggs and applesauce. Beat until smooth and well blended.
• Stir in walnuts. Pour into greased and floured 13 × 9 × 2″ pan. Press whole marshmallows into batter to bottom of pan—in 4 rows, 5 in each row.
• Bake in moderate oven (350°) about 50 minutes. Makes 20 servings.

Cake You'll Want to Bake

Fig trees grow in the yard of the hospitable Alabama woman who shares this fig cake recipe with you. She, like many of her neighbors, cans figs when they're ripe, to extend their season through winter. She uses her home-canned figs in this cake, but we had good luck in our Test Kitchens with canned figs from supermarkets.

You can bake, fill and frost this cake several days ahead and freeze it.

DEEP SOUTH FIG CAKE

Perfect-for-company, caramel-frosted, fig-filled, two-layer spice cake

½ c. butter
1 c. sugar
2 eggs
2 c. sifted flour
1 tsp. salt
1 tsp. baking powder
½ tsp. baking soda
½ tsp. cinnamon
¼ tsp. cloves
½ c. sour milk or buttermilk
½ c. fig juice
1 tsp. vanilla
1 qt. canned or 2 (1 lb. 1 oz.)
    jars figs, drained and
    chopped
1 c. chopped pecans
Fig Filling
Caramel Frosting (see Index)

• Cream butter and sugar together until mixture is light and fluffy. Beat in eggs.

• Sift together dry ingredients. Combine milk and fig juice and add alternately with dry ingredients to the creamed butter and sugar. Beat until smooth.

• Add vanilla and fold in figs, reserving ⅔ c. to use in the filling. Stir in the pecans.

• Pour the batter into two greased 8" round layer cake pans. Bake in slow oven (325°) 1 hour, or until cake tests done. Remove from oven, cool in the pan 10 minutes and then invert cake layers on racks and cool completely. Put together with Fig Filling and frost with Caramel Frosting.

Fig Filling: Cook 1½ tsp. cornstarch with ⅓ c. fig juice until mixture is clear. Fold in ⅔ c. chopped and drained figs. Spread between layers.

Versatile Prune Cake

When one of FARM JOURNAL'S food scouts visited California recently, several people told her about the best prune cake in the Golden State. That started our search for the originator of the recipe, who turned out to be a home economist and a former prune grower (the contributor, too, of the recipe for Prune Pudding in this cookbook). She loves to entertain her friends and this cake, stored in her freezer, comes in handy.

Here is what she said about Prune Cake de Luxe: "I like the cake best unfrosted, but sometimes for variety I spread a confectioners sugar frost-

Flower Wedding Cake looks beautiful and tastes delicious. A new bride—or one celebrating her Golden Wedding Anniversary—will be proud of it. Flowers are candy-coated plastic (*recipes and directions start, page 313*).

ing on it. Often, too, I reheat the foil-wrapped cake and top the servings with vanilla ice cream, hard sauce or lemon sauce.

"At Christmas time, I add 1 to 2 cups mixed candied fruits, cut up, to the batter. I prefer this cake to traditional fruitcake. Not long ago, I had to have something hurriedly for a tea. I was thankful for the prune cake in the freezer. I cut it in 1" cubes and gently rolled them in confectioners sugar. They won many compliments from the guests."

PRUNE CAKE DE LUXE

This cake has a chocolate flavor that complements raisins and prunes

2   c. sifted flour
1   tsp. baking soda
¼   tsp. salt
2   tsp. cinnamon
1   tsp. nutmeg
¼   c. cocoa
½   c. shortening
1½ c. sugar
1   egg
2   c. pitted, cooked prunes, chopped, and juice
2   c. seedless raisins
1   c. coarsely chopped walnuts

• Sift together flour, baking soda, salt, spices and cocoa.

• Cream shortening; gradually add sugar, creaming until mixture is light and fluffy. Add unbeaten egg and beat into mixture until well blended.

• Alternately add prunes and juice (there should be at least ½ c. juice) with flour mixture to the creamed shortening, sugar and egg. Start and end with flour mixture. Add raisins and nuts.

• Bake in well-greased 13 × 9 × 2" pan in moderate oven (350°) about 1¼ hours, or until done (test with a toothpick). Let stand in pan on rack to cool, or cool 10 minutes and then remove to rack to complete cooling. Frost with confectioners sugar frosting, if desired. Makes 12 to 16 servings.

PRUNE-THATCHED CAKE

Iowa-style prune cake has fruit inside and on top, with whipped cream

¾   c. butter
1   c. sugar
2   eggs
2   c. sifted flour
1   tsp. ground cinnamon
¼   tsp. ground cloves
¾   tsp. baking powder
¾   tsp. baking soda
½   c. prune juice
1   c. chopped cooked prunes, drained
Prune Topping
Whipped cream

• Cream butter and sugar until fluffy. Add eggs and beat until light.

• Sift dry ingredients together; add to the creamed mixture alternately with prune juice. Fold in soft, chopped prunes. Spread in a greased 13 × 9 × 2" pan.

• Bake in moderate oven (350°) 45 to 50 minutes. Remove from oven and cool. Spread with Prune Topping. Crown individual servings with topknots of whipped cream. Makes 12 servings.

Here's the perfect gelatin salad to carry to potluck suppers or to set out on a buffet. Three-Row Garden Salad sparkles with color and tangy good taste. Recipe (*page 132*) calls for vegetables available most of the year.

PRUNE TOPPING

Shiny black top on cake gives rich fruit flavor and is also a fine dress-up

2 tblsp. butter
1 c. sugar
1 egg, beaten
1 tblsp. flour
1 c. chopped cooked prunes
¾ c. prune juice
⅛ tsp. salt
½ tsp. vanilla

• Combine all ingredients except vanilla. Cook over medium heat, stirring frequently, until mixture thickens (about 10 minutes). Remove from heat, add vanilla; spread on top of cake.

HARVEST PRUNE CAKE

A California prune grower's wife shares this treasured hostess recipe

½ c. shortening
1 ½ c. sugar
3 eggs
2 ¼ c. sifted flour
1 tsp. baking powder
1 tsp. salt
¾ tsp. baking soda
½ tsp. nutmeg
⅛ tsp. cloves
2 tsp. cinnamon
1 c. liquid from cooked prunes
1 tsp. vanilla
1 c. chopped cooked prunes
½ c. chopped walnuts

• Cream shortening; add sugar and then eggs, one at a time, beating thoroughly.
• Sift together flour, baking powder, salt, baking soda and spices. Blend into creamed mixture, alternately with prune liquid. Stir in the vanilla, prunes and nuts.
• Spread batter into a greased 13 × 9 × 2″ pan. Bake in moderate oven (350°) 40 to 50 minutes, or until cake tests done in center.
• Remove from oven; set pan on wire rack to cool 10 minutes. Loosen cake around edges with spatula and invert on rack, lift off pan and cool thoroughly. Serve plain, à la mode or spread with Cream Caramel or Caramel-Nut Frosting.

CREAM CARAMEL FROSTING

Country hostesses make caramel frosting with cream. Guests approve

1 c. sugar
1 c. brown sugar, firmly packed
⅔ c. sweet or dairy sour cream
⅛ tsp. salt
1 tsp. vanilla

• Combine sugars, cream and salt in saucepan. Heat slowly, stirring until sugars dissolve. Cook without stirring to the soft ball stage (234°). Remove from heat. Cool without stirring until lukewarm.
• Add vanilla and beat until thick and creamy. If necessary, thin frosting with a few drops of cream. Makes enough to frost a 13 × 9 × 2″ cake.

VARIATION

Caramel-Nut Frosting: Add ¼ c. chopped walnuts to frosting just before spreading it on the cake.

DATE CAKE IRRESISTIBLE

A moist, rich cake—serve at dessert party with whipped cream on top

1 ½ c. boiling water
1 c. pitted dates, cut up
        (½ lb.)
1 tsp. baking soda
¼ c. butter or margarine
1 egg, beaten
½ tsp. salt
1 tsp. vanilla
1 c. sugar
1 ½ c. sifted flour
1 tsp. baking powder
Date Topping

• Combine boiling water, dates, baking soda and butter. Let stand while mixing remainder of cake.
• To egg add salt and vanilla; beat to mix. Combine sugar and flour sifted with baking powder. Alternately add dry ingredients with cooled date mixture to the egg, beating after each addition (batter is thin).
• Bake in greased, paper-lined 13 × 9 × 2″ pan in moderate oven (350°) 35 to 40 minutes. Cool on rack. Spread with Date Topping. Makes 12 servings.

DATE TOPPING

The Iowa farm woman who shares this recipe gathers black walnuts in her yard for this frosting

1 c. cut-up pitted dates (½ lb.)
¾ c. water
¾ c. sugar
⅛ tsp. salt
½ c. chopped walnuts or black
        walnuts

• Combine all ingredients except nuts; cook until smooth, stirring constantly, about 10 minutes. Add nuts. Spread on top of cooled cake.

14-CARAT CAKE

A blue ribbon cake—it will keep 2 to 3 weeks in refrigerator if covered

2 c. sifted flour
2 tsp. baking powder
1 ½ tsp. baking soda
1 ½ tsp. salt
2 tsp. cinnamon
2 c. sugar
1 ½ c. salad oil
4 eggs
2 c. finely grated carrots
1 (8 ½ oz.) can crushed
        pineapple, drained
½ c. chopped nuts
1 (3 ½ oz.) can flaked coconut
        (optional)
Cream Cheese Frosting

• Sift together flour, baking powder, baking soda, salt and cinnamon. Add sugar, salad oil and eggs; mix well. Add carrots, pineapple, nuts and coconut; blend thoroughly.
• Pour into 3 (9″) round layer cake pans that have been greased and floured.
• Bake in moderate oven (350°) 35 to 40 minutes. Remove from oven, cool a few minutes in pans. Turn out on wire racks and cool thoroughly. Fill layers and frost top and sides of cake with Cream Cheese Frosting.

When baking a cake for a sale or meeting, stir up a 3-layer recipe. Then you'll have one layer for the family plus a good-sized 2-layer cake to take out to your meeting.

CREAM CHEESE FROSTING

½ c. butter or margarine
   (¼ lb.)
1 (8 oz.) pkg. cream cheese
1 tsp. vanilla
1 lb. confectioners sugar, sifted
   if lumpy

• Combine butter, cream cheese and vanilla; cream well. Add confectioners sugar gradually, beating well. If mixture is too thick to spread, add a small amount of milk.

UPSIDE-DOWN
SWEET POTATO CAKE

This spicy, moist gold cake freezes well. Wrap in foil and reheat to serve

1 c. water
2½ c. granulated sugar
3 oranges, sliced ⅛" thick
¼ c. butter
¼ c. brown sugar, firmly
   packed
1¼ c. lard
4 eggs, separated
1 tblsp. vanilla
1½ c. grated raw sweet
   potatoes
1 c. chopped walnuts
2½ c. sifted flour
1 tblsp. baking powder
½ tsp. salt
1 tsp. cinnamon
1 tsp. nutmeg
¼ c. milk
Orange Sauce

• Bring water and ¼ c. granulated sugar to a boil. Add orange slices. Cover and cook over medium heat 20 minutes. Drain, reserving liquid, and cool. Cut each orange slice in half.

• Melt ¼ c. butter in a 13 × 9 × 2" pan. Add ¼ c. granulated sugar and the brown sugar; spread mixture evenly over the pan. Arrange orange slices in 3 rows lengthwise in the pan.
• Cream lard and the remaining 2 c. granulated sugar until light. Beat in egg yolks; add vanilla and continue beating until fluffy; stir in potatoes and nuts.
• Sift together the flour, baking powder, salt, cinnamon and nutmeg; add alternately with the milk to the potato mixture. Beat egg whites until stiff and fold into the potato mixture. Spoon evenly over the orange slices in the pan.
• Bake in a slow oven (325°) 1 hour. Cool in pan on rack 5 minutes; then invert on large plate or baking sheet. Serve warm with Orange Sauce. Makes 12 servings.

Orange Sauce: Add water to reserved orange liquid (from slices) to make 1 c. Blend in 1 tblsp. cornstarch. Add ¼ c. sugar and 2 tblsp. butter. Cook over medium heat, stirring constantly, until mixture thickens slightly. Serve warm over cake.

LEMON BUTTERMILK CAKE

Lemon-Butter-Egg Sauce highlights this wonderful country-kitchen cake

1 c. vegetable shortening
2¼ c. sugar
2 tsp. vanilla
1 tblsp. lemon juice
1 tsp. grated lemon peel
6 large eggs, separated
3 c. sifted flour
1 tsp. baking powder
½ tsp. baking soda
1 tsp. salt

¾ c. buttermilk
Lemon-Butter-Egg Sauce

• Beat together shortening and 1½ c. sugar. Blend in vanilla, lemon juice and peel. Add egg yolks, one at a time, blending just until smooth after each addition.
• Sift together flour, baking powder, baking soda and salt. Add alternately with buttermilk to batter, blending until smooth.
• Beat egg whites until frothy, then gradually beat in ¾ c. sugar until egg whites stand in stiff peaks. Fold into batter.
• Spoon batter into 10″ tube pan that has been greased and dusted with fine bread crumbs. Bake in moderate oven (350°) about 1 hour and 15 minutes, or until cake tests done. Makes 16 servings.

Lemon-Butter-Egg Sauce: In a small saucepan, combine ½ c. butter or margarine, 1 c. sugar, ¼ c. water, 1 well-beaten egg and 3 tblsp. lemon juice. Cook over medium heat, stirring constantly, just until mixture comes to a boil. Makes about 1½ cups.

Put the Spotlight on Fruitcake

Fruitcake can be both decorative and delicious. When you make our Holiday Fruitcake, you'll find it's tasty, and when cut thin you'll see that the colors in it resemble those in stained-glass church windows. Here are directions to follow if you want the brilliant reds, greens and golds in the cake actually to glow on the buffet.

Line a cardboard box with aluminum foil. Inside it, place a 60-watt light bulb, attached to an extension cord. Cut a hole in the side of the box and pull the cord through it. Then cover the sides of the box with white muslin; set on the buffet and hide the sides with small evergreen branches.

Arrange slices of Holiday Fruitcake on a glass plate—around a low red candle, if you like. Set the plate on the lighted box (it should be larger than square top of box, as it makes the "lid"). The glowing rich, clear colors of fruits in the cake always bring exclamations from the guests.

HOLIDAY FRUITCAKE

Bake it before you get Christmas-busy —wrap and put in the freezer

1   lb. mixed candied fruit
      (2 c.)
1   (4 oz.) can chopped citron
1   lb. dates, pitted
½   lb. whole candied cherries
      (1 c.)
1   c. raisins
1   c. pecan halves
1   c. walnut halves
4   c. sifted flour
1   tsp. salt
1   tsp. cinnamon
1   tsp. cloves
½   tsp. nutmeg
1   c. butter
2   c. sugar
4   eggs
1   tsp. baking soda
1½ c. buttermilk

• Prepare baking pans—you can use 1 (10″) tube pan or 3 (8 × 4¼ × 2¼″) foil pans: Cut parchment or brown paper liners for bottoms of pans; grease each paper with unsalted fat. Top with one layer waxed paper. Grease all paper inside pan generously.

• Prepare and measure fruit; cut it in pieces the size of dates. (Leave nuts, cherries and dates whole.)

• Sift together flour, salt and spices. Use enough of this flour mixture to coat all fruit pieces.

• Cream butter and sugar until light and fluffy; beat in eggs, one at a time. Add soda to remaining flour. Add flour alternately with buttermilk to the egg mixture. Spoon into prepared pan or pans.

• To decorate, lay nuts and large fruit pieces on top to form a design.

• Bake cake in a slow oven (300°). This amount in a 10″ tube pan bakes in 2½ hours; 1-pound amounts bake in about 1¼ hours.

• Cool cake out of pan on rack. When completely cool, apply orange juice or cider to entire cake with pastry brush. Wrap in waxed paper, then in foil. Store in covered container in cool place. After two weeks, unwrap and brush again with orange juice or cider.

VARIATION

Fruitcake Bonbons: Line tiny (1¼″) cupcake pans with paper bonbon cups. Fill cups three fourths full with batter. Bake in slow oven (300°) 40 to 50 minutes (place pan of water in oven so cakes will stay moist). Remove from pans. Cool on rack. When completely cool, cover with Tinted Bonbon Glaze.

• Remove paper cups from cakes. Set cakes on racks over foil or waxed paper. Spoon glaze over tops and

down sides of cakes. Let stand until glaze is firm. If first coat of glaze is too thin, repeat. The glaze that drips off may be scraped up, melted over hot water and reused. Makes 11 dozen.

Tinted Bonbon Glaze: Mix ¼ c. water, 1 tblsp. light corn syrup, 3 c. sifted confectioners sugar and ⅛ tsp. salt in top of double boiler. Heat just until lukewarm, stirring occasionally. Remove from hot water and add 1 tsp. vanilla. Divide and tint different colors with food color. Cool slightly.

ORANGE CANDY CAKE

Sweet and moist with the flavor of fruitcake, but easier on the budget

1 c. butter
2 c. sugar
5 eggs
1 tblsp. vanilla
1 (8 oz.) pkg. dates, cut up
1 (1 lb.) pkg. orange slice candy, cut up
2 c. pecans, chopped
1 (4 oz.) can shredded coconut
4 c. sifted flour
½ tsp. baking soda
1 tsp. salt
¾ c. buttermilk
Syrup

• Cream butter and sugar until light and fluffy. Beat in eggs, one at a time. Add vanilla.

• Mix dates, candy, nuts and coconut with ¼ c. flour. Sift remaining flour with baking soda and salt. Alternately fold them into the creamed mixture with the buttermilk.

• Fold in the fruit-nut mixture. Spoon into a well-greased and floured 10″ tube pan.

• Bake in slow oven (300°) 2½ hours.

• Remove cake from oven and at once pour on the Syrup. Set pan on wire rack and let cool. When the cake is cooled thoroughly, remove it from the pan. Wrap snugly in aluminum foil and refrigerate 1 day or longer before serving. The flavors blend during the refrigeration and the cake slices more easily.

Note: If you do not have buttermilk, use soured milk. Put 1 tblsp. vinegar in a 1-cup measure and fill to the ¾ c. mark with sweet milk. Let stand a few minutes.

Syrup: Mix together 1 tsp. grated lemon peel, 1 tsp. grated orange peel, ¼ c. lemon juice, ¼ c. orange juice and ½ c. confectioners sugar, sifted.

Paper baking cups, set in the rims of self-sealing jar lids and placed on a cookie sheet, provide extra containers when you are making more cupcakes than your muffin tins will hold. Rims of a matching size will keep batter-filled paper cups from spreading.

Cake and Fruity Spread Go Together

Jubilee Cake is a luscious guest-pleaser. Pear Jubilee, a fruit spread, tops sponge cake; whipped cream decorates the sides. You can make Pear Jubilee with ripe Bartlett, Kiefer, Anjou or Bosc pears. With a few jars of it in the cupboard, you're ready to turn sponge cake into a glamorous country dessert. And quickly!

JUBILEE CAKE

A country hostess special—sponge cake with crown of gold, Pear Jubilee

1 (10″) sponge cake
½ pt. Pear Jubilee (1 c.)
1 c. heavy cream
3 tblsp. confectioners sugar

• Remove cooled cake from pan and turn upside down. Spread top with Pear Jubilee.

• Whip cream and blend in confectioners sugar. Spread on sides of cake. Cut into servings with a cake breaker or carefully pull in wedges with two forks. Serve the same day. Makes 12 servings.

PEAR JUBILEE

Keep a few jars of this fruit spread on the shelf. It will come in handy

1 c. dried apricots, cut in thin strips
1 lemon, cut in thin slices
¾ c. water
5 c. peeled, cored and finely diced fresh pears
4 c. sugar
1 tblsp. rum extract (optional)

• Combine apricots, lemon and water in saucepan. Cover; simmer 5 minutes and set aside.

• Combine pears and sugar in heavy 4-qt. kettle. Cook over low heat until clear and thick, about 1 hour. Stir often to prevent scorching. Add apricot mixture; stir well. Add rum flavoring.

• Ladle into hot sterilized jars. Seal. Makes 4 half pints.

COUNTRY SPONGE CAKE

Use this feather-light, high cake for Jubilee Cake, or serve plain or frosted

6	egg yolks
½	c. cold water
1 ½	c. sugar
½	tsp. vanilla
½	tsp. lemon extract
1 ½	c. sifted cake flour
¼	tsp. salt
6	egg whites
¾	tsp. cream of tartar

• Beat egg yolks until thick and lemon-colored. Add water and beat until very thick. Gradually beat in the sugar. Add the vanilla and lemon extract.

• Sift together flour and salt; fold into the egg yolk mixture, a little at a time.

• Beat egg whites with cream of tartar until stiff peaks form. Pour the egg yolk batter over the egg whites and, with a rubber scraper, fold it into the whites, just to blend. Use an over and under motion, turning the bowl gradually.

• Spoon into a 10" *ungreased* tube pan. Bake in slow oven (325°) about 1 hour, or until cake tester or wooden pick, inserted halfway between center and side, comes out clean.

• Invert and cool completely. It will take about 1½ hours. Loosen cake with spatula and remove from pan.

Note: You can omit lemon extract and use 1 tsp. vanilla. Or use orange extract instead of lemon extract, especially good when cake's top wears Pear Jubilee.

Keep Cherry Mix in Your Freezer

Country women often surprise and please their guests in January with foods that taste and look like June and July. They're downright clever at stretching the abundance and flavor of summer fruit through winter.

Frozen Cherry Mix is a classic example. It's a double fruit mixture of tart red cherries and crushed pineapple. The pineapple helps sweeten the cherries and stretches them—an advantage if your cherry supply is short. The mix retains its flavor and pretty red color for months if stored in the freezer. You can keep it in the refrigerator, too, for up to a month, but it will lose color.

You'll find many interesting ways to use Cherry Mix when you entertain. Partly thawed, it makes a gala topping for vanilla ice cream; it's colorful and tasty on slices of angel or sponge cake. Pass it with ham for a relish. You will find several recipes in this cookbook that call for Frozen Cherry Mix. Look for them in the Index.

For the cake section in this cookbook, we couldn't omit Cherry Upside-Down Cake. It's right for those occasions when you want to serve a dessert with coffee during the evening. And it's easy to make. You can serve it warm or cold, whichever is the more convenient; your guests will praise it either way.

CHERRY UPSIDE-DOWN CAKE

A country-kitchen top-favorite dessert

1   tblsp. butter
1   c. Frozen Cherry Mix
       (recipe follows)
1 ¼ c. sifted flour
¾   c. sugar
1 ½ tsp. baking powder
¼   tsp. salt
⅔   c. heavy cream (30 to
       35% butterfat)
2   tblsp. milk
½   tsp. vanilla
1   egg

• Melt the butter in an 8 × 8 × 2″ pan. Spread Cherry Mix evenly in the pan.
• Sift dry ingredients together into mixer bowl. Add remaining ingredients. Mix to dampen dry ingredients. Beat 2 minutes at medium speed of electric mixer, or 300 vigorous strokes by hand.
• Pour batter in pan over the Cherry Mix and spread evenly. Bake in a moderate oven (350°) about 45 minutes, or until cake tests done.
• Remove from oven; let stand 5 minutes. Invert pan over cake plate, let stand 1 minute, then remove pan. Makes 9 servings.

FROZEN CHERRY MIX

From our Complete Pie Cookbook— *good in pie, also in many other dishes*

5   qts. stemmed tart red
       cherries
2   (1 lb. 4 oz). cans crushed
       pineapple, drained
8   c. sugar
8   tsp. ascorbic acid powder
2   tsp. cinnamon
⅛   tsp. ground cloves
2   (1 ¾ oz.) pkgs. powdered
       fruit pectin

• Pit cherries and chop coarsely. (Fruit and juice should measure about 12 cups.) Drain juice from cherries to use later.
• Add pineapple to cherries.
• Combine sugar, ascorbic acid powder and spices. Add to cherries and pineapple; mix well. Let stand to dissolve sugar.
• Combine pectin and cherry juice in large saucepan. Heat to a full rolling boil; boil 1 minute, stirring constantly; remove from heat. Add to cherry mixture; then stir for 2 minutes. Ladle into freezer containers and seal. Let stand at room temperature until set (about 8 to 10 hours). Freeze. Makes 10 pints.

Note: Recipes using Frozen Cherry Mix are: Cherry Upside-Down Cake, Cherry-Coconut Ice Cream Pie, Cherry Mix Salad and Peachy Relish Cups.

The Cake That Is an Angel

Give a farm woman a big angel food cake and watch what happens. Without a fairy's wand, she transforms it into a spectacular dessert. And what a variety of flavors she can add—peach, lemon, mocha and pineapple are classics.

The hostess prides herself on tricks to use when she wants to dress up an angel cake especially for company. Here are recipes for some special sauces culled from files in FARM JOURNAL Test Kitchens and from farm hostesses.

LEMON JELLY CAKE

Yellow and white ribbon cake with fresh lemon taste—good make-ahead

1   (9 or 10") angel food cake
1   envelope unflavored gelatin
1½ c. sugar
4   tblsp. cornstarch
⅛   tsp. salt
⅓   c. water
2   egg yolks, beaten
2   tblsp. butter or margarine
¼   tsp. grated lemon peel
⅓   c. fresh lemon juice
½   c. dairy sour cream
½   c. chopped nuts
7-Minute Frosting

• Cut cool cake in 3 equal layers.
• Combine gelatin with ¼ c. sugar and set aside. Combine remaining 1¼ c. sugar, cornstarch and salt. Add the water; cook over low heat, stirring constantly, until the mixture thickens and boils. Stir ½ c. hot mixture into egg yolks; stir this back into hot mixture. Return to heat and cook 1 minute, stirring constantly.
• Remove from heat and add the gelatin-sugar mixture. Stir until gelatin dissolves; stir in butter. Continue to stir until mixture starts to set but is still "soupy." Add lemon juice and peel; fold in sour cream and nuts. Cool. Spread between layers of cake. Frost top and sides of cake with 7-Minute Frosting, tinted yellow.

7-Minute Frosting: In double boiler, combine 1 egg white (2 tblsp.), ¾ c. sugar, ⅛ tsp. cream of tartar or 1½ tsp. light corn syrup and 3 tblsp. water. Place over boiling water and beat with rotary beater or electric mixer until mixture stands in stiff peaks. Scrape bottom and sides of pan occasionally. Fold in 2 tsp. grated lemon peel and tint a delicate yellow with food color. Spread on cake.

HAWAIIAN ANGEL CAKE

Pastel pink and green fillings make this delectable party cake glamorous

1   (10") angel food cake,
         split into 3 layers
1   (1 lb. 13 oz.) can crushed
         pineapple
2   envelopes unflavored gelatin
Mint extract
Green food color
2   (2 oz.) pkgs. dessert topping
         mix, whipped according
         to package directions
¾   c. drained and chopped
         maraschino cherries
3   tblsp. maraschino cherry juice
Red food color

• Drain pineapple well; reserve syrup. Soften gelatin in pineapple syrup; place over low heat until gelatin is melted. Mix with drained pineapple.
• Remove ⅓ (about 1 c. plus 2 tblsp.) of pineapple mixture to separate bowl. Flavor this amount with a few drops of mint extract and color a delicate green. Fold in ⅓ of whipped topping mix.
• To remainder of pineapple mixture, add chopped cherries and cherry juice. Fold in the remaining whipped topping mix. Color pink.
• Spread bottom layer of angel food cake with half of the pink cherry whip, add second layer and spread with green mint whip. Add top layer and spread with last of pink cherry whip. Leave sides of cake bare. Re-

frigerate 1 hour or more to firm. Makes 12 servings.

MOCHA FROSTED CAKE

For hostesses who like to stay out of the kitchen to visit with their guests

1 (3¾ oz.) pkg. chocolate pudding mix
1½ tblsp. instant coffee powder
1⅓ c. milk
1 c. heavy cream, whipped
1 (10") angel food cake, split into three equal layers
2 (¾ oz.) chocolate-coated toffee bars, crushed

• Blend pudding mix, coffee and milk. Prepare pudding as directed on package. Chill. Beat smooth; fold in half of the whipped cream. Spread half of the chocolate-cream mixture between the cake layers.

• Fold second half of whipped cream into remaining chocolate-cream mixture. Spread on top and sides of cake. Sprinkle with crushed candy bars. Chill several hours before serving. Makes 12 servings.

Note: This cake freezes well. First, freeze it uncovered. When firm, wrap and return to freezer. To serve, place cake, uncovered, in refrigerator 3 hours to reach serving temperature.

PEACH CAKE PUDDING

This refrigerator dessert is stunning with peach sunbursts on top

½ (9 or 10") angel food cake, cut into 1" squares
½ c. orange juice
1 (3¾ oz.) pkg. vanilla pudding mix, prepared with 3 c. milk

1 tsp. grated orange peel
1 tsp. vanilla
¼ tsp. salt
1 tblsp. butter
1 (10 oz.) pkg. frozen peach slices, thawed and drained, or 1 c. drained canned sliced peaches
¼ c. flaked coconut
¼ c. maraschino cherries, finely chopped and drained

• Arrange cake pieces in an 8 × 8 × 2" dish. Sprinkle with ¼ c. orange juice.

• Combine hot pudding, remaining orange juice, orange peel, vanilla, salt and butter. Pour over the cake; cover and refrigerate 3 hours or longer.

• At serving time, arrange peach slices on top; sprinkle with coconut and cherries. Makes 9 servings.

CHERRY-ALMOND SAUCE

Red-black cherries, almonds and lemon peel blend flavors deliciously

2 (1 lb. 1 oz.) cans pitted dark sweet cherries
2 c. cherry juice and water
2 tblsp. cornstarch
¼ c. sugar
¾ c. whole almonds, toasted
1 tsp. grated lemon peel

• Drain cherries, reserving juice. To cherry juice, add water to make 2 cups.

• Blend cornstarch and sugar in a saucepan; gradually add the cherry juice. Cook over medium heat until mixture thickens, stirring frequently. Remove sauce from heat.

• Meanwhile stuff each cherry with an almond. Stir lemon peel into sauce;

add the stuffed cherries. Serve while warm. Makes 4 cups, about 16 average-size spoon-on toppings.

ORANGE CREAM SAUCE

Keep this tangy, smooth sauce in your refrigerator, an angel cake in freezer—your refreshments are ready

6 egg yolks
⅔ c. sugar
⅔ c. orange juice
2 tsp. grated orange peel
1 tsp. grated lemon peel
⅛ tsp. salt
2 tblsp. lemon juice
½ pt. dairy sour cream (1 c.)

• Lightly beat egg yolks in top of double boiler. Blend in the remaining ingredients except the sour cream. Cook, stirring constantly, over simmering (not boiling) water until thick, about 15 minutes. Chill.
• Stir until smooth; blend in sour cream. Spoon on sliced cake. Garnish with orange slices. Makes about 3 cups.

Note: If you want to serve a thicker sauce, refrigerate it several hours after you add the sour cream.

FAST-FIX FRUIT TOPPING

Topping keeps well in refrigerator—handy to dress up cake slices

1 (1 lb. 4½ oz.) can pineapple chunks
1 (11 oz.) can mandarin oranges
1 c. orange marmalade

• Drain fruits; stir in marmalade. Heat and serve warm or cold on angel cake slices. Makes 3 cups.

PINK PARTY TOPPING

Pretty pink fluffy sauce on white cake makes a festive party dessert. It's so good and so easy to fix

1 c. miniature marshmallows
1 (10 oz.) pkg. frozen red raspberries or strawberries
1 c. heavy cream, whipped

• Pour marshmallows and frozen berries in a bowl. Cover; refrigerate overnight. Before serving, fold in whipped cream. Makes 3 cups.

SPICY CHERRY GLAZE

For a showy dessert spoon glaze on a whole cake—also pretty on slices

1½ c. drained, pitted tart canned cherries, 1 (16 to 17 oz.) can
Juice drained from cherries
8 whole cloves
3 sticks cinnamon
2 tblsp. cornstarch
¼ c. sugar
¼ tsp. salt
⅓ c. light corn syrup
1 tblsp. butter
Red food color

• Combine cherries, ½ c. cherry juice and spices in a saucepan. Bring to a boil. Reduce heat; simmer 5 minutes.
• Stir together cornstarch, sugar and salt. Stir in 2 tblsp. cold cherry juice and corn syrup. Gradually stir in the hot liquid drained from the heated cherries. Remove whole spices from cherries; pour cornstarch mixture over cherries in saucepan. Cook, stirring frequently, over low heat until mixture thickens. Reduce heat and simmer 5 minutes. Remove from heat and stir in butter and enough

food color to make sauce a regal red.

• Cool slightly. Spoon over a 10" angel food cake. Let glaze set about 2 hours before cutting. Makes 2 cups sauce.

Note: If you use sweetened frozen cherries, use 2 tblsp. sugar in making sauce instead of ¼ cup.

Pudding Cakes They'll Like

Some hostesses call them cakes, while others refer to them as puddings. Regardless of name, they're good, hearty eating and sure to win guest approval. Perhaps the cue to their popularity is that so frequently they fit the season in which country women serve them.

Here are two recipes that illustrate the point—Rhubarb Pudding Cake, as springlike as tulips and iris, and Pumpkin Pudding Cake, as much a part of autumn as golden oak trees.

RHUBARB PUDDING CAKE

Serve warm in dessert bowls with cream—pretty if made of tender, pink rhubarb

4   c. diced fresh rhubarb
1   c. sugar
¾   c. water
¼   c. vegetable shortening
½   c. sugar
1   egg
½   tsp. vanilla
1   c. sifted flour
2   tsp. baking powder
¼   tsp. salt
½   c. milk

• Cook rhubarb, sugar and water until rhubarb is tender; keep hot.

• Cream shortening and sugar; beat in egg and vanilla. Sift dry ingredients together; add alternately with milk to creamed mixture.

• Pour batter into greased 9" square baking pan. Spoon hot rhubarb sauce over batter. Bake in moderate oven (350°) 40 minutes. Makes 9 servings.

PUMPKIN PUDDING CAKE

You can bake, cool, wrap in foil and freeze this easy-to-make, moist spice cake. Reheat in foil before serving

1 ⅔   c. sifted flour
1 ⅓   c. sugar
¼   tsp. baking powder
1   tsp. baking soda
1   tsp. salt
1   tsp. cinnamon
¼   tsp. ginger
⅓   c. soft shortening
1   c. cooked, mashed or canned pumpkin
⅓   c. water
1   egg
⅔   c. raisins
⅓   c. walnuts or pecans

• Sift dry ingredients together into mixing bowl; add shortening, pumpkin and water. Beat 2 minutes on medium speed of electric mixer or until ingredients are all well mixed. Add egg, beat 2 minutes longer. Stir in raisins and nuts.

• Pour into a 1½-qt. ring or Turk's head mold that has been well greased and lightly dusted with fine, dry bread crumbs. Bake in moderate oven (350°) about 45 minutes, or until cake tests done. Serve warm with whipped cream or lemon sauce. Makes 8 servings.

APPLE PUDDING CAKE

Serve this sweet pudding cake faintly warm with whipped cream on top

Cake:
- ½ c. butter or margarine
- 1 c. sugar
- 1½ c. grated peeled apples
- 2 c. flour (unsifted)
- 1 tsp. baking soda
- 1 tsp. cinnamon
- 1 tsp. allspice
- 1 tsp. salt
- 1 c. walnuts, chopped
- 1 c. raisins

Topping:
- 1 tblsp. butter
- ½ c. sugar
- Grated peel and juice of 1 orange

• Cream butter and sugar until light and fluffy. Blend in grated apples. Sift together dry ingredients and stir into apple mixture.
• Stir in nuts and raisins. Spread in a lightly greased and floured 13 × 9 × 2" baking pan. Bake in moderate oven (350°) 40 minutes.
• Combine topping ingredients and bring to a boil over moderate heat. Reduce heat and simmer until sugar is dissolved. Pour hot topping over cake when it comes from the oven. Cut in individual servings. Makes 12 servings.

Fancy, Easy-to-Make Cake

Italian Cream Cake will be the talk of a celebration on Mother's Day, or any party for that matter. It's a tall, handsome cake, covered with whipped cream. When you cut it, the choc-olate and lemon fillings, spread alternately between five layers, are colorful. Easy to make: Use a packaged mix, bake the batter in a tube pan and split the cooled cake into layers. Make the fillings with packaged pie and pudding mixes. The cake tastes extra-good because the combination of chocolate-spice and lemon-fruit fillings is so luscious.

ITALIAN CREAM CAKE

Here's the fancy but easy cake for Daughter to bake for Mother's Day

- 1 (1 lb. 3 oz.) pkg. lemon chiffon cake mix
- Chocolate-Spice Filling
- Lemon-Fruit Filling
- 1½ c. heavy cream
- 4 tblsp. sifted confectioners sugar

• Prepare cake mix according to package directions. Bake in 10" tube pan.
• When cake has cooled, remove from pan and slice in 5 layers. Fill layers alternately with Chocolate-Spice and Lemon-Fruit Filling.
• Whip heavy cream with confectioners sugar; frost top and sides of cake. Chill several hours. Makes 12 to 16 servings.

Chocolate-Spice Filling: Prepare 1 (4 oz.) pkg. chocolate pudding and pie filling mix as directed on package, using 1½ c. milk and adding ½ tsp. cinnamon. Cover and cool to room temperature. Whip ½ c. heavy cream; fold into pudding. Add 2 tblsp. slivered toasted almonds. Chill 15 minutes.

Lemon-Fruit Filling: Prepare 1 (3¼ oz.) pkg. vanilla pudding and pie filling mix as directed on package, using 1½ c. milk. Cover and cool to room temperature. Add 2 tsp. lemon juice and 1 tblsp. grated lemon peel. Whip ½ c. heavy cream; fold into pudding. Add ⅓ c. drained pineapple tidbits and ¼ c. drained, quartered maraschino cherries. Chill 15 minutes.

Desserts for Junior Cooks

Smart mothers let their children help fix food for company—to make them feel they're a part of the entertaining. And they learn what goes on in the kitchen beforehand, too!

What girl wouldn't enjoy making Easter Cake by herself? Junior cooks also can fix Mincemeat-Lemon Stack Cake. Both desserts taste good, look attractive and are neither too difficult nor too easy to challenge a young cook.

EASTER CAKE

Looks like eggs, sunny side up, on toast—a fine Easter season dessert

1 pkg. chocolate or spice cake
  mix
1 (1 lb. 14 oz.) can apricot
  halves
Whipped cream

• Bake and cool cake in a greased 13 × 9 × 2″ pan as directed on package.
• Drain apricot halves (save and refrigerate juice to use later in a gelatin dessert, salad or in fruit drinks).
• To serve, cut the cake in squares and place on serving plates. Place a heaping spoonful of whipped cream

on each, then put a drained apricot half, cut side down on the center of the cake square. Serve at once. Makes about 9 servings.

MINCEMEAT-LEMON STACK CAKE

A frozen dessert to keep on hand ready for last-minute company

1 pkg. lemon cake mix
Confectioners sugar
1 c. mincemeat
1 qt. vanilla ice cream, softened

• Prepare cake as directed on package. Bake in paper-lined 15½ × 10½ × 1″ jelly roll pan. Chill or let stand several hours so tender cake may be easily handled. Invert onto a piece of heavy aluminum foil, dusted with confectioners sugar; carefully remove paper from cake. Cut cake crosswise in half.
• Blend mincemeat into softened ice cream. Quickly spread on one cake half. Invert other cake half onto ice cream; use foil to assist in turning one half over the other.
• Quickly cut cake into 12 servings. Freeze; wrap well. Move dessert from freezer to refrigerator a half hour before serving. Serve with a tart lemon sauce, warmed.

Super-Cheese Cake

You'll make a smart decision if you choose to serve this impressive cheese cake for a company dessert after a light meal. Or pair it off with coffee for a dessert luncheon or evening refreshment. With chocolate, almond and cheese flavors in combination, it couldn't taste better. Dramatic it is, too, with fluffy sour cream hugging its edges and making a medallion on the center-top.

CHOCOLATE-ALMOND CHEESE CAKE

A jackpot of good flavors—chocolate, cheese and almonds—in this dessert

1 ¼ c. graham cracker crumbs
     (18 crackers)
¾   c. very finely chopped
     unblanched almonds
     (about 3 ½ oz.)
½   c. melted butter or
     margarine
1   c. plus 3 tblsp. sugar
4   eggs
3   (8 oz.) pkgs. cream cheese
2   squares unsweetened
     chocolate
2   tsp. vanilla
1   c. dairy sour cream
Glacé fruit mix
Toasted slivered almonds

• Combine crumbs, chopped almonds, butter and 2 tblsp. sugar; mix well. Line sides and bottom of 9″ springform pan with mixture, pressing firmly against pan with back of spoon.
• Beat eggs well; gradually add 1 c. sugar, beating until mixture is lemon-colored. Add cheese in small amounts, mixing until smooth after each addition.
• Melt chocolate over hot water; blend into egg mixture along with vanilla.
• Pour into crumb-lined pan. Bake in moderate oven (350°) 35 to 40 minutes, or until cake is set in center. Remove from oven and cool thoroughly. Loosen up ring and remove side of pan.

• Blend sour cream with remaining 1 tblsp. sugar. Spread over torte, making wreath around the edge and a medallion in the center. Garnish with glacé fruit and slivered almonds. Makes 16 servings.

Little Cakes for Big Occasions

There's something flattering about a cake baked just for you. That's what a cupcake is—a single serving. If you know small children will be among your dinner guests, serve cupcakes. Much easier for youngsters to eat them than cake slices. And little cakes are both decorative and tasty.

If you bake the little cakes in paper baking cups, you cheat the dishwasher (human or electric) because the muffin cups require no washing. You'll find, too, that cakes baked in them hold their shape better than those baked in muffin pans.

We also give suggestions for tea-time and party dainties in this section.

CHOCO-APPLE CUPCAKES

They're good without frosting, wonderful with caramel or fudge frosting

½   c. shortening
1   c. sugar
1   egg
1 ¾ c. sifted flour
1   tsp. baking soda
½   tsp. salt
1   tsp. cinnamon
½   tsp. allspice
1 ½ squares unsweetened
     chocolate, grated
1 ¼ c. unsweetened applesauce

• Cream shortening and sugar until light and fluffy. Add egg; beat well.
• Sift dry ingredients together. Stir in grated chocolate. Add to creamed mixture alternately with applesauce, mixing after each addition.
• Fill greased cupcake pans two thirds full. Bake in moderate oven (375°) 20 minutes. Makes 18.

CARAMEL FROSTING

Press a pecan half in each frosted cake—quick dress-up that's inviting

½ c. butter (1 stick)
1 c. dark brown sugar, firmly packed
¼ tsp. salt
¼ c. milk
2 c. sifted confectioners sugar

• Melt butter in a saucepan over low heat, but do not let it brown. Stir in brown sugar and salt. Bring to a boil over medium heat and boil hard 2 minutes, stirring all the time. Remove from heat.
• Add milk and stir vigorously. Return pan to heat and bring mixture to a full boil again. Remove from heat at once and set aside to cool to lukewarm; it will take about 20 minutes.
• Stir the confectioners sugar into the lukewarm mixture and beat until smooth. If the frosting hardens too much to spread, beat in a few drops of milk. Makes enough to frost about 18 cupcakes or 2 (8 or 9") layers.

Make a candlewick cake by tinting white frosting a pastel color. Before icing hardens, imbed miniature marshmallows in the icing, to imitate a candlewick pattern.

PETITS FOURS

Make ahead and freeze to simplify last-minute preparations for party

1 pkg. white cake mix
Petits Fours Frosting
Decorations

• Prepare cake mix as directed on package. Pour batter into greased and floured 15½ × 10½ × 1" jelly roll pan. Bake 25 to 30 minutes. Cool.
• Use a sharp knife or cookie cutters to cut cake into small fancy shapes, such as hearts, triangles, circles, squares and diamonds.
• To frost, place the cakes, one at a time, on a rack over a large bowl. With a small pitcher or measuring cup, pour Petits Fours Frosting over top so all the cake is covered at one time. The frosting or glaze that drips off the cakes can be reheated and used again. Decorate tops of cakes with silver dragées, candy flowers or as you like. For an effective tray, divide the frosting into 3 parts; leave one part white and tint one a delicate green, the other a pastel pink. Makes about 54 (1½") squares, or 34 (2") squares.

PETITS FOURS FROSTING

This frosting glazes cakelets and is not sticky when guests pick them up

9 c. sifted confectioners sugar
½ c. water
½ c. light corn syrup
1 tsp. vanilla
½ tsp. almond extract

• Combine ingredients in top of double boiler; heat until just lukewarm. (Be careful not to overheat frosting or it will have a dull look.) Remove from heat, but leave frosting over hot water so it will remain thin. If frosting gets too thick, add a few drops of hot water at a time until you get the proper consistency.

Note: Trim edges from cake before cutting. To make squares, cut a lengthwise strip of cake 1½ or 2″ wide. Cut the strip crosswise to make squares. Cut squares diagonally to make triangles. Use a sharp knife. Cut other shapes with sharp, small cookie cutters. Wipe crumbs from knife or cutter each time after cutting.

ANGEL PARTY CUPCAKES

After you arrange these little cakes on a tray or platter, take a minute to see what a lovely picture they make. Certainly they're in tune with flowers, gleaming silver and pretty teacups.

ANGEL CAKELETS

• Prepare 1 pkg. angel food cake mix by package directions. You will have enough batter to make 48 medium-size cupcakes.
• Carefully spoon the batter into ungreased muffin-pan cups or paper baking cups. If you use paper cups, set them on a baking sheet before filling. Fill cups two thirds full.
• Bake in moderate oven (375°) 15 to 20 minutes. Remove, set on rack and let cool 10 to 15 minutes before removing from the cups.
• Meanwhile make Seven-Minute Frosting (recipe follows), or use package mix for fluffy white frosting. Dip tops of cooled cupcakes in frosting, or spoon frosting on tops of cakes.

• Tint ⅓ c. flaked coconut a delicate pink with a drop of red food color, a second ⅓ c. coconut with green food color and tint a third ⅓ c. coconut a pastel yellow (see Index for directions for tinting coconut).
• Hold frosted cupcakes on a fork, one at a time, and sprinkle 12 of them with pink coconut, 12 with green coconut, 12 with yellow coconut and the last 12 with a mixture of pink, green and yellow coconut; add a little white coconut if you like.

Note: You can divide the frosting in fourths, delicately tint one with pink, one with green, and one with yellow food color. Leave the fourth portion white. Frost tops of 12 cupcakes with each of these four frostings and decorate with flaked coconut, chopped nuts, chocolate sprinkles, crushed peppermint candy or silver dragées.

SEVEN-MINUTE FROSTING

    2   egg whites, unbeaten
    1½ c. sugar
    2   tsp. light corn syrup
    ⅓   c. cold water
    ⅛   tsp. salt
    1   tsp. vanilla

• Place all ingredients except vanilla in top of double boiler. Beat 1 minute with electric beater; then cook over hot water, beating constantly, until frosting forms stiff peaks, *about 7 minutes. Be careful not to overcook.*
• Remove top of double boiler and pour frosting into mixing bowl. Add vanilla and beat until of spreading consistency, about 2 minutes. Makes enough to frost tops and sides of 4 dozen medium-size cupcakes.

Talk-of-the-Party Cakes

Mug Cakes will get a lot of attention at teen-age parties. You bake the batter in empty 1 lb. cans (#303) to get the right shape. Frost the sides of the mugs with chocolate frosting and heap fluffy white frosting on top. Then add a candy handle to one side of each cake and insert a stick of candy, to represent a drinking straw. Our recipe tells in detail how to make these conversation cakes.

MUG CAKES

Serve these at graduation parties— they'll make a hit with the gang

2 pkgs. pound cake mix
1 pkg. chocolate creamy-type
    frosting mix (2-layer cake
    size)
1 pkg. white fluffy-type frosting
    mix (2-layer cake size)
Cake decorations (8 red licorice
    "twisters," white mint patties
    and peppermint sticks)

• Line bottoms and sides of 4 empty 1 lb. cans with waxed paper, allowing paper to extend 1″ over tops. Prepare 1 package pound cake mix according to package directions. Pour about 1 c. batter into each can.
• Bake in slow oven (325°) 55 minutes, or until lightly browned. Cool 15 minutes in can, pull out cakes, remove papers.
• Repeat, using second package of pound cake mix.
• Prepare frosting mixes according to package directions. Frost sides with chocolate frosting, then tops with

fluffy white frosting. Stick white mint patties on sides of mugs and insert peppermint sticks.
• Make mug handles by forcing ends of red licorice twisters into side of each cake.
• To serve, cut each cake into vertical quarters. Makes 32 small pieces.

Use a clean string for slicing pinwheel rolls or jelly rolls. Place center of string under roll where you want to slice. Bring ends up over top, cross string, and pull quickly to cut down through the roll. Slices more cleanly than the sharpest knife.

Multipurpose Country Cookies

Few foods equal cookies in their adaptability to many occasions. "The children think it's like going to Grandmother's house," says a young mother, "when I take them with me to visit neighborhood friends who keep homemade cookies in their freezers." Older children like to express their hospitality, when friends stop in, by serving cookies and a drink. And for a treat for grown-up callers, both men and women, cookies and coffee or tea have few equals.

Dainty cookies are at home on fashionable tea party tables along with flowers and candlelight. And at a picnic, a tray of cookies gets a big reception.

What a knack cookies have for supporting desserts that need a bit of bolstering, like fruit compotes, ice cream, sherbet and light puddings. Hostesses are mindful, too, of the help cookies give in Yuletide entertaining.

CRACKLED SUGAR COOKIES

An old-fashioned cookie with subtle lemon flavor, pretty, crinkled top

1   c. shortening (part butter)
1 ½ c. sugar
6   egg yolks, or 3 eggs, beaten
1   tsp. vanilla
½   tsp. lemon extract
½   tsp. orange extract
2 ½ c. flour
1   tsp. baking soda
1   tsp. cream of tartar

• Cream shortening and sugar until fluffy. Add yolks and flavorings; beat. Combine dry ingredients; add to creamed mixture.
• Shape into 1" balls. Divide into three piles.
• Roll one third of the balls in a mixture of ¼ c. sugar, 1 tsp. grated orange peel and ½ tsp. grated lemon peel; the second third in a mixture of 2 tblsp. finely chopped black walnuts, ½ tsp. nutmeg, 1 tblsp. brown sugar and 2 tblsp. granulated sugar; and roll the remaining third in ¼ c. chocolate cookie decorations.
• Place cookie balls on ungreased baking sheet. Bake in moderate oven (350°) 12 to 15 minutes. Cool on racks. Makes about 5 dozen big flat 3" cookies.

ANGEL COOKIES

A Cedar County, Iowa, hostess, who entertains big in her country home, keeps these in her freezer ready to serve with coffee or tea

1   c. butter or margarine
1   c. lard
1   c. granulated sugar
1   c. brown sugar
2   eggs
2   tsp. vanilla
4 ½ c. sifted flour
2   tsp. baking soda
2   tsp. cream of tartar
2   tsp. salt
1   c. chopped nuts

• Cream together butter, lard and sugars. Add eggs one at a time and mix thoroughly. Add vanilla.
• Sift together flour, baking soda, cream of tartar and salt. Add to creamed mixture. Stir in nuts. Chill dough until easy to handle.
• Shape in balls the size of walnuts and dip tops in sugar. Arrange on baking sheet about 2" apart.
• Sprinkle several drops of water on each ball of dough. Bake in moderate oven (350°) 15 minutes. Makes 9 dozen cookies.

Note: Divide the ingredients in half to bake 4¼ dozen cookies.

BROWN SUGAR-NUT BARS

Cut these chewy cookies in small bars—they're really rich, satisfying

1   lb. brown sugar
1   c. butter
2   eggs
2   c. flour
1   tsp. baking powder
½   tsp. salt
1   c. walnuts, coarsely chopped

• Cook sugar and butter in top of double boiler over hot water until sugar dissolves. Cool. Add eggs, one at a time, beating thoroughly after each addition. Stir in remaining ingredients. Spread in ungreased 15½ × 10½ × 2" pan. Bake in moderate oven (350°) 25 minutes. While hot, cut into squares. Makes 40 cookies.

JIFFY CANDY COOKIES

They taste like chocolate candy bars

18 graham crackers, broken into
    small pieces
1 (15 oz.) can sweetened
    condensed milk
1 (6 oz.) pkg. semisweet
    chocolate pieces
½ c. pecans, chopped
½ c. flaked coconut

• Combine all ingredients. Pour into
a greased 8 × 8 × 2″ pan. Bake in
moderate oven (350°) 35 minutes.
• While warm, cut into squares and
place on cooling rack. Makes 25
squares. These will firm when cool.

CARAMEL APPLE COOKIES

*Good keepers in the freezer, but so
tempting they may disappear fast*

Cookies:
½ c. shortening
1 ⅓ c. brown sugar, firmly
    packed
1 egg
2 ¼ c. sifted flour
1 tsp. baking soda
½ tsp. salt
1 tsp. cinnamon
1 tsp. ground cloves
½ tsp. nutmeg
1 c. grated peeled apples
1 c. light raisins
½ c. apple juice
1 c. walnuts, chopped

Caramel Icing:
¼ c. butter
¼ c. brown sugar, firmly
    packed
1 ½ c. confectioners sugar, sifted
¼ tsp. salt
2 ½ tblsp. light cream

• To make cookies, cream shortening,
sugar and egg until light and fluffy.
Sift together dry ingredients and add
to creamed mixture. When well
blended, stir in remaining ingredients.
• Drop by level tablespoonfuls onto
greased baking sheet. Bake in moderate oven (350°) about 12 minutes,
or until lightly browned.
• Remove from pan and cool on
racks.
• To make icing, cook butter and
brown sugar until sugar dissolves,
about 3 minutes. Add remaining ingredients. Beat; spread on cooled
cookies. If too thick, thin frosting
with more cream. Makes about 4
dozen.

Note: To freeze, layer cookies in
waxed paper in pan; wrap tightly.

How to Cut an Egg in Two: *When
you divide a recipe in half, sometimes
the new recipe calls for less than 1
egg. To get the correct amount, beat
the egg slightly, just enough to mix
yolk and white, and measure with a
tablespoon. Divide the number of
tablespoonfuls by two.*

Chocolate Cookie Specials

Almost every country kitchen has
a bulging recipe file of chocolate
cookies. That's a sure sign of their
top rating.

The recipes that follow are from
many farm and ranch homes and
from our Test Kitchens. Turn the
pages to find some tempting new
kinds.

INDIAN BARS

They're extra-moist chocolate brownies, and that means they're wonderful

1   c. butter or margarine
2   squares unsweetened
      chocolate
2   c. sugar
4   eggs, slightly beaten
1 ½ c. sifted flour
1   tsp. baking powder
2   tsp. vanilla
1   c. chopped pecans

• Melt butter and chocolate over low heat. Add sugar and eggs; mix thoroughly.
• Sift flour with baking powder; stir into creamed mixture. Mix in vanilla and nuts.
• Bake in a greased 13 × 9 × 2″ pan in moderate oven (350°) 35 to 40 minutes. Cool completely in pan. Cut into bars. Makes 2 dozen cookies.

Note: You can cut the recipe in half to make 12 cookie bars. Use an 8 × 8 × 2″ pan for baking the cookie mixture.

ORANGE BROWNIES

The new twist in these brownies is the delicate fresh orange taste

2   squares unsweetened chocolate
½   c. butter
2   eggs
1   c. sugar
1   tsp. vanilla
½   tsp. grated orange peel
½   c. sifted flour
⅛   tsp. salt
1   c. chopped walnuts

• Melt chocolate and butter. Beat eggs; beat in sugar gradually. Beat in butter and chocolate, vanilla and orange peel.
• Stir in flour, salt and nuts. Pour into buttered 8″ square pan.
• Bake in moderate oven (350°) 20 to 25 minutes. Do not overbake. Cut into squares. Makes about 1 dozen.

VARIATION

Double Chocolate Brownies: Stir in ½ c. semisweet chocolate pieces along with the nuts.

APPLESAUCE FUDGIES

Cookies contain applesauce—they'll stay moist longer than most brownies

2   squares unsweetened chocolate
½   c. butter
½   c. sweetened applesauce
2   eggs, beaten
1   c. brown sugar
1   tsp. vanilla
1   c. sifted flour
½   tsp. baking powder
¼   tsp. baking soda
¼   tsp. salt
½   c. chopped walnuts

• Melt chocolate and butter together.
• Mix applesauce, eggs, sugar and vanilla. Sift dry ingredients into applesauce mixture. Stir until blended; add chocolate and stir well.
• Pour into greased 9 × 9 × 2″ pan. Sprinkle with walnuts. Bake in moderate oven (350°) 30 minutes. Cool; cut into 16 squares.

FUDGE NUT BARS

Luscious fudge nut filling bakes between two layers of cookie mixture

Cookie Dough:
1   c. butter or margarine
2   c. light brown sugar

2 eggs
2 tsp. vanilla
2½ c. sifted flour
1 tsp. baking soda
1 tsp. salt
3 c. quick rolled oats, uncooked

Fudge Nut Filling:
1 (12 oz.) pkg. semisweet chocolate pieces
1 c. sweetened condensed milk
2 tblsp. butter or margarine
½ tsp. salt
1 c. chopped nuts
2 tsp. vanilla

• Cream together butter and sugar. Mix in eggs and vanilla.
• Sift together flour, soda and salt; stir in rolled oats. Add dry ingredients to creamed mixture. Set aside while you make filling.
• In a saucepan over boiling water, mix together chocolate pieces, sweetened condensed milk, butter and salt. Stir until chocolate pieces are melted and mixture is smooth. Remove from heat, and stir in nuts and vanilla.
• Spread about two thirds of cookie dough in bottom of a greased 15½ × 10½ × 1″ jelly roll pan. Cover with fudge filling. Dot with remainder of cookie dough and swirl it over fudge filling.
• Bake in moderate oven (350°) 25 to 30 minutes, or until lightly browned. Cut into small (2 × 1″) bars. Makes 60 bars.

FARMHOUSE CHOCOLATE CRUNCH

These chewy cookies containing black walnuts are first cousins of candy

⅔ c. butter or margarine
½ c. light corn syrup

1 tsp. salt
3 tsp. vanilla
1 c. brown sugar
4 c. quick rolled oats, uncooked
2 (6 oz.) pkgs. semisweet chocolate pieces
½ c. chopped black walnuts

• Melt butter in a large saucepan. Add syrup, salt, vanilla, brown sugar and rolled oats; mix well. Press into a well-greased 15½ × 10½ × 1″ jelly roll pan.
• Bake in hot oven (425°) 12 minutes. During the last 2 minutes of baking, sprinkle on chocolate pieces. When they melt, remove pan from oven and spread chocolate evenly to cover top. Sprinkle with chopped nuts. Cut in squares while still warm. Recut when cool. Makes about 48 (1½″) squares.

3-LAYER CHOCOLATE SQUARES

The cookies to make when your oven is busy—they're good, no-bake treats

½ c. butter or margarine
¼ c. cocoa
½ c. sifted confectioners sugar
1 egg, slightly beaten
2 tsp. vanilla
3 c. graham cracker crumbs
½ c. chopped pecans
¼ c. butter or margarine
1 tsp. cornstarch
2 tsp. sugar
3 tblsp. light cream or evaporated milk
1 tsp. vanilla
2 c. sifted confectioners sugar
1 (9¾ oz.) sweet chocolate bar

• Melt ½ c. butter. Add the following ingredients, one at a time, stirring after each addition: cocoa, ½ c. confectioners sugar, egg, 2 tsp. vanilla, cracker crumbs and pecans. Stir until mixture is well blended, then press it into 13 × 9 × 2" pan.

• Melt ¼ c. butter. Combine cornstarch and 2 tsp. sugar; add to butter and blend thoroughly. Add cream; cook, stirring constantly, until thick and smooth. Cool; add 1 tsp. vanilla and 2 c. confectioners sugar. Blend well and spread over first layer. (Drop by teaspoonfuls and spread carefully —this is a stiff mixture.)

• Melt chocolate bar over hot water; spread it over the cream filling. Cool at room temperature and cut in small squares before chocolate sets completely. Makes 60 (1") squares.

NUT-CRESTED COOKIE SQUARES

Fine selection for Christmas cookie exchange. Candy-like cookies taste good with punch, hot coffee or tea

1 c. butter (½ lb.)
1 c. brown sugar, firmly packed
1 tsp. vanilla
1 egg
2 c. sifted flour
⅛ tsp. salt
1 (6 oz.) pkg. semisweet
    chocolate pieces
½ c. finely chopped nuts

• Cream butter until fluffy; add brown sugar and beat until light. Add vanilla and egg; then add the flour and salt. Blend well.

• Spread evenly about ¼" thick on baking sheet. Bake in moderate oven (350°) 15 minutes.

• Meanwhile melt chocolate pieces.

• Remove baking sheet from oven and at once spread melted chocolate pieces over top to frost evenly. Sprin-

kle with nuts. Cut in 2" squares while still hot. Cool on racks. Makes about 48 cookies.

HALLOWEEN 3-DECKER BROWNIES

Fudge-type brownies are the base of these festive orange-and-black treats

First Deck:

2 squares unsweetened chocolate
½ c. butter
1 c. sugar
2 eggs, beaten
½ tsp. vanilla
½ c. sifted flour
½ c. chopped pecans

Second Deck:

1 c. confectioners sugar
2 tblsp. soft butter
2 tsp. milk
½ tsp. vanilla
3 or 4 drops orange food color
    (or use mixture of yellow
    and red to make orange)

Third Deck:

¼ square unsweetened
    chocolate
1½ tsp. butter

• To make first deck, combine chocolate and butter; melt over hot water. Beat in sugar, eggs and vanilla. Stir in flour and nuts. Bake in a greased 8" square pan in slow oven (325°) 30 to 35 minutes. Cool in pan on rack.

• To make second layer, combine confectioners sugar, 2 tblsp. soft butter, milk and vanilla to make a smooth mixture. Tint orange with food color. Spread over brownies in pan. Chill 10 minutes.

• To make third deck, combine chocolate and butter; melt over hot water. Drizzle from small spoon over top of brownies. Cool and cut in squares. Makes 16 squares.

Note: When in a hurry, use packaged brownie mix for the first deck. For the Christmas season, tint second deck green.

Fresh-from-the-Oven Cookies

The contributor of the recipe for Oatmeal-Coconut Crisps and its variations keeps the dough in a tight container in her refrigerator for several days—sometimes a few weeks. It's a great recipe; she finds it easier to bake a few cookies at a time. And, in addition, she can always serve cookies with that wonderful fresh-from-the-oven aroma and taste.

OATMEAL-COCONUT CRISPS

Taste-testers voted these the best oatmeal cookies they've sampled

    2   c. butter or margarine
    2   c. brown sugar, firmly
           packed
    2   c. white sugar
    2   tsp. vanilla
    4   eggs
    3   c. sifted flour
    2   tsp. salt
    2   tsp. baking soda
    6   c. quick-cooking rolled oats
 1 ½   c. flaked coconut

• Cream butter and sugars together until fluffy. Stir in vanilla; then add eggs, one at a time, beating after each addition.
• Sift together flour, salt and baking soda. Add to creamed mixture. Stir in rolled oats and coconut.

• Drop by teaspoonfuls, about 2″ apart, onto well-greased baking sheets. Bake in moderate oven (350°) 10 to 15 minutes. Makes 14 dozen cookies.

Note: You can divide the dough into three equal parts and add ⅓ c. flaked coconut to one part, ⅓ c. raisins to the second part and ⅓ c. chopped walnuts to the third part.

VARIATIONS

Oatmeal Raisin Cookies: Use raisins instead of coconut.

Oatmeal Nut Cookies: Use chopped walnuts instead of coconut.

Oatmeal Butter Crisps: Omit flaked coconut.

OATMEAL-MOLASSES COOKIES

Watch the youngsters and their guests enjoy these really big, chewy cookies

 8 ½   c. sifted flour
    1   tblsp. salt
    2   tblsp. baking soda
    8   c. quick-cooking rolled oats
 2 ½   c. sugar
    1   tblsp. ground ginger
    2   c. melted vegetable
           shortening
    2   c. light molasses
    4   eggs, beaten
   ¼   c. hot water
    3   c. seedless raisins
    2   c. ground black walnuts or
           English walnuts

• Reserve ½ c. flour. Sift together 8 c. flour, salt and baking soda.
• In a very large bowl or dishpan, mix oatmeal, sugar and ginger. Stir in shortening, molasses, eggs, hot water, sifted dry ingredients, raisins

and nuts. Work dough with hands until well mixed. Add the ½ c. flour if needed to make dough workable.
- Roll dough to ¼" thickness; cut with 3½" cookie cutter.
- Place cut cookies on lightly greased baking sheets. Brush with water and sprinkle with sugar.
- Bake in moderate oven (375°) 8 to 10 minutes. Makes 6 dozen.

MEXICAN SESAME SEED COOKIES

Anise seeds give these thin sugar cookies a new unusual taste

1 tblsp. whole anise seeds
2 tblsp. boiling water
⅔ c. sugar
¾ c. butter or margarine
⅛ tsp. baking soda
1 egg
2 c. sifted flour
1 egg, lightly beaten
Toasted sesame seeds (see Index
    under Seed Seasoners)

- Combine anise seeds and boiling water and let stand. Beat together sugar and butter until fluffy. Beat in soda and 1 egg. Drain anise seeds and add to mixture.
- Stir in flour, a little at a time, and mix well. Wrap dough in waxed paper and chill overnight.
- When ready to bake, roll dough into ½" balls. Place on ungreased baking sheets about 3" apart. Flatten to 1/16" thickness with the bottom of a glass. Brush tops with lightly beaten egg. Sprinkle each with toasted sesame seeds.
- Bake in hot oven (400°) 7 to 8 minutes, or until lightly browned. Makes 6 dozen.

BUTTERSCOTCH STRIPS

Cookies three ways—strips, man-size squares and a 4-layer stack

½ c. butter
2 c. brown sugar, firmly packed
2 eggs
2 c. sifted flour
2 tsp. baking powder
½ c. chopped nuts
½ tsp. salt
2 tsp. vanilla

- Melt butter, add to sugar and cool. Blend in eggs. Stir in remaining ingredients.
- Spread in a 13 × 9 × 2" baking pan. Bake in slow oven (325°) about 30 minutes. While still warm, cut into 24 strips about 3 × 1½". Roll in confectioners sugar, if you wish.

Note: These may be cut in 12 (3 × 3") squares for man-size cookies.

VARIATION

Butterscotch Stack: Mix dough and divide into 4 equal portions. Roll or pat out each portion into an 8" circle between 2 pieces of waxed paper (draw an 8" circle on counter top for guide).
- Chill circles in refrigerator until top piece of paper can be peeled off easily; transfer circles on waxed paper to baking sheets.
- Bake in slow oven (325°) about 20 minutes. You may bake two at a time by using both oven shelves; be sure to exchange top and bottom baking sheets after 10 minutes in the oven for even browning.
- Remove from baking sheet and cool on rack. When cool, peel off paper. Stack circles, spreading each with filling of whipped cream or scoops of

softened ice cream. Freeze. To serve, let stand at room temperature about 15 minutes. Cut into wedges. Makes 10 to 12 servings.

Fruited Cookies That Please

If there is any one kind of cookies that farmers like most, it's those laden with fruit, and with nuts for good measure. Raisins, dates, figs, prunes, oranges and lemons, for instance, have an honored place in many country cookie doughs, as the following recipes indicate. All make mighty good eating.

RANCH HOUSE RAISIN COOKIES

You cook the raisins before you stir them into cookie mixture—ranchers call them Boiled Raisin Cookies

½ c. raisins
1 c. water
1 c. brown sugar, firmly packed
½ c. shortening
1 egg
½ tsp. vanilla
1 ¾ c. sifted flour
½ tsp. salt
½ tsp. baking powder
½ tsp. baking soda
½ c. chopped nuts

• Bring raisins to a boil with water. Cool thoroughly.
• Cream sugar and shortening until fluffy. Add egg and vanilla. Beat to mix.
• Sift together flour, salt, baking powder and soda. Alternately add to creamed mixture with cooled raisins (should be ½ c. liquid with raisins;

if not, add water to make ½ c.). Stir in nuts.
• Drop dough by teaspoonfuls onto greased baking sheets at least 2″ apart.
• Bake in moderate oven (350°) 10 to 12 minutes. Makes 4 dozen.

ORANGE-GLAZED PRUNE COOKIES

Brown cookies with yellow topknots combine spicy prune and orange flavors. Make them small for parties

2 c. brown sugar
1 c. butter or vegetable shortening
2 eggs, beaten
½ c. milk
3 ½ c. sifted flour
1 tsp. baking powder
1 tsp. baking soda
1 tsp. cinnamon
½ tsp. salt
2 c. cooked prunes, chopped
1 c. walnuts, chopped
1 tsp. vanilla
Orange Glaze

• Cream together sugar and butter; stir in eggs and milk.
• Sift together flour, baking powder, soda, cinnamon and salt; stir into brown sugar mixture. Add prunes, nuts and vanilla.
• Drop by small spoonfuls onto greased baking sheet. Bake in moderate oven (350°) 15 to 20 minutes, until lightly browned. Cool on wire rack.
• Spread tops of cooled cookies with a thin layer of Orange Glaze. Makes 8½ dozen cookies.

Orange Glaze: Blend together 3 c. confectioners sugar, grated peel of 1 orange and 4 tblsp. orange juice.

DATE SANDWICH BARS

When you're asked to bring cookies, carry these favorites in baking pan covered with foil—also store in pan

¼ c. granulated sugar
3 c. cut-up dates
1½ c. water
¾ c. soft butter or margarine
1 c. brown sugar, firmly packed
1¾ c. sifted flour
½ tsp. baking soda
1 tsp. salt
1½ c. quick-cooking rolled oats

• Mix granulated sugar, dates and water, and cook over low heat until mixture thickens. Stir to prevent scorching. Set aside to cool.

• Thoroughly mix butter and brown sugar. Beat until fluffy.

• Stir flour, baking soda and salt together. Stir into the brown sugar-butter mixture. Add rolled oats and mix well. Divide in half and spread one part into a greased 13 × 9 × 2″ pan. Flatten and press it down with hands so the mixture will cover the bottom of the pan.

• Spread the cooled date mixture on top. Sprinkle evenly with the second half of the rolled oat mixture. Pat it down lightly with hands.

• Bake in hot oven (400°) until a delicate brown, 25 to 30 minutes. Remove from oven and while the cookie is warm, cut it into bars the size you like. Remove the bars at once from pan to a wire rack to finish cooling. Makes about 30 (2 × 1½″) bars.

When making cookies, you can substitute 2 egg yolks and 2 tblsp. water for 1 whole egg. For custards, you can use 2 egg yolks for 1 whole egg.

FIG BARS

These butter cookies store well—the moist fig filling is not overly sweet

Dough:

1 c. butter
2 c. brown sugar, firmly packed
3 eggs
1 tsp. vanilla
1 tblsp. lemon juice
4 c. flour
1 tsp. salt
1 tsp. baking soda
1 tsp. baking powder

Fig Filling:

1½ c. ground figs
1 c. water
¾ c. sugar
3 tblsp. flour
¼ c. chopped walnuts
2 tblsp. orange juice

• To make dough, cream butter and sugar. Add eggs, vanilla and lemon juice; beat. Stir together dry ingredients; blend into creamed mixture. Chill.

• Meanwhile, prepare fig filling. Boil figs in water 5 minutes. Blend sugar and flour; stir into figs. Cook over low heat, stirring frequently, until thick. Stir in nuts and orange juice. Cool.

• Divide chilled dough in half. Roll each half in a rectangle 18 × 12 × ⅛″ on well-floured pastry cloth. Cut into four 3″ wide strips. Put cooled filling down center of strips. Using a spatula, fold dough over filling. Cut strips in half; transfer strips, seam side down, to ungreased baking sheet. Bake in moderate oven (375°) about 15 minutes. Cool. Cut; makes about 5 dozen (2″) bars.

LEMON LOVE NOTES

Brown-topped cookies have crunchy crust, rich and luscious lemon filling

½ c. soft butter (room temperature)
1 c. flour
¼ c. confectioners sugar
1 c. sugar
2 tblsp. flour
½ tsp. baking powder
2 eggs, beaten
2 tblsp. lemon juice
2 tsp. grated lemon peel

• Mix butter, 1 c. flour and confectioners sugar. Press into an 8″ square pan. Bake in moderate oven (350°). Cool in pan on rack.
• Combine sugar, 2 tblsp. flour and baking powder. Add eggs, lemon juice and peel. Mix well. Pour on baked, cooled mixture in pan.
• Bake in moderate oven (350°) 25 minutes. (Top puffs up in baking, but falls in cooling.) Cool and cut in squares. Makes 16 cookies.

LEMON-COCONUT SQUARES

Delicate texture, fresh lemon flavor —a favorite from our Country Cookbook

Cookie Dough:
1 ½ c. sifted flour
½ c. brown sugar
½ c. butter or margarine

Filling:
2 eggs, beaten
1 c. brown sugar, firmly packed
1 ½ c. flaked or shredded coconut
1 c. chopped nuts
2 tblsp. flour
½ tsp. baking powder

¼ tsp. salt
½ tsp. vanilla

Frosting:
1 c. confectioners sugar
1 tblsp. melted butter or margarine
Juice of 1 lemon

• Mix together ingredients for cookie dough; pat down well in buttered 13 × 9 × 2″ pan. Bake in very slow oven (275°) 10 minutes.
• To make filling, combine eggs, sugar, coconut, nuts, flour, baking powder, salt and vanilla. Spread on top of baked mixture. Bake in moderate oven (350°) 20 minutes.
• While still warm, spread with frosting made by combining confectioners sugar, melted butter and lemon juice. Cut in squares. Makes about 24 (2″) squares.

Cookies to Share with Friends

"Here are three of the best cookies I've ever tasted," says a Utah home economist, the mother of three sons and a daughter. That is her recommendation for Sand Balls, Frosted Drop Brownies and Best-Ever Butterscotch Cookies. She especially likes to pass a plate of the brownies and butterscotch cookies to guests. "This pair of cookies always wins praise," she adds. Make them for a special occasion and see if you don't get the same reactions.

SAND BALLS

Honey enhances flavor; double roll in sugar produces snowy white coating

- 1   c. butter
- ½   c. confectioners sugar
- 2   tblsp. honey
- 2¼ c. sifted flour
- ¼   tsp. salt
- 1   tsp. vanilla
- ¾   c. chopped walnuts

• Cream butter, confectioners sugar and honey together thoroughly. Add flour, salt, vanilla and nuts. Mix with hands, if necessary, to blend well.
• Form into balls 1″ in diameter and chill thoroughly.
• To bake, place cookie balls 2½″ apart on a greased baking sheet. Bake in moderate oven (375°) 14 to 17 minutes. While still warm, roll in confectioners sugar. Cool. Then roll in confectioners sugar again. Makes 4 dozen cookies.

FROSTED DROP BROWNIES

Frost some cookies white, some with chocolate for contrast. Serve on tray

- ½   c. butter or margarine
- ¾   c. sugar
- 1   egg
- 2   squares unsweetened chocolate
- 1¾ c. sifted flour
- ½   tsp. baking soda
- ½   tsp. salt
- ½   c. milk
- 1   tsp. vanilla
- ½   c. chopped nuts

Shiny White Icing or Chocolate Icing

• Cream butter and sugar until fluffy.

Add egg and beat well. Stir in melted chocolate.
• Sift together flour, baking soda and salt. Add alternately with the milk to the chocolate mixture. Stir in vanilla and nuts.
• Drop by teaspoonfuls 2″ apart onto ungreased baking sheet; bake in hot oven (400°) 8 to 10 minutes. Cool; then frost with Shiny White Icing or Chocolate Icing. Makes 3 dozen cookies.

Shiny White Icing: Add enough cream or top milk to 2 c. sifted confectioners sugar to make icing of spreading consistency. Add ½ tsp. vanilla. Drop 1 tsp. icing onto center of each cookie and swirl with a fork. Top with walnut or pecan halves. (Tint part of the icing a delicate pink with a few drops red food color. Flavor with peppermint extract, if you like.)

Chocolate Icing: Add 1 square unsweetened chocolate, melted, to 1 c. sifted confectioners sugar; beat in enough cream or top milk to make icing of spreading consistency. Add ½ tsp. vanilla.

BEST-EVER BUTTERSCOTCH COOKIES

About the best cookies you can bake

- ½   c. butter or margarine
- 1½ c. brown sugar, firmly packed
- 2   eggs, beaten
- 2½ c. sifted flour
- 1   tsp. baking soda
- ½   tsp. baking powder
- ½   tsp. salt
- 1   c. cream, soured (evaporated milk with vinegar)
- 1   tsp. vanilla

⅔ c. chopped nuts
Butter Brown Icing

• Cream together butter and sugar until well blended. Add eggs (well beaten); beat until fluffy. Alternately add flour, sifted with baking soda, baking powder and salt, with sour cream (see note for directions for souring evaporated milk). Stir in vanilla and nuts.

• Drop on greased baking sheet about 2½" apart. Bake in moderate oven (350°) 10 to 12 minutes, or until lightly brown and barely firm to touch. Frost with Butter Brown Icing. Makes 5 dozen cookies.

Note: You can use sour cream, but best results (according to women who use this recipe) are obtained by pouring 1 tblsp. vinegar into a 1-cup measuring cup and filling cup with evaporated milk. Let stand 15 minutes at room temperature before using.

Butter Brown Icing: Melt ¼ c. butter (must be butter) in small saucepan and cook over medium heat, stirring constantly, until butter stops bubbling and is nut-brown in color (do not scorch). Combine with 2 c. confectioners sugar and 2 or 3 tblsp. boiling water; beat until smooth and of spreading consistency.

Dainty Party Cookies

Size can determine the occasion for which cookies are appropriate. For parties—especially teas—small, dainty cookies are the order of the day, while for picnics, larger or man-size cookies get top billing. You can bake or cut most of the cookies in this section in small, medium or large sizes.

The recipe for Peppermint Kisses comes from a 12-year-old Indiana farm girl, the daughter of a member of FARM JOURNAL's Test Group, who bakes them for her mother's parties. Like many other junior cooks, this young lady is a great cookie baker. Leaf through the collection of cookie recipes in this cookbook and then point out to your daughter some she'll like to try. That's one way to bring up a good cook. Interest and encouragement are fine teachers.

GRAPEFRUIT SUGAR COOKIES

These dainty cookies make talk at tea parties—guests want to know why they're so good. Candied peel is the secret

1   c. butter
1 ¼ c. sugar
2   eggs
3   c. sifted flour
2 ½ tsp. baking powder
½   tsp. salt
¾   c. finely chopped candied grapefruit peel (see Index)

• Cream butter and sugar; add eggs and beat until fluffy. Sift dry ingredients together; mix chopped grapefruit peel into dry ingredients. Combine the mixtures. Divide dough in half; put in covered container and refrigerate several hours.

• Roll about ¼" thick on floured board, cut with floured cutter.

• Place on greased baking sheets and bake in moderate oven (375°) 8 to 10 minutes. Makes 60 cookies.

PECAN COOKIES

Jewel-like centers make these a pretty addition to the party tray or plate

2 c. ground pecans
⅔ c. sugar
½ tsp. salt
2 egg whites
⅓ c. strawberry preserves
18 candied or maraschino
   cherries, cut in halves

• Combine pecans and sugar. Add salt and egg whites and mix until mixture is completely moistened.
• Form into small balls (mixture will be moist). Place on ungreased baking sheet. Press a small hole in center of each ball with your finger tip. Fill with strawberry preserves. Top with cherry halves, cut side down.
• Bake in moderate oven (350°) about 15 minutes. Remove from baking sheet at once to prevent sticking. Makes 36 cookies.

DEBBIE'S PEPPERMINT KISSES

A 12-year-old Hoosier farm girl bakes the dainties for her mother's parties

4 egg whites
¼ tsp. salt
¼ tsp. cream of tartar
1 tsp. peppermint extract
1½ c. brown sugar, firmly packed
1 (12 oz.) pkg. semisweet
   chocolate pieces

• Beat egg whites, salt, cream of tartar and peppermint extract together until soft peaks form.
• Add brown sugar gradually, beating all the time. Beat until stiff peaks form.
• Set aside 48 chocolate pieces and fold remaining pieces into the egg white mixture.
• Drop teaspoonfuls on plain paper spread on a baking sheet. Top each with a chocolate piece.
• Bake in slow oven (300°) 20 to 25 minutes, or until set and slightly brown. Remove from paper while slightly warm. Makes 48 kisses.

Note: To remove kisses from paper easily, remove paper from baking sheet, spread a wet towel on the hot baking sheet and place the paper of kisses on top. Let stand only 1 minute. The steam will loosen the kisses and they will slip off easily on a spatula.

ALMOND CIRCLES

These dainty rich cookies sometimes are called Finnish shortbread

2 c. butter
1 c. sugar
4 c. sifted flour
⅛ tsp. salt
Chopped almonds
Sugar

• Cream butter and 1 c. sugar thoroughly. Add flour and salt. Shape in long, slender rolls 1" in diameter. Wrap rolls in waxed paper and chill thoroughly.
• To bake, cut in slices ½" thick. Press each circle down with your thumb. Sprinkle with almonds, then with sugar. Bake in hot oven (400°) 7 to 10 minutes. Cookies should not brown. Makes about 14 dozen.

Note: You can take the dough from the refrigerator and bake cookies whenever convenient. It's a good idea to chill the dough at least 24 hours.

CREAMY SATIN FILLING

So smooth—it deserves its name

½ c. sugar
3 tblsp. cornstarch
3 tblsp. flour
½ tsp. salt
2 c. milk
1 egg, slightly beaten
½ c. heavy cream, whipped
1 tsp. vanilla

• Combine sugar, cornstarch, flour and salt in saucepan.
• Gradually add milk, stirring until smooth. Cook, stirring constantly, until mixture is thick and bubbling.
• Stir a little of this hot mixture into egg, then add to hot mixture and cook until just bubbling hot again.
• Cool, then chill thoroughly. This mixture will be very thick. Beat with mixer or rotary beater until smooth.
• Fold in whipped cream and vanilla.

Shiny Glaze: Crush ½ c. fresh strawberries. Add ½ c. water and cook 2 minutes; strain through sieve. Combine ¼ c. sugar and 1 tblsp. cornstarch in small saucepan; stir in berry juice. Cook, stirring constantly, until thick and clear. Cool; spoon carefully over strawberries in the pie.

New and Old Company Pies

You might call this pie section a postscript to *Farm Journal's Complete Pie Cookbook*, which you probably have. The book contains almost all the really good pie recipes available when it was published. But because pie is extremely popular in country entertaining, our Test Kitchens constantly develop new recipes. Here are some new, choice ones, plus a few from the *Complete Pie Cookbook* and several from the personal files of farm women.

STRAWBERRY SATIN PIE

What makes a June day more perfect? This gorgeous pie, which we score 100% (see photo in this book)

Baked 9" pie shell
½ c. sliced toasted almonds
Creamy Satin Filling
1½ c. fresh strawberries
Shiny Glaze

• Cover bottom of baked pie shell with almonds.
• Cover almonds with Creamy Satin Filling. Chill thoroughly at least 3 hours, or overnight.
• Slice strawberries in halves, reserving a few perfect berries for center of pie. Arrange on filling in layers, starting at outer edge. Place some berries cut side up to make a pattern. Cover with Shiny Glaze. Refrigerate 1 hr. or until serving time. Makes 8 servings.

Frosted Fruit Centerpiece: *Select two or more kinds of fruit, such as red apples, pears, lemons, oranges and different kinds of grapes, divided into small clusters. Dip in egg white and roll in granulated sugar. Place on wire racks to dry thoroughly. (Lay waxed paper under racks to catch drip.) Arrange fruit with a few green leaves in a bowl or on a tray.*

TWO-TIERED STRAWBERRY PIE

Another make-ahead dessert to chill until time to serve your guests

Baked 9" pie shell
½ c. sifted confectioners sugar
½ tsp. vanilla
¼ tsp. almond extract
1 (3 oz.) pkg. cream cheese
½ c. heavy cream, whipped
⅓ c. sugar
2 tblsp. cornstarch
⅓ c. water
⅓ c. grenadine syrup
1 tblsp. lemon juice
2 c. fresh whole strawberries

• Add confectioners sugar, vanilla and almond extract to cheese and beat until smooth and creamy.
• Fold in whipped cream. Spread evenly over bottom of baked pie shell. Chill thoroughly several hours.
• Combine ⅓ c. sugar and cornstarch in saucepan. Add water slowly, stirring to make a smooth mixture. Add grenadine and lemon juice.
• Cook, stirring constantly, until thick and clear. Cool.
• Add to strawberries, stir to coat with glaze. Spread over top of chilled cheese layer. Chill before serving.

CREAM CHEESE PIE

Pie can have red or gold trim—strawberries in summer, dried apricots in winter. A bake-ahead-and-chill pie

1 c. graham cracker crumbs
6 tblsp. butter
3 tblsp. sugar
12 oz. cream cheese
½ c. sugar
2 eggs
1 tblsp. vanilla
1 c. dairy sour cream
3 tsp. sugar
1 tsp. vanilla
16 whole strawberries, or cooked dried apricots

• Mix crumbs, butter and sugar; press into 9" pie pan; chill.
• Blend well the cheese, sugar, eggs and 1 tblsp. vanilla. Pour into crust.
• Bake in very slow oven (250°) 20 to 25 minutes. Cool slightly. Cover with mixture of cream, sugar and 1 tsp. vanilla. Return to oven and bake 10 minutes. Chill. To serve, decorate top with fruit. Makes 8 servings.

PEACH PECAN PIE

The crunchy nut top gives this peach pie a new look and extra-good flavor

¼ c. soft butter or margarine
¼ c. sugar
2 tblsp. flour
½ c. light corn syrup
¼ tsp. salt
3 eggs
1½ c. diced fresh peaches
1 unbaked (9") pie shell
Nut Crumb Topping (see recipe)

• Cream together butter, sugar and flour. Stir in syrup and salt. Mix well. Beat in eggs, one at a time, until just blended. Add peaches; pour into pie shell. Sprinkle with topping.
• Bake in hot oven (400°) about 35 minutes or until knife comes out clean when inserted halfway between center and edge of pie. Serve chilled.

Nut Crumb Topping: Combine ¼ c. flour and ¼ c. brown sugar; work in 2 tblsp. soft butter until crumbly; add ½ c. coarsely chopped pecans.

PEACH CUSTARD PIE

Custard pie with a delicate peach flavor—filling has pumpkin pie texture

Unbaked 9" pie shell
1   c. sugar
3   tblsp. flour
½   tsp. salt
½   tsp. ginger
½   tsp. cinnamon
½   tsp. nutmeg
1 ½   c. fresh Peach Purée
3   eggs, slightly beaten
1   c. milk
1   (6 oz.) can evaporated milk

• Combine sugar, flour, salt and spices. Add peach purée and stir well. Add eggs, milk and evaporated milk; blend.

• Pour part of mixture into unbaked pie shell. Place in oven and then carefully pour in the remaining mixture. Bake in very hot oven (450°) 10 minutes, then in slow oven (325°) about 45 minutes, or until knife comes out clean when inserted halfway between center and outer edge of pie. Cool to serve.

Peach Purée: Peel soft, ripe peaches and put through a sieve, colander or food mill. Or purée them in an electric blender.

REFRIGERATOR CUSTARD PIE

When you want a different, extra-good dessert to make ahead, try this

1   (8 ½ oz.) pkg. chocolate
      wafers, crushed into fine
      crumbs
½   c. melted butter or margarine
1   envelope plus 1 tsp.
      unflavored gelatin
¼   c. cold water

4   eggs, separated
⅔   c. sugar
1 ⅓   c. milk
1   tsp. vanilla
¼   tsp. almond extract
1   c. heavy cream

• Reserve 2 tblsp. wafer crumbs for topping. Mix rest of crumbs with melted butter, and press into two 9" pie pans. Bake in moderate oven (375°) 6 to 8 minutes. Cool.

• Soften gelatin in cold water.

• Combine egg yolks and sugar in saucepan. Stir in milk. Cook over medium heat about 5 minutes, or until mixture forms a very thin custard sauce that coats the spoon. Do not overcook. Add softened gelatin and stir until dissolved. Cool custard quickly to room temperature (over ice water).

• Beat egg whites until stiff but not dry. Fold into cooled custard mixture along with vanilla and almond extract. Whip heavy cream and fold into custard.

• Pour filling into cooled crusts; top with reserved crumbs. Refrigerate until firm. Makes 2 (9") pies.

MARSHMALLOW CREAM PEACH PIE

From our Let's Start to Cook *cookbook—a big success with junior bakers*

9" graham cracker crust
18   marshmallows
¼   c. milk
1   c. heavy cream, whipped
3   c. diced peaches (5 to 6
      medium peaches)

• Melt marshmallows in milk in top of double boiler. Cool until set. Beat until smooth; fold into whipped cream.

• Fold peaches into marshmallow-cream mixture. Pile into graham cracker crust. Chill several hours, or until firm.

PEAR ORCHARD PIE

Pears accented with orange juice bake in 1-crust pie with crisp brown top

Unbaked 9" pie shell
5 large Bartlett pears
3 tblsp. frozen orange juice concentrate
½ tsp. grated lemon peel
¾ c. flour
½ c. sugar
⅛ tsp. salt
1 tsp. cinnamon
½ tsp. ginger
½ c. butter or margarine

• Peel, core and slice pears thinly. Toss lightly with undiluted orange juice concentrate and lemon peel. Arrange in pie shell.

• Mix remaining ingredients until crumbly. Sprinkle evenly over pears.

• Bake in hot oven (400°) 40 minutes, or until fruit is tender.

SPICY APPLE CRUNCH PIE

New, unusually delicious apple pie— a FARM JOURNAL *5-star recipe*

Unbaked 9" pie shell
3 egg yolks
1½ c. sugar
1 tblsp. flour
1 tsp. cinnamon
⅛ tsp. cloves
1 tblsp. melted butter
1 tblsp. vinegar
1 c. pared and grated apples (2 to 3 medium)

½ c. chopped pecans
3 egg whites

• Beat egg yolks until thick and lemon-colored.

• Combine sugar, flour, and spices. Add to egg yolks alternately with butter and vinegar; mix well.

• Stir in apples and pecans.

• Beat egg whites until stiff peaks form. Fold into apple mixture, blending well.

• Pour into unbaked pie shell.

• Bake in moderate oven (350°) about 50 minutes, or until knife inserted 1" from edge of pie comes out clean.

DEEP-DISH PEAR AND MINCEMEAT PIE

Cheese pastry tops mincemeat and pears in this unforgettable dessert

Filling:
4 large pears (3 c. sliced)
¼ c. sugar
1 tblsp. flour
¼ tsp. salt
1½ c. mincemeat
1 tblsp. lemon juice
2 tblsp. butter

Pastry:
1 c. sifted flour
½ tsp. salt
⅓ c. shortening
¼ c. grated Cheddar cheese
2 tblsp. water

• Arrange pear slices in bottom of an 8 × 8 × 2" baking dish. Combine sugar, flour and salt; sprinkle over pears. Cover with mincemeat; sprinkle with lemon juice and dot with butter.

• Prepare pastry: Combine flour and salt; cut in shortening until mixture resembles coarse meal. Add cheese and toss to blend. Add water gradually to form soft dough. Roll out to fit top of fruit in dish. Place pastry on fruit. Crimp edges and cut slits for steam to escape. Bake in hot oven (425°) 35 to 40 minutes. Serve warm. Makes 6 servings.

Apple Pie That's Different

When you want to serve guests a dessert that's beautiful and exceptionally good, select this company-special apple pie. It's a favorite of a Minnesota home economist, whose friends rate her a gracious hostess who always serves exciting, distinctive food.

You'll need time to make this dessert, but the reception your guests give it will repay you for every minute you spend. Choose the right occasion to offer this pie—when men are among the guests. You'll be proud of your dessert and the compliments it will get.

SCHLOSS HERBLINGEN PIE

An open-face pie with apple slices showing through a butter-sugar glaze

Pastry for 1-crust 9" pie
1 tblsp. fine dry bread crumbs
1 tblsp. crushed toasted
   almonds (optional)
Thinly sliced tart apples, about 4 c.
1 egg
1 egg yolk
1 c. heavy cream
½ c. sugar
⅛ tsp. salt
¼ tsp. cinnamon
¼ tsp. nutmeg

1½ tblsp. melted butter or
   margarine
3 tblsp. sugar

• Line pie pan with pastry. Sprinkle crumbs and almonds over pastry; arrange apple slices in pie pan, layering evenly; do not heap. Use enough apples to level across the top.

• Bake in moderate oven (350°) 5 minutes.

• Meanwhile combine egg and egg yolk. Beat slightly. Blend in cream and sugar. Add salt, cinnamon and nutmeg, and stir until sugar dissolves. Pour half of egg mixture over apples and bake until custard is firm, about 30 minutes.

• Pour remaining egg mixture evenly over partially baked filling. Bake again until knife inserted near edge comes out clean, 30 minutes.

• Remove pie from oven and pour melted butter over top. Sprinkle evenly with the 3 tblsp. sugar. Return to oven long enough to glaze topping, about 8 minutes. Cool slightly before cutting. Makes 8 servings.

NO-CRUST APPLE PIE

Help guests cut calories—serve them this tasty pie without pastry. The weight-watchers will appreciate it

6 medium-size tart peeled
   apples, cut in eighths
½ c. sugar
1 tsp. cinnamon
½ c. water
3 tblsp. butter or margarine
¼ c. brown sugar
½ c. sifted flour
½ tsp. baking powder
½ tsp. salt

Mix apple slices with sugar, cinnamon and water in saucepan. Cook about 10 minutes, or until apples are partially cooked. Turn into a 9" pie pan.

• Cream butter; gradually cream in brown sugar. Sift together flour, baking powder and salt. Add to creamed mixture and mix thoroughly with a spoon. Sprinkle mixture over the apples.

• Bake in moderate oven (350°) until apples are tender and top is nicely browned, about 45 minutes. Serve with a spoonful of whipped packaged dessert topping mix. Makes 6 to 8 servings.

APPLESAUCE MERINGUE PIE

Tall, gold-tipped meringue tops lemon-flavored apples touched with cinnamon

Baked 9" pie shell
2 c. sweetened applesauce
Juice of 1 lemon
2 tsp. grated lemon peel
¼ tsp. salt
¼ tsp. cinnamon
1 tblsp. cornstarch
3 eggs, separated
¼ tsp. cream of tartar
¼ tsp. salt
6 tblsp. sugar
½ tsp. vanilla

• Combine applesauce, lemon juice, peel, salt, cinnamon, cornstarch and slightly beaten egg yolks in saucepan; cook until thick and smooth. Cool slightly. Pour into baked pie shell. Spread filling to level.

• Cover warm filling with meringue made of beaten egg whites, cream of tartar, ¼ tsp. salt, 6 tblsp. sugar and

vanilla. Spread to cover entire filling; seal to pastry.

• Bake in hot oven (425°) 10 to 12 minutes, until meringue is nicely browned. Makes 8 servings.

Pie Bakers Extend Cherry Season

Farm people for generations have heeded the old saying, "make hay while the sun shines." Here is one way the pie baker does it. When trees are red with tart pie cherries, she freezes the juicy, top-quality fruit to use for months ahead in pies.

Here is a new recipe for Cherry Purée Mix, which home economists in our Test Kitchens developed. We also repeat, for those of you who do not have our *Complete Pie Cookbook*, recipes for Frozen Cherry Mix and Mincefruit Pie Filling. Many farm hostesses can the Mincefruit Filling when the harvest season for pears and apples is at its peak.

RIPE RED CHERRY PURÉE

Chill cherries in refrigerator at once after picking, until you purée them —helps keep their red color bright

10 c. ripe, red cherries
¾ to 1 c. sugar for each 4 c. purée

• Wash cherries and drain well. (You don't need to pit the cherries.) Place in heavy saucepan; cover. Heat 5 to 10 minutes until cherries are steaming and soft. Do not cook.

• Place cherries in a colander, a small quantity at a time, and purée (cherry pits remain in the colander). Skim off the foam. Add sugar and stir to dissolve. (Riper cherries require the smaller amount of sugar.) Allow to cool to room temperature.

• Freeze purée in 1 and 2 c. portions. Makes 4 cups.

Note: Desserts that use Ripe Red Cherry Purée are: Cherry Meringue Pie, Cherry Ice and Cherry-Cheese Dessert.

CHERRY MERINGUE PIE

Just the pie for the Christmas season —flavor of fruit fresh-from-the-tree

Baked 9" pie shell
¼ c. cornstarch
¼ c. sugar
¼ tsp. salt
2 c. thawed Ripe Red Cherry Purée
2 tblsp. butter or margarine
3 egg whites
¼ tsp. salt
¼ c. sugar

• Combine cornstarch, ¼ c. sugar and ¼ tsp. salt in saucepan. Add thawed Cherry Purée gradually to cornstarch mixture; stir until smooth.
• Cook, stirring constantly, until thick and bubbling rapidly.
• Remove from heat. Reserve ½ c. of thickened mixture.
• Add butter to remaining mixture; stir until melted. Pour into pie shell. Cool 15 minutes.
• Add salt to egg whites; beat until frothy. Add ¼ c. sugar gradually, beating until stiff peaks are formed.
• Stir the ½ c. of reserved cherry filling until smooth. Gently fold it into the egg white mixture in 3 parts. Pile lightly on filling, carefully covering to the edges.

• Bake in moderate oven (350°) about 25 minutes. Cool completely away from drafts. Makes 8 servings.

CHERRY-COCONUT ICE CREAM PIE

Good! Cherry-red topping in a crisp coconut crust with ice cream between —from our Complete Pie Cookbook

1 ⅓ c. flaked coconut (3 ½ oz. can)
2 tblsp. butter, melted
¼ c. graham cracker crumbs
2 tblsp. sugar
1 qt. vanilla ice cream
1 c. Frozen Cherry Mix (see Index)

• Combine coconut and butter; mix well. Add crumbs and sugar, mixing thoroughly. Press firmly on bottom and sides of an 8" pie pan. Bake in moderate oven (375°) 10 to 12 minutes, or until lightly browned. Cool in pan on rack.
• Soften ice cream and spread in the coconut pie shell. Spread slightly thawed Frozen Cherry Mix over the top; freeze until ready to serve.

MINCEFRUIT PIE FILLING

You'll be ready for pies all winter if you can this fruity mix. It also makes wonderful filling for cookies, cakes

4 lbs. pears
3 lbs. apples
4 medium oranges
2 (15 oz.) pkgs. seedless raisins
5 c. sugar
1 tblsp. salt
4 tsp. cinnamon
1 tsp. cloves

• Cut unpeeled pears, apples and oranges in quarters. Remove cores and seeds. Run through food chopper, using medium blade.

• Add remaining ingredients; stir to combine. Bring to a boil over medium heat. Simmer until thick, about 1 hour. Stir frequently.

• Pack at once in hot pint jars. Adjust lids. Process in boiling water bath (212°) 25 minutes.

• Remove jars from canner and complete seals unless closures are the self-sealing type. Makes 8 pints.

Mincefruit Pie: Use 4 c. filling to make a 2-crust 9″ pie. Bake in hot oven (400°) 25 to 30 minutes.

MINCEFRUIT PASTRY SQUARES

Pan dessert easy to carry and cut at serving time—great coffee go-with

2 ½   c. sifted flour
1   tblsp. sugar
1   tsp. salt
1   c. lard
1   egg, separated
Milk
3   c. Mincefruit Pie Filling
1   c. confectioners sugar
2   tblsp. lemon juice

• Sift together flour, sugar and salt; cut in lard with pastry blender or two knives, until mixture resembles coarse meal.

• Beat egg yolk in measuring cup and add enough milk to make ½ c. Add to lard mixture; mix just enough so dough shapes into ball. Roll out half to 15 × 11″ rectangle; transfer to baking sheet. Spread evenly with filling to within ¾″ of edges.

• Roll out rest of dough for top crust; place over filling; seal edges.

• Beat egg white until stiff; spread on

top crust. Bake in hot oven (400°) 25 to 30 minutes.

• Mix confectioners sugar and lemon juice. Drizzle over top of crust while hot. Makes 12 to 14 servings.

MINCEMEAT-PUMPKIN PIE

Flatter your guests with pie that boasts of the flavors of two fillings

Unbaked 9″ pie shell
1   c. cooked pumpkin
½   c. brown sugar
½   tsp. salt
¾   tsp. cinnamon
¾   tsp. nutmeg
3   eggs
½   c. heavy cream
1   c. mincemeat

• Combine pumpkin, sugar, salt, spices, eggs and cream and beat only until blended. Stir in mincemeat. Pour into unbaked pie shell. Bake in hot oven (425°) until filling is set, about 35 minutes. Serve warm.

Note: See Index for Country-Kitchen Mincemeat recipe.

BLACK AND WHITE DATE PIE

Rich 2-layer pie—serve with coffee

Baked 9″ pie shell

Bottom Layer:
1   c. chopped fresh dates
     (8 oz. pkg.)
½   c. water
⅛   tsp. salt
½   c. sugar
1   tsp. cornstarch
1   tsp. butter
1   tblsp. lemon juice

Top Layer:
¾ c. sugar
4 tblsp. flour
2 tblsp. cornstarch
¼ tsp. salt
2 c. milk
3 egg yolks, beaten
½ tsp. lemon juice
½ tsp. vanilla
¾ c. heavy cream, whipped

• To make bottom layer, cook dates with water and salt until they are very soft. Combine sugar and cornstarch; add to dates. Simmer 1 minute. Add butter and lemon juice. Cool; then spread in baked pie shell.
• For top layer, combine sugar, flour, cornstarch and salt. Scald milk; gradually add to dry mixture, stirring constantly. Cook over boiling water until mixture thickens. Cool.
• Add egg yolks, beaten until foamy. Cook over boiling water 3 minutes. Remove from heat; add lemon juice and vanilla. Partially cool. Spread on top of date mixture in pie shell. Cool thoroughly.
• Serve topped with whipped cream. Makes 8 servings.

OREGON WALNUT PIE

A rich pie that's highly favored by walnut growers' families and guests

Pastry for 1-crust pie
1 c. sugar
1 c. dark corn syrup
¼ c. melted butter
3 eggs, beaten
1 tsp. vanilla
1 c. broken walnut meats
½ c. flaked coconut

• Line a 9" pie pan with pastry.
• Mix together all the other ingredients and pour into the pastry-lined pan.
• Bake in moderate oven (350°) 50 to 60 minutes. Makes 6 to 8 servings.

GOURMET CHEESE PIE

One of the make-ahead desserts that's an easy winner with most guests

Crust:
20 graham crackers, finely crushed
¼ c. sugar
½ c. butter or margarine, melted
1 tblsp. water

Filling:
2 (3 oz.) pkgs. cream cheese
2 eggs
1 c. small curd creamed cottage cheese
½ c. sugar
1 tsp. vanilla
⅛ tsp. salt

Topping:
⅔ c. dairy sour cream
2 tblsp. sugar
½ tsp. vanilla

• To make crust, combine cracker crumbs and sugar in a medium bowl; stir in butter and mix thoroughly. Add water; stir to mix well. Press mixture evenly over the bottom and side of a 9" pie pan; do not make a rim.
• Bake in moderate oven (350°) 10 minutes. Remove from oven and cool.
• To make filling, beat cream cheese until fluffy; combine with remaining ingredients for filling, and beat to mix thoroughly. Pour into the cooled crust.
• Bake in moderate oven (350°) 20 minutes. Remove from oven and cool.

• Blend together ingredients for topping. Spread over the cooled pie. Refrigerate at least 4 hours (8 hours even better). Makes 8 servings.

MERINGUE CRUNCH PIE

Unusual pie—filling and crust in one

3 egg whites, at room
   temperature
1 c. sugar
½ tsp. baking powder
½ tsp. salt
10 dates, cut up
1 tblsp. flour
1 c. pecans, chopped
10 macaroon cookies, crumbled
Almond-Flavored Whipped Cream

• Beat egg whites until foamy.
• Sift together sugar, baking powder and salt. Gradually beat into egg whites to make a stiff meringue.
• Cut dates into flour so pieces won't stick together. Mix in nuts and macaroon cookie crumbs, then gently fold in meringue. Pour into 9″ buttered pie pan; bake in moderate oven (350°) 30 minutes.
• Cool; cut into wedges and serve with Almond-Flavored Whipped Cream.

Almond-Flavored Whipped Cream: Whip 1c. heavy cream with 1 tblsp. sugar and ½ tsp. almond extract.

Take Your Pick of Tarts

A Minnesota hostess says a "Tart Bar" delights her guests for evening dessert with coffee or for the final course in a progressive dinner. Here is how she prepares for and sets up this unusual buffet-style dessert.

Bake tart shells ahead and chill or freeze. The day of the party, make pie fillings. At serving time, arrange rows of empty tart shells on a tray and place them on a serving cart or side table. Surround with bowls of pie fillings and garnishes—chopped pecans, flaked coconut, sliced strawberries, whipped cream.

Invite guests to give you their choice of fillings for their tart shells. Fill the shell, place it on an individual plate and hand it to the guest.

"Don't be surprised," warned the Minnesota hostess who originated this style of service for tarts, "if some guests come back for seconds. Many people want to try more than one kind." Then she added: "None of the leftovers are wasted. I store the empty tart shells and covered pie fillings in the refrigerator and use them next day to the delight of my family."

In our Test Kitchens, we developed some new recipes for tart fillings which we recommend.

The cream fillings—so light and delicious—are perfect for the hostess who likes to work ahead, making use of her freezer. They're 2-part recipes: first you make basic pastes (lemon, chocolate, pumpkin) which you refrigerate or freeze.

On the morning of your party, defrost as many portions of basic paste as you will need to serve guests. (Each portion yields enough filling to fill 6 to 8 (2½″) party tart shells.) Whip the pastes with dessert topping mix to make a filling which is light and airy and can be easily spooned into tart shells. Chill them for several hours before serving.

For your tart bar selection, we also offer a fruit filling which you can make ahead. It's a combination of canned peaches and frozen blueberries with orange marmalade—colorful and delicious.

Here are recipes for tart shells and fillings.

TART SHELLS

2 c. sifted flour
1 tsp. salt
¾ c. vegetable shortening, or
    ⅔ c. lard
4 or 5 tblsp. cold water

• Combine flour and salt in mixing bowl. Cut in shortening with pastry blender or with two knives until mixture is the consistency of coarse cornmeal or tiny peas.

• Sprinkle on cold water, 1 tblsp. at a time, tossing mixture lightly and stirring with fork. Add water each time to the driest part of mixture. The dough should be just moist enough to hold together when pressed gently with a fork. It should not be sticky.

• Divide pastry into 6 parts. Shape into smooth balls and roll out each ball to make 4½ to 5″ circles.

• Fit pastry circles over backs of inverted 3½″ muffin-pan cups. Make pleats so pastry will fit snugly. Prick entire surface with 4-tined fork. Or fit pastry over inverted custard cups, prick well and set on baking sheet. Refrigerate 30 minutes before baking.

• Preheat oven to very hot (450°). Bake tart shells 10 to 12 minutes, or until golden. Cool on wire racks. Then carefully remove from pans, or custard cups. Fill as desired. Makes about 6 (3″) tarts, depending on how thin the pastry was rolled.

Note: Regardless of the size of your muffin-pan cups, you can bake tart shells on them. With a string, measure one of the inverted cups up one side, across the bottom and down on the other side. Cut the string this length. Find a bowl, saucer or small plate in the kitchen that has the same diameter as the string. Or cut a cardboard this size. Use for a pattern to cut the rolled pastry in circles. Fit pastry rounds on alternate muffin cups—6 on a pan with 12 cups. Pleat pastry to fit snugly.

CHOCOLATE CREAM TART FILLING

Strong chocolate flavor—delightful with a snowy drift of flaked coconut

½ c. Cocoa Paste (recipe
    below)
1 (2 oz.) pkg. dessert topping
    mix

• Thaw Cocoa Paste.

• Prepare topping mix according to package directions. Add Cocoa Paste; continue beating until creamy and smooth. Chill in refrigerator several hours before serving. Makes filling for 6 (3″) tarts.

COCOA PASTE

1 ⅓ c. cocoa
1 c. sugar
2 c. boiling water

• Combine cocoa and sugar in heavy saucepan. Add water slowly, stirring to make a smooth mixture.

• Cook and stir over high heat until

mixture boils. Reduce heat to low and continue cooking for 15 minutes, stirring occasionally.

· Pour into bowl; cool. Package in ½ c. portions; freeze, or store in refrigerator. (May be stored up to 4 weeks in refrigerator or freezer.) Makes 2 cups.

PUMPKIN CREAM TART FILLING

True pumpkin flavor—spicy! Garnish filled tarts with toasted pecans

1 ⅓ c. Pumpkin Paste (recipe below)
1 (2 oz.) pkg. dessert topping mix

· Thaw Pumpkin Paste.
· Prepare topping mix according to package directions. Add Pumpkin Paste; continue beating until creamy and smooth. Chill in refrigerator several hours before serving. Makes filling for 6 (3") tarts.

PUMPKIN PASTE

1   c. sugar
½   c. brown sugar, firmly packed
⅓   c. sifted flour
1 ½ tsp. cinnamon
1 ½ tsp. nutmeg
¾   tsp. salt
3   c. canned pumpkin
¾   c. water

· Combine sugars, flour, spices and salt. Add to pumpkin in heavy saucepan; mix thoroughly. Add water.
· Cook 15 minutes over low heat, stirring occasionally.
· Pour into bowl; cool. Package in 1⅓ c. portions; freeze. (May be stored up to 4 weeks in freezer.) Makes 4 cups.

LEMON CREAM TART FILLING

Light and lemony—and so good when topped with sliced strawberries

½ c. Lemon Paste (recipe below)
1 (2 oz.) pkg. dessert topping mix
Few drops yellow food color

· Thaw Lemon Paste; keep cold.
· Prepare topping mix according to package directions. Add Lemon Paste; continue beating until creamy and smooth. Add more milk for thinner mixture, if desired. Add food color to give lemon color.
· Chill in refrigerator several hours before serving. Makes filling for 6 (3") tarts.

LEMON PASTE

½   c. butter
⅓   c. sifted flour
1   c. sugar
1   c. boiling water
½   c. lemon juice
1   tblsp. grated lemon peel

· Melt butter in heavy saucepan. Add flour and stir to make smooth paste. Mix in ¼ c. sugar. Add water slowly, stirring to make a smooth mixture. Add remaining sugar, lemon juice and peel.
· Cook and stir over high heat until mixture boils. Reduce heat to low and continue cooking for 15 minutes, stirring occasionally.
· Pour into bowl; cool. Package in ½ c. portions; freeze, or store in refrigerator. (May be stored up to 4 weeks in refrigerator or freezer.) Makes 2 cups.

PEACH AND BLUEBERRY TART FILLING

Sparkling, colorful fruit filling, not too sweet. Offer whipped cream topping

1 (1 lb. 13 oz.) can sliced
   peaches
1 (10 oz.) pkg. frozen
   blueberries
1 tblsp. cornstarch
¼ c. orange marmalade

• Drain peaches; reserve 1 c. juice. Defrost blueberries; drain well.
• Gradually add 1 c. peach juice to cornstarch in small saucepan to make smooth mixture.
• Cook and stir until mixture is thick and clear. Add orange marmalade.
• Pour over peaches and mix. Add blueberries and mix gently. Chill in refrigerator several hours before serving. Makes filling for 6 (3") tarts.

Letter Pastry for Birthdays

If you want to help a friend celebrate her birthday, give a coffee party for her. Instead of serving a conventional cake, borrow a trick from our overseas Danish neighbors and make Letter Pastry.

Shape the filled pastry in the guest of honor's initial. It will create a lot of conversation at the party because it's different. And it's unusually good.

It does take time to make the pastry—elegant puff pastry, sometimes called French pastry, and no one can turn it out in a hurry. You'll want to make it on a day when you'll be at home so you can dovetail the work with other household tasks. Or you can fill and shape the pastry and freeze it to bake the day of the party. Bake it a few minutes longer if frozen.

Perhaps you'll prefer to take a short cut and use Quick Puff Pastry. It's surprisingly quick and easy to make, but handle it gently. While it is not quite as flaky as the best puff pastry, it's a compliment winner every time.

You can bake a large Letter Pastry, which you cut to serve, or small initials for individual servings. We give you the directions for both.

LETTER PASTRY

Pastry is tender, golden and crisp; it contains many flaky layers—fillings are luscious and distinctive

2¼ c. sifted flour
¼ tsp. salt
1 c. cold butter
½ c. cold water (about)
Pastry Filling
1 egg white, slightly beaten
Confectioners sugar

• Sift flour and salt together into mixing bowl. Cut in 6 tblsp. of the butter with pastry blender or two knives until particles are fine.
• Sprinkle with just enough water to moisten, a little at a time, and toss with fork to mix. Gather together into dough; chill 30 minutes to 1 hour in refrigerator.
• Roll out dough on floured board to 14 × 8" rectangle.
• Divide remainder of butter into 3 parts. Using one part of butter, dot two thirds of dough surface with small dots or very thin sheets of butter. Fold uncovered third of pastry over the middle third. Then fold butter-covered pastry end over the top, like an envelope and roll out to a 14 × 8" rectangle. Fold over twice again (same envelope-style fold, but in the opposite direction) and then roll out

once more to 14 × 8″ rectangle. Chill dough 30 minutes to 1 hour.

• Repeat procedure outlined above two more times, using each of the two parts of remaining butter—dot with butter, fold, roll, fold, roll, chill. Use no more flour than necessary. During the last rolling, roll dough ⅛″ thick; cut into strips 4″ wide and as long as necessary to form letters you plan to make. Chill dough slightly.

• To assemble, place a ½″ diameter log or strip of filling down length of dough strips to within 1″ of ends. Don't overfill. Roll pastry around filling like a jelly roll so that pastry encircles filling about 1½ times. Pinch pastry together at ends and down open edges to seal.

• Shape letters, sticking together filled strips of pastry if necessary to form your letters. Roll lightly with rolling pin to ⅜″ thickness.

• Lift onto ungreased baking sheet. Chill if dough is very soft. Brush with egg white.

• Bake in hot oven (400°) until golden, about 20 to 25 minutes. Remove to wire rack to cool.

• Sprinkle with confectioners sugar. Cut into pieces to serve. Makes 2 or 3 letters or 8 breakfast-size (coffee party) pastries.

Small Pastries: Shape some of dough into crescents, logs or turnovers.

Cranberry Turnovers: Roll out dough ⅛″ thick. Cut into 5″ squares; place 1 tblsp. drained cranberry sauce on each square. Fold diagonally to make triangle; press edges together firmly to seal. Reduce baking time for small pastries to 15 minutes.

Note: For a larger amount of pastry, double the recipe and roll dough out each time to 16 × 14″ (about) rectangle.

PASTRY FILLINGS

Traditional Almond: Beat 1 egg white with fork until foamy. Add ⅔ c. sugar, 1½ tsp. almond extract, 1 tblsp. grated lemon peel and 2 c. ground blanched almonds. Stir to mix well. Wrap or cover tightly and chill thoroughly.

Note: For best flavor, make this filling at least 1 or 2 days ahead of the time you plan to use it—to let it chill and blend thoroughly. It will keep in refrigerator in tightly covered jar as long as 6 months.

Preserves: Use raspberry, apricot or other flavorful fruit preserves.

Sugar-Nut Whip: Beat 1 egg yolk with ¼ c. sugar and ½ tsp. vanilla. Stir in ⅓ c. toasted slivered almonds and ¼ c. golden raisins.

Prune Paste: Stir together ½ c. finely cut-up, cooked and well-drained prunes, 3 tblsp. sugar and 1 tsp. grated fresh lemon peel.

QUICK PUFF PASTRY

Sour cream puff pastry is new—much easier to make than traditional kind

     1   c. butter
     1 ¾ c. sifted flour
     ½   c. dairy sour cream

• Cut butter into flour with pastry blender until completely mixed. With a fork, stir in sour cream until thoroughly blended. Wrap dough securely and refrigerate 8 hours or overnight. Roll out ⅛″ thick; cut and shape as for regular Letter Pastry.

PASTRY HATS

Dainty Washington's birthday pastries

¼ c. sugar
½ c. water
1 tsp. cinnamon candies (red hots)
2 medium apples
1 stick pie crust mix
½ c. shredded process cheese
2 tblsp. hot water
2 tblsp. melted butter
⅓ c. chopped walnuts or pecans
3 tblsp. sugar
½ tsp. ground mace (or cardamom)
¼ tsp. grated lemon peel
⅛ tsp. salt

• Combine ¼ c. sugar, water and cinnamon candies. Bring to a boil and simmer 10 minutes. Peel and core apples; slice in 18 slices. Cook a few apple slices at a time in the simmering syrup until just tender, about 10 minutes, adding a little water as necessary.

• Combine pie crust mix, cheese and hot water; blend until mixture cleans the bowl. Roll out ⅛″ thick. Cut in 3″ circles with scalloped cookie cutter. Brush lightly with 2 tblsp. melted butter.

• Combine nuts, 3 tblsp. sugar, mace, lemon peel and salt. Dip apple slices in this spiced sugar mixture and cut each slice in 3 pieces; lay on pastry circles. Pinch and fold edges of pastry to form colonial tri-cornered hats.

• Bake in hot oven (425°) 5 to 8 minutes, or until pastries are golden brown. Makes approximately 18 pastry hats.

CHAPTER 7

GREAT COUNTRY DESSERTS

The dessert is a hostess's final chance to have her guests leave the table in a happy, satisfied frame of mind. The recipes in this chapter achieve this.

Apple desserts are favorites of many people—notice the desserts made with them—Apple-Apricot Torte, Baked Apple Tapioca, Big Apple Bars and Apple Macaroon. Our big-pan apple desserts are another special— just right to carry to a church supper.

Country-Kitchen Mincemeat is the homemade kind that, while cooking, wafts that wonderful come-hither aroma. The desserts you make with it are extra-good, hearty, winter favorites. Our fruit cobblers have distinctive touches. For instance, one of the peach cobblers bakes in a ring, while another has a cheese biscuit crust.

No chapter on country desserts would be complete without recipes for homemade ice creams, electrically or hand turned. From our basic recipe for Homemade Vanilla Ice Cream you can also make Chocolate, Peanut Butter, Strawberry and Peach. We include Frozen Vanilla Custard, made with skim milk, for weight-watchers—surprisingly good. And from this recipe you also can make Frozen Coffee, Banana, Peppermint Stick and Strawberry custards. Coconut Honey Ice Cream is such a treat that we reprint the recipe from our *Freezing & Canning Cookbook,* just in case you don't have it. Notice, too, Crispy Sundae Crunch to freeze in a large pan to have ready when company comes.

Do look at our directions for making a Dessert Tree (see picture in this book). This is a dramatic way to serve fruit and cheese. We help you get acquainted with many of the world's natural cheeses now available in our supermarkets. This chapter contains a list of the great dessert cheeses; look for them when you are shopping. Cheese, crackers and fruit are a favorite European meal ending being adopted by many American families, especially when there are guests.

and cook, stirring constantly, until mixture comes to a boil and is clear. Cool slightly. Pour over crust. Chill.

• To make topping, place marshmallows and milk in a saucepan; cook over low heat, stirring frequently, until marshmallows are melted. Cool. Fold whipped cream into marshmallow mixture; spread over chilled raspberry filling. Chill. Makes 12 servings.

Tortes—Beautiful and Luscious

Mention tortes and everyone thinks of parties and other gala occasions where fancy-looking desserts match the festivities. The hostess knows not only how lovely and delicious tortes are, but also that you can fix them ahead and either freeze or chill them. And she knows that when she serves a torte for dessert, she'll get compliments.

RASPBERRY TORTE

Taste-testers rated this "blue-ribbon"

Crust:
1 ¼ c. flour
¼ c. sugar
¼ tsp. salt
1 c. butter or margarine

Filling:
3 tblsp. cornstarch
1 c. sugar
2 (10 oz.) pkgs. frozen red
   raspberries, thawed

Topping:
45 large marshmallows
1 c. milk
1 c. heavy cream, whipped

• To make crust, combine flour, sugar and salt in bowl. Cut in chilled butter until mixture resembles coarse crumbs. Pat in bottom of a 13 × 9 × 2″ pan. Bake in moderate oven (350°) until lightly browned, 15 to 18 minutes. Cool.

• For filling, combine cornstarch and sugar in saucepan. Add raspberries

APPLE-APRICOT TORTE

Tart apricots contrast with apples and crunchy nuts in a superb dessert

1 ½ c. sifted flour
1 tsp. baking powder
2 tblsp. sugar
1 egg, slightly beaten
½ c. soft butter
3 c. finely chopped peeled
   apples
1 c. dried apricots, cut in thin
   strips with scissors
1 tsp. cinnamon
1 ½ c. sugar
3 eggs, slightly beaten
1 c. dairy sour cream
¼ c. finely chopped blanched
   almonds

• Sift flour, baking powder and 2 tblsp. sugar together. Add egg and butter; work into flour mixture until smooth dough is formed. Press dough into thin layer on bottom and sides of buttered 9″ spring-form pan, making sides 2″ high.

• Combine apples, apricots, cinnamon and 1½ c. sugar.

• Combine eggs and sour cream; blend until smooth. Add to apple mixture; mix well. Pour into dough-lined pan. Sprinkle with almonds. Bake in moderate oven (350°) 1 hour and 15 minutes. Cool. Remove from spring-form pan to serve. Cut into wedges. Makes 12 servings.

CHERRY TORTE

Takes a little time to fix this three-layer dessert, but results are worth it

Crust:

2   c. sifted flour
½   tsp. salt
¼   c. confectioners sugar
¾   c. butter or margarine
1   tsp. grated lemon peel
½   c. finely chopped walnuts

Filling:

1   (1 lb. 8 oz. or 1 lb. 5 oz.) jar cherry pie filling
1½ tsp. cornstarch, dissolved in 1 tblsp. water
1   tblsp. butter or margarine

Meringue:

4   egg whites
⅛   tsp. salt
⅛   tsp. cream of tartar
½   tsp. vanilla
8   tblsp. sugar

• Sift together dry ingredients for crust; cut in butter or margarine to make a mixture the consistency of coarse cornmeal. Toss with lemon peel and nuts. Press into shallow 2-qt. glass baking dish. Bake in moderate oven (375°) 20 minutes, or until lightly browned.

• Combine pie filling and cornstarch mixture; cook over medium heat, stirring constantly, until thickened. Remove from heat; stir in butter. Pour hot filling into hot crust; top with meringue.

• To make meringue, combine egg whites, salt, cream of tartar and va-nilla; beat until foamy. Beat in sugar, 1 tblsp. at a time, beating thoroughly after each addition. Swirl on pie filling. Brown in moderate oven (350°) about 15 minutes. Makes 10 to 12 servings.

PINEAPPLE MERINGUE TORTE

Beautiful show-off for table

8   egg whites, beaten stiff
1½ tsp. vanilla
1   tsp. vinegar
2   c. sifted sugar
1   pt. heavy cream, whipped
1   c. canned crushed pineapple, drained
¾   c. maraschino cherries, drained and cut in eighths

• Beat egg whites (which are at room temperature) until foamy; add vanilla and vinegar and continue beating until mixture forms peaks. Add sugar, 1 tblsp. at a time, and continue beating until mixture is stiff and all sugar is dissolved.

• Spread mixture gently into 2 (9") round layer cake pans. (A pan with a blade scraper will help loosen the meringue; otherwise line pans with plain paper.)

• Bake in slow oven (300°) 1 hour and 15 minutes. Cool thoroughly before turning out of pan. (Do not be alarmed if the meringues crack or break a little.)

• Whip cream and fold pineapple and cherries into it. Spread filling over bottom layer; adjust top layer and spread top and sides with remaining whipped cream mixture. Chill at least 12 hours, or overnight. Makes 10 to 12 servings.

FROZEN PINEAPPLE TORTE

Refreshing light dessert to make and freeze the day before you entertain

3   egg yolks
⅛   tsp. salt
½   c. sugar
1   (9 oz.) can crushed
       pineapple (save juice)
2   tblsp. lemon juice
3   egg whites
2   tblsp. sugar
1   tsp. grated lemon peel
1   c. heavy cream, whipped
1   c. vanilla wafer crumbs

• Beat egg yolks slightly; add salt and ½ c. sugar and beat a little more. Add pineapple juice (drained from crushed pineapple) and lemon juice. Cook over hot, not boiling, water until custard coats the spoon; stir constantly while cooking. Add the pineapple and cool.

• Make a meringue with egg whites and 2 tblsp. sugar. Fold in the pineapple custard, lemon peel and whipped cream.

• Coat the sides of a greased 13 × 9 × 2″ baking pan with ½ c. vanilla wafer crumbs. Pour custard into pan and sprinkle remaining vanilla wafer crumbs over the top. Cover and freeze.

• Place dessert in refrigerator about 30 minutes before serving. It then will cut easily. Makes 8 to 10 servings.

Plan to entertain guests several days in a row. Silver, best glassware and dishes need to be taken out, polished and stored away only once. Same flowers and centerpieces can be used for all events.

Pinking shears help with holiday decoration. Cut place mats from red oilcloth or plastic-coated fabric, and use them over tablecloths. Mats are festive and eliminate some of the laundry at this busy season.

Spectacular Holiday Tortes

Many people, at some time during the Christmas season, tire of fruitcake. That's because they've had it so often. Take your cue from the reactions of friends and when they reach this stage, leave the fruitcake in the freezer the next time you entertain. It will come in handy later. (One Southern hostess serves thin slices of fruitcake and iced lemonade for guest-pleasing Fourth of July refreshments.)

Both of the two gorgeous tortes, Fruit-Nut or Orange Angel, are handsome holiday desserts. Fruit-Nut Torte is chewy; it is topped with a baked-on meringue. Orange Angel Torte has a delicate baked meringue crust filled with luscious orange filling garnished with whipped cream. Both are elegant, says the Virginia home economist who likes to serve them when she entertains.

Neither torte is especially difficult to make. And both freeze successfully so you can bake them ahead. It's important, if you do not freeze them, to let the tortes stand a day after baking so they will be firm enough to cut easily.

Even though these holiday specials contain the same fruits and nuts as fruitcakes, they taste different. That's because the tortes have a base rich in sugar and eggs.

FRUIT-NUT TORTE

Nut curls for garnish: Shave nuts thin with vegetable parer or knife

Torte:

1	c.	Brazil nuts, halved, or ¾ c. whole blanched almonds
2	c.	walnut or pecan halves
1	c.	whole candied red and green cherries, mixed
1	c.	raisins or sliced dates
1½	c.	sifted flour
1	tsp.	salt
4		eggs
2		egg yolks
1¼	c.	sugar
1	tblsp.	vanilla

Topping:

2		egg whites
¼	c.	plus 1 tblsp. sugar
¼	c.	sifted confectioners sugar
¼	c.	Brazil nut curls

• Fit two lengths of brown paper into a 9 × 9 × 2″ pan; allow 1½″ extension beyond pan edges. Grease lightly to settle papers into the pan.
• Combine nuts and fruit in a large bowl. Toss with ½ c. flour.
• Sift remaining 1 c. flour with the salt.
• Beat eggs and egg yolks until thick and lemon-colored. Gradually beat in sugar and vanilla, beating until cream-colored. Fold in dry ingredients. Pour over the fruit-nut mixture; fold until completely mixed. Turn into prepared pan.
• Bake in moderate oven (375°) 50 to 60 minutes, or until cake tester comes out clean when inserted in center of the torte. (When the torte is a medium brown, cover it with paper or foil for remainder of baking time.)

• Meanwhile, prepare topping. Beat egg whites until peaks form. Gradually beat in ¼ c. sugar and the confectioners sugar; continue beating until stiff and glossy.
• Take torte from the oven, remove paper cover and spread the topping evenly over crust. Be sure to cover edges. Sprinkle with remaining 1 tblsp. sugar and Brazil nut curls. Return to oven for 15 minutes, or until lightly browned.
• Cool in pan 30 minutes. Lift from pan by paper liner onto wire rack. Loosen paper from meringue edges. When cold, cut paper off sides, but leave it on the bottom of the torte. Serve cut in slices or small squares, plain or topped with whipped cream. Makes 24 servings.

ORANGE ANGEL TORTE

You can fix the base for this lovely torte one day, the filling the next

1	c.	thinly sliced candied red and green cherries
1½	c.	chopped nuts
2	c.	flaked coconut
¾	c.	fine soft white bread crumbs
6		egg whites (⅞ c.)
1	tsp.	cream of tartar
½	tsp.	salt
2	c.	sugar
1	tsp.	vinegar
1	tsp.	vanilla
Orange Filling		
2	c.	heavy cream, whipped, or 1 (4 oz.) pkg. dessert topping mix, whipped
Cherry Flowers		

• Line a 15½ × 10½ × 1″ jelly roll

pan with brown paper; grease and lightly flour paper.

· Combine fruit, nuts, coconut and crumbs in a large bowl; mix to coat fruit, nuts and coconut with crumbs.

· Bring egg whites to room temperature. Add cream of tartar and salt. Beat at high speed of electric mixer or portable beater to soft peak stage. Slowly beat in sugar, vinegar and vanilla. Beat 10 minutes to the stiff peak stage. Fold into the fruit-nut mixture.

· Turn mixture into the prepared pan. Spread evenly over paper, building the edges higher. Bake in moderate oven (375°) 25 minutes, or until lightly browned. Cool. Transfer torte to a tray; cut paper from edges, but not from bottom.

· Spread chilled Orange Filling over the top to the raised edges. Cover with whipped cream or dessert topping mix, prepared by package directions. Decorate with Cherry Flowers. Refrigerate overnight before serving, or freeze unwrapped, then wrap for storage. Thaw 30 minutes before serving frozen torte. Makes 24 servings.

Orange Filling: Mix ½ c. flour, 1½ c. sugar and ½ tsp. salt in saucepan. Gradually add 2½ c. orange juice, then 6 slightly beaten egg yolks (½ c.) and 2 tblsp. butter or margarine.

· Cook over medium heat until thick. Cover and cool, then refrigerate.

Cherry Flowers: Cut 12 red candied cherries in quarters, 3 green candied cherries in eighths. Group 2 red slices and 1 green slice together on top of Orange Angel Torte to make 24 flowers, one for each serving.

Baked Prune Pudding Surprise

Here's a dessert that tastes royally rich even though it isn't. Notice how simple the ingredients in the recipe are and how easy it is to put them together for an outstanding dessert.

This pudding recipe comes from California prune-growing country. It's a top favorite of a home economist, who keeps a supply of the dark baked puddings in her freezer ready to heat in the oven when she wants to serve something special. She finds the dessert ideal for a crowd. In fact, she has baked and frozen enough of it at one time to serve 100! (See also Prune Cake de Luxe, a recipe from this same home economist.)

PRUNE PUDDING
Guests never dream this dessert is so simple—it tastes rich and elegant

1   c. sifted flour
1   tsp. baking soda
¼   tsp. salt
¼   tsp. cinnamon
1   c. seedless raisins
1   c. chopped walnuts
1   c. sugar
1   c. cooked, mashed prunes
1   tblsp. butter, melted
1   tsp. vanilla
¾   c. milk
Whipped cream or Sherry Sauce

· Sift together flour, baking soda, salt and cinnamon; combine with raisins and nuts.

· Add sugar to soft, mashed prunes;

add melted butter and vanilla and mix well.

· Combine dry ingredients with prune mixture and milk, blending thoroughly.

· Pour into greased 8" pan; bake in slow oven (325°) 1 hour. Serve warm with whipped cream, lemon sauce or Sherry Sauce. Makes 8 servings.

VARIATIONS

Apricot Pudding: Substitute dried apricots for the prunes.

Apricot-Prune Pudding: Use ½ c. each cooked, mashed prunes and dried apricots.

SHERRY SAUCE

Success secret: don't let sauce boil

2 eggs
2 c. sugar
1 c. sherry wine
½ c. butter or margarine

· Beat eggs well in top of double boiler. Add sugar and mix. Stir in sherry and butter. Cook over simmering (not boiling) water, stirring constantly until fairly clear and thickened. Serve hot. Makes 3 cups, or 12 servings.

Note: The sauce may be cooked in a heavy saucepan over low heat, stirring constantly. Bring just to a boil (do not let boil).

FLAMING PLUM PUDDING

Trim pudding with sugar cubes tinted red and soaked in lemon extract, then light for a flaming spectacular

½ c. butter, softened
1 ½ c. brown sugar, firmly packed

2 eggs
1 tsp. vanilla
1 c. grated peeled carrots
1 c. grated peeled apples
½ c. raisins
1 c. pecans, coarsely chopped
1 c. sifted flour
1 tsp. baking soda
½ tsp. salt
1 c. fine dry, white bread crumbs
Caramel Sauce

· Cream butter and sugar. Beat in eggs and vanilla; stir in carrots, apples, raisins and nuts. Sift together flour, soda and salt; stir into creamed mixture. Add crumbs and mix well.

· Spoon into well-oiled 1½-qt. mold. Cover securely with mold lid or several thicknesses of waxed paper tied in place with string.

· Place mold on a rack in covered kettle of boiling water. (Water should come halfway up on the mold.) Steam for 3 hours. Unmold pudding onto serving plate; flame if you wish (directions follow). Serve hot with warm Caramel Sauce. Makes 8 to 10 servings.

Caramel Sauce: Combine ½ c. brown sugar, firmly packed, 1 tblsp. cornstarch and ⅛ tsp. salt in small saucepan. Add 1 c. boiling water; cook until thickened and clear, stirring constantly. Remove from heat and stir in 2 tblsp. butter and 1 tsp. vanilla.

To Flame Pudding: Soak sugar cubes in lemon extract tinted with red food color. Just before serving, place 2 or 3 cubes on top of pudding or several around sides, not touching pudding (use a metal or flame-proof dish). Light the cubes.

SWEET POTATO PUDDING

When you want to glamorize this hearty, spicy and easy-to-make dessert, spoon ice cream on each serving

4 c. cooked, mashed sweet
    potatoes
½ c. heavy cream
1 tsp. grated lemon peel
Juice of ½ lemon
½ tsp. ground cinnamon
½ tsp. ground ginger
¼ tsp. ground cloves
3 eggs, separated
1 (3½ oz.) can flaked coconut
⅓ c. brown sugar
⅓ c. slivered almonds

• Beat potatoes, cream, lemon peel, juice, spices and egg yolks until smooth. Reserve ⅓ c. coconut; fold remaining coconut into sweet potato mixture.
• Beat egg whites until soft peaks form; gradually beat in brown sugar to make a stiff meringue. Fold into sweet potato mixture. Spoon into buttered 2-qt. casserole; top with ⅓ c. coconut and almonds.
• Bake in moderate oven (375°) 55 minutes, or until inserted knife blade comes out clean. Serve warm. Makes 8 servings.

HOOSIER PERSIMMON PUDDING

If Indiana has a state dessert, here it is—made with small native fruit

2 c. mashed and sieved
    persimmon pulp (fresh
    or frozen)
3 eggs, beaten
1¾ c. milk
2 c. sifted flour
½ tsp. baking soda

1 tsp. salt
1½ c. sugar
1 tsp. ground coriander
3 tblsp. melted butter
Heavy cream, whipped

• Mix persimmon pulp, eggs and milk.
• Sift together flour, baking soda, salt, sugar and coriander.
• Pour persimmon mixture into dry mixture; add butter. Stir briefly.
• Pour into a greased 13 × 9 × 2″ pan; bake in slow oven (325°) about 1 hour. Serve warm or cold with whipped cream. Makes 12 servings.

Custard Bread Pudding

A Montana ranch woman, whose son is a medical doctor, entertains several young doctors during the autumn hunting season. Of all the dishes she serves these hungry men, her Glorified Bread Pudding gets the most praise. It holds its place of honor, year after year, among favorite country desserts. Since few women make it often, many guests consider it a wonderful new discovery.

GLORIFIED BREAD PUDDING

An outstanding custardy pudding

2⅔ c. milk
¼ c. butter
3 eggs
¾ c. sugar
1¼ tsp. vanilla
¼ tsp. salt
3 c. (1″) day old bread cubes,
    top crusts removed
⅛ tsp. nutmeg
¼ tsp. cream of tartar

• Scald milk; add butter and cool.

• Add 3 egg yolks and 1 egg white to ½ c. sugar; beat to mix well. Add 1 tsp. vanilla and salt.

• Place bread cubes in buttered 1½-qt. casserole. Pour egg-milk mixture over bread. Sprinkle nutmeg on top.

• Set casserole in a pan containing at least 2″ warm water. Bake in moderate oven (350°) 45 to 60 minutes, until knife inserted halfway between center and edge comes out clean. Remove from oven.

• Make meringue by beating remaining 2 egg whites with remaining ¼ tsp. vanilla and cream of tartar until soft peaks form; gradually add remaining sugar, beating constantly. Beat until stiff peaks form and all the sugar is dissolved. Swirl on warm pudding, making sure meringue covers pudding edges. Bake in moderate oven (350°) about 15 minutes, until meringue is golden brown. Serve warm or cool. (Cool out of drafts.) Makes 6 servings.

Note: You can omit vanilla from pudding and add 1 tblsp. lemon juice and ½ tsp. grated lemon peel.

LEMON CUPS

We top these with whipped cream and garnish the servings with coconut

1	c. sugar
2	tblsp. salad oil
⅛	tsp. salt
¼	c. sifted flour
2	tsp. grated lemon peel
⅓	c. lemon juice
1 ½	c. scalded milk, cooled until lukewarm
3	egg yolks, beaten
3	egg whites, beaten stiff

• Combine sugar, oil, salt and flour.

Add lemon peel and juice. Stir milk into egg yolks; add to lemon mixture. Fold in egg whites.

• Pour into 8 ungreased custard cups (or a 1-qt. casserole). Set in pan of warm water and bake in slow oven (325°) 40 minutes, or until set when tested with a knife. Serve warm or chilled, unmolded and with sweetened whipped cream on top. Makes 8 servings.

Note: If you wish to chill this custard dessert, cover with foil or plastic wrap while warm and place in refrigerator.

Molded Desserts to Make Ahead

Gelatin desserts rate top priority in country entertaining not only because they are delectable showpieces, but also because you get them ready in advance for thorough chilling. Once you've done this, you can dismiss them from your mind until serving time.

Our collection of these gelatin meal enders contains some specials. For instance, the children of a Minnesota member of FARM JOURNAL's Family Test Group ask for Lime-Chocolate Fascination when they have guests and on their birthdays. They prefer it to cake.

Peel peaches the easy way. Hold peach in sieve or large spoon; immerse in boiling water for 1 minute. Plunge in cold or iced water to cool quickly. Break peach skin with the point of a knife and slip off the skin.

LIME-CHOCOLATE FASCINATION

Let's have the "green dessert," beg the children of one of our Testers. This is their favorite meal ending

1 (14½ oz.) can evaporated
    milk
1 (3 oz.) pkg. lime flavor
    gelatin
2 c. hot water
1 c. sugar
¼ c. lime juice
2 tsp. lemon juice
About 4 drops green food color
2 c. chocolate wafer crumbs
    (an 8½ oz. pkg.)
½ c. melted butter

• Chill milk at least 1 day in refrigerator.
• Dissolve gelatin in hot water. Chill until mixture is partly congealed (consistency of unbeaten egg whites). Then whip until fluffy. Stir in sugar, lime and lemon juices and food color to tint a delicate green.
• Whip milk until light and fluffy; fold into gelatin mixture.
• Combine cookie crumbs and melted butter. Reserve ½ c. crumbs; press remaining crumbs into bottom of a 9″ square pan. Add whipped gelatin-milk mixture. Sprinkle reserved ½ c. crumbs on top. Chill overnight or until firm. Makes 9 servings.

HOLIDAY CHARLOTTE PUDDING

A delicate custard dessert that's just right for holiday entertaining

1 tblsp. unflavored gelatin
⅓ c. cold water
6 tblsp. sugar
1 tblsp. cornstarch
2 egg yolks, or 1 egg

2 c. milk
1 c. heavy cream, whipped
½ c. confectioners sugar
1 tsp. vanilla
¼ c. slivered toasted almonds
Royal Red Sauce

• Soften gelatin in cold water. Mix together sugar and cornstarch.
• Beat egg yolks in medium saucepan; blend in sugar mixture and milk.
• Cook to the consistency of cream over low heat, stirring constantly. Add gelatin and stir to dissolve. Cool until consistency of unbeaten egg whites, watching carefully that custard does not get too firm.
• Sweeten whipped cream with confectioners sugar; add vanilla. Fold in the custard mixture and almonds.
• Rinse a 1-qt. mold with cold water; drain. Pour mixture into mold. Chill several hours or overnight. Unmold and serve with Royal Red Sauce. Makes 6 to 8 servings.

ROYAL RED SAUCE

It's berry-sweet and gorgeous in color

1 (10 oz.) pkg. frozen red
    raspberries
Sugar to taste
2 tsp. cornstarch

• Thaw berries; put through sieve. (You should have about 1 c. juice.) Add sugar to taste (amount depends on how much raspberries were sweetened).
• Mix cornstarch with a little of the juice to make a smooth paste.
• Combine with remaining juice and cook mixture over low heat, stirring constantly, until clear and slightly thickened. Cool and pour over unmolded pudding. Makes about 1 cup.

MOLDED RHUBARB SWIRL

Use pink-red rhubarb so tender the stalks won't string when cut. Your reward—a dazzling spring dessert

1 c. graham cracker crumbs
4 tsp. sugar
3 tblsp. melted butter or margarine
3 c. finely diced fresh rhubarb
½ c. sugar
1 (3 oz.) pkg. strawberry flavor gelatin
1 c. boiling water
½ c. sugar
¼ c. flour
1 c. milk
1 tsp. vanilla
2 tsp. unflavored gelatin, softened in 2 tblsp. cold water
2 c. heavy cream, whipped

• Combine crumbs, sugar and butter; press into the bottom of 2-qt. oblong casserole or 8″ round spring-form pan, greased on bottom only. Bake in moderate oven (350°) 7 minutes. Cool. Line sides of spring-form pan with waxed paper.

• Meanwhile, cover fruit with sugar; let stand 1 hour. Then simmer in a heavy saucepan only until rhubarb loses crispness. Drain, reserving liquid. Add cold water to liquid to make ¾ c.

• Dissolve strawberry gelatin in boiling water. Stir in the ¾ c. water-fruit liquid. Chill until syrupy.

• Combine ½ c. sugar, flour and milk in a heavy saucepan. Bring to a boil; then reduce heat and cook, stirring constantly, 2 minutes, or until thickened. Remove from heat. Stir in vanilla and gelatin; let stand 5 minutes. Then fold in whipped cream.

• Whip strawberry gelatin mixture until fluffy. Fold in rhubarb; then fold in half of whipped cream mixture. Alternately spoon the strawberry gelatin mixture and the remaining whipped cream mixture into crust-lined pan; swirl with a knife. Chill overnight. Makes 9 servings.

LEMON DAFFODIL DESSERT

Cheerful as sunshine, lemony and light—perfect after a hearty meal

6 eggs, separated
1 c. sugar
⅓ to ½ c. lemon juice
1 tsp. grated lemon peel
1 envelope unflavored gelatin
½ c. cold water
1 (11 oz.) loaf angel food cake
1 c. heavy cream

• In top of a double boiler, combine slightly beaten egg yolks, ½ c. sugar, lemon juice and peel. Cook over simmering water, stirring constantly, until mixture thickens. Remove from heat; stir in gelatin, which has been softened in cold water. Cool until partially set.

• Meanwhile, rub cake gently with clean dish towel to remove loose outside crumbs. Tear cake into bite-size pieces. Set aside.

• Beat egg whites until foamy, gradually beat in remaining ½ c. sugar to make soft meringue that holds a peak. Whip ½ c. cream and fold into meringue; carefully fold this mixture into gelatin mixture. Fold in cake pieces.

• Spoon into shallow oblong 3-qt. glass dish. Refrigerate overnight to set. Cut into squares; top with remaining ½ c. cream, whipped. Makes 10 to 12 servings.

PUMPKIN PARFAIT

Delicious light dessert to make ahead.
Recipe can be doubled to serve 12

1 tblsp. unflavored gelatin
¼ c. cold water
3 eggs, separated
½ c. sugar
1¼ c. cooked or canned pumpkin
½ c. milk
¼ tsp. salt
½ tsp. cinnamon
½ tsp. nutmeg
¼ tsp. salt
½ c. sugar
1 c. heavy cream, or 1 (2 oz.)
    pkg. dessert topping mix
1 tsp. sugar
½ tsp. rum extract
Chopped nuts

• Soak gelatin in cold water. Beat egg yolks (save the whites for later). Add ½ c. sugar, pumpkin, milk, ¼ tsp. salt, cinnamon and nutmeg. (For added flavor, grind your own cinnamon and nutmeg.)
• Cook in a heavy saucepan over low heat, stirring constantly, until thickened. Mix in gelatin until completely dissolved. Chill about 2 hours in refrigerator.
• Beat egg whites and ¼ tsp. salt until stiff.
• Remove pumpkin mixture from refrigerator and beat until fluffy. Add ½ c. sugar while beating.
• Fold in beaten egg whites and return to refrigerator for 1 hour.
• Whip the cream or dessert topping mix. Add 1 tsp. sugar and rum extract. Fold whipped cream into pumpkin mixture, reserving a bit of the cream for topping.
• Place the mixture in sherbet or parfait glasses and return to the refrig-

erator until ready to serve. Top each with a spoon of whipped cream and a sprinkle of chopped nuts. Makes about 6 servings.

STRAWBERRY WHIP DESSERT

The electric blender speeds the making of this light and airy molded dessert

½ c. boiling water
1 (3 oz.) pkg. strawberry flavor
    gelatin
15 marshmallows, cut in halves
½ c. cold water
1 (10 oz.) pkg. frozen
    strawberries in syrup,
    partially defrosted
1 tsp. lemon juice
1 c. heavy cream

• Place boiling water and gelatin in blender. Cover; blend on "low" until gelatin is dissolved. Add marshmallows, cold water, strawberries and lemon juice. Cover and blend on "low" until smooth (rest hand on container lid). Remove contents from the container; chill until partially set.
• Fold in blender-whipped heavy cream and refrigerate in 6 to 8 individual serving dishes or an 8" square pan. Chill until firm. Serve with crisp cookies. Makes 6 to 8 servings.

Heirloom Dessert Recipes

Many women treasure recipes for a few dishes their mothers used to make. While they adopt many new combinations of foods and new ways of cooking, they still hold on to the best of the old. Two examples, shared with us by a Utah home economist with four children of her own, are Elegant Chocolate Log and Sweetheart Party Cake. Both of these make-ahead desserts appear on her table or buffet when she entertains.

"I make Mother's chocolate roll for special company," she says. "It's the prettiest and most delicious of all cake rolls. When we're having quite a few guests, I fix two rolls and put them together on an antique fish platter. They make a long log and a stunning service.

"Sweetheart Party Cake is a favorite of my family and friends. Once I carried one of these lovely pink cakes, with a bouquet of violets tucked in the center, to a friend for a birthday gift. I've never made a gift in my kitchen that was appreciated more.

"My sons often ask for my Lemon Cheese Torte on their birthdays. It's an interesting dessert containing cottage and cream cheeses and packaged vanilla pudding mix, with a cherry-red glaze."

Here are the three prized recipes, two of them old and one of them new, but on the way to becoming a family heirloom.

SWEETHEART PARTY CAKE

Luscious pink cake to grace a party

1 (10 oz.) pkg. frozen strawberries
1 envelope unflavored gelatin
2 c. heavy cream
2 tblsp. sugar
1 (9 or 10") angel food cake

• Thaw strawberries and drain well. Over juice in dish, sprinkle gelatin; let stand until it softens. Set dish in pan of hot water and stir until gelatin dissolves. Combine with berries. Barely cool—do not let mixture congeal.

• Whip cream; add sugar. Fold in strawberry mixture. (Strawberry mixture may appear too thin, but it will mix well into whipped cream.)

• Cut angel food cake in two layers. Spread strawberry-cream mixture generously over the bottom layer. Adjust top layer and spread remaining strawberry-cream over top and sides of the cake. Refrigerate at least 2 hours before serving. Makes 10 to 12 servings.

ELEGANT CHOCOLATE LOG

Share the beauty of this chocolate roll by serving it at the table

1 ¼ c. sifted confectioners sugar
¼ c. plus 1 tblsp. sifted flour
½ tsp. salt
5 tblsp. cocoa
6 eggs, separated
¼ tsp. cream of tartar
1 ¼ tsp. vanilla
1 tblsp. water
1 c. heavy cream, whipped
Granulated sugar
8 to 12 marshmallows, cut up
1 square unsweetened chocolate
2 c. confectioners sugar
Light cream
¼ c. finely chopped pecans

• Sift 1¼ c. confectioners sugar, flour, salt and cocoa together 3 times.

• Beat egg whites with cream of tartar until stiff.

• Beat egg yolks until thick and lemon-colored; beat in vanilla and water. Add sifted dry ingredients and beat into egg yolks until well blended. Fold in beaten egg whites.

• Bake in greased, paper-lined jelly roll pan (15½ × 10½ × 1") in moderate oven (375°) 15 to 20 minutes. Lightly dust clean dish towel with confectioners sugar; loosen cake around edges with spatula. Invert on towel. Lift off pan and carefully peel off paper. With a sharp knife, cut off cake's crisp edges. Roll up cake gently, from narrow end, by folding edge of cake over and then tucking it in; continue rolling cake, lifting towel higher with one hand as you guide the rolling with the other hand, rolling the towel in the cake (to prevent cake sticking). Let cool on rack (wrap tightly in towel to hold it in shape).

• Unroll cake on towel; spread with whipped cream, sweetened to taste with granulated sugar (about 2 tblsp.) and with marshmallows added. Roll like jelly roll.

• For frosting, melt chocolate; add 2 c. confectioners sugar with enough light cream to make it spreadable. Spread over cake and immediately sprinkle with chopped nuts. Makes 8 to 10 servings.

LEMON CHEESE TORTE

Count on this cake with its shiny red top to give pleasure to guests

¾ c. finely ground graham
    cracker crumbs
1 tblsp. sugar
2 tblsp. melted butter
1 (3½ oz.) pkg. lemon pudding
    and pie filling mix
⅔ c. sugar
1 c. light cream
2 c. cottage cheese
1 (8 oz.) pkg. cream cheese
4 egg yolks
¼ tsp. salt
4 egg whites, beaten to soft
    peaks
Cherry Glaze

• Combine crumbs, 1 tblsp. sugar and butter; mix well. (This amount may be doubled for a thicker crust.) Press mixture firmly into bottom of a 9″ spring-form pan (or a 3-qt. casserole, but it's easier to remove in good shape from a spring-form pan).

• Combine pudding mix, ⅔ c. sugar and light cream in saucepan. Cook and stir until mixture comes to a full boil and is thickened. (This takes about 5 minutes.) Mixture may curdle while cooking, but it will be smooth when it boils. Remove from heat.

• Combine cottage and cream cheeses (both should be at room temperature). Mix well; add egg yolks, one at a time, mixing well after each addition. Add salt and cooked pudding; blend well. Fold in beaten egg whites and pour over crumb mixture in pan.

• Bake in slow oven (300°) 1 hour. Cool to room temperature. Chill thoroughly. Spread on Cherry Glaze. The cake is best when chilled overnight before serving. Makes 8 to 10 servings.

CHERRY GLAZE

½ (3 oz.) pkg. strawberry flavor
    gelatin (4 tblsp.)
½ c. boiling water
¼ c. sugar
½ c. juice drained from cherries
1 (16 to 17 oz.) can pitted tart
    cherries (water pack)

• Dissolve gelatin in boiling water; stir in sugar. Add juice drained from cherries. Chill until slightly thickened.
• Spread well-drained cherries over top of chilled Lemon Cheese Torte.
• Pour gelatin mixture over cherries. Chill until ready to serve.

Big-Pan Desserts That Carry Well

When you take desserts to potluck and community suppers, you want them big enough to serve a crowd. And you want them so inviting that everyone will take notice. From good country hostesses come recipes for big-pan desserts that meet these qualifications deliciously.

Cherry-Crested Torte and Lemon-Chocolate Dessert are favorites of an Illinois member of FARM JOURNAL's Family Test Group. Sometimes she substitutes golden apricots or blueberries for the cherries. In summer, she says, the Lemon-Chocolate Dessert is a stay-at-home treat, but it carries successfully when the weather is cold.

An Iowa Test Group member rates Raspberry Dessert her best one for carrying to suppers. All three of these meal-endings are "covered dishes," in the true sense if you make and carry them in pans with slide-on lids. If your pans do not have covers, make your own with aluminum foil.

CHERRY-CRESTED TORTE

One of the best-tasting and easiest to fix cheese cakes, with a change of toppings to make the dessert different

    2   c. graham cracker crumbs
    ½   c. butter, melted
    ¼   c. chopped nuts (optional)
    3   (8 oz.) pkgs. cream cheese
    1½   c. sugar
    5   eggs
    3   tblsp. lemon juice

    1   (1 lb. 8 oz.) jar cherry
         prepared pie filling

• Mix graham cracker crumbs, butter and nuts in a 13 × 9 × 2" pan. Press firmly into bottom of pan.
• Beat cream cheese and sugar together until fluffy; add eggs, one at a time, beating well after each addition. Stir in lemon juice.
• Pour filling over crumbs and bake in moderate oven (350°) until set in the center, about 45 minutes. Cool. Spread pie filling (or apricot topping, see below under Apricot-Crested Torte) over top; refrigerate until ready to serve or carry out. Makes 15 to 18 servings.

VARIATIONS

Blueberry-Crested Torte: Prepare like Cherry-Crested Torte, but substitute 1 (1 lb. 8 oz.) jar blueberry prepared pie filling for the cherry filling.

Apricot-Crested Torte: Prepare like Cherry-Crested Torte, and substitute the following topping for the pie filling: Drain 1 (1 lb. 14 oz.) can apricot halves, reserving liquid. Cut halves lengthwise in slices and drain well on paper towels. Add enough water to the liquid to make 2 c. Place liquid in saucepan with ¼ c. sugar mixed with 2 tblsp. cornstarch, 1 tblsp. lemon juice, ¼ tsp. ginger and ⅛ tsp. cloves. Cook until slightly thickened, stirring constantly. Cool to room temperature. Arrange apricot pieces on torte; pour apricot sauce on top.

Milk Figures: *1 c. fresh milk is equal to ½ c. evaporated milk plus ½ c. water or 1 c. reconstituted non-fat dry milk plus 2 tblsp. butter.*

LEMON-CHOCOLATE DESSERT

Weight-watchers vote for this airy, light dessert that does not tax the budget—women especially like it

1	(14½ oz.) can evaporated milk
1	(3 oz.) pkg. lemon flavor gelatin
¾	c. sugar
1½	c. boiling water
3	tblsp. lemon juice
1	tblsp. grated lemon peel
25	chocolate wafers (thin, icebox type, 2⅜″ in diameter), finely crushed
¼	c. butter, melted

• Chill can of evaporated milk overnight in refrigerator.

• Mix gelatin and sugar; dissolve in boiling water. Chill until almost completely set; stir in lemon juice and peel.

• In a large mixing bowl whip milk until it resembles soft whipped cream. Add gelatin mixture, continue whipping about 2 minutes.

• In a 13 × 9 × 2″ pan, place chocolate wafer crumbs, reserving about 1 tblsp. crumbs. Add melted butter, mix, press firmly into bottom of pan. Pour in whipped lemon mixture, sprinkle on remaining chocolate crumbs. Refrigerate until serving time. Makes 15 to 18 servings.

RASPBERRY DESSERT

Marshmallow-cream base crowned with berries that sparkle like garnets

2	(10 oz.) pkgs. frozen red raspberries in syrup
1	c. water
½	c. sugar
2	tsp. lemon juice
4	tblsp. cornstarch
¼	c. cold water
50	large marshmallows
1	c. milk
2	c. heavy cream, whipped, or 2 pkgs. dessert topping mix
1¼	c. graham cracker crumbs
¼	c. chopped nuts
¼	c. butter, melted

• Heat raspberries with water, sugar and lemon juice. Dissolve cornstarch in ¼ c. cold water; stir into raspberries and cook until thickened and clear. Cool.

• Melt marshmallows in milk over boiling water; cool thoroughly.

• Whip heavy cream or dessert topping mix and fold into marshmallow mixture.

• Mix graham cracker crumbs, nuts and butter in a 13 × 9 × 2″ pan. Press firmly into bottom of pan.

• Spread marshmallow-cream mixture over crumbs. Spread raspberry mixture over top. Refrigerate until firm. Makes 15 to 18 servings.

Desserts That Feature Mincemeat

When frost sparkles on autumn fields and sunrise is noticeably later, that's the time for golden-crusted mincemeat pies. Many farm women cook a supply of mincemeat to freeze or can for these fall and winter treats.

Here is a treasured family recipe for mincemeat from a Pennsylvania member of FARM JOURNAL's Family Test Group. It's a meaty, fruity concoction without a vinegar tang.

We also give you recipes for exceptionally good desserts in which mincemeat is an important ingredient. If you don't want to make mincemeat, you can use the kind on supermarket shelves. And most successfully!

COUNTRY-KITCHEN MINCEMEAT

A bountiful blending of chopped meat and fruit spiced to perfection

1½ lbs. beef, trimmed of fat
    and cut in chunks
1½ lbs. pork, trimmed of fat and
    cut in chunks
½ lb. suet
2 oranges, quartered
2 lemons, quartered
½ lb. citron
8 c. peeled chopped, tart
    cooking apples
2 (15 oz.) pkgs. seedless
    raisins
3 (11 oz.) pkgs. currants
4 c. sugar
1 lb. brown sugar
1 c. molasses
2 tsp. cloves
1 tblsp. cinnamon
1 tblsp. ginger
1 tsp. nutmeg
3 c. apple juice
2 c. meat broth

• Cook beef and pork in gently simmering water until tender, about 1½ hours. Drain, reserving 2 c. broth. Put meat, suet, oranges, lemons and citron through food chopper using coarse blade. (Chop apples by hand.)
• Combine all ingredients in a large kettle. Bring to a gentle simmer over low to medium heat; stir occasionally. Cover; simmer 1 hour. Stir mixture occasionally.
• Remove from heat, cool immediately. Package in airtight containers; refrigerate or freeze. If you can mincemeat, reduce cooking time to 30 minutes; follow canning instructions in instruction book which came with your pressure canner. Makes 7 quarts.

Note: If mincemeat seems dry when you use it, add apple juice. Recipes using Country-Kitchen Mincemeat are: Mincemeat Refrigerator Dessert, Mince-Streusel Coffee Cake, Mincemeat-Pumpkin Pie, Mincemeat-Lemon Stack Cake and Mincemeat-Apple Betty.

MINCEMEAT-APPLE BETTY

Fast-fix spicy fruit dessert with crunchy bread and cheese topping

1 (1 lb. 8 oz.) jar apple pie
    filling
2 c. mincemeat
8 slices white bread
½ c. butter, melted
1 c. shredded American process
    cheese

• Combine pie filling and mincemeat. Spread in buttered, shallow 2-qt. baking dish.
• Trim bread crusts; cut bread into small cubes. Toss bread in butter. Sprinkle over fruit. Top with cheese. Bake in hot oven (400°) 20 minutes, or until cheese bubbles and bread cubes are toasted. Serve warm. Makes 8 servings.

Sugared or glazed Square Doughnuts (*recipe, page 162*) will be the talk of your coffee party. They're easy to make. Use a knife to cut dough in squares and any small cutter for centers. Also try our Raisin Doughnuts.

MINCEMEAT REFRIGERATOR DESSERT

Creamy, light filling in crisp ginger-snap crust; an easy-to-make dessert

Crust:
- 2 c. gingersnap crumbs
- ⅓ c. melted butter

Filling:
- 1 ½ tblsp. unflavored gelatin
- 2 c. mincemeat
- 4 eggs, separated
- ¼ c. butter
- ½ c. lemon juice
- ½ c. sugar
- 1 c. heavy cream, or 1 (2 oz.) pkg. dessert topping mix, whipped

• To make crust: Combine crumbs and melted butter; mix thoroughly. Reserve ½ c. for topping; pat remaining crumbs in bottom of a 13 × 9 × 2″ pan and refrigerate while you make the filling.

• To make filling: Soften gelatin in 5 tblsp. cold water. Combine mincemeat, slightly beaten egg yolks, butter and lemon juice in heavy saucepan. Cook over low heat, until slightly thickened, about 15 minutes. Stir constantly. Remove from heat; add gelatin, stir until dissolved. Refrigerate.

• When mincemeat mixture chills and begins to thicken, prepare a soft meringue of the egg whites and sugar. Fold meringue and whipped cream or topping mix into mincemeat mixture. Gently pour into crumb-lined pan. Sprinkle with remaining crumbs. Chill several hours. Makes 12 to 15 servings.

Apple Blossoms to Dumplings

Apple growers believe no one has lived until he walks through an orchard in full bloom. Their wives insist that no woman excels as a cook until she can fix at least a half-dozen superb apple dishes.

This explains why the food editors of FARM JOURNAL, when they wanted to locate some exceptional apple recipes, turned to orchard women's favorites—from New England and upstate New York to Virginia, Michigan and across country to Washington State. This cookbook contains many of their treasures, tested and tasted in our Test Kitchens. (Be sure to check Index—more good apple recipes appear in other chapters.)

Apple-Cranberry Dumplings is one of the desserts from the Pacific Northwest. It's a substantial windup for dinner in autumn.

APPLE-CRANBERRY DUMPLINGS

Biscuit dough winds around apples, black walnuts and cranberries. Pinwheels bake in a spiced syrup

Syrup:
- 2 c. water
- 2 c. sugar
- ½ tsp. cinnamon
- ½ tsp. cloves
- ½ c. butter

Glamorize your angel food cakes with these colorful dress-ups: Cherry Glaze (on uncut cake) and (top to bottom) Mocha Frosting, Fast-Fix Fruit and Pink Party Toppings (*see recipes for these and other toppings, page 188*).

Biscuit Dough:

2 c. sifted flour
1 tblsp. baking powder
1 tsp. salt
2 tblsp. sugar
½ c. shortening
¾ c. milk

Filling:

4 c. grated, peeled apples
1 c. drained cooked whole
   cranberries, or canned
   whole-cranberry sauce
½ c. black walnuts, chopped

• Combine first four ingredients for syrup and boil together 5 minutes. Remove from heat and add butter.
• Sift together dry ingredients and cut in shortening. Gradually add milk, tossing dry ingredients to make a soft dough. Roll out on a floured board to a rectangle 18 × 12″.
• Spread with apples, cranberries and nuts. Roll up like a jelly roll. Cut in 1″ slices and place in lightly greased 13 × 9 × 2″ baking pan.
• Pour over hot syrup and bake in a hot oven (425°) for 40 minutes. Serve warm. Makes 12 servings.

Autumn Blush Dessert

This cousin of the all-time favorite, apple crisp, is made with cranberries, which, with nuts, give the dessert a distinctive taste as well as appearance. It's a rather tart dessert. For a touch of sweetness, top with vanilla ice cream when serving. An especially good ending for a meal featuring poultry or pork.

Slip it into the oven late enough so that your guests can share a few minutes of the baking. The aroma is heavenly and should be shared.

APPLE-CRANBERRY CRISP

Apples bright with cranberries bake to make this fragrant treat

2 c. cranberries
3 c. unpeeled red apple slices
¾ c. sugar
½ c. butter
1 c. quick-cooking rolled oats
½ c. flour
½ c. brown sugar
½ c. chopped nuts

• Combine cranberries, apple slices and sugar in bottom of 2-qt. casserole.
• Melt butter; stir in remaining ingredients. Spread over cranberries and apples.
• Bake in moderate oven (350°) 1 hour. Makes 6 servings.

Note: Make 2 casseroles of this dessert for more or larger servings.

BAKED APPLE TAPIOCA

Country dessert of apple slices in a rosy sauce—good end to an oven meal

5 c. sliced peeled, firm
   cooking apples
2½ c. water
¼ tsp. cloves
½ c. quick-cooking tapioca
½ c. red cinnamon candies
   (red hots)
½ c. sugar
½ tsp. salt
¼ c. butter
¼ c. lemon juice

• Arrange apples in a greased 3-qt. casserole. Combine water, cloves, tapioca, candies, sugar and salt and

bring to a boil over medium heat, stirring constantly. Continue cooking at hard boil for 1 minute.
· Remove from heat; add butter and lemon juice; stir until butter melts.
· Pour over apples. Cover and bake in moderate oven (375°) about 45 minutes, or until apples are tender. Serve warm with whipped cream or vanilla ice cream sprinkled lightly with cinnamon. Makes 8 servings.

APPLE MACAROON

Guests will ask for the recipe for this dessert—apple slices topped with a crisp, golden cookie crust

4 medium-size peeled apples
¼ to ½ c. sugar (depending on tartness of apples)
½ tsp. cinnamon
½ c. pecan pieces
½ c. coconut
¼ c. shortening
¼ c. butter, softened
½ c. sugar
1 egg, well beaten
¾ c. sifted flour
½ tsp. vanilla

· Thinly slice apples into 10″ pie pan. Sprinkle with ¼ to ½ c. sugar and cinnamon. Top with pecan pieces and coconut.
· Make a batter of remaining ingredients by creaming together shortening and butter until fluffy. Add sugar gradually. Stir in well-beaten egg, blending well. Add flour and stir in gently but thoroughly. Stir in vanilla. Spread batter over top of apples.
· Bake in moderate oven (375°) until top is crisp and golden, about 35 minutes. Top with whipped cream, if desired. Makes 8 servings.

BIG APPLE BARS

Take your pick of Apple-Apricot or Apple Bars—both are delicious

1 c. sifted flour
½ tsp. salt
½ tsp. baking soda
½ c. light brown sugar
1 c. quick-cooking rolled oats, uncooked
½ c. vegetable shortening
2 tblsp. butter or margarine
2½ c. tart apple slices
¼ c. sugar
Butter pecan or vanilla ice cream

· Sift flour with salt and baking soda. Stir in brown sugar; mix in rolled oats. Cut in shortening until mixture is crumbly. Press half of this mixture firmly into bottom of greased 8″ square pan or dish. Dot with butter. Add apple slices and sprinkle with ¼ c. sugar. Cover with rest of crumbs.
· Bake in moderate oven (350°) until top is golden, 45 minutes.
· Cut in 6 large bars. Serve cold or faintly warm with ice cream or your favorite sauce. Makes 6 servings.

VARIATION

Apple-Apricot Bars: Substitute 1 c. canned drained and chopped apricots for 1 c. of the apple slices.

Use small quantities of fresh fruit (one kind or a combination) for frozen ice cream toppings. To make raspberry, strawberry or blackberry topping, wash fruit and crush until the juice begins to run. Add sugar to taste and mix thoroughly. Pack, label and freeze. To serve, spoon over vanilla ice cream before topping is completely thawed.

PEARS CARDINALE

Delightful! This light fruit dessert won bouquets from taste-testers

1 (10 oz.) pkg. frozen red
     raspberries in syrup
1 (1 lb. 13 oz.) can *large* pear
     halves, chilled
¼ c. sugar
2 tblsp. cornstarch
2 tblsp. toasted slivered almonds

• Defrost raspberries. Drain well, reserving liquid. Drain pear halves, reserving liquid.
• Pour liquid from drained raspberries into a 1-cup measure. Add enough pear liquid to make 1 c.
• Mix cornstarch and sugar in a small saucepan. Gradually stir in the 1 c. fruit liquid. Cook over moderate heat, stirring constantly, until clear and thickened. Simmer gently for 3 minutes. Cool to room temperature.
• Fill cavities of pear halves with well-drained raspberries and invert in individual glass serving dishes. Allow 1 pear half per serving.
• Spoon raspberry glaze over pear halves. Sprinkle toasted almonds over glazed pears. Refrigerate until serving time (up to 2 hours). Makes about 7 servings, depending on number of pear halves in can.

Fruit Basket

Assorted melon balls served in a watermelon basket make an attractive centerpiece for the buffet table. Select a rather small, round melon that weighs about 12 lbs. (Use a larger melon for more than 8 servings.)

• Cut a slice from one end of the melon to make a steady base. To make a handle for basket, stand melon upright and mark center of top. Measure ¾" from center on two sides (opposite each other) to make a handle 1½" wide. Cut a wedge from top half of the melon on both sides of handle; cut fruit from rind at top to free the handle. Then, with a sharp knife, cut points around top of basket (top of melon after removing wedges).
• Scoop out remaining fruit; you have a basket with a handle and a scalloped edge. Cut balls from melon; heap basket high with watermelon and cantaloupe or honeydew balls. In addition to watermelon balls, you will need about 4 c. cantaloupe or honeydew balls, or a combination of the two. Refrigerate basket until serving time.
• Set basket on buffet table. Twine ivy around handle and the base of the basket. Set a plate of lemon and lime wedges nearby for guests to squeeze over their servings of melon balls. Let guests help themselves. Makes 8 servings.

Summer's Superb Dessert— Peaches Melba

The wise hostess often plays safe on desserts by serving a dish that has stood the test of time. Peaches Melba is a classic example. It delights guests just the way it did in 1905, when a French chef created the dessert and named it for Melba, the opera star. The season for fresh peaches and red raspberries is so brief that scarcely anyone ever has a chance to tire of the combination.

To extend the season for this famous dish, make the purée with frozen raspberries and use well-drained canned peach halves. But it's the fresh fruit and berries that make the superb Parisian treat that's now revered around the world. The purée also makes a tasty sundae sauce when served on vanilla or peach ice cream or lemon sherbet.

One advantage of Peaches Melba is that you fix the peaches and purée hours ahead so that they'll have a chance to chill thoroughly. It takes little time to assemble the dessert when you're ready to serve it. You can depend on getting compliments every time you serve peaches the French way, or American style.

PEACHES MELBA

A luscious dessert of brilliant colors. Double the recipe for 12 servings

1 c. sugar
1 c. water
¼ tsp. vanilla
6 ripe freestone peaches
1 qt. vanilla ice cream
Raspberry Purée

• Place sugar and water in a saucepan with high sides; bring to a boil and let boil 2 minutes. Add vanilla.
• Peel peaches carefully, cut in halves and discard pits. Add peach halves, 4 at a time, and simmer gently in the syrup, spooning some of the hot syrup over the peaches while they cook. Cook only until tender—it takes only a few minutes. (Don't overcook or peaches will lose their shape.) Lift

from syrup with a slotted spoon; drain thoroughly and chill.
• To serve, place a layer of ice cream on each serving plate. Top each serving with 2 peach halves, cut side up. Fill peach centers with ice cream. Spoon Raspberry Purée over the desserts. Makes 6 servings.

VARIATION

American Peaches Melba: Place uncooked halves of 3 chilled, large, ripe peeled peaches in a medium bowl. Sprinkle ½ c. orange juice over peaches. Pour Raspberry Purée over, cover and refrigerate an hour or several hours. To serve, remove peach halves with a slotted spoon; place one half on each plate. Arrange a scoop of ice cream on each peach half. Spoon Raspberry Purée over the top. Makes 6 servings.

FRESH RASPBERRY PURÉE

2 c. very ripe red raspberries
½ c. sugar

• Strain the ripe raspberries through a sieve. Add sugar and stir to mix well. Chill thoroughly. Makes about 2 cups.

VARIATION

Frozen Raspberry Purée: Mash 1 (10 oz.) pkg. frozen red raspberries, thawed, in a saucepan. Add ½ c. currant jelly; bring to a boil. Add 1½ tsp. cornstarch mixed with 1 tblsp. cold water. Stir and cook until sauce is clear. Chill. Makes about 2 cups.

PEACH MELBA PARFAIT

*New version of Peaches Melba—
mold this beauty in glass dishes*

1 (3 oz.) pkg. raspberry flavor
   gelatin
2 c. hot water
1 (10 oz.) pkg. frozen
   raspberries (1 ¼ c.)
1 (3 oz.) pkg. peach flavor
   gelatin
½ c. cold water
1 pt. vanilla ice cream
1 ½ c. diced fresh peaches

· Dissolve raspberry gelatin in 1 c.
hot water in bowl. Add unthawed
raspberries. Stir occasionally to separate berries. Let thaw (it will begin to
set).
· Pour 1 c. hot water over peach
gelatin in another bowl; stir to dissolve. Add ½ c. cold water. Add ice
cream in eight chunks; stir to melt.
Refrigerate until thick enough to
mound up.
· Spoon slightly thickened raspberry
mixture into 8 dessert dishes.
· When ice cream mixture has thickened, fold in peaches and spoon over
raspberry mixture. Chill at least 30
minutes before serving. Makes 8 servings.

Cobblers Are Country Fare

When the branches of peach trees
bend and a blue haze covers blueberry patches, that's summer signal-
ing that it's time to make cobblers.

Cobblers continue in favor after
the fruit harvest ends, when canned
fruit becomes the basic ingredient.

Cream is the traditional accompaniment for this juicy fruit dessert with
its flaky pastry crust. Pass the cream
so guests can help themselves. This
gives them a chance to take as little
or much as they think advisable. It
all depends on how serious they are
about weight watching.

Here are recipes for a few specials.
Remember, while cobblers are acceptable when cold, they're tops in
flavor when freshly baked and still
faintly warm.

FRESH PEACH COBBLER

*An all-time-great country dessert in
summer—cheese topping is new*

Filling:
2 qts. fresh peach slices
1 ½ c. sugar
2 tblsp. cornstarch
½ tsp. salt
2 tblsp. lemon juice
½ tsp. almond extract
3 tblsp. butter

Cheese Topping:
2 c. all-purpose biscuit mix
1 c. grated sharp cheese
4 tblsp. melted butter
⅔ c. milk (about)

· Place peach slices in a greased
13 × 9 × 2″ (3-qt.) baking pan.
· Mix sugar, cornstarch and salt;
sprinkle evenly over peaches. Sprinkle
on lemon juice and almond extract;
dot with butter.
· Place in a preheated hot oven
(400°) until hot and bubbly, about 15
minutes.
· In the meantime, mix cheese topping. Measure biscuit mix into a small
bowl; stir in grated cheese. Add

melted butter and enough milk to make a soft dough. Stir with fork until well blended.
• Remove peach mixture from oven. Drop dough onto hot peaches, making 12 biscuits.
• Place in hot oven (400°) about 20 minutes, or until biscuits are golden. Makes 10 to 12 servings.

Note: The amount of sugar required depends on the sweetness of the peaches. If peaches are tart, increase the sugar slightly.

PEACH COBBLER RING

This cobbler bakes in a ring—plain, it's a marvelous breakfast bread; with cream and sliced peaches, it's dessert

Dough:
2 c. flour
4 tsp. baking powder
1 tblsp. sugar
½ tsp. salt
½ c. shortening
⅔ c. milk

Filling:
2 tblsp. soft butter
¼ c. brown sugar
1 tblsp. flour
1 tsp. cinnamon
1 c. diced fresh peaches

• For dough, sift dry ingredients together; cut in shortening until mixture resembles coarse crumbs. Add milk all at once; stir to form soft dough. Turn out on lightly floured board and knead 6 to 8 times. Roll into 18 × 9" rectangle.
• To fill, spread dough with butter. Sprinkle with mixture of brown sugar, flour and cinnamon; cover with peaches.

• Roll up like jelly roll. Place on ungreased baking sheet and form into circle. Make slits from outside edge of circle almost into center every 2". Turn each cut on its side. Brush with butter. Bake in hot oven (400°) 25 to 30 minutes. Serve warm with cream, and spoon sliced peaches over top.

FRESH BLUEBERRY COBBLER

Lemon accents delicate berry taste

Filling:
1½ c. sugar
½ c. flour
1 tsp. salt
2 qts. fresh blueberries
3 tblsp. lemon juice
3 tblsp. butter

Topping:
2 c. sifted flour
4 tsp. baking powder
2 tblsp. sugar
1 tsp. salt
½ c. shortening
⅔ c. milk
1 egg, slightly beaten

• Mix sugar, flour and salt; combine with blueberries and lemon juice. Pour into a greased 13 × 9 × 2" (3-qt.) baking pan; dot with butter.
• Place in a preheated hot oven (400°) about 15 minutes; be sure that mixture is hot and bubbling.
• In the meantime, mix the topping. Sift together flour, baking powder, sugar and salt. Cut in shortening until mixture resembles coarse meal. Add milk and slightly beaten egg to dry ingredients. Stir with fork to blend well.
• Remove hot blueberry mixture from

oven. Drop topping onto hot blueberries, making 12 biscuits. Return to hot oven (400°); bake about 20 minutes, or until biscuits are browned. Makes 12 servings.

WINTER CHERRY COBBLER

Keep canned cherries in the cupboard to make this quickie dessert

1 ½ c. sugar
3 tblsp. cornstarch
3 (1 lb.) cans pitted tart cherries
¼ c. butter or margarine
3 c. sifted flour
¼ c. sugar
4 ½ tsp. baking powder
1 ½ tsp. salt
½ c. plus 1 tblsp. butter
1 ½ c. milk

• Stir together 1½ c. sugar and cornstarch in a saucepan. Drain fruit, reserving juice; arrange in 13 × 9 × 2″ baking pan. Stir juice into dry ingredients in saucepan. Bring to a boil; boil 1 minute. Stir constantly. Pour 1½ c. hot sauce over fruit. Save rest of sauce. Dot fruit mixture with ¼ c. butter.

• Sift dry ingredients. Cut in butter as for pastry. Lightly stir in milk; spoon batter over hot fruit. Sprinkle with sugar and cinnamon.

• Bake in hot oven (400°) 30 minutes, or until topping is golden brown. Serve warm with reserved sauce. Pass a pitcher of dairy half and half or heavy cream. Makes 12 servings.

VARIATION

Winter Peach Cobbler: Prepare as directed for Winter Cherry Cobbler, except substitute 4 (1 lb.) cans sliced peaches for the cherries and decrease the sugar to ½ c.

JIFFY PEACH CRUMBLE

Take it hot and fragrant from oven, cool it just a little and serve

2 (16 to 17 oz.) cans sliced peaches, drained (about 3 c.)
¾ c. brown sugar
1 ½ c. graham cracker crumbs
½ tsp. cinnamon
3 tblsp. melted butter or margarine
1 tblsp. lemon juice
Light cream or whipped cream

• Drain peaches.
• Combine brown sugar, cracker crumbs and cinnamon. Combine melted butter and lemon juice; pour over cracker mixture and mix thoroughly. Add peaches and blend gently.
• Pour into a greased 13 × 9 × 2″ pan.
• Bake in moderate oven (350°) 30 minutes. Serve with light cream, heavy cream, whipped, dairy half and half or vanilla ice cream. Makes 8 servings.

APPLE GINGERBREAD

For a crowd stack two of these gingerbreads—a dramatic dessert

½ c. whole bran cereal
½ c. light molasses
¼ c. softened shortening
¼ c. boiling water
1 egg
1 c. sifted flour
½ tsp. baking soda
½ tsp. baking powder

½ tsp. ginger
¼ tsp. cloves
¼ tsp. salt
6 c. thin slices peeled apple
¼ c. melted butter
¼ c. light corn syrup

· Mix bran, molasses, shortening and water. Add egg, and beat with rotary beater; let stand 5 minutes.
· Sift together flour, soda, baking powder, spices and salt; add to bran mixture and stir only until blended. Pour into greased 8 × 8 × 2″ pan. Bake in moderate oven (350°) 20 minutes.
· Arrange apple slices in layers over top. Brush with mixture of butter and syrup. Bake 10 minutes longer, or until apples are tender.
· Remove from oven, brush apples with milk and broil just a few minutes to brown edges of apple slices (for a change, sprinkle chopped walnuts over apple slices). Serve warm. Makes 12 servings.

New Homemade Ice Cream

Guests enjoy no dessert more than homemade ice cream unless it's homemade ice cream and cake—the kind of cake you're sometimes lucky enough to find at country ice cream socials. The ice cream recipes are in this section. Look in another chapter for the excellent cake recipes (see Index).

Ice cream is at home on many occasions—company meals, at picnics, cookouts and parties, and for evening refreshments. You can make it ahead, pack it in ice and salt (directions follow) and forget about it un-

til serving time. Flavors ripen and mellow while it waits. Or you can store it in the freezer. All you need do at serving time is dish it and graciously accept the compliments.

We share with you several remarkably good ice cream recipes. They come from farm and ranch kitchens across the country. The rich, velvety Homemade Vanilla Ice Cream is the specialty of a Hoosier farm family; the Fast Mix Ice Cream comes from a Georgia country kitchen. We first tasted Fruited Velvet Ice Cream on a Colorado ranch. And mindful of weight-watchers, one of the ice creams contains skim milk instead of cream, to cut down on calories. We include a popular recipe, Coconut Honey Ice Cream, with its rewarding tropical flavors. It's an original recipe from the wife of a California "honey farmer."

Try also the many exciting variations which we developed in our Test Kitchens.

How to Freeze and Ripen Ice Cream

1. Pour the cool ice cream mixture into the freezer can. Fill can two thirds to three fourths full to leave room for expansion. Fit can into freezer; follow manufacturer's directions if using an electric freezer.
2. Adjust the dasher and cover. Pack crushed ice and rock salt around the can, using 4 parts ice to 1 part rock salt. Turn the dasher slowly until the ice melts enough to form a brine. Add more ice and salt, mixed in the proper proportions, to maintain the ice level.

Turn the handle fast and steadily until it turns hard. Then remove the ice until its level is below the lid of the can; take the lid off. Remove the dasher.

3. To ripen the ice cream, plug the opening in the lid. Cover the can with several thicknesses of waxed paper or foil to make a tight fit for the lid. Put the lid on the can.

4. Pack more of the ice and salt mixture around the can, filling the freezer. Cover the freezer with a blanket, canvas or other heavy cloth, or with newspapers. Let ice cream ripen at least 4 hours. Or put the can in the home freezer to ripen.

Note: If you buy ice by the pound, you can use these proportions of ice to salt: 20 lbs. ice to 5 c. rock salt for a 1-gal. freezer; and 25 lbs. ice to 7 c. rock salt for a 6-qt. freezer. Use half the salt to freeze the ice cream, the other half to ripen it.

HOMEMADE VANILLA ICE CREAM

Velvety, rich, delicious—perfect go-along with your best homemade cake

1   qt. milk
2   c. sugar
¼   c. flour
½   tsp. salt
4   eggs, slightly beaten
1   tblsp. vanilla
1 ½ qts. light cream, or dairy
      half and half

• Scald milk. Mix sugar, flour and salt. Add enough hot milk to sugar-flour mixture to make a thin paste. Stir paste into hot milk. Cook over low heat, stirring constantly, until mixture thickens slightly, about 15 minutes.

▸ Add hot mixture gradually to beaten eggs and cook over low heat, stirring constantly, until mixture thickens slightly, about 2 minutes (do not cook longer or eggs may curdle).

• Cool quickly in refrigerator. Do not allow mixture to cool at room temperature.

• Add vanilla and light cream to cooled mixture. Pour into freezer can; fill only two thirds full to allow for expansion. Freeze and ripen by basic directions for freezing ice cream. Makes 1 gallon.

VARIATIONS

Chocolate Ice Cream: Add 4 squares unsweetened chocolate to milk before scalding. After scalding, beat with rotary beater until chocolate flecks disappear. Increase sugar by ½ c. and prepare according to directions for freezing Homemade Vanilla Ice Cream.

Peanut Butter Ice Cream: Omit 1 c. light cream. Stir a small amount of the custard mix gradually into ½ c. peanut butter to blend well. Add to rest of the mixture in the freezer can.

Strawberry Ice Cream: Omit 3 c. light cream. Add 1 qt. washed and hulled strawberries which have been mashed and sweetened with ½ c. additional sugar. Add a few drops of red food color if you wish.

Peach Ice Cream: Omit 3 c. light cream. Add 1 qt. crushed fresh peaches mixed with ¾ c. additional sugar.

You can substitute 3 tblsp. cocoa plus 1 tblsp. fat for 1 (1 oz.) square unsweetened chocolate.

FROZEN VANILLA CUSTARD

It's made with skim milk and contains fewer calories than many ice creams

3 qts. skim milk
2 c. sugar
6 tblsp. flour
2 tsp. salt
8 eggs, slightly beaten
2 envelopes unflavored gelatin,
    softened in ¼ c. cold water
3 tblsp. vanilla

• Scald milk in top of double boiler. Mix sugar, flour and salt and add a little of the hot milk. Blend well and add to milk in double boiler. Cook over boiling water until bubbles form at the edge of the pan.
• Remove from heat. Add the hot mixture gradually to the eggs. Return to double boiler and cook over simmering, not boiling, water, stirring constantly, until mixture coats a wooden spoon.
• Remove from the heat; gradually stir the hot mixture into the gelatin, stirring until the gelatin completely dissolves. Refrigerate until custard thickens, about 2 hours, or until it reaches 70°. (You can cook the custard a day ahead and refrigerate it). Add vanilla to cooled custard.
• Pour into freezer can. Freeze and ripen by basic directions for freezing ice cream. Makes 1 gallon. 105 calories per ½ cup serving.

VARIATIONS

Frozen Coffee Custard: Omit vanilla. Reserve 1 c. custard and add ¼ c. instant coffee powder. When custard is partly frozen, add coffee-custard mix and continue freezing until firm. 105 calories per ½ cup serving.

Frozen Banana Custard: Add 5 large, very ripe bananas, mashed (about 2 c.), and ¼ tsp. yellow food color. Freeze. 117 calories per ½ cup serving.

Frozen Peppermint Stick Custard: Add ¼ tsp. green food color to chilled custard. Partially freeze. Add 1 c. crushed green and white peppermint stick candy, or omit food color and add red and white peppermint stick candy; freeze. 125 calories per ½ cup serving.

Frozen Strawberry Custard: Omit 1 tsp. salt and 1 c. milk when making custard. Partially freeze. Add 2 c. sliced, fresh strawberries sweetened with 2 tblsp. sugar. Freeze until firm. 109 calories per ½ cup serving.

FRUITED VELVET ICE CREAM

A pretty ice cream with luscious fruit flavors—surprisingly simple to make

Basic Mix:
1½ qts. light cream
1 c. eggs, beaten
1½ c. sugar
1 tsp. vanilla

Fruit Mix:
½ c. chopped nuts
½ c. diced banana
½ c. drained diced pineapple
    (canned)
½ c. chopped maraschino
    cherries
½ c. chopped fresh strawberries
¼ c. sugar
2 tsp. fresh lemon juice
½ tsp. salt

• Combine cream, eggs and sugar for basic mix. Cook over very low heat, stirring constantly, until mixture coats the back of a metal spoon. Cool quickly in refrigerator. Add vanilla. Pour into freezer can; fill two thirds full.

• Combine nuts, fruits, ¼ c. sugar, lemon juice and salt. Let stand 5 minutes. Add to mixture in freezer can. Freeze and ripen by basic directions for freezing ice cream. Makes 1 gallon.

FAST MIX ICE CREAM

No cooking of custard—this refreshing frozen dessert tastes like ice milk

    5 eggs, beaten
 2½ c. sugar
    1 tblsp. vanilla
    1 (14½ oz.) can evaporated
        milk
    2 qts. whole milk

• Mix all the ingredients. Pour mixture into freezer can; fill it about two thirds full. Freeze and ripen following basic directions for freezing ice cream. Makes about 1 gallon.

COCONUT HONEY ICE CREAM

Ice cream, from the Freezing & Canning Cookbook—*too good to leave out of this collection of hostess ice creams*

 1½ c. honey
    4 eggs, slightly beaten
    3 c. heavy cream
    2 tsp. vanilla
   ½ tsp. lemon extract
   ½ tsp. salt
    3 c. milk
    1 (3½ oz.) can flaked
        coconut
    2 (8½ oz.) cans crushed
        pineapple

• Add honey to eggs; mix well. Add cream, flavorings, salt and milk; stir until well blended. Chill.

• Pour into freezer can; put dasher and cover in place. Pack chopped ice and rock salt around can, 4 parts ice to 1 part salt. Turn dasher.

• When partly frozen, add coconut and pineapple; continue freezing until crank turns hard. Remove dasher. Pack in same ice mixture until serving time. Or spoon into freezer containers; seal, label, date and store in freezer. Makes 1 gallon.

Note: To intensify coconut flavor, add 2 tsp. coconut extract with lemon extract and vanilla.

CRISPY SUNDAE CRUNCH

Simply delicious make-ahead dessert with ice cream between crisp crusts

    2 tblsp. butter
   ¼ c. light brown sugar
    1 c. oven-toasted rice cereal,
        crushed
   ⅓ c. walnuts
   ⅓ c. flaked coconut
    1 qt. vanilla ice cream

• Melt butter in skillet; add sugar and heat slowly, stirring until blended. Add crushed rice cereal. Toss well to coat with butter-sugar mixture. Remove from heat; add nuts and coconut.

• Reserve ⅔ c. cereal mixture for topping. Spread remaining cereal mixture into an 8 × 8 × 2″ pan. Spread ice cream on top. Sprinkle the ⅔ c. cereal mixture over the ice cream. Freeze. Cut in squares to serve. Makes 9 servings.

Crispy Sundae Crunch for a Crowd:
Double the recipe; use a 13 × 9 ×
2″ pan. Reserve 1⅓ c. cereal mixture
to spread over top of ice cream.
Makes 18 servings.

AVOCADO SHERBET

*This recipe came from Hawaii by way
of California. Sherbet has a buttery
taste, is refreshing and smooth*

1 envelope unflavored gelatin
2 tblsp. cold water
½ c. sugar
½ c. milk
⅔ c. mashed avocado
⅛ tsp. salt
¼ c. chopped pecans
½ c. orange juice
¼ c. lemon juice
1 egg white, stiffly beaten

• Soften gelatin in water; dissolve
over boiling water. Dissolve sugar in
milk. Add avocado, salt, pecans and
juices. Stir in the gelatin.
• Fold in beaten egg white. Freeze
in refrigerator tray, stirring occasionally. Makes 4 to 6 servings.

LEMON PINEAPPLE SHERBET

*When our taste panel sampled this,
they said: "Excellent. Outstanding"*

2 c. sugar
1¼ c. lemon juice
1 (8½ oz.) can crushed
      pineapple, undrained
1½ qts. milk
1 c. heavy cream, whipped
2 egg whites, stiffly beaten

• Dissolve sugar in lemon juice by
heating slightly and stirring; add pineapple and cool.

• Pour this mixture and milk into a
1-gallon crank-style electric ice cream
freezer container. Pack chopped ice
and rock salt around can. Churn until
mixture reaches slush stage, about 10
minutes.
• Meanwhile, fold whipped cream into
beaten egg whites; open freezer container and fold into partially frozen
sherbet mixture. Freeze. Remove
dasher. Let sherbet ripen 1 hour before serving. Makes about 3½ quarts.

PARTY SHERBET MOLD

*Don't-eat-the-daisies dessert—that is
what a Kansas Guest Cook calls this
treat she serves at women's luncheons*

12 ladyfingers
3 pts. orange sherbet
1 pt. lemon sherbet
Chocolate Whipped Cream
Semisweet chocolate, shaved or
   grated

• Wash and dry a clay flowerpot, 8″
in diameter, 4¼″ deep. Line with
aluminum foil, making a double thickness of foil in the bottom of the
flowerpot. Grease foil lightly.
• Line bottom and sides of flowerpot
with ladyfinger halves (about 12
whole ladyfingers).
• Soften orange sherbet and lemon
sherbet with a fork to spreading consistency (two other flavors of sherbet
or ice cream, if you prefer) in separate bowls; stir until smooth.
• Spoon half of orange sherbet into
pot, make a layer of lemon sherbet
on top and then spread remaining
orange sherbet over the lemon. Insert about 6 large drinking straws,
cut in 4″ lengths, into sherbet and
place flowerpot in freezer overnight.

• Remove straws, turn out and then invert on serving plate. Replace straws. Spread top with Chocolate Whipped Cream. Sprinkle with semisweet chocolate. Place dessert in freezer to firm. When ready to take to the table, insert fresh daisies or other flowers in the straws. (Let stand at room temperature about 15 minutes for easier cutting.) 8 servings.

Chocolate Whipped Cream: Mix ¼ c. confectioners sugar and 2 tblsp. cocoa; add ½ c. heavy cream and ¼ tsp. vanilla. Chill thoroughly. Whip until light and fluffy.

CHERRY ICE

Intriguing frosty red dessert that's a refreshing ending for a heavy meal

2   c. frozen Ripe Red Cherry
    Purée (see Index)
¼   c. sugar
1   envelope unflavored gelatin
2   tblsp. water
2   tblsp. lemon juice
1   egg white
2   tblsp. sugar

• Thaw Cherry Purée just enough to remove from freezer container. Add ¼ c. sugar to purée in saucepan; heat to just below boiling point.
• Soften gelatin in water and lemon juice. Add to hot purée and stir until gelatin is dissolved. Cool. Pour into freezer trays and freeze until mushy (about 45 minutes). Remove from freezer, turn into bowl and beat well.
• Beat egg white until frothy; add sugar and beat until stiff peaks form. Fold into cherry mixture.
• Return to freezer tray. Freeze 3 hours, stirring every 30 minutes. Makes 1 quart.

TUTTI-FRUTTI ICE

When it's hot and humid, give your meal a cool start with this tart red ice; or serve it as a refreshing relish in main-dish course

1   qt. cranberries
2   c. water
1   c. sugar
1   (10 oz.) pkg. frozen
    raspberries
¼   c. lemon juice
1   tsp. grated orange peel
½   c. orange juice

• Combine cranberries, water and sugar; bring to a rapid boil over high heat. Cook 10 minutes or until cranberry skins pop. Remove from heat; add raspberries. Stir until raspberries are thawed.
• Run mixture through a food mill to make a smooth pulp. Stir in remaining ingredients; pour into large mixing bowl. Put in freezer. When mixture is partially frozen, beat at high speed in mixer. Return to freezer.
• Before ice is firm, beat once more, at high speed (beat until ice becomes lighter in color; don't expect fine crystals). Put into freezer containers, cover and freeze. Makes 2 quarts.

Note: For individual servings, quickly spoon Tutti-Frutti Ice into paper cups, set in shallow pans and freeze. Then package and return to freezer.

FROZEN STRAWBERRY SQUARES

Here's a dessert to fix ahead. It's luscious, says the Texas Test Group member who sent the recipe

1   c. flour
½   c. chopped nuts
¼   c. brown sugar

½ c. melted butter
2 egg whites
2 c. sliced fresh strawberries,
   or 2 (10 oz.) pkgs. frozen
   strawberries, thawed
1 c. sugar (use ⅔ c. for frozen
   berries)
2 tblsp. lemon juice
1 c. heavy cream, whipped

• Mix together flour, nuts, sugar and butter. Spread in a 13 × 9 × 2″ pan. Bake in moderate oven (350°) 20 minutes, stirring every 5 minutes. Remove from oven and stir again. Remove crumbs from pan and cool. Sprinkle two thirds of crumbs, about 1⅓ c., back in pan to cover bottom.
• Combine egg whites, berries, sugar and lemon juice in large mixer bowl. Beat at high speed until stiff peaks form, 10 to 15 minutes. Fold in whipped cream. Spread lightly over crumbs in pan. Sprinkle remaining crumbs on top. Freeze until firm. Cut in squares to serve. Makes 12 to 16 servings.

FROZEN STRAWBERRY WHIP

A pleasing, make-ahead dessert

Crust:
2 ⅔ c. graham cracker crumbs
  ½ c. sugar
  ½ c. melted butter or margarine

Topping:
3 egg whites
1 c. sugar
1 (10 oz.) pkg. frozen
   strawberries, thawed
1 c. heavy cream, whipped

• To make crust, combine graham cracker crumbs, sugar and melted butter. Save out ⅔ c. crumbs; press remaining crumbs in bottom of a 13 × 9 × 2″ pan.
• Beat egg whites until stiff; add sugar and berries. Beat with electric mixer 15 minutes. Fold in whipped cream. Pour on crust in pan; sprinkle top with reserved ⅔ c. crust mixture.
• Cover with aluminum foil; freeze. Makes 15 servings.

FROZEN STRAWBERRY FLUFF

Smooth as cream, fresh as just-picked berries and frosty as icicles

1 ¼ c. crisp cookie crumbs
  ⅓ c. butter
  2 egg whites
  1 tblsp. lemon juice
1 ⅓ c. sugar
  2 c. fresh strawberries
  1 c. heavy cream, whipped

• Mix crumbs and butter; press into bottom of buttered 9″ square pan or 7″ round spring-form pan. Bake in moderate oven (350°) 8 minutes. Cool.
• Beat egg whites and lemon juice slightly in large bowl of electric mixer; gradually beat in sugar and berries. Beat at high speed 12 to 15 minutes, until mixture is fluffy and has large volume.
• Fold in whipped cream. Spread over crumb crust. Freeze overnight. Cut in squares or wedges to serve. Garnish with fresh berries. Makes 9 servings.

VARIATIONS

Peach Fluff: Use 2 c. sliced ripe peaches instead of strawberries. Garnish with peach slices.

Raspberry Fluff: Use fresh raspberries instead of strawberries.

Blueberry Fluff: Use fresh blueberries instead of strawberries.

Calorie-Cutting Fruit Fluff: Substitute whipped nonfat dry milk for whipped cream. Sprinkle ½ c. nonfat dry milk over ½ c. ice water. Add 1 tblsp. lemon juice and beat until stiff.

Double-Frozen Fluff: Instead of fresh berries or peaches, use 1 (10 oz.) pkg. sweetened frozen berries or peaches; use 1 c. sugar instead of 1⅓ cups.

Short-Cut Strawberry Fluff: Omit the buttered crumbs. Prepare the Strawberry Fluff as directed and spread in a 9″ pan. Freeze. Cut in squares or wedges and serve with angel food cake.

24-HOUR CHOCOLATE DESSERT

Chill or freeze, whichever is easier

3 eggs, separated
2 tblsp. water
2 tblsp. sugar
2 (4 oz.) bars sweet cooking
     chocolate, melted and
     cooled
1 pt. heavy cream, whipped
18 ladyfingers
Whipped cream
Maraschino cherries

• Beat egg yolks; beat in water, sugar and chocolate. Fold in beaten egg whites. Fold in whipped cream.
• Arrange 9 ladyfingers in 10 × 6″ dish; put half of chocolate mixture over top; place 9 more ladyfingers over chocolate; cover with remaining chocolate mixture.
• Chill in refrigerator 24 hours. Cut in squares to serve. Garnish with whipped cream and maraschino cherries. Makes 8 to 10 servings.

Note: Angel food cake or sponge cake may be used instead of ladyfingers.

CHERRY CHEESE DESSERT

Two-layer, make-ahead frozen dessert

1 c. graham cracker crumbs
1 tblsp. sugar
¼ c. melted butter or margarine
1 (2 oz.) pkg. dessert topping
     mix
1 (8 oz.) pkg. cream cheese
1 c. Ripe Red Cherry Purée,
     slightly thawed (see Index)
½ c. sugar
Few drops red food color

• Combine crumbs, 1 tblsp. sugar and butter. Reserve ¼ c. of this mixture. Pat remaining mixture in bottoms of 2 (10 × 4″) refrigerator trays or a 9 × 9 × 2″ pan.
• Prepare dessert topping mix according to package directions. Set aside.
• Soften cheese at room temperature. Add purée to cheese gradually, beating until smooth and creamy. Beat in ½ c. sugar and food color.
• Fold cheese mixture into whipped topping a little at a time, until well blended. Pour into the crumb-lined trays; sprinkle on the ¼ c. crumb mixture. Freeze.
• Let frozen dessert stand at room temperature 5 minutes before cutting. Makes 12 servings.

RHUBARB-PINEAPPLE SAUCE

Serve this warm on ice cream and unfrosted cake slices—gorgeous color and luscious. Keeps well

3 c. diced rhubarb
1 (8½ oz.) can crushed
     pineapple

½ c. sugar
½ c. water
¼ c. red cinnamon candies
    (red hots)
2 tblsp. cornstarch
2 tblsp. water
¼ tsp. salt
2 tblsp. lemon juice
2 tblsp. butter or margarine

• Combine rhubarb, pineapple, sugar, water and candies. Bring to a slow boil.

• Meanwhile dissolve cornstarch in 2 tblsp. water and add to hot fruit. Cook gently 5 minutes. Remove from heat. Stir in salt, lemon juice and butter. Cool slightly before serving. Makes about 4 cups.

BOUNTIFUL DESSERT TREE

Guests like to "pick" dessert from this tempting tree—several times

One perfect way to end a holiday (or company) feast is with fruit and cheese. This combination is popular in Europe and many American restaurants offer it at gourmet prices. At your holiday dinner, let guests choose their favorite fruits from a bountiful tree (see picture).

Place your fruit tree on a low coffee table or buffet where you can see it from the dining table.

To build your tree, assemble trays, cake stands and footed dishes, graduated in size; place the heaviest pieces on the bottom. Roll florist's clay (available from a florist) into long thin strips. Use clay to anchor each dish firmly to the one below it. If your trays and dishes don't match in color and material, cover glass or metal pieces with contact paper and spray with copper or gold paint.

Begin at the bottom to stack fruits and work up (we've used five layers). Intersperse fruits with green leaves from your yard—ivy, holly, laurel, or whatever you have.

Supplement your own homegrown fruits with an assortment from the food store. Add color with a few out-of-season strawberries or cherry tomatoes. Quarter fresh pineapple by cutting right through the crown (leaves). Remove the core with a sharp knife, loosen fruit from rind, then cut in bite-size pieces to spear with toothpicks.

Try cheeses for dessert that you've not tasted before. (A list of Important Natural Cheeses follows.) We recommend Pineapple Cheese, Blue or Roquefort, Neufchatel, Liederkranz and an aged Cheddar. Set a basket of interesting crackers nearby. Some of your guests may prefer to eat them instead of fruit with the cheese.

Keep your tree to replenish throughout the holiday season. Refrigerate perishable fruits and most cheeses until guests arrive.

Important Natural Cheeses

• *Blue (spelled bleu when imported)*: A creamy white cheese with blue-green threads, called veins. Most of the imported supply in the United States comes from Denmark. This cheese is especially tasty when added to green salads, but it has many other uses.

• *Brick:* A native of the United States. It is something like Muenster and has the same kind of openings or holes (man-made), but is more moist. It is a sandwich favorite.

• *Camembert:* A French original that comes divided into serving portions. It is soft and a creamy yellow inside with a white or gray-white crust that's good to eat. It's excellent for dessert with crackers and/or fresh fruit.

• *Cheddar:* This cheese was first made in Cheddar, England. It varies from pale yellow to a medium orange in color and from mild to sharp in flavor. (New York State Cheddar cheese is a pale yellow, while Wisconsin's Cheddar is a deeper yellow or orange. The color is due to the food color added by the cheese maker.) It has few or no holes. You can buy it in many shapes—cylinders, cubes, blocks, bars, slices, wedges and spreads. Cheddar is used in many kinds of dishes, both hot and cold, and you'll find it listed often in this book's recipes.

• *Colby:* A cheese born in the United States. It is mild to mellow in taste and is softer and more open (has more holes) than Cheddar Cheese. Many people like it in sandwiches, especially in cheeseburgers, and for snacks.

• *Cottage Cheese:* No one knows where this *uncured* cheese was first made. Our grandmothers made it in their kitchens and they almost always added salt and cream to it. You can buy either the creamed or dry cottage cheese in cartons, usually 1 pint.

• *Edam:* You'll recognize this ball-shaped cheese that is red-coated (wax). It was first made in the Netherlands. The cheese has a mild, slightly salty taste. You can scoop out the inside of the ball, cut the cheese in pieces and put it back in the red ball. Served on a big plate, surrounded with crackers, the cheese invites guests to help themselves.

• *Gorgonzola:* A creamy white Italian cheese that has blue-green threads. On the outside, the cheese is clay-colored. Sometimes the cheese is crumbly, other times it is semisoft. It contains less moisture than blue cheese. It comes in cylinders, wedges and oblongs. This cheese makes good salads, dips and sandwiches and is a satisfying dessert when served with crackers and/or fresh fruit—especially pears.

• *Gouda:* Invented in the Netherlands, this cheese is mellow and has a nut-like, slightly acid taste. There are small, uneven or round holes throughout the cheese, which ranges in color from a creamy yellow to a medium orange yellow inside. It is shaped in a ball, flattened at top and bottom, and usually is coated with red wax. The American-made Gouda is somewhat softer than the cheese from the Netherlands and it does not have the openings—"a closer body," cheese makers call it. It is used in the same ways as Edam.

• *Gruyère:* A Swiss-type cheese that is sharper than American Swiss-type cheese. It has small holes throughout and is semihard. The cheese is a light yellow and has a light brown coat covering. Nibblers like it with crackers or fruits, especially apples.

• *Limburger:* It was first made in Belgium. During the curing it develops a strong flavor and odor. Sandwiches made with it and dark rye bread have many friends.

• *Mozzarella:* A soft, *uncured*, mild and delicate-flavored Italian cheese that is used especially in making pizzas and other Italian-style main dishes. It was first made with buffalo milk, but now is made with whole or partly skimmed cow's milk. You can buy packaged slices or grated mozzarella.

• *Muenster:* This creamy white German cheese has mechanical, manmade openings or holes. It is semisoft and mild to mellow in taste, and is used in sandwiches and in snacks.

• *Mysost:* An *uncured* Norwegian cheese made from cow's milk. It has a sweetish, caramel taste and is firm and buttery. It is white to light brown and often is served with a dark bread for snacks and desserts. It is marketed in cubes, cylinders and wedges.

• *Neufchatel:* A soft, *uncured* French cream cheese that contains less milk fat than American cream cheese. It is smooth and is used like cream cheese. Usually it comes in 4- and 8-ounce packages.

• *Parmesan:* A hard, dry, creamy white Italian cheese that's often grated and added to cooked dishes, especially to spaghetti. It is lower in milk fat and moisture than Romano. You can buy it grated, shredded, in wedges or in cylinders.

• *Port du Salut:* A smooth buttery, semisoft cheese that originated in France. The cheese is creamy white and has small openings. You can buy it in wheels (rounds) and wedges. Usually it is a dessert cheese and often is served with fresh fruits.

• *Provolone:* A firm, smooth Italian cheese with a sharp, mellow or smoky flavor. It is used in sandwiches, snacks and cooking, and is often served with crackers. When fully cured and dried, it often is grated. The cheese is sold in pear and sausage shapes and in packaged wedges and slices.

• *Ricotta:* An *uncured* Italian cheese with a sweet, nut-like flavor. Usually sold in pint and quart plastic containers, it is used in making lasagne,

ravioli and other Italian dishes. This cheese is something like a very dry cottage cheese.

• *Romano:* A family of hard cheeses made with goat's milk in Italy, with cow's milk in the United States. Yellowish white inside and greenish black on the outside, it's fine for seasoning soups, casseroles, sauces and breads. When it has been cured a year, it often is grated.

• *Roquefort:* A French cheese with blue-green threads. The blue-green color comes from molds added in the curing and often give the cheese a marbled look. Made of sheep's milk, the cheese is sharp and slightly peppery in taste and is made only in France. It's often crumbled and added to salad dressings, green salads and dips, but it has many other uses.

• *Sapsago:* A cheese imported from Switzerland. It is not made in the United States. Very hard and light green in color due to the addition of dried and powdered clover leaves, it has a sharp, clover-like taste and comes shaped in cones and in shakers (grated cheese). Usually it is grated and added to soups, meats, macaroni and hot vegetables, although it sometimes is mixed with butter and spread on crackers.

• *Swiss:* Named for the country in which it was born, this cheese was imported by Caesar to Rome about 2000 years ago. In Switzerland it is called Emmentaler cheese. It is firm and smooth and has large, round holes, called eyes. Sweet and nutlike in taste, it is a great favorite in sandwiches, snacks, sauces, fondues, cheeseburgers and many other dishes. It is sold in packaged slices, segments and pieces.

CHAPTER 8

BEVERAGES, SNACKS AND APPETIZERS

If you're going to have a party, company for dinner or supper, or friends over for evening refreshments, you'll find many good ideas in this chapter. And in great variety.

There are recipes for fruit drinks which guests, dressed in their Sunday-best, sip fom glass cups; Old-Fashioned Lemonade to serve on the porch during a summer evening; rich, hot French Chocolate to pour at a tea party and Lemon-Lime Fizz teen-agers like to whip up.

Look over the tempting party dips you can serve in the living room before a meal. Guests like to nibble on them while visiting. Many men enjoy this pre-dinner socializing because they have a chance to host and so help the hostess while she attends to last-minute details in the kitchen. There are many kinds of good meal openers in this chapter, such as Tomato Soup Piquant, to serve hot in mugs along with dips in the living room, or in cups or bowls at the table. Men especially like small Mock Reuben Sandwiches, a hot appetizer. And Golden Glow Fruit Cocktail gives the sit-down dinner a royal send-off.

You'll surely want to make our Christmas Snack Tree for your next holiday—directions in this chapter. It always gets lots of attention and admiration. And don't miss Sandwiches on Sticks, stuck in polished red apples, for the young set. Among the snacks are candies that melt in the mouth, sugared and salted nuts and superior candied Grapefruit Peel. Then there's Honey Crackerjack, regular country-kitchen kind.

No family of recipes creates greater enthusiasm among country hostesses than our fruit accompaniments for meats and poultry. Spiced Apples Glacé, Orange Slices, Blushing Peaches, Pear Chutney and Refrigerator Spiced Prunes are excellent examples. Their beauty and exciting flavors flatter other foods in the meal. Turn the pages in this chapter for marvelous hostess ideas.

Something Good to Sip

Some people like drinks hot and some like them cold, but every hostess agrees that something to sip is essential in company meals and refreshments. Good coffee is the first choice in many country homes. Tea and chocolate beverages have staunch followers too. And there are occasions when fruit drinks and punches have no substitute.

Here are some of the country specials, both icy cold and steaming hot. You'll have no trouble making your selections, for the collection includes drinks to please all tastes.

FRENCH CHOCOLATE

If you have an antique chocolate pot and cups in your cupboard, use them to serve this rich, warm drink at a tea party (see menu chapter), or serve in your prettiest teacups

½ c. semisweet chocolate pieces
½ c. light corn syrup
¼ c. water
1 tsp. vanilla
1 pt. heavy cream
2 qts. milk

• In saucepan over low heat, stir chocolate pieces, corn syrup and water together until chocolate is melted. Pour into a small pitcher or cup, cover and chill until cool. Add vanilla.
• In a large bowl, beat the cream, while gradually adding the chocolate mixture. (Use electric mixer at medium speed.) Continue beating until mixture just mounds; spoon fluffy chocolate whipped cream into a crystal serving bowl and refrigerate. (You can fix this in the morning for the afternoon tea, or an hour ahead.)
• Just before serving, scald the milk and pour into a warmed serving pot. Place on tray with cups and saucers and crystal bowl of chocolate whipped cream.
• To serve, spoon some of the whipped cream mixture into each cup; fill cups with hot milk. Let guests stir the two together before sipping. Makes 16 servings in teacups, about 35 servings in chocolate cups.

Cocoa—Piping Hot or Iced

Girls enjoy hot cocoa topped with whipped cream tinted delicate pink or green, with stirrers of pink or red and white peppermint stick candy. Boys will settle for melting marshmallow floats. In the iced cocoa season, plastic drinking straws of bright colors add a festive note in the glasses. Use two or three straws in each glass—of the same color or contrasting.

INSTANT COCOA

Keep this on hand for teens after-game—float marshmallows in cups

1 (1 lb.) pkg. nonfat dry milk
1 c. sugar
¾ c. cocoa
¼ tsp. salt

• Sift all ingredients together three times; place in a tightly covered container. Store in a cool place. Makes 27 to 30 servings with hot water added.

To Use Instant Cocoa: Combine ⅓ c. of the mix with hot water in serving cup and stir to mix. Or combine 1⅓ c. of mix with 1 qt. hot water.

HOT COCOA, PARTY STYLE

After ice skating or sledding, warm up the youngsters with this hot drink

6 c. milk
¾ c. Cocoa Syrup (recipe below)
Pink whipped cream
Peppermint candy sticks

· Heat milk until bubbles form around edge of saucepan. Add Cocoa Syrup, stirring until well mixed with milk.
· Pour into mugs or cups and top with whipped cream, tinted a delicate pink with a drop or two of red food color. Put a stick of candy in each serving for a stirrer. Makes 6 servings.

VARIATION

Iced Cocoa: Beat cold milk with Cocoa Syrup to combine. Pour over ice cubes in tall glasses. To make 1 glass, use 2 tblsp. Cocoa Syrup to 1 c. milk.

COCOA SYRUP

Handy for youngsters' entertaining

½ c. sifted unsweetened cocoa
1 c. sugar
⅛ tsp. salt
1 c. boiling water
1 tsp. vanilla

· Combine cocoa, sugar and salt in saucepan. Add the water gradually, stirring until mixture is smooth.
· Cook over medium heat, stirring until mixture comes to a boil. Boil 1 minute without stirring.

· Remove from heat and cool. When cool, stir in vanilla. Pour into jar or other container, cover and refrigerate until needed. Makes 1¼ cups.

Grape Float: *Add a scoop of lemon or lime sherbet to each glass of cold grape juice.*

Banana-Chocolate Milk: *Slice a ripe banana into a bowl and beat until creamy. Add 1 c. cold milk and 2 tblsp. chocolate malted milk powder and ¼ tsp. vanilla. Beat to mix well; pour into a tall glass and add a scoop of vanilla ice cream.*

Apple Punch—Hot and Fragrant

Over the years, as you might imagine, FARM JOURNAL has printed quite a collection of recipes. Like mothers with their children, our food editors are proud of them. We are including several of the most praised recipes in this cookbook to give some of you a chance to renew old friendships and others, who had had no introduction to them, the opportunity to serve them.

Hot Apple Punch, which we collected in Utah, rates as one of our great recipes. Women write us that this steaming, fragrant-with-spice beverage is one of their all-time favorites. They say its aroma greets guests in a friendly way, and that sips of it always bring three comments in this order: It's wonderful. How do you make it? May I have your recipe?

So here it is, a refreshing hot fruit drink, with our guarantee.

HOT APPLE PUNCH

A famous FARM JOURNAL *recipe*

2 ¼ c. sugar
1 qt. water
2 (2 ½ ") sticks cinnamon
8 whole allspice berries
10 whole cloves
1 whole piece ginger root
    (about size of a quarter)
1 qt. orange juice (fresh,
    canned or reconstituted
    frozen)
1 pt. lemon juice, or a 16 oz.
    bottle
2 qts. apple cider or juice

• Combine sugar and water and boil 5 minutes. Remove from heat; add spices. Let syrup stand, covered, 1 hour. Strain.

• Just before serving, combine syrup, fruit juices and cider; bring quickly to a boil. Remove from heat; serve at once. Makes 4½ quarts.

SPICY HOT GRAPE PUNCH

Guest-pleasing on a cold evening

2 c. grape juice
½ c. sugar
1 stick cinnamon
1 tsp. whole cloves
1 tblsp. lemon juice
1 (6 oz.) can frozen orange
    juice concentrate,
    reconstituted by
    directions on can

• Combine all ingredients. Bring to a boil. Strain and serve hot in teacups. Makes 8 servings.

Tea for Two—or More

When you wish to entertain women in the afternoon, consider having a tea. It has many merits. You can expand your guest list from one dear friend to a few or many guests. With a little planning, giving a tea for a crowd is comparatively easy. You can fix practically all the food ahead and refrigerate or freeze it.

Making good tea is simple. So simple, in fact, that some hostesses slight it. Remember that tea tastes only as good as the care you take in brewing it.

Different teas have different flavors and bouquets. So experiment with various kinds until you find types you like best. To make tasting of new teas an adventure, ask a friend to share the experience with you. Try one kind, then sample another. You'll want to get acquainted with the three basic tea families—black, green and oolong.

Black teas obtain their flavors from a full fermentation of the leaves before drying. These teas grow mainly in India, Ceylon and Indonesia. Darjeeling tea (from Northern India) is the favorite black tea of many expert tea sippers.

Green teas are dried without fermentation. They grow in Formosa and Japan.

Oolong teas consist of leaves briefly fermented; they have some of the characteristics of both black and green teas. Our supply comes from Formosa. Connoisseurs consider oolong the champagne of teas.

You can buy these teas loose in packages or in tea bags. Most of the teas on the market are blended—they contain several kinds and qualities. That's why teas have such a variety of colors, flavors and fragrances. Regardless of which tea you select— plain, scented with jasmine flowers, delicate oolong, smoky Chinese or robust English breakfast—you brew the leaves the same way. Here are the directions for perfect tea:

How to Make Perfect Hot Tea

· Use a glass, china or earthenware pot; some metals change the color of tea brews. Wash it with heavy suds, rinse thoroughly and fill with hot water to heat teapot (good tea is always made in a preheated teapot). The warmer the water, the warmer the tea when served. Empty just before adding tea.

· Use rapidly boiling water to extract full flavor from the tea leaves. Water that has just reached a full boil contains the most air bubbles and makes the most sparkling brew. Heat freshly drawn cold tap water to a full rolling boil and use at once. Do not use water that has been boiled previously. And never boil tea in water.

· Measure loose tea accurately (or count the tea bags). Add 1 tsp. loose tea (or 1 tea bag) for every ¾ c. (*measuring* cup) boiling water. Pour the water on the tea and cover.

· Let tea steep no less than 3 minutes, no longer than 5. Watch the clock or set the timer. Don't guess, for oversteeping makes tea bitter.

After steeping, stir the tea and strain into warmed pot or into teacup. If you like a weaker tea, add hot water —always after steeping and straining. (See Index for Tea for 30 to 35 and Tea for 200.)

One of the mistaken ideas about tea is that the color of the brew indicates its strength. Instead, it is due largely to the kind of tea. The darker amber brew may be weaker than the light colored brew. Another wrong impression quite prevalent is that "orange-pekoe" is a variety of tea. Instead, it designates the size of the tea leaf and the part of the leaf used. "Pekoe" teas have larger leaves than "orange-pekoe."

HOT SPICED TEA

Fruited, spiced and fragrant—a good choice when you want something unusual

6	c. water
1	tsp. whole cloves
1	(1″) stick cinnamon
2½	tblsp. black tea
¾	c. orange juice
2	tblsp. lemon juice
½	c. sugar

· Place water in saucepan; add cloves and cinnamon. Bring to a boil and remove from heat. Add the tea at once, stir to distribute and immerse leaves. Cover and steep 5 minutes. Strain.

· While tea steeps, heat orange and lemon juices, with sugar added, to a boil. Stir into the hot tea and serve at once in teacups. Makes 7 or 8 servings.

Note: See Index for Hot Spiced Tea for 100.

TOMATO SOUP PIQUANT

Colorful and light start for a big meal. Serve in living room in mugs

2 (8 oz.) cans tomato sauce
2 cans condensed beef bouillon
5¼ c. water
2 (1 pt.) cans tomato juice
½ tsp. prepared horse-radish
4 drops Tabasco sauce
1½ tsp. salt
¼ tsp. pepper
¼ tsp. dried basil
12 thin lemon slices

• Combine all ingredients except lemons; simmer 10 minutes, or until thoroughly heated.
• Garnish individual servings with lemon slices. Makes 12 servings.

ZUPPA VERDE

You'll have chicken and broth left over to freeze or use in casseroles

1 (4 lb.) chicken
4 qts. water
1 large onion
2 stalks celery with leaves
1 tblsp. salt
½ tsp. pepper
1 carrot, scraped
1 medium-size head endive
Grated Parmesan or Romano
   cheese

• Place all ingredients except endive and cheese in large kettle. Bring to a boil and simmer, loosely covered, until chicken is tender, about 2 hours. Strain and cool broth; skim off fat. Save carrot.
• Remove and discard skin from chicken breasts. Cut breast meat into slivers to make 2 c.
• Cook endive in boiling salted water

10 minutes. When tender, drain and squeeze dry. Chop.
• Add carrot, diced, and slivered chicken to 2 qts. chicken broth. Heat; add endive and serve. Garnish with grated Parmesan or Romano cheese. Makes 8 servings.

HOT SPICED PUNCH

Float a clove-studded orange slice in each cup of this refreshing drink

1 tblsp. whole cloves
½ tblsp. whole allspice
3 sticks cinnamon
½ c. brown sugar
2 c. water
¼ tsp. salt
2½ c. pineapple juice
2 c. cranberry juice

• Combine spices with brown sugar and water in saucepan. Simmer 15 minutes. Strain through several layers of cheesecloth.
• Combine salt and fruit juices. Add strained spice mixture. Heat and serve from warmed punch bowl or electric coffee maker. Makes about 6½ cups, or 8 servings.

Note: To serve a larger crowd, double the recipe.

Christmas Cranberry Drinks

Tulip-red cranberries make the perfect base for hospitable chilled drinks during the Yuletide season. Here's a recipe for Basic Cranberry Syrup which our food editors developed. You can keep this in the refrigerator handy for making pretty punches quickly. Here are the directions.

BASIC CRANBERRY SYRUP

With this on hand, you'll always be ready to serve stop-in guests

3 lbs. whole cranberries
5 c. sugar
2 qts. water
5 sticks whole cinnamon

• Combine ingredients in a large kettle; bring to a boil. Mash cranberries with potato masher; simmer 15 minutes. Strain through several layers of cheesecloth or muslin. Stir in enough water to make 2½ quarts syrup. Store in refrigerator. Serve iced or very cold, mixed with other fruit juices, ginger ale or iced tea, as desired.

VARIATIONS

Zippy Cranberry Cooler: Mix 1 part Basic Cranberry Syrup with 2 parts chilled ginger ale.

Cranberry-Apple Drink: Mix equal portions of Basic Cranberry Syrup, apple juice and carbonated water.

Cranberry-Lemon Sparkle: Combine 2 (6 oz.) cans frozen lemonade concentrate and 1 qt. Basic Cranberry Syrup. Add 1½ qts. water and 1½ qts. ginger ale. Makes about 18 cups.

Cranberry Tea: Mix equal portions of Basic Cranberry Syrup, carbonated water and iced tea.

CHRISTMAS PUNCH

Festive red two-fruit holiday drink. Add ginger ale if you like the bubbles

1 qt. apple juice
1 (1 qt.) bottle cranberry juice cocktail
½ c. lemon juice

• Mix juices. Chill. Garnish with canned pineapple chunks, drained. Makes 12 servings.

GOLDEN PUNCH

This punch is on the tart side. It's refreshing, colorful, easy to fix

1 (6 oz.) can frozen orange juice concentrate
1 (6 oz.) can frozen lemonade concentrate
1 (12 oz.) can apricot nectar
2 c. pineapple juice
½ c. lemon juice
1 qt. lemon-lime carbonated beverage, or 1 qt. ginger ale
Sherbet

• Reconstitute orange juice and lemonade as directed on cans. Combine in punch bowl with apricot nectar, pineapple juice and lemon juice.
• Pour bottled carbonated beverage or ginger ale slowly down side of bowl. Drop scoops of pineapple, orange, lime or raspberry sherbet into punch. (Sherbet is not necessary, but it is decorative and delicious.) Makes about 3½ quarts without sherbet.

CARDINAL PUNCH

Tea and fruit juices join in this— float a thin lemon slice in each glass

2½ c. boiling water
2 tblsp. black tea
¼ tsp. allspice
¼ tsp. cinnamon
⅛ tsp. nutmeg
¾ c. sugar
1 (1 pt.) bottle cranberry juice cocktail
½ c. orange juice
⅓ c. lemon juice
1½ c. water

• Pour the rapidly boiling water over tea; add spices. Cover and let steep 5 minutes. Strain and stir in sugar. • Add the cranberry, orange and lemon juices and cold water. Cover and chill thoroughly. Makes 8 servings.

CRANBERRY-LEMON CUP

Refreshing and color-bright! Skip lemon slices for a less tart drink

1 (32 oz.) bottle chilled
    cranberry juice cocktail
2 (10 oz.) bottles chilled lemon-
    lime carbonated beverage
1 lemon, cut in thin slices

• Mix cranberry juice and lemon-lime carbonated beverage in a pitcher. Pour into small glasses and float a thin slice of lemon in each glass. Serve as first course with crackers. Makes about 8 servings.

OLD-FASHIONED LEMONADE

Press lemon slices to extract juices and oils, which give fine flavor. No squeezing of lemons for this ade

4 lemons
¾ c. sugar
1 qt. water
1 tray ice cubes

• Wash fruit. Cut into thin slices; remove seeds. Place lemon slices in a large bowl. Cover fruit with sugar. Let stand 10 minutes, then press firmly with potato masher to extract juice. Add water, continue to press fruit with masher until liquid is well flavored. Add ice cubes.
• Taste lemonade for sweetness when it's chilled. If you wish, add more sugar and stir to dissolve. Pour over

two ice cubes in tall glasses; add lemon slices to each glass. Makes about 7 servings.

VARIATIONS

Lemon-Limeade: Use 2 limes and 2 lemons. Increase sugar to 1 c. Prepare according to the directions for Old-Fashioned Lemonade.

Lemon-Orangeade: Use 2 oranges and 3 lemons. Decrease sugar to ½ c. Prepare according to directions for Old-Fashioned Lemonade.

PINEAPPLE FROST

Tangy, refreshing, subtle-flavored, unusual spring drink that keeps people trying to guess what they're sipping. Repeat recipe for more than six

2 c. pineapple juice
1 bunch watercress
3 tblsp. sugar
2 tblsp. lemon juice
1 c. finely cracked ice

• Put all the ingredients in the blender. Blend thoroughly. Makes about 6 servings.

LEMON-LIME FIZZ

Expand the kinds of these drinks you make by using different sherbets

1 qt. lime sherbet
2 (6 oz.) cans water
1 (6 oz.) can frozen lemonade
    concentrate
2 (7 oz.) bottles carbonated
    water, chilled

• Spoon sherbet into 6 tall (10 oz.) glasses.
• Mix water with lemonade concen-

trate. Pour over sherbet in glasses. Fill glasses with carbonated water. Makes 6 servings.

VARIATION

Lemon Fizz: Use lemon sherbet instead of the lime.

STRAWBERRY ADE

The color and bubbles of this drink please youngsters at birthday parties

2 (3 oz.) pkgs. strawberry flavor
    gelatin
2 c. boiling water
5 c. ginger ale

· Dissolve gelatin in water; cool at room temperature (do not chill or let set). If it starts to thicken, set bowl in pan of warm water.
· Add ginger ale and pour into 8 tall glasses filled with ice cubes or crushed ice. Makes 8 servings.

STRAWBERRY SODAS

These country-good sodas contain jam from fruit closet or refrigerator

1 ½ qts. strawberry ice cream
½ c. strawberry jam
3 (7 oz.) bottles ginger ale

· Divide the ice cream between 8 tall (10 oz.) glasses. Add 1 tblsp. strawberry jam to each glass. Fill with ginger ale. Stir with a long spoon to mix. Makes 8 servings.

Use your 30-cup coffee maker for serving cold drinks to a large crowd. With the coffee basket removed, there's plenty of room for ice. Turning the spigot is easier than dipping from a punch bowl or pouring from a pitcher.

Iced Tea—Great American Beverage

On a hot day during the St. Louis World's Fair in 1904, the thirst of a visitor inspired a new drink, iced tea. It caught on at once and has been highly prized ever since.

In making iced tea, you add more tea or tea bags to boiling water than when you make hot tea. This is because ice cubes dilute the brew.

Sometimes iced tea has a cloudy look. Cloudiness does not affect the taste, but you can restore the clarity by stirring a little boiling water into the tea just before pouring it into the glasses. Cloudiness usually develops if you chill hot tea in the refrigerator.

ICED TEA FOR 8 OR 10

· Pour 1 qt. freshly boiling water over ⅓ c. loose tea or 15 tea bags. Cover and steep 4 minutes. Stir; strain into a pitcher containing 1 qt. cold water. Pour into ice-filled glasses.

Packaged instant tea is available. Make it by label directions. Iced tea mix is ready to serve; it contains sugar and lemon juice. Just add water and ice.

Iced Tea Accompaniments: Lemon eighths, quarters or slices and sugar are traditional. Sprigs of fresh mint in the glasses contribute good flavor and looks. Other favorites are: small scoops of lemon or pineapple sherbet, pineapple chunks and fresh strawberries strung on sippers, and sticks of fresh pineapple in the glasses to stir the tea and to eat.

Set Out the Dips—
Guests Are Here

For first courses to serve in the living room before dinner, dips have few rivals. Guests like to gather round them to dip, eat and talk.

Bowls of dips with assorted crackers, potato chips, corn chips and crisp raw vegetables are great favorites. Most of our recipes for them are for the type you can make several hours ahead, put in serving bowls and chill in the refrigerator. Actually, their flavors blend and improve during the chilling.

Get out your shiny chafing dish for the hot ones, or set them on an electrically heated tray to keep warm. Or cover toast with Clam-Crab Spread and run under the broiler for a minute or two.

PARTY CHEESE DIP

Three kinds of cheese contribute flavor to this well-seasoned party dip. One taste and its popularity zooms

¼ c. milk
8 oz. cottage cheese
3 (1″) cubes blue cheese
2 (3 oz.) pkgs. cream cheese, cut in 1″ cubes
½ small clove garlic
¼ tsp. salt
½ tsp. paprika
2 tsp. Worcestershire sauce

• Pour milk into the electric blender container. Add cottage cheese; cover and blend on "low" about 20 seconds, or until smooth.

• Add blue cheese, cream cheese, garlic, seasonings and Worcestershire sauce. Cover and blend on "high" until smooth, about 20 seconds. Refrigerate until serving time. Makes about 1 pint.

Note: You can use the electric mixer to make this dip if you don't have a blender.

SMOKY COTTAGE CHEESE DIP

Serve this with carrot, celery and cucumber sticks and cauliflowerets

1 c. cottage cheese
1 (3 oz.) pkg. cream cheese
2 tblsp. light cream or milk
¼ tsp. monosodium glutamate
1 tsp. minced onion
½ tsp. liquid smoke
¼ tsp. garlic salt
½ c. ripe olives, minced

• Beat together cottage cheese, cream cheese and cream. Blend in remaining ingredients. Makes 1⅔ cups.

BLUE CHEESE WHIP

Wonderful for vegetables or crackers

2 (3 oz.) pkgs. cream cheese
1 tblsp. milk
1 (3 oz.) pkg. blue cheese
1 tblsp. minced onion
1 c. heavy cream, whipped

• Soften cream cheese. Blend in milk, then blue cheese and onion. Fold in whipped cream. If you wish, garnish with thinly sliced green onions. Makes 2½ cups.

CORN 'N' BACON CHIP DIP

Garlicky good dip for crisp crackers

1 (8 oz.) pkg. cream cheese
1 c. dairy sour cream
¼ c. mayonnaise
2 cloves garlic, minced
½ tsp. Tabasco sauce
1 (8 oz.) can whole kernel corn
8 slices crumbled, crisp-fried
    bacon

• Soften cream cheese; gradually blend in sour cream and mayonnaise. Stir in remaining ingredients. Chill several hours to blend flavors. Makes 3 cups.

TEXAS CHILI DIP

Watch men and boys dip into this—they'll like that hot chili taste

1 (15½ oz.) can chili with beans
1 c. cottage cheese
2 tblsp. chopped chili peppers,
    fresh or canned, or bottled
    hot-pepper sauce
2 tblsp. lemon juice

• Turn chili, cottage cheese and peppers into mixer bowl; beat together at low speed until blended, adding lemon juice. (If you use hot-pepper sauce, sometimes called tacos sauce, omit chopped peppers and add sauce with lemon juice.)
• Chill about 4 hours. Serve as a dip for cucumber slices, cauliflowerets, celery and carrot sticks, or with toasted wedges of cornmeal tortillas, slices of party rye bread, crackers or corn and potato chips. Makes 2⅔ cups.

QUICK MUSTARD SAUCE

Right for vegetable and meat dippers

1 pt. dairy sour cream
3 tblsp. horse-radish
½ c. prepared mustard

• Combine ingredients. Serve cold, or heat until mixture simmers and serve warm. Makes 2½ cups.

GREEN GODDESS DIP

Substitute this tasty dip for salad dressing on lettuce for a real treat

2 soft ripe avocados
1 c. dairy sour cream
¼ c. mayonnaise
1 tblsp. lemon juice
½ c. finely chopped parsley
¼ c. finely chopped green onions
    and tops
1 tsp. seasoned salt
¼ tsp. dried dill weed
⅛ tsp. pepper

• Mash avocados well with a fork; add sour cream, mayonnaise and lemon juice. Blend thoroughly and add remaining ingredients, mixing well.
• Chill at least 1 hour so flavors will blend. Serve with crackers or potato or corn chips. Makes about 3 cups.

BACON AND EGG DIP

Rather bland in flavor, but at a party some guests always favor it

3 slices bacon
6 hard-cooked eggs
2 tsp. Worcestershire sauce
1 tblsp. soft butter
1 tsp. lemon juice
1 drop Tabasco sauce
1 tsp. prepared mustard

½ tsp. salt
2 tsp. grated onion
½ c. mayonnaise or salad
    dressing

• Cook bacon until crisp; drain on paper toweling and break in tiny bits.
• Chop eggs fine; add bacon and remaining ingredients. Mix well. (Use the blender to mix this dip if you have one.)
• Chill in refrigerator at least 4 hours before serving. Whip to soften just before serving. Makes 2 cups.

HOT CRAB DIP

Quick and easy, guest approved

1 (5 oz.) jar sharp process
    cheese spread
1 (8 oz.) pkg. cream cheese
1 (7½ oz.) can crabmeat,
    flaked
2 tblsp. cream
½ tsp. Worcestershire sauce

• Combine ingredients in top of double boiler. Cook, stirring occasionally, until mixture is blended and hot.
• Serve hot in chafing dish or other heated casserole with potato chips or crackers. Makes 2½ cups.

BEAN DIP

Good with corn chips—easy to fix

1 can condensed bean soup
1 (8 oz.) can tomato sauce
1 c. shredded sharp cheese
¼ tsp. chili powder

• Heat together soup, tomato sauce, cheese and chili powder.
• Keep hot on electrically heated tray, in chafing dish or over candle warmer. Makes 2¼ cups.

CLAM-CRAB SPREAD

Sea food fans at parties gather around canapés made with this and toast

2 (3 oz.) pkgs. cream cheese
¼ c. soft butter or margarine
1 tblsp. Worcestershire sauce
Few drops Tabasco sauce
¼ c. mayonnaise or salad
    dressing
1 (7 oz.) can minced clams,
    drained
1 (7 oz.) can crabmeat, drained

• Blend cream cheese, butter, mayonnaise, Worcestershire sauce and Tabasco sauce. Stir in clams and crabmeat, broken in flakes.
• Spread mixture on toasted rounds of rye bread or melba toast; set under the broiler 1 or 2 minutes, until mixture is hot and bubbly. Serve at once. Makes 2¼ cups.

Snack Tree Says
Merry Christmas

Let our Christmas Snack Tree help put you and your party guests in a festive party mood. Fix the tree base a few days ahead, the appetizers to stick on it and the bowls of dips to set under it a few hours before the party. Keep them in the refrigerator until it's almost time for guests.

The tree is easy to make. You can use it another year, or by changing the food decorations, you can make it fit into another season. Here are directions for making the tree and the appetizers to fasten on it with toothpicks. See recipes for Blue Cheese Whip, Corn 'n' Bacon Dip,

Quick Mustard Sauce and other dips in this chapter. And don't overlook the picture of Christmas Snack Tree.

CHRISTMAS SNACK TREE
Tree shows off snacks for dipping

• Select a Styrofoam cone, 12" to 18" high, at a variety store or florist shop. Give it a firm base by forcing the center part of an 8 or 10" angel food cake pan two inches into the bottom of cone. Anchor pan base to a heavy plate with florist's clay so the tree is secure.
• Cover the cone and the base with green foil. Stick toothpicks into appetizers and "trim the tree." Snacks are easier to remove for eating if you make holes in the covered tree with ice pick or skewer, then insert toothpicks. Use Tomato Roses (instructions follow) and evergreens to decorate the base.

How to make Snack Tree dippers
• *Meat and cheese dippers:* Cut 3 × 1½" rectangle of thinly sliced, cooked ham; roll lengthwise and fasten with toothpick. Use small cookie cutters to make salami and bologna cutouts. Cut small cubes of semihard cheeses; insert toothpicks carefully.
• *Vegetable dippers:* Wash and separate cauliflower into small flowerets; chill in ice water. For celery fans, cut celery into 1½" lengths. Slit parallel strips one half the length of each piece; chill in ice water until curled. To make carrot daisies, cut pared carrot crosswise into three pieces. Cut

five or six lengthwise notches around the carrot; slice into ½" rounds. Place green pepper square atop carrot slice and insert toothpick. For radish accordions, wash radishes; cut out root ends. Make crosswise parallel notches the length of the radish; crisp in cold water.

TOMATO ROSES
Red roses to make at Christmas time

• Select a large, bright red tomato. Rose is made from outer shell of tomato. With stem end up, insert knife ¾" from stem and cut a crosswise slice only two thirds of the way through (slice serves as base of rose). From this cut, continue peeling tomato in an unbroken spiral, ¾" wide and ⅛" thick.
• To form rose, place stem end on plate, skin side down. Starting at free end, roll up spiral toward stem. Secure with a toothpick.

Party Appetizers Guests Like

Bring out an attractive tray of before-dinner tidbits to put your guests in a sociable mood. They'll enjoy nibbling while they chat, until dinner is ready to serve. A tart fruit drink or chilled tomato juice tastes good with these snacks. Or, with hot broth, tea or coffee, they're fine for light refreshments during a winter evening.

You won't want to serve more than two or three kinds at a time. So take your pick of the recipes that follow.

Build a Snack Tree for the appetizer course to serve in your living room. Guests like to pick the trimmings—bite-size raw vegetables, cheese and meats—to dunk in dips. Directions for tree and snacks are above.

CHEESE CRACKERS

Serve these nippy crackers with dips and soup—they'll please your guests

1 ½ c. sifted flour
½ tsp. salt
1 tblsp. chopped chives
½ c. butter or margarine
½ lb. sharp process cheese, grated (2 c.)

• Combine flour, salt and chives.
• Cream together butter and cheese. Add flour mixture and mix well.
• Roll into 1″ balls; place on baking sheet. Flatten to about ¼″ thickness (bottom of glass tumbler is good for this). Prick top with a fork.
• Bake in moderate oven (350°) 12 to 15 minutes. Makes 5 dozen.

SPICED SHRIMP

Another shrimp dish to boost the sea food's popularity in country kitchens

1 lb. cooked, peeled and deveined shrimp (4 c.)
3 medium onions, thinly sliced
1 lemon, sliced
½ c. white vinegar
¼ c. water
2 tsp. salt
1 tsp. sugar
½ tsp. dry mustard
¼ tsp. ginger
½ tsp. whole black pepper
1 bay leaf
⅛ tsp. Tabasco sauce
¼ c. lemon juice
½ c. salad oil

• Fill a bowl with alternating layers of shrimp, sliced onions and lemon.

• Combine vinegar, water, salt, sugar, dry mustard, ginger, pepper, bay leaf and Tabasco sauce in a saucepan. Bring to a boil; cover, simmer 5 minutes. Cool.
• Strain; add lemon juice and oil. Pour over shrimp. Cover, and refrigerate 24 hours. Stir occasionally. Drain before serving. Have wooden picks for spearing. Makes 1 quart.

Frozen Fish Sticks: Cut each fish stick in half and prepare according to package directions. Serve hot. A bowl of tartar sauce is good for dunking.

Meat Roll-Ups: Use thin slices of cold cuts like cervelat, spiced ham or bologna. Overlap edges of 2 slices. Spread with seasoned cream cheese or a soft cheese spread. Roll up. Wrap in waxed paper or foil. Chill. Cut into 1″ slices and spear each with a wooden pick.

Salmon or Tuna Cubes: Soften 1 tblsp. unflavored gelatin in ¼ c. cold water; dissolve over hot water. Drain a small can (about 7 oz.) salmon or tuna; reserve liquid. Discard skin and bones from salmon. Flake fish. Add fish liquid, a finely chopped hard-cooked egg, 2 tblsp. finely chopped celery, 2 tblsp. chopped green pepper and 1 tblsp. chopped onion. Add 2 tblsp. lemon juice, ½ c. mayonnaise or salad dressing, ¼ tsp. salt and dissolved gelatin. Mix well. Spoon into an 8½ × 4½ × 2½″ loaf pan to make a layer 1″ thick. Chill. Cut into 1″ squares. Top squares with a slice of pickle or olive. Spear with a wooden pick. Makes about 2 dozen.

For a gorgeous dessert that tastes wonderful, make Strawberry Satin Pie (*recipe, page 209*). Cut berries in half, arrange them cut side up on cream filling in a pretty design; then spoon on clear strawberry glaze.

Little Pizzas: Bake 1 can ready-to-bake refrigerator biscuits according to package directions. Cool and split each in half. Spread each half with a little tomato paste. Sprinkle with a little orégano. Top with a thin slice of mozzarella or natural sharp American cheese; add a drop or two of salad oil. Sprinkle with Parmesan cheese. Bake in hot oven (450°) 6 to 8 minutes. Top each with a piece of anchovy. Serve whole or cut in half, but serve hot. Makes 20 whole pizzas.

Ham-Mushroom Canape: Drain 1 (4 oz.) can mushroom stems and pieces; chop finely. Add 1 small can deviled ham, ½ tsp. prepared mustard, 1 tsp. pickle relish and 1 tblsp. mayonnaise. Mix well. To serve, remove crusts from light or dark bread. Cut into strips or desired shapes using cookie cutters. Spread lightly with butter, then with filling. Decorate with slices of mushrooms. Makes ¾ cup spread.

Curried Egg Canapé: Chop 2 hard-cooked eggs finely. Add 1 tblsp. mayonnaise, ¼ tsp. salt and ¼ tsp. curry powder. To serve, cut bread into rounds or desired shapes. Butter lightly. Spread with egg mixture. Decorate some with carrot wedges and a slice of green olive; top others with ripe olive slices. Makes about ½ cup spread.

Roquefort or Blue Cheese Mold: Place 1 (8 oz.) pkg. cream cheese in a mixing bowl. Let it come to room temperature. Add 6 oz. Roquefort or blue cheese, ½ tsp. vinegar, ½ tsp. prepared mustard and ⅛ tsp. Worcestershire sauce. Cream or beat until smooth. Chill; form into a ball. Roll in ¼ c. chopped salted peanuts. Refrigerate. Serve as a spread for crackers. Makes 1½ cups.

Peppy Onion Dip: Combine 1 (1½ oz.) pkg. onion-soup mix, 1 c. dairy sour cream, ¼ c. milk and 1 tsp. prepared mustard in a bowl. Cover and let stand in refrigerator 1 hour or more to thicken, overnight if you wish. Makes 1 cup.

Clam Dip: Drain 1 (7 or 8 oz.) can minced clams. Reserve liquid. Have 1 (3 oz.) pkg. cream cheese at room temperature. Combine cheese, 1 tsp. Worcestershire sauce, ½ tsp. prepared mustard, 1 tblsp. chopped parsley, 1 tsp. finely chopped onion and the minced clams. Mix well. Add clam liquid (about 2 tblsp.) to give consistency for dunking. Cover; store in refrigerator until ready to use. Good on potato chips or crackers. Makes 1 cup.

Franks in Hot Sauce: Combine 1 (8 oz.) can tomato sauce, ½ c. chili sauce, ½ c. chopped onion, 1 beef bouillon cube and 2 tblsp. chopped celery leaves. Cook 10 minutes. Cut ½ lb. frankfurters into pieces about 1″ long. Add to sauce. Simmer 5 to 10 minutes. Serve hot. Makes 1 cup sauce. You can double the recipe and serve in an electric skillet or chafing dish.

VIENNA LOGS

Fix these ahead and chill thoroughly

1 (5 oz.) jar process pimiento cheese spread
1 tblsp. mayonnaise
2 (5 oz.) cans Vienna sausages
¾ c. crushed potato chips

• Blend together cheese and mayonnaise. Run cold water over sausages to wash off liquid from can. (This makes them easier to coat with cheese mixture.) Cut each sausage crosswise in half.

• Spread cheese mixture over sausage halves. Roll in crushed potato chips. To serve, spear each sausage with wooden pick. Makes 28 appetizers.

MOCK REUBEN SANDWICHES

Men really like these hot appetizers

1 loaf party rye bread
1 (1 lb.) can sauerkraut, drained
1 (15½ oz.) can corned beef hash
Swiss cheese slices (about 3 oz.)

• If you are unable to buy party rye bread, cut regular slices of rye bread in quarters. Top each with 1 heaping tsp. sauerkraut, 1 scant tblsp. corned beef hash and a strip of cheese.

• Place on baking sheet, run under broiler just long enough to melt cheese. Makes 26 open-face sandwiches (appetizers) when made with party rye bread.

PARTY ROLL-UPS

Predinner party pickups—serve hot. You'll find them a big success

12 thin slices white bread
8 slices bacon, cooked, drained and crumbled
2 (3 oz.) pkgs. cream cheese, softened
12 cooked asparagus spears
Melted butter

• Trim crusts from bread slices; roll with rolling pin to flatten slightly. Blend bacon bits with cream cheese and spread mixture on bread slices.

• Lay a cold, cooked asparagus spear on each slice of bread and roll up.

• Place on baking sheet, seam side down. Cover and refrigerate until serving time.

• Then brush with melted butter and toast in broiler until lightly browned. Serve hot. Makes 12 appetizers.

Snacks for the Nibblers

In the country, when company comes you often hear: "Let's pop some popcorn." Sometimes instead of popcorn, the request is for candy, nuts or other confections.

These time-honored snacks have high popularity ratings. They are refreshments teen-agers especially like to fix and to eat. The young (and grown-up) crowd also likes to make, serve and eat cereal snacks when they include such things as peanut butter, raisins, nuts and dates along with the cereals. And many women keep in the cupboard a few packages of the many tasty snacks now available in supermarkets.

HONEY CRACKERJACK

Honey makes these different. Nice to pass to children who come to visit

3 qts. popped corn
1½ c. sugar
½ c. honey
1 tsp. salt
2 tblsp. butter or margarine
1 tsp. vanilla

• Turn popped corn into bowl. Combine sugar, honey and salt in small saucepan. Heat and stir to dissolve sugar. Boil to hard ball stage (260°). Add butter and vanilla. Pour syrup over corn, stirring gently to coat kernels.

· Drop by tablespoonfuls onto waxed paper. When popcorn is cool enough to handle, butter hands and quickly shape into bite-size balls. Store in airtight container at room temperature. Makes 24 balls.

SUGARED NUTS

Nibblers like these candied nuts because they're so good—hostesses like them because they're so easy to fix

3 c. walnut halves
1 ½ c. pecan halves
2 c. sugar
1 c. water
¼ tsp. cinnamon

· Mix ingredients in a heavy skillet. Cook until water disappears and nuts have a sugary appearance. Remove from heat and pour nuts onto a greased baking sheet. Separate quickly with 2 forks. Makes 4½ to 5 cups.

SALTED WALNUTS

· Spread walnuts over bottom of baking pan in one layer. Dot with butter, 1 tblsp. butter to 1 c. nuts. Bake in slow oven (325°) 15 minutes, stirring occasionally, or until nuts are lightly browned. Remove from oven. Salt generously, ½ tsp. salt to 1 c. nuts, and stir well. Spread on paper towels to cool. The nuts become crisp as they cool.

APRICOT NUGGETS

These easy-to-make candies add a tasty note to the plate of confections

1 lb. confectioners sugar
6 tblsp. melted butter or margarine
2 tblsp. orange juice
½ tsp. vanilla
1 (11 oz.) pkg. dried apricots, ground (about 1½ c.)
1 c. chopped pecans

· Combine sugar, butter, orange juice and vanilla. Add apricots. Mix, then knead in bowl until ingredients are well mixed.
· Form into 1" balls. Roll in chopped nuts. Store in refrigerator or freezer in covered container. Flavor improves with storage. Makes 6 dozen candies.

Note: If you like, you can omit the pecans and roll the candy balls in 1½ c. shredded coconut.

COCONUT KISSES

Sweet sensations is what one hostess calls these party confections. Watch the baking to avoid overbrowning

1 c. sweetened condensed milk
3 c. flaked coconut
1 tsp. baking powder
1 (6 oz.) pkg. chocolate chips

· Combine milk, coconut and baking powder. Add chocolate chips; drop from teaspoon onto well-greased wrapping paper on baking sheet.
· Bake in slow oven (325°) until they begin to brown around edges, about 10 minutes. Cool 5 minutes, then remove to racks. Makes about 6 dozen.

CHOCOLATE-COCONUT
BONBONS

*Professional-looking and so easy to
make and eat—a tea party favorite*

1 (15 oz.) can sweetened
  condensed milk
½ c. butter
2 lbs. confectioners sugar
2 (8 oz.) pkgs. flaked coconut
  (4 c.)
2 (12 oz.) pkgs. semisweet
  chocolate pieces
⅛ lb. household paraffin
  (½ bar)

• Mix condensed (not evaporated)
milk, butter, confectioners sugar and
coconut together. Mixture will be
very stiff. Cover and chill several
hours or overnight. Shape into small
balls.
• Melt chocolate pieces and paraffin
together over hot water. (Paraffin
comes in 1-lb. pkgs., 4 bars to a package. Use half a bar. This is the kind
of paraffin used to top jelly.)
• Place each coconut ball on a fork
and dip in chocolate mixture to coat.
Use a toothpick to help slide the
coated bonbons off the fork onto
waxed paper. (If chocolate refuses to
cling to candy, let it cool slightly.)
• Store candies in a cool place, or
freeze. Makes 95 to 100 bonbons.

*Add Flavor
with Grapefruit Peel*

Here are directions for fixing the
best candied grapefruit peel you'll
ever taste. It's tender, piquant, sparkling. This method of making the
delicacy comes from the bluegrass
section of Kentucky, a region famed
for gracious hostesses and fine food.

The peel, carefully candied, is a
marvelous, out-of-the-ordinary gift
for friends. It's a tasty confection; set
out a plate of it for nibblers. A hostess with imagination, who keeps a
supply of it in her freezer, will find
many ways to use it in cooking,
especially in baking (see Index for
Grapefruit Sugar Cookies).

How to Candy Grapefruit Peel

• Select and wash thick-skinned
grapefruit. Cut into quarters and remove pulp. Put peel in saucepan;
cover with cold water. Weight down
peel with a plate. Let stand several
hours or overnight. Drain.
• With scissors, cut peel into strips
about ¼″ wide.
• Cover peel with cold water and
slowly bring to a simmer (180°) in a
saucepan. Remove from heat, cover
pan and let stand about 1 hour; drain.
Repeat process until peel no longer
tastes bitter (about 3 times).
• Cover again with water and boil
until yellow peel is tender, about
15 minutes. Drain well in colander.
Press out water. Pack peel firmly into
measuring cup to measure.
• Return peel to saucepan. For each
cup of peel, add 1 cup of sugar. Place
over medium heat; stir until sugar
has dissolved (peel forms its own
liquid).
• Cook peel over medium heat, stirring frequently, until sugar syrup is
concentrated; reduce heat to low
(syrup should boil gently). Continue
cooking until the grapefruit peel is

semitransparent and most of the sugar syrup has boiled away.

• Drain in colander. Separate pieces of peel on baking sheets and allow to stand until it feels fairly dry. Sprinkle with enough sugar to give a crystalline look.

• Store in tightly covered cans, or in plastic bags in the freezer.

Ways to Use
Candied Grapefruit Peel

Apple Pie: Sprinkle ½ c. finely chopped candied grapefruit peel over apples before adding top crust to pie. Bake as usual.

Cake Frosting: Add candied grapefruit peel to your favorite recipe for confectioners sugar cake frosting (⅓ to ½ c. finely chopped peel to 2 c. confectioners sugar).

Tea Biscuits: Add ⅓ c. finely chopped candied grapefruit peel to 2 c. biscuit mix. Make and bake as directed; serve hot.

HOLIDAY LOGS

Professional-looking and easy to make. The candy logs make a hit when shared with friends

⅓ c. soft butter or margarine
¼ c. light corn syrup
1 tsp. vanilla
½ tsp. salt
1 lb. confectioners sugar
Red and green food color
Few drops of oil of cinnamon
      or peppermint, or of rum
      extract
1 lb. candy caramels
3 tblsp. cream or evaporated
      milk
1½ c. chopped pecans, toasted

• To make fondant center, combine butter, syrup, vanilla and salt in a large mixing bowl. Add confectioners sugar; mix together with a fork, then knead with hands. Mixture will be very dry, but softens with kneading.

• Divide in thirds. Knead on board, blending green color and mint flavoring into one third, red food color and oil of cinnamon into another third and rum extract into last third. (Adjust flavorings to taste.)

• Form into rolls 1″ in diameter. Cut fondant rolls in half crosswise to make 6 rolls. Wrap individually in waxed paper and store overnight in freezer or refrigerator.

• Make caramel nut coating next day by heating caramels and cream in double boiler. Dip chilled fondant rolls into warm caramel mixture, spooning to cover. (Work quickly so rolls don't soften.) Immediately roll in chopped pecans; wrap in aluminum foil and chill. Store logs in refrigerator or freezer until ready to serve. Slice just before serving. Makes 2⅓ pounds.

Try These Company Cereal Snacks

Among the important guests in many homes are the children who come with their parents or on their own. They always welcome something good to eat. Cookie-like snacks with glasses of fruit juice or cold milk, and fruit, such as apples, are great favorites.

These snacks contribute more than calories and marvelous flavors; they're nutritious and they are easy to fix—

require no baking. They cost less than many other kinds of refreshments. And they taste so wonderful that people of all ages enjoy them. Here are three of the best cereal snacks you'll ever encounter. They are from FARM JOURNAL's Test Kitchens.

PEANUT CHEWS

Peanut butter fans will like these crunchy snacks, cousins of cookies

9   c. corn flakes
1 ½ c. sugar
¼   tsp. salt
¾   c. light corn syrup
¼   c. butter or margarine
¾   c. water
2   tsp. vanilla
½   c. chunk style peanut butter

· Place the corn flakes in a bowl.
· Combine sugar, salt, syrup, butter and water. Bring to a boil and reduce heat.
· Cook to the hard ball stage (250°), using care not to overcook.
· Remove from the heat and stir in the vanilla and peanut butter. Pour over the corn flakes.
· Toss with a fork to completely cover the corn flakes with the syrup. Work quickly.
· Drop the mixture in clusters onto waxed paper. Makes about 40 (2½″) clusters.

SPICY CRUNCH

Raisins and nuts make this a real treat

3   c. puffed oat cereal
2   c. shredded rice, bite-size
     biscuits
2   c. shredded corn, bite-size
     biscuits

2   c. shredded wheat, bite-size
     biscuits
1   c. raisins
1   c. pecan halves
½   c. butter or margarine
1 ⅓ c. brown sugar, firmly
     packed
¼   c. light corn syrup
2   tsp. cinnamon
½   tsp. salt

· Butter a large bowl and toss the cereals, raisins and pecans in it to mix.
· Combine butter, brown sugar, corn syrup, cinnamon and salt in a heavy skillet. Stir constantly over medium heat until boiling. Boil 3 minutes.
· Pour the hot syrup over cereal mixture in the bowl; stir to coat thoroughly.
· Spread on two buttered baking sheets. Cool. When firm, break into pieces. Makes about 2½ quarts.

COCONUT CRISPS

Cookie-like bars, luscious with dates, nuts and snowy coconut topknots

6   c. oven-toasted rice cereal
1   c. chopped walnuts
¾   c. butter or margarine
1 ¼ c. sugar
2   tblsp. milk
¼   tsp. salt
1   c. chopped dates
1   tblsp. vanilla
2   tblsp. lemon juice
1   (3 ½ oz.) can flaked coconut

· Combine the cereal and walnuts in a greased 13 × 9 × 2″ pan.
· Combine butter, sugar, milk, salt and dates. Cook to the soft ball stage (240°); stir occasionally. Remove

from heat and add the vanilla and lemon juice.

• Pour the hot syrup over the cereal-nut mixture and stir lightly to coat cereal. Spread the mixture evenly in the pan. Sprinkle the coconut over the top and press the mixture firmly into the pan.

• Let set 4 hours or longer. When firm, cut into 3 × 1¼" bars. Makes 30 bars.

SANDWICHES ON STICKS DELIGHT CHILDREN

For a children's snack, serve tiny sandwiches on red apples. Polish the apples until they're as shiny as if they were going to the teacher. Allow 1 apple and 1 sandwich, made with 2 slices of bread, for each serving.

• Choose a firm sandwich filling, such as any favorite one made with peanut butter. Use a slice of white and one of dark bread (such as whole wheat) for each sandwich. Cut sandwich in 1" squares. Stick toothpicks into apple and fasten tiny sandwiches on the other ends of the picks. Serve with glasses of milk.

SNACKS ON PICKS

• A big grapefruit makes a cheerful "pin cushion" for snacks on wood picks.

• Choose a large, shiny green avocado to hold snacks on picks. Especially attractive for shrimp.

• Humble cabbage glorifies the appetizer tray if stuck with picks holding snacks. Select a big head of red, green or Savoy cabbage with a broad flat base so it will be steady.

• Polished red apples make gay holders for snacks.

Relishes Perk Up Meals

Country kitchens are famous for their relishes. These are the remarkable foods that brighten the flavor and color of meals. Some of them are double-duty foods, which means they're equally at home in the dessert course—beauteous crimson Spiced Apples Glacé, Apple-Pineapple Scallop and Poached Pears, to name a few.

SPICED APPLES GLACÉ

Serve in a crystal compote to display fruit's glistening red beauty. Ideal meat accompaniment to set on a buffet, also an excellent dessert

6   large apples
2   c. sugar
3   c. water
6   thin lemon slices
3   whole cloves
1   tblsp. grated orange peel
1   (1") stick cinnamon
6   maraschino cherries
2   tsp. cornstarch
¼   c. cold water
Red food color

• Peel and halve apples; remove stem ends. (You can remove cores easily with a melon ball scoop.)

• Combine sugar and water in a large skillet. Bring to boil. Add lemon slices, cloves, orange peel and cinnamon. Add apples. Simmer, uncovered, over moderate heat until apples are tender but still firm, about 15 minutes. Turn apples once during cooking.

• Remove apple halves and lemon slices to serving dish. Garnish with maraschino cherries.

• Bring syrup to a rolling boil and boil until it forms a very thin syrup, about 5 minutes. Stir in 2 tsp. cornstarch dissolved in ¼ c. cold water. Cook about 2 minutes more until slightly thickened. Add a few drops red food color. Cool slightly and pour over apples. Makes 6 dessert servings; more as meat accompaniment.

APPLE-PINEAPPLE SCALLOP

Unusually good fruit-cheese combination; serve hot, as a tangy-sweet meat accompaniment, or warm as dessert

1 (1 lb. 4½ oz.) can
   pineapple chunks
¼ c. sugar
1 tblsp. cornstarch
¼ tsp. salt
¼ c. lemon juice
3 c. sliced, tart cooking apples
4 slices dry bread, broken
   into coarse crumbs
¼ lb. pasteurized process
   cheese spread, shredded

• Drain pineapple; reserve ¾ c. liquid. Combine dry ingredients in heavy saucepan; add pineapple liquid. Cook, stirring constantly, until thickened. Remove from heat; stir in lemon juice and set aside.

• Layer fruit, crumbs and cheese in buttered 2-qt. casserole. (Pour on sauce before adding last layer of crumbs and cheese.) Cover; bake in moderate oven (350°) about 1 hour or until apple slices are tender. Makes 8 servings.

SPICED ORANGE SLICES

Sweet-tart pork, chicken or duck go-with to keep in refrigerator ready to perk up company meals

8 whole medium-size oranges,
   unpeeled
5 c. sugar
3 c. water
1 ¼ c. vinegar
24 whole cloves
2 sticks cinnamon

• Select oranges with unblemished skins. Simmer whole oranges in enough water to cover, until tender, about 20 minutes. Drain, cool and slice fairly thin.

• Combine sugar, water, vinegar and spices. Bring to a boil. Add sliced oranges and simmer 20 minutes. Remove cinnamon sticks.

• Spoon orange slices into 6 hot, sterilized pint jars. Pour on cooking liquid to cover. Place 2 or 3 cloves from liquid in each jar. Seal. Store in refrigerator. Makes 6 pints.

GOLDEN GLOW
FRUIT COCKTAIL

Fix-ahead appetizer for a guest dinner—good breakfast eye opener

4 large grapefruit, peeled
4 large oranges, peeled
1 (1 lb. 4½ oz.) can
   pineapple chunks
½ c. sugar
½ c. lemon juice
4 tsp. grated horse-radish, or
   ¾ tsp. peppermint extract

• Section grapefruit. Cut oranges in ¼" slices, then cut slices in halves. Drain pineapple; reserve syrup. Mix fruit in large mixing bowl.

- Add sugar to reserved pineapple syrup; bring to boil. Stir until sugar dissolves. Remove from heat and cool.
- Stir in lemon juice and horse-radish. Pour over fruit. Cover; refrigerate overnight. Makes 12 generous servings.

Note: To substitute dried mint flakes for peppermint extract, steep 1½ tsp. mint flakes in 3 tblsp. boiling water for 10 minutes. Strain; add mint-flavored liquid to fruit.

GOURMET PRUNES

Prunes reach gourmet status when you add tea, spice and citrus, and refrigerate them after cooking

1 lb. prunes
4 c. strong black tea
Peel of ½ orange, cut in strips
Small piece of stick cinnamon
2 tblsp. sugar
¼ tsp. salt

- Wash prunes and drain; soak overnight in the tea. Add orange peel and stick cinnamon; simmer 30 minutes. Add sugar and salt; cook 5 minutes longer.
- Cool, cover and refrigerate. Makes 12 servings.

PEACH AND NUT CONSERVE

With jars of this luscious conserve in the cupboard, you have the perfect dress-up for vanilla ice cream. Or use for cake filling

6 c. chopped, peeled peaches
Juice of 2 lemons
25 maraschino cherries, cut in quarters

3 ¾ c. sugar
1 ¼ c. chopped walnuts

- Combine all ingredients, except nuts, in heavy preserving kettle; cook, stirring frequently, until thick (about 30 minutes). Add nuts and stir in well.
- Ladle into hot, sterilized canning jars, filling to top of jars. Seal immediately. Makes 3 pints.

PEAR CHUTNEY

Guests will want to come into the kitchen when you make this meat accompaniment—aroma is inviting

5 lbs. firm pears, peeled and chopped coarsely
1 lb. light brown sugar
2¼ c. white sugar (1 lb.)
1 (15 oz.) pkg. golden raisins
3 cloves garlic, minced
2 tblsp. salt
2 tblsp. mustard seeds
¼ c. minced fresh red hot pepper pods
6 oz. preserved ginger (sugar rinsed off), chopped (⅔ c.)
1 ½ qts. cider vinegar

- Combine pears and sugars in large kettle. Cook slowly over low heat until mixture is thick, about 2 hours. Stir frequently to prevent scorching.
- Add remaining ingredients and let mixture come to a boil. Remove from heat; cover and let stand overnight at room temperature.
- Bring to a boil over medium heat and simmer until thick, about 1 hour. Stir frequently.
- Pour hot chutney into hot sterilized jars and seal. Makes 5 pints.

POACHED PEARS

*Keep in refrigerator to use in salads
and desserts and as lovely garnishes
for meat platters—also try variations*

4 firm pears
1½ c. sugar
1½ c. water
½ lemon, sliced

• Cut pears in halves lengthwise. Peel
and core.
• Combine sugar and water in saucepan. Bring to a boil. Add lemon and
pears. Simmer until pears are tender,
about 10 minutes. Remove from heat.
Chill to serve.

VARIATIONS

Ginger Pears: Poach pears as above,
except use 1 c. brown sugar, ½ c.
water, ½ lemon, 1 tsp. ginger and 4
whole cloves. Turn occasionally while
cooking. Chill. Serve as salad on
lettuce with scoop of cottage cheese
in cavity. Top with sour cream.

Rosy Pears: Sprinkle 2 tblsp. strawberry flavor gelatin over poached
pears when you remove them from
heat. Turn gently to get color into
pears. Chill. Spoon cranberry sauce
into cavities and serve as a garnish
for meats, or top with ice cream and
chocolate sauce for dessert.

RHUBARB-ORANGE JELLY

*Spread the colorful jelly on cinnamon
toast for an informal tea or coffee*

4 c. diced rhubarb
2 c. water
1 (6 oz.) can frozen orange
    juice concentrate
⅓ c. water

1 (1¾ oz.) pkg. powdered
    pectin
4 c. sugar

• Simmer rhubarb and water 15 minutes. Drain rhubarb, reserving liquid;
press rhubarb through a food mill.
Combine sieved pulp and liquid to
measure 2 c. Mix with orange juice
concentrate and water. Bring to a
boil.
• Add pectin; bring to a rolling boil.
Add sugar; boil 1 minute.
• Pour into hot sterilized glasses; seal.
Makes 5 half pints.

TOMATO-APPLE CHUTNEY

*Apples, tomatoes and raisins star in
relish—good with rice main dishes*

18 medium-size ripe tomatoes,
    peeled and chopped
4 lbs. apples, peeled and
    finely chopped
2 c. chopped onions
1 c. chopped green pepper
2 lbs. light brown sugar
2 c. dark, seedless raisins
1 qt. cider vinegar
4 tsp. salt
4 to 6 tsp. ground ginger
½ tsp. ground allspice
4 large cloves garlic, minced

• Combine all ingredients in a large
(12-qt.) kettle. Bring to a boil and
cook uncovered over low heat until
mixture thickens, 2 to 2½ hours.
Stir frequently to prevent sticking.
• Pour while boiling hot into clean,
hot jars. Fill to within ½" of top.
Adjust jar lids. Process in boiling
water bath 5 minutes (start to count
the processing time when water in

canner returns to boiling.) Remove jars and complete seals if necessary. Cool jars on a wire rack.

· This chutney can also be kept in the refrigerator without processing. Or freeze it in pint freezer containers. Allow to defrost at room temperature about 3 hours before serving. Makes 8 to 10 pints.

UNCOOKED TOMATO RELISH

Let this fresh-tasting, bright refrigerator relish add interest to guest meals

18   medium-size ripe tomatoes
2   stalks celery
2   green peppers
2   sweet red peppers
4   medium onions
½   c. finely ground horse-radish
⅓   c. salt
2½   c. sugar
½   tsp. pepper
½   tsp. ground cloves
2   tsp. ground cinnamon
3   tblsp. whole mustard seeds
3   c. cider vinegar

· Scald tomatoes; remove skins and as many seeds as possible. Chop into small pieces; should make about 3 quarts chopped tomatoes.

· Put celery, peppers and onions through food chopper, using coarse grind. Use the finest grind for horse-radish.

· Combine vegetables and salt; let stand overnight in refrigerator. Drain thoroughly in a strainer. Add sugar, spices, mustard seeds and vinegar. Mix well.

· Pack in sterilized jars; seal and store in the refrigerator. Should keep for several months. (Do not store at room temperature.) Makes about 4 quarts.

BLUSHING PEACHES

Peaches cook rosy in jelly syrup—serve hot as a companion to beef, pork or lamb

1   c. water
½   c. sugar
3   tblsp. currant jelly
2   tblsp. lemon juice
1½   tsp. grated lemon peel
4   large peaches

· Combine water, sugar, jelly, lemon juice and peel in fry pan. Cover, and simmer 5 minutes until jelly is dissolved.

· Peel and cut peaches in halves. Place cut side down in syrup in fry pan. Cover and simmer 10 minutes. Turn cut side up, cover, and cook 5 minutes more.

· Remove peaches from syrup into a dish. Cook syrup, stirring constantly, until it begins to jell (2 drops run together in a sheet when mixture is dropped from edge of spoon). Pour mixture over peaches in dish. Makes 8 servings.

REFRIGERATOR SPICED PRUNES

They'll keep in refrigerator for weeks, actually improve in flavor

1   lb. prunes (about 42)
4   c. water
⅓   c. vinegar
⅓   c. dark brown sugar
3   sticks cinnamon
1   tblsp. whole cloves

· Combine all ingredients in a saucepan (tie cloves in a piece of cheesecloth). Bring to a boil and simmer 7 minutes. Remove cloves.

· Cool, cover and chill in the refrigerator 24 hours or longer. Serve as a relish or garnish with meats or poultry. (Allow 2 prunes to a serving.)

CRANBERRY CONSERVE

Good take-along relish to add flavor and color to co-operative meals

1 lb. whole, fresh or frozen cranberries
3 oranges, cut in quarters
¾ c. dried currants
1 c. seedless raisins
2 finely cut, peeled tart apples
2 (8½ oz.) cans crushed pineapple
1 c. boiling water
5 c. sugar
½ c. slivered blanched almonds

• Put cranberries through food chopper, using coarse blade; chop oranges, using fine blade.
• Mix all ingredients except almonds in heavy saucepan. Cook, stirring occasionally, over medium heat until thick, about 45 minutes. Stir in almonds.
• Spoon into hot, sterilized jelly glasses. Cover with paraffin. Makes 12 (6 oz.) glasses.

PEACHY RELISH CUPS

Stunning, warm relish for meat platters—colors are red and yellow. You can fix it in a few minutes

6 canned cling peach halves
½ c. Frozen Cherry Mix (see Index)
¾ c. miniature marshmallows

• Drain peach halves quite dry. Spoon thawed Frozen Cherry Mix into center cavities.

• Arrange the tiny marshmallows in circles around mix in peach halves. Broil several minutes, or until marshmallows are lightly browned. Serve as a garnish on the meat platter. Especially good with ham, pork or chicken. Makes 6 servings.

PICKLED CARROT APPETIZER

Perfect accompaniment for shrimp. Fix several days before serving and chill. A popular Texas hostess special

1 lb. carrots, peeled
3 cloves garlic, minced
2 tblsp. coarsely chopped onion
3 tblsp. salad oil
¼ c. vinegar
1½ tsp. salt
½ tsp. dry mustard
⅛ tsp. pepper
1 tblsp. whole pickling spices
1 medium-size onion, peeled and thinly sliced

• Cut carrots lengthwise in ¼" slices; then cut in strips about ¾" wide and 3" long.
• Cook garlic and chopped onion in salad oil until almost tender, about 5 minutes (do not let brown).
• Stir in vinegar, salt, dry mustard, pepper, pickling spices, tied in a cheesecloth bag, and carrots. Cover and simmer about 5 minutes (carrots should be crunchy and crisp). Remove pickling spices.
• Arrange the carrot mixture in a shallow dish; top with a layer of sliced onions. Cover and refrigerate until time to serve, spooning some of liquid over carrots from time to time.
• Serve cold on plate, surrounded with short lengths of celery and cherry tomatoes. Makes 10 to 12 servings.

APPLE-CRANBERRY RELISH

Applesauce and cranberry combination pays big taste dividends. Soft jellied sauce is excellent with poultry and meats

1   (1 lb.) pkg. fresh cranberries
¾   c. sugar
1 ½ c. boiling water
1   (3 oz.) pkg. lemon flavor
     gelatin
1   c. sweetened applesauce

• Combine cranberries, sugar and water; bring to a boil. Continue boiling rapidly 5 minutes, or until cranberries pop.
• Pour hot cranberry mixture over gelatin in 2-qt. casserole; stir to dissolve gelatin. Blend in applesauce. Cover and refrigerate overnight. Makes 8 servings.

CHAPTER 9

COOKING FOR A CROWD

When women talk of food for a big gathering, you can be sure a happy time is on the way. It may be a family reunion, church supper, club celebration, picnic or other meals that country people share.

Food is of great importance on these occasions. That's why the chairman of the food committee, or the hostess if the event is in a home, searches for new and interesting quantity recipes. This chapter is full of suggestions. Many of the recipes come from the collection of a home economist who has successfully managed tearooms, club dining rooms and other kinds of first-class restaurants across the whole country. They are her favorites that have proved to please a crowd.

Take Smoky Mountain Barbecued Ribs, for example. If you're looking for a recipe for really good barbecued ribs, try them—we predict your quest is at an end. Fresh lemon slices on the russet red ribs provide top appetite appeal. Notice the unusual seasoning in the Mountain Cabin Barbecue Sauce—cinnamon. We want also to call special attention to the Beef Stroganoff that contains potatoes. Really good.

Orange-Ginger Punch, in a bowl garlanded with flowers and fruit, has made many parties memorable. It will perform the same way for you—simple to make, beautiful to look at and so luscious to sip.

Try Fruit and Nut Charlotte, heaped in sherbet glasses, and don't overlook some of the country-kitchen classics, such as Honey Cup Custard and Purple Plum Cobbler. Puffed-Up Apple Turnovers are a little work to make, but you can freeze them and have them ready to bake on party day.

Since a number of the recipes originated in tearooms, you may find the servings somewhat smaller than those for most FARM JOURNAL recipes—allow for this when counting the people you will serve. If you have household scales, you'll find they'll help you use some of these large-quantity recipes—we list some ingredients by weight. And if you're planning a large affair, do consult our "Buying Guide for 50 Servings," at the end of this chapter.

Smoky Mountain Barbecued Ribs

Giant snowflakes danced lazily in the air and glittered on trees aglow with bright autumn leaves. A premature unwelcome snow, exclaimed tourists, who came to mountain country to enjoy sunshine and the season's high coloring. On that stormy evening, a FARM JOURNAL food scout, who is an experienced home economist, tasted what she considers the best barbecued ribs ever to come to a table. Excited by her discovery, she complimented the hospitable mountain cook, who graciously gave her the recipe.

Returning home with her prize, the home economist began to experiment in her kitchen. She wanted to duplicate the shiny, russet-red look of the ribs and their superlative flavor. She succeeded, and we share the recipe with you.

"It's important," she says, "to use lean, small ribs, the kind that people often call pencil-ribs, because they are about the size of large pencils (they have more meat and less bone). If you use larger ribs, you will need to allow ¾ to 1 lb. for a serving." Here is the recipe geared to serve different size crowds. Cook the ribs in water and make the sauce a day ahead if possible. Then pour the sauce over the ribs and refrigerate overnight. Bake next day. This divides the work and enhances flavors.

SMOKY MOUNTAIN BARBECUED RIBS

To serve, remove cooked lemon slices, top with fresh ones. It's surprising how their fresh look glamorizes the ribs and adds appetite appeal

Number of Servings	20	40	60	120	240
Spareribs, lean	10 lbs.	20 lbs.	30 lbs.	60 lbs.	120 lbs.
Water					
Salt	4 tsp.	8 tsp.	4 tblsp.	½ c.	1 c.
Flour	½ c.	1 c.	1½ c.	3 c.	6 c.
Paprika	2 tblsp.	4 tblsp.	6 tblsp.	¾ c.	1½ c.
Chili powder	2 tsp.	4 tsp.	2 tblsp.	4 tblsp.	½ c.
Black pepper	1 tsp.	2 tsp.	1 tblsp.	2 tblsp.	4 tblsp.
Dry mustard	2 tsp.	4 tsp.	2 tblsp.	4 tblsp.	½ c.
Onions	1½ lbs.	3 lbs.	4½ lbs.	9 lbs.	18 lbs.
(will make)	20 slices	40 slices	60 slices	120 slices	240 slices
Lemon slices					
(8 to 1 lemon)	20 slices	40 slices	60 slices	120 slices	240 slices

Mountain Cabin Barbecue Sauce (see recipe)

• Have spareribs cut in ½ lb. squares (1 serving).
• Cover ribs with water; add salt. Simmer 45 minutes, removing film as it rises to surface. Cool ribs in liquid. Drain and save liquid for sauce.
• Combine flour, paprika, chili powder, pepper and mustard; mix thoroughly. Roll cooled ribs in mixture to coat; place them in a roasting pan (or pans)— stand them on an angle in pan, like cards in a file.
• On each serving of ribs place 1 onion slice and top with 1 lemon slice. Secure with toothpicks.
• Pour hot Mountain Cabin Barbecue Sauce over ribs.
• Bake in moderate oven (350°) until ribs brown, about 1 hour. Baste occasionally if sauce does not cover ribs. If allowed to stand 1 hour before serving, most of the fat will rise to the top and may be spooned off. Return to oven long enough to reheat.

MOUNTAIN CABIN BARBECUE SAUCE

What a great sauce! No wonder the ribs look and taste so good

Number of Servings	20	40	60	120	240
Worcestershire sauce	1⅓ c.	2⅔ c.	1 qt.	2 qts.	1 gal.
Ketchup	1 qt.	2 qts.	3 qts.	1½ gals.	3 gals.
Tabasco	1 tsp.	2 tsp.	1 tblsp.	2 tblsp.	4 tblsp.
Wine vinegar	¾ c.	1½ c.	2¼ c.	4½ c.	2¼ qts.
Stock (liquid in which ribs cooked)	2 qts.	1 gal.	1½ gals.	3 gals.	6 gals.
Brown sugar	¾ c.	1½ c.	2¼ c.	4½ c.	2¼ qts.
Unsulphured molasses	4 tblsp.	½ c.	¾ c.	1½ c.	3 c.
Cinnamon	2 tsp.	4 tsp.	2 tblsp.	4 tblsp.	½ c.
Grated orange peel	½ tsp.	1 tsp.	1½ tsp.	3 tsp.	2 tblsp.
Lemon juice	1 c.	2 c.	3 c.	1½ qts.	3 qts.

• Combine all ingredients and heat to boiling point. Pour hot mixture over spareribs and bake as directed.

TURKEY ALMOND LOAF

Ideal dish for a company luncheon

4½ c. Medium White Sauce
6   eggs, beaten
2   tblsp. grated onion
6   tblsp. chopped parsley
1½ tsp. salt
¾   tsp. pepper
¾   tsp. celery salt
3   c. soft bread crumbs
3   qts. finely chopped cooked
      turkey (or chicken)
3   c. blanched almonds,
      toasted and chopped

• Make white sauce (directions follow). Combine eggs, white sauce, onion, parsley, salt, pepper, celery salt and bread crumbs.
• Add turkey; mix until well blended.
• Turn into greased 9 × 5 × 3" loaf pans; set in pans or a large pan of hot water. Bake in slow oven (325°) about 30 minutes. Slice to serve. Sprinkle with toasted almonds. Pass thickened chicken broth (gravy) to ladle over. Makes 18 servings.

To Toast Almonds: Spread almonds in one layer in a shallow pan. Heat in slow oven (300°), stirring occasionally, until lightly browned, 20 to 25 minutes. Remove from pan at once and chop. (It's a good idea to remove almonds before they're as dark as desired, for they continue to brown a little after they're removed.)

Medium White Sauce: Melt ½ c. butter in saucepan, add ½ c. plus 1 tblsp. flour and stir until smooth. Add ¾ tsp. salt and ¼ tsp. white pepper. Gradually add 1 qt. plus ½ c. milk, stirring constantly. Cook and stir over low heat until smooth and thick. Makes about 4½ cups.

BARBECUED BEEF FILLING

Please the crowd—take a big kettle of this to the Sunday school picnic

4½ lbs. boneless beef
3   tblsp. melted shortening or
      beef fat, more if needed
3   c. water
4   tblsp. Worcestershire sauce
1   c. tomato sauce
1   c. ketchup
4   c. chopped onions, cooked
      tender in melted
      shortening
1½ tsp. salt (or to taste)
¼   tsp. pepper

• Cut beef in 4" pieces; brown well in shortening or beef fat. Add to 3 c. water and simmer until tender, about 2 hours. Remove beef from cooking liquid and put through coarse food grinder.
• Combine beef with remaining ingredients. Add enough of the cooking liquid to make filling moist but spreadable (about 2 c.).
• Heat filling and serve between hamburger buns. Makes enough filling for 50 sandwiches.

Sesame Burgers: *Toast sesame seeds by placing them in a small, heavy skillet. Heat slowly, stirring constantly, until seeds turn a light golden brown. Remove from heat at once. Butter split toasted buns and sprinkle buttered surface with toasted sesame seeds. Fill with cooked hamburger patties.*

BEST-EVER BARBECUED HAMBURGERS

Watch and stir if you cook this on your range top—it scorches easily. Better still, bake it in moderate oven (350°), stirring occasionally

    20 lbs. ground beef
    1 ¼ c. lard
    20 large onions, peeled
    20 green peppers, seeds
          discarded
    2 ½ c. sugar
    2 ¼ c. cider vinegar
    3 ¾ qts. ketchup (15 c.)
    1 ¼ c. dry mustard
    6 ⅔ tblsp. salt (3 oz.)
    Buns

• Brown beef in lard, stirring constantly until mixture is crumbly.

• Put onions and peppers through food chopper. Combine with sugar, vinegar, ketchup, mustard and salt. Add to meat.

• Simmer slowly 30 minutes, stirring occasionally with a wooden spoon. Serve in buns. Makes 4 gallons.

Note: If you serve ½ c. meat mixture in each bun, you get 128 servings; if you use ¾ c. you get about 106 servings. If you bake the mixture instead of cooking on top of the range, first rinse out the pan or pans with cold water but do not dry. This will help prevent the meat mixture from sticking to the pan.

Stroganoff Made with Roast Beef

Farm women like to swap good recipes. Home economists, who manage superior tearooms and other eating establishments, often consider their recipes trade secrets. That's because the food they serve attracts paying customers and duplications of their dishes might affect their own business. The Indiana woman who shares this recipe had adventures in locating it. For years she tried to locate the best stroganoff in the country. One evening in New York, at a dinner party given by a hostess of Russian birth, she took one bite and said to herself: "This is it."

Later in the evening, she had a chance to discuss the tasty main dish with her hostess. She asked why it was so exceptionally tasty. The hostess replied: "I always make it with rare roast beef." Then she added: "This means I entertain dinner guests two evenings in a row. The first day I serve a large rib beef roast. The second day I use the leftover beef to make stroganoff. It's really important that you use *rare* beef and raw potatoes. Allow 1 potato, cut in strips, for every pound of beef."

Returning to Hoosier country, the jubilant home economist started to serve guests, in the tearoom she managed, stroganoff made by this method. It quickly became famous locally, boosted business by making customers happy. You can make your guests happy by serving this dish, too.

You may want to make it first for a comparatively small group. That's why we give you a recipe you can use to make 6, as well as 18 servings.

BEEF STROGANOFF

Try buttermilk instead of sour cream in this dish. The taste is slightly different —many people prefer it to cream—and it contains fewer calories

Number of Servings	6	18
Chopped onions	3 tblsp.	½ c. plus 1 tblsp.
Diced mushrooms	2 c. (1 lb.)	1½ qts. (3 lbs.)
Butter or margarine	4 tblsp.	¾ c.
Rare roast beef, cut in strips ¼" wide, 1" long	1 lb. (about 2 c.)	3 lbs.
Raw shoestring potatoes	1 large baking (7 oz.)	3 lbs. (3 large baking)
Flour	4 tblsp.	¾ c. (12 tblsp.)
Beef stock	1 c.	3 c.
Chili sauce	½ tsp.	1½ tsp.
Salt	to taste	to taste
Dry red wine	1½ tblsp.	4½ tblsp.
Dairy sour cream	2 c. (1 pt.)	1½ qts.

• Cook onions and mushrooms (cut in large dice) in butter; add beef and potatoes.

• Blend flour with a little of the cold beef stock to make a smooth paste; then stir into remaining beef stock. Add chili sauce and salt to taste. Combine with the beef mixture. Add red wine.

• Bake, covered, in slow oven (325°) 1 hour, or until potatoes are cooked. Fold in sour cream and heat, but do not let come to a boil.

Note: You can use a gravy-soup mix, or bouillon cubes to make the beef stock; or make it from scratch in your kitchen (see Index for Beef Stock recipe).

BOHEMIAN STEAK

Serve this tempting, frugal meat with brown gravy containing mushrooms or plain—tastes delicious either way

1 lb. plus 14 oz. noodles
13 lbs. plus 2 oz. ground beef
⅓ c. finely chopped onion
    (4½ oz.)
Salt
Pepper
1½ qts. chicken stock
1½ qts. tomato purée

• Crumble noodles before cooking. Cook in salted water by package directions; drain and rinse in lukewarm water.

• Add noodles to ground meat and other ingredients. Shape in 60 patties. Spread in greased baking pans.

• Bake in moderate oven (350°) until browned, about 30 minutes. Makes 60 servings.

Note: You can use canned chicken broth, bouillon cubes with hot water or cook a hen to make the stock.

COUNTRY CLUB LASAGNE

The meat topping always tempts the men. Pass shakers of Parmesan cheese

Number of servings	10	20
Ground beef, pork or Italian sausage	1 lb.	2 lbs.
Olive or salad oil	1 tblsp.	2 tblsp.
Cloves garlic, minced	1	2
Dried parsley flakes	1 tblsp.	2 tblsp.
Dried basil	1 tblsp.	2 tblsp.
Salt	2 tsp.	4 tsp.
Tomatoes	1 (1 lb. 11 to 13 oz.) can (2½ c.)	2 (1 lb. 11 to 13 oz.) cans (1¼ qts.)
Tomato paste	1 (6 oz.) can	2 (6 oz.) cans
Lasagne noodles	1 (10 oz.) pkg.	2 (10 oz.) pkgs.
Large curd creamed cottage cheese	2 (12 oz.) cartons (3 c.)	4 (12 oz.) cartons (6 c.)
Eggs, beaten	2	4
Salt	2 tsp.	4 tsp.
Pepper	½ tsp.	1 tsp.
Dried parsley flakes	2 tblsp.	4 tblsp.
Grated Parmesan cheese	½ c.	1 c.
Mozzarella cheese, very thin slices	1 lb.	2 lbs.

• Brown meat in oil; add next six ingredients. Simmer, uncovered, until thick, about 1 hour. Stir occasionally while cooking.

• Cook noodles as directed on package; drain.

• Meanwhile combine cottage cheese with eggs, salt, pepper, parsley flakes and Parmesan cheese.

• Place half of the noodles in a greased 13 × 9 × 2" pan for 10 servings, in two pans of the same size for 20 servings. Spread on half the cottage cheese mixture; then add half of the mozzarella cheese. Top with the meat mixture. Repeat layers.

• Bake in moderate oven (375°) 30 minutes. Spoon into individual casseroles or on serving plates. Pass shakers of Parmesan cheese.

Note: When arranging the bottom layer of noodles in the pan, lay half of the noodle ribbons in one direction, the other half in the opposite direction (crisscross). Repeat with second layer of noodles.

GENUINE SWEDISH MEAT BALLS

Meat balls make their own rich brown gravy while they bake—perfect on rice

Number of Meat Balls (Small)	75	150	300
(Medium)	50	100	200
Ground round steak	6 lbs.	12 lbs.	24 lbs.
Ground lean pork	3 lbs.	6 lbs.	12 lbs.
Eggs, beaten	6	12	24
Brown sugar	1 tblsp.	2 tblsp.	4 tblsp.
Mashed potatoes	3 c.	1½ qts.	3 qts.
Dry bread crumbs	3 c.	1½ qts.	3 qts.
Salt	1½ tblsp.	3 tblsp.	6 tblsp.
Black pepper	1½ tsp.	1 tblsp.	2 tblsp.
Ground ginger	1½ tsp.	1 tblsp.	2 tblsp.
Ground cloves	1½ tsp.	1 tblsp.	2 tblsp.
Allspice	1½ tsp.	1 tblsp.	2 tblsp.
Milk	3 c.	1½ qts.	3 qts.
Flour (for coating)	½ to 1 c.	1 to 2 c.	2 to 3 c.
Fat			
Light cream	1½ qts.	3 qts.	1½ gals.

· Combine meats, eggs, brown sugar, potatoes, bread crumbs, salt, pepper, spices and milk; mix thoroughly. (This mixture will be so soft that you can barely handle it.) Shape into balls the size of *small* walnuts, or larger if you wish.

· Roll meat balls in flour to coat.

· Pan-fry in small amount of fat (enough to prevent sticking to skillet) until brown on all sides. Pour on cream; cover and bake in slow oven (325°) 40 minutes, or simmer on top of range about 30 minutes. The cream makes gravy around the balls. Serve over cooked rice, allowing 3 to 5 meat balls per serving. One pound (2 c.) processed or converted rice makes about 16 c. when cooked.

Teriyaki Sauce from Hawaii

You don't have to live in the beautiful, palm-fringed Hawaiian Islands to enjoy Teriyaki Sauce. We've imported the recipe. Brush the sauce on any meat or chicken that you are going to broil, either over coals or in the oven. It's the right touch for ham slices or steaks. Marinate the ham in the sauce 30 minutes (no longer or it will get too dark). Then grill it. Also try the sauce on lamb!

The one ingredient you may have trouble locating is fresh ginger root, although more supermarkets now have it than formerly. Sometimes you can get it from a Chinese restaurant.

Or you can call on friends in California to send some to you. Once you get fresh ginger root, keep it, wrapped in foil, in your freezer ready for use.

HAWAIIAN TERIYAKI SAUCE

Sauce gives grilled meats fine flavor

1   qt. soy sauce
⅔ c. sherry wine
⅔ c. sugar
⅛ tsp. monosodium glutamate
2   cloves garlic, crushed
2   pieces fresh ginger root, crushed

• Combine all the ingredients. Store in refrigerator in screw-top bottle. Shake before using. Brush sauce on ham slices, lamb or beef before broiling or pan-broiling. Makes 5⅓ cups.

Note: This recipe comes from a native Hawaiian educated on the mainland, who is an excellent cook. If you like a sauce of lighter color and with less soy taste, you can reduce the amount of soy sauce.

CHEESE-OLIVE RICE

Welcome hot dish for a party

For 6 Servings:

1   c. uncooked long grain rice
2   c. milk
1   lb. process cheese (yellow)
2   eggs, beaten
¾ tsp. pepper
2   c. sliced pimiento-stuffed olives
½ c. buttered bread crumbs

For 18 Servings:

3   c. uncooked long grain rice
1½ qts. milk
3   lbs. process cheese (yellow)

6   eggs, beaten
2¼ tsp. pepper
1½ qts. sliced pimiento-stuffed olives
1½ c. buttered bread crumbs

• Cook rice.
• Scald milk, add cheese and stir until it melts. Add eggs and seasoning. Fold in cooked rice.
• Spread in a greased baking dish, 9" square for 6 servings, 13 × 9 × 2" for 18 servings. Spread olives evenly over top. Cover with bread crumbs.
• Set pan in another pan containing warm water. Bake in moderate oven (350°) 15 minutes. Scoop out individual servings and arrange on plates or in individual casseroles, crumb side up. Serve at once.

Note: This dish cannot wait long after you remove it from the oven. Put it in to bake when the remainder of the meal is ready.

CHICKEN VELVET SOUP

Rich, tasty—almost a meal in a bowl

¾ c. butter
¾ c. flour
1   c. warm milk
1½ qts. hot chicken broth (stock)
1   c. warm light cream
1½ c. chopped cooked chicken
¾ tsp. salt
⅛ tsp. white pepper

• Blend butter and flour until well mixed.
• Combine milk, 1 pt. chicken broth and cream; heat, but do not let boil. Add butter-flour mixture and stir and cook until mixture thickens.
• Add remaining 1 qt. chicken broth, cooked chicken, salt and pepper. Heat

piping hot, but do not boil. Serve at once. Makes 18 to 20 cups, or 12 bowls.

Note: To make chicken broth or stock, simmer a 5 lb. fowl in 2½ qts. water until tender.

VEGETABLE CHOWDER

A thick, full-bodied, pink soup which, with salad and dessert, makes a meal

For 2½ Gallons:

2 c. diced salt pork or bacon
2 c. diced onions (1 pt.)
2 c. chopped celery (1 pt.)
2 c. diced carrots (1 pt.)
2 c. diced turnips (1 pt.)
6 qts. Beef Stock (see Index)
4 c. diced potatoes (1 qt.)
1 qt. tomato purée
1 c. flour
½ c. butter (4 oz.)
1 gal. milk
½ tsp. baking soda

For 5 Gallons:

4 c. diced salt pork or bacon
4 c. diced onions (1 qt.)
4 c. chopped celery (1 qt.)
4 c. diced carrots (1 qt.)
4 c. diced turnips (1 qt.)
12 qts. Beef Stock (see Index)
8 c. diced potatoes (2 qts.)
2 qts. tomato purée
2 c. flour
1 c. butter
2 gals. milk
1 tsp. baking soda

• Cook salt pork and onions together until lightly browned. Add celery, carrots, turnips and Beef Stock. Cook until vegetables are almost tender; then add the potatoes and cook until they are just tender. Add tomato purée.

• Meanwhile, combine flour and butter and blend thoroughly. Scald milk and add flour-butter mixture. Cook, while stirring, to make a thin sauce. Add baking soda; slowly add to the vegetable mixture to prevent curdling. Heat and serve at once.

Specialty-of-the-House Eggplant

Shiny, purple eggplant is beautiful in markets and gardens and tasty in many dishes. It's a pity that more people don't appreciate what it can do for company meals.

Our recipe for Cheese-Eggplant Scallop comes from the Midwest, where it was a drawing card in a popular eating establishment. Do try it and see if your guests don't especially enjoy it. While this vegetable dish is a fine companion to most meats, it's simply wonderful with fried chicken and other poultry specials. Some people believe it has a faint taste akin to scalloped oysters.

CHEESE-EGGPLANT SCALLOP

They'll like eggplant fixed this way

¼ bushel fresh eggplant (8¼ lbs.)
1 lb. butter or margarine, melted
1 (2 lb.) loaf sandwich bread, cut in cubes
6 eggs, beaten
1 lb. Cheddar cheese, grated
Salt
Pepper

• Peel eggplant, cut into chunks and cook in water barely to cover until soft, about 30 minutes. Drain and mash to a coarse consistency.

• Add butter to bread cubes, then divide them in half. To one half add eggs, half of the cheese and salt and pepper to taste. Add eggplant.

• Place half of remaining bread cubes in bottom of greased pans (the number depends on their size) and add eggplant mixture to the depth of 2". Top with remaining bread cubes. Sprinkle with remaining half of cheese. Cover and bake in hot oven (400°) about 30 minutes. Remove cover, and bake just long enough to brown top. Makes 50 servings.

Note: You can double the recipe for 100 servings. Bake in 5 (18 × 14 × 2½") pans.

SCRAMBLED CABBAGE

This dish adds color and flavor to the meal—vegetables are tender-crisp

2	tblsp. salad oil
1½	qts. finely shredded cabbage
1	pt. finely sliced celery
2	onions, thinly sliced
1	green pepper, chopped
4	tomatoes, peeled and diced
2	tsp. salt
½	tsp. pepper

• Pour salad oil into skillet or skillets, depending on size. Add other ingredients, tossing to mix. Cover; cook 5 minutes. Makes about 15 servings.

Individual Potato Salads: *Press potato salad into custard cups and chill. Turn out onto large tomato slices. Garnish salads with chopped chives or quarters of small tomatoes.*

Vegetable Medley
A bargain in good eating

Treat your guests to color-bright Vegetable Medley that's five times as good as most vegetable dishes. That's because all five vegetables in it contribute their flavors.

You can get the vegetables ready for cooking a few hours ahead, cover and refrigerate. The cooking is brief, for the secret to the success of Vegetable Medley is that you don't overcook any vegetable. But you cook them in three separate portions.

Undertake this dish when you have a helper in the kitchen to give it undivided attention. Or select it for a co-operative meal and ask one woman to fix it. If you tote Vegetable Medley or must hold it for a tardy guest, cover it and keep warm in a moderate oven (350°). In case it starts to dry out a little in the oven, pour on some tomato juice, which provides both moisture and flavor.

VEGETABLE MEDLEY

Bring a new dish to your table

6	lbs. green cabbage, shredded fine
3	lbs. celery, sliced
6	green peppers
3	lbs. medium onions, peeled and separated into rings
4	lbs. tomatoes, peeled and quartered
4	tblsp. salt
1	tblsp. pepper
1	c. salad oil

• Cook cabbage, uncovered, in boiling water to cover 7 minutes. Drain.

• Cook celery in 2" water in covered saucepan until just tender; drain.
• Cut green peppers in strips (like French fries) and then cut in very small pieces.
• Combine onion rings and tomatoes. Cook together until onion rings are soft.
• Combine vegetables; add salt and pepper.
• Heat salad oil in large kettle and add vegetables. Cook 1 minute. Taste for salt. Serve hot. Makes 35 servings.

SCALLOPED POTATOES

Always especially enjoyed by men

6½ lbs. potatoes
1½ tblsp. salt
 ½ c. grated or chopped onion
8   c. Medium White Sauce
     (2 qts.)
1½ c. buttered cracker crumbs

• Wash, peel and thinly slice potatoes. Place in a 20 × 12 × 2½" pan (or two smaller pans) and sprinkle with salt.
• Stir onion into white sauce; pour over potatoes. Bake in moderate oven (350°) 1 hour; then cover with cracker crumbs. Continue baking another hour. Makes 25 servings.

Note: To shorten baking time, cook the potatoes in their jackets the day before. Peel and slice on serving day; add to white sauce, cover with cracker crumbs and bake until tender, about 1 hour.

Medium White Sauce: Melt 1 c. butter or margarine; remove from heat. Add 1 c. flour and stir until smooth. Add ½ tsp. salt and ½ tsp. pepper. Scald 2 qts. milk; add gradually, stir-ring all the time, to the butter-flour mixture; cook over low heat until smooth and thick. Makes 2 quarts.

CANDIED SWEET POTATOES

They add a touch of gold to serving plates and almost everyone likes them

16 lbs. sweet potatoes,
     cooked and peeled
 ½ c. butter or margarine
2½ lbs. brown sugar
1   tblsp. salt
 ½ c. orange juice

• Slice potatoes lengthwise into ¾" slices. Place in single layer in baking pans.
• Melt butter; stir in sugar, salt and orange juice. Cook over low heat, stirring all the time, until sugar dissolves and makes a syrup. Pour over potatoes.
• Bake uncovered in moderate oven (350°) 40 to 45 minutes, spooning syrup over potatoes occasionally. Makes 50 servings.

Note: For a more distinct orange flavor, cook 2 tsp. grated orange peel with brown sugar-butter mixture.

VARIATION

Pineapple Candied Sweet Potatoes: Substitute pineapple juice for the orange juice.

BEET PICKLES

These pickles add color and zest to meals. Be sure to chill them

5   (1 lb. 4 oz.) cans sliced
     or whole beets
2½ c. beet juice and water
2½ c. cider vinegar
 ⅔ c. sugar

2 ½ tsp. salt
10 whole cloves
15 peppercorns
1 ½ bay leaves

• Drain beets, reserving juice. Add enough water to juice to make 2½ c. Bring to a boil with all the ingredients, except beets. Remove from heat.

• Add beets; cool. Chill thoroughly before serving. Makes 25 servings.

Note: Add 1 tblsp. prepared horseradish with spices for peppy pickles.

COUNTRY HOLLANDAISE SAUCE

Spoon this on hot vegetables, broiled fish and other cooked foods—especially good on asparagus and broccoli. Sauce stands without separating

For 1 Quart:
3 oz. butter or margarine
    (6 tblsp.)
¼ tsp. paprika
½ c. sifted flour
1 qt. milk
3 egg yolks, beaten
2 tsp. salt
¼ tsp. pepper
Juice strained from 4 lemons

For 1 Gallon:
12 oz. butter or margarine
    (1 ½ c.)
1 tsp. paprika
2 c. sifted flour
1 gal. milk
12 egg yolks, beaten
2 tblsp. plus 2 tsp. salt
1 tsp. pepper
Juice strained from 16 lemons

• Melt butter; sift together paprika and flour and add to melted butter. Stir and cook until well blended, but do not let brown. Heat milk until lukewarm and slowly add to the flour-butter mixture. Cook and stir until smooth. Stir a little of this hot mixture into the egg yolks; stir yolks into the hot sauce. Combine salt and pepper; add to sauce. Cook and stir until thickened.

• Add lemon juice strained through a fine sieve. Then strain hot sauce through a coarse sieve or a fine colander. Keep warm over hot water. Allow ¼ to ½ c. for each serving. Add to hot food just before serving.

Note: To make 25 servings of fresh asparagus, order 8 to 9 pounds. Cook, drain and add Country Hollandaise Sauce.

Tossed Green Salad to Remember

There are all kinds of tossed green salads—many good, some quite ordinary and a few superb. Here is one that can't be surpassed. The unusual ingredient is Creole mustard, available in the New Orleans area and in many food specialty and gourmet shops across the country. If you cannot find it, you can substitute any good prepared mustard, but the results will not be quite the same. Creole mustard has an elusive flavor that does something special to this salad. The most like it is Dijon mustard.

It's important to pat the greens dry with clean dish towels after you wash and drain them. Chill them until they are so crisp that they crackle when you break them in bite-size pieces to measure (do this as near serving time as possible). Use at least three kinds of greens. Follow the recipe carefully and see if you don't turn out a green salad your guests will remember.

TOSSED GREEN SALAD

Put this on your gourmet list to use when you want an impressive salad

1	clove garlic
2	qts. mixed greens (spinach, leaf lettuce, bibb lettuce, endive or celery cabbage)
1	qt. head lettuce
1½	tsp. salt
¾	tsp. freshly ground peppercorns
1	c. salad oil
4	tblsp. Creole mustard
4	tblsp. wine vinegar

· Rub salad bowl with crushed garlic clove and discard.
· Break dry salad greens in small pieces before measuring; do not cut them. Sprinkle salt and pepper over greens in bowl. Add salad oil and turn with fork until leaves are coated with oil.
· Mix mustard and wine vinegar. Pour over greens just before serving. Toss lightly to distribute. Makes 12 servings (individual salad bowls).

Note: Make 12 servings at a time. It works out better than trying to toss a larger quantity of leaves.

PERFECTION VEGETABLE SALAD

This salad is named correctly—make the recipe 4 times to serve 60, or if easier, multiply ingredients by 4

2	(3 oz.) pkgs. lemon flavor gelatin
¼	c. lemon juice
2	tsp. salt
2	c. finely shredded cabbage
2	c. diced celery
2	(2 oz.) cans pimientos, chopped
12	small sweet pickles, chopped

· Prepare gelatin by package directions. Add lemon juice and salt. Chill until partially set. Add remaining ingredients.
· Pour into a 13 × 9 × 2" pan. Chill until firm. Cut in individual servings. Serve on lettuce leaves; garnish with salad dressing. Makes 15 servings.

For a child's party, use a bouquet of lollipops for a centerpiece.

SCARLET BEAUTY SALAD

Expertly seasoned, bright-color aspic deserves the praise it gets

4	envelopes unflavored gelatin
1⅓	c. sugar
1	c. lemon juice
1½	qts. tomato juice
½	bay leaf
½	c. chopped onion
1	c. chopped celery tops
½	c. cider vinegar
¼	tsp. salt

· Combine gelatin, sugar and lemon juice.
· Heat tomato juice with bay leaf, onion and celery tops. Strain over gelatin mixture. Add vinegar and salt.
· Pour into molds and chill until firm. Makes 24 servings.

Note: This salad of gorgeous color is attractive if molded in paper serving cups with pleated sides (see Index for Mauve Frozen Fruit Salad with directions for removing salads from paper cups).

SALMON BOWL SALAD

Tearoom sales of this tripled when shaped with an ice cream scoop

Number of Servings	12	18	72
Salmon (canned)	2 lbs.	3 lbs.	12 lbs.
Lemons	⅓	½	2
Paprika	1 tsp.	½ tblsp.	2 tblsp.
Dry mustard	1 tsp.	½ tblsp.	2 tblsp.
Salt	⅔ tsp.	1 tsp.	4 tsp.
Mayonnaise	1 c.	1½ c.	6 c.
Diced celery	1 qt.	1½ qts.	6 qts.
Sweet pickle relish	½ c.	¾ c.	3 c.
Hard-cooked eggs	4	6	24
Lettuce			

• Remove salmon from cans; separate with fork into *large* flakes. Squeeze juice from lemons over salmon.

• Mix paprika, mustard and salt with mayonnaise in large bowl. Add celery and pickle relish; mix well.

• Add eggs, coarsely diced, and salmon. Mix gently to avoid making mixture mushy. Chill and serve in bowls on crisp lettuce.

Note: A pretty garnish for this salad consists of hard-cooked egg slices, tomato wedges and the sprigs of small top celery leaves.

VARIATION

Tuna Bowl Salad: Substitute canned tuna for the salmon.

Distinctive Vegetable Salad

What's in a name? If it's for food to sell, the name is of great importance. "When we called this colorful vegetable salad 'Spinach Salad' on our menu," says the manager of a tearoom, "the sales were low. When we changed the name to 'Mixed Vegetable Salad,' the orders skyrocketed."

Be sure to select young, tender spinach leaves and to wash them through enough waters to remove all the grit and sand.

MIXED VEGETABLE SALAD

This is a good-for-you salad if there ever was one—delicious, too

4 qts. tender spinach leaves, thoroughly washed
6 medium carrots
2 green onions
1 green pepper
½ c. celery
Creamy Spring Dressing (see Index)

• Wash young spinach leaves through several waters. Pat dry with towels, break in small pieces and measure.

· Grate carrots and chop green onions very fine. Finely chop green pepper and celery. Mix vegetables with Creamy Spring Dressing. Makes 50 servings.

JEWEL SALAD MOLDS

A delicate salad that looks like jade. Good cool main dish for summer

For 24 Servings:

4 (3 oz.) pkgs. lime flavor
    gelatin
1 qt. hot water
1 qt. grated peeled cucumber
1 c. grated onions
1 qt. cottage cheese
1 qt. mayonnaise
1 qt. heavy cream, whipped
Lettuce

For 48 Servings:

8 (3 oz.) pkgs. lime flavor
    gelatin
2 qts. hot water
2 qts. grated peeled cucumber
2 c. grated onions
2 qts. cottage cheese
2 qts. mayonnaise
2 qts. heavy cream, whipped
Lettuce

· Dissolve gelatin in hot water (boiling). Cool until mixture starts to set.
· Fold in remaining ingredients *lightly* except lettuce (method of mixing affects the consistency of the salad). Pour into individual salad molds. Chill until firm. Serve, fringed with lettuce, on salad plates.

Mold gelatin for potlucks in cupcake liners or paper cups. The individual servings are easy to handle and keep the gelatin separate from other food.

Stars and Stripes Salad

You'll have exciting Jellied Pear Salads if you take the serving suggestions offered by a Kentucky farm woman. She says: "Stick the pole of a tiny American flag in each salad just before mealtime. Have the salads on the tables before the guests arrive. It's a glorious sight, especially if there are 50 or more place settings.

"I've used this decoration many times at church suppers and I've yet to see the man, woman or child who isn't moved by it. Sometimes I serve the cheese-stuffed pear halves on drained canned pineapple slices, omitting the gelatin. Even then, the salads are a triumphant success, partly because they display our flag."

JELLIED PEAR SALAD

Pears and cheese team together in this make-ahead salad for a crowd

6 (1 lb. 13 oz.) cans small
    pear halves (about 50)
4½ qts. juice drained from pears
8 (3 oz.) pkgs. lemon flavor
    gelatin
1¾ lbs. creamed cottage cheese
    or cream cheese
6 heads lettuce
1 qt. mayonnaise

· Drain pears. Measure pear juice and add enough water to make 4½ qts. Heat to boiling; pour over gelatin and stir to dissolve. Chill until slightly thickened. Pour a thin layer over bottom of 6 (8") square pans, or other pans to obtain about 50 servings.
· Fill cavities in pear halves with drained cottage cheese (or cream

cheese). Divide filled pear halves equally in pans containing gelatin layer and arrange pear halves, cut side down. Pour remaining slightly thickened gelatin mixture over pears. Chill until firm.

• To serve, cut salad so each serving contains a pear half. Serve cheese side up on lettuce leaves. Garnish with spoonfuls of mayonnaise or salad dressing. Sprinkle with finely chopped nuts or candied ginger, if desired. Makes 50 servings.

Note: You can add a little crushed pineapple, drained, to the cheese, if you like. A maraschino cherry on each salad makes a festive trim. If you cut the lettuce in ribbons before placing salads on plates, you'll retain the desired green color and almost everyone will eat it.

MOLDED VEGETABLE SALAD

For pretty garnish, use yellow-green leaves from tops of celery hearts

1½ c. unflavored gelatin
2 qts. cold water
2 qts. boiling water
¼ c. salt (scant)
2 qts. sweet pickle juice
2 qts. assorted fruit juices
   (from canned fruit or
   canned juices)
2 to 3 medium onions, grated
2 c. diced celery
2 c. diced green pepper
4 c. diced carrots (raw)
2½ qts. shredded cabbage
1 qt. cooked, diced beets (or
   canned)

• Sprinkle gelatin over cold water. Let stand 10 minutes. Add boiling water and salt; stir until gelatin is dissolved. Chill until mixture thickens slightly, or to consistency of uncooked egg whites.

• Add pickle juice, fruit juices and onions; stir occasionally until mixture is partly congealed. Stir in celery, green pepper, carrots and cabbage. Then stir in beets (it is important to add the beets as late as possible to prevent their color running).

• Pour into individual molds, or long, shallow pans (first rinse pans or molds in cold water and shake out water). Place in refrigerator to set. Top individual servings with spoonfuls of mayonnaise or salad dressing. Makes 96 servings.

Note: Try this experiment in serving gelatin salads. Cut in squares, place on salad plate and instead of putting mayonnaise or salad dressing on center of each salad, place it on the upper right-hand corner. Tuck just a little lettuce under salad—one leaf is enough. Such treatment shows off the beauty of the salads.

Big-Batch Hospitality Salad

A smart hostess works out ways to serve superior food to friends on short notice. One excellent plan is to fix a large fruit salad and freeze it. Then when guests come, all you have to do is make coffee or tea and slice the salad.

We share with you the salad-dessert recipe of an Iowa extension home economist who makes nine quarts of the luscious fruit mixture every year right after Thanksgiving. Then she's ready to welcome guests throughout the holiday season. She calls it Hospitality Salad-Dessert. Her friends call it good!

FROZEN FRUIT SALAD-DESSERT

Serve attractive slices of this luscious frozen treat to holiday drop-in guests

4 (1 lb. 4 oz.) cans crushed
    pineapple
2 (1 lb.) cans sliced peaches
2 c. fresh white seedless
    grapes, halved, or 2
    (1 lb. 4 oz.) cans
1½ c. maraschino cherries, cut
    in eighths
½ lb. marshmallows, quartered
    (30)
2 tsp. crystallized ginger,
    finely chopped
1 envelope unflavored gelatin
¼ c. cold water
1 c. orange juice
¼ c. lemon juice
2½ c. sugar
½ tsp. salt
2 c. coarsely chopped pecans
2 qts. heavy cream, whipped,
    or 10 pkgs. dessert
    topping mix, whipped, or
    1 qt. heavy cream and 5
    pkgs. dessert topping mix,
    whipped
3 c. mayonnaise

• Drain fruit; save 1½ c. pineapple

syrup. Cut peaches in ½" cubes. Combine fruit, marshmallows and ginger.

• Soften gelatin in cold water.

• Heat pineapple syrup to boiling. Add gelatin; stir to dissolve. Add orange and lemon juices, sugar and salt; stir to dissolve. Chill.

• When mixture starts to thicken, add fruit mixture and nuts. Fold in whipped cream and mayonnaise.

• Spoon into 1-qt. cylinder cartons (paper, plastic or metal). Cover and freeze. Makes 9 quarts.

• To serve, remove from freezer and thaw enough to slip out of carton. Cut in 1" slices. Serve salad on lettuce; garnish with cherries. For dessert, top with whipped cream. Each quart makes 6 to 8 servings.

Note: You can substitute 1½ c. ground raw cranberries or 3 (1 lb.) pkgs. frozen whole strawberries for the cherries. Thaw, drain strawberries. Substitute juice for some of the orange and pineapple juices.

MAUVE FROZEN FRUIT SALAD

Dark cherries marbleize salads—paper cups give molds decorative sides

To Make 1 Quart:

2 tblsp. confectioners sugar
½ c. Golden Salad Dressing
    (see Index)
½ c. mayonnaise
¼ tsp. grated lemon peel
½ c. pitted canned white
    cherries (Royal Anne),
    cut in halves and drained
1½ c. fruit cocktail (canned)

Put our big 9-quart Frozen Fruit Salad (*recipe, above*) into your freezer and you'll have a tasty salad or dessert always ready for company. Slice it on lettuce for salad. Whipped cream topping makes it a proud dessert.

½ c. heavy cream, whipped
½ c. diced marshmallows
½ c. pitted dark sweet
     cherries (Bing) cut in
     halves and drained
Lettuce

To Make 4 Quarts:

½ c. confectioners sugar
2 c. Golden Salad Dressing
    (see Index)
2 c. mayonnaise
1 tsp. grated lemon peel
2 c. pitted canned white
    cherries (Royal Anne),
    cut in halves and drained
6 c. fruit cocktail (canned)
1 pt. heavy cream, whipped
2 c. diced marshmallows
2 c. pitted dark sweet
    cherries (Bing), cut in
    halves and drained
Lettuce

• Combine the sugar, Golden Salad Dressing, mayonnaise and lemon peel. Stir until sugar is dissolved. Fold in white cherries and fruit cocktail, drained, whipped cream and marshmallows. Fold in drained dark sweet cherries last (they will streak the salad with their color, giving salad a distinctive look).

• Pour into 4 or 8 oz. pleated paper serving cups, depending on size of salads desired. Freeze. To serve, run metal blade of knife (without pointed end, which might pierce paper cup) around edge of salad cups to loosen sides. Then pull paper cups from opposite sides, pulling out pleats (the cups will look something like saucers). Run knife under bottom of salads to loosen them. Turn out. The salads will have a design on sides made by pleats.

• Serve top side (rough side) up on plates. Serve in lettuce hearts or garnish with sprigs of watercress.

Note: If you cannot get paper serving cups, you can use individual molds. The paper cups are the kind used by hotels and restaurants for serving foods, such as cranberry sauce, on dinner plates with other foods. They are called portion cups.

Cape Cod Slaw: *To 1 qt. finely shredded cabbage add 2 c. finely shredded peeled yellow turnips and 1 small apple, cored and chopped fine. Toss with salad dressing. Serve on green cabbage leaves, garnished with mounds of peeled, shredded raw beet. An end-of-the-garden favorite—good with baked beans or a brown, tender pot roast.*

Consider Salad Dressings

Clever hostesses know that the dressing can make or break the salad. Many women have a variety of dressings to introduce change and intriguing flavors to their company salads. Here are recipes for several exceptionally fine ones. You also can use the bottles and jars of superior dressings and packages of salad dressing mixes on supermarket shelves. Experiment with different kinds to find out which ones rate highest with your company.

When peaches are ripe, mold and serve this luscious, make-ahead Peach Melba Parfait (*recipe, page 246*) in dessert glasses to display its rich color and sparkling beauty. Also make classic Peaches Melba (*page 245*).

CREAMY SPRING DRESSING

*It's thin as pour cream and a perfect
dressing for young, tender greens*

⅔ c. sugar
4 egg yolks
1 tsp. salt
4 tblsp. flour
2 c. vinegar
2 tsp. dry mustard
⅔ tsp. paprika
Light cream or dairy sour cream

• Combine sugar, egg yolks, salt,
flour, vinegar, mustard and paprika.
Cook over water in double boiler until mixture thickens. Cool; add light
cream or dairy sour cream (about
2 c.) so dressing will be the consistency of light cream. Makes enough
for 50 individual salads.

GOURMET COLESLAW DRESSING

*Guarantee: This superior dressing
makes ordinary cabbage salad special*

2 small onions
1 qt. dairy sour cream
2 c. tarragon vinegar
½ c. sugar
2 tsp. celery seeds
½ tsp. white pepper
2 tsp. salt
1 c. heavy cream, whipped

• Grate onions into sour cream. Add
remaining ingredients, except heavy
cream, and stir to blend.
• Fold in whipped cream. Keep in refrigerator until ready to use. Makes
1½ quarts.

Note: Allow ½ to ¾ c. of this dressing to 1 qt. finely shredded new cabbage. Shred cabbage and spread ice
cubes over it. Just before serving coleslaw, drain cabbage and fold in the
dressing, allowing about 1 c. coleslaw
for a serving. To garnish, sprinkle top
of coleslaw with a little celery seed
and very finely diced green pepper.

RED CLOVER SALAD DRESSING

*Bright red color and ketchup flavor
make this a great favorite of men*

1 c. honey
1½ tblsp. salt
1 tblsp. dry mustard
1½ tblsp. paprika
½ c. ketchup
½ c. lemon juice
1 c. vinegar
2 c. salad oil

• Mix all ingredients, except salad oil,
with electric mixer until well blended.
• Gradually add salad oil, beating
constantly, to blend well and to obtain the consistency of mayonnaise.
Serve with greens or fruits. Makes
about 5 cups.

CELERY SEED DRESSING

*You heat paprika to give dressing a
lovely orange color—good with fruit*

To Make ½ Gallon:
4½ c. confectioners sugar
2 tblsp. dry mustard
2 tblsp. salt
1 c. plus 2 tblsp. cider
   vinegar
1½ qts. salad oil
2 tblsp. paprika
2 tblsp. celery seeds

To make 1 Gallon:
2 qts. plus 1 c. confectioners
   sugar
4 tblsp. dry mustard
4 tblsp. salt

2 ¼ c. cider vinegar
3 qts. salad oil
4 tblsp. paprika
4 tblsp. celery seeds

• Mix confectioners sugar, mustard, salt and vinegar. Let stand 3 hours, stirring mixture every half hour, or until mixture is the consistency of honey.
• Heat 1 c. salad oil with paprika added. Strain through cheesecloth and cool (otherwise it will not be smooth). Add to the remainder of salad oil. Then slowly add enough oil, drop by drop, to the sugar-vinegar mixture, beating all the time until the mixture forms an emulsion (thickens). Slowly pour remainder of oil into mixture. Add celery seeds and let stand 24 hours before serving.

VARIATION

Poppy Seed Dressing: Omit paprika. Substitute poppy seeds for celery seeds. This dressing is especially wonderful on grapefruit salads. Also on grapefruit-avocado salad.

COOKED SALAD DRESSING

Using this dressing is the secret to making coleslaw or potato salad with that like-mother-used-to-fix taste

For 1½ Gallons:
1 qt. water
3 c. sugar
2 c. flour
2 tblsp. salt
2 tblsp. dry mustard
2 c. water
2 qts. cider vinegar
1 ½ qts. egg yolks, beaten
1 ½ lbs. butter or margarine

For 3 Gallons:
2 qts. water
6 c. sugar
4 c. flour
4 tblsp. salt
4 tblsp. dry mustard
1 qt. water
1 gal. cider vinegar
3 qts. egg yolks, beaten
3 lbs. butter or margarine

• Bring 1 qt. or 2 qts. water to a boil, amount depending on how much dressing you are making. Combine dry ingredients and mix to a smooth paste with 2 c. or 1 qt. water, depending on quantity of dressing you are making. Add paste gradually to boiling water, stirring constantly. Add cold vinegar to egg yolks; stir into first mixture.
• Cook over hot water until dressing thickens. Add butter and stir to mix. Cool, cover and store in refrigerator. This makes a thick dressing; to use, mix equal amounts of the salad dressing and light or dairy sour cream.

Note: If you want to use this dressing for a fruit salad, you can substitute fruit juice for vinegar.

GOLDEN SALAD DRESSING

Perfect quantity dressing for fruit

1 c. pineapple juice
1 c. orange juice
½ c. lemon juice
8 eggs, separated
1 ½ c. sugar

• Combine pineapple, orange and lemon juices in top of double boiler; heat.
• Beat egg yolks slightly; gradually add ¾ c. sugar. Stir into the heated

juices; cook until thick and smooth, stirring constantly.

· Beat egg whites until stiff; fold in remaining ¾ c. sugar. Then fold into mixture in double boiler. Cool. Part of this may be refrigerated and used from time to time. Makes 2 quarts.

· When you use dressing, add 1 part heavy cream, whipped, to 2 parts cold salad dressing.

BLUE CHEESE CREAM DRESSING

A Florida dress-up for greens— creamy, thick Grecian type dressing

```
1   c. lemon juice (8 oz.)
2   qts. mayonnaise
2   qts. light cream
3   lbs. blue cheese, crumbled
```

· Combine all ingredients and blend in electric mixer or with a wire whisk. Makes 4½ quarts.

Homemade Breakfast Rolls Typify Christmas in the Country

Homemade rolls, especially if they have shiny brown tops dotted with nuts, are welcome at holiday coffee parties. And a pan of them makes a most appropriate and appreciated Christmas gift for a neighbor. A member of FARM JOURNAL's Family Test Group, who lives in Ohio, gave us her choice recipe for Pecan Rolls, which she makes in large quantity for Christmas gifts. (She puts packages of them in cars of friends attending church services on Christmas Eve.)

She bakes the rolls in disposable aluminum pans, turns them out while hot into other disposable pans of the same size, and lets them cool. They then are ready to wrap and deliver. Her recipe makes 144 rolls, but home economists in our Test Kitchens reduced it to yield 72 rolls. The dough is easier to handle than in the larger quantity.

You can wrap the cool rolls and freeze them for reheating just before serving or taking to friends. At breakfast time they are a merry Christmas greeting from one family to another.

PECAN ROLLS

Pecan topping makes them irresistible

Dough:

```
1 ½  c. milk, scalded
1 ½  c. sugar
4    tsp. salt
¾    c. shortening
5    pkgs. active dry yeast
2    c. warm water (105–15°)
6    eggs, beaten
15   to 16 c. sifted flour
```

Pecan Syrup:

```
1    c. butter
3    c. brown sugar
½    c. light corn syrup
3    c. broken pecan pieces
```

· Scald milk, stir in sugar, salt and shortening; cool to lukewarm.

· Dissolve yeast in warm water. Stir in lukewarm milk mixture, beaten eggs and half of the flour.

· Work in remaining flour. Knead about 8 minutes. Divide dough and place in 2 greased bowls, then invert dough. Cover; let rise in warm place until doubled in bulk, about 1½ to 2 hours.

• To make syrup, place butter, brown sugar, corn syrup and pecans in heavy saucepan. Heat until butter melts. Stir together.

• Grease a dozen 8″ aluminum pie pans, round cake pans or disposable aluminum pans. Spread about ⅓ c. of the pecan syrup in the bottom of each pan. Punch down dough, form into round rolls. Place 6 rolls in each pan on top of the syrup. Cover with a clean dish towel, and allow to rise in a warm place until doubled in bulk, about 1 hour.

• Bake rolls in moderate oven (350°) until nicely browned, about 30 minutes. While still hot, turn out of pan. Cool on rack. Makes about 72 rolls.

Pancakes for Money-Making Suppers

If you belong to a church or club group that wants to have a pancake supper to raise funds, you'll welcome this recipe for Pancake Supper Cakes. At one time this very same recipe delighted after-theater crowds in New York and Washington and other big cities. The recipe, much sought after, was a guarded trade secret. The tender, brown cakes puffed up in baking and were served so hot that butter quickly melted into golden pools.

The famous restaurant chain is now closed, but we have resurrected the recipe because we think it's so good. It will provide a change from most griddle cakes now served at money-making suppers. We believe both you and your customers will be well satisfied.

PANCAKE SUPPER CAKES

Many good pancakes come from a mix, but these are homemade. The pancake supper crowd will get their money's worth

8	c. flour
10	tblsp. baking powder
4⅔	tsp. sugar
1	tblsp. salt
8	eggs, separated
2	qts. milk
1	c. melted butter or margarine

• Mix and sift together flour, baking powder, sugar and salt.

• Beat egg yolks; add to milk. Pour slowly on flour mixture. Beat thoroughly.

• Beat egg whites until stiff and fold into batter; add melted butter.

• Drop by spoonfuls onto hot griddle. Cook on one side over medium heat, until bubbles appear on top of cakes. Turn and bake on the other side. Serve with butter and maple or other table syrup. Makes 1 gallon of batter, or 20 servings, 3 (5″) cakes to each serving.

Note: Keep batter at room temperature. If it becomes thick before all of it is used, add a little tap water to thin.

Nut Bread Party Sandwiches

Thin nut bread slices, spread lightly with butter or softened cream cheese, make delightful sandwiches to serve at tea and coffee parties. And they're a fine accompaniment to salads. It's a good idea to bake the bread a day ahead, cool, wrap in foil and set in a cold place. It will slice more easily and neatly. Or, you can bake the bread several days before the party, cool, wrap and freeze.

If you'd like to serve dainty round sandwiches, bake the batter in cans you've washed and saved after using the contents in cooking. Bake the batter for Cranberry-Nut Bread 45 to 50 minutes in 3 well-greased 1 lb. 4 oz. cans, or about 40 minutes in 5 well-greased soup cans. The batter should fill the cans a little more than halfway.

Don't worry about the crack that usually forms on top of the bread in baking. This is its trademark. And do slice nut breads thinly to give them a glamorous party look.

CRANBERRY-NUT BREAD

This foolproof recipe makes festive bread. Bake 3 loaves for 50 servings

¾ c. sugar
1 egg
1 ¼ c. orange juice
3 c. biscuit mix
¾ c. chopped nuts
1 c. chopped fresh cranberries, or chopped, unthawed frozen cranberries

• Mix sugar, egg, orange juice and biscuit mix. Beat vigorously ½ minute (batter still may be slightly lumpy).
• Stir in nuts and cranberries.
• Bake in well-greased 9 × 5 × 3″ loaf pan in moderate oven (350°) 55 to 60 minutes, or until toothpick inserted in center comes out clean. Cool thoroughly before slicing. Makes 1 loaf, 16 to 17 servings.

VARIATION

Apricot-Nut Bread: Use chopped dried apricots for the cranberries.

GARDEN SANDWICH FILLING

Texture contrast, flavor and gala color appeal—a clever way to put lots of vegetables in the menu

1 qt. frozen peas (undercooked)
1 qt. peeled cut-up carrots (undercooked)
1 qt. finely cut celery (raw)
1 pt. cut-up peeled, firm tomatoes
Mayonnaise
50 slices bread

• Cook peas by package directions in salted water, only cook less time (they should be slightly *undercooked*).
• Cut carrots in small squares (size of peas) and slightly undercook. Cut celery in pieces of the same size; do not cook.
• Mix peas, carrots and celery like marbles (mix to distribute vegetables evenly). Cover, refrigerate overnight.
• At serving time, add tomatoes, cut in pieces the size of peas, to vegetable mixture and toss lightly with just enough homemade or other mayonnaise to moisten vegetable mixture.
• Spread on 25 whole wheat or other bread slices; top with remaining bread slices. Cut sandwiches diagonally in fourths. Makes 25 sandwiches.

Note: Serve Garden Sandwiches this way. Arrange sandwich triangles on serving plate, pointed ends in (toward center of plate), to show the attractive sandwich filling. Two or three ripe olives in center of plate make a pretty garnish.

Make grated chocolate for garnish by dropping chocolate bits into your nut-meat grinder. Just a few turns of the handle and your garnish is ready.

Yellow Butter Cake for Birthdays

Butter cakes are in demand by customers of exclusive tearooms and other eating establishments that cater to the party trade. Yellow Butter Cake is called "Yellow Birthday Cake" in one such tearoom, operated by the home economist who shares the recipe.

"When someone calls and asks that a birthday cake be served for luncheon or dinner, this is the cake we usually make," she says. "We buy decorations for the frosted cake, as a rule. That's a good way to save time (to cut down on labor costs) and there are so many attractive inexpensive decorations available." Among them are small flags, candies of different colors and shapes, candles, marshmallows, animal crackers and small toys, dolls for girls and soldiers for boys.

YELLOW BUTTER CAKE

Most cakes today start as a mix, but here's an old-fashioned layer cake that has a fine grain and a buttery taste

For 5 (9″) Layers:
¾ lb. butter
3 c. sugar
6 eggs
1 tblsp. vanilla
1 pt. milk (2 c.)
1 ½ qts. sifted cake flour
¼ tsp. salt
3 tblsp. baking powder

For 10 (9″) Layers:
1 ½ lbs. butter
1 ½ qts. sugar
12 eggs
2 tblsp. vanilla
1 qt. milk
3 qts. sifted cake flour
½ tsp. salt
6 tblsp. baking powder

• Cream butter and sugar until light; add eggs and vanilla and beat until mixture is fluffy. Alternately add milk and flour, salt and baking powder, first sifted together.

• Pour batter into lightly greased 9″ layer cake pans. Bake in moderate oven (350°) 35 to 40 minutes. Remove from pans and cool on racks. Put two layers together with frosting of your choice to make a cake. Five layers make 2½ (2-layer) cakes (cut the remaining layer in half and frost to make half of a 2-layer cake); ten layers make 5 (2-layer) cakes. You can cut each full-size 2-layer cake in 14 servings.

MARSHMALLOW FROSTING

A dual-purpose recipe. It's frosting on cake, sauce on ice cream

2 lbs. sugar (4 c.)
1 ¼ c. water
1 tsp. cream of tartar
1 c. egg whites
1 tblsp. vanilla
1 ½ tsp. almond extract

• Combine sugar, 1 c. water and cream of tartar in saucepan. Stir over low heat until sugar is dissolved. Bring to boiling point. Cover saucepan the

first 2 or 3 minutes of boiling; uncover and boil, without stirring, to 240° on candy thermometer. Wipe crystals from pouring surface with a damp cloth or swab of cheesecloth.
• Meanwhile, when syrup is almost cooked (236° on thermometer) start beating egg whites. Beat in a large bowl until stiff, but not dry, peaks form, adding remaining ¼ c. cold water when half beaten.
• Pour hot syrup in a fine stream over egg whites, beating steadily; add vanilla and almond extract. Continue beating until frosting stands in peaks. Makes about 2 quarts. After frosting cake, put any remaining frosting in a tightly covered jar; refrigerate and use for sauce on chocolate and other ice creams.

A Wedding Cake Good to Eat

A gorgeous, tall wedding cake . . . a table aglow with silver . . . a room full of friends extending warm wishes . . . the reception is off to a good start. The cake is the important food for this festive occasion. And no other cake in the bride's life will ever mean so much to her. She wants it lovely to look at and delicious to taste. Too many wedding cakes, even though beautiful, are dry and tasteless.

To develop a recipe for a wedding cake that is handsome and delicious was the ambition of the home economists in our Test Kitchens. They wanted to perfect a recipe that is easy to follow and does not require the purchase of special pans for baking. Our Flower Wedding Cake is the result.

Along with the cake recipe, you will find two fillings (take your choice), and Fluffy White Frosting to cover the filled cake. Included are directions for assembling the cake in three tiers and for coating artificial flowers, the kind you buy at dime stores, by dipping them in a special frosting. The flowers provide the final touch of glory, the decoration.

You need no good luck charm to bake and decorate the cake sucessfully. Just follow the recipes and directions carefully and you'll find your production will rival the creations of the best and most expensive caterers. Here are suggestions on how to organize the work.
• Dip the flowers in the sugar glaze (Dipping Frosting) a week before you bake the cake. Spread them in a box lined with waxed paper and store in a dry place.
• Bake the cake and cool. Wrap at once in waxed paper to prevent drying.
• Build the cake with your choice of fillings and spread with Sealing Frosting to keep down the crumbs. You can do this the day before the wedding. Or you can freeze the filled and sealed cake a week before frosting it.
• Decide on the placement of the flowers. Then add the Fluffy White Frosting and the flowers on the wedding day.

This wedding cake is easy to cut, but here's a gracious way to do it. Lift off the top tier and save it for the bride and bridegroom. Cut the middle tier into 14 pieces; then cut the bottom tier into 36 rectangular pieces. Add them together and you'll have 50 servings.

Here are the recipes.

FLOWER WEDDING CAKE

You'll need to make two recipes of this cake to make the 3-tier beauty (see picture). Cake serves 50

3 ⅓ c. sifted cake flour
4 tsp. baking powder
1 ½ tsp. salt
7 egg whites
½ c. sugar
½ c. butter
½ c. vegetable shortening
1 ¾ c. sugar
1 egg yolk
1 ⅓ c. milk
2 tsp. vanilla
1 tsp. almond extract

• Pans are important. This cake *must* bake in shallow layers. Do not try to bake deeper cakes. Line 15½ × 10½ × 1″ jelly roll pan and 8 × 8 × 2″ baking pan with plain brown paper. (*Do not* grease and flour pans, since this makes a crust that's too heavy.)
• Sift cake flour, baking powder and salt together 3 times.
• Beat egg whites until foamy. Add ½ c. sugar gradually; continue beating only until meringue will hold *soft* peaks. Set aside.
• Cream butter and shortening together until well blended and smooth. Gradually add 1¾ c. sugar; beat until light and fluffy. Add the egg yolk and beat until well blended.
• Add extracts to milk. Add milk alternately with dry ingredients to the creamed mixture, a small amount at a time; beat after each addition until smooth.
• Add meringue and beat throughly into batter.
• Spread batter in the two pans, about

½″ deep in each pan. Spread batter out to corners, leaving a slight depression in center. Tap pans sharply on counter top several times to remove large air bubbles.
• Bake in moderate oven (350°) 25 to 30 minutes.
• Cool on racks 10 minutes. Remove from pans and finish cooling on racks. To keep from drying, wrap as soon as cool.

ALMOND CREAM FILLING AND SEALING FROSTING

Take your pick of this or the fruity Orange-Raisin Filling—both luscious

4 egg yolks, slightly beaten
1 ⅓ c. evaporated milk
1 ⅓ c. sugar
½ c. butter or margarine
2 tsp. vanilla

• Blend yolks and milk in saucepan; stir in sugar and butter. Cook over medium heat, stirring constantly, until thick and bubbling. Add vanilla.
• Remove 1½ c. of above cooked mixture and add to it 2 c. of finely chopped, toasted almonds. Cool; stir occasionally until of spreading consistency.

Sealing Frosting: Cool remainder of filling. Add 1½ to 2 c. sifted confectioners sugar and beat until of thin spreading consistency.

Use your camera to make a gift any bride would treasure. When invited to a shower, take camera and flashbulbs; snap candid pictures of the bride-to-be, the gifts and the serving table. Mount the pictures in a white or pastel-colored album.

ORANGE-RAISIN FILLING

Golden raisins and orange candy teamed deliciously with almonds

½ c. sugar
2 tblsp. flour
2 c. golden raisins, ground
1 c. water
1 c. finely cut orange gumdrops
1 c. finely chopped toasted almonds

• Combine sugar and flour. Add to raisins in saucepan. Add water and stir to dissolve. Cook, stirring constantly, until thick.
• Add gumdrops and cook 3 minutes.
• Add almonds and cool thoroughly before using.

Sealing Frosting: Blend 2 slightly beaten egg yolks with ⅔ c. evaporated milk in saucepan. Stir in ⅔ c. sugar and ¼ c. butter or margarine. Cook over medium heat, stirring constantly, until thick and bubbling.
• Remove from heat; add 1 tsp. vanilla and cool.
• Stir in 1½ to 2 c. sifted confectioners sugar and beat to thin spreading consistency.

Bottom Tier: Trim crusts from the two 15½ × 10½ × 1" cakes to make smooth straight sides.
• Cut 9½" square and 4" square from each cake. Reserve the 4" squares for top tier. (You'll have some scraps.)
• Cut 9½" square of cardboard and cover with foil. Place 9½" square of cake on cardboard. Spread desired filling evenly over cake top. Place other 9½" cake square on filling and press firmly.
• Spread thin layer of Sealing Frosting

over sides and top of this tier. Pull spatula over surface to make smooth straight sides.

Middle Tier: Trim crusts from the two 8 × 8 × 2" cakes to make 6½" squares.
• Cut 6½" square of cardboard and cover with foil. Place 6½" square of cake on cardboard. Spread with desired filling. Top with other 6½" square of cake. Center 6½" tier on bottom tier. Cover top and sides with Sealing Frosting.

Top Tier: Repeat procedure (using cardboard and foil) for two 4" squares. Center this tier on middle tier. Seal top and sides with frosting.

FLUFFY WHITE FROSTING

Looks like a white satin cloud

2 egg whites
1 ½ c. sugar
⅓ c. water
¼ tsp. cream of tartar
1 tsp. vanilla

• Combine all ingredients, except vanilla, in top of double boiler. Beat 1 minute on high speed with electric mixer.
• Place over boiling water. Cook 7 minutes, beating all the time on high speed with electric mixer.
• Remove from hot water. Turn frosting into bowl. Add vanilla; beat until of spreading consistency.

TO DECORATE CAKE

• Let Sealing Frosting set before you apply Fluffy White Frosting.
• Decide on placement of flowers before you apply final frosting.

• Apply Fluffy White Frosting, starting with sides of bottom tier. Hold spatula perpendicular to tray and pull along carefully to make smooth sides and square corners. Apply to ledge of tier, building a ridge along outer edge (see color picture). Repeat for each tier.
• When frosting just begins to set, arrange flower design.

TO MAKE DECORATIONS

• Select plastic flowers in pastel colors such as yellow or pink. For an orderly and attractive design, use no more than three varieties of flowers. Flowers that have definite form and petals that outline sharply show off best when dipped.
• Wash plastic flowers in warm suds and rinse in clear water; dry. Cut individual flowers from stalk with a wire cutter, leaving a stem to hold when you dip it.
• Dip plastic flowers in Dipping Frosting (recipe follows). Twirl in hand to distribute frosting evenly. Hold in hand a few minutes until frosting begins to set. Place on rack to dry. For thicker coating, you will probably want to dip again after first coating dries. When final coating is dry, snip off remaining stems.
• Work out your desired arrangement for flowers before applying Fluffy White Frosting. Then when this final frosting is applied and just beginning to set, place flowers in desired spots.

DIPPING FROSTING

2 c. sugar
1 c. water
⅛ tsp. cream of tartar

1 to 1½ c. sifted
   confectioners sugar

• Combine 2 c. sugar, water and cream of tartar in saucepan. Cook to a thin syrup (226°). Remove from heat and cool to lukewarm (112°).
• Add confectioners sugar gradually, stirring until smooth. Mixture should be of pouring consistency.
• Place over warm water to keep frosting at right consistency for dipping. If too hot, plastic flowers will soften.
• A little experimenting will determine the best consistency for coating. If you don't like appearance of flowers on first dipping, wash off frosting, pat dry with dish towel and redip.

Sleight-of-Hand with Pie

Frequently the food committee for a church or other community supper has leftover cherry and apple pies. You can sell them to guests if you tell them how to serve the pies next day so that they'll taste fresh baked:

Mix 1 c. brown sugar and 2 tblsp. melted butter. Spread mixture evenly over top of a day-old cherry, apple or other 2-crust fruit pie in pie pan. Set in another pie pan—the double pan keeps the bottom crust from browning too much. Bake in hot oven (425°) until topping melts and browns.

You can depend on compliments when you serve this pie. Many guests are so impressed with it that they ask for the recipe, never dreaming the pie was once a leftover. But don't try this with fresh-baked pie. You'll be disappointed if you do.

Apple Pie, Best Seller

Southern Apple Cream Pie quickly moves to the list of best sellers on any restaurant menu—and stays there. That's the report of a woman who has served it in several exclusive public eating places. Many of her friends have begged her for the recipe, which she always has had to refuse. This makes FARM JOURNAL especially proud to present it in this cookbook.

Do make it both with buttermilk and dairy sour cream to find out which is your choice. The difference in flavor is slight, yet noticeable to taste-testers.

SOUTHERN APPLE CREAM PIES

Luscious open-face apple pies—be sure to chop peeled apples very fine

```
2    unbaked 9" pie shells
1    qt. finely chopped peeled
     apples (or drained canned)
1½   c. sugar
4    tblsp. flour
2    c. buttermilk, or dairy sour
     cream
2    eggs, beaten
1    tsp. vanilla
```

Topping:

```
1    c. sugar
2    tsp. ground cinnamon
4    oz. butter (1 stick)
⅜    c. flour (6 tblsp.)
```

• Chop apples fine; add sugar and flour and mix thoroughly. Add buttermilk or sour cream and beaten eggs. Stir in vanilla.

• Place in pie shells. Bake in hot oven (400°) 30 minutes. Remove from oven and sprinkle topping over pies (topping will heap up on pies). Bake 10 minutes longer. Makes 2 pies.

• To make topping: Cream together sugar, cinnamon, butter and flour until mixture is crumbly. Sprinkle all of this mixture on pies (it will be heaped).

Note: To make 4 pies, double the recipe.

Caramel Whipped Cream: *To surprise your guests, sweeten whipped cream for desserts with brown instead of white sugar. Especially good on apple and other fruit pies, pumpkin pie and apple crisp. Put ⅔ c. brown sugar, firmly packed, 1 c. heavy cream and ½ tsp. vanilla into bowl; chill 1 hour or longer. Then beat until mixture holds its shape, but use care not to overbeat. You can add ¼ tsp. nutmeg or ½ tsp. cinnamon for a spicy taste. Makes about 2 cups.*

New Trick with Old Favorite Chocolate Pie

Originally black walnuts flavored this superb country pie. Now that these nuts of high quality are not widely available, pecans can substitute for them in the Frosty Fudge Pie. Black walnut flavoring and vanilla team together to maintain the taste. This is a good example of the wonders of recipe development in Test Kitchens across country.

FROSTY FUDGE PIE

A good-looking chocolate pie with frosted top—popular wherever served. Flavor is best if made a day ahead. Pie is rich, sweet and inviting

Number of Pies	3	6	12
Unbaked 10″ pie shells	3	6	12
Chocolate squares	8 oz.	1 lb.	2 lbs.
Medium brown sugar	11 oz.	1 lb. 6 oz.	2 lbs. 12 oz
Margarine, room temperature	½ lb.	1 lb.	2 lbs.
White sugar	1 lb. 6¾ oz.	2 lbs. 13½ oz.	5 lbs. 11 oz.
Eggs	12	24	48
Salt	1 tsp.	2 tsp.	4 tsp.
Milk	2 c.	1 qt.	2 qts.
Light corn syrup	1 c.	2 c.	1 qt.
Vanilla	2 tsp.	4 tsp.	2 tblsp. plus 2 tsp.
Black walnut extract	2 tsp.	4 tsp.	2 tblsp. plus 2 tsp.
Pecans, broken in pieces	1 c.	2 c.	1 qt.
Confectioners sugar frosting			

• Melt chocolate in double boiler, stir in margarine until melted, add brown sugar and white sugar; stir until all ingredients are blended. Remove from heat and cool.

• When chocolate mixture is cool, add eggs, one at a time, beating after each addition. Add salt, milk and corn syrup. Combine vanilla and black walnut extract and add to chocolate filling; stir to blend well.

• Scatter nuts evenly in bottom of pie shells. Add pie filling.

• Bake in slow oven (325°) 1 hour and 15 minutes or until knife inserted 1 inch from edge comes out clean. Do not be disturbed if top crust cracks. Cool. Spread with thin layer of your favorite white confectioners sugar frosting to give top of pie a frosty look. To serve, cut each pie in 8 wedges. Garnish, if you like, by placing a bouquet or fluff of whipped cream on the upper right side of the pie (more attractive than if placed on center of pie wedge).

VARIATION

Frosty Fudge Walnut Pie: Substitute black walnuts for the pecans.

CORN FLAKE PIE CRUST

Match the delicacy of chiffon pie filling by using this unbaked crust

3 c. crushed corn flakes
6 tblsp. confectioners sugar
1 c. melted butter

• Combine corn flakes and sugar. Add melted butter; gently blend.
• Press into 2 (9") pie pans, saving out a little of the mixture to sprinkle over top of the chiffon pie. (This mixture is very moist.) Refrigerate until time to add pie filling.

APPLE TURNOVERS

Handy to keep in your freezer to bake and frost when company comes

1 lb. butter
4 c. flour
1 lb. creamed cottage cheese
     (2 c.)
2 tsp. sugar
3 tblsp. lemon juice
8 c. finely chopped peeled
     apples
1 ½ tsp. ground nutmeg
1 ½ tsp. ground cinnamon
6 tblsp. sugar

• Cream butter with flour. Add cottage cheese and 2 tsp. sugar. Beat until mixture is smooth. Wrap in waxed paper and chill overnight.
• Next morning, roll dough very thin and cut in 5" squares. (Divide flour mixture in fourths and roll and cut each fourth, keeping unrolled mixture in refrigerator.)
• Sprinkle lemon juice on apples (peeled and *chopped very fine*). Add spices and sugar.
• Put apple mixture on half of each pastry square and fold over to make triangles. Seal edges with tines of fork. Freeze on trays, then wrap and return to freezer. The recommended storage time is two to three months.
• To serve, take the desired number of turnovers from freezer and bake on a lightly greased baking sheet in hot oven (400°) about 18 minutes, or until turnovers puff up and brown. Watch that edges do not get too brown. While hot, frost with confectioners sugar frosting (1 tblsp. soft butter and 2 tblsp. cream to 1 c. confectioners sugar). It takes about 4 c. confectioners sugar to frost all the turnovers, but you may not bake all of them the same day. Makes about 34 turnovers, depending on how thin you roll the pastry.

Note: You can bake turnovers without freezing. Bake in hot oven (400°) about 15 minutes, or until turnovers puff up and brown.

Start a Betty Jar

Ever hear of a Betty Jar? That's what the manager of many successful tearooms calls the covered container in which she places remnants of leftover pies, cake, homemade rolls and coffee cakes. Stored in the refrigerator a few days, or in the freezer for a longer time, it provides tasty crumbs for baking a brown betty. Here's a recipe for Fruit Betty, which shows what can be done (also see recipe for Date-Nut Torte in this chapter). The dessert tastes wonderful, sells well.

FRUIT BETTY

Sweet, rich and delicious version of your old friend, Brown Betty dessert

Number of Servings	32	40	64
Leftover fruit pies and crusts, finely cut	3 qts.	4 qts.	6 qts.
Brown sugar	¾ qt.	1 qt.	1½ qts.
Lemons, juice and grated peel	1	1⅓	2
Butter	½ c.	⅔ c.	1 c.
Hot water, or syrup drained from canned fruit	½ c.	⅔ c.	1 c.

• Chop leftover fruit pies, both filling and crust, very fine. Use crumbs from cake or homemade rolls if you do not have enough pie. Mix with sugar, lemon juice and grated peel. Put mixture into pans or casseroles greased with shortening.

• Add butter to hot water (if you have syrup drained from fruit, heat and use it instead of the water); pour over pie mixture in pans. Cover; set in pans of hot water and bake in moderate oven (350°) 1½ to 2 hours.

• Spoon warm dessert into serving dishes, top side up (this makes a more attractive dessert); serve with Zippy Lemon Sauce or other tart sauce.

Note: If you have cherry pie, save some of the cherries in the filling to scatter over top of dessert before baking. Their bright color gives the pudding eye appeal.

ZIPPY LEMON SAUCE

Vinegar joins with lemon to give this sauce an intriguing tart taste or zip

Number of Servings	8 (3 c.)	24 (1½ qts.)	48 (3 qts.)
Sugar	2 c.	1 qt.	2 qts.
Flour	2 tblsp.	4 tblsp.	½ c.
Boiling water	2 c.	1 qt.	2 qts.
Cider vinegar	¼ c.	½ c.	1 c.
Grated lemon peel	1 tblsp.	2 tblsp.	4 tblsp.
Lemon juice	1 tblsp.	2 tblsp.	4 tblsp.
Egg yolks	2	4	8
Margarine	½ c.	1 c.	2 c.

• Combine sugar and flour; blend thoroughly. Add to boiling water, stirring constantly. Cook until mixture thickens. Add vinegar.

• Add lemon peel and juice to egg yolks; beat together. Stir into hot mixture. Remove from heat. Add margarine and serve warm over Fruit Betty and other pudding desserts.

PURPLE PLUM COBBLER

Old-fashioned country dessert that's kind both to the budget and guests

For 24 Servings:

1   qt. sugar
½   c. butter or margarine
2   c. milk
3   c. sifted flour
4   tsp. baking powder
½   tsp. salt
1   qt. drained canned purple plums
1   qt. plum juice and water
2   tblsp. butter, melted
2   lemons, juice and peel

For 48 Servings:

2   qts. sugar
1   c. butter or margarine
1   qt. milk
1½   qts. sifted flour
2   tblsp. plus 2 tsp. baking powder
1   tsp. salt
2   qts. drained canned purple plums
2   qts. plum juice and water
4   tblsp. butter, melted
4   lemons, juice and peel

• Cream half the sugar with butter. Stir in milk and add flour sifted with baking powder and salt. Grease a 14 × 9 × 2½″ pan for 24 servings, 2 pans of the same size for 48 servings. Add the batter and spread in pan or pans.
• Top batter with plums, pitted and cut up.
• Add enough boiling water to juice drained from plums to make 1 qt. for 24 servings, 2 qts. for 48 servings. Stir in last half of sugar; stir until dissolved. Add melted butter, lemon juice and peel. Stir to mix.

Pour over fruit and batter in pan(s).
• Bake in moderate oven (375°) 40 to 45 minutes. Serve warm or slightly cooled.

Note: Top with scoops of vanilla ice cream for an extra-good treat.

CHEESE APPLE CRISP

A pan dessert that has an attractive yellow and brown top. Serve it warm

For 20 servings:

3¼   qts. apples, peeled and thinly sliced
1½   tsp. cinnamon
3½   c. sugar
¾   c. water
1½   tblsp. lemon juice
2   c. sifted flour
¾   tsp. salt
½   lb. butter
12   oz. grated cheese, aged Cheddar or process American

For 40 Servings:

6½   qts. apples, peeled and thinly sliced
1   tblsp. cinnamon
7   c. sugar
1½   c. water
3   tblsp. lemon juice
1   qt. sifted flour
1½   tsp. salt
1   lb. butter
1½   lbs. grated cheese, aged Cheddar or process American

• Arrange thinly sliced apples in shallow *greased* baking pans. Sprinkle with cinnamon mixed with a little sugar so it will be smooth. Add water and lemon juice.
• Combine remaining sugar, flour and

salt; work into butter to form a crumbly mixture. Lightly stir in grated cheese (do not use brick cheese). Spread mixture over the apples.
• Bake in moderate oven (350°)

30 to 35 minutes, or until apples are tender and top is brown and crisp. Cut in squares to serve. If dessert is served hot, it is quite moist; it thickens as it cools.

DATE-NUT TORTE

A prize-winning dessert when topped with Lemon Foamy Sauce. Serve at room temperature. You can bake it 2 or 3 days ahead

Number of Servings	8	16	32
Egg whites	½ c.	1 c.	2 c.
Water	1½ tsp.	1 tblsp.	2 tblsp.
Sugar	⅝ c. (10 tblsp.)	1¼ c.	2½ c.
Cake crumbs	1 c.	2 c.	4 c.
Baking powder	¼ tblsp.	½ tblsp.	1 tblsp.
Chopped walnuts or pecans	½ c.	1 c.	2 c.
Chopped dates	1 c.	2 c.	4 c.
Lemon Foamy Sauce			

• Combine egg whites and water; whip until stiff. Add sugar.
• Combine cake crumbs with baking powder. Mix in nuts and dates. Fold into egg white mixture.
• Place in greased 9″ square pan, 1 pan for 8 servings, 2 pans for 16 servings and 4 pans for 32 servings, and bake in slow oven (325°) 25 to 30 minutes. Remove from oven and set on rack to cool quickly. The torte will continue to bake if not cooled quickly. Overcooking makes it dry. To serve, cut in squares and top with Lemon Foamy Sauce. Or omit sauce and sprinkle torte with confectioners sugar. Or serve topped with whipped cream.

LEMON FOAMY SAUCE

Pale yellow, fluffy sauce that tastes so good. It complements desserts

1 c. water
¼ c. lemon juice
Grated peel of 1 lemon
2 tblsp. cornstarch
½ c. cold water
2 egg yolks
1 c. sugar
2 egg whites, beaten
1 c. heavy cream, whipped

• Combine 1 c. water, lemon juice and grated peel. Heat.
• Meanwhile stir cornstarch with ½ c. cold water until smooth.
• Beat together egg yolks and ¾ c. sugar until light. Add to cornstarch mixture. Stir in a little of the hot lemon juice. Then stir yolk mixture into the remainder of the hot lemon juice.
Cook, stirring, until mixture thickens. Cool slightly. Fold remaining ¼

c. sugar into beaten egg whites, and fold into lemon mixture. Cool.

• Just before serving over puddings, cake or other desserts, fold in whipped cream. Makes 16 servings.

Note: The color of the sauce depends on how yellow the egg yolks are. If more color is needed, add a little yellow food color to the sauce before folding in whipped cream.

How to Add Food Color: Insert a toothpick in bottle of food color. Dot food mixture with pick in zigzag lines. Then fold in color. Repeat until you get the desired depth of color.

Honey Cup Custard— Delicate Flavor

Custard is an old-fashioned country dessert that's just as popular today as when our grandmothers served it to guests. This particular custard contains a special ingredient, honey, but it still has grated nutmeg splashed over its top. If you have a nutmeg grater, use it on the whole spice for a fresh flavor touch. The ground spice, of course, is satisfactory and quicker.

The recipe for Honey Cup Custard originated in the Midwest, which explains why it calls for clover honey, the top favorite in our heartlands. You need not use clover honey if you prefer other nectar tastes. If you live in areas adjacent to the Tennessee and North Carolina mountains, sourwood honey may be your choice, or if in California, you may choose orange blossom honey.

It's interesting to try several kinds of honey in your kitchen to find out which ones your family and friends like best. One general rule—the lighter the color of honey, the milder its flavor is likely to be.

HONEY CUP CUSTARD

Serve this velvety custard in baking cups on colorful china or pottery plates with fancy paper doily liners

For 18 Servings:
8 eggs, *slightly* beaten
1 c. honey (clover)
2 qts. milk
Nutmeg (for garnish)

For 27 Servings:
12 eggs, *slightly* beaten
1 ½ c. honey (clover)
3 qts. milk
Nutmeg (for garnish)

• Combine eggs, honey and milk; pour into 5 oz. custard cups. Grate a little nutmeg (or sprinkle ground nutmeg) on top of each custard. Set in pan of warm water that reaches almost to the top of cups (covers about ⅞ of cup).

• Bake in slow oven (350°) 45 to 60 minutes, or until a metal knife inserted in custard comes out clean.

Note: Remember that the water bath around custard evaporates during the cooking. Replenish it if necessary to keep the water level high. Add only hot water. Take out of water immediately after removing from oven or the custards will continue to cook.

Cover fruitcakes with brown paper or foil during the last hour of baking to keep tops from getting hard and dry.

REFRIGERATOR PLUM PUDDING

Keep batter for this wonderful plum pudding on hand during holidays for quick use. Puddings are extra-good

2 c. chopped dates
3 c. raisins
2 c. currants
2½ c. mixed candied fruits (for fruit cakes)
2 c. candied cherries
4 candied pineapple slices, cut in small pieces (1½ c.)
½ c. candied grapefruit peel, cut in small pieces
⅔ c. candied orange peel
3 c. chopped suet
9 c. flour
2 tsp. cinnamon
6 tsp. baking soda
3 c. sugar
3 c. molasses
6 eggs, beaten
Apple juice or cider (about 1½ c.)
Chopped nuts

• Put all chopped fruit, peels and suet in a large bowl. Sift together flour, cinnamon and baking soda. Add 1 c. flour mixture to fruit and stir to distribute flour and separate pieces of fruit.
• Add remaining ingredients, except nuts, to fruit mixture and stir to mix well.
• Put in covered container and store in refrigerator, or put in freezer. (If you freeze batter, divide and store in meal-size portions.) Makes 5 quarts.
• To use, butter custard cups; cover bottoms of cups with broken nuts. Add 1 heaping tablespoon of the batter. Steam 30 minutes; then place in moderate oven (350°) a few minutes

to dry tops. Invert puddings to serve. Serve warm with hard sauce or your favorite pudding sauce. Makes about 100 puddings.

Luscious and Lovely Charlottes

Charlottes are delightful dessert choices. We give you two splendid examples, Peanut Brittle and Fruit and Nut Charlottes. The success of these desserts rests on two things— folding, instead of stirring, the peanut brittle, fruit and nuts and other ingredients into the whipped cream and transferring the charlotte to the stemmed glasses for serving with two spoons. Dip the dessert with one spoon and push it off this spoon into the glass with the second spoon. You get a serving that stands high, proud and inviting.

PEANUT BRITTLE CHARLOTTE

Grate orange over marshmallows so oil from peel will fall into bowl and add its full flavor to this dessert

1½ lbs. marshmallows, cut in small pieces
1½ c. orange juice
1 tblsp. grated orange peel
1½ lbs. peanut brittle, crushed in plastic bag with rolling pin, or put through food chopper
⅜ c. confectioners sugar (½ c. minus 2 tblsp.)
1 tblsp. vanilla
5½ c. heavy cream, whipped

• Place marshmallows in bowl and

pour on orange juice. Grate orange peel over marshmallows (grated peel of 1 orange makes 1 tblsp.). Let stand 30 minutes in refrigerator. At serving time save out a little peanut brittle for garnishing and *fold* re-maining peanut brittle, confectioners sugar and vanilla into whipped cream. Then *fold* in marshmallows. Serve heaped in stemmed dessert glasses. Sprinkle with crushed peanut brittle. Makes 32 servings.

FRUIT AND NUT CHARLOTTE

Always a favorite and easy to make—whether for family or a crowd

Number of Servings	12	24	50
Marshmallows, cut in small pieces	4 oz.	8 oz.	1 lb.
Canned pitted, dark sweet cherries, drained and cut in fourths	1¾ c.	3¼ c.	6½ c.
Canned pineapple tidbits, drained	1 c.	2 c.	4 c.
Orange juice	¼ c.	½ c.	1 c.
Grated orange peel	2 tsp.	4 tsp.	2 tblsp. plus 2 tsp.
Finely chopped toasted pecans	1 oz.	2 oz.	¼ lb.
Dates, chopped (optional)	2 oz.	4 oz.	½ lb.
Heavy cream, whipped	1 pt.	1 qt.	2 qts.

· To marshmallows add cherries, cut in fourths with scissors, pineapple, orange juice and orange peel. Stir to mix. Let stand in refrigerator 30 minutes or longer.

· When ready to serve, fold in pecans and dates. Fold ¼ c. this mixture at a time into the whipped cream (adding more at a time will "loosen" or break down cream). Scoop with spoons into stemmed dessert glasses.

To Toast Pecans: Melt enough butter in shallow pan to cover bottom. Spread nuts, before chopping, in a single layer in pan. Place in slow oven (300°), stirring occasionally, until nuts are a light golden brown, 10 to 15 minutes. Salt very lightly and turn at once into a cold pan so cooking will not continue. Cool thoroughly. Chop fine and sprinkle on top of Fruit and Nut Charlotte.

Russian Cream Luncheon Special

This is an appropriate luncheon dessert. It's rich and colorful—looks like a party. But, it does not hold from one day to the next. Make it early in the morning and refrigerate to serve at midday.

The amount of cranberry sauce or frozen raspberries or strawberries you'll need to dress it up depends on how much you wish to pamper your guests. You can get by with as little as one or two tablespoons for a serving, but a more generous topping will please.

RUSSIAN CREAM

Crimson and creamy white beauty

3 ½ c. heavy sweet cream
2 c. plus 2 tblsp. sugar
3 tblsp. unflavored gelatin
1 ½ c. cold water
3 ½ c. soured heavy sweet cream
1 tblsp. plus ½ tsp. vanilla
Cranberry sauce

• Heat 3½ c. heavy sweet cream with sugar until lukewarm.
• Meanwhile, combine gelatin and cold water. When gelatin is softened, add to warm cream-sugar mixture. Stir until gelatin and sugar are dissolved; then remove from heat.
• Chill until mixture starts to thicken. Then add soured cream, whipped until fluffy. (To sour cream, pour 4 tblsp. lemon juice into a 1-qt. container. Add 3¼ c. heavy cream. Let stand a few minutes before whipping.) Beat entire mixture to blend; add vanilla and pour into 2 (9") square pans. Chill until firm. Cut in squares to serve and top with spoonfuls of cranberry sauce or partly defrosted frozen red raspberries or strawberries. Makes 18 servings.

VARIATION

Summer Raspberry Sauce: Substitute this sauce for frozen raspberries or strawberries or cranberry sauce. To make it: Combine 2 tblsp. cornstarch with 2 tblsp. cold water; stir to make a smooth paste. Melt ½ c. butter in saucepan; stir in 2 c. sugar, 2 c. fresh raspberries, crushed, and cornstarch mixture. Bring to a boil, stirring constantly. Boil 1 minute. Remove from heat and stir in 2 tsp. lemon juice. Cool. Makes 2½ cups.

HOLIDAY FRUIT COMPOTE

Eye-catching but easy-to-fix dessert for buffet meal. Serve in frosty bowl

1 (1 lb. 4 oz.) can pineapple slices
2 (1 lb. 4½ oz.) cans pineapple chunks
3 (10 oz.) pkgs. frozen peach slices
4 c. frozen Bing cherries
5 bananas, sliced slantwise
4 c. frozen strawberries
2 (11 oz.) cans mandarin oranges
1 c. shredded coconut

• Partially thaw frozen fruit; drain all fruit. Treat bananas with ascorbic acid (or sprinkle with lemon juice) to prevent darkening.
• Layer fruit in large glass bowl, beginning with pineapple slices and ending with coconut. Chill 3 or 4 hours before serving. (For a frosty appearance, place bowl in freezer 30 minutes before serving.) Makes about 30 servings.

Note: This is a light dessert, often desirable after a heavy meal. Serve with Christmas cookies if you like.

So Easy to Fix— Pretty Punch

"After I once served Orange Ginger Punch at a party," reflects a food consultant to a business concern, "it never left the top of my list of party fruit drinks." The recipe is so simple that the results are almost unbelievably rewarding, both in looks and flavor.

It's important always to chill the punch bowl itself in advance. Since space in refrigerators is seldom adequate for a big punch bowl, it's a good idea to fill the bowl with cracked ice. Remove it just before you pour in the punch.

When you add the bottles of chilled ginger ale to this special punch, hold them high above the bowl, pouring in a steady stream on the sherbet. The force of the liquid sloughs off the frozen sherbet to give the drink an interesting appearance.

Fruit and flower decorations on the punch bowl entrance guests. This punch, which is orange in color, is perfect for autumn parties. Fasten tiny clusters of little purple asters and green grapes (use small grapes and only a few in a cluster) here and there on the outside of the punch bowl with transparent tape. Then you omit garnishes in the bowl. If fresh flowers are unavailable, artificial may be used, but be sure they're tiny ones.

For the Christmas season, use cranberry sherbet instead of orange and decorate the outside of the bowl with sprigs of holly and mistletoe.

ORANGE GINGER PUNCH

Refreshing easy-to-fix party punch

3 qts. orange ice (or sherbet)
5 qts. chilled ginger ale

• Place large chunks of orange ice in chilled punch bowl.
• Pour ginger ale over, holding the bottles some little distance above the bunch bowl. Garnish with fresh mint leaves and maraschino cherries, if desired, or with seedless green grapes

when in season. Makes 55 punch cups or servings.

Note: Use different kinds of sherbet instead of the orange if you prefer a different color and flavor.

SWEDISH COFFEE

Superb coffee for a crowd—you can make it in a big kettle and pour from pitchers or regular coffee makers

2 eggs
2½ lbs. regular grind coffee
2 c. cold water
18 qts. cold water

• Mix eggs and broken shells with coffee. Add 2 c. water. Divide in two equal parts; place each part in a cheesecloth bag and tie securely. Leave room for the coffee to swell.
• Measure 9 qts. water into each of two large coffeepots or kettles. Immerse a cheesecloth bag of coffee in water in each container. Bring to a boil. Stir and then remove from heat.
• Leave bags in pots at least 3 to 4 minutes, up to 10 minutes if you like a beverage of greater strength. Makes about 96 (6 oz.) cups.

Note: Usually about half the guests (48) like sugar and cream in coffee; you will need 3 c. cream and 50 cubes of sugar.

HOT TEA FOR 30 TO 35

You have to alter your regular system of tea making when you wish to make a larger quantity than your pot will hold. First, you make a Tea Concentrate, then you add hot water:
• Bring 6 c. (1½ qts.) freshly drawn cold water to a full boil; remove from heat and add ¼ lb. loose tea. Stir to

distribute and immerse leaves; cover.
· Let steep 5 minutes exactly. Strain
into a warmed teapot or pitcher. You
will have about 1 quart Tea Concentrate.
· To serve, have ready a pot of very
hot water. Add about ¼ c. Tea Concentrate to each teacup and fill with
hot water. (Or put the same proportions in a teapot.)

HOT TEA FOR 200

· Make the Tea Concentrate as for
Tea for 30 to 35, but use 1 lb. loose
tea and 1½ gallons freshly boiling
water. Steep 10 minutes instead of
5 minutes.

While you can use either loose tea
or tea bags, most women believe it is
economical and less messy to use
loose tea for making the brew for a
crowd.

Instant teas also are available. Follow package directions when using
them. Some of these quick teas are
the dried extract of freshly brewed
tea, while others contain equal parts
of the dried extract and carbohydrates, which protect the flavors. Read
the label.

Additions to Hot Tea in Brewing:
Add a little grated orange peel to the
pot when steeping tea. Or add a rose
geranium leaf, a few whole cloves or
sprigs of fresh mint.

What to Serve with Hot Tea: Lump
sugar, thin lemon slices and a pitcher
of light cream or milk are the
traditional accompaniments. (Some
tea experts, especially the English, say
that milk does not mask the tea taste
the way cream does.) Some people
like the flavor of whole cloves stuck
in the lemon slices.

Among other excellent accompaniments to hot tea are a small pitcher
of orange juice or pineapple juice to
add to the poured tea; sugar-dusted
fresh mint leaves; clove-studded thin
lime or orange slices; and stick cinnamon to use for stirrers.

ICED TEA FOR 200

· Make the Tea Concentrate as for
Hot Tea for 200. Add 1 c. of Concentrate to every 6 c. cold water.

Note: Sometimes iced tea has a cloudy
look. Cloudiness does not affect the
taste, but you can restore the clarity
by stirring a little boiling water into
the tea just before pouring it into the
glasses. Cloudiness usually develops if
you chill hot tea in the refrigerator.

Big Yuletide Dinner

Hospitality and the Christmas spirit
go together. Neighborliness reaches
new highs in the country during the
holidays, and big dinners give family
and friends an opportunity to get together and visit. Many farm women
work together to prepare and serve
these meals, either for a crowd at
home or for community gatherings.
To help you meet the problems involved, our Test Kitchens developed
a menu and recipes for such occasions. See the menu for "Feast for
Fifty or for the Family" in the menu
chapter (see Index). Turkey Stacks
are the main dish, a surprisingly different one. You can keep them warm
in electric servers if you wish. No last-minute carving.

Days ahead of the holiday meal, you bone the turkey, slice and freeze it. Then all you'll have to do the day of the dinner is put a ham filling between two slices and bake. Here's the recipe that makes either 12 or 50 servings.

TURKEY STACKS

The ham filling is excellent, but you can use your favorite bread stuffing

For 50 Servings:
    5   (12 lb.) turkeys
 7½   lbs. ground smoked ham
 3¾   c. fresh bread crumbs
    5   eggs
 2½   c. milk
 1¼   tsp. salt
    ¾   tsp. pepper
    ¾   tsp. ground cloves
    ¾   tsp. ground allspice
 2½   lbs. butter or margarine

For 12 Servings:
    1   (12 lb.) turkey
 1½   lbs. ground smoked ham
    ¾   c. fresh bread crumbs
    1   egg
    ½   c. milk
    ¼   tsp. salt
    ⅛   tsp. pepper
    ⅛   tsp. ground cloves
    ⅛   tsp. ground allspice
    ½   lb. butter or margarine

• Cut up raw turkey, leaving breast whole and thighs attached to legs. Freeze necks, wings, backs and giblets for future meals.
• Strip meat from bones on breast, thighs and legs. Slice breast meat into 3½ × 5″ pieces about ¼″ thick. (Part of meat peels off in narrow filets; for larger pieces, slit sideways almost through and pull flat to butter-fly.) Cut meat from each leg and each thigh in two pieces; pound flat; sprinkle with meat tenderizer; let stand as directed on bottle. Wrap; freeze slices.

Day of the Dinner:
• Mix rest of ingredients except butter.
• Thaw turkey slices; sprinkle with salt and pepper to taste.
• Melt butter about ⅜″ deep in large shallow baking pans in moderate oven (375°); remove pans from oven.
• To make stacks, place slices of turkey in one layer in pan. Top each slice with ¼ c. ham mixture, then with another turkey slice; brush with butter in pan. (Make some stacks all white meat, some all dark and some mixed.)
• Bake in moderate oven (375°), covered 30 minutes, uncovered about 1 hour, until tender and browned (if meat curls, slit edges with scissors). Spoon liquid in pan over stacks often (pour off and reserve some liquid if more than ¼″ deep). Remove meat to warm place, and make gravy.

Note: If turkey has been frozen previously, do not refreeze raw slices or parts; follow directions for preparing raw slices one or two days prior to serving day; refrigerate. Cook remaining parts, then freeze.

GRAVY

Rich cream gravy adds crowning touch to Turkey Stacks

For a Crowd: Pour off drippings from all pans to make 2 c.; return to one baking pan; add 2 c. flour, blend and simmer until browned. Add 2 qts. hot chicken bouillon; cook, stirring constantly with wire whisk, until gravy thickens. Add 2 qts. heated milk. Add salt, pepper and paprika to taste. Cook, stirring constantly, until thickened. Spoon over Turkey Stacks. Makes 50 servings.

For Family: Follow above directions, except use ½ c. drippings, ½ c. flour, 2 c. hot chicken bouillon and 2 c. heated milk. Makes about 3¼ cups.

SCALLOPED ONIONS

Red and green pimiento bits and parsley spark this Yuletide vegetable dish —start it day before holiday feast

For 50 Servings:
20 lbs. small white onions
1   c. butter or margarine
2   c. flour
4   qts. milk
2   tblsp. salt
1   tsp. pepper
2   qts. grated sharp cheese
    (1 ¾ lbs.)
5   (4 oz.) jars pimientos,
    chopped
1 ¾ c. chopped parsley
2   c. bread crumbs
¼   c. butter

• Peel onions (day ahead of dinner); cook in salted water 15 minutes until just tender; drain. Divide equally in 2 (10 × 15") pans. Refrigerate.
• Day of dinner, melt the 1 c. butter in 6-qt. kettle, add flour; blend until smooth, then cook 5 minutes.
• Heat milk; add to flour mixture slowly, stirring. Bring just to boil and cook about 20 minutes, stirring constantly with wire whisk. Add salt and pepper.

• Stir in cheese until melted; add pimiento and parsley; mix. Pour over onions, dividing sauce equally between two pans. Mix crumbs with ¼ c. softened butter; divide in half and sprinkle as border for each pan. Brown in moderate oven (375°) 15 minutes.

For 8 Servings:
2   lbs. small white onions
¼   c. butter or margarine
¼   c. flour
2   c. milk
½   tsp. salt
¼   tsp. pepper
1   c. grated sharp cheese
¼   c. chopped pimiento
¼   c. chopped parsley
½   c. bread crumbs
1   tblsp. butter

• Place cooked onions in 1½-qt. pan.
• Make sauce as directed above, except cook flour mixture only 3 minutes and white sauce only 5 minutes. Pour over onions; sprinkle on border of crumbs mixed with 1 tblsp. butter.
• Bake in moderate oven (375°) 15 minutes.

When you entertain dinner guests, use your automatic oven timer to remind you to look at potatoes, check the roast or put on vegetables. It saves extra trips to the kitchen and eliminates clock watching.

Keep a file of company meals on small cards. Record the date, names of guests and complete menu. This way you avoid repeating meals and your guests will say, "You always have a surprise for us."

MUSTARD STAR SALAD

Delicate, fluffy mustard-egg mixture on the make-ahead salads substitutes for dressing. Salads handle easily

For 50 Servings:

16	eggs
1	qt. water
2	c. white vinegar
3	c. sugar
4	envelopes unflavored gelatin
¼	c. dry mustard
2	tsp. ground turmeric
1	tsp. salt
1	qt. heavy cream, whipped
14	(3 oz.) pkgs. lime flavor gelatin
3 ½	qts. hot water
10 ½	c. cold water
3 ½	c. diced cucumber
3 ½	c. shredded cabbage
3 ½	c. shredded carrots
3 ½	c. sliced celery

• To make the first layer: Beat eggs in top of large double boiler or pan which will fit into another pan to form hot water bath.

• Heat water and vinegar together; slowly stir into eggs and blend.

• Mix sugar and unflavored gelatin; stir in mustard, turmeric and salt. Stir into egg mixture; cook over boiling water until slightly thickened, about 20 minutes, stirring constantly. Cool; fold in whipped cream. Divide into 3 (13 × 9 × 2″) pans or 3 (1½-qt.) star molds; spread. Chill until set.

• To make the second layer: Dissolve lime gelatin in hot water; add cold water; chill until mixture mounds when dropped from a spoon. Fold in remaining ingredients. Pour on top of first layer. Chill until set; turn out on large trays.

For 8 Servings:

2	eggs
½	c. water
¼	c. white vinegar
6	tblsp. sugar
1 ½	tsp. unflavored gelatin
1 ½	tsp. dry mustard
¼	tsp. ground turmeric
⅛	tsp. salt
½	c. heavy cream, whipped
2	(3 oz.) pkgs. lime flavor gelatin
2	c. hot water
1 ½	c. cold water
½	c. diced cucumber
½	c. shredded cabbage
½	c. shredded carrots
½	c. sliced celery

• To make the first layer: Beat eggs in top of double boiler; add water and vinegar; stir in mixture of sugar, unflavored gelatin, dry mustard, turmeric and salt. Cook as above 15 minutes. Cool. Fold in the whipped cream; pour into 1½-qt. mold.

• To make the second layer: Dissolve lime gelatin in hot water; add cold water; chill until mixture mounds when dropped from a spoon. Fold in remaining ingredients. Pour on top of first layer. Chill until set; turn out on large plate or tray.

EGGNOG TARTS

Make this holiday dessert a day ahead —instant pudding eliminates cooking and foil cups cut dishwashing

For 50 Servings:

3 ½	qts. graham cracker crumbs
1 ½	c. brown sugar
3	c. butter or margarine, softened

12 (3¾ oz.) pkgs. instant
   vanilla pudding and pie
   filling
6 qts. reconstituted nonfat dry
   milk
1½ tsp. rum extract (optional)
¾ tsp. ground nutmeg

For 9 Servings:
2⅓ c. graham cracker crumbs
¼ c. brown sugar
½ c. butter or margarine,
   softened
2 (3¾ oz.) pkgs. instant
   vanilla pudding and pie
   filling
1 qt. reconstituted nonfat dry
   milk

¼ tsp. rum extract (optional)
⅛ tsp. ground nutmeg

• The day ahead of the party, mix graham cracker crumbs and sugar; cut in butter with a pastry blender.
• Place ⅓ c. mixture into each 3" foil (or glass) custard cup; mold to sides and bottom with small spatula or fingers; chill several hours.
• Add pudding slowly to milk, beating at low speed just until blended; add extract and nutmeg. Continue beating at low speed just to blend well (mixture thickens on standing). Pour ½ c. mixture into each crumb-lined foil cup. Chill overnight. To serve, top with whipped cream.

BUYING GUIDE FOR 50 SERVINGS (APPROXIMATE)

For 100 servings, multiply quantities by 2; for 25 servings, divide by 2

Bread, Butter and Sandwiches:	*Quantity*
Sliced bread	4 to 6 (about 1 lb.) loaves
Bread for sandwiches	2 (3 lb.) loaves
Crackers	1 lb.
Rolls	7 doz.
Butter for 50 squares	1 lb.
Cheese slices	3¼ lbs.
Sliced baked ham	5 lbs.

Desserts:	
Apples for pie	20 lbs.
Apples for sauce (or salad)	15 lbs.
Cherries, fresh, for pie	7 qts. or 15 lbs.
Cream, heavy, to whip for dessert topping	1 qt.
Ice cream with No. 12 dipper	2½ gals.
Pies	9 (9") pies
Sherbet with No. 16 dipper	6 qts.

Drinks:	*Quantity*
Coffee, instant	1½ small jars
Coffee, regular	1¼ lbs.
Cream for coffee	2½ pts.
Frozen fruit juice concentrates	9 (6 oz.) cans
Lemonade, frozen concentrate	13 (6 oz.) cans
Lemons (to slice for tea)	6 large
Milk	3 gals.
Punch	2 gals.
Sugar (cube) for coffee or tea	1⅛ lbs.
Tea	¼ lb.
Tomato or fruit juice (canned)	4 (46 oz.) cans

Fish:	
Frozen fish filets	13 to 14 (1 lb.) pkgs.
Oysters for stew	6 qts.
Salmon for salad	8 (1 lb.) cans
Tuna for salad	16 (6 to 7 oz.) cans

Meats and Poultry:	
Bacon (2 slices)	6 lbs.
Frankfurters	100
Ground beef for hamburgers	15 lbs.
Ground beef for meat loaf	12 lbs.
Ham (canned, boned)	1 (14 lb.) can
Ham, ground for loaf	12 lbs.
Lamb, leg to roast	25 lbs.
Pork chops, ¾" thick	17 lbs.
Pork loin to roast	25 lbs.
Rolled beef roast (before boning)	25 lbs.
Sausage, bulk or link	12½ lbs.
Standing rib roast (beef)	35 lbs.
Veal chops, loin	14 to 15 lbs.
Chicken to roast (drawn)	40 lbs.
Chicken to stew and cut up	25 lbs.
Turkey to roast and cut up to use in dishes	16 to 17 lbs.
Turkey to roast and slice	40 lbs.

Relishes:	*Quantity*
Carrots for sticks	6 large
Celery	5 to 6 bunches with 12 stalks each
Cranberries for sauce	3 lbs.
Cranberry sauce	6 (1 lb.) cans
Jam and Jelly	8 (8 oz.) glasses
Ketchup	3 (14 oz.) bottles
Olives	2 qts.
Pickles	2 qts.
Radishes	8 to 16 bunches

Salads and Salad Dressings:	
Cabbage for coleslaw	15 lbs.
Chicken	6½ qts.
French dressing	1½ qts.
Fruit	9 qts.
Lettuce, head for salad	10 to 12 heads
Lettuce, leaves for garnish	6 large heads
Mayonnaise or salad dressing	1 qt.
Potato	6½ qts.
Tomatoes, small	15 to 18 lbs.

Vegetables:	
Carrots without tops	16 lbs.
Instant potatoes	1 family-size and 1 regular-size pkg.
Potatoes to mash	25 lbs.
Potatoes to scallop	12 to 16 lbs.
Squash to mash	10 to 12 lbs.
Sweet potatoes to "candy"	25 lbs.
Vegetables, canned	14 (1 lb.) cans, or 11 (1 lb. 4 oz.) cans
Vegetables, frozen	15 to 18 (10 to 12 oz.) pkgs.

CHAPTER 10

COOKING OVER COALS

Cooking over coals is like cooking on an old-fashioned wood and coal stove—you're on your own. No automatic heat controls make decisions for you. You have to build the fire, decide when it's right for the food you want to cook and figure out how long to cook it. These uncertainties challenge the outdoor chef. If he (or she) conquers the problems and turns out really good food, he has a gratifying sense of accomplishment.

Instead of using a thermometer to judge the degree of heat, follow the rules of successful outdoor chefs and test the fire with the palms of your hands like this: Hold your hand at the cooking level and start counting at a normal speed; one thousand and one, one thousand and two, one thousand and three. If you can count only to one thousand and one or two, the coals are hot (high heat), to one thousand four or five, you have medium heat and to one thousand five or six, the heat is low. This system corresponds to grandmother's plan of testing the oven heat in her big black stove. She put a small pan containing flour in the oven and timed the minutes required to brown it. By this method, she was able to bake those beautiful, tasty loaves of bread, cakes, pies and cookies that are unforgettable!

Remember that the most carefully tested recipes for outdoor cooking may not be letter perfect for you. Equipment varies greatly—even the grills themselves. While we describe different kinds of equipment in this book, none of it may fit your grill. Read and follow the cooking directions that came with your grill. And experiment! If you're a beginner in outdoor cooking, grill only the meat over the coals for the first experiment. Give it your undivided attention so you'll be proud to serve it. Fix rest of the meal in the kitchen and have it ready to carry out.

The menus and recipes that follow will be a guide to you, but experience will be your teacher. To acquire skills, try the recipes and heed the directions in this chapter; they come from expert outdoor cooks and can bring you and your guests wonderful food, cooked over coals.

Pointers for Outdoor Cooking

• Keep meals simple with few dishes and generous amounts of what you serve.

• Organize the food for easy carry-out (from kitchen to patio or barbecue spot) to save steps. Large trays and baskets are helpful.

• If there are outdoor electrical sockets, take advantage of them for coffee making, grilling (when a charcoal fire isn't practical) and for making pancakes and waffles for supper or breakfast. Put the electric skillet to work.

• Use simple table appointments (adequate but held to a minimum). A varnished table, with or without place mats, can be wiped clean quickly with a sponge and soapy water. Stainless steel flatware and plastic and/or paper dishes add up to casual meals.

• Acquire the habit of cooking vegetables in heavy aluminum foil. Pack them in individual servings so they can go directly from grill to table.

• Buffet service from table or tray is modern and practical and guests like to help themselves.

• Desserts to eat out of hand are a fine choice. Ice cream cones or bars, cookies, one-layer cakes with baked-on frosting and fruits in season are good examples. Pass a plate of candy for an after-dinner treat.

• One-bowl vegetable or fruit salads make excellent help-yourself foods. Or have a tray of assorted vegetable relishes, with pickles and olives, instead of salad. Wedges of cantaloupe make a marvelous salad substitute.

• Sometimes assemble a smorgasbord supper on a big tray or two, such as cold cuts, potato salad, crackers or chips, rye bread and butter, and cookies with plenty of hot coffee. An ideal meal for a hot day!

• Add ice to tea or the ade drinks, made with frozen fruit juice concentrates, and place in the refrigerator an hour or two before mealtime. Bring them out at the last minute; they will require no last-minute icing.

Types of Favorite Grills

Vertical Grill: The simplest form is a two-sided, hinged appliance, similar in appearance to an old-fashioned bread toaster, that you clamp together and hang in the fireplace indoors or outdoors. You set a drip pan underneath to collect juices and excess fat. A crane, the kind colonial cooks hung their teakettles on, is the handy device some outdoor chefs use for the vertical broilers. A modern version has a center compartment for charcoal; it is either round or rectangular in shape and has clamp-type grills and drip pans on the outside. Some of these grills have skewers for "brochette" broiling.

Rotisseries and Basket Grills: These are attachments, with electric motors, on the more elaborate portable braziers or grills. The rotisserie is a long skewer with clamps; it fits on the sides of the grill and turns slowly. Meats and poultry placed on it must be balanced on the skewer or the spit will not turn smoothly. Basket grills also rotate and are ideal for cooking pieces of chicken or heating frozen French fries or onions and rolls.

Smoke Cooking Grills: They are similar to hooded portable grills except the hood completely covers the grill and imparts a smoky flavor (much favored by many people) to all foods cooked under it. You can make your own smoke cover this way: Press heavy aluminum foil into the empty firepot of an open-type grill so that it takes the shape of the grill. Remove it and when ready to cook the food use aluminum foil as a cover or hood for the grill.

Fireplace Grill: Families who do much outdoor cooking and dining in a spot protected from wind like built-in fireplace grills the best of all. The taste of charcoal broiled meats is so enjoyable that many people continue to cook them outdoors after summer ends. New homes frequently have fireplace grills built into the kitchen or family room. And one of FARM JOURNAL's readers utilized an old chimney in her kitchen that could not be removed when the kitchen was remodeled to install a fireplace for grilled foods. Broiled meats now are an around-the-year specialty in this Iowa farm home.

Cookout Stroganoff Supper

Bring out a heavy skillet and kettle and cook supper on the grill. All you have to fix in the house, when you use this menu, is the bread, which you can bake days ahead and store in the freezer. The homemade bread, cut in thick slices, makes this supper distinctive, but you can eliminate it and spoon the Stroganoff over crisp Chinese noodles (canned) or cooked rice.

Outdoor chefs highly prize heavy, cast-iron skillets for cooking the main dish, but the electric skillet may be used instead. Then you'll cook only the vegetables and dessert dumplings on the grill. There's something fascinating about a dessert cooked over coals and spooned into serving dishes with everyone watching. It's a type of showmanship most guests enjoy. And so do the chefs!

MENU

Skillet Stroganoff*
Vegetables in Foil*   Melon Wedges*
Homemade Bread   Crab Apple Jelly
Huckleberry Dumplings*

SKILLET STROGANOFF

When cooking beef, stir with a fork, try to keep in marble-size pieces

¼ c. butter or margarine
⅔ c. minced onion
1 large clove garlic, minced finely
2 lbs. ground chuck beef
1 tsp. salt
½ tsp. pepper
2 (8 oz.) cans mushrooms, drained (save ½ c. liquid)
4 tblsp. flour
1 can condensed cream of mushroom soup
2 c. dairy sour cream
⅓ c. minced parsley

The perfect way to end a feast is with fruit and cheese—and here's a spectacular way to serve it. Build the Fruit Tree from trays, cake stands and footed dishes; then load it with fruit. *Directions, page 257.*

• Melt butter in large cast-iron skillet. (Use 10″ size, or better still, a cast-iron stew kettle.) Add onion and garlic and cook until delicately browned. (Or cook in an electric skillet.)

• Have coals banked at front part of grill so that you do not have to reach over hot spots in working. Add beef to the onion-garlic mixture; stir and cook only until red color disappears. Add seasonings, mushrooms, ½ c. liquid, blended with flour, and soup. Stir thoroughly; cook slowly 20 minutes with pan pushed to back of grill where reflected heat will do the cooking.

• At serving time, add the sour cream (do not cook) and parsley; mix well and heat. Serve hot off the grill in individual casseroles or soup plates. Makes 8 to 12 servings.

VEGETABLES IN FOIL

• Make individual servings of vegetables, such as sliced carrots, sliced zucchini with chopped onion and a slice of tomato; or green beans with sliced carrots; or sliced carrots and peas. Place on 12 × 10″ squares of heavy foil. Season carrots with a little sugar, salt and pepper, and add ½ tsp. butter. Season other vegetables as you do when cooking them in the kitchen. Bring up the sides of the foil squares and twist at the top to close. Cook 15 to 20 minutes on grill set low (4 to 6″ from coals) or near coals in the firebox.

HUCKLEBERRY DUMPLINGS

Add dumplings to hot berries soon after the Stroganoff starts to simmer

1 qt. fresh or frozen huckleberries
1 c. sugar
¾ c. water
½ tsp. mace
¼ c. sugar
2 c. prepared biscuit mix
¾ c. milk

• Put huckleberries in a 3-qt. stew pan, preferably one with a heavy bottom, a snug-fitting lid and wide enough to hold 8 dumplings. Add 1 c. sugar and water, and cook on grill until berries are tender and bubbling. Add the mace.

• To make dumplings, add ¼ c. sugar to biscuit mix, stirring with fork to mix. Then stir in the milk. Drop rounded teaspoons of mixture on top of hot berries. Cook uncovered 10 minutes; then cover and cook 10 minutes longer.

• Serve warm from grill in bowls. Pass a pitcher of milk or dairy half and half. Makes 8 servings.

VARIATIONS

Blueberry Dumplings: Substitute fresh or frozen blueberries for the huckleberries. Omit mace and add 1 tsp. lemon juice.

Raspberry Dumplings: Substitute fresh or frozen red raspberries for huckleberries, using a little less water. Omit the mace and add ⅛ tsp. cinnamon.

Lollipop lion, egg-carton witch, housewarming matches, flowers made from cone-shaped paper drinking cups or plastic bottles—all our party favors are easy to make from everyday materials. *Directions begin on page 383.*

Canned Berry Dumplings: Substitute canned huckleberries, blueberries or red raspberries instead of the fresh or frozen berries. Heat without adding water. Add dumplings and cook like Huckleberry Dumplings.

MELON WEDGES

· Chilled melon is a happy addition to this meal. A combination of two melons is pretty and tasty. To make 8 to 12 servings, allow 1 cantaloupe (or Crenshaw melon) and half a small watermelon. Cut cantaloupe in quarters, remove seeds and peel, and cut each quarter in half again for serving-size pieces. If you use a large Crenshaw instead, half of it is adequate; cut in eighths, remove seeds and peel, and then cut in serving-size pieces. Cut the heart of the watermelon in balls or chunks. Arrange melon pieces on a large salad tray or plate and garnish with sprigs of fresh mint. Or use a combination of melons and fresh fruits, such as peaches, pears and bananas, peeled and cut in serving-size pieces, and grapes.

Easygoing Fish Barbecue

You don't have to be a successful fisherman's wife to treat friends to a fish barbecue. And you don't have to spend hours fixing food for the feast. You can buy halibut steaks—wonderful when grilled over coals, and quick and easy to cook.

Baked potatoes are the only food in the following menu that requires cooking time (see Index). You can shorten cooking time by putting them on top of the coals for 45 to 60 min-

utes, or until they test soft when pinched. Or you can use frozen French fries. Put them in a corn popper and shake over coals until they are piping hot. Add salt and serve.

If you have baked potatoes, wait until they're tender before you start grilling the halibut.

MENU

Grilled Halibut Steaks*
Baked Potatoes in Foil*
Coleslaw   Sliced Tomatoes
Honeyed Fruit Compote*
Cookies

GRILLED HALIBUT STEAKS

The smoky flavor makes fish especially good; lemon, parsley add color

8 halibut steaks (about ¼ lb.
    each)
2 small cloves garlic, cut in
    halves
6 tblsp. salad oil
6 tblsp. lemon juice
Salt
Paprika
4 to 6 tblsp. toasted sesame
    seeds

· Rub halibut on both sides with cut garlic clove; brush with salad oil. Sprinkle with lemon juice (bottled lemon juice is easy to use) and salt. Place on grill about 4″ above medium-hot coals.

· Cook about 5 minutes; turn. Sprinkle top of steaks with paprika and toasted seasame seeds. Cook 5 minutes longer, or until the fish is done. Test for doneness with a fork; if the fish flakes easily, it is ready to serve. Serve at once with lemon wedges and chopped parsley. Makes 8 servings.

Note: See directions for toasting sesame seeds in Index under Seed Seasoners.

HONEYED FRUIT COMPOTE

Serve in a big bowl and let everyone help himself. Set a filled cookie jar on table. Supper's a success

1 cantaloupe
1 honeydew or casaba melon
2 large peaches
2 Bartlett pears
1 c. strained honey
2 c. canned apricots
1 c. juice from apricots (about)

• Cut each melon in half, remove seeds and peel off rind and unedible portions. Cut each melon half in eighths. Peel peaches, remove pits and cut in serving-size pieces. Cut pears in halves (no need to peel) and remove cores; cut in serving-size pieces.
• Add honey to canned apricots. Stir in liquid drained from apricots. Mix all the ingredients together with a light hand, cover and let stand 30 minutes to 1 hour. Let guests help themselves. Makes 8 servings.

Barbecued Chuck Roast Jardinaire

Giving pot roast with vegetables the French name makes it sound glamorous, but this is an easy-to-fix meal. Be sure to use a beef chuck cut no thicker than 2″ (some meatmen cut chuck roasts especially for cooking over coals), and to make a tight package. Then, if your fire is right, you'll have a moist, brown roast complete with tender vegetables that invite everybody to pitch in with knife and fork.

MENU

Barbecued Chuck Roast
with Vegetables*
Garlic Bread
Green Applesauce   Brownies

BARBECUED CHUCK ROAST WITH VEGETABLES

Outdoor excitement in foil

1 (4 to 5 lb.) chuck beef pot roast (1 to 2″ thick)
2 tsp. salt
1 large onion, sliced
12 medium potatoes, peeled
12 carrots, peeled
Beef Barbecue Sauce

• Rub beef with salt; place on a large sheet of heavy-duty aluminum foil (large enough to surround meat and vegetables). Cover meat with onion; lay potatoes and carrots around meat. Cover with Beef Barbecue Sauce, turning up foil to hold sauce.
• Fold foil around meat and vegetables to make a package; close tightly with a drugstore fold, but leave a little space for expansion of the steam. (A tight seal is desirable to retain the steam, which tenderizes the meat.)
• Turn package once or twice if the fold does not leak. If it leaks, place a second piece of heavy foil under the meat to collect any savory juices that may escape. Cook 2 to 2½

hours; test for doneness. Cook a little longer if necessary. Makes 8 to 12 servings.

Note: For long cooking, as for this pot roast, have a generous bed of coals—25 to 30 briquettes of charcoal. Start them in the usual cone shape and when they develop a gray ash and are so hot you cannot hold the palm of your hand near the cooking level, spread them out under the cooking area. Place 6 to 8 more briquettes in a fringe around the hot ones to add later in the cooking. After spreading out the coals, place the roast over them.

BEEF BARBECUE SAUCE

Best-ever sauce for vegetables and browned fork-tender beef

¼ c. salad oil
½ tsp. garlic powder
¼ to ½ tsp. dried thyme
1 tsp. salt
½ tsp. pepper
1 tsp. dry mustard
1 tblsp. brown sugar
½ c. ketchup
¼ c. bottled steak sauce
2 tblsp. wine vinegar

• Combine all ingredients; cook, stirring constantly, until mixture boils. Set aside until ready to use. Makes about 1 cup.

Chickens Turn on the Spit

It's that marvelous, come-hither aroma and shiny brown beauty of whole chickens turning over coals that builds up appetites and friendly talk.

If your grill has a rotisserie, you can cook 2 (3 to 3½ lb.) fryers on the spit. When you want to broil a larger amount of chicken to feed more than 8 hungry people it's wise to cut the birds in halves or quarters, clamp them in toaster-type grills and turn them over coals frequently, basting after each turn with Sweet-Sour Sauce. The chef provides the power for turning, which is one reason spits are popular with many barbecue fans.

MENU

Chilled Tomato Cream Soup*
Sweet-Sour Rotisserie Chicken*
New Potatoes in
Parsley-Chive Cheese Sauce*
Celery and Carrot Sticks
Pickles   Olives
Chilled Watermelon

CHILLED TOMATO CREAM SOUP

Chill mugs or cups in refrigerator so they'll be frosty when you serve this

1 (46 oz.) can tomato juice,
    chilled (6 c.)
1 c. instant nonfat dry milk
¾ tsp. dried dill weed, or
    1 tblsp. chopped fresh dill

• Combine tomato juice with milk; pour into blender or large bowl of electric mixer. Add dill weed or fresh dill; blend or beat to mix well. Makes 8 or more servings.

SWEET-SOUR ROTISSERIE CHICKEN

• Select 2 fryers, each weighing 3 to 3½ lbs. Rinse well; dry inside and out. Place on the spit in the head-to-tail formation, meshing them firmly together at equal distance from the ends of the spit so that they are balanced on the rod. Force the forked prongs well into the birds, one set at the front to penetrate and hold the meaty breast, the other prongs at the back to penetrate and hold the meaty thighs. Use pliers to turn screws firmly on the prongs so the chickens will rotate with the motor-driven spit, not by themselves.

• Truss chickens after placing them on the rotisserie. Tie the feet of the end bird together; then make a wrap with light wire (or string, but it may scorch) that includes the wings of this bird and the feet of the one in front of it. Tie wings of front bird close to the body.

• Start the cooking with the chickens set about 6" above the coals. Have two layers of coals that will last through the 2 hours of cooking, or until chicken is done. More charcoal may be added during the cooking if necessary, but burn it first at the back of the grill until covered with gray ashes. Push it forward as needed.

• Start basting chickens as soon as their skins are warm. Brush them with Sweet-Sour Sauce and continue throughout the roasting or until all the sauce is used. Makes 8 servings.

SWEET-SOUR SAUCE

This gives chicken gorgeous brown color, delightfully elusive flavor

½ c. butter or margarine
⅓ c. brown sugar
¾ c. pineapple juice
¼ c. lemon juice
1 tblsp. soy sauce
1 tsp. salt

• Combine all the ingredients and bring to a boil in a small saucepan. Keep on warming oven or some convenient spot for brushing on chicken. Makes about 1½ cups.

Note: For added flavor, brush the sauce inside the chickens before placing them on the spit.

NEW POTATOES IN PARSLEY-CHIVE CHEESE SAUCE

Since the grill will be busy with chicken, this is a good meal in which to feature a hot vegetable cooked in the kitchen. Potatoes in flavorful creamy sauce are an ideal choice because they are tasty and will hold successfully until serving time.

• Allow 2 or 3 small new potatoes for each serving. Scrub them and cook just until tender in salted water. (You can peel them before or after cooking, whichever is most convenient.) Drain thoroughly and add to Parsley-Chive Cheese Sauce.

PARSLEY-CHIVE CHEESE SAUCE

A wonderful cheese sauce—it's the seasonings that make this so good

½ c. butter or margarine
½ c. flour
1 tsp. dry mustard
5 c. milk
1½ c. shredded Cheddar cheese
(medium or aged)
½ c. chopped fresh parsley, or
1 tblsp. dried parsley
flakes
½ c. chopped fresh chives, or
1 tblsp. dried chives
Salt

• Melt butter in large saucepan; blend

in flour and mustard to make smooth mixture. Add the milk, stirring constantly, and cook until sauce is thickened. (Sauce will be medium-thin until cheese is added.)

• Stir in cheese, parsley and chives; cook over low heat, stirring constantly to blend and thicken. Taste for salt, adding enough to season (amount varies somewhat with different kinds of cheese).

• Add cooked potatoes and hold in a warm place until serving time. Makes enough sauce to dress 16 to 24 small new potatoes.

Country-Style Bean Barbecue

Beans and frankfurters get together in this homespun, substantial supper. The beans are well seasoned and contain tomatoes in the true Midwestern and Western tradition. Coney buns (the long ones) are a thoughtful addition to the menu because many guests like to make sandwiches when the franks come hot and brown from the grill. Better set out prepared mustard and tomato ketchup for the sandwich fans. This menu appeals especially to men and boys.

MENU

Home Baked Beans*
Grilled Franks*
Coney Buns   Crisp Lettuce Relish*
Cheese and Fruit Tray*

HOME BAKED BEANS

Hungry guests like this—proof is the speed in which beans disappear

2 lbs. navy or pea beans
1 lb. salt pork

1 lb. brown sugar
1 (1 lb. 13 oz.) can tomatoes
2 medium onions, chopped
      (about ¾ c.)
2 tblsp. prepared mustard
½ tsp. salt
½ tsp. pepper

• Wash and pick over beans; cover generously with water and soak overnight. Next morning, simmer beans in salted water until they test done. (An easy test is to bite into a bean to find out if it's tender.) Drain beans and save liquid.

• Put salt pork through food chopper. Place it in the bottom of a large bean pot or deep casserole. Alternately layer cooked beans with a mixture of brown sugar, tomatoes, onions, mustard, salt and pepper on top of salt pork. Pour on the water in which beans cooked and add enough hot water to cover beans. Adjust the lid, or cover with aluminum foil.

• To cook beans in the kitchen, bake in slow oven (300°) 6 to 8 hours, stirring occasionally and adding more hot water if necessary.

• To cook outdoors, set the beans on the cooking shelf at the side of the fireplace (if it has a shelf). Or set them on bricks in the fireplace, to the side and front. Keep a low wood fire all the time. If the fireplace has a swinging crane, cast-iron kettles, hung on it, are excellent to use. (Many antique shops have old kettles of this type for sale.)

• This recipe makes 15 to 25 generous servings. Put the leftover beans in a freezer container and store in the freezer to reheat for the next barbecue.

GRILLED FRANKS

· Allow 2 frankfurters for each serving. A good way to heat them is to place them in a clamp-type grill (like an old-fashioned toaster) and cook and turn them over coals until they brown all over. They will have a pleasing smoky flavor. Or cover them with cold water and bring to the boiling point.

CRISP LETTUCE RELISH

It's cut fine like a relish—a change from regular mixed vegetable salad

1 ½ qts. shredded head lettuce (iceberg)
3   lemon cucumbers, or 2 medium regular cucumbers, peeled and finely diced
1 ⅓ c. diced radishes
¾   c. thinly sliced green onions
1   c. oil or vinegar salad dressing (equal parts oil and vinegar with salt and pepper to season)

· Cut head lettuce on board, using a French chef's knife, into ½" slices; then cut crisscross to make of relish consistency (not too fine). Add prepared cucumbers, radishes and onions; chill until ready to serve. At the last minute, toss lightly with salad dressing (you can use bottled French dressing). Makes 8 servings.

CHEESE AND FRUIT TRAY

· Use fresh fruits in season with any favorite cheese. A pretty tray for help-yourself service is this: Place an Edam cheese or a wedge of blue cheese in the center of a cutting board. Encircle cheese with polished red and yellow apples (whole or quartered) and assorted grapes, divided into individual-size bunches. If you like, serve a plate of assorted crackers with the cheese and fruit.

Grill Chicken with Pineapple

Pineapple is to barbecued chicken what strawberries are to shortcake. And that means they're a superlative flavor team. Use canned or fresh pineapple. If you select the fresh fruit, serve it cooked or uncooked, whichever is easiest. It's right with chicken either way.

Be sure to allow ample time for the potatoes to bake. And if you want everyone to get excited about the dessert coming up, make a freezer of homemade ice cream on the barbecue scene. You may prefer to have dish-saving ice cream cones instead of the Sundae Bar. Remember, though, that homemade ice cream often is not firm enough for cones unless you make it ahead and put it in the freezer to harden.

MENU

Barbecued Chicken with Pineapple*
Baked Potatoes*
Peas and Onions in Foil Baskets*
Relish Tray of Crisp Vegetables,
Sweet and Dill Pickles
Toasted Buns with Sesame Butter*
Ice Cream Sundae Bar*

BARBECUED CHICKEN WITH PINEAPPLE

· Cook chicken pieces directly on the grill or in a rotating wire basket designed especially for barbecuing chicken.

- *For the Grill Method:* Use 2 lb. fryers or broilers. Cut chickens in halves, allowing a half for each serving. Grease the grill lightly and place the chicken, skin side down, on it. Sprinkle with salt.
- Melt a stick of butter or margarine. Turn the chicken frequently until done, brushing on butter with every turn. Allow about 45 minutes for thorough cooking.
- Dip drained, canned pineapple slices in melted butter with a little lemon juice added, and broil quickly on the hot grill while the chicken is being served.
- *For the Basket Method:* Use 3 (2½ to 3 lb.) fryers to make 8 servings. Disjoint chickens, salt and flour lightly. Dip in melted butter or margarine, or in Teriyaki Sauce (see Index).
- Place in basket with grill removed; basket should be about 6" from a generous bed of coals. Use ½ to ⅔ c. Teriyaki Sauce or butter for basting. Allow 1½ hours for cooking, but check for doneness after 1 hour.
- Fresh pineapple wedges may be broiled with chicken in a rotisserie basket. Dredge them lightly with flour and put in basket the last 30 minutes of cooking, basting lightly from time to time with butter or margarine.

BAKED POTATOES

- Select medium baking potatoes; brush lightly with salad oil and wrap individually in heavy aluminum foil so they will be easy to turn two or three times while cooking. Place them in a wide circle, toward the outside of the grill, where they will be par-
tially cooked by reflected heat from the hood of the grill. Allow 1½ to 2 hours for baking. Pinch to test for doneness; if potatoes are soft and yielding, they are done. Make a criss-cross cut in top of foil package, push on ends to fluff, add a spoonful of butter and serve in the foil wrapping. Pass butter or margarine, whipped until fluffy, or dairy sour cream. Also pass chopped chives or green onions.

PEAS AND ONIONS IN FOIL BASKETS

- Allow 3 (10 oz.) pkgs. frozen peas and pearl onions in butter sauce for 8 servings. Let thaw at room temperature, removing outer packages but leaving vegetables in their plastic bags. Place each bag on a sheet of heavy aluminum foil large enough to surround vegetables and allow for a twist at the top.
- Allow 20 minutes for cooking time. Place the foil bundles at the outside of the edge of the coals and toward the back where they will partly cook in reflected heat. If the grill is the brazier type without a shield at the back, place a large sheet of heavy aluminum foil in the bottom of the brazier before the charcoal is added. Allow 10 to 12" foil to provide a heat shield; this will furnish some reflected heat for cooking the whole meal. (Many barbecue chefs like to crinkle the foil used under the bed of charcoal because any fat that accumulates runs down into the grooves and there is less flare-up.)

BUNS WITH SESAME BUTTER

- Toast hamburger buns on the grill at the last minute. Spread with fluffy, whipped butter with a little seasoned salt and toasted sesame seeds added (see Index, under Seed Seasoners, for directions for toasting sesame seeds). Serve this butter on baked potatoes for a delightful change.

ICE CREAM SUNDAE BAR

· For a special treat, make a crank freezer full of ice cream. Have ready a tray holding a selection of sundae toppings, such as chocolate and butterscotch sauces or syrups, sliced or crushed fresh strawberries or peaches when in season, or strawberry or peach preserves when fresh berries and fruit are out of season. Whole bananas that guests can peel and use to make their own banana splits and chopped nuts also are a happy addition to the help-yourself Sundae Bar.

South-of-the-Border Barbecue

Bean suppers west of the Mississippi River, especially in Colorado, the Southwest and the Pacific Coast states, differ from those in New England. They show Mexican and Indian influences. Even the bean varieties are not the same, and dishes made with them often carry the taste and scent of chili powder. The sauces are really hot. That's why the Oregon hostess who shares this menu suggests that the hostess provide pitchers of ice water or very cold milk.

If your store doesn't carry peppermint ice cream, you can make your own. A simple way is to crush peppermint candy and stir it into vanilla ice cream, two sticks of candy to each quart of ice cream.

MENU

Refried Beans*
Tortilla Sandwiches*
Grilled Minute Steaks* Hot Sauce*
Sliced Tomatoes
Chopped Head Lettuce
Sweet Onion Rings
Peppermint Stick Ice Cream

REFRIED BEANS

A bean favorite of the Southwest borrowed from neighbors to the south

1 ½ lbs. pinto or pink beans
 3   slices bacon
1 ½ tsp. chili powder
Salt
Pepper
1 ½ lbs. ground chunk beef

· Wash beans and soak overnight, or at least 4 hours, in water to cover. Bring to a boil in water in which beans soaked; simmer until tender, about 2 hours, adding more water during cooking if necessary. (The beans should be cooked to a mushy consistency.) Mash beans with a potato masher or put them in the blender, adding enough water to make a loose consistency.
· Meanwhile, cut bacon in slivers; fry until barely crisp. Add bacon and 3 tblsp. bacon drippings to mashed beans. Season with the chili powder and salt and pepper to taste.
· Turn ground beef into a skillet, mixing and crumbling it with a fork while it cooks over a quick heat. (This may be done on the grill over coals just before cooking the steaks.) Season beef lightly with salt and pepper; cook only until red color of meat

disappears. Add to the bean mixture and heat, adding more water to make a mixture of loose consistency. (The beans thicken on standing, so hot water may be added from time to time.) Ground chuck usually adds the right amount of fat, about 4 tblsp., but if there is more, spoon it off. Place on or in warming oven, depending on type of grill. With some hooded types, the best place to keep food warm is on the top of the hood. Keep hot until serving time. Makes 8 servings.

TORTILLA SANDWICHES

Simplified American version of sandwich enjoyed South-of-the-Border

18 to 24 cornmeal tortillas
Butter or salad oil
Refried Beans
1½ c. shredded soft Cheddar
     cheese

• Tortillas may be found packaged in dozen lots in the freezer cases of many food stores. They are from 6 to 7″ in diameter. Hold them at room temperature until limp before handling to avoid breakage.
• Brush melted butter or salad oil over each tortilla; cut in half and lay on a greased baking sheet or in a greased shallow pan. Place in extremely hot oven (500°) 5 minutes, or until edges start to curl and brown slightly. Turn off heat and leave oven door ajar so the soft parts of tortillas will become crisp.
• To make open-face sandwiches, have guests place tortilla halves on their plates, spoon Refried Beans on them, sprinkle with grated cheese, and garnish with finely chopped or

shredded lettuce and tomato slices. Makes 8 servings.

Note: Some supermarkets carry canned tortillas, as well as the crisp and folded taco shells for filling and eating out of hand.

GRILLED MINUTE STEAKS

They're really 2-minute steaks. You broil them 1 minute on each side

8 (6 oz.) minute steaks
Salad oil
Sweet onion rings

• While guests are making their Tortilla Sandwiches, brush steaks lightly on both sides with salad oil. Grill them over hot coals, allowing 1 minute broiling time on each side. (A hand grill, like old-style toasters, into which you clamp the steaks, is excellent to use in grilling steaks. You can turn and remove the steaks from it easily.)
• Serve on the same plates with Tortilla Sandwiches. Garnish steaks with onion rings. Makes 8 servings.

HOT SAUCE

Go easy—the sauce is really hot

2 c. canned tomatoes
4 to 5 (2″) chili peppers,
     finely chopped
1 (8 oz.) can tomato sauce or
     paste
1 tsp. sugar
⅛ tsp. orégano

• Put tomatoes through a coarse sieve to break up chunky pieces; retain as much of pulp as possible. (Or put in blender, add chili peppers, seeds discarded, and blend finely.)
• Add chopped chili peppers, tomato

sauce, sugar and orégano. Bring barely to a boil. Hold in a warm place.

· Let guests ladle a little of this sauce over their steaks and Tortilla Sandwiches. Makes enough for 8 steaks and sandwiches made with 18 to 24 tortillas.

Note: Bottled hot sauces are available in many supermarkets if you don't want to make your own.

Lamb Chops en Brochette with Vegetables

When it comes to barbecue showmanship, nothing excels shiny brown lamb chops strung on skewers with colorful vegetables. As they come off the grill, the excitement of the guests matches the pride of the chef. If the feast is for eight people, the host can ask someone to take over two of the skewers. When it's time to thread the vegetables on the skewers, he will welcome two more pairs of hands to speed up the work.

Ice cream cones eliminate dishes and almost everyone enjoys this informal dessert, but if you prefer, you can serve the ice cream in dessert dishes and pass a plate of brownies. Have plenty of hot coffee to go around!

MENU

Skewered Lamb Chops with
Vegetables*
Cantaloupe with Mint*
Toasted Buns   Jelly or Jam
Ice Cream Cones

SKEWERED LAMB CHOPS WITH VEGETABLES

This main dish is colorful—yellow, red and shiny brown. And so tasty

8 sirloin lamb chops, 1 ½ " thick
Marinade for Lamb
8 ears sweet corn, cut in pieces
    (large ears in 4 pieces, small
    ones in 3)
8 plum tomatoes, or 16 tomato
    wedges (large tomatoes)
2 large green peppers, cut in 8
    pieces

· Trim excess fat from chops and arrange in container, such as a roaster, and pour on Marinade for Lamb (recipe follows). Let marinate 3 to 4 hours, turning at least 4 times.

· Four 20" metal skewers, two servings on each, are needed for holding the meat and vegetables. Leave the barbecue grill in place, set 6 to 8" above a good bed of coals. Run the skewers lengthwise through the chops, avoiding blade bone. Lay them on the grill and turn by hand. Broil 10 to 12 minutes on each side, brushing meat frequently with marinade. Remove from the heat long enough to add vegetables to each skewer.

· Arrange the vegetables alternately on each skewer, starting skewers through the cut ears of corn (lengthwise through the cobs), using a slightly twisting motion.

· Return meat and vegetables to grill; brush all over with marinade and broil 10 to 15 minutes, turning skewers frequently. Check lamb by cutting into it to determine its stage of doneness. Push chops back on skewer, if necessary, to prevent overcooking.

· To serve, place point of skewer on

plate and with a fork, use lamb chops to push the vegetables off the skewer. Makes 8 servings.

MARINADE FOR LAMB

This imparts superior flavor to lamb

1　envelope onion-soup mix
　　(1 to 1 ½ oz.)
1　c. water
½　c. salad oil
⅓　c. vinegar
3　tblsp. sugar
2　tsp. hickory-smoked salt

· Combine all ingredients and pour over the lamb chops. Makes about 2 cups.

CANTALOUPE WITH MINT

· Refrigerate cantaloupe quarters with sprigs of slightly bruised fresh mint for 1 hour or longer. Serve as a salad-appetizer on the plate with the lamb and vegetables.

Flank Steak Barbecue Special

Grilled steak, mashed potatoes and apple pie! You couldn't have a meal Americans like better—especially the men. Use packaged instant potatoes, following label directions. They're ideal for dining outdoors. (Better allow larger servings for outdoor appetites.) When the hot, fluffy potatoes are in the serving dish or on serving plates, make depressions in them with the back of a spoon. Fill with melted butter and sprinkle the yellow pools with chopped parsley or chives.

And here's another tip—the wise hostess bakes two 9″ pies for 8 to 12 guests. Plenty of this favorite dessert sends everyone home raving about the meal.

MENU

Grilled Flank Steak*
Mashed Potatoes
Vegetable Salad Tray*　Garlic Bread
Latticed Apple Pie with Cream*

GRILLED FLANK STEAK

So good you'll fix this steak again and again when you have company

2　unscored flank steaks, about
　　1 ½ lbs. each
3　c. Special Marinade

· Two hours before barbecue time, place the steaks in Special Marinade. (Two hours is the minimum time; a little longer is satisfactory.) It should cover the steaks. Turn steaks at least two or three times while in the marinade.
· Set grill about 6″ above hot coals. (Hold your hand, palm down, over the grill near the cooking level. If you can keep it there only about 2 seconds, it is hot enough for the steaks.)
· Grease grill lightly, place steaks on grill and cook to desired doneness. For total cooking time, allow about 8 minutes for rare to medium (4 minutes for each side); 10 to 15 minutes for medium to well done (5 to 8 minutes on each side). Turn once during grilling. Serve hot, cut diagonally across the grain. Makes 8 servings.

SPECIAL MARINADE

Give this sauce its share of credit for the wonderful flavor of the steak

1 ½ c. salad oil
¾ c. soy sauce
4 tblsp. Worcestershire sauce
2 tblsp. dry mustard
2 tsp. salt
2 tsp. coarse black pepper
½ c. wine vinegar
2 tsp. dried parsley flakes
2 cloves garlic, crushed
⅓ c. lemon juice

• Combine all ingredients; stir to blend. Make this sauce the day before using if possible. Makes 3 cups.

VEGETABLE SALAD TRAY

• Use carrot and celery sticks, cauliflowerets, quartered tomatoes or cherry tomatoes, and thick cucumber slices. Have a dip available for dunking vegetables. One of the easiest and best is mayonnaise with lemon juice added.

LATTICED APPLE PIE WITH CREAM

America has many excellent apple pies and this is one of the best. Try sour cream and brown sugar on top

Pastry for 2-crust 9″ pie
4 large quick-cooking apples, peeled and cut in eighths
1 c. sugar
½ tsp. cinnamon
½ tsp. allspice
3 tblsp. butter or margarine
Dairy sour or sweet cream

• Arrange apples in pastry-lined pan. Sprinkle with ½ c. sugar mixed with cinnamon.

• Sift together remaining ½ c. sugar and allspice. Cut into butter with pastry blender or fork until mixture is crumbly. Sprinkle over apples and top with pastry lattice; flute edges.
• Bake in hot oven (425°) 40 minutes. Turn off heat and leave pie in oven another 10 minutes. Serve pie at table and pass a bowl of brown sugar that pours and a bowl of dairy sour cream, or a pitcher of sweet cream to pour over pie.

Note: Serve pie slightly warm if possible. A good way to handle it is to slip it into, or on top of, the warming oven when you sit down to eat the main course. If the grill has no oven, place the whole pie in pan on grill as far from the cooking area as possible, raising the grill to its highest point.

Barbecued Ribs— Beef or Pork

Glistening ribs sizzling and browning over coals—what an invitation to supper! Take your choice of beef or pork ribs. We give you directions for grilling both kinds.

Use lean ribs if available and trim off excess fat. But remember, you want a little fat to drip on the coals to give the meat that wonderful smoky flavor. Another precaution you may want to take is to make a dripping pan of heavy aluminum foil, mitering the corners and forming sides 2″ high. Place this directly on the coals under the ribs (should cover same area as meat on grill). If you make the pan large enough, one end can extend downward and away from the fire to drain off the fat so it won't pop out on the coals and cause flare-ups.

Brush the ribs with sauce frequently while they broil. This gives them flavor and rich coloring. Notice that the sauces recommended for marinating and basting shortribs and spareribs are different, one to complement beef, one for pork. The flavors are not the same. But both are wonderfully good!

MENU

Barbecued Shortribs* or Spareribs*
Tossed Green Salad
Toasted Hard Rolls
Green Apple Cake* with
Rum Sauce* or Whipped Cream

BARBECUED SHORTRIBS

• Select the meatiest ribs available. Have ribs cut in 3″ lengths, allowing ¾ to 1 lb. for each serving. Trim off excess fat and pour Special Marinade (see Index) over them, adding an extra ½ c. ketchup to the marinade. Let stand 1 to 2 hours.

• Place ribs in a rotisserie basket if you have one; if not, place directly on grill over medium-hot coals, with grill set 6″ above coals.

• Baste several times during the cooking with Special Marinade, turning ribs when necessary to obtain even browning and cooking. Use tongs to turn ribs.

• Allow 20 to 30 minutes cooking time, but test for doneness. Do not overcook. A slight pinkness should show when you cut into the meat.

Note: The time of cooking depends on the meatiness of the ribs and the degree of heat.

VARIATION

Barbecued Spareribs: Substitute spareribs for shortribs in the menu. Use Peppy Barbecue Sauce instead of Special Marinade. Here are the directions to follow.

• If possible, select country or farmstyle spareribs that have a generous portion of back meat attached (they have less exposed surface). Allow ¾ to 1 lb. ribs per serving.

• Marinate spareribs 20 to 30 minutes in Peppy Barbecue Sauce, layering the ribs and sauce in a large container, such as a roaster, and turning them at least once while marinating.

• Cook over medium-hot coals with grill set about 6″ above coals. Brush ribs several times while cooking with the sauce. Turn with tongs as for Barbecued Shortribs. Allow 20 to 30 minutes for cooking. Cook until the lean meat shows no pink when cut into, or until ribs are browned, but do not overcook.

PEPPY BARBECUE SAUCE

Highly seasoned—right for pork ribs

1	tsp. salt
1	tsp. chili powder
1	tsp. celery salt
⅓	c. brown sugar
¼	c. cider vinegar
¼	c. Worcestershire sauce
1 ¼	c. ketchup
Few	drops Tabasco sauce
2 ⅓	c. water

• Combine ingredients and cook over low heat a few minutes until sugar is dissolved. Set aside until ready to use. Sauce may be packaged and frozen for later use. Makes enough sauce for 8 servings spareribs.

GREEN APPLE CAKE

Quick, easy, tasty dessert we found in the Pacific Northwest's apple country

1 c. sugar
¼ cup shortening
1 egg, beaten
3 c. finely chopped apples
1 c. flour
½ tsp. cinnamon
½ tsp. nutmeg
1 tsp. baking soda
Rum Sauce, or whipped cream

• Cream sugar and shortening together until fluffy; add beaten egg and blend mixture with apples.
• Mix flour, spices and baking soda. Add to first mixture.
• Turn into a greased 9″ square pan and bake 45 minutes in moderate oven (350°). Cut in individual servings and serve with Rum Sauce or whipped cream.

RUM SAUCE

Pour this sauce, heated, over cake; or top cake squares with whipped cream

1 c. sugar
½ c. cream
½ c. butter
1 tsp. rum extract, or 2 tblsp. dark rum

• Combine sugar, cream and butter in top of double boiler. Cook over simmering water 10 minutes. Just before serving, stir in rum extract or rum; pour hot over Green Apple Cake.

Pepper Steak: *Just before you lay steaks on the rack over coals, sprinkle them generously with freshly ground pepper or cracked pepper and press pepper into meat. A Western barbecue favorite.*

Use a wire corn popper to heat canned French-fried onion rings over hot coals. Onions are done in a hurry and add a gourmet touch.

A Lamb Barbecue to Remember

Take a look at the following menu and see if reading it doesn't make you hungry. As guests watch the meaty lamb chops bathed in minted pineapple sauce turn brown over coals, their appetites sharpen noticeably.

When the lamb chops are being served, it's time to toast the split English muffins on the grill. Pass them in a napkin or foil-lined basket and let everyone butter his own.

Pass a tray of brownies for dessert. Serve vanilla ice cream with them or, if you prefer, serve the brownies unfrosted and cut in larger than usual squares with scoops of vanilla ice cream on top.

No one goes home hungry after this barbecue. And the guests say goodbys with compliments.

MENU

Pineapple-Mint Lamb Chops*
Buttered Zucchini*   Sliced Tomatoes
Toasted English Muffins
Frosted Brownies and
Vanilla Ice Cream

PINEAPPLE-MINT LAMB CHOPS

Mint, pineapple do wonders for lamb

8 shoulder lamb chops, ¾ to
   1″ thick
2 (8½ oz.) cans crushed
   pineapple
½ c. clover honey (or other
   favorite kind)
¼ c. ground or chopped fresh
   mint leaves
¼ c. butter or margarine
1 tsp. salt or seasoned salt
¼ tsp. pepper
¼ tsp. dried thyme
⅛ tsp. garlic powder (optional)

• Trim excess fat from lamb chops.
• Combine all the other ingredients
is a saucepan (do not drain pineapple); bring to a boil, stirring constantly. Reduce heat and cook 5 minutes; let stand until ready to grill the
chops.
• Dip chops in the pineapple-mint
sauce and broil them 5 to 7 minutes
on each side (over hot coals), or
until the desired stage of doneness
is reached. Spread more of the sauce
on the chops while they cook. (Cut
into a chop with a steak or other
sharp knife to determine if meat is
rare, medium or well done.) Keep the
sauce hot while the lamb is cooking.
Serve it with the chops (may be
passed at the table). Makes 8 servings.

BUTTERED ZUCCHINI

*Use young, tender squash and scrub,
but do not peel. Cook in foil or pan*

5 c. thin zucchini slices
   (crosswise)
3 tblsp. butter or margarine
1 tsp. salt
⅛ tsp. pepper
⅓ c. water
1 clove garlic, cut in half

• Place all ingredients in a saucepan,
cover and cook on grill while chops
are broiling. (Or if grill space is
crowded, cook in an electric skillet.)
Cook only a few minutes, or until
squash slices are barely tender. Set
aside in a warm place until serving
time. Remove garlic before serving.
Makes 8 servings.

FOIL-GRILLED ZUCCHINI

• Slice zucchini in ¼″ crosswise
slices; allow about ⅔ c. per serving.
Place individual portions on 10 to
12″ lengths of heavy aluminum foil
(or doubled lighter weight foil).
Sprinkle each portion with a little
salt, pepper and grated Parmesan
cheese; add 1 tblsp. water and 1 tsp.
butter. Fold foil over squash to make
bags, twisting at the top to close. Cook
on grill (or in firebox a little away
from coals) 15 to 20 minutes.

Charcoal Broiled Pork Chops

Pork chops, beautifully browned
and smoky in flavor, occupy the spotlight in this supper menu. The go-
withs are wonderful, too; they're
kitchen-made and toted to the barbecue area. The hostess does much
of the fixing ahead to reduce mealtime work. Here's what she can have
ready before guests arrive:
• The tomato juice goes into the refrigerator for hours of chilling.
• The salad, too.

• Ice cream packed in paper serving cups goes in the freezer as much as a day ahead. The thoughtful hostess packs three kinds separately, such as vanilla, chocolate and strawberry ice cream, brings them out on a tray at dessert time and lets everybody take his choice.

• Hot Orange Marmalade Buns add a nice note and are a cinch to fix. Here's how: Split sandwich buns and spread cut sides with butter or margarine, then with orange marmalade. Sprinkle lightly with cinnamon. Broil, cut side up, on grill about 5 minutes, or until butter melts and buns are hot.

MENU

Chilled Tomato Juice
Charcoal Broiled Pork Chops*
Potato or Macaroni Salad
Hot Orange Marmalade Buns*
Ice Cream Cups

CHARCOAL BROILED PORK CHOPS

Always good—applesauce with pork chops—pass a big bowl of it

8 pork loin or rib chops, 1½"
    thick
½ tsp. powdered sage
Salt
Pepper

• Slit edges of pork chops to prevent curling. Rub both sides with sage.
• Place over a low charcoal heat so the chops will cook slowly and brown without burning. Turn once while cooking.
• Cook until no pink color shows when cut is made near the bone.

Season with salt and pepper and serve at once. Makes 8 servings.

Pig Roasts
for Summer Entertaining

Pig roasts, called luaus, are traditional in Hawaii. Adapted versions of the feast are becoming popular on the mainland in farm communities. One reason is that country homes usually have the necessary makings —a young pig, space to dig a pit, the necessary rocks, wood and corn leaves—and room for many guests. The food is different and satisfies outdoor appetites.

One of FARM JOURNAL's Family Test Group members, who lives in Indiana, says the luau that she and her husband gave for members of their Gourmet Club was a tremendous success—"the best party we ever had." The directions we give come from two Illinois country couples who fixed a pig roast for a community gathering. There were 80 guests, among them FARM JOURNAL's food editor. Here is the way the Illinois farm couples roasted the pig.

WHOLE PIT-ROASTED PIG

You will need:
Whole young pig, dressed and
    shaved
Rock-lined pit dug ahead of time
Several rounded rocks from a
    stream, in 1 to 4 lb. weights.
    (Sun dry them for a week.)
3 bushels or more of dry hard
    wood

Green corn stalks and leaves
Big tongs for handling hot rocks
Chicken wire or fencing—enough
    to encircle pig
2 baling hooks to carry roasted
    pig
12 clean burlap sacks
Canvas large enough to cover pit

• Allow 1 lb. dressed meat per person.
• Dig hole about 2½' deep at center, with diameter of 5½ to 8' depending on size of pig. Line with rocks.
• Stack wood on rocks, Indian-tepee style. Light fire. Place round rocks in fire where they will get most heat.
• While fire burns down, wet the burlap, and prepare pig. Rub inside of pig with salt and pepper, and garlic if desired. Place pig on chicken wire. Under legs, make slits big enough to insert round rocks. When fire has burned down and rocks are very hot, use tongs to fill abdominal cavity and slits in legs with hot rocks. Tie front legs together, then back legs. Wrap pig in wire, fastening well (so it can be lifted).
• Completely cover ashes and rocks with corn stalks and leaves. Lower pig right onto leaves. Cover it generously on top and sides with more leaves.
• Place wet burlap over leaves (this will hold heat and steam).
• Cover with large canvas; shovel gravel over canvas to keep steam in.
• Cooking time starts now. For 25 lb. pig, allow about 2 hours; for 50 lb. pig, 2½ hours; anything heavier, figure on at least 4 hours. If in doubt about doneness, leave pig in longer (because of steam, it won't burn).

• To uncover, remove gravel, canvas, burlap and covering leaves. Lift and carry wire-wrapped pig with hooks. Remove wire to serve.
• In Hawaii, the servers dip their hands frequently in cold water as they pull pork apart for individual servings. On the mainland, the servings of hot, juicy pork often are best liked when served in buttered buns, with barbecue sauce.

What to Cook with the Pig:

About 1 hour before the pig is cooked, partly uncover pit and add apples, wrapped in foil, and corn on the cob. Either wrap corn ears individually in foil or peel back husks, remove silks, replace husks and soak in cold water about 15 minutes before adding to pit. (In Hawaii, whole sweet potatoes are roasted with the pig.) Cover the pit at once after adding apples and corn.

PINEAPPLE REFRIGERATOR CAKE

Pineapple in the dessert is delicious, right for a luau or Hawaiian feast

½ c. butter
⅔ c. sugar
2 eggs, well beaten
1 c. chopped pecans
1 c. nut-like cereal kernels
1 (9 oz.) can crushed pineapple
1 (7¼ oz.) box vanilla wafers

• Cream butter and sugar; add eggs, pecans, cereal and pineapple with juice. Crush vanilla wafers to make crumbs.
• In an 8" square pan, make alternate layers of crumbs and pineapple mixture (start and end with crumbs). Chill at least 8 hours. Cut in squares; makes 6 to 8 servings.

Main Dishes to Grill over Coals

Certainly the easiest and perhaps the most popular outdoor meals feature only one grilled food, usually meat or poultry. The hostess fixes the remainder of the food in the kitchen and everyone helps carry it to the barbecue area. Some barbecue chefs like also to toast bread slices or split buns on the grill after the meat or poultry is done. Here are favorite main dishes around which to build your menu:

JUMBO PIZZA STEAK

Use steaks cut ⅛" thick from sirloin or tip, or bottom of round. Keep in freezer for last-minute cookouts

8   hard rolls or buns
8   chip steaks
8   slices American cheese
16 tomato slices
Orégano
Salt
Pepper

• Toast split rolls on back of grill.
• Grill one side of steaks over hot coals 1 to 2 minutes; turn steaks and immediately lay 1 cheese slice and 2 tomato slices on each. Sprinkle with orégano, salt and pepper; grill 1 to 2 minutes longer to melt cheese and finish cooking steak. Serve in buns. Makes 8 servings.

THICK BARBECUE SAUCE

Heat frankfurters in this and serve in buns. Youngsters really like them

2   medium onions
2   tblsp. vinegar
2   tblsp. Worcestershire sauce
¼   tsp. red pepper
¾   c. water
¾   c. ketchup
1   tsp. chili powder
½   tsp. salt

• Peel and shred onions. Mix all ingredients together in heavy skillet or saucepan. Cover and simmer about 45 minutes. Makes about 1 pint.

PENNY-SAVER STEAK

Here's your steak if you're not on a T-bone budget. Tenderizer makes chuck ideal for grilling; soy sauce darkens beef but gives it flavor

3   to 4 lb. chuck or round, cut
     1½ to 2" thick
1   tblsp. mixed Italian herbs
½   tsp. pepper
1   tblsp. ketchup
1   tblsp. salad oil
3   tblsp. soy sauce
Instant meat tenderizer

• Trim most of fat edge from meat; slash remaining fat at 1" intervals to prevent curling.
• Blend remaining ingredients except tenderizer; brush on meat; place in shallow dish. Cover and refrigerate overnight.
• Bring meat to room temperature; 30 minutes before grilling, apply tenderizer (follow directions on jar).
• Place meat on greased grill 4 to 5"

above hot coals; grill 10 to 15 minutes per side, depending on doneness you want; turn only once. (You can make a slit along the bone to check doneness.)

• Remove meat to a cutting board; carve out any bones; carve into ¼" slices to serve. Makes 6 to 8 servings.

To Broil in Oven: Preheat broiler; place steak on unheated broiler rack so top of meat is 4 to 5" from heat (for 2" steaks, or well done meat, increase distance); for medium, broil 18 to 20 minutes per side.

GLAZED HAM SLICES

Cider-honey mixture forms a glaze on ham slices while they heat over coals

1 c. cider
½ c. honey
½ c. brown sugar
1 tblsp. cornstarch
4 (¾" thick) center-cut slices
    ready-to-eat ham

• Combine cider, honey, brown sugar and cornstarch; bring to a boil and cook 5 minutes.

• Trim fat from ham slices; score them lightly with a knife. Brush on both sides with honey glaze.

• Place on grill over hot coals. Turn often and brush with the glaze until heated through and crusty brown, about 20 minutes. Makes 8 servings.

COMPANY LAMB BARBECUE

Lamb turning on a spit whets appetites. So roast two legs for big gatherings. Meat is expertly seasoned

5 lb. leg of lamb
1 tsp. dried tarragon
2 cloves garlic, cut in slivers
½ c. cooking oil
1 (7 oz.) bottle lemon-lime
    carbonated beverage
1½ tsp. paprika
1 tsp. salt
1 tsp. Worcestershire sauce
½ tsp. pepper

• Remove 3" of leg bone at shank end, leaving enough skin to fold over end; pin with skewer. Make at least a dozen ¼" slits in the fat covering with point of knife; insert pinches of tarragon and slivers of garlic; rub remaining tarragon over outside. Place roast in shallow dish.

• Mix remaining ingredients; pour over roast, coating all sides. Cover and refrigerate at least 6 hours or overnight (turn several times).

• Let stand at room temperature 1 hour before roasting.

• Insert spit from shank end of roast, aiming it to emerge beside bone at butt end. Fasten spit forks firmly in place. (Be sure roast does not shift on spit by its own weight.) Insert meat thermometer in thick end of roast, parallel to spit.

• Build up coals to back of fire basket; put spit in place; place drip pan (or trough of foil) directly beneath turning roast.

• Baste with remaining marinade every 15 minutes for best flavor.

• Roast to internal temperature of 175° for medium, 182° for well done. (Allow about 35 minutes per lb., or 2½ to 3 hours altogether.) Let stand 15 minutes before carving. Makes 6 to 8 servings.

VARIATIONS

Oven Rotisserie Lamb: Follow range manufacturer's directions.

Oven Roast Lamb: Roast uncovered on rack in shallow pan in slow oven (300°), 30 to 35 minutes per lb. Baste frequently with sauce.

LAMB KABOBS

Lamb fixed this way always goes over

1 tsp. ground ginger
1 tsp. dry mustard
1 tsp. monosodium glutamate
2 tsp. sugar
½ c. soy sauce
¼ c. salad oil
3 cloves garlic, minced
½ c. pineapple juice
2 to 3 lbs. lamb shoulder or
    leg, cut in 1½" cubes

• Combine all ingredients, except lamb, in a glass or pottery bowl. Cover this marinade and let stand at room temperature 24 hours.

• Add lamb cubes and stir to coat all lamb pieces with the marinade. Cover and let stand in refrigerator 6 to 8 hours.

• Arrange meat cubes on skewers at least 12" long. Allow space between every two pieces of lamb so it will cook evenly.

• Broil over coals 3 to 5" from source of heat about 20 to 30 minutes, turning frequently. To serve, rest end of each skewer on plate and push lamb off skewer with a knife. Serve at once. Makes 6 servings.

Note: Add small, not too ripe tomatoes to skewers during the last 5 minutes of cooking. If desired, thread small onions and canned whole mushrooms on skewers alternately with the meat. Brush them with leftover marinade.

BRANDED CHICKEN BUNWICH

Cookout goes Western with initials branded on top of buns. Expand this recipe to fit the size of the crowd

3 c. diced cooked chicken
1 onion, sliced
1½ c. bottled barbecue sauce
6 hamburger buns
2 tblsp. Parmesan cheese

• Combine chicken, onion and sauce; heat over grill until bubbling hot.

• Toast split buns on back of grill; fill each with ½ c. chicken mixture; sprinkle with 1 tsp. cheese. Makes 6 servings.

To Brand: Unwind metal coat hanger; form one end of wire into an initial. Heat in coals until red hot. Apply to top of bun long enough to burn initial.

COOKOUT HASH

This filling skillet meal is a cookout version of Spanish rice with beef

1 lb. ground beef
1 c. uncooked brown rice
1 c. chopped onion
½ c. chopped green pepper
2 tblsp. fat
1 tblsp. chili powder
1 tsp. salt
1 (1 lb.) can kidney beans
3 c. boiling water
8 slices sharp Cheddar cheese

• Brown beef, rice, onion and green pepper in hot fat in a deep skillet (for easy cleaning rub outside of skillet with soap).

• Add chili powder, salt, beans and water. Bring to a boil over coals; cover and simmer 30 minutes until rice is cooked. Remove cover; top with cheese. Cover; let stand on back of grill until cheese is melted. Makes 8 servings.

CAMP-STYLE HUSH PUPPIES
Help satisfy outdoor-size appetites

1 c. white cornmeal
1 tblsp. flour
1 tsp. baking powder
⅛ tsp. baking soda
1 (8½ oz.) can whole kernel
    corn, drained
2 tblsp. finely chopped onion
⅔ c. buttermilk
1 tblsp. water
Salad oil

· Combine dry ingredients; mix in corn and onion (green onion if available). Stir in buttermilk and water.
· Meanwhile, pour oil ½" deep in a heavy skillet (or 8" square of heavy-duty aluminum foil with edges turned up) set on grill over very hot coals.
· Drop batter by tablespoonfuls into hot oil. Bake until hush puppies are puffy and browned on bottom; flip over to brown other side. Drain. Makes 20 hush puppies.

PEACH TURNOVERS
These little pies taste twice as good baked over coals. For a change, use canned tart cherries or apples

Pastry for 2-crust pie
16 to 24 canned peach slices,
    drained
1 tsp. cinnamon
¼ c. sugar
3 tblsp. butter

· Divide pastry in half and roll out ⅛" thick.
· Cut in 5" squares. Place 2 or 3 peach slices on half of each square; sprinkle with cinnamon and sugar and dot with butter. Moisten edges and fold to make triangles; seal well by pressing around edges with a fork.
· Wrap each in foil with drugstore fold on edges. Chill until ready to bake. Place on burned-down coals, about 5 minutes per side. Watch carefully, they burn easily. Makes 8 turnovers.

Hostess How-to

HOW TO PLAN
COMPANY MENUS

The first step to a successful company meal is a good carefully-thought-through menu. That's why we're giving over a whole chapter to menus for every occasion—from a holly-decorated Christmas open house to share-the-load co-operative meals, informal ranch suppers, Sunday dinners or women's dessert luncheons. For summer entertaining, also look in the chapter *Cooking over Coals* for unforgettable outdoor meals —including complete directions for a Hawaiian pig roast.

Nothing gives you a better start than to jot down on paper the combination of foods you want to serve. Then you can work out the strategy for fixing the different dishes so you can get them ready on time without being too tired to enjoy guests.

You will find hundreds of exciting recipes in this book from which to make your selections. This chapter gives you a sample of some of them put together into meals that are sure to please and refresh guests and family. If you were building a new house and the architect brought you plans he drew for it, nine chances out of ten, you'd suggest a few changes. That's exactly what you may want to do with our menus that follow. We mean them to be a guide to foods that complement one another in texture, color and flavor, and that allow for convenient meal management. Make changes to fit the season, your food supplies, your time, your family's and guests' preferences.

Make-ahead dishes show up in many of the menus. Nothing strange about this, for today's women—especially farm women—are do-ahead hostesses, who fix part of the company food before the day they entertain. Freezers and refrigerators make this possible. Many women further simplify their guest meals and refreshments with intelligent use of some of the partly prepared foods their supermarkets offer. Many of these conveniences become ingredients in otherwise elaborate dishes—we give you recipes (for example, Lemon Cheese Torte with its cherry crown).

You can add an appetizer course to the dinners and suppers, if you wish. Just turn to Chapter 8 and select dips and dippers or other meal beginnings. It's fashionable to serve them in the living room with the host taking over, while the hostess attends to last-minute details in the kitchen.

Our menus do not always suggest beverages. The choice between coffee and tea brings no complications. Neither do we always list breads, knowing that a farm hostess, with home-baked rolls and loaves in her freezer, needs no reminder that they are praise-winners. (We do give you many exceptional bread recipes in a separate chapter.)

You'll find recipes in this book for all the dishes marked with an *. Please check the Index for page numbers.

Come to Dinner

When you invite friends to dinner, you compliment them because country company dinners are special. You can go to a lot of effort fixing the food— you want it to be letter-perfect. But if you choose your menu thoughtfully, you can spread out the work so it's almost easy—and still serve a wonderful meal. There are two important secrets: Include one or two make-ahead dishes and at least one more that requires almost no attention while it cooks. You'll find such recipes represented in the dinner menus that follow. Also, remember that a vegetable or fruit that seems "everyday" to you becomes company-special to town guests—the country hostess is smart to feature home-grown produce. Country surpluses often can yield the meal's most outstanding dish.

SUMMER DINNER

Oven-Fried Pecan Chicken*
Corn on the Cob
Summer Squash with Dill*
Superb Fruit Salad*
Brown Mountain Cake* Ice Cream

A dinner like this one makes people wish for summer never to end. It takes 1 hour to cook the chicken, but if you have no automatic timer and are away from the kitchen—at church, for instance—you can lower the oven temperature and let the chicken bake during your absence.

The gorgeous melon and fruit salad of brilliant colors needs a good chilling. Put the fruits and marsh-mallows in the refrigerator an hour or several hours before serving; add the melon later.

It takes little time to get the quick-cooking corn and squash ready. The cake has a fudge frosting. Maybe you'll want to bake it a few days ahead and put it in the freezer for quick use. (Fudge frosting sometimes becomes brittle and cracks, especially if you store it longer than a month.)

AUTUMN DINNER

California Pot Roast*   Gravy
Cheese Potato Puff*
Autumn Tomato Skillet*
Rye Bread or Rolls
Red and Green Cabbage Salad*
Apple Macaroon*

Here is a delightful dinner for the first chilly days of the season, but before frost nips the last of the garden vegetables. The expertly seasoned pot roast cooks slowly about 3 hours. So get it on the range in time. You won't have to pay much attention to it until mealtime. Bake the Apple Macaroon to free the oven for the Potato Puff, which takes 35 minutes. Dovetail fixing the tomato dish and salad making into your last hour of cooking. To fancy up the dessert, serve scoops of vanilla ice cream or fluffs of whipped cream on each serving.

WINTER PORK DINNER

Stuffed Pork Pockets*
Walnut Carrots*
Potatoes au Gratin*
Tomato Aspic with Vegetables*
Spicy Crunch Apple Pie*

Put the pork in the oven 1½ hours before you want to serve dinner. Then forget about it. Make the aspic several hours or a day ahead so it will chill until firm. Since carrots appear as a hot dish, omit them from the aspic. In fact, you can omit all the vegetables from this jellied salad if you like. But do serve the red aspic in lettuce cups.

Boil the potatoes a day ahead and store them in the refrigerator. You can peel them, mix them with the cheese and put them in the oven with the pork 50 minutes to 1 hour before dinnertime rather than the 35 minutes specified in the recipe. The oven temperature (325°) required by the pork chops is lower than that given in the recipe for Potatoes au Gratin.

COMPANY DINNER WITH VEAL

Company Special Veal*
Olive-Rice*
Cheese-Creamed Spinach*
Peach Pickles   Radish Roses
Stay-Crisp Cabbage Salad*
Pumpkin Pudding Cake*

You can fix the veal ahead to reheat at serving time. If it is easier for you, cook the rice, place it in a casserole, top with the veal and refrigerate to reheat at mealtime. But the rice will be fluffier if you cook it just before dinner, and use it to border the veal on the platter.

The salad comes from the refrigerator so is easy to serve. You can make it a day ahead. Serve the pudding cake warm; it needs to bake 1 hour. Unless your guests are weight-watchers, they'll enjoy their dessert topped with either whipped cream or vanilla ice cream.

AFTER-CHURCH DINNER

Mazetti*

Squash and Vegetable Sauté*

Hot Rolls   Jelly or Jam

Pineapple-Cheese Salad*

Mocha Frosted Cake*

Have Mazetti, a ground beef and noodle casserole, in the refrigerator ready to tuck in the oven to bake 1 hour after you return from church. Heat the rolls in the oven with Mazetti during the last few minutes. You can cook the squash dish, get out your best jelly or jam and arrange salad from refrigerator on individual serving plates while the main dish bakes. Remove dessert from refrigerator about 30 minutes before time to serve it.

AFTER SUNDOWN BUFFET

Rosy Ham Ring*

Western Baked Beans*   Garlic Bread

Garden Salad Bowls*

Cottage Blue Cheese Dressing*

Apple Gingerbread*

Men especially like this dinner. The cooking time for it is about 1½ hours. If you hurry, you may be able both to fix the food and cook it in 2 hours. Serve the ham on a chop plate and fill the center with a fluffy bouquet of parsley so it will look festive on the buffet table. (Or serve baked ham if you prefer.) You can mix and shape the ham loaf several days ahead and freeze it to bake the day you have company. You will need to bake the frozen loaf a few minutes longer.

You'll be thankful for an electric can opener, if you have one, when you get the different kinds of canned beans ready to bake. Serve the gingerbread warm. You can bake it at the same time you bake the ham and beans if your oven is large enough. Otherwise, put it in the oven before you bake the beans, set it in a warm place until time to serve.

COUNTRY CHICKEN DINNER

Parmesan Chicken*

Rice Pilaf*   Broccoli Platter*

Overnight Refrigerator Rolls*

Frozen Cranberry Salad*

Crispy Crunch Sundae*

If you serve guests this chicken dinner on a wintry day, they will compliment you on the food. You can easily get the dinner in 1 hour and 15 minutes. Both the salad and dessert are frozen; you can fix them at least a day ahead. You may wish to buy rolls and heat them. If you bake Overnight Refrigerator Rolls, increase the oven temperature when you take the chicken out and bake them while you are arranging the other food for serving. Then you'll serve the rolls piping hot fresh from the oven.

DINNER FOR A COLD DAY

Fresh Pork Pot Roast*   Dumplings*

Tomato-Lima Beans*

Cabbage-Onion Salad*

Applesauce Meringue Pie* or

Apple-Pineapple Scallop*

Farmers like this hearty dinner. The pork cooks about 2½ hours on top of the range, but requires little attention. You can make the salad a day or two ahead and refrigerate it. It's especially attractive made with red-purple onions. Bake the pie several hours ahead if you decide to serve pie. Apple-Pineapple Scallop is a lighter dessert, but you do need to serve it at least faintly warm. It can bake while the dumplings steam.

ITALIAN DINNER

Antipasto Salad Bowls
Zuppa Verde*   Lasagne Roll-Ups*
Roast Pork with Flavor Pockets*
Green Beans with Garlic Butter
Pears Cardinale*

Here's a hearty dinner inviting with color and tempting aromas. And it tastes simply wonderful. You can omit either the lasagne or pork roast for a less hearty meal, but they're so good you'll want to have both of them. Serve the lasagne first in true Italian style. You can fix it a day or longer ahead and freeze for quick reheating at mealtime. The soup cooks on top of the range while the pork roasts in the oven. While they cook, you can make the luscious dessert, toss the salad and cook the green beans. Dress the hot beans, cooked in salted water and drained, in butter in which you heated a crushed garlic clove (do not let garlic brown and remove before adding butter to beans). Have the salad on the table when you seat your guests. Toss mixed greens with Italian salad dressing. Place in individual salad bowls or on salad plates and garnish each salad with slices or slivers of pickled beets, a ripe or green olive, a quarter tomato, lightly salted, and shredded carrots.

Supper's Ready

Suppers on the farm often are much like dinners, but they usually are less pretentious. And that means they are easier to get. When you use our supper menus, you'll find the meals are attractive, tasty and will please guests.

AMERICAN SUPPER BUFFET

Pork Cantonese*   Fluffy Rice*
Herb Buttered Beans*
Strawberry Salad*
Mincemeat Pastry Squares*

This menu is an example of how we use a version of an international recipe. The main dish is of Chinese origin. You can serve it from your electric skillet or a bowl and let guests spoon it over the hot rice. (People like to help themselves.) The jellied salad is colorful and tasty, strictly American. Bake and glaze Mincemeat Squares in the morning for our popular adaptation of English tarts.

SUPPER FOR UNEXPECTED COMPANY

Chilled Tomato Juice
Woodstock*
Baked Potatoes   Buttered Corn
Homemade Pickles and Relishes
14-Carat Cake*

This is the kind of supper you can serve an unexpected guest. If you're in luck, you'll have the 14-Carat Cake (or another cake) in your freezer or refrigerator, the tomato juice and canned corn in the cupboard. And almost all country kitchens have a supply of potatoes to bake and cheese and eggs ready to use in Woodstock. Bake the potatoes, cut a cross in their tops with a fork, press both ends to fluff. Add a pat of butter to opening in each potato. Pass the Woodstock to ladle over the potatoes. Raid your fruit closet and serve your choicest pickles and relishes, such as pickled peaches, cucumber pickles and corn salad or other mixed vegetable relish.

COUNTRY SUPPER

Spaghetti Soufflé*   Cold Meat
Ripe Tomato Salad*
Crusty Brown Rolls*
Strawberry Whip Dessert*
Oatmeal Crisps*

The soufflé bakes 1 hour. This means you'll need 1¼ hours to get the entire meal. You make the dessert and bake the cookies ahead. If you bake yeast rolls, you'll want to try our fine European-type rolls with brown crusts. They are good insurance for tasty meals if you keep a supply in the freezer.

SPRING SUPPER

Asparagus and Egg Casserole*
Tart Rhubarb Salad*
Hot Rolls
Vanilla Ice Cream   Assorted Cookies

If you want to have a more substantial meal, add a platter of cold cuts. The only hot food is the casserole, so it has no competition for oven space. It takes 40 to 50 minutes

to cook the asparagus and to bake the casserole. If fresh strawberries are in season, crush and sweeten a few and serve over the ice cream, or pass a sundae sauce.

SUMMERTIME SUPPER

Frosted Vegetable Soup*
Seville Rice and Chicken*
Crusty Rolls or Bread
Lemon Daffodil Dessert*

It takes time to make the delicious soup of fresh vegetables with a recipe we borrowed from Spain, but one sip of the soup and you'll agree it's worth the effort. The minute-consuming task is chopping the vegetables fine. Make the soup in the morning and chill it thoroughly. It takes the place of salad, so there's one less dish to make.

Seville Rice and Chicken is another Spanish treat. It's almost a meal in itself. You need to allow 1¼ hours for it to cook.

Make the dessert the day before you have company and chill it in the refrigerator. If you prefer, serve slices of almond-flavored Country Sponge Cake (see Index for recipe), topped with sugared fresh strawberries and whipped cream, for dessert.

SUMMER FISH SUPPER

Halibut au Gratin*
Dilly Potato Salad*
Pineapple Beets*
Hot Rolls   Cantaloupe Salad*
Marshmallow Cream Peach Pie*

The two hot foods, halibut and beets, are quick. The halibut bakes in 45 minutes and you use canned beets, which are ready to fix with the turn of a can opener. (You can cook fresh beets from your garden if you have them.) Get the potato salad ready in the morning, cover and chill it; this gives the flavors a chance to blend.

The salad of melon and green grapes is refreshing and may take a double role, that of both salad and dessert. If you omit the pie, a tray of cookies from the freezer will provide a sweet ending. (Bake one or two kinds of cookies from the collection of recipes in this cookbook.) If you decide to have the pie, make it in the morning before your kitchen gets warm. Chill it until serving time.

AUTUMN SANDWICH SUPPER

California Pot Roast on Buns*
Cheese Scalloped Corn*
Dill Pickles   Radish Roses*
Celery   Carrot Curls*
Frozen Pumpkin Torte*

Instead of serving California Pot Roast sliced, with a bowl or boat of gravy, shred the meat, add it to the gravy and serve it between or on heated split buns. Cheese Scalloped Corn is a fast-fix dish; it bakes only 35 minutes. You use canned corn. Arrange the relishes on a tray to display their color. The dessert is one of those "hostess friends" that you can put in the freezer days ahead.

QUICK-AND-EASY SUPPER

Chicken-Broccoli*
Orange Carrots*
Relish Tray of Celery, Pickles, Olives
Mincemeat Refrigerator Dessert*

Try this meal on a winter day. Since you make the main dish with cooked chicken and frozen broccoli, it need bake only 30 minutes. When you have it in the oven, cook the carrots. If you have the relishes in the refrigerator, you can assemble them on a tray in a few minutes. The hearty dessert is a make-ahead special. Fix it either several hours or a day ahead. If you wish to serve a heartier meal, set a platter of cold baked ham, sliced, on the table.

SPECIAL-OCCASION SHRIMP SUPPER

Shrimp Marengo*   Fluffy Rice*
Bermuda Tossed Salad*
Crusty Rolls
Lemon-Chocolate Dessert*

If your guests like shrimp, this supper will please them. Allow an hour to get the meal, although, if you work fast, you can shave a few minutes off this time. Cleaning the shrimp is the most tedious task. Put the rice on to steam; then fix the shrimp main dish. The dessert must be made several hours early to chill. Better still, make it the day before you want to serve it.

CHICKEN SUPPER

Chicken Pizzas*
Catalina Tossed Salad*
Honey French Dressing*
Fresh Peach Cobbler*

If you have cooked chicken in the freezer or refrigerator, it won't take long to make and bake the pizzas.

You'll need to make our recipe (see Index) twice. For a heavier meal, top cobbler servings with vanilla ice cream or with lemon ice cream.

SOUP SUPPER

Herbed Potato Soup*
Crackers   Carrot-Chive Salad*
24-Hour Rum Rolls*
Molded Rhubarb Swirl*

This meal illustrates a good menu planning rule: When hearty soup is the main course, have an interesting bread and a glamorous dessert. Serve the soup at the table from a tureen or attractive bowl to add a special touch. Take the frosty-cold dessert from refrigerator to table. It's a beauty. The whole meal is so cheerful that it makes a rainy evening seem bright.

BUFFET SUPPER

Hot Crab Dip*   Blue Cheese Whip*
Crackers   Potato Chips
Carrot Sticks
Sweet-Sour Meat Balls*
Dilly Potato Salad*
Lima Beans with Cheese*
Rye Bread   Green Salad
Raspberry Torte*

The dessert needs to chill several hours. Try to get it in the refrigerator in the morning so you can dismiss it from your thoughts. Make the potato salad early in the day, too; cover and refrigerate until serving time.

Fix Blue Cheese Whip, place in a serving bowl, cover and refrigerate. Cut the carrot sticks, rinse in cold water and wrap them in waxed paper without drying (sprinkle first with a little garlic salt if you like), and refrigerate. Or leave carrot sticks in cold water; drain before serving.

Make the Hot Crab Dip just before time for your guests to arrive. Put the meat balls in the oven to bake while guests enjoy talk and appetizers. The lima beans are quick to fix because you use the frozen vegetable. If you bake bread and have our Heidelberg Rye Bread in your freezer, by all means serve it, thinly sliced. Your guests will appreciate it.

SHARE-THE-LOAD SUPPER

Golden Chicken Casserole*
Indiana Succotash*
Sun Gold Fruit Salad*
Mocha Frosted Cake*

You can successfully tote all the dishes in this meal. Make the salad a day ahead, or in the morning, to give it time to chill. Add the frosting shortly before you tote the salad. You'll not have to bother with salad dressing at serving time. You can fix the dessert a few days ahead and freeze it. If you take it from the freezer before you leave home, it will thaw enough by serving time. Succotash answers for two vegetables; the corn-green bean combination always holds up well if it has to wait but do serve it hot. You can use cooked chicken from the freezer or cook the chicken a day early so that getting the casserole in the oven will be quick. It bakes only 30 minutes.

COVERED DISH SUPPER

Glazed Spareribs with Apples*
Cheese 'n' Potato Casserole*
French Bread   Sauerkraut Salad*
Beet Pickles*   Carrot Curls*
Prune Cake de Luxe*
Vanilla Ice Cream

This is a hearty meal that's just right for a frosty day. Allow 1½ hours for the spareribs to bake, 1 hour for the potatoes. You can get the potato casserole ready to bake in the morning and refrigerate it until time to put in the oven. The salad is a refrigerator special. Make it a day ahead if you like. If you try to eliminate as much work as possible the day you entertain, bake the cake a day or several days ahead and freeze it. Top each serving with a dollop of vanilla ice cream.

Entertaining at Luncheon

Women's luncheons are happy occasions—a time for friends to gather for conversation before a purposeful committee meeting or club program. Because the menu is less substantial than supper, it's an easy way to entertain. Look through our suggestions for some out-of-the-groove recipes that are especially attractive without being fancy or tedious to prepare.

WOMEN'S LUNCHEON

Regal Chicken Salad*
Hot Sweet Potato Biscuits*
Chilled Grapefruit Halves

Nothing surpasses a really good chicken salad for the main dish in a women's luncheon. And Regal Chicken Salad is superior—attractive, too. Make it ahead and chill so the flavors will mellow. Serve it in Lettuce Baskets or Lettuce Cups (see Index). For dessert, cut chilled jumbo pink grapefruit in halves, and serve with a garnish of rosebuds and fresh mint, if available. Tuck a tiny pink sweetheart rose in center of each grapefruit half and stick two or three fresh mint leaves around it. Bake the biscuits after your guests arrive so you can serve them piping hot.

WOMEN'S SUMMER LUNCHEON

Salad Niçoise*
Toasted French Bread Slices
Chilled Cantaloupe

You'll want to serve a hot drink with this cold luncheon. Get the pretty and substantial French potato salad ready to serve before guests arrive. Then you'll have no worry about the food. You might like to have lemon sherbet instead of melon for dessert, or to top each wedge of orange melon with a little scoop of orange or mint sherbet.

SOUP AND SANDWICH LUNCHEON

Chicken Velvet Soup*
Garden Sandwiches*
Olives   Pickles   Celery
Raspberry or Orange Sherbet

You can use this menu for luncheon or supper. The soup is rich so you'll want to serve it in cups. If you make the chicken stock, cook the chicken a day ahead and refrigerate it and the chicken separately. Or perhaps you have a supply in the freezer. When making the Garden Sandwiches, be sure to read the note with the recipe that tells how to serve the sandwiches so their gala colored filling will show. The home economist who shares the recipe fixes homemade mayonnaise to use in filling.

LUNCHEON OR SUPPER

Italian Eggplant*
Tossed Green Salad*   Garlic Bread
Refrigerator Custard Pie*

Here's a meatless meal that guests enjoy, but you can add strips of crisp bacon or cooked ham slices if you want to serve meat. You'll find it takes less than an hour to brown the eggplant slices and bake them with cheese and tomato sauce. Make the pie in the morning and chill it in the refrigerator. You end up with a rather unusual meal, but one that always wins friends, especially new ones for eggplant, a vegetable too often neglected.

LUNCHEON ON THE LIGHT SIDE

Tomato Soup   Jellied Egg Salad*
Southwestern Corn Bake*
Ranch House Raisin Cookies*

With the salad main dish in the refrigerator, you have little cooking to do at the last minute before serving your guests. Heat the soup (you can use vegetable soup from your freezer). The Southwestern Corn Bake is extremely popular with hostesses and guests in our Southwest. You can buy the canned chilis in many sections of the country now, and in practically every market in Southwestern and some Western states. Get acquainted with these South-of-the-Border peppers, which are perfect seasoning for many corn dishes. Introduce your friends to them. The cookies are men favorites. Their old-fashioned name was Boiled Raisin Cookies.

EASY-TO-FIX LUNCHEON

Cashew Tuna Luncheon*
Buttered Green Peas
Savory Baked Tomatoes*   Hot Rolls
Jewels-in-a-Ring Salad*

Put the tuna casserole in oven to bake. Then fix the tomatoes. Just before it's time to take the tuna from the oven, cook frozen peas and butter them (be careful not to overcook and destroy their bright green color). When you're ready to take the tuna to the table, scatter snipped parsley over it. If you fix the salad, which also is the dessert, a day ahead, you can get this meal in an hour. You can buy and heat rolls, but homemade Oatmeal Rolls (see Index) make the meal special.

Special Occasion Menus

Every homemaker will at sometime during the year make a special occasion out of a holiday by entertaining. And, wisely, she'll let tradition help shape her plans for food and table decorations—people expect it! Turkey at Thanksgiving, red-and-green trimmings on the Christmas table, an orange-and-black color scheme at a Halloween party, cherries for Washington's birthday, Company Corned Beef on St. Patrick's Day. We think, however, that our recipes for traditional foods will lift your menus out of the ordinary. Here is a sampler for these happy social gatherings—everything from an especially pretty tea table to a complete Christmas dinner.

LARGE TEA OR RECEPTION

Party Roll-Ups*
Cucumber-Cheese Sandwiches*
Petits Fours*   Almond Circles*
Salted Nuts   Candy Mints
Hot Tea*   French Chocolate*

This food is pretty . . . be sure the table matches it in good looks. Have two friends pour, one the tea and the other (seated at the opposite end of the table), the hot chocolate. Make the sandwiches ahead, cover and keep them in the refrigerator until teatime.

GOLDEN WEDDING RECEPTION

Orange-Ginger Punch*
Flower Wedding Cake*
Yellow and White Candy Mints
Salted Nuts

Fill the punch bowl with ice to chill it. Decorate outside of bowl by taping tiny corsages or bridal bouquets on outside of punch bowl. (Use small flowers: If flowers are too heavy, the tape will not hold them.) Decorate the Flower Wedding Cake with yellow frosted flowers (as recipe

directs). If you do not wish to have a big wedding cake, use Petits Fours (see Index).

WOMEN'S DESSERT BRIDGE

Sweetheart Party Cake*
Salted Nuts
Tea or Coffee

This strawberry-and-cream cake is a valentine special. Use showmanship and serve the cake from a buffet table; tuck a bouquet of little flowers in the center. It might be a corsage to give for a bridge prize.

WASHINGTON'S BIRTHDAY DESSERT

Lemon Cheese Torte*
Coffee

Choose this superb torte for evening party refreshments. The cake has a red-cherry crown that glistens under lights. It's filling—sends everybody home in a happy frame of mind.

CHILDREN'S BIRTHDAY PARTY

Candy Birthday Cake
Ice Cream
Strawberry Ade*

Nothing pleases youngsters more at a birthday party than cake or cupcakes, ice cream and a colorful cold drink. If cake decorating isn't your forte, we have an easy solution: Go to your supermarket and see what you can find on the candy shelves— hard candy circle mints make gala candle holders, for example.

Or you can arrange flat round mints in pastel colors on top and sides of cake . . . or decorate the cake with a confetti effect, using different sizes and colors of candy.

You can do many things with gumdrops, such as make flowers (see Index for Cake Garnishes). Gold foil-wrapped chocolate coins, little sticks of candy and small lollipops—all have possibilities.

You'll delight the youngsters if you scoop two kinds of ice cream, like chocolate and vanilla, in each serving. And Strawberry Ade has the bright color and taste that make it popular at birthday parties.

ST. PATRICK'S DAY DINNER

Company Corned Beef*
Browned Creamed Potatoes*
Buttered Peas
Lettuce Salad   Hot Rolls
Lime-Chocolate Fascination*

Company Corned Beef is a favorite of a California hostess and her friends. You can serve it hot or cold, so take your choice. You simmer the beef from 3 to 3¾ hours, or until tender, then stud it with cloves, pour the sauce over it and bake 30 minutes.

Boil the potatoes a day ahead, cool and refrigerate; peel and chop them when it's time to combine them with cream and other ingredients (1 hour before dinnertime) to brown and heat in the oven. Sprinkle a wreath of chopped chives around edge of potatoes just before taking them to the table. Make the luscious green-and-chocolate dessert a day ahead and refrigerate.

HALLOWEEN EVENING REFRESHMENTS

Cider or Orange Juice
Colorado Spudnuts*
Halloween 3-Decker Brownies*

Teen-agers can fix the drink and take the doughnuts and cookies from the freezer. Let them serve the refreshments, but offer help if they need it. Suggest they place a bowl of polished apples on the table so guests can help themselves.

THANKSGIVING DAY DINNER

Roast Turkey with Stuffing*
Mashed Potatoes   Gravy
Orange Carrots*   Glazed Onions*
Cranberry Sauce
Relish Tray
Pumpkin Parfait*

Thanksgiving Day is one time many families refuse to tamper with their traditional menu. We suggest a minimum of changes. For instance, because the turkey occupies the oven, we give you a refrigerator pumpkin dessert instead of pumpkin pie. You can make it a day ahead, and put in the refrigerator. Holds better than pie.

You can substitute mashed yellow turnips (rutabagas) for the carrots if turnips are a traditional vegetable at your house for this occasion. Cook 2 large turnips in salted water, drain, mash and season with ¼ lb. butter. Taste for salt. Arrange mashed turnips in a ring on a large plate and fill center with Glazed Onions. If you want an appetizer course, try Tomato Soup Piquant (see Index).

ROAST BEEF
CHRISTMAS DINNER

Cranberry-Apple Drink*
Beef-Eaters' Favorite Roast*
Brown Potatoes*
Green Beans with Almonds*
Baby Beet Salad*
Flaming Plum Pudding*

Many people's first choice for Christmas dinner is a standing beef roast. Get it in the oven first. Add the potatoes in time to bake and brown them.

Instead of a big plum pudding, you may prefer Individual Plum Puddings (see Index). For them, you get the batter ready a few or several days ahead and refrigerate or freeze. You steam the desired number of servings in custard cups the day of the dinner. Divide the batter, if you freeze it, in portions for one meal so that you will need to thaw only the amount required. Serve plum puddings with your favorite pudding sauce (see Index for Hard Sauce Snow Men). If fresh beets are not available for the salad, you can use canned small, whole beets.

YULETIDE CHICKEN DINNER

Iced Tomato Juice
Roast Young Chickens*
Honey-Glazed Carrots*
Brussels Sprouts with Lemon*
Cranberry-Marshmallow Salad*
Fruitcake Bonbons*   Orange Sherbet

Precook the chickens in a hot oven 30 minutes; cool and freeze them.

Roast them only 1 hour just before dinner, basting them with lemon juice while cooking. With the chicken in the oven, cook vegetables on the top of the range. Make the salad ahead and refrigerate or freeze. Serve our Fruitcake Bonbons, or substitute thin slices of fruitcake.

CHRISTMAS BUFFET DINNER

Christmas Snack Tree*
Green Goddess Dip*
Clam-Cheese Dip*
Country-Style Beef Wellington*
Buffet Cheese Potatoes*
Buttered Peas
Hot Rolls
Cinnamon Apple Salad*
Date Cake Irresistible*

One of the advantages of building a Christmas Snack Tree is that your guests and the host can enjoy it while you put the finishing touches on the dinner.

Roast a whole beef tenderloin the day before Christmas. On the day of the dinner, wrap it in its pastry jacket and bake. Give the host a sharp carving knife or an electric slicing knife and let him carve the roast after the guests have a chance to admire its beauty.

Get the potatoes ready to bake the day before, too, and run them in the oven to heat and brown 45 to 50 minutes before the roast is done. Make the salad a day ahead and refrigerate it. You can bake the cake a few days early and freeze it. Serve it topped with whipped cream.

SNOWY DAY OPEN HOUSE

Hot Apple Punch*
Fruitcake Bonbons*
Lemon-Coconut Squares*
Candied Grapefruit Peel*
Sugared Nuts*

Serve punch from an attractive teapot or pitcher and use your prettiest teacups. Drop a half clove-studded orange slice in each cup. If you have time to bake small Grapefruit Sugar Cookies (see Index), serve them instead of Candied Grapefruit Peel. You can bake them ahead and freeze.

CHRISTMAS OPEN HOUSE

Hot Spicy Grape Punch*
North Carolina Bishop's Bread*
Chocolate-Coconut Bonbons*
Orange Brownies*

Keep the electric coffee maker filled with the steaming hot punch. Its aroma will please your guests. Arrange accompaniments, from freezer, around it on the table. Guests make their own selections.

What to Serve a Crowd

You'll find a mouth-watering collection of quantity-size recipes in the chapter on Cooking for a Crowd. Look them over and consider which combination of dishes will best suit the people you will entertain. Or start here with these menu suggestions; they have proved themselves on many occasions.

SUPPER FOR A CROWD

Smoky Mountain Barbecued Ribs*
Candied Sweet Potatoes*
Coleslaw   Garlic Bread
Southern Cream Apple Pies*

You can't miss with this menu. Make the sauce for the ribs, and also cook the ribs in water a day ahead. Cool and refrigerate. Then you need bake them in the sauce only an hour before serving. Instead of sweet potatoes, you can have Scalloped Potatoes (see Index for recipe). Bake the pies early in the afternoon or in the morning so they will not require attention during the busy minutes before you serve the meal. Substitute a green salad for the coleslaw if you like.

BUFFET SUPPER FOR 18

Beef Stroganoff*
Scrambled Cabbage*
Lettuce Salad*
Red Clover Dressing*
Date-Nut Torte*
Lemon Foamy Sauce*

It's difficult to imagine a supper more festive with color or more bountiful in fine flavors than this buffet menu. Since the Stroganoff contains rare roast beef, you can cook the roast a day ahead. Potatoes team with the beef, which means the dish pleases most men. You tuck it in the oven to bake the last hour before supper.

Scrambled Cabbage cooks in 5 minutes, but it takes longer than that to shred it for cooking! Serve wedges of iceberg lettuce on a tray and a pitcher of the salad dressing nearby to pour over the salads. (Or add the dressing to the salad before serving if you like.) The torte and sunny sauce are make-ahead specials. You can fix them a day before you entertain.

BUFFET SUPPER FOR A CROWD

Genuine Swedish Meat Balls*
Fluffy Rice   Vegetable Medley*
Rye Bread
Olives   Pickles
Fruit and Nut Charlotte*

If you're serving supper for 25, you'll need to shape the meat balls and refrigerate them until cooking time. Also you can make the lovely fruit dessert in the morning and chill. Getting the vegetables ready for Vegetable Medley is time-consuming, but you can peel, slice, shred and dice them an hour to two ahead and store them, covered, in the refrigerator until cooking time. Why not let your helper (perhaps a daughter) take charge of cooking the vegetable dish and getting it on the buffet in good form?

A little more than an hour before supper, brown the meat balls and get them in the oven. Put the rice on to cook about 30 minutes before you want to serve it (follow package directions). Bring out the chafing dish, if you have one, and serve the meat balls and their self-made brown gravy in it. Heap the fluffy rice in a big Chinese or other colorful bowl.

Arrange olives and the best pickles from your fruit closet on a large tray or platter. Make a showpiece of the relishes. (Of course you can buy an assortment of interesting pickles at your supermarket, too.) You can

place the bread loaf on a board and let everyone cut his own slice, but be ready to help guests reluctant to do their own slicing. You can depend on the dessert, refrigerator chilled, to make a hit.

CHRISTMAS FEAST FOR 50

Turkey Stacks*
Scalloped Onions*
Mustard Star Salad*
Eggnog Tarts*

This big holiday meal, which appeared in FARM JOURNAL, was so popular with our readers that we include it in this cookbook. See Index for recipes—we give complete directions for getting this holiday meal. Home economists in our Test Kitchens worked them out in great detail.

CO-OPERATIVE DINNER

Bohemian Steak*
Buffet Cheese-Potatoes*
Scarlet Beauty Salad*
Southern Cream Apple Pies*

If you're looking for a frugal meal, here it is. And what's more, the food really tastes wonderful. Ground beef takes the spotlight in the main dish that makes 60 servings. It needs to bake only 30 minutes, but it does fill the oven. Since the potato casserole makes only 12 servings, assign more than one woman to fix this dish— enough for your size crowd. Scarlet Beauty Salad is a gourmet-type tomato aspic—it deserves its name. Of course, you make it ahead. And the apple pies, baked a few hours before you serve them, are one of the best you and your guests will ever taste.

A DINNER TO TOTE

Best-Ever Barbecued Hamburgers*
Scalloped Potatoes*
Mixed Vegetable Salad*
Creamy Spring Dressing*
Frosty Fudge Pie*

While this is a simple meal, it usually pleases people more than many elaborate dinners. And you can feed 100 or more guests. Since it's easier to cook the hamburger mixture in the oven than on top the range, you'll need to substitute potato salad for the Scalloped Potatoes if you fix all the food in your own kitchen. This is a good menu for several women to share in cooking. The hostess, or one of the group, can make the hamburger mixture and the other women bake the potatoes and prepare the vegetables for the salad, and the salad dressing.

The salad takes time, but it's worth it. Perhaps you have a young salad maker in your home to help. Girls enjoy taking the responsibility for the pretty salad. The pie always is a huge success and, fortunately, it's best when baked a day ahead. To glamorize the dessert servings, spoon a small bouquet of whipped cream on each wedge and add a colorful candy flower.

SUMMER SALAD LUNCHEON

Salmon Bowl Salad*
Hot Rolls
Peanut Brittle Charlotte*

When the weather is hot, it's fine to serve this meal. The salad is attractive, substantial and tasty. (You can make it with tuna instead of salmon.) When it comes to surprises, the dessert wins on all counts. It's so much more delicious and tempting than its name indicates. Be sure to fold the peanut brittle and other ingredients into the whipped cream rather than stirring them into it. The recipe makes 40 servings, but you can cut it in half. See the directions for spooning this dessert into sherbet glasses.

ITALIAN-STYLE SUPPER

Country Club Lasagne*
Tossed Green Salad*
Garlic Bread
Spumoni   Coffee

Serve this supper when you haven't much time for cooking. Get the lasagne in the oven and forget about it during the 30 minutes it cooks while you fix the bread, salad and coffee. Have the bread ready to go in the oven when you take the lasagne out. Buy the ice cream. If spumoni is not available, put a scoop each of vanilla, strawberry and chocolate ice cream in an individual serving dish. This is a good menu to use for a crowd of 12 to 24 people.

Between-Meal Refreshments and Snacks

Two-part menus add up to easy hospitality . . . fresh hot bread to go with coffee at 10 o'clock in the morning, or the glamorous dessert you bring out at the end of an evening of visiting with friends. Among our suggestions, we include some heartier snacks, too: Men's Favorite Evening Lunch and Hayrack Ride Refreshments. Our bread and dessert chapters will provide more ideas for making guests happy.

EVENING DESSERT PARTY

Elegant Chocolate Log*
Coffee

The dessert is rich and luscious; your guests will wish for nothing more. Both men and women like it. For a crowd, put two of the logs together on a long platter and serve from a buffet. Handsome, appropriate for Lincoln's birthday.

COLD WEATHER DESSERT BUFFET

Assorted Tarts*
Coffee

Follow directions for serving different kinds of tarts (see Index). You'll find your guests like to make their own filling selections in this colorful and distinctive service.

WOMEN'S CLUB DESSERT

Mauve Frozen Fruit Salad*
Melba Toast
Tea or Coffee

Our recipe for the lovely, luscious salad makes 12 or 24 servings. Freeze it in paper cups (portion cups is what restaurants call them) with pleated sides, if you can find them in your supermarkets. Restaurant supply stores have them. The cups leave an interesting design when peeled off their individual salads. You can buy melba

toast or make your own. To make melba toast, cut day-old bread in 1/8" slices. Remove crusts if you like. Cut slices diagonally to make triangles. Spread in a large shallow pan and bake in slow oven (325°) until crisp, golden and curled, about 15 minutes. Turn at least once while baking. Serve hot or cold.

AFTERNOON TEA

Company Cinnamon Toast*
Sand Balls* Lemon Love Notes*
Hot Tea*

When some of the neighbors stop by in the afternoon, invite them to have a cup of tea. Bring cookies, like Sand Balls and Lemon Love Notes, from the freezer, and make some cinnamon toast at the last minute so you can serve it hot. It's easier to be hospitable if you have some good cookies in the freezer.

NEIGHBORHOOD COFFEE

Square Doughnuts*
Coffee

Have plenty of doughnuts and coffee. Little glasses of chilled orange or other fruit juice are always welcome.

MORNING COFFEE FOR UNEXPECTED GUESTS

Pineapple Juice
Prune Cake de Luxe*
Coffee

Keep the prune cake in freezer so you can rise to the occasion when there are unexpected guests. Cut it in small bars and roll in confectioners sugar.

HAYRACK RIDE REFRESHMENTS

Grilled Franks*   Buns
Mexican Relishes   Potato Salad*
Homemade Vanilla Ice Cream*
Cookies

Country people like to entertain their town friends with a hayrack ride. Choose a moonlight night for this party. Serve the refreshments on the picnic table in the yard or on the porch. Let everyone grill his frankfurters if you have a charcoal fire ready. Or carry out the grilled franks along with heated buns to hold them. Set these five relishes on the table to invite guests to take their choice for topping frankfurters in buns—tomatoes, green onions, green chili peppers, all finely chopped and served separately, prepared mustard and dairy sour cream.

Have hot coffee, iced tea or lemonade ready to pour. Serve the dessert before or after the ride, whichever your guests seem to prefer. Nothing causes more excitement than a freezer full of homemade ice cream. A tray of cookies always attracts the nibblers, but they're not indispensable in this meal.

Roast wieners in an old-fashioned corn popper instead of on a stick. They'll keep their juices better, and you can roast several at once.

MEN'S FAVORITE EVENING LUNCH

Sliced Tender Sirloin Tip Roast*
Big Crusty Rolls   Prepared Mustard
Horse-radish Pickles
Bowl of Cherry Tomatoes
Tossed Green Salad*
Apple-Cranberry Dumplings*

Roast the beef a day ahead and chill. Slice cold roast thin shortly before serving. Arrange on platter. Set meat and large crusty rolls on table, along with relishes and salad. Let guests make their own sandwiches. Have salt shaker nearby for seasoning tomatoes. (Leave stems on tomatoes.) At dessert time, serve the dumplings with or without topping of vanilla ice cream. For a heartier meal, serve Baked German Potato Salad (see Index) instead of the tossed salad.

BLACK AND WHITE DESSERT PARTY

Black and White Date Pie*
Whipped Cream Topping
Coffee

The two-layer pie filling is rich, luscious and satisfying. The country hostess who serves this dessert says that both men and women praise it. She covers her buffet table with a black cover, embroidered delicately in white, uses black or white napkins, and serves the dessert on her white tableware. Her guests go to the buffet table and pick up their own servings, napkins and silver.

HOW TO SET AN ATTRACTIVE TABLE

As a background for the food you serve, your table should be as inviting as you can make it. For a company dinner, that used to mean setting the table with your very best china, silver and damask—lovely, but a lot of work.

Today's hostesses are much more casual. Often their invitations are spur of the moment . . . their menus hearty, homey fare . . . and their tables imaginative. They mix-match dishes—don't worry about "complete place settings." They sew table mats from brilliant yard goods, invent centerpieces that will spark conversation.

When you toss out comfortable old rules about what goes with what, you need some new guideposts to take their place. Here are some suggestions to help you meet the challenge to be "different"—to make your table more interesting, your table service more adaptable.

Mix-Matching China and Glass

Even if you own complete place settings in your china pattern, don't serve your entire dinner on them—it's not necessary, and it tends to be monotonous. Instead, show your individuality by using little pewter or glass plates for bread and butter if you have them; frosted glass plates or antique bone dishes for salad; your grandma's ornate pattern for dessert.

Trying new recipes will often start you wondering what new or different dishes you might serve them in. With a mix-match table, you're free to collect unusual pieces—scallop shells to serve sea food appetizer; little covered casseroles for individual servings of stew or chowder; fragile white Chinese rice bowls for ice cream and berries.

A bride might consider this way of collecting tableware for her new home: Instead of planning for complete place settings of good china, silver, stemware—and complete sets of everyday dishes, stainless, tumblers—a shorter list actually will help her set a more interesting table. For example, she might buy (or register her wish for) dinner plates only, with different salad bowls, glass dessert plates. Using the same dinner plates for company and for everyday is practical if she chooses one of the new durable china patterns. Some are even guaranteed against breakage—yet they look formal in a dressed-up setting. Another advantage: she can have two dozen plates to serve a crowd—all in her pattern choice, rather than one dozen "complete" settings.

Her cups and saucers should be the same type of china, but she might want them in a contrasting color—or maybe a solid color to match design in the plates. Tip: For every dozen plates, it's smart to get 18 or more cups and saucers—handy when entertaining a group, and as replacements for cups that get broken. "Open stock" doesn't guarantee "open forever." It means you can buy separate pieces, but only so long as the store carries the pattern.

Tablecloths and Place Mats

As background for your food and tableware, you have a choice of tablecloths, runners and place mats—or of serving on the table surface itself. You'll always be serenely safe with white linen or damask for a formal dinner. But why not try some sew-your-own covers?

Look at yard goods—everything from dress fabric to burlap—for colors and patterns that will be harmonious in your dining room. Show restraint —if your china is highly patterned, choose a plain fabric (although certainly it may be a colorful one). Use plain napkins with patterned cloths, in colors to accent or contrast sharply with the print. Try a bright floral print or stripe for napkins with plain homespun table mats— or straw mats. Table runners laid over cloths (print over plain, or vice-versa) or on the bare table make an interesting setting . . . and they're easy to make from yard goods; easy to wash and iron, too.

Tablecloths should have a drop of at least 10″ over the edge of the table; anything less will look skimpy. Bridge tables need only a 3 or 4″ drop. A buffet table set against the wall may be covered to the floor—very dramatic! Minimum size for place mats, if you make them, is 11 × 15", but bigger is better. Dinner mats need to be 12 × 18". Luncheon-size napkins should be at least 12" square, and dinner napkins 16" square—or larger.

You may, for a special occasion, want to cover your table with a cloth made of deep-colored, patterned fabric—such a cloth can be dramatic if it looks well in your room. With a patterned cloth, do use a one-color centerpiece: a bouquet of leaves; an arrangement of green apples, green grapes, green pears; or a bowl of yellow lemons.

Every Company Table Rates a Centerpiece

When your garden is in bloom, collecting your centerpiece is easy—and there's no better table decoration than fresh flowers arranged in an attractive bowl or basket. What you need are ideas to help you when the garden's bare.

Here are some suggestions for last-minute arrangements you can make from materials you are likely to have on hand:

Five-Minute Centerpieces
• Start collecting baskets in a variety of sizes, deep enough to accommodate potted plants. When you need a quick centerpiece, line one of your baskets with two tones of pink/purple tissue paper to make a nest for several of your blooming African violets.
• Keep dried lunaria (silver pennies) or dried babies' breath on hand; stick small branches of it into potted green plants.
• Set a sparkling kerosene lamp or lantern on a block of wood and arrange small plants or nosegays around the base. For nosegays, arrange parsley or flowers in juice glasses or tumblers. Or use empty spice jars.

• Fill a large brandy snifter or other footed glass container half full of red cherry tomatoes, walnuts or sourballs.
• Arrange fresh fruit or scrubbed vegetables in a basket or bowl. You might want to spray-paint part of your basket collection in different colors, to use at different seasons: rich gold in the fall; new-leaf green for spring. When you put arrangements together, think of strong color contrasts: lemons, oranges or big white eggs in a black bowl or basket are dramatic.
• Store your dried beans, peas and lentils in attractive-shaped bottles and jars; set them out on a colorful tray or mat for an intriguing centerpiece.
• Set a potted plant on a tray sur-

rounded with rocks, or large smooth pebbles. To dress up clay pots, paint them or "slipcover" them with covers in bright colors—plastic, metal or basketry.

· Keep an idea file: clip pictures from magazines, write file card notes about arrangements you see at garden shows.

Ever-Ready Centerpieces

There are a number of long-lasting or permanent objects you can store on a closet shelf, to bring out whenever you need a table decoration and have no time and no flowers to make one. Some of these ideas would make unusual party or banquet decorations, too:

· Collect candlesticks of various heights and save half-used candles in different colors. Massed in the center of the table, they'll give a festive look —quickly!

· Make an egg centerpiece: blow out white egg shells, glue them together in a pyramid and, for drama, place the arrangement on a footed stand or pedestal. Twine a branch of ivy around the base.

· With black India ink, paint op-art designs on white egg shells for a year-round (but not Easter time) arrangement; display them in a white or black bowl. Designs can be spirals, concentric circles, squares, stripes, zigzag stripes, bull's eyes, checks, polka dots.

· Make permanent flowers from pine cones. Choose large cones; cut or saw them off near the stem end, leaving about 3 rows of scales, which will be the "petals." Paint the centers yellow; the petals in different colors. For an interesting effect, antique your flowers by rubbing them with stain or raw umber, or brighten them with rub-

on or spray-on gold. Coat with shellac to give them a sheen. Use wire, wrapped with florist's tape, for stems. Arrange in bowl; or cut a block of Styrofoam to fit a painted pot or container, and insert stems in foam.

· Find a "branchy" branch, one that's a good size and a decorative shape. Anchor it in a bowl or pot (perhaps in plaster of Paris), spray it if you like or leave it natural color, and decorate it for special parties. You might use: tassels of bright-colored wool; red paper valentine hearts; gift ribbon bows; tiny packages; coins (with branch set in a base of coins—real coins or foil-wrapped candy); birds (made of feathers, or pine cones, or carved from wood and painted); snowballs (from ball fringe, or use cotton balls); doll-size pots and pans and utensils (for a kitchen shower).

· On a walk in the woods or along the road, collect seed pods, thistles and other attractive materials for dried arrangements. Add materials from a florist shop if needed and make permanent bouquets in two or three sizes. Between appearances on your table, keep your bouquets dust-free by covering with plastic bags. For a Thanksgiving table, arrange dried thistles in a basket, make cornhusk dolls for each guest's place setting; use a homespun cloth in brown plaid.

· Make huge flowers from crepe paper for drama on a big buffet table— or set a big bouquet of them in a butter churn on the ground near your picnic table. Use vivid, shocking color combinations: pink and orange; blue and green; purple and aqua; gold and tangerine. (For a teen party, use school colors.) Make flower centers first; they should measure 2½ to 3" across. Use any of these materials: heavy yarn, looped or with cut ends; a tight bunch of tiny artificial or dried flowers; a wad of paper covered with colored crepe paper and tied with twine in a contrasting color—as you would tie up a box. This center should be long enough to give you a handle around which to wrap petals—about 5" long. To make petals: Cut packages of crepe paper in half; scallop one edge on each half before unfolding it—or slash it to look feathery, like fringe. Wrap flower center with crepe paper petals, first a layer of one color; then the contrasting color; and finish with the first color. Bunch the paper to make petals look full, and tie tightly around centers. Add heavy wire stems, wrapping them with green crepe paper or florist's tape.

• Cover card tables with white tablecloths (or paper tablecloths). Cut daisies, stars or snowflakes in two or three sizes from tissue paper in many colors; lay the cutouts flat, overlapping them, in the center of the table. Add a colored candle, a figurine, a favor, a single flower (real or paper) or at Christmas, a miniature tree.

Where to Put Centerpieces

At most sit-down dinners, the centerpiece goes, as its name suggests, in the center of your table. However, if one side of your table is pushed against the wall, a better place for your flowers will be at the back of the table. If you're serving buffet, and the table is loaded, you may even want to hang your decoration on the wall behind the table—perhaps hanging baskets of flowers and greens, or displaying colorful sombreros at a

Mexican dinner. You can also save a little space on your table by raising the decoration in some way above the serving surface—on a pedestal or stand.

If your main dish (an enormous casserole of Company Beef Stew, or a platter of ribs, for instance) must occupy the center of the table for serving, you can still enjoy flowers on the table. Place four small bouquets around the serving dish or platter, or nosegays at each place setting.

Use new materials—and your ingenuity—in arranging flowers. For example: fill a cake pan with the water-absorbent material that florists use (Oasis) and cover it with short-stemmed flowers, making a flat or mounded arrangement. You might place flower heads in such a way that they form stripes of different colors—or surround a birthday "7" (or whatever the appropriate year) made of red zinnias in a bed of white button chrysanthemums.

Party Favors You Can Make

For a very special party, you may want to decorate your table with individual party favors at each place setting. We offer ideas that are easy to make from everyday materials; you will find them pictured in color in this book. Here are the directions:

Lollipop Lion: His yarn mane is sandwiched between two cardboard circles. Staple loops of pink and orange yarn to one circle to make a fringe all around. Cover other circle with pink felt face; glue on orange felt nose and draw features with a fine felt marking pen. Glue face over mane; glue wrapped lollipop behind mane. Push lollipop stick into a large gumdrop for base.

Housewarming: Decorate matchboxes to look like houses. Glue white or colored paper on both sides of box (turn some boxes on side for different shaped houses). Let paper extend over one end of box on both sides—snip to form gables. From contrasting color paper, cut roof, windows, shutters, doors and glue on house; add details with pen or fine brush and black ink.

Bluebird: Base is a cross-section of tree limb (leave bark on). Drill hole in base and fill with glue—insert small twig. To make pine-cone bird: wrap 4″ length of wire around cone twice, twist ends. (When you finish bird, use wire ends to secure it to twig.) Shape head from paste (¼ cup flour, ¼ cup salt, 1 tablespoon water) and secure on broad end of cone; let dry. Cut paper wings and tail; glue to cone. Paint bird bright blue. Bird's nest is an acorn cap filled with small pebbles or candy.

Egg Basket: Tint a blown egg and snip away shell at one end to make a larger opening. Glue on rickrack trim. Tuck in Easter grass and insert flowers. Make small versions of paper cup flowers (see below) and mix them with artificial ones. Set in painted egg carton cups, cut high in back to hold egg upright.

Easter Bonnet: Paint face on blown egg. Cut off rim of nut cup to use as base. For bonnet, glue yarn hair inside another nut cup; glue lace doily

brim around edge; tie ribbon and posy around crown.

Paper Cup Flowers: Fill a paper cup with tightly rolled corrugated cardboard—this makes a base to hold flower stems. Paint. Make flowers from cone-shaped paper cups. Snip tip, insert green drinking straws for stems; cut cone in petal shapes and curl. Flower centers are tips of cones painted yellow. Leaves are plastic drinking straws, too, slit and spread out, with pointed ends.

Witch: Cut two egg cups from molded pulp egg carton; glue edges together. Cut feet from cardboard—a rounded heart shape about 1½″ long; glue to body. Paint face orange, add map tack eyes and nose. Paint rest of body black. When dry, glue on cord hair. Make hat from shiny black paper: shape a cone 2″ tall, ¾″ diameter at base. Cut 2¼″ circle for hat brim; cut 1″ hole in center, snip to within ⅝″ of edge; push snipped edges into cone and glue. Trim with orange yarn; fasten to head with straight pin.

Valentine Hearts: Paper hearts threaded together with beads make a stand-up cover hiding a tiny bottle of perfume. Cut 8 hearts 3″ long from construction paper. Stack evenly; draw center line on top heart; poke holes through all 8 hearts, one hole on each side of center line, near top of heart and near point. Fold each heart in half. Run a needle and thread through top holes—and through a small bead inserted in *fold* of each heart; tie ends. Repeat for holes near point, using a small bead in the *fold* of each heart and a large bead *between* each heart. Glue ribbons to top; attach a small flower. For base, glue lace doily to cardboard; glue a small perfume bottle in center and place heart over bottle. Nice touch: tiny heart stickers on ends of ribbon streamers.

Plastic Flowers: Cut a circle of Styrofoam 1½″ diameter, ¾″ deep. Cut petals 2″ long from plastic bottles. Stick petals into sides of foam with glue. Glue felt or paper center and trim with map tacks.

HOW TO DRAMATIZE FOOD
WITH GARNISHES

Garnishes catch the eye and tempt the appetite. Your menu should include foods that contrast with each other in shape and color. But you can also depend on garnishes to make each platter or plate look like a picture when you place it before your guests.

Think about garnishes while you work in your kitchen; what do you have in pantry or refrigerator that would contrast in color and shape with the dish you are preparing—red radishes, a long orange peeling coiled to look like a rose, a sprinkling of chopped green onion tops? Give your imagination full play; it's exhilarating to create a new idea. And prime your imagination by observing intriguing food trims wherever you eat. A file of attractive garnishes is almost as helpful as a recipe file when you fix food for guests. Make one and see if you don't agree.

We have quite a collection of garnishes that we've evolved in our Test Kitchens, noticed in public eating places, or admired in homes of friends. We'll share some of them here, but don't miss, too, the many suggestions we give you right with the recipes.

First, here are the good-to-eat garnishes. We have organized them from Main Dishes to Beverages in this chapter, just as our cookbook is organized.

GARNISHES FOR STEAKS, CHOPS AND OTHER MEATS

• Sprinkle sizzling hot steaks or chops with crumbled blue cheese, snipped chives, drained pickle relish or snipped parsley, sprinkled on thin lemon slices.
• Surround meat on warm platter with overlapping fried onion rings (canned or frozen, heated). Add parsley sprigs and radish roses.
• Wreathe meat on platter with drained cling peach halves (canned) filled with cranberry jelly. Fill peaches or drained pears with mint jelly to accompany lamb chops.
• Cut small holes in center of individual chicken pies. Insert a cluster of parsley in each hole.

• Spoon a border of fluffy, hot rice around creamed chicken, Swedish meat balls in gravy and other meats in sauce. Or fill custard cups with hot rice; pack firmly. Unmold at once to make border on platter or chop plate.

TEMPTING TOPS FOR CASSEROLES

• Spoon hot, cooked and seasoned frozen peas on casserole at serving time.

• Arrange pimiento, cut in strips or other shapes, and grated yellow process or Parmesan cheese on top of casserole just before taking to table. Run cheese-crowned casserole under broiler just long enough to melt process cheese slightly.

• Select a few large potato chips to decorate casserole top when you take it from the oven. Make a border, or cover entire top; poke one edge of chips into casserole, so they'll stand up, looking like brown "ruffles."

• Place three large green pepper rings, arranged like a three-leaf clover, in the center of a baked dish; add a few small red and white onion rings if you like.

• Dot hot casserole top with dabs of dairy sour cream.

• Arrange deviled egg halves or triangles of yellow process cheese on baked casserole. Run the cheese-topped dish under broiler for a minute or two to melt the cheese slightly.

• Use pretzels of all sizes and shapes, different kinds of crackers, chopped nuts or croutons (tiny toasted bread cubes) to give casseroles a crisp, crunchy top.

• Keep packaged instant mashed potatoes on hand for garnishing casseroles. Make a collar of mashed potatoes around the edge of the casserole, sprinkle with grated cheese, dot with butter and run under broiler briefly.

• Place bacon curls over top of casserole at the last minute before you carry it to the table. To make curls, cook bacon slices, but not until crisp. Take from skillet at once and curl each slice around tines of a fork. If necessary, fasten with toothpicks until ready to serve. Drain on paper towels. Place on casserole with seam side down.

CHEESE GARNISHES FOR MANY FOODS

• **Cornucopias:** Cut square slices process yellow cheese diagonally in halves. Start at long side of each and roll to make a cornucopia. Fasten with a whole clove. Serve with apple pie, one to each pie wedge.

• **Cheese curls:** With vegetable peeler shave thin slices from a block of process cheese. Roll each strip or slice around your finger. Remove carefully and chill until serving time. Good with apple pie and to garnish plate of cold cuts.

• With a tablespoon, scoop cream cheese and shape into balls with hands. Then roll balls in finely chopped nuts, grated orange peel, flaked coconut, chopped parsley—whatever color and flavor seems appropriate. Use to garnish salads.

• Thread three balls of cream cheese on a kabob stick, a large one in center and a small one on each side. Use tablespoon to measure cream cheese for large balls, a teaspoon for small balls. Stick one in each serving of fruit salad, fruit cup or gelatin desserts.

• Shape soft Cheddar cheese, mashed with fork, into apple-shaped balls. Stick a whole clove, bud end down, to simulate the stem. Then stick another whole clove in opposite end to represent bud end. Dust apple lightly with paprika or brush with a little red food color to provide red cheeks. Insert a watercress leaf in stem end. Serve on top or at side of apple pie servings. Or use to garnish salads.

• Cut-out cheese apples also are appealing on apple pie wedges and apple crisp. Cut apple shapes from process yellow cheese slices. Dust lightly with paprika.

• Trim open-face apple, cherry or strawberry pies or tarts with cheese petals. Scoop level teaspoonfuls cream cheese. Push out of spoon with thumb. Place these petals, rounded side up, in a double wreath (two rows) in center of pie.

• Center relish or dessert tray with a cheese flower. Cut petals in a small red-coated Gouda or Edam cheese but leave attached. Ring with assorted crackers, if you like, and celery fans. Provide knives for guests to cut out petals or servings of cheese.

GLAMORIZE GARDEN VEGETABLES

• Sprinkle cooked and seasoned vegetables with paprika, snipped chives or parsley, sieved hard-cooked egg yolk or grated hard-cooked egg white, cut-up pimiento, narrow strips or sticks of green pepper, thin lemon slices, crumbled crisp bacon, chopped toasted almonds or grated cheese. (The vegetable should be hot enough to melt the cheese a little.)

• Combine two separately cooked and seasoned vegetables of different colors and shapes. They make their own garnish. Here are some tasty partners.

Carrots (sliced, slivered or in sticks) and peas

Cauliflowerets and peas or green beans

Green beans and lima beans

Peas and tiny new potatoes or onions

Lima beans and yellow corn (succotash)

Whole kernel yellow corn and sliced zucchini

Carrot strips and green lima beans

Small white onions (whole) and green beans

Mashed winter squash, in mounds with depression in center filled with peas

A head of cauliflower, cheese sauce spooned over, surrounded with slivered carrots

Peas in center of ring of mashed potato or yellow or white turnips (formed in ring mold and turned out)

• Serve fluffy mashed potatoes in a shallow bowl. Indent surface with teaspoon and fill holes with dabs of butter to melt in yellow pools.

• Top baked potatoes with butter rolled in poppy seeds, snipped chives or parsley, or sprinkle with paprika. To open baked potatoes, cut across on top with fork; press ends, push up and fluff; then add butter.

• Cut top of baked sweet potatoes crisscross; press ends. Top each potato with a little orange marmalade and butter.

VEGETABLE GARNISHES FOR MANY DISHES

• **Radish Roses:** Cut roots from crisp radishes; then with four or five knife cuts down the radish, form thin petals (use tip of paring knife). Chill in ice water.

• **Radish Accordions:** Cut slightly elongated red radishes in thin slices, but not quite through. Chill in ice water. The radish slices will spread apart.

• **Scalloped Radishes:** Cut off both ends of large red radishes. Outline scallops near top with tip of paring knife. Peel off red skin within scallops. Chill in ice water until ready to use.

• **Carrot Curls:** Peel large carrots. Hold the large end of a carrot on cutting board and shave off long slices with vegetable peeler. Roll each strip around your fingertip; place in bowl of ice cubes for at least 1 hour.

• **Carrot Holders:** Tuck perky sprigs of parsley in carrot curls just before serving. Makes a pretty garnish on cold cut and other meat platters.

• **Celery Fans:** Cut celery stalks in 3″ lengths. Make several slits in each end almost to the center. Or make slits only in one end almost to the other end. Place in ice water until celery fans out.

• **Celery Hearts:** Remove outer stalks. Wash remainder of celery and trim root. Cut bunch in half lengthwise; then cut each half in three lengthwise pieces. Slash sides of celery pieces, using a sharp knife. Chill in ice water.

• **Caulifloweret Slices:** Separate cauliflower head into individual flowerets. Cut each floweret into thin slices with a sharp knife. Dip in lemon juice to retain whiteness. Chill on ice.

• **Fluted Cucumber Slices:** Score a peeled or unpeeled cucumber by running sharp tines of a fork down the length of cucumber from one end to the other. Lay on cutting board and cut thin crosswise slices. Chill on ice cubes or in refrigerator. Pretty garnish for potato salads and fish salads and fine to include in relish tray.

• **Cherry Tomato Blossoms:** With sharp knife start at stem end of cherry tomatoes and cut in wedges half way down. Pull petals apart and fill with a bit of pickle relish, drained, or seasoned cream cheese. Alternate pickle-filled baby tomatoes with bacon and carrot curls on platter of fish. Use cheese-filled flowers to perk up salads.

HOW TO DRESS UP SALADS

• Fill lettuce cups with fruit and vegetable salads. Fit two large lettuce leaves to form the cup. If you lay a strip of green pepper across the salad to edges of cup, you have a salad basket.

• Cut canned cranberry jelly in thick slices, then into shapes with small, fancy-shaped cookie cutter. These cutouts add color and flavor to fruit salads and to meat and poultry dishes.

• Arrange lemon, orange or lime twists on top of fruit salads and many main dishes. Cut a lemon, orange or lime in very thin slices; then cut a slit from the center of each slice through the edge. Pick up each slice, with one hand on one side of the slit, the other hand on the other side. Twist in opposite directions.

• Make corkscrew olives to place on top fruit, vegetable, chicken, fish and sea food salads. Hold pitted olive upright in hand with index finger and thumb. Turn olive counterclockwise while you slice a thin continuous strip from the top to the bottom of the olive.

Tossed Green Salads

• Add one of the following for a taste change: whole seedless green grapes (or red grapes, cut in halves and seeded), avocado slices, pitted ripe olives, sliced pimiento-stuffed olives, cherry tomatoes, whole or cut in halves.

• Sprinkle on pomegranate seeds.

• Scatter carrot daisies over the top. To make them, cut four shallow wedges the full length of peeled fat carrots. Cut the carrot in thin crosswise slices (the wedges make notches in the slices). Chill in ice water until carrots curl up into a flower.

Stuffed Tomato Salads

• Stick an onion-radish kabob on top of each stuffed tomato this way: Thread three radish slices, with holes cut in the center, on a small green onion. This also is a good garnish for deviled eggs and to serve on sandwich plates.

• Serve the salad in tomato blossoms. Start at the cored end of the tomato and cut in wedges half way down. Use a sharp paring knife. Gently pull petals open and fill tomatoes with mixed vegetable salad, coleslaw, cottage cheese, fish, meat, chicken, shrimp or egg salad.

Fruit Salads

• Top salad with perky fresh mint or watercress sprigs, balls of creamy cottage cheese stuck with toasted almonds, or tiny clusters of seedless green grapes.

• Make sugared grapes for special garnishes. Dip little bunches of seedless green grapes in slightly beaten egg white. Roll in superfine granulated sugar, dry on cake racks. For added color, contrast, frost both red and green grapes. A plate of sugared grapes also makes a delightful light dessert.

• Serve fruit salad in grapefruit or melon bowls. Cut grapefruit or small cantaloupes or honeydew melons in halves. Scoop out seeds and fruit. Reserve fruit in refrigerator to use in salad. Cut small wedges from edges of grapefruit and melon shells to make scallops; chill. Make fruit salad from the reserved grapefruit or melon, mixed with frozen fruits or berries, partly thawed. Either mix salad dressing with fruits or top each serving with it when you pile fruit into the scalloped "bowls." Serve on plates lined with paper doilies. Lay a small flower on each plate.

Potato Salad

• Top with sprigs of fresh dill, shredded yellow cheese, bunches of tiny leaves from celery hearts, pickle rings, tomato wedges or deviled eggs.

• Make egg daisies to lay on the top of a bowl of potato salad. Cut hardcooked eggs in half lengthwise through white only. Leave the yolk whole. Separate white from yolk. With tiny hors d'oeuvre cutters or the point of a sharp paring knife, cut oval petals from egg white; trim them until they are the same thickness. Slice egg yolk with egg slicer; use a slice for center of daisy and lay white petals around it. If you do not have an egg slicer, use sieved egg yolk to make flower centers and grated egg white for petals.

To sieve hard-cooked egg yolk, push it through a fine sieve with the back of a spoon. To grate hard-cooked egg white, rub it gently against a fine grater. These make attractive toppings.

TRIMMINGS FOR CAKES AND COOKIES

• Arrange a wreath of small marzipan fruits on top of white frosted cake or glazed fruit cake.

• To make spiral design in frosting, hold spatula in center of cake you've just frosted. Draw it slowly to you, while slowly turning cake. Use a cake turntable if you have one.

• Press tip of inverted spoon in freshly frosted cake to make a scallop. Make scallops in rows or other designs over entire top of cake.

• Melt 1 square chocolate combined with ½ teaspoon shortening and drizzle from teaspoon around edge of frosted cake. Let some of chocolate run down cake sides to form uneven drips. Effective on a white frosted cake, or on white frosting tinted orange for Halloween.

• Trim frosted cupcakes with silver dragées or tiny colored candies, heart-shaped for Valentine's Day.

• Trim a frosted cake with gumdrop roses. To make roses, sprinkle board and rolling pin with granulated sugar to prevent candy from sticking. Roll 4 to 5 big pink gumdrops about ¼" thick. Cut each oval in half to make petals. Roll up one half-oval to make center of rose. Then fit and press other half-oval petals around it. Press together at the base, trim base flat. Place on frosted cake. Roll green gumdrops in the same way and cut leaves and stems from the ovals. Arrange around the rose on the cake.

• Arrange colored miniature marshmallows on tops of frosted cupcakes to make flower designs. You can cut stems and leaves from rolled green gumdrops (see directions above).

• When you take cupcakes from the oven, put a marshmallow on top of each cake; return to oven until marshmallow begins to melt. Quickly remove from oven and press a nut or chocolate piece in center of each marshmallow.

• Cut tall, narrow triangles or petals of rolled red gumdrops and arrange 5 of them like points of a star or poinsettia on frosted Christmas cake. Put a tiny gumdrop in center.

• Gather 24 green leaves of different sizes and shapes, wash and dry. Melt 2 squares semisweet chocolate with 1 teaspoon butter. With clean watercolor brush, paint one side of each leaf with chocolate. The chocolate should be about ⅛" thick on leaf and it should *extend just to edge of leaf.* Chill. With the point of a paring knife, separate chocolate from the leaf at one place. Then carefully peel off and discard leaves. Decorate top and sides of frosted cake with chocolate leaves as you like. Press them in frosting with care. It's a good idea to have the frosted cake chilled and to keep the cake, once you trim it, in the refrigerator until ready to serve.

• Spread cooled, rolled cookies with frosting, tinted in delicate colors. Pink frosting is especially festive on chocolate and molasses cookies.

• When cookie dough balls are on baking sheet, make small indentations in them with your little finger. Bake and cool. At serving time dot with your most colorful jelly. Or fill, after baking and cooling, with dabs of tinted frosting.

• Press half a candied cherry on top of each cookie ball before baking. Use both red and green cherries for color contrast.

• Put cookies, cut in fancy shapes, together like sandwiches with tinted frosting for the filling.

• Cut brownies in fingers instead of squares.

• Spread cookies with chocolate frosting and sprinkle half of them with flaked coconut, white or tinted green. Sprinkle other half with chopped nuts.

DECORATIVE TOUCHES FOR PIES

• Arrange 5 big tablespoonfuls of whipped cream on center of cool pumpkin pie like the petals of a flower. Sprinkle flower with chopped walnuts.

• Omit top from cherry or other fruit pie; bake. Cut rolled pastry (for top crust) in fancy shapes with small cookie cutter. Brush with cold water and sprinkle with white or colored sugar. Lay on baking sheet and bake in a very hot oven (475°) a few minutes, or until cutouts are browned. Watch carefully to avoid overbrowning. Cool; place on top of baked pie, one cutout for each serving.

• Glamorize pies by giving them fancy edges and tops. Here are suggestions from our *Complete Pie Cookbook:*

• **Fancy Lattice Top:** Twist strips of pastry placed over pie to make the lattice; cut strips with rippled pastry wheel to give a pretty edge.

• **Sparkle Tops:** With fingers, moisten top crust with cold water and sprinkle evenly with a little sugar.

• **Shiny Tops:** Brush top pastry crust lightly with beaten egg or egg yolk, cream, milk, undiluted evaporated milk or melted butter, margarine, shortening or salad oil. Sprinkle with sugar if desired.

• **Decorative Vents:** Use tiny cookie cutters or cut around homemade patterns with sharp knife to make steam vents in the shape of the fruit in the pie—cherries, apples or a cluster of grapes, for instance.

• **Flutes:** Trim pastry ½″ beyond rim and fold under to make double rim. Make a stand-up rim. Place left index finger inside pastry rim. With right thumb and index finger on outside of rim, press pastry into V-shapes ½″ apart. Pinch flutes to make points, if desired. For 1- or 2-crust pies.

• **Scallops:** Form like flutes but do not make points. Flatten each flute with a 4-tined fork. For 2-crust pies.

• **Sawtooth:** Cut pastry overhang with scissors in sawtooth design; moisten rim and fold the triangles of pastry up on rim, pointing to center of pie; press down.

• **Quarter Moon:** Trim pastry even with pan edge; cut long strip of pastry same width as pan edge and press down onto moistened pastry on pan edge; with inverted ½ teaspoon measuring spoon, press design of two semicircles (one inside the other) around edge.

SIMPLE TRIMS FOR DESSERTS

• For a change from maraschino cherries, use a single strawberry, unhulled, to top desserts.

• Serve slices of red-coated Gouda or Edam cheese with apple pie. Leave the red color on the cheese and let guests remove it.

• Drift flaked or grated coconut on chiffon pies.

• Surround warm plum or other steamed puddings with hard sauce shaped like snowmen. Chill hard sauce and shape in balls, about 1½″ balls for bodies, ¾″ balls for heads and ½″ balls for feet. Put together to make snowmen. Fasten together with short pieces of toothpicks if necessary. Add whole cloves for eyes, strips of drained maraschino cherries for mouths, cinnamon candies (red hots) for buttons and maraschino cherry halves for hats. Freeze until time to serve. Put a snowman on each serving.

• Drizzle maple syrup on baked custards and vanilla puddings to make checks or any design you like.

• Tint vanilla puddings pale pink or green with food color.

• Spread flaked coconut on baking sheet; toast in moderate oven (350°) until golden brown, about 8 minutes. Watch carefully to prevent over-browning. Sprinkle on puddings and other desserts.

• Tint flaked coconut green for St. Patrick's Day, pink for Valentine's Day. Quick trick: Place 1 cup flaked coconut in a plastic bag. Mix 1 or 2 drops food color with 1 teaspoon cold water and add to coconut. Fold over top of bag and shake until coconut is evenly tinted.

• Almond flowers are attractive on many desserts. Spoon a small mound of whipped cream on top of individual dessert; arrange 5 toasted almonds around whipped cream to make flower petals (poke their pointed ends into the cream).

DRESS UP ICE CREAMS AND SHERBETS

• Spoon bright-red cranberry sauce over vanilla ice cream.

• Spoon colorful frozen mixed fruits, partly thawed, in sherbet glasses and top with scoops of vanilla ice cream.

• Chop and sprinkle chocolate-coated peppermint mints (candy) over chocolate or vanilla ice cream.

• Drizzle maple or other bottled syrup over vanilla ice cream.

• Spoon heated, prepared mincemeat over vanilla ice cream and top with chopped nuts and maraschino flowers. Cut drained cherries three fourths of the way down, with scissors or sharp knife, and pull apart to make petals.

• Serve two flavors and colors of ice cream or sherbet in the same glass. Vanilla ice cream and raspberry sherbet are congenial; so are chocolate and pink or green peppermint stick ice creams.

• Top orange sherbet with flaked coconut and garnish each serving with 1 to 3 orange sections (or mandarin orange sections). To section an orange (or grapefruit), peel off rind in strips, cutting deep enough to remove all the white membrane. Then insert knife blade along the dividing membrane, cutting around single section and lifting it out with blade.

• Sprinkle vanilla ice cream with a bit of powdered instant coffee.

GARNISHES FOR PUNCH AND TALL DRINKS

• Thread a whole strawberry and a wedge of thin-sliced orange on a cinnamon stick for punch stirrer.

• In each cup of punch, place a short stick of red-and-white peppermint candy or a candy cane.

• Add a scoop of vanilla ice cream to each mug or glass of root beer and insert a stick of candy for stirring.

• Prepare lemonade, orange juice and Concord grape juice from frozen concentrates. Pour into three ice cube trays; refrigerate remaining juices for use in making punch. Use these cubes instead of regular ice cubes to keep punch from diluting.

• Slice an orange and a lemon; cut each slice in four or five pieces. Drop fruit pieces and tiny seedless green grapes into sections in filled ice cube trays, one piece of fruit or grape in each section. Freeze. Serve in punch or fruit juice coolers.

• Pour pineapple juice into ice cube trays; add a mint leaf or small sprig of mint and small strawberries to the sections. Freeze and serve in punch or fruit drinks.

• Add strawberry halves, raspberries or blueberries to glasses of fruit coolers.

• Tint water for ice cubes with red or green maraschino cherry juice and freeze.

• Add melon balls to fruit punch or drinks. Cut melon in half, remove seeds and scoop out balls with melon ball cutter or measuring spoons with rounded bowls.

• Add decorative ice floats to punch bowl. Pour ½ to 1″ water (distilled or boiled and cooled water makes clearer ice) into a ring or fancy shaped mold. Arrange maraschino cherries (rinsed in cold water to remove excess color and prevent "bleeding"), orange or lemon slices, mint sprigs, strawberries, green seedless grapes or raspberries in mold; freeze. Add water almost to top of mold and freeze. Unmold by dipping in hot water just until ice will drop out. Invert float in bowl of punch. Use a heart-shaped mold for Valentine parties, a star-shaped one for Yuletide punch. Decorate the float, if you wish, with a few tiny flowers, such as sweetheart roses, or a small corsage. Or use orange or lemon slices on the float instead of flowers.

• Add small scoops of lemon sherbet to glasses of iced tea.

• Borrow a trick from Hawaii and insert a stick of pineapple in each glass of iced tea.

• String pineapple cubes and fresh strawberries on drinking straws and place in glasses of iced tea.

• Put an umbrella of fresh mint (stems down in tea) in each filled iced tea glass.

RELISH AND GARNISH TRAYS

• Proudly display your sparkling homemade jelly in footed sherbet glasses. Set two or three kinds and colors of jelly on tray or large plate and surround with assorted crackers and cheese slices. Use currant and mint jellies at Christmastime.

• Fill a large, shallow bowl about two thirds full of crushed ice. Stick tiny, trimmed green onions in the center. Arrange overlapping slices of small tomatoes and thin fluted cucumber slices around onions.

• Fix a black and white tray of shiny black olives and white celery fans. To give ripe olives a glossy look, roll them in a little salad oil or olive oil.

• Heap your best small cucumber pickles in the center of a shallow, flat bowl. Ring with sliced cauliflowerets and carrot curls.

• Serve cranberry-orange relish in grapefruit bowls. Arrange three or more bowls on a tray for buffet table.

• Serve stuffed celery and carrot curls on a bed of watercress.

GIVE SOUPS A NEW LOOK

When soup is in bowls ready to serve, add one of the following garnishes:
Popped corn
Snipped chives
Chopped tender, small celery leaves
Paper-thin carrot or radish slices
Spoonfuls of whipped cream flavored
    with a little prepared horse-radish
Tiny cubes of firm, ripe tomatoes
Grated cheese
Small cheese cubes
Frankfurter slices
Sliced pimiento-stuffed olives
Crumbled crisp bacon
Spoonfuls of dairy sour cream
Thin lemon slices
Shoestring potatoes
Slices of hard rolls sprinkled with
    Parmesan cheese

HOLIDAY SPECIAL GARNISHES

• Surround roast turkey, chicken, ducks or geese with your choice of: tiny bunches of red and green grapes, cranberry-orange relish heaped on thick orange slices, drained spiced crab apples nestled in fluffy parsley, bunches of kumquats or spiced peaches or apricots (drained) on greens.

• Cut core from stem end of two spiced crab apples and fit over ends of roast drumsticks just before serving.

• Decorate top of whole baked Easter ham with peach sunburst. Overlap slices of drained, canned, sliced peaches in a ring on glazed ham to make a golden sunburst. Place a green maraschino cherry in center of sunburst.

• Garnish Easter ham with carrot flowers. Use thin slices of small, peeled carrot for petals, strips of green pepper for stems and leaves and a bit of ripe olive in center of flowers.

• Buffet Service of Ice Cream Balls: The day before your party, scoop ice cream balls (several colors and flavors) onto a cool metal tray; return to freezer to firm up. Chill your prettiest *metal* bowl; fill it with ice cream balls; put bowl in the freezer. At serving time let guests make their own sundaes—surround bowl of ice cream with small bowls of sauces, fruit, nuts on a tray. (It's a good idea to set the bowl of frozen desserts in another bowl containing crushed ice.)

• For a Halloween party, place sugared doughnuts and mounds of sugared doughnut balls alternately around a bowl of apple cider or orange punch.

• Use heart-shaped candies, cakes, cookies and molded salads for Valentine's Day garnishes. For molded hearts, make cherry flavor gelatin by package directions. Pour ¼" deep in shallow pan and chill until firm. Cut in small heart shapes for dessert and salad garnish. Use tomato aspic hearts for green salad garnish.

• Garnish with green for St. Patrick's Day: mint jelly, pickle relish, pickle fans (small cucumber pickles cut in thin slices from one end almost to other end), snipped chives and parsley.

• Dip ends of stuffed celery or celery fans in parika for the Fourth of July.

• Garnish Fourth of July fruit salads and desserts with watermelon balls.

• Cut Fourth of July stars from slices of cranberry jelly.

• For Fourth of July desserts top vanilla ice cream with whole ripe strawberries.

• Crown New Year's desserts with drifts of snow—whipped cream, or flaked or fine grated coconut. Trim with silver dragées.

• Kumquat flowers add a festive touch to Christmas platters. Cut fresh (or preserved) kumquats in 6 sections with scissors; cut about ¾ way down. Spread petals apart to resemble flowers. Arrange them in clusters in parsley.

• Bake cherry pie for Washington's Birthday with a peekaboo crust (lattice top).

GARNISHES TO LOOK AT— NOT TO EAT

There are times when you'll want to trim food platters with inedible decorations. Here are a few suggestions from our garnish file—many of them seasonal, or for specific parties:

Tiny colored Christmas tree balls

Sprigs of holly

Big red candle in the center of a Christmas tube cake—light the candle when you bring cake out for guests to see.

Candles on cupcakes

St. Patrick's Day clay pipes, handles tied with green ribbons

Tiny pine cones or acorns

Leaves—choose decorative leaves such as geranium, ivy, galax, when you want the garnish to hold up for a long time. Place leaves on platters with food, on plates or trays under food containers, or around edge of serving dishes.

Flowers—an especially festive garnish. For example, into the center of a grapefruit half tuck a tiny nosegay made from a pink sweetheart rosebud and two or three mint leaves.

Artificial flowers (see Index for Flower Wedding Cake—use the idea for other special-occasion cakes.)

Candied violets and other flowers (from candy stores) to top puffs of whipped cream.

Ribbons, tiny flags, paper leis, miniature parasols

Paper doilies—white, silver, gold

Colored drinking straws

Paper frills—you can make your own frills to cover lamb bones and drumsticks. Use ordinary typing paper or onionskin, or lightweight gift wrapping paper in pretty solid colors, silver or gold, or baking parchment (avoid non-sticking or silicone parchment—you won't be able to fasten frills). Cut paper 3 × 5″ for small chop bones, proportionately larger for larger bones. Fold it to make rectangle 2½ × 3″. Snip every ⅛″ all along folded edge; make snips about ¾″ deep. Then coil paper (still folded in half) around your little finger and fasten with a bit of cellophane tape or glue.

SERVING DISHES MAKE A DIFFERENCE

When food is colorful, or distinctive, you may find it needs no more garnish than the right serving dish to set it off. Clever hostesses look for unusual dishes to get dramatic effects. Here are a few ideas:

• Chill and serve fruit flavored gelatin in your thinnest glasses to show off its sparkling beauty.

• Serve custard sauce for desserts in glass pitchers to emphasize its sunny yellow.

• If you have a long, narrow platter, tray or old-fashioned celery dish, arrange overlapping slices of fruitcake in it to display fruits in the cake. Garnish with a few marzipan fruits.

• Serve ice cream and fresh, ripe strawberries layered in goblets instead of concealing their beauty in bowls.

• Line a basket with a bright bandanna or checkered napkin and heap fried chicken in it for an informal supper.

• Serve baked beans in your homey bean pot. Or set out individual servings in brown earthenware custard cups or little casseroles. Garnish tops with pickle slices and bacon curls. Keep warm on buffet by using an electric hot tray.

• Give the gorgeous brown loaf of homemade fruit or yeast bread the spotlight on a buffet. Place it on a bread board, cut a few slices, lay electric slicing knife nearby. Let guests (adults) have the fun of cutting their own servings.

• See Index for Glazed Fruit Salad and the way a member of FARM JOURNAL's Family Test Group glamorizes it by serving it in a footed dish.

• Collect a variety of baskets (straw and metal) in sizes in which your most frequently used baking or cooking dishes will fit. They'll dress up your table and make it possible for you to serve in the same dish you cook in— saves dishwashing. When you buy new pots and pans, look for attractive range-to-table ware, practical as it is pretty—and such a timesaver.

• Look around for a black or near-black platter, plate, tray or bowl. A black background intensifies food colors; pale-colored foods, especially, benefit by displaying them in or on a black serving dish.

HOW TO SERVE GUESTS GRACIOUSLY

When you invite guests to dinner or supper, you'll have to decide first what style of service to use—commonly a choice between sit-down or self-serve buffet. Your guest list may decide for you—few homes have room to seat more than twelve people around the main dining table. With buffet service, you can entertain a crowd—and still seat them, at small tables.

If you're planning a sit-down meal, you have three types of service to choose from: English style, banquet or plate service (originally Russian style) and country style—the kind many families use daily. We describe all three services in detail below, so you will know which plan you want to use. Many hostesses like to combine styles—for example, they'll serve one course at the table (English style) and another course on plates filled in the kitchen (banquet style). Choose the one (or combination) easiest for you; then it will also be the most pleasant for your guests.

How to Serve English Style

The host has the starring role in the English service. From platters and dishes placed in front of him, he serves the meat and vegetables. At the opposite end of the table, the hostess serves the salad, and later, the dessert and coffee. Or the host may also serve the dessert, while the hostess pours the coffee. Our grandparents of European ancestry often used this service; if the host enjoys serving and does it well, it is a gracious service—and especially appropriate when children are at the table.

When soup is the first course, the hostess serves it from a tureen. Then, of course (unless the children are old enough to take over), she has plates to remove and platters to bring in while guests sit at the table. That is why, today, most smart hostesses serve an appetizer or first course in the living room. The host—or the children—may pass mugs of hot soup to the guests, or glasses of fruit juice or tomato juice cocktails, often with "dippers and dips" (see Index). They visit with guests during this course, giving the hostess these needed minutes in the kitchen to finish dinner and arrange food before inviting guests to the table.

For the main course, place the platter of meat or other main dish directly in front of the host's place, with vegetable dishes to his left or right within easy reach. Stack the dinner plates at his place setting, and put the serving silver alongside the dishes of food (never in the food), with the carving knife to the right of the platter, the fork to the left and the spoons near the vegetables. (In this service, if you prefer, you may put plates at each place instead of stacking them in front of the host. Then the host fills the plate in front of him and passes it. The person who receives it passes his empty plate to the host.)

Order of Serving: Both host and hostess follow this pattern from their opposite ends of the table. The host serves the hostess first (and she serves him first from the dishes at her end). He passes the filled plate to the left and everyone on that side of the table passes it on to the hostess. The next plate is passed down to the guest on the hostess' right and continues in this pattern until everyone on this side of the table is served. Then he serves the people on the other side of the table in the same manner, starting with the guest at the hostess' left. He serves himself last.

While the host serves the meat and vegetables, the hostess serves the salad from a bowl or tray placed in front of her, with serving plates and silver to her left.

When it's time to offer second helpings, the host, starting with the guest at his right, asks everyone (the hostess last) to have a second helping. If someone desires another helping, he passes his plate (with his knife and fork side by side on it near the center so they won't fall off) to the host, who serves the food and passes the plate back.

To insure warm second helpings, the hostess or a helper may return food to the kitchen after the first serving and bring it back for the second helpings.

At dessert time, the hostess or a helper removes all serving dishes from the table first, then all dinner plates (guests lay their used silver, knife and fork parallel, across their plates near the center). The hostess or helper also removes unused silver (except dessert silver and coffee spoons) and condiments. Dishes may be removed from left or right; both ways are permissible. But once you decide to "remove left," all dishes should be removed consistently from the left, so as not to confuse guests.

When the table is cleared, the dessert is placed in front of the hostess' place setting along with the serving silver and china. It's often convenient for the hostess to arrange the dessert on a serving cart, a nearby small table or buffet ahead of time and transfer it to the table when it's time to serve—or serve from the cart. If you do not serve coffee or tea with the main course, bring it to the table for the hostess to pour after she passes desserts. Arrange the coffee maker or teapot, cream, sugar and cups and saucers in front of the hostess' place. She pours and serves it like any other food.

How to Serve Banquet Style

Many women vote the Russian Service (better known in America as banquet or plate service) the easiest way to serve. They bypass serving dishes entirely, filling plates in the kitchen and carrying them in to seated guests. (One of the older children can help.) If you've served a church or school banquet, you've probably served it "Russian style."

The plate is placed before each guest from the left, removed from the left or right. The very correct (European) way is to serve left and remove left, too. But it is quite all right to serve left, remove from the right—the main thing is to be consistent, removing all plates from the same side. However, something like a bread and butter plate, on guest's extreme left, should be removed left so you don't reach in front of a guest.

Banquet service can be even more formal. In elegant hotels or dining rooms, waiters offer food in serving dishes to each person. The waiter serves from the left, always, holding platter low enough for the guest to help himself easily; the serving silver is placed face down in the dish, with handles toward the person being served.

How to Serve Country Style

The easiest service for both host and hostess is country style—where everyone helps himself to food passed around the table. Most families use it daily, and many guests especially enjoy it. Even though it's informal, it can be gracious.

For country-style service, place all the food in serving dishes on the dining table, with serving silver alongside—the main dish nearest the hostess. She may serve herself first, or she may pass the dish to the guest at her right or left. Other foods follow in order of their importance —vegetables, gravy, salad, rolls or bread and relishes. Whoever sits nearest the different dishes, frequently a member of the family, puts the serving silver in them, helps himself and passes the food.

If a country-style meal is to run smoothly, all the food should be passed in one direction, to the left or to the right. It's a good idea in family meals always to pass the food the same direction—then you establish a habit, and everyone will know what to do when there's company. Suppose you decide to pass to the right. The dish continues around the table until it returns to its original position. The success of this service depends on how alert the hostess, host and other members of the family are to the needs of the guests.

Having a side table or serving cart near the hostess will be a big help. Set a pitcher of ice water, a pot of coffee and some extra rolls on it. This will save the hostess running to and from the kitchen during the meal. Leave the dessert in the kitchen, or if it doesn't require refrigeration and space permits, arrange it on the side table or cart, or on the buffet.

When all have finished the main course, the hostess asks everyone to pass his plate to her, along with serving dishes. She can stack them on a serving cart or side table, but it's usually best if her helper carries them to the kitchen.

The hostess may serve the dessert on individual dishes (English style) or she may continue country style, passing dessert dishes and then the dessert, letting each person help himself.

Experienced hostesses will use different combinations of service, depending on the menu, or their situation (will son or daughter be there to help serve, for instance). Here's an especially popular combination: Place the first course, such as fruit cup or soup, and individual salads on the table before you seat the guests (banquet style). Remove the first course silver and dishes and bring in the main course. Let the host serve the meat, vegetables and gravy (English style). Clear the table of everything except what the dessert course requires. Bring the dessert to the dining table on individual plates filled in the kitchen (banquet style).

HOW TO SERVE CORRECTLY

· Place dishes before guests from the left with your left hand; remove from left or right (see banquet service, above).

· Offer foods, such as relishes and hot rolls, from the left with your left hand.

· Pour and serve coffee and other beverages from the right with your right hand. Refill water glasses or goblets from the right without removing glasses. Carry a napkin in the left hand to wipe up spills if they occur.

· Always handle dishes and plates by their outer edges, taking care not to place thumb or finger over the rim. Hold goblets by their stems.

· If you serve a meal in courses, remove everything belonging to one course before serving the next one. When you serve coffee with the main course, leave the cups and saucers on the table for second servings.

· Remove food first when clearing the table. Then remove soiled dishes from the individual place settings, along with the clean or unused silver for that course.

· Clean one place completely before moving to the next. To remove left, stand at the guests' left and with your left hand, remove his dinner plate and put it in your right hand. Pick up his salad plate and place it on the dinner plate in your right hand. If there's a bread and butter plate, remove it last and place it on the salad plate.

HOW TO SET THE TABLE

Allow 24 to 30" of space at the table for each person if you can; 18 to 20 is the minimum for comfort. This space for each person, along with the necessary china, silver, glassware and napkin, is called a *cover*.

The dinner plate occupies the center of the cover. Arrange the flat silver next to it in the order in which it will be used. Place the knife, cutting edge toward the plate, to the right. Place the spoons, bowls up, to the right of the knives. Place the forks, tines up, to the left of the plate parallel with the knife. If you use a salad fork, place it nearest the dinner plate. When the salad is served with the main course, it is correct to eat it with the dinner fork—you do not have to pick up first one fork, then the other. See that the handle ends of all silver pieces are 1" from the table edge.

Place bread and butter plates (if used) at the left, near the tip of the dinner fork. The usual position for the spreader is straight across the upper edge of the plate but you can place it in any position on the plate that you wish, except in the center.

Salad plates can occupy one of three positions. Take your choice of the spot above the dinner fork, above the dinner plate or to the left of the forks. It is correct to let the salad plate double as the bread and butter plate—a good compromise if your table seems crowded.

Place the water glasses or goblets at the tip of dinner knife. If you wish to serve tomato or fruit juice cocktail or wine with the dinner, place the cocktail or wine glasses to the right of water glasses. The host may open the wine bottle at the table. He pours a little wine into his own glass, just in case there are bits of cork floating in it. Then he fills the glass of the woman at his left and repeats, walking around the table, ending with his own glass. He does not serve all the women guests first.

Place the folded napkins at the left of the forks or on the dinner plate. Put the chairs around the table, their front edges flush with the table edge.

WHEN IT'S TIME TO SERVE DINNER

Fill water glasses a little over three fourths full. Pour the milk, if you want to serve it, just before you seat the guests.

The hostess announces dinner in a simple, friendly manner, often by asking: "Won't you come to dinner?" She plans the seating arrangement ahead, leads guests to the dining table and promptly tells every person, when he enters the dining room, where to sit.

Traditionally, the host sits at one end of the table, the hostess at the opposite end (the one nearest the kitchen). The most important woman guest sits to the host's right, and another woman to his left. The most important man guest sits at the hostess' right, another man to her left, except when a child helps her serve the meal. Such a child sits at the left of the hostess, who guides her in what to do.

If the guests include children, seat the youngest child at the left of one parent, the next youngest, to the left of the other parent. Separate husbands and wives in seating arrangements, but if dating teen-age couples are present, seat them together.

The hostess stands directly behind her chair while everyone finds his place around the table and does the same. When the hostess sits down (always from the left side of her chair), it's the signal for guests to sit. Guests also sit from the left of the chair.

If grace will be said, the hostess makes advance arrangements for it; no guest or child should be surprised at table by the request to say grace. When guests are seated, the hostess bows her head and places her hands in her lap, before unfolding her napkin. What she does tells everybody what to do; no one picks up his napkin until the hostess does.

BUFFET MEALS— THE HELP-YOURSELF STYLE

Buffet meals are extremely popular —the hostess likes them because she can entertain a bigger crowd than she can manage at a sit-down dinner party, often with less work—dishwashing, for example. And she can fix most of the food ahead so she can visit with the guests as soon as they arrive. The host is happy not to have to serve the food. Guests enjoy moving around freely and visiting.

While most buffet suppers are informal, the refreshments for weddings, birthdays and other anniversary receptions can be quite elaborate, even on the fancy side. For such occasions, you bring out your best linens, china, and silver, and you arrange a lovely centerpiece on the table.

Visiting with farm women all over the country, we find more and more of them turning to buffet style to serve refreshments for bridge and luncheon clubs, as well as evening refreshments and coffee parties. And they tell us there's no better way to serve church and other community meals. Buffet style service adapts to any occasion.

Originally, in bigger homes, these help-yourself meals were placed on a buffet or sideboard. That's how they got their name. But when hostesses serve a crowd today, they often use the dining room table to serve the food. When it's crowded, the buffet or a side table takes the overflow—perhaps the dessert or coffee.

Here are some pointers to help you; they come from farm women who are experienced in giving buffet suppers— who have become famous in their communities for the meals they serve.

· Arrange a charming table. Think of it as the background for your food. A theme, such as a holiday, birthday or after-the-game get-together, will be your incentive to make fascinating decorations—and guests will appreciate your festive touches. (See Index for Table Setting and Decoration.)

· Use colors that harmonize, and also complement your food—set it off.

· If possible, set up card tables or individual tray tables in the living room. Men don't like to hold plates or trays on their laps. If you use card tables, cover them with pretty linens and set with silver, napkins, salt and pepper sets and cream and sugar for coffee. Let the young crowd sit on the floor, stairs, or where they like.

· When you plan your menu, think how your guests will manage it. Choose fork foods if possible; then your guests won't need knives. Avoid creamy foods that run all over the plate. Casseroles are excellent choices because they hold the heat, but do have extras keeping warm in the oven, and bring them in as needed. Butter bread and rolls in advance.

· A two-course menu, main and dessert courses, is manageable, and all that's expected, for a buffet. If you want to have an appetizer, serve it in the living room beforehand.

· Always think of your guests—be a thoughtful hostess in planning a buffet. Try not to have too many different dishes or foods—remember, the dinner plate must hold all the main course. The ideal menu would include one or two main dishes, at least one vegetable, salad and rolls, all to go on the dinner plate. Dessert and coffee will follow later. If there's room on the buffet table, leave some empty places where guests can put down their plates while helping themselves. Have serving silver alongside each food—not in the food—when the guests start serving themselves.

· If you're serving a large crowd, arrange the buffet so your guests can move around the table. For a small party, you can push one side of the table against the wall and arrange a decorative centerpiece on the wall side.

• Place serving dishes and accessories on your table so that guests will find it easy to serve themselves—and strive for balance. Don't overcrowd one part of the table while another part looks bare or empty.

• Set out the main course before inviting guests to help themselves.

• Stack the dinner plates at the starting point, at one end of the table. For a large crowd, replenish dinner plates as needed; don't stack them all up at once. Set the main dish or dishes next to the plates, to the left. Continue around the table to the left, placing the vegetables, salad, and finally the rolls. Fit the relish dishes in among the larger serving dishes, all within convenient reach.

• If you have room, arrange the water pitcher, glasses, the coffee maker, cream and sugar at one end of the table. Or put beverages on a side table or on the buffet. If you do not seat guests at tables, omit saucers so guests can put their filled cups on their dinner plates. Or you may prefer to pass the coffee, cream and sugar after guests are seated at card or tray tables.

• To keep the buffet table appealing, promptly refill empty dishes with food or bring in new ones. Many guests return for seconds. It's customary for men to offer to refill women's plates with food they desire.

• You'll avoid traffic jams if you help your guests move clockwise around the table, from left to right. This puts the right hand next to the table and makes it easy for a right-handed guest to help himself. Have forks, spoons and overlapping napkins in rows at the last stop so they can be picked up after the plate is filled.

• When everyone has eaten the main course, ask a friend to take the dinner plates and used silver to the kitchen while you, the hostess, clear the buffet table and bring out the dessert, with its silver. You can place the dessert on the buffet or on a side table or bring it on individual serving plates directly to your guests.

Generally, buffet service is easy and casual; there are no hard and fast rules. The clever hostess adapts the service to her guests and her home. But a good cook with her reputation to uphold does make one absolute rule: She serves hot foods really hot and cold ones cold.

BUFFET SERVICE IS IDEAL FOR POTLUCK MEALS

Potluck buffet-style meals are a sign of the times. They enable busy women and their families to get together more often for friendly talk as they enjoy wonderful home-cooked food. That's because everybody shares both the work and the cost of the meal.

Where to serve the potluck supper depends largely on the size of the crowd. You can accommodate smaller groups at home; church, club, and other more spacious quarters will be better for large crowds. Regardless of where friends meet to visit and dine together, the meal will run more smoothly, if you appoint a food chairman. If it's a home-served buffet, the hostess automatically becomes the chairman. For larger groups, the women who bring the food select their chairman.

Once appointed, the food chairman asks other women to help her. Usually for big affairs she asks two women to serve on each committee. She finds out (or she may suggest) what food the different women plan to bring—at least what type of food, such as main dish, vegetable, salad, dessert, relishes, breads, etc. Experience shows that a fully or partially planned potluck menu is desirable to pure "potluck."

Another duty of the chairman is to provide or arrange for the centerpiece and decorations, tablecover, napkins, dishes, and silver. And when the meal is ready, it is she who invites everybody to come to the buffet and help himself. If there are guests of honor, she asks them to serve themselves first.

Here are the committees and their duties:

Table Committee: These women arrange an attractive buffet and supervise the placement of food on it, except for the dessert. That is, they tell the women who bring the food where to place it. They try to keep the table looking neat—uncluttered. If there are many dishes of the same type (often the case with a big crowd) the committee will be wise to hold back all but two or three main dishes, vegetables and salads. They will see that there's one tray of rolls and another of relishes on the table. When this food is served, the committee members bring in replacements from the dishes held back.

Coffee Committee: These women help the hostess make the coffee or they make it. They also serve the coffee, sugar and cream.

Dessert Committee: The women responsible for dessert service will cut pies or cakes; they arrange desserts and necessary plates and silver on the buffet as soon as it has been cleared of main course dishes. Or they set it up in advance on a side table.

Clean-Up Committee: The two women on this committee oversee the clearing away after supper. They make sure the kitchen is put back in order. If in a home, they stack the hostess' dishes. They also ask guests who brought food to collect their dishes, pans, and tools so they will be ready to take home.

SEMIFORMAL AND FORMAL BUFFETS

Most buffet-style meals in country communities are delightfully informal. For special occasions, such as wedding breakfasts and luncheons and anniversary celebrations, or when you entertain in honor of an important guest, you may want to have a semiformal or formal buffet. Guests help themselves to part of the food at the semiformal buffet, to none of it at the formal kind. The hostess does the serving and needs help with this type of entertaining. Ask two of your friends to assist you. These hostess helpers, when they serve all the food, fill their own plates and join the other guests.

Semiformal Buffets: Ask one assistant hostess to sit at one end of the table, the other opposite her. One assistant serves the main dish and salad, the other pours the coffee or other beverage. Guests help themselves to the other foods, napkins and silver, and carry them to their tables.

You can serve the dessert from the cleared buffet table, with guests returning to serve themselves, or you can ask young friends to carry dessert directly to the guests from the kitchen. First, the helpers remove the main course plates from the tables, two at a time, and take them to the kitchen. They return with the desserts, bringing them in two servings at a time. This speeds up the service.

Formal Buffet: Use your most beautiful linens, china and silver, and set the buffet table with great care. Be sure the centerpiece is most attractive.

Seat your guests as for semiformal buffets. Place cards will help them find their seats quickly.

To avoid overcrowding the buffet table, place the plates, silver, and napkins on a side table, called a service table, or on the sideboard.

Set out duplicate services of the food at the ends of the table, where you will ask two assistant hostesses to serve. The plates they fill will be carried to seated guests by young friends of the hostess. This is how they do it.

The waitress carries two empty plates from the service table to one of the assistant hostesses. She places the plate in her left hand in front of the woman who serves the food (from her left side). The waitress picks up the filled plate and places the empty plate in her right hand before the assistant hostess. While the assistant fills the second plate, the waitress takes the filled plate to the service table, places a napkin under it and a fork on it. She gives the plate to a guest, from the left, with the fork handle to the guest's right. She then takes an empty plate from the service table to the buffet table and picks up her second filled one. She continues to exchange empty for filled plates until she serves all the guests.

Another waitress passes buttered rolls. She passes them twice during the main course. She, or another waitress, sets small glasses of ice water on a tray and passes them.

The waitresses pass filled coffee cups on a tray or trays. Another waitress follows with a tray holding coffee spoons, sugar, and cream. Coffee may be served during the main course or only with dessert. In refilling the cups, the waitress pours the coffee from a pretty pot without removing cups from the tables.

While guests eat the main course, clear the buffet table. Arrange the desserts on it, and serve them as for the main course. Or serve the desserts from the kitchen. Waitresses remove the plates from the main course, two at a time. If they take desserts to the guests, they carry two at a time. This speeds up the service.

Waitresses pass candy mints and salted nuts during the dessert course.

After the waitresses serve all the desserts, they remove dessert dishes from the buffet table, leaving only the centerpiece and decorations.

And when guests finish with desserts, waitresses carry their plates and napkins to the kitchen.

GOOD TABLE MANNERS

The person who learns how to behave at home, as a child, has a decided social advantage. He will be poised and comfortable wherever he goes. Here are the established rules to teach your family.

• Stand behind your chair at the table

until the hostess sits down. Then sit down in your chair from the left.

• Start eating when everyone is served and the hostess unfolds her napkin and takes up her silver to eat.

• Don't reach in front of another person.

• Take part in the table conversation, but try not to monopolize it. Stick to cheerful subjects.

• Don't talk about your food dislikes or the cost of food. If you confront food you do not like, eat at least a few bites of it.

• Keep your silver on your plate; never put it back on the table. And avoid motioning or playing with your silver.

• If you're offered a choice of food, like dark or light chicken meat, state your preference promptly, but quietly.

• Keep all food off the table. If your dinner plate is full, place relishes, rolls and butter on your bread and butter plate if you have one or on your salad plate.

• Don't talk when you have food in your mouth. Don't hold food on your fork. Try not to ask a question of a person who has food in his mouth.

• Avoid tipping dishes to get the last bite (but you can tip a soup or dessert dish if you tip it away from yourself).

• Never stir foods like ice cream, sherbet, custards before eating them.

• Sit erect about six or seven inches from the table edge. Bending forward or lounging is bad form—and no elbows on the table while eating.

• Sit quietly without wiggling.

• Keep your mouth closed while chewing food.

• Drink coffee or other drinks only when you do not have food in your mouth.

• Leave the last bit of food, such as gravy or fruit preserves, on your plate rather than trying to mop it up with bread.

• If you must cough or sneeze, place a handkerchief or tissue or your hand over your nose and mouth; don't use your napkin.

• If you must leave the table, ask your hostess to excuse you.

• When you've finished eating, leave your dishes in place instead of stacking them.

• The hostess keeps on eating until all the guests finish their meal. Leave your napkin on your lap until she places her napkin on the table just before she arises. You do not refold your napkin; just gather it loosely and lay to the left of your plate.

• Rise from the left side of your chair. If necessary for others to pass, push your chair close to the table.

• Watch your own table manners, not those of other people.

USE TABLE TOOLS CORRECTLY

Knives, forks, and spoons are the common mealtime tools in our country. Learn to use them correctly and teach your children how to do so. Here are a few suggestions:

• To cut with a knife, hold it in the right hand, cutting edge down; hold the fork, tines down, in the left hand. Hold the handles so that little of them shows (the ends are in the palms of the hands). Place the index finger along the handles of both knife and fork to guide and steady them.

• Cut only enough meat at a time for two or three bites.

• Change the fork, tines up, to the right hand to take the food to the mouth. (This is our American style—in Europe, diners keep the fork in the left hand, tines down).

• Use a fork instead of a spoon whenever possible. For soft desserts, like ice cream, custards and puddings, use a spoon.

• It is proper to use a knife to cut lettuce salad if necessary.

• Use a knife or butter spreader to spread butter or jam on bread or rolls. Break off a small piece of bread, butter and eat it. Never butter a whole slice of bread at a time nor eat it without first breaking it into small pieces.

• Don't mash foods on your plate with a fork nor stir foods together.

• When you are not using silver, lay it across the back of the plate. When you finish eating, lay the knife and fork on the plate near the center, with the knife's cutting edge toward the center and the fork tines up.

• Use a spoon to test the temperature of a beverage—one sip—but drink the beverage from the cup.

• Never leave a spoon standing in a cup or dessert glass. Place it on the saucer or liner plate.

• Never drink a beverage with a spoon in the cup.

• When eating food with a spoon, dip toward you, except with soup. Dip soup away from you.

• Remove pits from fruit (plums and prunes) in the dish with a spoon. With small fruits, like cherries, you may need to remove the pits from the mouth. Use your spoon to transfer them from the mouth to the edge of the plate.

• Remove small fish bones, cleaned in the mouth, bird shot and other foreign bodies accidently taken into the mouth with the thumb and forefinger.

• Do not spit food from the mouth into the napkin. If you take food that's too hot into the mouth, immediately take a drink of water to cool it. If you find you've taken spoiled food, such as a bad clam, into the mouth, remove it using your fork (just as you remove cherry pits with a spoon), and place on the side of your plate.

• How to serve and eat artichokes: Serve cooked artichokes on salad plates so discarded leaves will not clutter dinner plates. Arrange small bowls of melted butter or sauce on each plate. To eat, pull off the leaves, one at a time, and dip the light-colored end into the butter or sauce. Scrape off the pulp with the teeth and discard the rest of the leaf. When all the outer leaves are eaten, cut out the "choke" or fuzzy center with a knife and fork and discard. The heart or the most delicious part of the vegetable remains. Cut it into bite-size pieces and use a fork to dip it in sauce and eat.

• When eating corn on the cob, butter and season a row or so at a time, never the whole ear at once; eat with fingers holding the ear firmly. Make a mixture of butter, salt and pepper on the side of the plate, to smear on corn as needed.

• Use the fingers to take whole pickles, radishes, celery and olives from the serving dish; put them on the side of your plate or on the butter plate—

never put them directly from serving plate into the mouth. Large olives are eaten in bites and the stone put aside but not cleaned in the mouth.

• Eat potato chips with the fingers; eat French fries with a fork, halving them if necessary.

• How to eat fresh fruit served at the table: Peel, quarter and core apples and pears and eat the quarters with fingers or with a fork. Peel oranges, pull apart segments and eat with fork or fingers; cut large segments in half with a fruit knife. Halve, then quarter peaches, pull off the skin of each quarter and eat in small sections with a fork. Peel bananas and break off small pieces to eat with fingers. Eat watermelon with a fork; take the fruit, seeds and all, into the mouth, clean the seeds in the mouth and drop them into your cupped hand to place on the side of the plate. Eat grapes one at a time after placing the bunch on your dessert plate, dropping seeds (and skins if necessary) into your cupped hand, as with watermelon seeds.

How to Give a Tea

Large teas continue to be important to compliment a guest speaker, to welcome new members into an organization, and to share a guest of honor with many friends. With flowers and candlelight, the dainty food and refreshing hot tea make a party so enchanting that to most women, teas have a glamour that cannot be equaled.

When you prepare to serve tea, cover the dining table with your choicest cloth. Add a lovely centerpiece—flowers and candles are almost ritual. Always light the candles on your table—even in the daytime. They will brighten the scene.

Set the tea service, arranged on a tray, at one end of the table and a similar service for coffee at the other end. Or instead of coffee, serve hot, spicy fruit punch from a pot or prepare French Chocolate (see Index) with whipped cream.

Place the pouring pots and cream pitchers on the trays to the right, with handles turned to the right (for right-handed women, who pour). At the left of the tray, set your prettiest teacups and saucers and/or tea plates, teaspoons, and a neat pile of napkins. Have loaf sugar, with tongs turned to the right, and a plate of thin lemon slices within easy reach of the tea service. Near the coffee service, set a plate of candied nuts or Candied Grapefruit Peel (see Index).

On each side of the table, arrange plates of two or three kinds of small sandwiches and a variety of small cookies or teacakes. For a large party, arrange silver and napkins on each side of the table instead of near the tea and coffee services, so guests can pick up their own.

Ask two friends to pour. They serve the tea (made to the strength most people like) and coffee, with sugar, cream and lemon slices, as the guests suggest. They set the filled cups on saucers or tea plates, and for smaller teas, also place the napkins and teaspoons on the saucers or plates. Then they hand the tea (or coffee) to each guest. The guests help themselves to the food. They sit or stand in groups and visit.

How to Give a Coffee Party

"Won't you come over for coffee?" That familiar invitation over the telephone is a sign of hospitality in country neighborhoods. No refreshments give greater pleasure than cups of coffee with one go-with—or several accompaniments.

Coffee parties are very informal. You can give one in the morning, afternoon or evening. And you can serve the steaming, fragrant beverage and luscious food anywhere—in the kitchen around the table (for kitchens are pretty these days), in the breakfast nook, at the dining room table, or in the living room.

Arrange your food, coffee, cups, saucers or plates, spoons, cream and sugar and napkins on a large tray or a small table. Since coffee parties are casual, the food need not be as dainty as you'd serve for teas. You may serve coffee cake, sweet rolls, or doughnuts. Or you can serve freshly baked breads or breads from the freezer, reheated so they'll have that fresh-from-the-oven taste. You may also want to have a tray of nibbles, like candied nuts, celery, carrot sticks and other fresh vegetables, stuffed dates or prunes, your best small pickles, relishes, olives, and wedges of cheese or cream cheese spreads.

You can use colorful pottery, if you have it, or your best dishes. A small bouquet on the tray or table, perhaps a rosebud in a slender glass vase, contributes to the party mood. The hostess pours the coffee and the guests help themselves to the other food.

Children's Birthday Parties

We have two rules for Small Fry parties:

Keep them simple, but make them memorable. Little children like best the food they normally have. Give them a hand in fixing it, such as spreading their own sandwiches and filling their own glasses with fruit juice or milk. Tint the milk pink for a change. Chocolate milk is a great favorite.

If you have bright colored dishes and tablecovers, use them for children's parties. One FARM JOURNAL reader covers her party table with a red oilcloth—the children adore it. Another has a red and white checked plastic tablecover that looks festive.

Add some imaginative frills to your food service. Cut the bread for sandwiches in fancy shapes with cookie cutters—animal cutters make a hit.

Do the same with cookies. One ranch mother has swimming parties for her little girl. She takes the guests to a swimming pool in a park, which means a trip to town. After swimming, she hands each guest a picnic lunch packed in a box.

Another farm woman puts different kinds of sandwiches and cookies in individual plastic bags which she ties to low trees or shrubs with bright colored ribbons. She trims a cookie tree and a sandwich tree. The children like to pick their own refreshments. The mother of the young host, at a nearby picnic table, pours the cold fruit or milk drink.

Snacks Please at Teen-Age Parties

Teen-agers like to plan and fix their own refreshments. Keep snacks they like in the cupboard, ice cream in the freezer. Have ground beef or Multi-Purpose Hamburger Mix (see Index) in the refrigerator or freezer and try to have buns on hand.

A jar of homemade cookies rates as a treat, as do fruit drinks, bottled soft drinks and plenty of milk.

Make suggestions if youngsters ask for them, but let them fix the food themselves.

Index